Also by Robert J. Donovan

. . .

THE ASSASSINS

EISENHOWER: THE INSIDE STORY

MY FIRST FIFTY YEARS IN POLITICS (WITH JOSEPH W. MARTIN, JR.)

PT-109: JOHN F. KENNEDY IN WORLD WAR II

THE FUTURE OF THE REPUBLICAN PARTY

ROBERT J. DONOVAN

CONFLICT
AND
CRISIS

The Presidency of Harry S Truman,
1945–1948

———

W · W · NORTON & COMPANY · INC · NEW YORK

FIRST EDITION

DESIGNER: MARJORIE J. FLOCK

Library of Congress Cataloging in Publication Data
Donovan, Robert J.
  Conflict and crisis.
  Bibliography: p.
  Includes index.
  1. United States—Politics and government—1945-1953.
2. World politics—1945-1955. 3. Truman, Harry S,
Pres., U.S., 1884-1972. I. Title.
E813.D6 1977   973.918′092′4   77-9584

ISBN 0 393 05636 8

1 2 3 4 5 6 7 8 9 0

To L. L. Engelking
and other old colleagues on the
New York Herald Tribune

Contents

III
COLD WAR

IV
1948

Photographs appear following page 252

Preface

————

On April 12, 1945, Harry S Truman was in his eighty-third day as vice-president of the United States. He and President Franklin D. Roosevelt had been inaugurated—Roosevelt for a fourth term—the previous January 20. Because the Second World War was then at its height and also because Roosevelt's strength was ebbing, the ceremony was a simple one held on the south portico of the White House instead of in the traditional elaborate setting in front of the Capitol.

Like many other men who had come to the vice-presidency after years of action, Truman found himself reduced to the state of "a political eunuch," as he said. Yet, considering his antecedents, he had come an incredibly long way in life.

At the age of thirty-four, his formal education having consisted of high school and some night law-school courses, he was still a farmer in Missouri. At thirty-eight he was washed up on the rocks by the failure of a haberdashery he had opened with a friend in Kansas City after serving as a captain of Battery D, 129th Field Artillery, Thirty-fifth Division, in the First World War.

Truman had long been tempted to enter politics. In the army he had become friendly with James Pendergast, son of Mike Pendergast, a Democratic leader in the rural parts of Jackson County, Missouri. The county also embraced Kansas City and nearby Independence, where Truman lived. Truman mentioned his interest, and young Pendergast passed the information on to his father. The latter was the brother of Thomas J. Pendergast, boss of the corrupt Kansas City Democratic machine and a power throughout Missouri.

Truman was popular and particularly well liked by veterans, and Mike Pendergast talked to him about running for judge (commissioner) of Jackson County. In 1922 Truman, in need of a job after his business failure, decided to run; and, supported by Mike Pendergast, he won. When it came time to run for a second term, two years later, he lost. Hence, at forty he was out of a job and in debt. Then he ran again two years later, this time with the support of Tom Pendergast, and was elected presiding judge—an administrative, not a judicial, post. While conforming with the ways of the organization and even liking its seedy bosses ("You can't get anywhere in politics around Kansas City unless you work with the machine," he once said[1]), he did his own job honestly and competently. He was well enough regarded to have been chosen president of the Greater Kansas City Plan Association and director of the National Conference on City Planning. Despite the corrupt machine to which he belonged, no scandal ever tarnished him. As a politician he began to attract attention throughout Missouri.

In the election for United States senator in 1934 the political situation in Missouri was such that Tom Pendergast needed a winning candidate in order to sustain his own position. When some of the state's senior Democrats turned him down, he picked Truman. Truman won because the race became divided three ways; because he ran better than his opponents in the rural areas; and because the Kansas City machine was as ingenious in tabulating 90 percent of the vote for him in Jackson County as the St. Louis bosses were in tabulating 90 percent of the vote for his rivals in the eastern end of the state.

When he came up for reelection to the Senate in 1940, however, Tom Pendergast was in jail; and Truman's chances of winning were considered so meager that Roosevelt tried to lure him out of the race in favor of another Democrat with an offer of a seat on the Interstate Commerce Commission.[2] But Truman ran and won. In the ensuing years he gained national prominence and esteem as chairman of the Senate Special Committee to Investigate the National Defense Program, or Truman Committee, as it was called. By 1944, finally established as a power in the Senate, he was mentioned with increasing frequency as a possible choice for the Democratic vice-presidential nomination. Happy in his role in the Senate, he said he did not wish to be vice-president. His preference was Rayburn, but a split in the Texas delegation killed Rayburn's chances. Truman, therefore, went to the Democratic National Convention in Chicago prepared to nominate Senator James F. Byrnes of South Carolina at Byrnes's request. Instead, by incredibly roundabout dealings, Roosevelt and the big city bosses contrived to get the nomination for Truman.

The combination of events that had decided his destiny was extraordinary. The plot began in the previous spring and summer of 1944 with discussions about a running mate for Roosevelt in the election to be held that November. The circumstance that enabled all others to fall into place was Roosevelt's decision not to try to dictate the selection of a particular vice-presidential candidate, notably the incumbent vice-president, Henry A. Wallace, or Byrnes, the two front-runners.

Ailing and preoccupied with the war, Roosevelt vacillated. Thus the usual political forces were allowed free play in the party—to the detriment of Wallace and Byrnes, as it developed. For Vice-President Wallace, who traditionally would have been renominated, was anathema to the powerful southern faction of the party and to the northern bosses. Without Roosevelt's insistence he could not have been renominated in any case; and Roosevelt, while saying kind things about him, did not insist. Furthermore, Byrnes, basically a conservative southerner, was unacceptable to the powerful labor faction. Although Roosevelt had encouraged him to seek the vice-presidential nomination, telling him he was the best qualified for it, Roosevelt—in the face of labor's opposition—looked the other way when Byrnes needed his help at Chicago. Finally, Truman was liked by the southerners and was acceptable to labor: a rare combination of blessings in 1944 and one that worked steadily to bring him to the fore.

As the convention approached, the party was in a state of tension, caused mainly by disagreement over the direction a Democratic administration should take after the war. The South and the business interests were passionately opposed to Wallace because they feared he would lead the country to the left. Party leaders warned Roosevelt that Wallace's nomination would hurt the Democratic ticket and drive away large contributors.

On the other hand, the potent labor faction headed by Sidney Hillman, president of the Amalgamated Clothing Workers of America and chairman of the Political Action Committee of the Congress of Industrial Organizations (CIO-PAC), opposed Byrnes, fearing he would lead the country to the right. Byrnes had other political liabilities too—especially among some Catholic voters, because he had abandoned his native Catholicism. But labor's opposition weighed most heavily with Roosevelt.[3]

A small band of New Dealers promoted the candidacy of Associate Justice William O. Douglas of the Supreme Court, which pleased Roosevelt. However, Douglas lacked an appreciable number of delegates.

For months Truman's name had kept popping up in the speculation over the vice-presidential nomination. Behind the scenes, Democratic National Chairman Robert E. Hannegan, a Missourian, was scheming to get him on the ticket. As the then chairman of the Democratic Central Committee in St. Louis, Hannegan had helped Truman win renomination and reelection to the Senate in 1940. In 1943, at Truman's urging, Roosevelt had appointed Hannegan United States collector of internal revenue in Missouri. Thereafter Hannegan had moved up in Democratic politics and was now using his influence as national chairman on Truman's behalf. Edwin W. Pauley, treasurer of the Democratic National Committee, also was trying to get Truman the nomination.

Dissembling as the time of decision approached, Roosevelt questioned whether Truman was too old. Then he wrote a letter to Hannegan saying he would be glad to run with Truman or Douglas, thereby providing a large opening for Truman's supporters. But, after that, even though Roosevelt had in effect dropped Wallace, he wrote another letter to be read to the convention saying that if he were a delegate he would vote for Wallace. Still he did not insist that the delegates do so. "I hardly know Truman," he told Byrnes. According to Byrnes, Roosevelt once said he had no preference, then told black leaders that Byrnes was his choice and finally instructed party leaders: "Clear it with Sidney"—Sidney being Sidney Hillman.[4] Hillman vetoed Byrnes.

Arriving in Chicago, Truman wrote his nominating speech for Byrnes. The cocky, quizzical-looking Irishman from Spartanburg already had become an important figure in the Senate when Truman first came to Washington. He was five years older than Truman, and Truman looked up to him, as the two became good friends. Ironically, Byrnes helped Truman in certain ways that kept Truman going as a politician and built him up finally to vice-presidential stature. In 1940, for example, when Truman was involved in the fight of his life for reelection to the Senate and hard up for money, Byrnes persuaded his friend, Bernard M. Baruch, the financier, to contribute $4,000 to Truman's campaign.[5]

After years as the President's chief operative behind the scenes in the Senate, Byrnes was nominated by Roosevelt as associate justice of the Supreme Court. When the country went to war he left the bench to become Director of War Mobilization, or "Assistant President," as exaggerated newspaper stories called him. In comparison with this prestigious and colorful South Carolinian, Truman was a minor figure, even in 1944.

Through hard work, friendliness, good sense, and a knack for investigation, however, Truman had risen in the Senate not to the inner circle but to a position of respect and influence. It had been a slow climb, for in his early days as a senator he had been treated with a good deal of contempt as the supposed tool of Pendergast—indeed, someone had dubbed him "the gentleman from Pendergast." Whatever favors he may have done for Pendergast in the Senate in Missouri affairs, however, he became a regular of the national Democratic party in his votes on the main issues. Finally, he stepped onto what proved to be the escalator of the Truman Committee.

With mixed motives, compounded of his own critical view of waste in the rearmament program and the dissatisfaction he was hearing from Missouri contractors over their share of defense work, he had proposed a Senate investigation. At first it was not an auspicious proposal. But then the administration felt a need to head off a threatened unfriendly investigation of defense spending in the House. Roosevelt and Byrnes, then still a senator, put their heads together, and the upshot was the creation of the Truman Committee in the Senate. Again Byrnes had been instrumental in giving Truman a boost—this one providing, as it developed, the vehicle to the vice-presidency.

The Truman Committee was popularly credited with having saved the taxpayers billions of dollars, though there is no accurate accounting of this. It was a valuable means of keeping the spotlight on defense officials and contractors and providing public review of all phases of the war mobilization. The committee did expose wrongdoing. Undoubtedly it was responsible for some improvement in war production.

As chairman, Truman was praised for his fairness. His role brought other political assets too. Coming from a border state, he had been close to the leading southern conservatives in the Senate. This was all the more natural because of his warmth for the South, acquired from his mother in particular. She had been a rabid Rebel ever since her girlhood exposure to Yankee depredations in Missouri during the Civil War. The work of the Truman Committee, on the other hand, drew him into a closer relationship with the liberals than he had previously enjoyed.

Truman had conducted the investigations in such a way that Roosevelt was protected from criticism over war production. The president, who had rather snubbed him earlier in his Senate career, now warmed up to him to a degree and spoke approvingly of his work, though it would be much too much to say that Roosevelt ever regarded Truman as being in his own class.

Another consideration that attracted Roosevelt to Truman was the help that Truman as vice-president might give him in the Senate when it came time to send up the peace treaties and the United Nations Charter. Mindful of what had happened to Woodrow Wilson in the Senate after the First World War, Roosevelt recognized the value of a vice-president who, unlike Wallace, would be popular in the Senate and who might be able to line up votes for the treaties.[6]

Piece by piece, Truman's credentials fell into a pattern that fit the description of a compromise candidate. His border-state ties with the South appealed to conservatives. At the same time, though he had deserted Roosevelt on some lesser issues, he had been a consistent supporter of the New Deal and backed Roosevelt's war policies. That made him acceptable to the liberals. He had no trouble being cleared by Sidney, nor by such other labor leaders as William F. Green, president of the American Federation of Labor, and A. F. Whitney, president of the Brotherhood of Railroad Trainmen. Furthermore, he had made few enemies of consequence, a fact that impressed Roosevelt. Roosevelt did not believe any vice-presidential candidate could help him on election day. His interest was in a running mate who would be least likely to hurt the ticket, and Truman best matched that qualification.[7] Finally Truman's own background in machine politics and his popularity in the Senate made him a comfortable choice for the city bosses.

After Roosevelt had been renominated, Truman was called to a meeting of party leaders in the Blackstone Hotel. The group included Hannegan, Pauley, former Democratic National Chairman Edward J. Flynn of the Bronx, Mayor Edward J. Kelley of Chicago, Mayor Frank Hague of Jersey City, and Postmaster General Frank Walker. By this time Truman had been told by Hannegan that he was the president's choice, but he was unconvinced.

As Truman recounted the Blackstone meeting in his memoirs, Hannegan made a long-distance call to the president, who was visiting San Diego on his way to Hawaii. Hannegan held the telephone far enough from his ear so the others could hear both ends of the conversation.

"Bob, have you got that fellow lined up yet?" Truman heard Roosevelt ask.

"No," Hannegan replied. "He is the contrariest Missouri mule I've ever dealt with."

"Well, you tell him," Roosevelt retorted, "if he wants to break up the Democratic party in the middle of a war, that's his responsibility."

With that, Roosevelt hung up.[8] "Oh, shit," Truman said.[9]

"Well, if that is the situation, I'll have to say yes," he told the leaders, "but why the hell didn't he tell me in the first place?"

He then went after the nomination in earnest, Byrnes having already withdrawn, bitterly. Truman won on the second ballot, but only after a struggle with Wallace and with the indispensable help of the bosses and the South.

Without a doubt many of the delegates who voted for him were fed up with the New Deal and were gratified to be able to cast their ballots for a man they believed would move the Democratic party and the country in a more conservative direction if given the chance.

Afterward Truman came to say out of modesty that a million men might better have stood next in line of succession to the presidency than he, and surely he had in mind more than the machinations in Chicago. What he meant was that there were other men in the United States whose education, whose background in both national and international affairs, whose standing in high places and demonstrated capacity for leadership would have made them more likely candidates for this role than he.

International relations were in flux because of the war. Yet Truman had not had a single day's experience in the conduct of foreign affairs. On the contrary, his work as a senator had been concentrated on domestic problems.

Once when he was chairman of the investigating committee his interest had been aroused by the Hanford Works near Pasco, Washington, which was connected with the atomic bomb project, of which he had no exact knowledge. Knowing at least that it was a great and secret undertaking, he got in touch with Secretary of War Henry L. Stimson and asked that a member of the committee staff, General Lowe, be taken into Stimson's confidence. On March 13, 1944, the latter wrote Truman, declining. According to Stimson, Truman did not take this rebuff lightly. "He threatened me with dire consequences," Stimson wrote in his diary March 13. "I told him I had to accept the responsibility for those consequences because I had been directed by the President to do just what I did do. Truman is a nuisance and a pretty untrustworthy man. He talks smoothly but he acts meanly."[10] This pique did not surface again and seems not to have obstructed future cordial relations between the two men. But even on April 12, 1945, Truman still did not know the exact nature of the great project.

Throughout Truman's brief tenure as vice-president, Roosevelt had excluded him not only from discussions about the bomb but from all conferences within the executive branch on foreign policy, except as it arose in the cabinet. Thus, at a time of some of the greatest diplomatic crises in history, Truman's knowledge of events derived mostly from what he read in the newspapers and heard around Capitol Hill.

Since the onset of the war the White House had been the center of stirring events. Statesmen journeyed there from all over the world. Daily, the braided hats of admirals and generals lay on the tables in the waiting rooms. Congressional leaders of both parties often came to confer with President Roosevelt. In this drama and spectacle Harry Truman had not participated.

Nevertheless, as a senator from 1935 to 1945 he had been involved in a number of the principal domestic issues of that tempestuous period. He had a hand in the writing of some major legislation, including the Civil Aeronautics Act of 1938 and the Transportation Act of 1940.[11]

He had been a member of the Senate Appropriations Committee under the eminent Carter Glass of Virginia and of the Senate Interstate and Foreign Commerce Committee under Burton K. Wheeler of Montana. It was Wheeler who, during the investigation of the railroads in the 1930s, tutored Truman in the skills of congressional investigation. Truman had also been a member of the Senate Military Affairs Committee.

These committees were a veritable school on the mechanics of government. Truman was knowledgeable, therefore, in critical areas such as the process of appropriations, the preparation and composition of the budget, the structure and functions of the armed services and the relationship between the executive branch and Congress. The inquiries of the Truman Committee into the affairs of industries and unions had taught its chairman a good deal about the workings of the economy. As a county commissioner overseeing the construction and maintenance of roads and public institutions, he had had a limited but useful experience in managing, delegating authority, making practical decisions, and observing how the system works on one important level. As an officer under fire in the First World War, he had found within himself a capacity to lead other men.

His role on the Truman Committee had brought him into a wider range of political activity and had won him favorable national publicity. He was increasingly in demand as a speaker at political dinners. His picture was on the cover of *Time*. *Reader's Digest* featured an article on him entitled "Billion-Dollar Watchdog." A poll of Washington correspondents conducted by *Look* named him (alone among members of Congress) as one of the ten civilians in Washington most useful to the war effort.

Thus, on the eighty-third day of his vice-presidency Harry Truman was a gregarious, popular, highly experienced, methodical politician, who had been well established in the Senate, was familiar with government operations, conscientious about detail, accustomed to the needs for compromise, and schooled in domestic issues. Candid within the limits of a devious profession, he was endowed with an unpretentious but strong character, a clear and retentive mind, an independent spirit, a large measure of common sense and self-reliance, and a formidable capacity for indignation and anger. Being a man of strong likes and dislikes, he was often slow to forgive anyone who had displeased him.

Vigorous, hardworking, simple, he had grown up close to the soil of the Midwest and understood the struggles of the people on the farms and in the small towns—a larger segment of America then than now. After ten years in the Senate he had risen above the Pendergast organization. Still he *had* come from a world of two-bit politicians, and its aura was one that he never was able to shed entirely. And he *did* retain certain characteristics one often sees in machine-bred politicians: intense partisanship, stubborn loyalty, a certain insensitivity about the transgressions of political associates, and a disinclination for the companionship of intellectuals and artists. Mostly, his personal friends were plain, obscure, even mediocre men who shared his love of politics and poker. On the other hand, he had won the esteem and friendship, not easily given, of Associate Justice Louis D. Brandeis, who regularly invited him to his home.

A collateral descendant of President John Tyler (of whom he came to hold no high opinion), Truman was born into a Baptist family in the town of Lamar, Missouri, on May 8, 1884. His parents were ardent Democrats. His father, John A. Truman, who died in 1914, was a combative, unschooled farmer, livestock and mule trader, and unlucky grain speculator who nevertheless provided a comfortable life for his family. Harry loved and respected him, but was closer to his mother, Martha Ellen Young Truman, a spirited woman who was well educated for her day. Harry and his brother and sister grew up in a disciplined home where great emphasis was placed upon right and wrong. However modest, it was also a home with music and books. Harry learned to play the piano.

Partly because his defective eyes kept him from sports, he also became an insatiable reader, delving into a remarkable miscellany from Plutarch and the Bible to military lore and American history. He had absorbed a good deal of knowledge about the presidency. On the whole, though, Truman was more steeped in history than subtle about it. He had a great repertoire of tales about battles and generals, kings and presidents, and admired strong men of action. His store of historical anecdotes made him an engaging conversationalist. In his particular way, Truman was an educated man.

He had had by all signs a happy boyhood in the pleasant town of Independence, a few miles off the dead center of the country, where his family had settled in 1890. The lives of his family and neighbors had been filled with experiences of the frontier and the Civil War, and he had a good sense of the roots and traditions of American democracy. Imbued with the optimism of his time, he was a product of a generation that believed in the limitless possibilities of progress.

He attended the public schools. Poor eyesight frustrated his ambition to enter West Point. Then, with his family pressed for money, he passed up the idea of going to college. He took odd jobs in a drug store, in the mail room of the *Kansas City Star,* and as a bookkeeper on the Atchison, Topeka, and Santa Fe Railroad. He settled down for a time as a bank clerk, but then worked on the farm when his family needed him. He joined the National Guard. He went off to war, patriotically. On his return he opened the haberdashery with his friend, Edward Jacobson, at Twelfth and Baltimore in Kansas City. He took a pass at studying law at night, doing well enough in class but finally losing interest in a legal career. He spent a good deal of time in the Masonic Lodge, the American Legion, and the National Old Trails and Roads Association. He liked the songs of Stephen Foster.

He enjoyed goodfellowship with men. He was profane, although usually in outbursts of anger or levity. Characteristically, his discourse was quite sober.* He laughed at barnyard and barracks jokes, but his own preference as a raconteur ran to political yarns. An unseemly joke in public offended him. Truman was a light eater. He never smoked. He enjoyed his bourbon—sometimes he started the day with a shot—but drinking was not a problem for him in his active years. He was uncomplicated, at peace with himself, proud of his origins, and secure in the affections of his family.

In his beliefs, his ideals, his outlook, his reaction to things, Truman came close to being the typical self-made, white, middle-class, sixty-year-old American man of 1945.

He had married his childhood sweetheart, Elizabeth Virginia Wallace, known as Bess, and elevated her and their only child, Mary Margaret, to a plane somewhere above the rest of humanity. He seemed shy about other women. Once, when he was fifty, he jotted on a piece of paper in the middle of the night after Pendergast had offered him the Senate nomination: ''I have come to the place where all men strive to be at my age. . . . In reading the lives of great men, I found that the first victory they won was over themselves and their carnal urges. Self-discipline with all of them came first.''[12] He must have been one of the few soldiers in the American Expeditionary Force who had found the Folies Bergère ''disgusting.''[13]

His political views were a mixture of Wilsonian and Rooseveltian liberalism, Midwestern progressivism, and border-state conservatism, all contained, however, within narrow enough limits to stamp him as a moderate. He believed in a balanced budget. He was skeptical about social experimentation, although he thought the government had a responsibility to help solve social and economic problems. He also distrusted concentrations of economic power, whether in business or labor, even though he was regarded as a friend of the unions. He had been considered a rather typical middle-of-the-road senator. Recently, he had indicated that his favor-

---

* Evidently in retirement he grew increasingly profane with age, to judge from Merle Miller's *Plain Speaking: An Oral Biography of Harry S Truman.*

ite position was "a little left of center"[14]—scarcely far enough so, however, to qualify him as a reformer, let alone a crusader. He was a doer, not a dreamer.

Truman had gone to Europe only once—on a troopship in 1918—but otherwise had no firsthand knowledge of the world beyond the oceans nor acquaintanceship with any of the leaders of other countries. In manner, speech, and scope of interests he was rather provincial, yet he knew far more about the United States and its people than most persons more sophisticated than he. Furthermore, his capacities had yet to be tested to the full.

Acknowledgments

THE RECORDS of the Harry S Truman Library at Independence, Missouri, were researched for this book by Lawrence A. Yates, a candidate for the degree of Ph.D. in history at the University of Kansas.

The idea for this work was conceived by Evan W. Thomas, editor of W. W. Norton & Company. From start to finish his brilliant mark is upon it both as to style and content. Indispensable help on the composition of the manuscript came from Sara Blackburn, the critic, and on its structure from Sterling Lord. Newspaper colleagues, Donald M. Irwin, Marianne and Dennis Britton, and Joseph R. Slevin, gave me valuable editorial help. Men who were on the Washington scene with President Truman, whom I have known all these thirty years, cooperated with me beyond the call of duty in reconstructing events. Among those who helped me were Benjamin V. Cohen, John W. Snyder, Clark M. Clifford, Dr. John R. Steelman, Robert A. Lovett, Henry J. Nicholson, Charles S. Murphy, James E. Webb, Oscar R. Ewing, the late Samuel I. Rosenman, the late Charles E. Bohlen, Major General Harry H. Vaughan (retired), W. Averell Harriman, W. Stuart Symington, Richard E. Neustadt, George D. Aiken, Tom C. Clark, and Leon H. Keyserling. George M. Elsey, an administrative assistant to President Truman, with an academic background in history, who is now president of the American National Red Cross, not only provided similar help but read the manuscript and steered me away from pitfalls. Above all, I am indebted to a generation of scholars, whose names appear in the References, without whose labors on different aspects of postwar history the story of the Truman presidency could not possibly be told.

I

TAKING OVER FROM F. D. R.

1. *Call from the White House*

THE HOUSE OF REPRESENTATIVES adjourned early on the rainy afternoon of Thursday, April 12, 1945, after a light calendar. As Speaker Sam Rayburn stepped down from the rostrum, he invited the parliamentarian, Lewis Deschler, for a drink in his private office.

"Be there around five," Rayburn said. "Harry Truman is coming over."[1]

Although the Second World War was then at a momentous turn in Europe and the Pacific, it was a quiet afternoon in Washington.

President Franklin Delano Roosevelt was in Warm Springs, Georgia, resting after his recent journey to the Big Three conference at Yalta in the Crimea. Secretary of War Henry L. Stimson was having tea at home with Lord Halifax, the British ambassador. At the State Department, Dean Acheson, assistant secretary of state for economic affairs, was sitting for a photograph.

At the White House it was humdrum, too. Eleanor Roosevelt had had lunch with Nila Magidoff, a lecturer for Russian War Relief. At three o'clock, before leaving for an affair at the Sulgrave Club, she received Charles W. Taussig, a friend and State Department official, to discuss the impending United Nations Conference on International Organization in San Francisco.

The Senate was debating a water treaty with Mexico. In his constitutional role of president of the Senate, Vice-President Harry S Truman was presiding. Bored by what he thought a fatuous speech by Senator Alexander Wiley of Wisconsin, he jotted a note to his mother and his sister, Mary Jane Truman, on the family farm in Grandview, Missouri: "Turn on your radio tomorrow night at 9:30 your time, and you'll hear Harry make a Jefferson Day address to the nation. I think I'll be on all the networks, so it ought not to be hard to get me. It will be followed by the President, whom I'll introduce."[2]

Deschler arrived at Rayburn's hideaway across a corridor from the Speaker's Lobby before five. The Speaker had already made himself a drink, and the parliamentarian put some glasses, ice, and soda around for other guests. While he and Rayburn were chatting, James M. Barnes, a congressional liaison man on the White House staff, came in. The telephone rang. Deschler was curious, for few persons knew the Speaker's private number. Deschler offered to answer, but Rayburn took the call.

"Yes, Steve," Deschler heard him say. "I'll tell him."

"That was Steve Early at the White House," Rayburn said, hanging up. "He wants the vice-president to call him right away when he gets here."

Presently, the Senate having adjourned, Harry Truman sauntered in.

Seen at a distance he had an unassuming air and, at sixty, a rather gray look. He was dressed neatly in a double-breasted gray suit with a white handkerchief in the breast pocket, white shirt, and blue polka-dot bow tie. He wore a First World War discharge button in his left lapel, a triple-band gold Masonic ring on his left hand. Five feet and ten inches tall, weighing one hundred and sixty-seven pounds, he was compactly built, with a light complexion, down-pointed nose, high forehead topped with short gray hair combed flat and parted on the left, and blue eyes behind thick, steel-rimmed glasses. Judging by his appearance, he might have been an insurance salesman paying a call, or the family physician.

As he drew nearer, the image changed from bland to crisp. The man who was nondescript from afar exuded a glow of vitality at closer range. The backs of his hands were covered with fine dark hairs, and when he shook hands his grip was strong. His bearing was erect, his shoulders sturdy. Though his voice might sound nasal and lacking in cadence when he read a speech, it could be deep and resonant in conversation. Magnified by his glasses, his eyes seemed to take in everything at once. When he spoke, a caustic streak was apt to show through his mild manner. His explosive laughter obliterated the gray look, revealing a warm and friendly man.

Shooting the breeze with political friends like Rayburn and Deschler was something made-to-order for putting Truman in a hearty mood. He poured himself some bourbon and sat on the arm of an overstuffed black leather chair beside Rayburn's desk. Deschler took a seat directly opposite Truman.

"Mr. Speaker," the parliamentarian said, "wasn't the vice-president supposed to call the White House?"

"Oh, yeah, Harry, Steve Early wants you to call him right away," Rayburn said, as Deschler later recalled the conversation that afternoon.

Stephen T. Early, formerly the House press secretary, was currently a principal assistant to President Roosevelt.

"Want me to get him for you?" Rayburn asked.

"No, I'll get it," Truman said, taking the telephone and putting through the call.

When Early came on the line, his voice sounded so strange that Truman was startled. Evidently under great tension, Early asked him to come to the White House quickly and to enter by way of the north portico on Pennsylvania Avenue, the main entrance.

Deschler, who was scanning Truman's face, saw him turn pale. Truman hung up the phone.[3]

"Jesus Christ and General Jackson!" he said.

Turning to Rayburn: "Steve Early wants me at the White House immediately." Truman made for the door, and while his hand was still on the knob, he turned around and said, "Boys, this is in the room. Something must have happened."

The vice-president's office as well as his limousine, were on the Senate side at the other end of the Capitol, the length of a long city block from Rayburn's quarters. Instead of picking up the Secret Service agent regularly assigned to guard him and walking through the main corridor and rotunda, Truman darted by himself down a nearby staircase to the basement and a long, narrow passageway that traverses the length of the building.

It was now around five o'clock and the basement was deserted. Instead of walking, Truman broke into a run.[4]

What a remarkable sight it would have been on that April afternoon to see the vice-president of the United States racing alone through a dim deserted stone passage underneath the Capitol! Why was Vice-President Truman running? Was he running merely to elude his Secret Service agent? Was he running because he was desperate to be alone at that moment? Was he running out of sheer nervous tension? Was he running because he was in frantic haste to get to the White House to learn why Early's voice was strained and to discover what this might mean for him?

He ran for the same reason that Eleanor Roosevelt was just then clenching her hands in her car riding back to the White House from the Sulgrave Club on Massachusetts Avenue, near Dupont Circle. While she was at the club, knowing that her husband had fainted at Warm Springs but given to understand that his condition was not serious, she too had received a call from Early. In a distressed voice he had asked her also to return immediately. He gave no reason for his request then, either; but Mrs. Roosevelt kept her hands clenched all the way back to the White House.

"In my heart of hearts," she said afterward, "I knew what had happened, but one does not actually formulate these terrible thoughts until they are spoken."[5]

No less awesome for the vice-president, these thoughts swirled, yet did not take definite shape.

Harry S Truman *president of the United States?* If Roosevelt was dead—yes, incredibly. But, no—Roosevelt was not dead. As he ran, Truman allowed himself to believe that he would be back at the Capitol again that evening.

Yes, he knew that Roosevelt's health was precarious. He had begun worrying about it right after the Democratic National Convention and had been aghast at the president's haggard appearance when Roosevelt had to sit at a desk in the House of Representatives while addressing a joint session March 1 on the results of the Yalta Conference.

But, no, the president must suddenly have returned from Warm Springs. Because wartime secrecy shrouded presidential travel, Truman would not have known of the journey. Perhaps Roosevelt came back on account of the death in Washington of his old friend, the Right Rev. Julius W. Atwood, retired Episcopal bishop of Arizona.[6] Maybe, Truman thought, the president just wanted to talk over some things with him before going back to Warm Springs. Nevertheless Truman ran, and what impelled him was hardly a vision of a brief business meeting with Roosevelt.

Although he had not actually formulated such thoughts, events everywhere were moving swiftly, inexorably now. As life was never to be the same again for Harry Truman, neither was it to be for the Poles, the Rumanians, the Bulgarians, the Germans, the Chinese, the Japanese, the Americans.

Already, as he ran toward his fate, the Soviet Union was becoming the greatest power in Europe. Having swept across Eastern Europe, the Red Army was fighting on the approaches to Berlin that very day.

Already nationalism was glowing in the embers of Asia.

Already the well-fed, well-clothed, hardened Eighth Route Army of Mao Tse-tung was established in Shensi Province in northern China, invincible against the forces of Generalissimo Chiang Kai-shek.

Already the rot that had begun in the British and French empires between 1914 and 1918 was far advanced, weakening their foundations everywhere and opening the way to massive revolt against colonialism.

Already a revolution had occurred in United States foreign policy. In contrast to recent isolationism, the country was involved in military, political, and economic commitments around the world.

Already the decline in the farm population and the migration of black and white workers from rural areas to the war plants had accelerated urban congestion, hastening the change in the character of American civilization.

Already social changes caused by the war had alarmed the South and moved race relations to the forefront of American politics.

Already the outburst of technology and the dislocation caused by the war were affecting the way people thought and lived, and revolutionary changes were occurring in education.

Already, with millions of women working for the first time and American society becoming increasingly mobile, the old family structure was giving way.

Already the country was on the verge of a huge population growth, for which not enough housing was available.

Already too, though Truman did not know it, enriched U-235 was being shipped from Oak Ridge, Tennessee, to Los Alamos, New Mexico, where scientists were hastening an implosion program, with consequences that would forever alter the terms on which men lived.

On the way to his limousine Truman stopped at his office just off the Senate floor to get his hat, of all things. Colonel Harry H. Vaughan, his military aide, and Matthew J. Connelly, his secretary, were there.

"Steve Early wants you to—" Vaughan began, when Truman cut him short.

"I talked to him. He wants me at the White House right away. I'm going. I'm worried about the President."

As he often did when he was alone with Truman, a friend of many years, Vaughan cracked a joke.

"If anything has happened to the President," he said, "don't let them swear you in until Matt and I get there, or it won't be legal."

Too late, he could tell by the vice-president's agitation that the joke had fallen flat.[7]

The limousine, driven by a chauffeur, rolled down Capitol Hill and, without a police escort, dodged through the rush-hour traffic. Street cars were bunched along Pennsylvania Avenue. Sprinkled among the crowds going home were hundreds of military and naval uniforms. At the busy newsstands the headline on the *Evening Star* said: 9TH ARMY CROSSES ELBE: WINS BRIDGEHEAD.

When Truman had gone to the White House on business in the past he had used the East Executive Avenue entrance. Now, complying with Early's request, he directed the chauffeur to the northwest gate on Pennsylvania Avenue. The wet grass was fresh, and the blossoms and the tulips were in bloom. It was about 5:25 P.M. when the limousine pulled up to the north portico. Ushers were on hand to escort

Vice-President Truman inside. They told him Mrs. Roosevelt was awaiting him in her sitting room on the second floor.

He stepped into a small elevator furnished in oak panels. He and Mrs. Roosevelt did not know each other well. She had favored the renomination of Vice-President Wallace at the Democratic National Convention in 1944. When he was defeated by Truman she tried to console Wallace: "I had hoped that by some miracle you could win out, but it looks to me as though the bosses had functioned pretty smoothly. I am told that Senator Truman is a good man, and I hope so for the sake of the country."

Evidently she grew more encouraged, for a week later she wrote to a friend, "I am much more satisfied with Senator Truman than I would have been with some of the others who were seriously considered."[8]

It was quiet on the second floor. The vice-president walked solemnly into Mrs. Roosevelt's sitting room, where she waited, grave and calm. With her was her daughter, Mrs. Anna Roosevelt Boettiger, her husband, Colonel John Boettiger, and Stephen Early. Truman knew at a glance that his premonition had been true. Mrs. Roosevelt came forward directly and put her arm on his shoulder.

"Harry, the President is dead."[9]

"This is the White House calling."

The call came into the Washington offices of the three press-wire services as the White House switchboard set up a conference call, enabling the White House to talk with all of them simultaneously.

In each office—the Associated Press, United Press, and International News Service—there was a scurry to get dictationists on the line for a White House announcement. When all three reported ready a click was heard at the other end. Then:

"This is Steve Early. I have a flash for you . . ."

INS moved it fastest, at 5:47 P.M.:

FLASH   WASHN—FDR DEAD

In seconds radio network programs were cut. "We interrupt this program to bring you a special bulletin . . ."

Within minutes a woman jumped on a Washington streetcar, fairly screaming, "Listen, President Roosevelt died!"[10] A secretary opened Acheson's door: "The president is dead!" An aide hastened to Prime Minister Winston Churchill's study at 10 Downing Street in London: "Sir, President Roosevelt died a short time ago!"

"Here, read it! Here! You never wanted to believe it. Here it is!" shouted Adolf Hitler, waving a paper. "Here we have the miracle I always predicted. Who was right? The war isn't lost. Read it! Roosevelt is dead!"[11]

"Hey, Roosevelt's dead!" a young American soldier yelled, running through the corridor of a schoolhouse in Belgium being used as a billet for troops on furlough. In one room perhaps twenty GIs sat up in the cots, astounded. "Hey, Wallace is president now," one of them said. A murmur of amazement and assent ran through the room. Suddenly an older soldier said, "No, Wallace isn't president—Senator Truman is." The others gaped at him, then turned away in scornful disbelief.[12]

The telephone rang in the modestly furnished, five-room, $120-a-month apartment at 4701 Connecticut Avenue in Washington. Margaret Truman, an undergraduate at the George Washington University in the capital, who was getting ready for a dinner date, answered.

"Hi, Dad."

"Let me speak to your mother."

"Are you coming to dinner? *I'm* going out."

"Let me speak to your mother."

"I only asked you a civil question."

"Margaret, *will you let me speak to your mother?*"

Pouting, she turned the phone over to Bess Truman and retired to her room. In a few moments her mother appeared in the doorway in tears.

"Mother, what's the matter? What is it?"

"President Roosevelt is dead."

"*Dead?*"[13]

In China Generalissimo Chiang Kai-shek retired to meditate. In Moscow Premier Joseph V. Stalin told Foreign Minister Vyacheslav M. Molotov he wished to see the American Ambassador, W. Averell Harriman, in the morning.

In Hyde Park, New York, the bells of St. James Episcopal Church began to toll for the senior warden. At the Groton School in Massachusetts students assembled to pray for the famous alumnus of the class of '00. As funereal music poured from radios, people thronged into Times Square in New York and into Lafayette Park across from the White House.

When Eleanor Roosevelt had put her hand on his shoulder and had actually spoken the "terrible thoughts," the impact on Truman was paralyzing. At first he could not speak. He had to strain to hold back tears. "The overwhelming fact that faced me was hard to grasp," he later recalled.

"Is there anything I can do for you?" he asked Mrs. Roosevelt at last.

"Is there anything *we* can do for *you?*" she countered. "For *you* are the one in trouble now."[14]

A long silence. Then the world came tumbling in on Harry Truman.

Secretary of State Edward R. Stettinius, Jr., who barely knew Truman, entered in tears. Mrs. Roosevelt wondered if she might take a government plane to Warm Springs. Truman insisted she must. Steve Early returned from his office. He and Stettinius suggested that a cabinet meeting be called at once, and Truman agreed. The White House was swirling. Reporters, photographers, members of the vice-president's staff, Roosevelt's associates, people by the score, were rushing in from all over Washington.

Chief Justice Harlan Fiske Stone was summoned at Truman's request to administer the oath of office. Truman made his way to the cabinet room. "He looked like a little man as he sat waiting in a huge leather chair," Jonathan Daniels, Roosevelt's press secretary, recalled.[15] When members of the cabinet arrived Truman spoke to them briefly. Miss Frances Perkins, the Secretary of Labor, wept. Truman sought out Stimson and requested that he, Secretary of the Navy James V.

Forrestal, and the Joint Chiefs of Staff meet with the new president the next day. He said he wished to tell them formally that he wanted the conduct of the war to proceed as theretofore.

When the chief justice arrived he asked Truman if he had brought a Bible of his own.

"Oh, no . . . you see . . . I didn't know . . ." Truman replied.[16]

Joined by Mrs. Truman and Margaret, the vice-president stood before a portrait of Woodrow Wilson. The chief justice had not had time to fetch his robe. Dressed in a blue serge suit, he administered the oath of office at 7:09 P.M. to the thirty-third president of the United States—the first from Missouri, the man who had never sought the vice-presidency in the first place.

The chief justice began by intoning, "I, Harry Shippe Truman . . ."—Shippe being a family name—but the president responded correctly, "I, Harry S Truman . . ."[17] The *S* did not stand for anything; it was his parents' compromise between giving their son a middlename chosen after that of his paternal grandfather, Anderson Shippe Truman, and his maternal grandfather, Solomon Young.

Harry Truman was the seventh vice-president to succeed to the presidency on the death of a president. He had long sensed, or feared, that he would become president at some point during the four years starting on January 20, 1945, when Roosevelt was inaugurated for a fourth term.

Even before Truman had been nominated for vice-president, he was concerned that Roosevelt's health was such that he might die in office. Several weeks later he lunched with the president on the South Lawn of the White House. Truman was much disturbed by Roosevelt's appearance. Afterward he confided to Harry Vaughan that when Roosevelt poured cream in his coffee his hand shook so that as much cream went into the saucer as the cup.[18]

That September he had taken an old friend, Edward D. McKim, to a White House reception. When they were departing, McKim bade Truman look back at the mansion.

"That's where you are going to be living," McKim said.

"I'm afraid you're right, Eddie," Truman replied, "and it scares the hell out of me."[19]

Speaking with Vaughan after the election, Truman wondered whether Roosevelt would have won, or won so decisively, if the voters had been aware of his condition.[20] The American people had been deceived about the health of the Democratic candidate for president in 1944, and Truman was one of those who had gone along with the charade. To have done otherwise, of course, would have been to have acted wildly out of line. Particularly in time of war, for him to have said publicly what he confided in private would have caused a tremendous shock; but then, so did Roosevelt's death.

Whether or not Truman had rehearsed in his own mind how he would proceed if he ever did assume the presidency, certainly his remarks to the cabinet in the tense moment before the swearing in were exactly appropriate.

He said he would be pleased if the members would retain their posts.[21] Their experience gained under Roosevelt was necessary to him during this exigency. A change in administrations inevitably brings changes in the cabinet, he continued, but he would keep an open mind about each member until they had had a chance to work together.

While there would be continuity, Truman said, he would be president in his own right and would take responsibility for all decisions. He asked the cabinet officers to give him their advice unhesitatingly. In doing so they were free to differ with him. But once he had made a decision, he expected the cabinet to support him.

He would continue the domestic policies of President Roosevelt. He intended also, he said, to continue Roosevelt's foreign policies.

So much for what Truman said. What Truman did not realize, however, because of his exclusion from Roosevelt's inner circle, was that in a number of vital areas Roosevelt's policies were either riddled with ambiguity—much of it inevitable, perhaps—or had not yet had time to ripen. Hence they would not long sustain a new president in swiftly changing circumstances. On a number of difficult problems looming before Truman—Germany, Palestine, the future role of the Japanese emperor, international control of atomic energy, a postwar economic program—Roosevelt had bequeathed no definitive policies.

The United States was facing an unprecedented situation. It was altogether different from that of 1918. The Americans were not about to pack up and come home and let the world go by. This time the country was committed to joining in enforcement of the peace. Events from Munich to Pearl Harbor had convinced the United States that the way to avert another world war was to exert its influence abroad. Hence, it was already engaged in complex international negotiations. And now, suddenly, the responsibility fell to a typical American, unprepared for the burden, unschooled in the negotiating art.

Having been excluded from all diplomacy, Truman did not even know what Roosevelt had said in the secrecy of the Teheran and Yalta conferences. He knew, of course, that Roosevelt had returned from Yalta publicly voicing high hopes for postwar accord. But he did not know to what extent these hopes had been strained before Roosevelt's death.

In fact Truman had taken office at a moment when a change was occurring in the attitude of the American people and their officials toward the Soviet Union. The good will and generosity of the darkest days of the war were gradually yielding—now that the military situation had turned around—to scrutiny and suspicion. In Congress, opinion was tightening on further aid to the Soviets under Lend-Lease, the vehicle for providing America's allies with weapons and industrial equipment. The Roosevelt administration had been stiffening in its approach to a postwar loan to Moscow. Various segments of American opinion, notably the Catholic hierarchy and citizens of Polish descent, were openly condemning Soviet interference in Eastern Europe. A new president could not have been immune to such atmospheric changes.

That the Soviet Union would cooperate with the Western nations in maintaining a workable international order had been the assumption behind Washington planning for the postwar era. But Truman did not realize the crumbly character of his inheritance. No one had informed him how fragile were the Yalta accords that underlay the overall policy he had just promised to continue, particularly on the pressing and divisive issue of the political structure of Poland—in short, the extent of Communist control.

Above all, he was unaware of how far discontinuity already had progressed in the last weeks of Roosevelt's life. Even at the height of the war, particularly when the Allies delayed their invasion of France, relations with the Soviet Union had been difficult. Then, as Germany buckled in the early months of 1945, the wartime alliance between the Soviets and the Western democracies began to totter. The stark truth confronting Truman was that efforts to arrange postwar settlements were drifting alarmingly by the night of April 12, 1945.

Two weeks after Yalta, Ambassador Harriman had protested to Molotov about the way the Allied Control Commission in Rumania was being run by the Soviet chairman. Only days then passed before the Soviet Union, by ultimatum, forced a Communist regime on that country. After that Moscow began a campaign of intrigue and intimidation to establish Communist predominance in Czechoslovakia.

On March 13 Churchill, upset over developments in Poland, sent Roosevelt a warning of "a great failure and an utter breakdown of what we settled in Yalta."[22]

On March 16 Molotov protested to Washington and London against secret Anglo-American talks with German officers in Berne, Switzerland, exploring the possibility of the surrender of German forces in Northern Italy—an affair that had, except for arousing Stalin, no practical consequences.[23]

On March 17 Roosevelt protested to Stalin that American officers were being prevented from assisting American prisoners of war, some of them ill or wounded, in Soviet-held territories.[24]

On March 22 Molotov, returning to the Berne affair, sent another note, saying that "the Soviet government sees not a misunderstanding but something worse"—meaning that the Soviets suspected the Allies were trying to make a separate peace with Germany.[25]

On March 24 Roosevelt dispatched a message to Stalin saying that the Allies would not suspend the contacts in Berne.[26]

This same day Roosevelt lunched with Mrs. Anna Rosenberg, a friend and official of the War Manpower Commission. Presently he was handed a cable. "He read it and became quite angry," Mrs. Rosenberg recounted later. "He banged his fists on the arms of his wheel chair and said, 'Averell is right; we can't do business with Stalin. He has broken every one of the promises he made at Yalta.' He was very upset and continued in the same vein on the subject."[27]

At about this time Roosevelt learned with dismay that Molotov would not be sent to the United Nations conference in San Francisco. On March 24 he appealed to Stalin to send him, lest Molotov's absence appear a Soviet protest or dissent.[28] Stalin replied March 27 that other business would keep Molotov in Moscow in April, a worrisome development for FDR, who had aroused high hopes for the United Nations among the American people.[29]

On March 29 Stalin, answering Roosevelt's message of the twenty-fourth about the Berne affair, suggested that these talks had enabled the Germans to shift troops from Italy to the eastern front and added: "This circumstance is irritating to the Soviet command and creates grounds for distrust."[30]

On April 1 Roosevelt cabled Stalin: "I cannot conceal from you the concern with which I view the developments of events of mutual interest since our fruitful meeting at Yalta. So far there has been a discouraging lack of progress made in the carrying out, which the world expects, of the political decisions we reached at the conferences, particularly those relating to the Polish question. I am frankly puzzled as to why this should be and must tell you that I do not fully understand in many respects the apparent indifferent attitude of your Government."[31]

On April 2 Secretary Forrestal noted in his diary after a State-War-Navy meeting: "The Secretary of State advised of serious deterioration in our relations with Russia."[32]

On April 3 Stalin wrote Roosevelt saying that some of the president's advisers must have been ill-informed about Berne. Then this taunt: "I understand that there are certain advantages for the Anglo-American troops as a result of these separate negotiations in Berne or in some other place since the Anglo-American troops get the possibility to advance into the heart of Germany almost without any resistance on the part of the Germans."[33]

"Roosevelt was furious," Charles E. Bohlen, an American diplomat, recalled. "It was one of the few times that I saw him angry. He was seated at his desk at the White House, his eyes flashing, his face flushed, outraged that he should be accused of dealing with the Germans behind Stalin's back."[34]

On April 4 Harriman notified Stettinius (in paraphrase): "We now have ample proof that the Soviet government views all matters from the standpoint of their own selfish interests. . . . We must clearly recognize that the Soviet program is the establishment of totalitarianism, ending personal liberty and democracy."[35]

The same day Roosevelt, still angered by Stalin's intimations of Allied bad faith at Berne, replied to him: "Frankly, I cannot avoid a feeling of bitter resentment toward your informers, whoever they are, for such vile misrepresentations of my actions or those of my trusted subordinates."[36]

The next day Churchill cabled Roosevelt: "I am astounded that Stalin should have addressed to you a message so insulting to the honour of the United States and also of Great Britain."[37]

Twenty-four hours later—less than one week before his death—Roosevelt answered: "I am in general agreement with your opinion expressed in 934, and I am pleased with your very clear strong message to Stalin No. 935. We must not permit anybody to entertain a false impression that we are afraid. Our Armies will in a very few days be in a position that will permit us to become 'tougher' than has heretofore appeared advantageous to the war effort."[38]

On April 6 Harriman sent another message to Stettinius saying that Stalin was trying to create a security ring around the Soviet Union through control of the bordering states. Whenever the United States resisted, Harriman said, the Soviet Union would retaliate, as they had by refusing to send Molotov to San Francisco. Harriman suggested in effect a hardening of the American attitude.[39]

On April 7 Stalin rebuffed Roosevelt's letter of the fifth protesting "vile misrepresentations" about Berne. Stalin said: "It is difficult to agree that lack of resistance on the part of the Germans on the Western Front can be explained only that they have been defeated. . . . Don't you agree that such a behavior of the Germans is more than strange and incomprehensible.''[40]

The same day Stalin also sent Roosevelt another message: "Matters on the Polish question have really reached a dead end.''[41]

On April 11, the day before Roosevelt's death, Harriman cabled the State Department deprecating a Soviet request for a $6 billion loan and suggesting that "it certainly should be borne in mind that our basic interests might better be served by increasing our trade with other parts of the world rather than giving preference to the Soviet Union as a source of supply.''[42]

The statements cited in some of these messages represented their harder edge. The exchanges did not yet preclude conciliation. While Roosevelt may have blurted that he could not do business with Stalin, he continued to the end trying to do business with him. Nevertheless the tenor of the exchanges was evidence of, and contributory to, rapidly growing mistrust. They were handed to Truman to ponder in an atmosphere already heavily charged with suspicion about Soviet motives. The exchanges constituted an important part of his introduction to the state of the foreign relations he had inherited.

While the cabinet was still present, Early stepped in and told Truman that the reporters were asking whether the United Nations conference would convene as scheduled on April 25. In his first decision as president he authorized Stettinius to announce that it would. It was an obvious decision and not a particularly difficult one for Truman. He had believed in the League of Nations, had been convinced that the unwillingness of the United States to join it had contributed to the onset of the Second World War and had striven in the Senate to commit the United States to membership in the United Nations.

When the excitement at the White House finally quieted that evening, Truman would have been justified in feeling that he had had about enough for one day. On the contrary, however, a most momentous piece of intelligence still awaited him, though it was broached by Stimson so circumspectly that the implications were not immediately clear. The secretary of war informed the president that the Pasco project they had once discussed involved the development of a new explosive of incredible power. For the moment he left it at that, and Truman was merely puzzled.[43]

Afterward Stimson wrote in his diary for that day: "The new President on the whole made a pleasant impression, but it was very clear that he knew very little of the task into which he was stepping and he showed some vacillation on minor matters . . . as if he might be lacking in force. I hope not.''[44]

Stettinius asked Attorney General Francis Biddle and Secretary Forrestal if Truman's accession meant another Harding administration.[45]

Former Vice-President John Nance Garner wrote to a friend, "Truman is honest and patriotic and has a head full of good horse sense. Besides, he had guts. All of this can be made into a good President.''[46]

"Truman will not make a great, flashy President like Roosevelt," Rayburn said. "But, by God, he'll make a good President, a sound President. He's got the stuff in him.''[47]

"Truman has no background for the job," Secretary of the Interior Harold L.

Ickes wrote in his diary, "but I have never doubted his sincerity and conscientiousness. He is vigorous physically and mentally even if he doesn't have great depth mentally."[48]

Senator Arthur H. Vandenberg of Michigan wrote in his diary: "The gravest question-mark in every American heart is Truman. Can he swing the job? Despite his limited capacities, I think he can."[49]

David E. Lilienthal, chairman of the Tennessee Valley Authority, wrote in *his* diary: "Complete unbelief. That was first. Then a sick, hapless feeling. Then consternation at the thought of that Throttlebottom, Truman. 'The country and the world doesn't deserve to be left this way, with Truman at the head of the country at such a time.' "[50]

But in Missouri the president's ninety-two-year-old mother, Martha Ellen Truman, said, "Harry will get along."[51]

After Stimson had left, Truman wearily put in a call to his friend, McKim, who was in town, staying at the Statler. That noon—long ago as it must have seemed now—Truman had seen him at lunch and had suggested that they have a poker game that night in McKim's hotel room.

Wartime shortages had left McKim without any liquor, so Truman told him to drop by his office in the Senate Office Building and pick up some Scotch given to him by James Crowell, United States ambassador to Canada, and a case of bourbon, a gift (as McKim recalled) from Bernard Baruch.

Everything was still in readiness for a game when McKim answered the phone.

"I guess the party's off," the new president of the United States said. "They've got me fenced in out here."[52]

2. *Honeymoon for the "Missouri Gang"*

I'M NOT BIG ENOUGH. I'm not big enough for this job," Truman groaned, fairly clinging to his friend, Senator George D. Aiken of Vermont.[1]

It was the next day, Friday, April 13, and Truman was still staggered at the thought of being president in place of Franklin D. Roosevelt.

Soon after the puzzling talk the night before with Stimson he had left the White House in what struck Vaughan as a panicky mood.[2] When he reached the apartment Margaret Truman found him stunned, practically in a state of shock.[3]

After munching some food for the first time in hours, he talked with his mother on the phone and then called perhaps his best friend, John W. Snyder, vice-president of the First National Bank of St. Louis, who was visiting Mexico City. "I feel like I have been struck by a bolt of lightning," he said, sounding to Snyder like a man in need of help.[4] Truman asked him to come to Washington at once and appointed him Federal Loan Administrator.

When Truman was leaving the apartment for his first day on the new job, he spotted a reporter he knew, Tony Vaccaro, of the Associated Press, and gave him a lift to the White House. "I just want the folks I love to know," he said, "that if we can't get together in the old informal way, it is not of my choosing. Tell them that, will you? You know, if I could have my way I'd have them all come in without knocking. You know how it will be. My schedule will be busy every day."

Overnight F.D.R.'s famous knickknacks had been removed from the presidential desk, leaving it bare for his successor. When Truman entered the Oval Room* he sat down in Roosevelt's chair, squirming around to get accustomed to it. He rolled it to and fro, leaned back and then pushed forward with a sigh to the desk.[5]

Forthwith a stack of reports and correspondence was brought in by Fleet Admiral William D. Leahy, who had been chief of staff to the commander in chief under Roosevelt and was retained in that post by Truman. When Leahy that first morning placed papers, teeming with problems, on the president's desk, it struck him that the stack looked bigger than Truman sitting in the chair.

The country was unprepared for the sudden transfer of power in the White House, and people found it awkward even to *say* "President Truman." It was so difficult to disassociate the presidency from Roosevelt that when Truman telephoned former Secretary of Commerce Jesse H. Jones to tell him that "the president" had appointed his friend, Snyder, as Federal Loan Administrator, Jones asked, "Did he make that appointment before he died?" "No," Truman said, "he made it just now."[6]

* Now called the Oval Office.

Among the millions of American servicemen around the globe most were too young to remember any president but Roosevelt. He had been in the White House so long that he and the presidency were almost synonymous, not only to soldiers and sailors but to millions of their countrymen. After his urbane and even princely presence it was hard for people to visualize anyone else as president, let alone an obscure, prosaic politician from a small town in Missouri, who had no national following of any kind, no advisers of note, no familiar voice on radio, no program of his own and no popular mandate beyond the 1944 Democratic platform on which Roosevelt and he had run.

From the first Truman was worried about the reaction of the people and the armed forces to Roosevelt's death and his own succession. On Capitol Hill he had sensed the political tensions caused by war and abnormal conditions at home. He knew the importance of Roosevelt's personal power and prestige in maintaining equilibrium, and he was anxious about the effect Roosevelt's death might have on the prosecution of the war and the maintenance of controls and production.[7]

What he was told on this first morning did not lighten his worries. At his meeting with Stimson, Forrestal, and the Joint Chiefs, the military estimates given him were that the war with Germany would last for another six months and the war with Japan for another year and a half.[8]

"He made the impression on me," Stimson noted in his diary afterward, "of a man who is willing and anxious to learn and to do his best but who was necessarily laboring with the terrific handicap of coming into such an office where the threads of information were so multitudinous that only long previous familiarity could allow him to control them."

Stimson and General of the Army George C. Marshall, army chief of staff, discussed Truman while riding back to the Pentagon together.

"We shall not know what he is really like until the pressure begins to be felt," Marshall said.[9]

In these first hours of his presidency Truman kept telling friends that the people would have to rally behind him for the good of the country. It was before the days when a president could appear before millions on television, and Truman's natural instinct led him back to Congress for signs of support.

On this very first day in office he decided to go to Capitol Hill for lunch. He and the secretary of the Senate, Leslie L. Biffle, carefully drew up a list of seventeen of the leading senators and representatives of both parties, whose cooperation would be important to Truman in the future. His visit shattered all tradition, as Vandenberg was to note approvingly in his diary.

"But it was both wise and smart," Vandenberg observed. "It means that the days of executive contempt for Congress are ended; that we are returning to a government in which Congress will take its rightful place."

Surely this was the reaction Truman hoped for. He went even farther out of his way to court Vandenberg by having Vaughan take the influential Republican senator, ranking minority member of the Senate Foreign Relations Committee, the last box of cigars left in the old vice-presidential office.[10] He also took the unusual step of inviting Senator Kenneth D. McKellar, Democrat, of Tennessee, to sit with the cabinet in his capacity as president *pro tempore* of the Senate.

Although the pressures of the presidency were to alter his thinking soon enough, Truman entered the White House with a senatorial view of relations between the president and the Congress. As Richard E. Neustadt has said, "Truman never did like White House meddling in legislative *tactics* . . ."[11] For ten years Truman had seen and often felt the annoying effects of Roosevelt's prying and pressure, and Vandenberg was right in assuming that he intended to reestablish a more traditional relationship between the executive and legislative branches in hope of minimizing friction.

At the luncheon Truman was ill at ease. Still, his first meeting as president with Congressional leaders, many of them his old friends, was cordial, and nothing about it could possibly have foretold the long, frustrating ordeal that lay ahead of him in Congress. It was while he was on the Hill that he saw Aiken and humbly poured out his fears about his inadequacies. When he was leaving, he encountered a group of reporters and told them, "Boys, if you ever pray, pray for me now. I don't know whether you fellows ever had a load of hay fall on you, but when they told me yesterday what had happened, I felt like the moon, the stars and all the planets had fallen on me. I've got the most terribly responsible job a man ever had."[12]

"What a test of democracy if it works!" wrote one of his callers that day, Roy A. Roberts, managing editor of the *Kansas City Star*.[13]

Later Truman met with James Byrnes in the White House and on this first day moved toward a decision that was logical enough in the circumstances. He told Byrnes, according to Truman's memoirs, that he was considering nominating him as secretary of state, succeeding Stettinius, a minor figure in the Roosevelt administration. The actual offer of the post was made three days later, and Byrnes accepted. Because Stettinius was to head the United States delegation to the United Nations, however, Truman deferred any announcement of the change in order not to undermine Stettinius's authority at San Francisco.

Except for a minor role at Yalta, Byrnes had not had much more experience in foreign relations than Truman. His great popularity on Capitol Hill, however, seemed important to the new president. Byrnes was distinctly the Senate's preference for secretary of state. When the peace treaties and the United Nations Charter came along he could be helpful getting them through the Senate. As soon became apparent, Truman's choices for his cabinet leaned heavily toward men whom he supposed—often erroneously—could help him in Congress.

Another consideration in Byrnes's favor was that the law then designated the secretary of state as first in line of succession to the presidency after the vice-president. With Truman in the White House there was no vice-president. Hence the secretary of state would succeed him if he were to die. Truman said Stettinius did not represent either his or Roosevelt's political outlook.[14]

Furthermore, being a party man par excellence, he felt that Byrnes's long service to the Democratic party and his hurt at being sidetracked in favor of Truman for the vice-presidency argued for a major role for him in the new administration. Finally, since Truman had no staff of his own choosing qualified to deal with policy, he did desperately need help and advice in domestic as well as foreign affairs. Byrnes knew the workings of the executive branch much better than he, and Truman reached for his support.

"There was a general feeling," Ickes noted in his diary April 29, well before the appointment was announced, "that Jimmy was willing to take over and tell Truman how to run his job."[15]

On Saturday, April 14, a brief funeral service for Roosevelt was held in the White House.

"When President Truman came into the East Room," wrote Robert E. Sherwood, one of Roosevelt's speech writers, "nobody stood up, and I'm sure this modest man did not even notice this discourtesy or, if he did, understood that the people present could not yet associate him with his high office; all they could think of was that the President was dead. But everybody stood up when Mrs. Roosevelt came in."[16]

The next day Roosevelt was buried with simple ceremonies in the garden by his house in Hyde Park. Muffled drums . . . a volley of shots fired by West Point cadets . . . an elderly rector intoning, "Now the laborer's task is o'er" . . . then taps. As the coffin was being lowered into the grave, Merriman Smith of the United Press glanced over a bank of flowers and scanned Truman's face. He seemed, Smith wrote afterward, "tired and a little uneasy. He stared down at the lowering casket through his heavy glasses. A bright sun made his hair seem whiter than it actually was, and his wife and daughter by him looked uncomfortable and sad."[17]

Truman's feelings about Roosevelt oscillated. He had felt hurt at Roosevelt's slights in his early years in the Senate, yet he was proud to run on the same ticket with him in 1944. Now that Truman was president he resented Roosevelt's having excluded him from foreign affairs because it made his own task in the White House infinitely more difficult. "They didn't tell me anything about what was going on," he complained to Henry Wallace in May.[18] Even in his private notes the dichotomy persisted. Sometimes, as in notes he made in 1946, he would refer to Roosevelt privately as "that great humanitarian and world leader."[19] On the other hand, in 1948 he grouchily jotted on his calendar one day: "I don't believe the USA wants any more fakers—Teddy and Franklin are enough."[20] Nevertheless Truman admired Roosevelt as a political leader and readily espoused his causes.

On April 16 President Truman appeared for the first time before a joint session of Congress. George E. Allen, business man, man-about-town, secretary of the Democratic National Committee and friend of Roosevelt's and Truman's, had begun drafting the speech on the funeral train with the help of an associate.[21] Later Byrnes, Snyder, and Early added their ideas. When Truman ascended the rostrum he received such a rousing reception that, excitedly, he began to speak at once.

"Just a minute," rasped Speaker Rayburn, his voice audible on radio. "Let me present you, will you, Harry?"

With that formality out of the way, Truman said in his speech that there would be no relaxation in the efforts made under the New Deal "to improve the lot of the common people."[22]

He also promised there would be no drawing back from Roosevelt's military goal: "Our demand has been—and it *remains*—unconditional surrender!"

During the drafting of the speech someone had argued that unconditional surrender should now be abandoned because it played into the hands of German propaganda and, by hardening German resistance, prolonged the war.[23] Determined to follow Roosevelt's policy, Truman rejected the suggestion. And Congress proved to be in a mood for unconditional surrender; his pledge brought an ovation. With the Reich already being crushed from East and West, Truman's commitment was academic in the case of Germany. With respect to Japan, where the course of the war might conceivably have been altered by negotiation, it was a more significant decision.

Back in his office after the address Truman received British Foreign Minister Anthony Eden and Lord Halifax. Eden later cabled Churchill: ". . . my impression from the interview is that the new President is honest and friendly. He is conscious of but not overwhelmed by his new responsibilities. His references to you could not have been warmer. I believe we shall have in him a loyal collaborator, and I am much heartened by this first conversation."[24]

And Halifax cabled Churchill: "It may be of interest that Truman's hobby is history of military strategy, of which he is reported to have read widely. He certainly betrayed a surprising knowledge of Hannibal's campaigns one night here."[25]

That evening the Trumans moved from their apartment to Blair House, diagonally across Pennsylvania Avenue from the White House, to stay until Mrs. Roosevelt was able to pack.

"Good luck, Harry," a cab driver called to him as he was walking over to the White House one morning. The traditional honeymoon was on. On April 12 Truman had been a blank to some millions of people and an ominous question mark to others; now as the shock of Roosevelt's death passed, he was being showered with popularity.

Friends and office-seekers soon swarmed to the White House. "ALL MISSOURI'S HERE TO SEE HARRY," said a headline in the *Washington Daily News*. *Newsweek* reported that as one caller would depart, Truman would stick his head out the door and inquire, "Who's next in line? Bring him in." He worried about seeming "high-hat" to old friends. When it was impossible for him to see any of them, they were routed to Vaughan for apologies.[26]

The *New York Times* reported that Washington's reaction to Truman's first thirty days in office was good.

To be sure, many veteran New Dealers did not think much of him and some of them never would. To them nobody was worthy to succeed Roosevelt. The sudden appearance of Truman and his assistants was resented by some of the Roosevelt staff. "I just can't call that man President," Grace Tully, one of Roosevelt's secretaries, told Wallace.[27] Curiously, however, the contrast with Roosevelt put Truman in a pleasing light with many Americans in the early days of his presidency. By 1945 there were more than a few who found Roosevelt's grand style tiresome. The humbleness and folksy air of Truman and his family had a fresh appeal. His midwestern, small-town background was a novelty after Hyde Park. People warmed to Truman's simplicity and gregariousness. He had an endearing naturalness about him.

Rayburn cautioned him that people seeking favors "will say you're the greatest man who ever lived in order to make time with you. And you know and I know that it just ain't so.''[28] In the long run, of course, such counsel rarely prevails against the presidency. Exalting them, setting them apart, magnifying their strengths and weaknesses, leading them into different poses, the office affects most men who hold it. It was to affect Truman, however gradually. Three years were to elapse, for example, before anyone would dream of referring to him as ''Give-'em-hell Harry.'' Such a posture was utterly foreign to the modesty of his early period in office.

On succeeding Roosevelt he assumed no new airs.

''It was a wonderful relief to preceding conferences with our former Chief to see the promptness and snappiness with which Truman took up each matter and decided it,'' Stimson wrote in his diary on April 18. ''There were no long-drawn-out 'soliloquies' from the President and the whole conference was thoroughly businesslike so that we actually covered two or three more matters than we had expected to discuss.''

''When I saw him today,'' Under Secretary of State Joseph C. Grew wrote May 2, ''I had fourteen problems to take up with him and got through them in less than fifteen minutes with a clear directive on every one of them. You can imagine what a joy it is to deal with a man like that.''[29]

Another contrast with Roosevelt, whose legs were partially paralyzed by polio, was mentioned by Budget Director Harold D. Smith in his personal notes. After conferring with Truman for the first time on April 18 Smith, a holdover from the Roosevelt administration, observed: ''When I entered the President's office he was standing by the window looking out, but he quickly turned to come over and shake hands with me. This was a startling contrast to seeing President Roosevelt, who could not move from his chair.''[30]

Truman was up every day at dawn, as befitted the first president since Ulysses S. Grant who had worked part of his adult life as a dirt farmer. ''I have the reveille habit,'' he once explained.[31] After dressing without the services of a valet, he breezed outdoors before breakfast, cane in hand, and, accompanied by a Secret Service man, stepped along at a military gait of 120 paces a minute, heading for Dupont Circle or the Washington Monument or for some window-shopping on F Street. He delighted in waving to other surprised early risers and telling anyone who asked that he felt ''fine and dandy.'' One morning he stopped and shook hands with a street cleaner in Madison Place and complimented him on his tidiness.

From morning to night the president was filled with so much vim that Acheson was moved to write later: ''Some remote ancestor . . . bequeathed him the priceless gift of vitality, the lifeforce itself that within certain strains bubbles up through the generations, endowing selected persons with tireless energy. Mr. Truman could work, reading and absorbing endless papers, and at times play, until well past midnight and be up at six o'clock. . . . He slept, so he told us, as soon as his head touched the pillow, never worrying because he could not stay awake long enough to do so.''[32]

With the plain, straightforward man from 219 North Delaware Street, Independence, Missouri, in the White House, old hatreds kindled by Roosevelt began to subside. A certain tension went out of the political atmosphere. By mid-May thousands of friendly letters had flowed into the White House. ''I know of no better way

to communicate to you my profound good wishes for your Presidency,'' wrote
Henry R. Luce, editor-in-chief of *Time*, ''than to tell you of the confidence which,
among themselves, a great number of your fellow citizens already feel in your character and ability.''[33]

A Gallup poll showed that seven of every ten voters, Republicans and Democrats, approved of what the president was doing. His rating in the poll rose to 87
percent, three points higher than ever had been recorded for Roosevelt.[34] The *Nation* commented that Truman's decisiveness had had ''a wonderfully tonic effect
upon the whole government hierarchy.''

Almost everything the president did in these early weeks produced a favorable
reaction. His first press conference, for example, was no work of art; it was all
right. But Arthur Krock of the *New York Times*, who was then one of the reigning
pundits in Washington, gave it high praise. He reported that Truman was not afraid,
that in fact he had electrified the reporters and demonstrated that he was president
and meant to be. *Newsweek* chimed in: ''Overnight respect for him mounted.''

Truman was profiting from perhaps the overanxiety created by Roosevelt's
death. People were agreeably surprised that he knew how to go about being president.

More to the point, the war was going well and domestic issues were sidelined
momentarily, so that Truman had not yet had occasion to propose legislation on
major questions that had embroiled Roosevelt in controversy.

Informality notwithstanding, Truman had a pronounced sense of orderliness.
His characteristic view from the Senate was that Roosevelt had been a poor administrator, which was true only in a narrow sense. And as most presidents do on taking
office, Truman set about to draw firmer lines of organization in the executive branch
and revise procedures for making decisions.

He was not Roosevelt. Roosevelt had certain political skills in the manipula-
tion of men and use of presidential power that Truman could never match. Truman
went at things more directly, less subtly. Roosevelt's caginess about decisions was
foreign to Truman, who itched to make them on the spot, if possible. Roosevelt's
creative sense of seeking ideas and strength through deliberately fostered confusion,
conflict and personal rivalry in the White House struck Truman as incomprehensible. Truman was straightforward, not devious.

He elected to revive the cabinet from the doldrums of the Roosevelt administration. In contrast to Roosevelt's manner of personal decision making in informal
discussions with senior officials Truman preferred to work with the cabinet as a
body. Consequently the departments more consistently participated in the making of
presidential decisions under Truman than they had under Roosevelt. ''I am very
anxious,'' Truman wrote that summer, ''to get things set up as soon as we can so
that the Executive Branch of the Government can be operated through the Cabinet.''[35]

Truman was one of the last of the presidents, Dwight D. Eisenhower being the
other, to use the cabinet in the old American style as a body that met regularly—
Truman held weekly cabinet luncheons as well as the formal cabinet meetings—to
air views, offer advice and give shape to presidential decisions. The final voice on
policy, of course, was Truman's, as he gave his cabinet to understand in an anec-

dote he related May 18: a discussion of the impending Emancipation Proclamation was held in Abraham Lincoln's cabinet. When a vote was taken on whether to issue the proclamation, the cabinet voted no. Lincoln said he voted Aye, and the proclamation would therefore be issued.[36]

Several weeks after taking office Truman told the budget director that Roosevelt had not been able to keep track of his department heads during the last couple of years.[37] They were always quarreling and spreading stories about each other, Truman complained. He said he was going to end that kind of backbiting. Apropos no particular incident, he gave the cabinet a hard-boiled lecture May 4 about keeping interdepartmental differences out of the newspapers.[38] In fact the Truman cabinet became an arena of some drastic personal conflicts. In the stormy years ahead, twenty-four different men served in it.[39]

Truman told Budget Director Harold D. Smith he was going to give the department heads full responsibility in the interests of orderly procedure. If they did not discharge it properly, he would discharge them. It became his practice, with mixed results, to put a man in a cabinet post and then let him run his own department with a minimum of interference from the White House and with assurance of presidential support.

As a result of the depression and the war the office Truman inherited from Roosevelt was a far larger institution than had existed until the end of the 1930s. The Reorganization Act of 1939 had established the extended Executive Office of the President with its administrative assistants and powerful arms of the presidency, including the Bureau of the Budget, the Office of Emergency Management, and the Office of War Mobilization and Reconversion.

And as the dimensions of the office had expanded, the responsibilities had mushroomed. The depression and the war had thrown entire new burdens on the federal government, with a proliferation of agencies to handle them. After 1940 foreign affairs and defense took priority over domestic problems. Radio was already an immensely influential tool of the office, and television was on the way. As Roosevelt's successor, Truman was a pioneer of the powerful modern presidency we have come to know in the second half of the twentieth century.

In Truman's time the government departments still played a much more important role in initiating programs and dealing with Congress than has been the case in later years. The government was then less centralized in the White House. Often cabinet officers who headed these departments were figures of greater stature than their more recent successors and were Truman's principal advisers on policy. The White House staff served him more than it tried to orchestrate government activities. It did not decide which options Truman should consider. He usually made the choice among alternatives after listening to the arguments directly.

Truman's own White House staff (as distinct from the staffs of the other new arms of the Executive Office of the President) never exceeded 13, a fraction, for example, of President Ford's staff of 550 in 1975.[40] These were the men who arranged his schedule, dealt with the press, guarded his signature, drafted his speeches. They had ready access to him. Truman was anything but an isolated president. As Neustadt has recalled, Truman was his own chief of staff. He chaired the morning staff meeting in his office, parceled out assignments, gave directions, discussed the concerns of the different members, and watched the White House budget.[41]

In his first years, however, he had a largely mediocre staff and on many questions did not get the kind of advice he needed. Furthermore he was slow to develop the knack of using a staff well. Snyder, who was in a good position to know, said afterward that, especially in the hectic early months, Truman drew upon the rudimentary principles of administration he had learned at reserve army summer camps in the twenties and thirties.[42]

After Truman had been in office a few weeks a joke went around about two politicians discussing an issue. One shook his head and said, "I'm from Missouri," to which the other retorted, "Who the hell isn't, now?"

Snyder and Vaughan, who had been with Truman through his ups and downs, were the vanguard of the "Missouri Gang," the Truman "cronies" to whom the joke alluded.

One day in April Truman, Vaughan, and Snyder lunched together. As Snyder was to recall, "This was quite a reunion from old Fort Riley days during the 'Twenties and 'Thirties when, as colonels, Truman commanded the 379th Field Artillery Regiment, Vaughan the 380th and I the 381st for two weeks each summer."[43]

During the First World War Truman and Vaughan, young lieutenants, first met at Camp Doniphan, Oklahoma, in 1918. Truman and Snyder met at reserve officers' summer training at Fort Riley, Kansas, in 1928, when Snyder was cashier of the First National Bank of Blytheville in his native Arkansas. They attended summer camp together for the next dozen years, in the course of which Snyder moved to St. Louis and the Truman and Snyder families became good friends.

Another Missouri recruit in the White House was Charles G. Ross, who had gone through school with Harry and Bess in Independence, after which he had entered newspaper work, won a Pulitzer Prize for articles in the *St. Louis Post-Dispatch* on the depression and was in 1945 that newspaper's respected Washington bureau chief. With hometown fanfare Truman chose him as presidential press secretary shortly after taking office.

The results of the appointment were mixed. A lovable, sad-faced man, Ross, approaching sixty, was rather well along in years for such a strenuous job and accepted it reluctantly. Moreover, Truman burdened him with other chores too. Ross presided over a weak press office. He made little effort to coordinate the release of news throughout the government and seemed to have no particular scheme for legitimately presenting Truman and his policies in the best light. To reporters, he seemed rather lackadaisical about detail. And certainly, as time passed, he was unable to rescue Truman from a bad press much of the time, although circumstances were against him on this score.

On the other hand, he exerted a good influence on Truman on the side of dignity, liberalism, and good sense. And he played the news straight. He made his share of blunders, but to his honor no "credibility gap" developed under Charlie Ross.

Truman had fewer Missourians around him than Kennedy would have Bostonians, Johnson Texans, Nixon Californians, or Carter Georgians. In rank, Snyder rose highest. Most of the leading figures in the Truman administration came from other states, and many of them were promoted by the president from within their own departments. His Missouri friends, for the most part, held rather minor and confidential positions, but positions of influence nevertheless, positions from which favors could be granted or denied. Mostly, these were men who, because of the origins of the Truman administration, had never demonstrated, or had a chance to demonstrate, competence in high political affairs.

Schooled in machine politics, Truman craved loyalty and personal devotion in men around him in his trying circumstances. As a result he trapped himself with some poor appointments, haphazardly made.

Occasionally the hit-or-miss approach produced an outstanding staff man, as in the case of Clark M. Clifford, whose appearance evolved out of the resignation of Roosevelt's naval aide shortly after the new administration took office. Truman had had his fill of some of the brass around Roosevelt. He himself had come into the military service through the National Guard. His new military aide, Vaughan, was a reserve officer, to the everlasting annoyance of the Pentagon. In seeking a naval aide, Truman decided to pass over regular navy officers.

Out of the thousands of reserve officers he hit upon James K. Vardaman, Jr., who was, needless to say, a friend of his, Vaughan's, and Snyder's from Fort Riley days, and who also had helped out in one of Truman's Senate campaigns. In civilian life he had been a banker in St. Louis, and his attorney was Clark Clifford. Back from Okinawa after Truman had sent for him, Vardaman ran into Clifford in San Francisco, and when he needed an assistant in the White House that summer he chose Clifford, who was also on wartime navy duty. It was to be a year, however, before Clifford emerged as a top member of the White House staff.

While assembling his staff and struggling with the reins of office, Truman plunged from one thing to another with little hesitation. His decisiveness was surprising, even perplexing. "You could go into his office with a question and come out with a decision from him more swiftly than from any man I have ever known," Harriman recalled.[44]

Some of those who worked most closely with him thought his hastiness of decision was more pronounced in the early years of his presidency, when the pressure of events was enormous. In later years, they felt, he became more deliberate.[45] Being thrown into office as the successor to one of the foremost political figures of the age was a trial. In fact in his first term he had a portrait of Roosevelt in his office, and sometimes when he pondered a decision, he would glance at it and ask whoever happened to be with him, "Would he think this is the right thing?" [46]

No doubt Herbert Feis, a leading historian of that period, was right when he suggested that in the first, tense years Truman equated rapidity of decision with firmness. "His assurance was perhaps at times a subconscious cover for insecurity," Feis observed.[47]

After a talk with Truman April 27 Wallace noted in his diary: "It almost seemed as though he was eager to decide in advance of thinking."[48]

Some of the hard experience that lay ahead taught Truman the dangers of hasty decisions. He managed to place restraints upon himself, though without ever quite conquering the tendency of shooting from the hip, as Sam Rayburn used to say.

It was both his strength and his weakness that he had a simple view of right and wrong. It was a source of strength that he was able to view complex problems in simple terms. "I think this was the secret of Harry Truman," said Abe Fortas, who was in and out of government in those years before becoming a member of the Supreme Court.[49] It was partly a strong sense of what was right and what was wrong that made Truman decisive and emphatic—and, in no small measure, didactic.

Not infrequently Truman's problem was that he could be headstrong as well as decisive. Impulsiveness sometimes drove him into blunders and indiscretions. At times he sloughed off worry so easily it appeared to be a symptom of superficiality. But at other times, such as on the issues of a Jewish state in Palestine and postwar reconversion, he was tormented. Grave problems weighed on him, yet the agony of decision seldom seemed to linger.

If black and white came through to Truman clearly, nuances were not his cup of tea. He liked to look at a problem in concrete terms of action and to be able to ask, as Neustadt recalled, "What am I supposed to do about this?" He was less comfortable grappling with a problem in the abstract.[50]

At the moment plenty of concrete problems were at hand. Fortunately, too, he had recovered from the daze of taking office.

3. *Pro–New Deal; Anti–New Dealer*

TRUMAN HAD COME TO the White House as a practical, not an ordained New Dealer. In the Senate he had been a vote for the New Deal, not a voice, and certainly not an ideological voice. His primary allegiance, as Alonzo L. Hamby, the historian, has remarked, was to the party, not to an ideology.[1]

In his years in Washington he had not hung out with men like David Lilienthal, Henry Morgenthau, Jr., Chester Bowles, Leon Henderson, William O. Douglas, and other doctrinaire New Dealers. Most of his warmest friends in Congress were men of both parties who took a rather detached view of Roosevelt and his programs. Those he felt most at home with were pragmatic middle-of-the-road politicians.

Necessity had forced Truman to work as a farmer, but he had aspired to succeed in business. His outlook was more that of a middlewestern small-business-man than of a farmer. Though as president he often rejected their advice, he was quite comfortable with conservatives who upheld the role of business in American society. A number of his appointments reflected this, to the dismay of some New Dealers, even though in the Roosevelt administration antagonism toward business had waned during the war.

Truman liked the New Deal better than the New Dealers. He was put off by their style rather than their principles. "He seemed to have some distaste for persons who flaunted their liberalism," said Charles S. Murphy, a leading member of Truman's staff.[2] It was not that Truman felt the kind of inferiority toward Ivy League graduates that Lyndon Johnson manifested later. In fact Truman was not awed by their opinions and never would have dreamed of installing an intellectual-in-residence in the White House for display. But many of the Roosevelt crowd were different from Truman in background, wealth, education and social position. An outstanding liberal, David Lilienthal, a member of the Roosevelt and Truman administrations and—once he had recovered from the shock of Roosevelt's death—a staunch admirer of Truman, observed that the new president reacted against the vocabulary of the early New Deal intellectuals.

Lilienthal noted that Truman "came out of the Middle West kind of progressivism, a kind of twentieth-century version of Populism—against Wall Street, the railroads, Big Business, etc., and hence he used the words and ideas of Teddy Roosevelt, Norris, Bryan, the elder LaFollette, and could not communicate with the more recent progressives and with their great emphasis on language that seemed to him highfalutin and crackpot."[3]

A program of a character that his contemporaries called "liberal" Truman preferred to call "forward-looking."[4]

Lilienthal was a liberal in a good position to judge the difference between Truman's sarcasm and his actions. Lilienthal's term as chairman of the Tennessee Valley Authority was due to expire soon after Truman took office. The powerful, disagreeable, bulbous-nosed, squinting Senator Kenneth McKellar of Tennessee had for months been inveighing against Lilienthal's renomination. McKellar personally demanded of Truman that he not choose Lilienthal again and promised the worst Senate fight in twenty years if he did. McKellar was outraged by Lilienthal's refusal to place a dam in Tennessee where the senator thought it should be placed and to use TVA employment rolls for patronage. Such was McKellar's influence that Jonathan Daniels says in his memoirs that for fear of jeopardizing Senate consent to postwar treaties, Roosevelt had decided to nominate a different TVA chairman when Lilienthal's term expired.[5] Lilienthal realized that it would be difficult for the new president to get into a battle straight off. He understood that Truman could court Southern conservatives by nominating someone else. One day, however, Truman called Lilienthal to the White House and informed him that he was renominating him.[6] Despite McKellar's fulminations, the Senate confirmed the nomination.

Along with Truman's progressive outlook, he possessed, as Roy Roberts, a long-time acquaintance, wrote after he became president, "the innate, instinctive conservatism, in action, of the Missouri-bred countryman."[7] Even so, Truman stood in the tradition of Wilson and Roosevelt, but not at that time on its left flank. If he had, he would not have been nominated for vice-president. He knew that most of the leading New Dealers had not been for him as Roosevelt's running mate in 1944. In his diary of May 22, 1945, he did praise Roosevelt's confidential aide, Harry L. Hopkins, as an "advanced 'Liberal,' " but gave thanks that he was ". . . not a professional one (I consider the latter a low form of politician)."[8] He complained to Clark Clifford that Roosevelt had been surrounded by figures from the "lunatic fringe." "The American people have been through a lot of experiments and they want a rest from experiments," he added.[9]

Her father "had a very poor opinion of many members of Mr. Roosevelt's team," Margaret Truman recalled.[10] Indeed he once said that the cabinet he had inherited—a veritable pantheon of New Deal heroes—was a "mudhole."[11] Even among FDR's liberal admirers the Roosevelt cabinet was not universally esteemed.[12] It was perfectly right and natural for Truman to want his own men, as every president does; he knew Roosevelt holdovers inevitably would measure everything Truman did against what they supposed the old chief would have done.

Having come from Congress and witnessed Roosevelt's difficulties there, Truman wanted a cabinet that he hoped, overoptimistically, could help him on Capitol Hill. Thus he gave cabinet posts to four members or former members of Congress. Beside Byrnes, they were Secretary of Agriculture Clinton P. Anderson, Secretary of Labor Lewis W. Schwellenbach, and Secretary of the Treasury Fred M. Vinson. (After having replaced Secretary of Labor Frances Perkins with Schwellenbach—a disastrous choice—Truman remarked to his staff that he did not want a woman in the cabinet.[13])

Truman held Vinson in high esteem and to the end of his presidency had ever larger roles in mind for him. The new secretary of the treasury was a tall, somber-looking, but amiable man with a knowing air and voice to match, who had come to the House of Representatives from Kentucky in 1924 and eventually played an influential part in the passage of New Deal legislation. When the war came, Roosevelt made him an executive in mobilization agencies, and Vinson was already in the White House as director of the Office of War Mobilization and Reconversion when Truman arrived.

Like Truman, Vinson was a border-state middle-of-the-roader and practical New Dealer. In the White House the two became good friends. The impression the Kentuckian made on Truman may be gauged by this entry jotted by Truman in a personal memorandum June 17: ". . . Fred Vinson, straight shooter, knows Congress and how they think, a man to trust."[14] In the opinion of some who dealt with him he was also a quite fuzzy-minded man. He was a regular player—and inveterate loser—in Truman's poker games. In the early Truman cabinet he was probably the most influential member.

In the most controversial of his early cabinet appointments Truman replaced the liberal, Paris-born, Harvard-educated Attorney General Francis Biddle with Tom C. Clark, assistant attorney general in charge of the Criminal Division, a Texas lawyer who was close to the state's business and political interests and to Hannegan. An acquaintance of the new president, Clark had handled some of the fraud cases referred to the Department of Justice by the Truman Committee. Unlike Biddle, who had supported Justice Douglas, he had worked for Truman's nomination as vice-president at Chicago.

Truman handled the removal of Biddle badly. One day in May Stephen Early telephoned the attorney general and said Truman wanted his resignation. Biddle said he thought this was an abrupt, undignified way of doing business and a reflection on his record. He called the White House and requested an appointment with the president.

When the two met, Truman seemed stiff and self-conscious. Biddle quickly offered to submit his resignation and said only that he was surprised at the way it had been solicited. Truman conceded that he should have sent for the attorney general. "He had not felt like facing me, he said," according to Biddle. "I told him that I understood perfectly that he should want me to go—the relationship was a highly personal one, lawyer to client. He should have his own man."

The president seemed relieved.

"I got up, walked over to him and touched his shoulder," Biddle recalled. " 'You see,' I said, 'it's not so hard.' "

Truman smiled. Biddle asked if the president would mind telling him the name of the new attorney general.

"You'll be pleased," Truman replied. "He is someone in your department—Tom Clark."[15]

The degree of Biddle's pleasure may be inferred from the following story he subsequently told Dean Lloyd K. Garrison of the University of Wisconsin Law School, then a member of the War Labor Board: Shortly before Roosevelt's death Biddle had become dissatisfied with Clark's performance as assistant attorney general and decided to replace him. Clark went to Senator Tom Connally, Democrat, of

Texas, chairman of the Senate Foreign Relations Committee, and Connally got in touch with Roosevelt, who asked Biddle to hold off on Clark's case.[16]

Now, in one of those ineffable Washington contretemps, Biddle was out and Clark was becoming attorney general. Biddle told Truman coolly he would not have recommended Clark.*

About the only New Deal flavor left in the cabinet came from the retention of Harold Ickes as secretary of the interior and Henry Wallace as secretary of commerce.

Wallace, incidentally, had come to doubt Truman after the fight over the vice-presidential nomination. He did not charge Truman with having tried to get the nomination for himself. Rather his objection was that Truman publicly supported Rayburn and then Byrnes for the nomination after he had told Wallace on the Senate floor that, according to Wallace, Wallace was his candidate. "This kind of action," Wallace had confided to his diary in the midst of his disappointment after the convention, "convinces me beyond doubt that he is a small opportunistic man, a man of good instincts but, therefore, probably all the more dangerous. As he moves out more in the public eye, he will get caught in webs of his own making."[17] Truman, on the other hand, told an associate in June 1945, that Wallace was a "cat bastard," whatever that may have meant.

Truman's distrust of some former associates of Roosevelt took a serious turn in the case of Thomas G. Corcoran, an old New Dealer famed as "Tommy the Cork." Part legal wizard, part Machiavelli, part James Cagney brashly playing George M. Cohan, Corcoran was a bill-drafter, speech writer, and spectacular political operator for Roosevelt. His connivances often offended members of Congress and did not sit particularly well with Senator Truman. In league with Felix Frankfurter, Corcoran had funneled men into key jobs all over Washington as the government burgeoned during the New Deal. Before Roosevelt died Corcoran returned to private law practice in Washington.

When Truman became president he and some of his subordinates, possibly including J. Edgar Hoover, were suspicious that because of New Deal appointments, Corcoran remained a hidden power throughout the government. With whatever justification, it occurred to them that as a lawyer he might do handsomely for clients before federal regulatory agencies, some of whose members may have owed their jobs to him. The possibility that a scandal might arise and disparage the Truman administration seems not to have been overlooked. Corcoran already had, after his departure from the government in 1941, been questioned by a Senate investigating committee about charges that he was using his influence with government officials to benefit private clients. In later years this was to happen again, one instance involving a lucrative pipeline case before the Federal Power Commission.

---

* Thirty years later Truman told Merle Miller that Clark was a "damn fool from Texas" and "was no damn good as Attorney General." "Tom Clark was my biggest mistake," he said. While in office, however, Truman manifested no such feelings. The impression he conveyed about his relations with Clark was quite the opposite. Indeed he had even bigger things in store for him than the Department of Justice.

Corcoran was absolved of wrongdoing. The problem evidently was on Truman's mind, however. Associates recalled hearing him and Vaughan grumbling about Corcoran's throwing his weight around. They considered him a lobbyist. When some things happened in the government that the White House disliked there was a tendency to suspect his influence.

In June Truman informed Tom Clark that he was, in Clark's words, "particularly concerned" about the activities of Corcoran and his associates and, Clark said, wanted "a very thorough investigation" made "so that steps might be taken, if possible, to see that such activities did not interfere with the proper administration of government." The attorney general, therefore, authorized the Federal Bureau of Investigation to place a "technical surveillance"—a term usually referring to wiretapping and bugging—on Roosevelt's former aide.[18]

Strictly speaking, Truman did not order electronic surveillance of Corcoran. He instigated an investigation, and the recommendation of method was left to the attorney general. For three years, however—until May, 1948—General Vaughan, Truman's official liaison officer with Hoover, received reports from the wiretaps or bugs; and Truman must have known about them.

In furtherance of his promise to carry on Roosevelt's policies, Truman, soon after he took office, endorsed the Bretton Woods monetary program and continuance of the reciprocal trade agreements program, both then pending in the Senate. He said he would further Roosevelt's aims for public power. He expressed hope that Congress would extend the wartime price control and stabilization program for at least another year. He endorsed the idea of full employment, an outgrowth of Roosevelt's "economic Bill of Rights." He backed the main features of the Wagner-Dingell bill to expand Social Security. In line with Roosevelt's earlier requests, he asked Congress to assure unemployment benefits of $25 a week for twenty-six weeks for persons thrown out of work.[19] These positions were not the Truman program—there had been no time for that yet. In general, however, they were liberal positions, foreshadowing the nature of the Truman program when it was finally presented to Congress.

At the time he took office the civil rights issue was in ferment, largely as a result of the war and the migration of blacks from the South.

Truman had come to the presidency with a mixed but—by standards of 1945—a reasonably good record on civil rights, considering that he was a politician from a Jim Crow state. His position was the familiar one of a compassionate and fair-minded man caught between the devil and the deep on the race issue. Segregation was the way of life in Missouri, and Truman accepted this. On the other hand, 130,000 black voters lived in Missouri in those days, 20,000 of them in Jackson County. Truman needed their votes.

Despite its sins, the Pendergast organization was attentive to the needs of these voters. "Truman was politically astute on the race question before he ever came to Washington because the Pendergast machine was politically astute," wrote Roy Wilkins of the National Association for the Advancement of Colored People, who had once worked for the *Kansas City Call*, a black newspaper.[20]

While Truman's background was rural, his political career drew him early into the problems of urban minority groups around Kansas City. As county commissioner he was conscientious in caring for unfortunate blacks in public institutions. When he ran for the Senate he defended the right of blacks to education, welfare, and economic opportunity, and they supported him strongly. Injustices to blacks galled him. He sensed that endless indignities would lead to a crisis. As he said in a Senate campaign speech in Sedalia, Missouri, in 1940, he believed in the brotherhood of men and not merely of white men. "In giving the Negroes the rights that are theirs, we are only acting in accord with ideas of true democracy."[21]

What Truman was talking about were legal and constitutional rights as they were generally understood fourteen years before the Supreme Court decision in the school case and more than two decades before the social revolution of the 1960s. Like most of his contemporaries, he never dreamed of the rights yet to be asserted and probably would have been unhappy about them if he had. Characteristic of a white Missourian of his time, he opposed social equality for blacks.

On July 14, 1940, he addressed the National Colored Democratic Association in Chicago, saying:

I wish to make it clear that I am not appealing for social equality of the Negro. The Negro himself knows better than that, and the highest type of Negro leaders say quite frankly that they prefer the society of their own people. Negroes want justice, not social relations.[22]

This was the viewpoint, surely, of most enlightened white Americans of that period.

In 1944 many blacks were outraged at the dumping of Wallace. The *Pittsburgh Courier,* a black weekly, called Truman's nomination an "appeasement of the South." During the campaign Morris Milgram, national secretary of the Worker's Defense League, interviewed Truman. The vice-presidential candidate was quoted as having said that if blacks sat at a counter in a drugstore in Independence, "they would be booted out" because the management of such stores had a right to refuse to serve.

According to the account, Truman said that in St. Louis blacks had begun a "push day once a week" to shove whites out of bars. Because the same thing was starting in Washington, Margaret was not allowed to go downtown in the streetcar on Thursdays, he said, adding, "It is not safe—they push people off the streetcars."

When the interview appeared in the *Courier* Truman denied that he had ever made such statements.[23]

At his first presidential press conference a black reporter, Harry McAlpin of the *Atlanta Daily World,* asked him where he stood on civil rights—"on the fair employment practice, the right to vote without being hampered by poll taxes and all that?"

"I will give you some advice," he replied, sidestepping the question. "All you need to do is to read the Senate record of one Harry S Truman."[24]

The record showed that Truman usually had supported anti-poll tax legislation. He had backed funds for the Committee on Fair Employment Practices (FEPC). He had endorsed antilynching legislation, though, because of filibusters, he had never had an opportunity to vote for it. He had signed an unsuccessful petition to end a filibuster on an anti–poll tax bill. He also had supported an amendment to the Selective Service Act to outlaw discrimination against members of minority groups who wished to volunteer for service. On the other hand he voted against an anti-poll tax amendment to the soldiers' vote bill.[25]

In sum, considering his support for segregation, it was a record of compromise. Despite the dismay over the sidetracking of Wallace, however, some black publications spoke up for Truman when Roosevelt died. The *Crisis,* journal of the NAACP, said that Truman's record had been good enough so that he was "entitled to a chance to add to that record as President."[26]

The controversy over civil rights in the spring of 1945 centered on the FEPC. While for various reasons the FEPC never lived up to its promises, it was an issue of great importance at that period because the FEPC was the first open federal commitment to a policy of racial equality in employment—the most definite break that had ever occurred, as Gunnar Myrdal wrote, "in the tradition of Federal unconcernedness about racial discrimination."[27] As such, it incurred hostility in the South, which was already frightened by social changes being forced upon it by the depression and the war.

Threatened with a black march on Washington, Roosevelt had issued an executive order in 1941, directing employers and unions "to provide for the full and equitable participation of all workers in defense industries, without discrimination because of race, creed, color or national origin." He created the FEPC to enforce the order. The committee, however, had no police powers. Enemies sprang to life in Congress. For fear of getting his war measures entangled in the politics of civil rights Roosevelt rather ignored the FEPC, following his cautious practice of not intervening in congressional debates on racial problems.

When Truman took office two FEPC bills were pending in Congress. One was an appropriations bill on which the wartime FEPC depended for funds in the fiscal year starting July 1. The other was a bill to establish a permanent FEPC. On June 1 the House Appropriations Committee deleted all funds for continuing the wartime FEPC. Its excuse was that Congress should await developments on the second bill to create a permanent FEPC. But this bill was incarcerated in the House Rules Committee, dominated by Southerners.

Walter White, executive secretary of the NAACP, asked Truman to urge the Rules Committee to schedule floor debate on the permanent FEPC bill.[28] Abandoning Roosevelt's policy against intervening in a racial issue, Truman sent a letter to the chairman of the committee, Representative Adolph J. Sabath, saying that to abandon the principle on which the FEPC had been established was "unthinkable."[29]

He noted that the Appropriations Committee had omitted funds for the wartime FEPC because a bill for a permanent FEPC was pending. But unless the Rules Committee cleared the latter bill the House could not vote on it. He asked the Rules Committee, therefore, to schedule the legislation for debate. The permanent FEPC bill never did clear the Rules Committee, however. As for the wartime FEPC, Congress ultimately voted it a token sum of $250,000 but with a mandate to liquidate by June 30, 1946.

The South had expected something different from Truman than intervention on behalf of the FEPC. Southern states had insured his nomination as vice-president. With his Missouri background it had been assumed that he would be sensitive to Southern feelings on race. On the Roosevelt funeral train Senator Burnet R. Maybank, Democrat, of South Carolina, had confided to a southern friend, "Everything's going to be all right—the new President knows how to handle the niggers."[30] After the letter to Sabath, Representative Frank W. Boykin, Democrat, of Alabama, wrote Truman saying that a large delegation of congressmen wished to call on him before any other action, then or in the future, was taken on FEPC. The group wished to give Truman "our view of this terrible thing that is not only tearing *our Party* to pieces, but *the entire Nation.*"

"The answer is not enough time to get 'em in," Truman scribbled to his secretary on the bottom of the letter.[31]

4. *The Ominous Rift over Poland*

DINING ONE NIGHT with a friend from Kansas City, N. T. Veatch, in the early weeks in the White House, Truman said there was one thing he was not going to do—he was not going to let Stalin beat him at a poker game.[1] Already Stalin was an adversary of sorts. The opening hand was Poland—"first of the great causes," as Churchill was to say, "which led to the breakdown of the Grand Alliance."[2]

With Soviet-American tension rising, the Polish issue was Truman's first major test as president. However ill-prepared, he saw the problem in sharp hues and tackled it resolutely.

Throughout history Russian lands had been invaded from Poland, most recently by the Germans in 1941. When the Soviets had turned the tide against them and had themselves overrun Poland, they were determined that in their own defense and for the protection of the Soviet system Poland would be ruled by a regime responsive to and dependent on Moscow. With this end in view they fostered and, over Roosevelt's protest, recognized a Communist-controlled Warsaw Provisional Government. The Allies, on the other hand, recognized the Polish government-in-exile in London, ultimately headed by Stanislaw Mikolajczyk. The composition of a permanent Polish government, therefore, became a difficult issue at the Yalta Conference.

The best that Roosevelt and Churchill succeeded in doing was entering into an agreement with Stalin that the Communist regime should be reorganized so as to include other, democratic Polish leaders from (1) within the country and from (2) among the London exiles. The new government would be pledged to hold free elections. A Soviet-American-British commission was created to oversee the reorganization from Moscow.

The meaning of the agreement soon fell into dispute. To the Soviets reorganization meant the Communist Warsaw government modestly altered. To the Americans and British reorganization meant, ultimately, a new government to be elected by the people. Still, Roosevelt acknowledged that the Yalta agreement placed somewhat more emphasis on the Communists than on other elements. He did not accept the idea of an exclusive Soviet sphere achieved unilaterally through the blatant spread of Communist rule. Neither did he believe the United States should shirk the responsibility it had assumed at Yalta for a representative Polish government.[3] Before his death he warned Stalin that "any such solution which would result in a thinly disguised continuation of the Warsaw regime would be unacceptable."[4]

It was in this context—in this impasse, in which someone had to give way—

that Truman two weeks later took up the Polish issue. It was the immediate point on which his pledge to carry out Roosevelt's policies focused. In fact the problem was thrust upon him during his first full day in office, April 13, because of the need for the new president to deal with messages that had been sent to his predecessor by Stalin and Churchill.

On April 7 Stalin had cabled Roosevelt and Churchill, charging that their ambassadors were ignoring the Warsaw regime. He submitted a proposal that went even beyond Yalta, suggesting that the Warsaw government be expanded by adding one new minister for each four already in the cabinet. This so-called Yugoslav precedent would have created a ratio of one in five and would, of course, have assured the pro-Moscow Poles' predominant power.

Indignant, Churchill proposed to Roosevelt that they issue a joint statement letting the world know what was happening in Poland. On the day before his death Roosevelt replied, counseling that they "minimize the general Soviet problem as much as possible because these problems, in one form or another, seem to arise every day and most of them straighten out. . . . We must be firm, however."[5]

Churchill's proposal was placed before Truman on the thirteenth by Stettinius, who still hoped that the Yalta agreement would be carried out. Truman adhered to the cautious tenor of Roosevelt's final message, cabling Churchill: "Although with a few exceptions he [Stalin] does not leave much ground for optimism, I feel very strongly that we should have another go at him."[6] Truman suggested that instead of publicizing the dispute he and Churchill send Stalin a joint note, which they did, rejecting the application of the Yugoslav precedent to Poland.[7] In sum, the note continued the impasse, which also had become a heated political issue in the United States. Through their newspapers and spokesmen in Congress, several million Americans of Polish descent were putting pressure on the Truman administration to bring about an independent Poland.

When Stettinius had seen Truman on the thirteenth he gave him an estimate of the international situation specially prepared by the State Department. The paper was permeated with criticism of Soviet conduct and made no attempt to explain the Soviet viewpoint. Since Yalta, the summary said, the Kremlin had taken "a firm and uncompromising position on nearly every major question."[8] This and other similar accusations in the summary would have created anxiety for any president. If the disagreements as described were to continue, their ramifications obviously could jeopardize the peace for which Truman was now responsible to the American people. The next day he confided to Snyder that he had learned on the thirteenth for the first time that Stalin was not living up to the Yalta agreements.[9]

One thing the conflict reflected was that old and underlying differences between the United States and the Soviet Union that had been patched over in the military alliance of convenience against Hitler were breaking through to the surface again as victory over Germany drew closer and just as Truman was assuming responsibility for American policy.

Another was that since Pearl Harbor Roosevelt had insisted on fighting the war and postponing political settlements until near the end. Now Roosevelt was gone. Except for the agreement at the Dumbarton Oaks estate in Washington, laying the groundwork for the United Nations; and for the United Nations Monetary and Financial Conference at Bretton Woods, New Hampshire, creating the International Monetary Fund and the International Bank for Reconstruction and Development (World Bank), practically nothing of a permanent nature had been settled.

The tides of history would not wait for Truman to catch his breath. The main problems immediately confronting him were winning the war against Germany and Japan and consummating the negotiations between the Allies and the Soviet Union over postwar settlements, which were bound to shape the world for decades.

Because of the way he had come to office, the president-elect transition from one administration to the next was obviously out of the question. He had no interval before entering office when he could appoint task forces to ascertain the facts for him. He had no experts and advisers whose loyalty had been tested during an election campaign to assist him in a critical review of old policies and a systematic preparation of new ones.

Events around the world were moving with tremendous momentum. Even if he had wished to do so, Truman was too new to the presidency, too inexperienced, too lacking in prestige and command over the military and civilian bureaucracies suddenly to make a drastic change in the course of American policy. For the most part, in those frantic early days he made decisions on the recommendations of senior advisers.

As senator and vice-president, he had displayed no well-defined attitude toward the Soviet Union. He disliked communism, and more particularly the spread of communism, as had most Americans and their elected representatives ever since the Russian Revolution, the Comintern, the Moscow purges of the 1930s, the Molotov-Ribbentrop pact of 1939, and the Soviet invasion of Finland that same year.

He had not been rabid on the subject, however. He took no part in the Red-baiting that occupied some politicians in the 1930s and 1940s. But after Hitler had invaded the Soviet Union in June, 1941, he gave a reporter an off-the-cuff interview in which he was quoted as having said: "If we see that Germany is winning we ought to help Russia and if Russia is winning we ought to help Germany and that way let them kill as many as possible, although I don't want to see Hitler victorious under any circumstances. Neither of them thinks anything of their pledged word."[10] This attitude may have been cynical, but it was widely held at the time.

In any case Senator Truman steadfastly supported Roosevelt's foreign policy, with its element—after Pearl Harbor—of helping the Soviet Union defeat Hitler. Barely three months after talking with the reporter he voted for extending Lend-Lease aid to the Soviet Union. He acknowledged the Soviet people as a "brave ally."[11]

Nevertheless he had displayed no broad philosophical concept of future good relations between the two countries. He was not a natural friend of the Soviets. His forbearance was limited. As he pored over the diplomatic exchanges that had followed Yalta he was struck by the indignant tone of some of Roosevelt's comments to Stalin, and it did not take much to arouse righteous indignation in Truman. He agreed entirely with what Roosevelt had said (or had been said over Roosevelt's signature); it became his own attitude.[12] Stalin's blunt correspondence angered him.

"The insulting language of the recent Stalin telegrams was an affront to the solid, old-fashioned Americanism possessed by Harry Truman," Leahy recalled.[13]

During Truman's novitiate it was the men whose own sentiments were reflected in Roosevelt's messages—Leahy, Harriman, and Secretary of the Navy Forrestal—who took a leading part in informing and advising him. One of his earliest discussions on Soviet-American relations was with Major General John R. Deane, chief of the United States military mission in Moscow, whose attitude already had been communicated to General Marshall: "I feel certain we must be tougher if we are to gain their respect and be able to work with them in the future."[14] The influential Baruch, just back from a mission to London, spoke in similar terms.[15] The air the new president breathed was permeated with advice to be firm, to keep his commitments and demand that the Soviets keep theirs.

Fortunately, as it seemed, Stalin—upon the suggestion of Harriman—relented in his decision to keep Molotov home from the San Francisco conference.[16] He agreed with Harriman that Molotov not only should attend but should call on Truman on the way to the conference. Where Soviet-American relations were concerned, however, the bad news kept driving out the good. Before hurrying home to warn Truman about Soviet intransigence over Poland, Harriman cabled that Assistant Foreign Minister Andrei Y. Vishinsky had informed him that Moscow and the Warsaw regime were preparing to sign a treaty of mutual assistance even before the formation of the new Polish government. The State Department promptly asked that the treaty be deferred.

Truman was disturbed. He had come to regret, as he commented to Stettinius, that the Yalta terms on Poland were not more clear-cut.[17] To do otherwise than put up a fight for the American interpretation, however, would surely have seemed to him a show of weakness in a new president. After only five days in office, therefore, he decided to take the not inconsiderable step of "laying it on the line with Molotov" when the latter got to town.[18]

Beforehand Truman met April 20 with Harriman, who had preceded the Soviet foreign minister to Washington. It was the first time Truman and Harriman had met. A banker and industrialist of great inherited wealth deriving fom the Union Pacific Railroad, Harriman was a broad-minded, public-spirited, cultivated man, articulate and staunch in his opinions. Originally a Republican, he had turned Democratic upon voting for Alfred E. Smith for President in 1928. An acquaintance of both Roosevelt and Hopkins, he joined the New Deal as an official of the National Recovery Administration. With the outbreak of war in Europe Roosevelt sent him first to Great Britain and then to the Soviet Union to expedite American assistance to them in their struggle against Hitler. In 1943 Roosevelt named him ambassador to Moscow.

Harriman was well disposed toward the Soviets and hoped for a fruitful relationship between the United States and the Soviet Union after the war. As months passed, he began to feel frustrated by Soviet secrecy and Soviet obdurateness over Lend-Lease negotiations and joint military planning. He was annoyed too by the difficulties the Soviets placed in the way of conducting routine diplomatic affairs in

Moscow. The real assault upon his hopes for Soviet-American cooperation, however, came in the form of signs that Stalin would not tolerate Polish independence.[19]

In 1944 Harriman warned Washington that the Soviet Union coveted a sphere of influence in Eastern Europe and the Balkans. Without abandoning the goal of Soviet-American friendship, he urged that postwar American financial assistance be extended to the Soviets only "if they work cooperatively with us on international problems in accordance with our standards."[20] Dollars, he advised Secretary of State Cordell Hull, were "one of the most effective weapons at our disposal to influence European political events" and thwart a Soviet sphere of influence.[21]

A week before Roosevelt's death in April, 1945, Harriman had cabled Hull's successor, Stettinius, that United States interests must be protected from "selfish" Soviet aims by adoption of "a more positive" economic policy. In advice that was to carry weight in the Truman administration, Harriman recommended that economic aid should be oriented toward friendly countries. While the United States should try to cooperate with the Soviet Union, such collaboration should occur "always on a quid pro quo basis. This means tying our economic assistance directly into our political problems with the Soviet Union."[22] Of like mind, Roosevelt before Yalta had demurred at Secretary of the Treasury Morgenthau's wish that he discuss postwar credits with Stalin in the interest of improved relations. "I think it's very important," Roosevelt said, "that we hold this back and don't give them any promise until we get what we want."[23]

Truman and Harriman got on well in their talk about the troubles in Eastern Europe. Harriman told the president the Soviets were trying to do two things simultaneously: cooperate with the Allies and unilaterally extend their control over neighboring states. The Soviets did not wish to break with the United States, the ambassador continued, since they would need American help to rebuild after the war. In Harriman's opinion the United States had nothing to lose in standing firm on important issues.

In no sense, Truman interjected, was he afraid of the Russians. He said he intended to be firm but fair—a reasonable comment. He added that the Soviets needed the Americans more than the Americans needed the Soviets.

And yet, Harriman said, some people in Moscow believed that American business would have a vital need to export goods to the Soviet Union after the war.

Truman said he would make no concessions just to win the Soviets' favor. Give-and-take, he said, sensibly, was the only basis on which relations between the two countries could be established.

Then Harriman made a memorable observation: what the world was faced with was a "barbarian invasion of Europe." This was a theme that was being aired in the press and elsewhere even before Truman had taken office; the events that were now occurring gave it greater impact on the thinking in Washington. Obviously, Harriman acknowledged, some concessions would have to be made.

Of course, Truman replied, he did not expect the Soviets to yield 100 percent of the time. But, he said, ascending to the peak of delusion, on important matters the United States ought to be able to get 85 percent of what it wanted.

Harriman asked Truman how he felt about the Polish question in relation to the

San Francisco conference and American participation in the United Nations.

Truman answered that in his opinion the Senate would not approve the United Nations Charter unless the Polish question was settled along the lines of the Yalta agreement. He said he intended to tell Molotov just that in words of one syllable. Harriman asked: Would the United States go ahead with its plans for the United Nations, if the Russians dropped out?

Truman's reply was a thoughtful one. The truth of the matter was, he said, that without the Russians there would not be much of a world organization.[24]

Despite his annoyance, Truman was worried by the time Molotov arrived over the extent to which the amicable spirit of Yalta had evaporated.[25] He was given fresh cause for dismay April 21 with the news that Moscow had rejected the State Department's request and had a signed a mutual assistance treaty with Poland, thereby recognizing the present Warsaw regime as the legitimate government.

Truman's first meeting with Molotov occurred the next day in Blair House, where the foreign minister was staying. With the possible exception of a social chat at an embassy party or some similar affair, it was apparently the first time Truman had ever spoken with a citizen of the Soviet Union. In a cordial enough atmosphere he said he stood squarely behind all of Roosevelt's commitments. Molotov observed that the Yalta agreement was sufficiently clear to overcome any difficulties. This led Truman to the subject of Poland. It was, he said, the most important pending problem because of its effect on American opinion.

Molotov granted that the question was important to the United States. He said, however, it was vital to the Soviet Union because Poland was a bordering country.

In its larger aspects, Truman replied, the Polish question had become for the American people a symbol of foreign relations.

Molotov then asked Truman specifically whether the commitments made at Yalta with regard to the Far East still stood. It was a vital question.

Subject to later approval by Chiang Kai-shek, Roosevelt had offered Stalin certain territorial, political, and commercial concessions in the Far East. In return Stalin had pledged to attack Japan in two or three months after the German surrender. This guarantee had been long sought by Roosevelt. At the time of Yalta American forces were still battling on Luzon. The slaughter of Iwo Jima and Okinawa lay ahead. And beyond loomed the bloodshed of the contemplated invasion of the Japanese home islands. Japan still had a million men in China plus its million-man Kwantung Army in Manchuria and Korea, which might make a prolonged stand. To United States strategists at that period, therefore, the unleashing of Soviet forces against Japanese troops on the Asian continent was a matter of overwhelming importance if a long war with huge American casualties was to be averted. This was one reason—bringing the Soviets into the United Nations was another—why Roosevelt had been so accommodating to Stalin on other issues at Yalta.

In answer to Molotov's question, Truman replied that the Far Eastern commitments made at Yalta still stood.[26]

Next Molotov met with Stettinius and Anthony Eden. He reasserted the demand for the Yugoslav precedent as the basis for the new Polish government and insisted that this government be seated at the San Francisco conference.

This clinker was then dropped in Truman's lap on the afternoon of April 23 when he met with his advisers in preparation for his working session with Molotov that evening. Truman was exasperated. He was caught in a situation where the United Nations conference was at hand, but with basic disagreements unresolved in advance. Oblivious to concessions Stalin had made, even at Yalta, he said that so far agreements with the Soviet Union had been a one-way street.[27] The United States would go to the San Francisco conference, he said, and then, letting off steam, added that if the Russians did not wish to join, they could go to hell.

He asked for opinions around the table.

Secretary of War Stimson urged restraint. It was important, he felt, to learn what the Soviets were driving at. Without comprehending how seriously they regarded the Polish question, he noted, the United States might be heading into dangerous waters.

Contrary advice was offered by Forrestal, a tense, introspective, hard-driving man, whose Irish face was marred by a nose flattened in a boxing match at the Racquet and Tennis Club in New York. A talented administrator, Forrestal, Princeton '15, had made his way on Wall Street to the presidency of Dillon, Read and Company before becoming one of those administrative assistants to President Roosevelt who were required to have a "passion for anonymity." A conservative Democrat with no enthusiasm for the New Deal, he had moved from the White House to the Navy Department, first as under secretary and then secretary. He perceived that capitalism was under attack in the world, loathed communism, and distrusted Stalin.

Forrestal made the most dramatic statement of the afternoon. He told the president that if the Russians were going to pursue a rigid course, it would be better to force a showdown with them then rather than later.

Truman evidently was in a mood to hear some strong talk.[28] However, the suggestion of a showdown, whatever that might imply, gave him pause. He said he had no intention of delivering an ultimatum to Molotov. This was the essential point of the day. The president said he merely intended to make the American position clear to his visitor.

Leahy made the point that it would be a serious matter to break with the Soviet Union. Still, he believed the Soviets should be told that the United States stood for an independent Poland.

General Marshall also urged restraint, emphasizing the hope that the Soviets would enter the Japanese war in time to help American forces. The Soviets had it in their power, he warned, to delay their attack until the Americans had done all the dirty work. A break with the Soviet Union, he said, would be very serious.

Apart from Forrestal's lone mention of a possible showdown, the advice to Truman was anything but inflammatory. It boiled down to counsel to stand firm on the American position on Poland but to go slow on a break with the Soviet Union, particularly in view of the military situation in the Far East. Truman gave no indication that he would reject this advice. Obviously, however, he was indignant over Molotov's latest tactics and still quite ready to lay it "on the line" with him at 5 P.M.

Yet if ever there lived a man who could not easily be moved by words, it was the one who called on the president in the White House at that hour, fortified by a breakfast that morning of salad and soup.[29] In his rise to power in the Soviet Union Vyacheslav Mikhailovich Molotov had endured such struggles as Harry Truman had never dreamed of. His own wife had been banished by Stalin. He came as the representative of a nation that had survived four years of bloodshed and devastation beyond the imagination of most Americans. Superficially professorial in his blue serge suit, mustache, and pince-nez, he was hard and cold, a man "saturated with our blood," as Aleksandr I. Solzhenitsyn was to say.[30] To make his presence the more formidable he had a large bump on his forehead that seemed to swell when he grew angry.[31]

Truman, speaking through Bohlen, his interpreter, came right to the point: he regretted that no progress had been made on a Polish solution. The proposals that he and Churchill had sent to Stalin April 16, concerning the Poles whom they wished to have invited to Moscow, were fair, he said.

The United States, he told Molotov, would not be a party to the formation of a Polish government that did not represent all Polish democratic elements. As if hinting that the Soviet Union might be by-passed, if need be, Truman said that regardless of what differences might arise on other issues, the United States intended to go ahead with other countries in establishing the United Nations.

Then he made a point the meaning of which was not likely to be missed by a government hoping for American assistance in postwar reconstruction. Roosevelt, Truman recalled, had explained in a message to Stalin that no executive policy in the United States could succeed without public support. This applied in the case of economic assistance, Truman said. He noted that funds would have to be appropriated by Congress. Falling back on the Harriman-State Department strategy of using dollars to prevent a Soviet sphere in Eastern Europe, he said he hoped Moscow would bear all this in mind in connection with the Polish question.

Thereupon he handed Molotov a note for Stalin, which said that the Yalta agreement could be carried out only if a group of representative democratic Polish leaders were invited to Moscow for consultations. In a warning tone the message said failure to carry out the agreement "would seriously shake confidence in the unity of the three Governments and their determination to continue the collaboration in the future as they have in the past."

Molotov, speaking in Russian through his interpreter, told Truman that his government wanted to cooperate with the United States and Great Britain.

Of course, Truman replied—otherwise the two of them would not be talking together.

Molotov continued that the three governments had established a basis for settling their differences. The three, he said, had dealt as equals and there had been no time when one or two had tried to impose their will on the third. This was the only basis of cooperation acceptable to his government, Molotov said.

All he was asking, Truman said, was for the Soviets to honor the Yalta decision.

Molotov retorted that his government did stand by the decision as a matter of honor. He was sure the difficulties could be settled. But Truman, with an old senator's instincts about the keeping of commitments, was doubly firm. An agreement had been reached, he declared, and it only remained for Stalin to carry it out in accordance with his own word.

Molotov said he did not see why the matter could not be solved through application of the Yugoslav precedent, already rejected by Truman and Churchill. An agreement had been reached on Poland, Truman repeated. All that was needed was for the Soviet Union to carry it out.

Molotov now turned "a little ashy," Bohlen noted, but the vain dialogue continued, the two men simply talking past each other. Finally, Truman could stand it no longer.

"That will be all, Mr. Molotov," he snapped. "I would appreciate it if you would transmit my views to Marshal Stalin."[32]

Thus dismissed, Molotov disappeared in a hurry, appearing to be offended.[33]

Truman was obviously pleased with his performance, for he later told Joseph E. Davies, former ambassador to Moscow: "I gave him the one-two, right to the jaw."[34] And Leahy wrote: "Truman's attitude in dealing with Molotov was more than pleasing to me. I believe it would have a beneficial effect on the Soviet outlook."[35]

Harriman was more realistic. "I did regret that Truman went at it so hard," he recalled, "because his behavior gave Molotov an excuse to tell Stalin that the Roosevelt policy was being abandoned."[36]

Obviously, Truman did not have anything like the rapport with Soviet leaders that Roosevelt had enjoyed after years in office. Roosevelt's political skills, his relationship with Stalin, and his determination to get along with the Soviet Union might have improved postwar arrangements. In the passage from Roosevelt to Truman the presidential attitude undoubtedly hardened, partly because Truman had to rely on State Department advisers, who were much less sympathetic to cooperation with the Soviets than Roosevelt had been. Nevertheless, the climate had begun to change under Roosevelt.

How far would Roosevelt's policy of cooperation have extended as national interests clashed in the disputes over postwar settlements? Or, to cut closer to the bone, how tolerant would Congress have been toward tangible cooperation with the Soviet Union, especially on terms acceptable to Stalin? In any event Roosevelt's policy of cooperation had had quite definite limitations. He had not cooperated in informing Stalin about the development of the atomic bomb and in soliciting his partnership in atomic energy after the war. He had not cooperated in furthering negotiations for a postwar loan to the Soviet Union. These were no minor matters. Roosevelt had not cooperated either on the composition of the Warsaw regime, the problem in which Truman was now engaged. The choice between soft words and blunt words was not likely to have made a fundamental difference in resolving the conflict of objectives. Truman had not suddenly set off in quest of new aims at variance with Roosevelt's at that point. There had been no time for such an undertaking, nor had Truman conceived new objectives of his own. What he sought was a settlement on terms consistent with the American interpretation of Yalta as expounded to him by Roosevelt's chief advisers.

In areas in which Roosevelt had bequeathed clear policies Truman tried to carry them out as he understood them. This was the case in demanding unconditional surrender of Germany and Japan. It was the case in respecting zones of occupation in Europe. It was the case in withholding the secret of the atomic bomb from Stalin while the bomb was being developed. It was the case in supporting Chiang Kai-shek as against Mao Tse-tung.[37] It was the case (according to a recent study by the historian Walter LaFeber) in allowing restoration of French rule in Indochina.[38] It was the case in encouraging the Soviet Union to enter the war in the Far East, at least until the last moment when the successful test of the atomic bomb changed American minds, but to no effect. Albeit with considerable hesitation, it was the case in granting concessions to the Soviets in the Far East, agreed upon at Yalta. It was the case in insisting that the Soviets carry out their pledges in Poland, while still seeking general accord with Moscow. Demanding that Molotov live up to the Yalta terms on Poland undoubtedly struck a man of Truman's directness as the best way to fulfill Roosevelt's policy on that point. In these early days he was even more adamant against an exclusive sphere of influence in Eastern Europe than Roosevelt had been.

Like Harriman, he thought that by being blunt with the Soviets he could establish a workable basis for future relations. He believed—and would continue to believe—that the Soviets were wrong and the Americans right. The Russians, he told Henry Wallace, were like people from across the tracks whose manners were very bad.[39] Under the influence of Harriman he believed too that by exploiting American economic advantages he could do business with Stalin, which is what Roosevelt had thought in his last days.[40] The proposition that Stalin would in the end back down had been advanced by Harriman and others for months. With some lesser exceptions, it proved to be quite erroneous.[41]

Truman's words suggested that his opposition was not so much to communism as a way of life in the Soviet Union as it was to Stalin's foreign policy. This was viewed in Washington as expansionist, not simply because the Soviets had absorbed Estonia, Latvia, and Lithuania and had annexed parts of Poland, Ruthenia, and Bessarabia, but because of Soviet political, economic, and military dominance, in time, of all of Poland as well as Hungary, Rumania, Bulgaria, and Czechoslovakia. For ideological as well as strategic reasons Truman and his advisers did not wish to see communism installed beyond the Soviet borders because it then appeared a threat to democracy itself and not simply an instrument of Soviet security. Soviet feelings of insecurity in Eastern Europe were not something that registered with Truman to any great extent. Hence his tendency to exaggerate Soviet motives, granted that no one in the West knew exactly what those motives were.

A State Department memorandum informed him: "Basic United States policy has been to oppose spheres of influence in Europe."[42] The United States opposed formation of any bloc exclusively dominated by an alien power, just as it favored an open door to trade and travel. In the eyes of Truman and the men who were conducting American diplomacy these traditional principles were being assailed by Soviet probing in Eastern Europe, the Balkans, and the Middle East. On the other hand, making for a classic conflict, the Soviets, with their memories of Western intervention in the First World War, feared that if the capitalist nations dominated Eastern

Europe, they might exploit it eventually as a hostile base against the Soviet Union.[43]

The tough talk to Molotov did not end the negotiations over Poland. Truman continued to strive in the face of an intractable situation. In the political vacuum created by the destruction of Germany, an anticapitalist nation and an anti-Communist nation had begun to converge and compete. Each was a nation with a different historical experience. Each held an exclusive view of its own national interest and strong aspiration for world leadership. The two had mutually contradictory systems and contrasting cultures.

Truman was up against the fact that Stalin's conception of the postwar world was very different from his own. Stalin had his problems also. Obsessed with the future of national security and the preservation of the Soviet system, he too was tough and firm. Because of the Allied delays in opening a second front, Stalin felt that the Soviets had borne the brunt of the war against Hitler and that their blood had purchased the right to their own objectives in Eastern and Central Europe. As Harriman was to explain to Truman, it was hard for Stalin to understand "why we should want to interfere with Soviet policy in a country like Poland, which he considers so important to Russia's security, unless we have some ulterior motive."[44]

In Poland, unless Truman was ready for sterner measures, which he was not, partly because of the exigencies of the Japanese war, he was caught without much room for maneuver. In Teheran in 1943 Roosevelt had given tacit approval to the Curzon Line as the eastern boundary of Poland. This was agreed to at Yalta, leaving almost half of Poland's prewar territory in Soviet possession. Controversy or not, the puppet government in Warsaw was functioning. The Red Army was on the ground. Who was going to dislodge it?

Contrary to the terms of the Atlantic Charter and the dream of self-determination for all people, the war was ending with the Soviets engaged in imposing their authority on half of Europe. Old fears of revolutionary communism were reawakening in the West, while suspicion and xenophobia suffused the Kremlin, impeding mutual understanding. The Soviets asserted that the Americans and British were going back on the pledges at Yalta; Washington and London believed the same of the Soviets. A chasm was opening between the ways East and West viewed their common problems. Mutual confidence was cracked. What with the wreckage of the traditional European order and the decline of the British Empire, the war had left such a state of upheaval that it was beyond the capacity of the men involved on both sides to tidy it up in accordance with high ideals and principles.

At the same time the Japanese were still fighting furiously, and American casualties were heavy. Everything considered, it was a situation conducive to postwar international discord. All that was needed in the way of further mischief at that juncture to insure a world rife with suspicion, mistrust, and fear was something like the invention of an atomic bomb.

5. *"The Most Terrible Weapon"*

O<small>N APRIL</small> 24, the day after Truman's bout with Molotov, a note arrived at the White House from Stimson:

> Dear Mr. President,
>
> I think it is very important that I should have a talk with you as soon as possible on a highly secret matter.
>
> I mentioned it to you shortly after you took office, but have not urged it since on account of the pressure you have been under. It, however, has such a bearing on our present foreign relations and has such an important effect upon all my thinking in this field that I think you ought to know about it without much further delay.[1]

Not having known about the development of the atomic bomb before he became president, Truman had had no occasion to search his heart in advance about the advent of such a weapon. Because the bomb was being developed secretly, no public constituency against its use had formed to exert the kind of pressure that had been brought against, say, gas warfare. On the contrary a formidable array of senior presidential advisers believed that, if perfected, the bomb should be used. Even before Truman took office, as Barton J. Bernstein has noted, a committee had been studying how to drop atomic bombs on Japan.[2]

By the time Truman became president great momentum had developed behind the new weapon. A monumental scientific effort had gone into its production. Two billion dollars, a huge sum then, had been committed already. Everyone involved was straining forward with the task. The thought of failure was intolerable. The very fact that the United States was on the verge of an epochal feat, a turning point in history, spurred the scientists and governmental officials. The urge to reach final victory and peace was strong. To men like Stimson, as his biographer, Elting E. Morison, noted, the bomb loomed as "a force that could put an end to an evil situation that would otherwise continue."[3]

The weapon had appalling implications, but, as Stimson was to recall, "we were at war, and the work must be done . . . it was our common objective, throughout the war, to be the first to produce an atomic weapon and use it."[4]

If there was any matter on which Truman needed to rely on advice, it was, because of his unfamiliarity with the subject, the atomic bomb. He asked Stimson to come in the next day, April 25. A protégé of Theodore Roosevelt's and the quintessential eastern Republican lawyer, Stimson had been secretary of war under William Howard Taft and secretary of state under Herbert Hoover. Rather aloof and Olympian and an upholder of traditions and institutions, he was seldom addressed as Henry, but rather as Colonel Stimson—his rank in the field artillery during the First World War. As secretary of state he had halted secret code-breaking operations in the department because "gentlemen do not read each other's mail."

In 1940 Franklin Roosevelt, faced with the problems of reelection and war in Europe, chose two Republicans for his cabinet—Frank Knox as secretary of the navy and Stimson as secretary of war. Stimson was given ultimate responsibility for development of the atomic bomb. When Truman became president, Stimson was a somewhat rumpled-looking man with close-cropped hair and bangs, worn in imitation of those of his idol, former Secretary of War Elihu Root. Approaching his seventy-eighth birthday, Stimson was weary and in uncertain health.

On the twenty-fifth he brought with him to the White House General Leslie R. Groves, commanding general of the Manhattan Engineer District, code name for the army engineers' secret bomb project. Stimson told Truman that "the most terrible weapon ever known in human history" probably would be ready within four months—by August.[5] He and Groves recounted the history of the bomb and described the weapon. Truman appeared impressed but not overwhelmed.

The question of the atomic bomb was like many other great problems that had descended on him, in this respect: it did not come wrapped up in a settled policy, yet it had a history that pointed toward a certain future course of action. The most compelling attitude Truman had inherited about the bomb had been voiced by Roosevelt almost a year before. In a conversation with his secretary, Grace Tully, he said, "I can't tell you what this is, Grace, but if it works, and pray God it does, it will save many American lives."[6]

From its beginning in the Roosevelt administration the bomb was regarded as part of the war effort. The assumption was that it would be used when available. Indeed, in view of the heavy demand for materials and scientists the only reason the government was willing to allocate funds for the bomb in the first place was that it met the criterion of being of use in the war.[7] General Eisenhower, not directly involved in the question, once expressed to Stimson his hope that the United States would not be the first to use such a "horrible" weapon.[8] Under Secretary of the Navy Ralph A. Bard said in a memorandum that prior warning should precede use of the bomb.[9] General Marshall also thought the Japanese should be warned in advance. The overwhelming weight of opinion among policymakers, however, favored employing the bomb. Obviously that was what Stimson had in mind when he wrote later, "At no time, from 1941 to 1945, did I ever hear it suggested by the President, or by any other responsible member of the government, that atomic energy should not be used in the war."[10]

That was part of the history of the bomb, pertaining to its use in the war. Another part pertained to the diplomatic import of possession of an atomic bomb and consideration of how this might affect power alignment in the world, especially between the United States and Great Britain, partners in the development of the weapon, on the one hand, and the Soviet Union on the other.

As early as 1943 it was recognized by high Allied officials that the bomb would have strategic and diplomatic significance. Churchill was particularly outspoken in his concern that the Soviets or the Germans might produce the weapon first and use it for international blackmail. His assistant for atomic energy, Sir John Anderson, observed that the bomb "would be a terrific factor in the postwar world as giving an absolute control to whatever country possessed the secret." On orders from Roosevelt, the Manhattan Engineer District took precautions to keep the secret of the bomb from the Soviet Union as well as Germany. Churchill was dead set against informing the Soviets about the weapon, and Roosevelt concurred. At Quebec in August, 1943, he and Churchill formally agreed that "we will not either of us communicate any information about [the bomb] to third parties except by mutual consent."[11]

Roosevelt's policy was illuminated early in 1944 when Associate Justice Felix Frankfurter urged upon him proposals of Frankfurter's friend, Niels Bohr, Danish physicist and Nobel laureate. Concerned about future Soviet reaction to the secret Anglo-American development of the bomb, Bohr believed that the new weapon necessitated a new international order with international control of the bombs.

Frankfurter left a meeting with Roosevelt believing he had received a sympathetic hearing and encouragement by the president to have Bohr take up international control with Churchill. The truth was quite the opposite: Roosevelt and Churchill rejected Bohr's suggestions. The Quebec decision stood. And on June 13, 1944, Roosevelt and Churchill signed an Agreement and Declaration of Trust, providing that their two countries would cooperate in seeking to control available supplies of uranium and thorium, needed for the manufacture of the bombs, both during and after the war.[12]

On December 31, 1944, Stimson discussed the bomb with Roosevelt. The president had just protested to Stalin against the Soviets' decision to recognize the Communist regime in Poland. Stimson told Roosevelt that General Deane, head of the American military mission in Moscow, had warned that further easy concessions to the Soviets would accomplish nothing. The United States, Deane recommended, should be more forceful in demanding a quid pro quo. Stimson suggested to Roosevelt that this is where possession of the atomic bomb might come into play.[13] It was implicit in the concept of a quid pro quo that allied possession of the bomb would render the Soviets more manageable, since they would have to make concessions to benefit from information about or cooperation in the field of nuclear energy.

The idea had taken root, in other words, that possession of the bomb might be used for bargaining with Stalin and therefore ease difficult diplomatic problems. If the United States were to agree to international control of atomic energy, for example, Stalin might have to do something accommodating in Eastern Europe in return. For the moment, however, Stimson told Roosevelt it was not time to share any secrets with the Soviet Union, and Roosevelt agreed. He already had approved plans for training crews for a possible atomic bomb attack on Japan.[14] When he saw Stalin at Yalta in February, 1945, Roosevelt did not mention the bomb, though he knew the Soviets were spying on the project, supposedly without having yet obtained vital information.[15]

When the Truman administration came to power Byrnes was quick to sense a diplomatic potential of the weapon. He told Truman that the bomb might well put the United States in a position to dictate its own terms at the end of the war, although he may have been referring simply to Japanese peace terms.[16] At that stage

American planning had gone no further than the decision to keep the bomb an Anglo-American secret, to ready it for possible use against Japan and to continue the Anglo-American monopoly after the war.

When Stimson and Groves called on Truman April 25—the same day, curiously, that the United Nations conference opened in San Francisco—the secretary of war read a memorandum to the president. It said that the United States could not maintain its monopoly on the bomb indefinitely and that proliferation of the weapon among other countries could lead to the destruction of civilization. No known system of control could cope with the menace. Effective control, Stimson explained, "would involve such thoroughgoing rights of inspection and internal controls as we have never heretofore contemplated." While he did not mention it in his memorandum, Stimson had for some time been doubtful whether, as a police state, the Soviet Union would ever agree to international inspection.

He proposed, and Truman assented to, the appointment of an *ad hoc* committee to advise the president on future nuclear policy. Stimson became chairmen of the group, called the Interim Committee, and at Stimson's suggestion Truman named Byrnes as his own personal representative on the committee, which, of course, gave Byrnes a most influential voice in nuclear policy. No one versed in the ways of Washington is likely to suppose that such a committee was appointed to advise Truman not to use the bomb. On the contrary, its discussions assumed that it would be used.

The other members were Vannevar Bush, president of the Carnegie Institute and director of the Office of Scientific Research and Development; James Bryant Conant, president of Harvard University and chairman of the National Defense Research Committee; Karl T. Compton, president of the Massachusetts Institute of Technology; Under Secretary of the Navy Bard; William L. Clayton, Assistant Secretary of State for Economic Affairs; and, as Stimson's alternate, George L. Harrison, president of the New York Life Insurance Company and a wartime special assistant to the secretary of war.

Subsequently appointed to advise the committee was a scientific panel consisting of J. Robert Oppenheimer, director of the Los Alamos Scientific Laboratory, where the bomb was being assembled; Enrico Fermi, director of the Argonne National Laboratory, operated by the University of Chicago; and Arthur H. Compton and Ernest O. Lawrence, directors, respectively, of the atomic projects at the University of Chicago and the University of California at Berkeley.

If there was ever a logical juncture for reconsideration of the atomic bomb project, it was the moment when the matter was placed before a new president. Truman had the authority to set his own policy. Having no mandate to change Roosevelt's course, however, he did not raise the slightest question. Evidently, he never gave serious thought to interfering with the project. To have called a halt to it at this late date would have had a shattering effect in the government. Considering the bloody character of the war with Japan, such an action would have been thought irresponsible, even treasonous perhaps. In mid-April Marshall had given British Foreign Secretary Anthony Eden a grim forecast of a long war against Japan with heavy casualties "if conventional weapons only were used."[17] The general's estimates to Truman and Stimson ranged from five hundred thousand to more than a million American casualties.[18]

Truman surely knew instinctively what the consequences would have been for him and for the Democratic party if tens of thousands of Americans were killed or wounded in Japan while the atomic bomb lay in discard in a laboratory. Who would have understood the consequences better than the former chairman of the Senate Special Committee to Investigate the National Defense Program? Nothing less than a sweeping congressional investigation would have been launched into the $2 billion spent to build an atomic bomb. Shortly before Roosevelt's death, Byrnes, while still director of the Office of War Mobilization and Reconversion, had warned him in a memorandum: "If the project proves a failure, it will then be subjected to relentless investigation and criticism." In the War Department the prospect of a future congressional investigation was borne in mind during work on the bomb.[19]

Truman told Stimson and Groves that he fully agreed that it was necessary to develop the bomb.[20] Thereupon he let the matter rest for the time being with the decision to appoint the Interim Committee. After the meeting he spoke to J. Leonard Reinsch, a radio station director, who was on his staff briefly to coach him on speaking over radio. "Leonard," he said, "I have just gotten some important information. I am going to have to make a decision which no man in history has ever had to make." After a pause he continued, "I'll make the decision, but it is terrifying to think about what I will have to decide."[21]

From Washington that night Truman addressed the opening session of the San Francisco conference by radio, touching at one point on a theme that troubled him: the danger of a resurgence of isolationism.

"Man has learned long ago," he said, "that it is impossible to live unto himself. This same basic principle applies today to nations. We were not isolated during the war. We dare not now become isolated in peace."[22]

The next day he had an appointment with Budget Director Harold Smith. Reports were stacked on the president's desk. He said he never would have time to read them all. In fact in the fourteen days since taking office, he told a friend, he had taken home so many papers to read into the night that he feared he had seriously strained his eyes.[23] One of the documents on the desk was the Lend-Lease budget. Smith ventured that isolationism could come to the fore again and cause trouble in Congress over such issues as Lend-Lease. That was right, Truman replied. He said he was aware that a good deal of isolationist propaganda was floating around in various guises. The isolationist spirit might well come into the open, he ventured.[24]

In a speech in Kansas City two months later he was to say, in the euphoria over the recent signing of the United Nations Charter, that it would be "just as easy for nations to get along in a republic of the world as it is for us to get along in the republic of the United States."[25] Afterward the United Press reporter, Merriman Smith, asked him about this statement. Rather shyly, Truman replied that he had not originated the idea, whereupon he took from his wallet a worn piece of paper, on which were written ten lines from Tennyson's *Locksley Hall,* ending:

Till the war-drum throbb'd no longer, and the battle
flags were furled
In the Parliament of man, the Federation of the world.

Truman told Smith he had carried the piece of paper in his wallet since 1910.[26]

As a freshman senator, however, he had succumbed for a time to the isolationist argument, growing out of the Senate munitions investigation, that bankers and munitions makers had maneuvered the United States into war in 1917. Before the Second World War he voted for the Neutrality Act, passed on an isolationist tide. The unfolding events in Europe and Asia and perhaps the influence of Roosevelt's leadership changed Truman's mind. He favored revision of the Neutrality Act as well as supporting preparedness and collective security. He had hopes that by bringing nations together in open debate, the United Nations might keep the peace, though he did not place blind faith in the organization.[27]

6.   V-E Day: Triumph and Trouble

ON MAY 7, THE EVE OF V-E DAY, the Trumans moved from Blair House into the White House, forewarned by Mrs. Roosevelt that they would have trouble with rats.[1] Twenty army trucks were required to move the Roosevelts' possessions. One was all that was needed to bring the Trumans' belongings.[2]

The next day Truman celebrated his sixty-first birthday by announcing the German surrender, but not until after some difficulty with Churchill. As the president explained in a letter to his mother and sister:

Have had one heck of a time with the Prime Minister of Great Britain. He, Stalin, and the U.S. President made an agreement to release the news all at once from the three capitals at an hour that would fit us all. We agreed on 9 A. M. Washington time. . . . Mr. Churchill began calling me at daylight to know if we shouldn't make an immediate release without considering the Russians. He was refused and then be kept pushing me to talk to Stalin. He finally had to stick to the agreed plan—but he was mad as a wet hen. . . .[3]

In a V-E Day broadcast Truman said: "Our victory is but half-won. The West is free, but the East is still in bondage to the treacherous tyranny of the Japanese. When the last Japanese division has surrendered unconditionally, then only will our fighting job be done."[4] However, at the instigation of Stimson, Forrestal, and Grew, who hoped that the Japanese might be induced to stop short of resisting unconditional surrender to the end, he issued a separate statement giving assurance that unconditional surrender "does not mean the extermination or enslavement of the Japanese people."[5] Tokyo did not respond.

The end of the war in Europe brought difficult problems for Truman. When the fighting stopped, American forces were deep inside the previously determined Soviet zone of occupation. Appalled by Stalin's tactics and by the surge of the Red Army in Eastern and Central Europe, Churchill wanted Truman to order American forces to stand their ground until the Soviets changed their policies in Eastern Europe. Also the German surrender confronted Truman with the question of what to do about Lend-Lease shipments of wartime material and supplies to the Soviet Union and to the Allies. Both of these were highly sensitive issues, especially when the situation in Poland continued to deteriorate and quarrels between the Soviet Union and the Western nations had broken out at the United Nations conference in San Francisco. In other difficulties furthermore the president was brought into conflict with General Charles de Gaulle over the stationing of French troops in Germany, Italy, and the Middle East and edged toward hostilities with Marshal Tito of Yugoslavia over the occupation of Trieste.

Churchill's entreaties on behalf of using Allied military power on the ground to checkmate the westward thrust of the Red Army had first been made to Roosevelt. Shortly before Roosevelt died the prime minister had urged ''that we should join hands with the Russian armies as far to the east as possible and, if circumstances allow, enter Berlin.''[6] But with the approval of Roosevelt and the Joint Chiefs, Eisenhower—for purely military considerations—drove for the Elbe River south of Berlin, leaving the German capital prey to Soviet troops.

When Truman became president, Churchill renewed the pressure, urging that American troops liberate Prague before the Red Army arrived.[7] When Truman, following Roosevelt's course, supported Eisenhower's more limited advance in Czechoslovakia, Churchill resorted to recommending a prompt Big Three conference. He proposed it to Truman May 6, urging that meanwhile the allied armies hold fast in place. Truman agreed to a meeting. Because of domestic problems, he said he could not leave Washington until after June 30, end of the fiscal year. He also chilled Churchill's hopes of a forward stand by the troops by saying that pending the conference, which ultimately convened at Potsdam in mid-July, ''it is my present intention to adhere to our interpretation of the Yalta agreements.''[8] Even so, Churchill persisted.

''Surely,'' he pleaded with Truman, ''it is vital now to come to an understanding with Russia, or see where we are with her, before we weaken our armies mortally or retire to the zones of occupation.''[9]

The president's final word on the subject was sent to Churchill June 11: ''. . . I am unable to delay the withdrawal of American troops from the Soviet zone in order to use pressure in the settlement of other problems.''[10]

Three distinct threads ran through his motives that spring. He felt obliged to carry out Roosevelt's agreements, especially on the zones of occupation, believing that this was the best way to induce the Soviets to carry out their obligations. He hoped to preserve a working relationship with Moscow so that a decent peace could be achieved. He wanted to be able to move American troops from Europe to the Far East as quickly as possible and to make sure Stalin carried out his pledge to enter the Japanese war.

Like Roosevelt, he took the position that the tactical deployment of American troops in Europe was a military one and accepted the position of the military in opposing Churchill's strategy. Also the State Department warned that using occupation zones for bargaining purposes would only make it more difficult to get the Soviets to cooperate in the occupation of Germany. Finally, after talks with Stalin in Moscow as the president's emissary, the former Roosevelt aide, Harry Hopkins, warned Truman, as the latter recalled, that a delay in withdrawal of American troops from the Soviet zone ''is certain to be misunderstood by the Russians.''[11]

Still the situation in Eastern Europe deteriorated. The West was shocked when sixteen leading non-Communist members of the Polish underground were enticed to a conference with Soviet officials, arrested, and, despite British and American inquiries, held incommunicado for weeks. The Allies suspended negotiations in Moscow on the formation of a new Polish government. Discouraged by developments in Bulgaria and Rumania, Grew told Truman of the increasing ''difficulty of maintaining the position of this Government in an area where the Soviet Government considers its interests paramount.''[12] On May 4 Truman cabled Stalin demanding again that he carry out the Yalta agreement.

''I must tell you,'' he declared, ''that any suggestion that the representatives of the Warsaw Provisional Government be invited to San Francisco, conditionally or otherwise, is wholly unacceptable to the United States Government.''[13]

As in his meeting with Molotov Truman was still talking tough. ''We've got to teach them how to behave,'' he said at one point early in May.[14] As far as Poland was concerned, however, the game was about over. Tough talk was not doing the trick. Stalin would not budge, and Truman was in no position to make him budge. Whatever diplomatic chips may once have been on the American side of the table had long ago been spent. They had been used to shore up the military alliance with Stalin, to win his promise to enter the Japanese war, and to bring him into the United Nations. Now Stalin had his Curzon Line. His troops had inundated Poland. His puppet government ruled in Warsaw. As a practical matter, by the time Truman had taken office it was too late to change these circumstances. That which had been conceded at Teheran and Yalta could not be retrieved.

The heaviest pressures on Truman were in the direction of winning the war, bringing the troops home and getting back to normal. A military confrontation with the Soviet Union over Eastern Europe at that point was out of the question. Furthermore, like Roosevelt, Truman became diverted by larger questions than Poland, now that the war with Germany was finally at an end.

When the excitement of V-E Day ended Truman was faced with the question of curtailing Lend-Lease, another situation for which there had been inadequate planning before he came to office. During the war the United States had furnished the Soviet Union through Lend-Lease more than 17 million tons of supplies valued at more than $10 billion.[15] As the danger of a German victory receded, however, Roosevelt had come under increasingly heavy political pressure to curb lavish spending abroad. Suspicion grew in Congress that he was up to some kind of global New Deal. Hence a movement developed against any use of Lend-Lease assistance by a recipient country for postwar reconstruction. Conscious of the political appeal of this issue, Roosevelt agreed to Republican-sponsored legislation in the House declaring that Lend-Lease could not be used for postwar reconstruction or relief, with certain technical exceptions. Then Senator Robert A. Taft, Republican, of Ohio, proposed an amendment eliminating even these. So strong was the sentiment he reflected that the roll call ended in a tie and the measure was killed only by the vote of Vice-President Truman two days before Roosevelt died.

The experience was sobering to Truman. After becoming president he told Harold Smith that he understood what was bothering the senators and that if he were to consent to the use of Lend-Lease for reconstruction he would be in for a lot of political trouble.[16] With the United Nations Charter and the peace treaties presumably coming along soon for ratification, it was not a time to flout the Senate. Truman's advisers generally agreed that under the law Lend-Lease would have to be curtailed not only for the Soviet Union but for Britain and France, now that V-E Day had passed, though there has always been some question as to whether, technically, curtailment was required at that stage. Truman did not choose to put the issue to a test.

The situation in Congress was probably enough to have forced his hand. In addition, curtailment of Lend-Lease jibed with the policy of exerting economic pressure on the Soviets to mend their ways and of reducing overseas spending generally. On May 9 at the San Francisco conference Stettinius agreed with Harriman that curtailment of Lend-Lease to the Soviets should begin immediately and that future shipments would be scrutinized "with a view to our own interests and policies." They wanted curtailment handled, however, so as not to imply a threat or suggestion of political bargaining.[17] Still it was perfectly clear that the Soviets would resent the act, and nothing was done to prepare them for the blow.

Harriman and other officials drafted a memorandum dated May 11 for the president's signature, providing that only supplies needed for Soviet military operations in the Far East or for completing industrial plants already delivered in part were to be shipped. In presenting it to Truman, both Grew and Foreign Economic Administrator Leo Crowley explained the details and cautioned Truman that the Soviets would be dismayed.[18] Nevertheless he signed it without reading it,[19] and what followed was a mess.

The Subcommittee on Shipping of the President's Soviet Protocol Committee met to act on his directive. Noting that the memorandum said that supplies not needed for Far Eastern operations or for completion of plants were to be cut off immediately, Crowley's representatives, attentive to congressional sentiment, made a literal interpretation. The subcommittee issued orders not only to stop the loading of Soviet supplies at the piers but to turn about the ships that were already at sea, bound for Soviet ports with such cargoes.[20]

The effect on Soviet-American relations was dreadful. The order created the hostile impression in Moscow that Harriman and Stettinius had wished to avert. Hoping to mollify the Soviets and ease the cutback, Harriman obtained Truman's permission to turn the ships about at sea again. Loadings were resumed at the piers. But the repercussions went on. Outraged, Stalin told Hopkins that the action was "brutal"—something done in a "scornful and abrupt manner." If, he said, it was "designed as pressure on the Russians in order to soften them up, then it was a fundamental mistake."[21]

The popular euphoria surrounding the opening of the United Nations conference in San Francisco was soon shattered by quarrels between the United States and Soviet delegates. Following a custom that the host country should provide the presiding officer, Eden moved that Stettinius be named permanent chairman. Molotov demanded rotation among four coequal chairmen, representing the United States, the Soviet Union, Great Britain, and China. Truman and Stettinius fumed together over the telephone and decided that at least the secretary of state should be the senior of the four. Truman told Stettinius to stand his ground on this and tell Molotov to "go to hell" if he was not agreeable to such an arrangement.[22] Seniority turned out to be more or less the way the issue was resolved.

To win the friendship of the Latin American countries and their future support in the United Nations, the United States supported the admission of pro-Fascist Argentina as a founding member. With justification, Molotov objected. At Yalta it had been agreed that Argentina would be excluded.[23] Then the Americans were thrown into a funk when Molotov demanded the seating of the Warsaw regime as the sole representative of Poland. Moreover the conference seemed headed for the rocks over voting procedure in the Security Council. The Americans and British held that under an agreement at Yalta a veto could be exercised only when the council acted on a substantive question. The Soviets now insisted that a veto also could be invoked to prevent an item from appearing on the agenda.

The talk in San Francisco about Soviet-American irreconcilability and the gossip in Washington about the danger of war between the two countries worried Truman, and he called in Joseph E. Davies, former United States ambassador in Moscow, for chats. On one occasion he introduced him to his mother—''Mamma''—who was visiting. She told Davies she had come ''to see that Harry started right.''

The former ambassador was the Kremlin's best friend in Washington, the author of the popular book *Mission to Moscow,* which drew a benign picture of Stalin. In his talks at the White House Davies tried to soften Truman's attitude toward the Soviets, after Truman had provided an opening, by asking whether he had done the right thing in giving Molotov a ''straight one-two to the jaw.'' The Soviets, Davies said, were aware of the feelings against them at some levels of the State Department and the armed services. He cautioned Truman against giving Moscow the impression that he shared these sentiments.[24]

The antagonisms at San Francisco, however, chipped at the good will for the Soviet Union that had flourished in the United States during the war. The tinder of anti-Communism left over from the twenties and thirties had not been totally destroyed in the common effort against Hitler. The sparks from San Francisco did not have far to blow. The idea, nourished in the press, that the Soviets were fouling the peace plans and thus had to be dealt with firmly spread and eventually was carried back to Washington by Vandenberg, a member of the United States delegation, and others. It soon became part of the political climate in which Truman had to work.

At one of the lowest points in the conference Bohlen and Harriman conceived the idea, which Truman later agreed to, of having the President send Hopkins to Moscow to talk to Stalin in an effort to prevent a breakdown.[25] As Roosevelt's alter ego, Hopkins enjoyed a special relationship with Stalin dating back to the early days of the war, and a mission by him would symbolize Truman's desire to carry on Roosevelt's policies. As an adjunct to the mission Truman sent Davies to London to see Churchill, noting in a private memorandum:

''I told him I was having as much difficulty with Prime Minister Churchill as I was having with Stalin—that it was my opinion that each of them was trying to make me the paw of the cat that pulled the chestnuts out of the fire. . . . [I] said I did not want to give the impression I was acting for Great Britain in any capacity, although I wanted support of Great Britain in anything we do as far as peace is concerned. . . .''[26]

Truman did not wish Stalin to get the impression that the president and the prime minister were ''ganging up on him.''[27]

The Davies mission was a sideshow. Rightly or wrongly, Churchill got the impression from Davies that Truman intended to meet alone with Stalin before Potsdam. If that was the plan, Churchill squelched it by threatening to boycott the conference.[28]

The mission to Moscow proved a more substantial affair. Before Hopkins's departure Truman jotted in his diary on May 22:

"To have a reasonably lasting peace the three great powers must be able to trust each other, and they must honestly want it. . . . I want peace and I am willing to work hard for it. It is my opinion we will get it."

He had instructed Hopkins, he noted, to "make it clear to Uncle Joe Stalin that I knew what I wanted—and that I intend to get—peace for the world for at least 90 years."[29]

On the eve of the Hopkins mission Truman assured Stettinius that "Harry would be able to straighten things out with Stalin."[30] Some things, yes, as it turned out. But when it came to Poland things were straightened out Stalin's way.

Hopkins, to be sure, restated the American case.[31] The segment of American opinion that had consistently supported friendly relations with the Soviet Union, he told Stalin, was now so disturbed by events that these relations were threatened. Truman wished to continue Roosevelt's cooperative policies. But: "Without the support of public opinion and particularly of the supporters of President Roosevelt it would be very difficult for President Truman to carry forward President Roosevelt's policy." As things stood, the American people felt that the Soviets wished to dominate Poland.

Stalin brushed it all aside and countered with a proposal that had a familiar ring. The Warsaw regime would form the ruling majority of the future Polish Provisional Government of National Unity. Representatives from other Polish groups who were acceptable to the Allies and the Soviets would have four or five of the eighteen or twenty ministries in the government. Mikolajczyk would be welcome. But no interpretation of the Yalta agreement was possible other than that the Warsaw regime was to form the basis of the new government, the position Stalin had stuck to ever since Yalta.

Hopkins told Truman the list of new candidates for the Polish government, primarily selected by Stalin, was satisfactory; and urged Truman to approve it, which he did in a burst of hope.[32] More realistically, Churchill cabled Truman: "While it is prudent and right to act in this way at the moment, I am sure you will agree with me that these proposals are no advance on Yalta. They are an advance upon deadlock. . . ." But the United States and, at Truman's request, Great Britain recognized the Provisional Government in Warsaw.[33]

So after weeks of conferences, bluster, and handing Molotov his hat, things were back to about where they had stood when the Yalta conference ended as far as Poland was concerned. But having got his way on Poland, Stalin was conciliatory on other issues in his talks with Hopkins.

Before Hopkins left Washington, the president had bade him seek an agreement with Stalin on as early a date as possible for the Soviets' entry into the Japanese war. Stalin agreed that the Red Army would be deployed on the Manchurian border by August 8. In line with the Yalta agreement he pledged his help in unifying

China under Chiang Kai-shek, the Nationalist leader. He endorsed America's "Open Door" policy in China. He agreed to a Big Three meeting in July. Truman had favored Alaska as the site, but Stalin's preference for Potsdam prevailed. The president had asked Hopkins to try to settle with Stalin the question of voting procedure in the United Nations Security Council. Stalin agreed to the American position, thus averting a breakdown at San Francisco and assuring adoption of the Charter. The American position was sound in principle since it assured freedom of debate. If the Security Council was to be a world forum, it was important that problems could be discussed before it and not shunted aside in advance by a veto. Whether, after debate, an issue was vetoed was another matter. All the major powers insisted on that right.

The immediate effect on Truman of the Hopkins-Stalin talks was euphoric. In his first public report on the Hopkins mission at a press conference June 13 he called the results "completely satisfactory and gratifying." He praised Stalin's agreement on voting procedure and other non-Polish issues and said that "the Russians are just as anxious to get along with us as we are with them." A reporter asked if the first step of the new Polish government would be to hold free elections. "I hope so," Truman replied. "That is the reason for setting it up."[34]

Like Roosevelt, he continued to hope that the promised elections would bring to power a non-Communist government. But as time passed no one really took free elections seriously any longer. Eventually Mikolajczyk and some of his friends were forced to flee, the dream of democracy vanished, and Joseph Stalin was left master of Poland.

The troubles with Tito began before the surrender of Germany, when Yugoslav partisans overran much of Italy's northeastern province of Venezia Giulia and entered its port of Trieste. The Allies had plans to occupy the area, and the British especially feared the effect of a Yugoslavian occupation on the postwar settlement of the region. Churchill cabled Truman: "It does not seem to me there is a minute to lose."[35] Truman agreed that the Supreme Allied Commander in the Mediterranean, Field Marshal Sir Harold Alexander, should move troops into Venezia Giulia, risking the possibility of armed conflict.

Truman told Grew he did not intend to commit American forces to fight Yugoslavia.[36] When the situation between Tito and Alexander worsened, Grew erroneously suggested to Truman that the Soviets were behind Tito. Truman replied that he had finally come to the conclusion that clearing out Trieste was the only solution. He admitted this was a reversal of his earlier position, but said developments left him no alternative.[37]

Marshall, however, wanted to avoid military action, and Stimson persuaded Truman to go easy. Overcoming his indignation, Truman telegraphed Churchill May 16: ". . . I am unable and unwilling to involve this country in a war with the Yugoslavs unless they should attack us . . ."[38] Having drawn back from a potentially dangerous military solution, Truman asked Stalin May 20 to use his influence with Tito to resolve the incident. While Stalin's initial reply was disappointing, a compromise was reached eventually. The Allies retained Trieste; Tito held the bulk of the province outside it.

As for the troubles with the French, de Gaulle's troops had entered Stuttgart after the city had been enveloped by Allied forces. Previously drawn lines, however, had placed Stuttgart in the American sector. When American forces sought to relieve the French there, however, the local French commander refused to budge, obeying orders from de Gaulle, who wanted to occupy the city in furtherance of the bid for a French zone of occupation in Germany. Eisenhower appealed to de Gaulle, but de Gaulle would not relent. Eisenhower then turned the issue over to Washington. On May 1 Truman dispatched a note to de Gaulle, threatening to undertake "an entire rearrangement of command," which obviously might affect the flow of American equipment to the French.[39] "I don't like the son of a bitch," Truman told his staff two days later.[40]

De Gaulle backed down, but then other French troops occupied the Val d'Aosta area in northwestern Italy, near the French border. Reports circulated that de Gaulle might try to annex it. Again Eisenhower ordered the French to withdraw, and again they refused. Again Alexander wanted to move in his forces. Truman learned that the French were putting roadblocks in the way of American troops advancing into the area. Stimson told him that he had come to regard de Gaulle as a psychopath. Truman replied that this was his opinion of de Gaulle too.[41]

"The French are using our guns, are they not?" he asked Leahy.

"Yes, sir," Leahy replied.

"All right," Truman said, "We will at once stop shipping guns, ammunition and equipment to de Gaulle."[42]

A public statement to that effect was prepared, but again Stimson prevailed on Truman to tread softly and handle the matter privately with de Gaulle. With Stimson's help a letter was drafted and signed by Truman June 6, appealing to de Gaulle to withdraw the troops. The letter accused the local French commander of "an almost unbelievable threat that French soldiers bearing American arms will combat American and Allied soldiers whose efforts . . . have so recently . . . contributed to the liberation of France itself." Until the threat was withdrawn, the presidential letter said, "I regret that I have no alternative but to issue instructions that no further issues of military equipment or munitions can be made to French troops. Rations will continue to be supplied."[43]

De Gaulle withdrew the troops.

More trouble with the French was brewing, however. This time the scene was the Middle East. After the First World War, France had been given a League of Nations mandate over the Levant (roughly, present Syria and Lebanon) and maintained a garrison there. During the Second World War the Allies recognized Syria and Lebanon as independent nations. Nevertheless de Gaulle insisted on retaining special French rights. Roosevelt, on the other hand, assured King Ibn Saud of Saudi Arabia that if the French tried to thwart Syrian and Lebanese independence, the United States would assist the two countries with "all possible support short of war."

Determined to uphold French interests, de Gaulle landed a new detachment of French forces at Beirut in May. Disorders erupted among the Levantine peoples. French forces were engaged. On May 27 Grew prepared a note asking de Gaulle to change his policy and treat the Levant states as independent nations. Truman approved it. Then, on the advice of Stettinius, he approved a second warning to de Gaulle. The president was thoroughly aroused, and when Churchill asked him to support a British decision to intervene with force, he did so.

The appearance of Royal Air Force squadrons and British armor in Beirut persuaded the French to back down in a most embittered atmosphere. France gradually withdrew.[44] "Those French ought to be taken out and castrated," Truman said at a White House staff meeting May 31.[45]

Truman talked as though he were still living over the wartime disputes when de Gaulle was head of the Free French in London and the American and British invaded North Africa November 8, 1942, and were engaged by French defenders. "The President himself commented one morning recently," Eben A. Ayers, assistant White House press secretary, noted in his diary, "that de Gaulle had insulted President Roosevelt and his troops had killed Americans and he [Truman] could not forgive him for those things."[46] For military and political reasons Roosevelt had tried to keep de Gaulle out of the picture during the North African campaign. He patronized him and intimated that the general thought of himself as Joan of Arc. Returning from Yalta, Roosevelt had invited de Gaulle to meet him in Algiers, and de Gaulle declined, which may have been the "insult" to which Truman alluded.

With the world in turmoil that spring, therefore, Truman was dealing with an enormously complex interplay of events. Simultaneously, the problems of Eastern Europe, the German occupation, reparations, the atomic bomb, and the final form of the war and peace in Asia flowed into a stream that swirled around the Truman administration and eventually drained off to shape the swamp of the postwar world.

Rhetoric aside, Truman pursued a basically conservative course in Trieste, in Poland, in the positioning of American troops in the occupation zone and in relations with Stalin. He proceeded on the assumption that in time the United States and the Soviet Union could iron out their difficulties.

Entwined in these and other events of that crowded spring were developments that passed without much notice but that held the seeds of trouble for the future.

Thus a month after the German surrender Truman sent a telegram to Stalin about the withdrawal of troops to the respective zones of occupation. Among other things he proposed that the commanders make provision for free access for American forces to Berlin by rail, air, and highway.

As the zones had been drawn by the European Advisory Commission during the war and approved at Yalta, Berlin lay 110 miles inside the Soviet zone but was not, legally, a part of it. The Soviets, Americans, British, and later the French were each assigned a sector of the city. The assumption was that the Allies would have rights to access through the Soviet zone. At the time the United States Army wished to keep arrangements flexible and preferred to settle on details later. Thus no guarantee was put in writing concerning routes over which the army might send men and supplies to Berlin.

When Stalin replied to Truman's message he ignored the point about access rights.[47] Later Marshal Georgi K. Zhukov, head of the Soviet occupation, assured his American counterpart, General Lucius D. Clay, that access would be granted.

Yet, although provision was made subsequently for a corridor for American planes, no document was ever signed dealing with access by surface routes.

Serious as the trouble foreshadowed by lack of designated Berlin access routes was, events then occurring in another part of the world held the makings of a calamity for the American people.

With the atomic bomb nearing readiness, with continents in turmoil, with Truman swamped by urgent problems domestic and foreign, Vietnam was a rumble far away in the spring of 1945. Indochina had been a French colony for more than half a century until the Japanese overran it during the war. A question that had been posed before Truman took office was which alternative should be adopted after the defeat of Japan: restoration of French rule, trusteeship, or complete independence for the Indochinese? Struggling to achieve the last of these alternatives in Vietnam was a group of native Communists and nationalists who had organized in 1941 a League for the Independence of Vietnam, or Vietminh, and whose efforts were becoming increasingly effective under the leadership of Ho Chi Minh.

Annoyed by de Gaulle and desiring to eradicate colonialism, Roosevelt had proposed in 1943 that Indochina be placed under a United Nations trusteeship after the war. Churchill fought this policy, fearing that if Roosevelt was able to bar the return of the French to Indochina, the British Empire might someday follow the French Empire down the drain. Other influences weighed against Roosevelt's plan. The weakening of China lessened its chance of replacing the French as a stabilizing force in Southeast Asia. The State Department resisted trusteeship. Influential officials in the department were eager to see France restored as a counterweight to Soviet might in Europe and thus opposed a ban on French restoration in Indochina. The Joint Chiefs of Staff were willing to allow French agents into Indochina for military activities.

Gradually, according to Professor LaFeber, Roosevelt softened his position, saying that the French could retain their colonies if Paris would set independence as an eventual goal. Later he authorized American air forces in China to aid French resistance units combating the Japanese occupation. He acquiesced in the infiltration of French saboteurs into Indochina. On the eve of Roosevelt's death Churchill instructed Admiral Lord Louis Mountbatten, commander of the Southeast Asia Command, to conduct "minimum preoccupational activities in Indochina," even though Indochina lay outside the jurisdiction of the command. Roosevelt never objected. By the time Truman became president the trickle of French back into Indochina had begun without objection by the United States.[48]

Early in the Truman administration the State Department conducted a policy review. The Office of Far Eastern Affairs and the Office of European Affairs agreed that the United States should not seek trusteeship. At the San Francisco conference Stettinius informed the French foreign minister that "the record is entirely innocent of any official statement of this government questioning, even by implication, French sovereignty over Indochina." On June 22 the State Department issued a statement announcing formal recognition, while favoring eventual independence for the Indochinese.[49]

While this was in line with Roosevelt's course, it was a decision for which Truman was now responsible, and a momentous one. Soon the French returned in substantial numbers, frustrating the indigenous movement toward Vietnam independence.

The United States wanted peace and efforts by the French to win the support of the Vietnamese people, even if this meant settling with Ho Chi Minh. The French seemed to be complying by negotiating with Ho and other nationalist groups. The Truman administration, therefore, took a relaxed view, offering to lend assistance, if sought.[50]

The gathering problems were by no means limited to foreign affairs. Even as Truman took office the housing situation was buzzing like an overloaded transformer about to explode. Because of the lack of home construction stemming from the depression and the war, some veterans and their families were living in Quonset huts, chicken coops, boxcars, attics, basements, and even on front porches equipped with hot plates for cooking.

Truman for the first time, too, felt the gusts of the foul weather developing in the labor situation throughout the United States when on May 1 seventy-two thousand members of John L. Lewis's United Mine Workers of America struck the anthracite coal mines over new contract demands. After years of conflict with Roosevelt, Lewis was now embroiled with Truman. Truman thought Lewis's act inexcusable in wartime, an attempt to browbeat him and the federal government.[51] On the recommendation of his highest advisers he ordered the government on May 3 to seize the mines, as Roosevelt had done in earlier disputes, and called on the miners to return to work May 7. Lewis said, "No comment," and the miners refused Truman's request. In the end they won a favorable settlement, and Lewis came off well in his first skirmish with Truman.[52] Their great battles, however, lay ahead.

On June 7, meanwhile, a group of other labor leaders called on Truman and appealed for a relaxation of the "Little Steel" wage formula,* one of the Roosevelt administration's devices for "holding the line" against wartime inflation. By the time Truman took office labor was seething with resentment against it.

Although many Americans were getting rich in the war economy, the National War Labor Board had held that workers should be content to maintain a decent standard of living but not to improve it during the war. On July 16, 1942, the board promulgated the Little Steel formula, under which most workers were allowed a 15 percent wage increase to offset a similar increase in the cost of living since January 1, 1941.

Once the war against Germany was won, restlessness erupted among the unions. Resentment was spurred by rising prices on one hand and, on the other, by cutbacks in war production, reducing the number of hours of work, notably in overtime, and hence the size of the weekly paychecks. On April 29 the executive committee of the American Federation of Labor asked for revision of Little Steel. Then Philip Murray, president of the Congress of Industrial Organizations,† urged an increase of seventeen cents an hour for workers in steel and other heavy industries.

At a meeting with labor leaders June 7 Truman decided to retain the Little Steel

---

* "Little Steel" took its name from the settlement of a contract dispute between the United Steel Workers of America and five small steel companies.

† The AFL and CIO did not merge until 1955.

formula for the time being. "We will work out a survey of the situation at a later date, and then come to a conclusion," he told reporters.[53]

It was calm language for a man sitting on a time bomb. When Truman got around to his diary later in the day, however, he could at least console himself with the prospect of success at the San Francisco conference:

We may get a peace yet. . . .
There's no Socialism in Russia. It is the hotbed of special privilege. A common every-day citizen has about as much to say about his government as an average stockholder in a giant corporation. But I do not care what they do. They evidently like their government or they would not die for it. I like ours, so let's get along. But when Russia puts out propaganda to help our parlor pinks—well that is bad—and that must stop. . . .

His thoughts were still running along this line in his diary on June 13: "Propaganda seems to be our greatest foreign relations enemy. Russians distribute lies about us."[54]

Truman's political honeymoon continued through the spring, but war weariness, shortages of all kinds, and labor's resentment were enough to insure trouble ahead. In the first glow of the honeymoon Robert Taft, and a group of other leading Republican senators had called on their old colleague who was now in the White House and wished him well. Truman and Taft were poles apart politically. Still Truman esteemed Taft as intelligent, ethical, and trustworthy.[55] And Taft liked Truman, describing him to a friend at the time as "a straightforward man and much franker than Roosevelt." "He has the quality of decision which is a good thing in an executive," he added, though he was concerned about Truman's lack of "education or background to analyze soundly the large problems which are before him."

However, Taft made the mistake of surmising that the president "will go with the conservative side" in any split within the Democratic party.

By May 25 the positions the president had taken on various issues had disillusioned the senator. Truman "will be as much a New Dealer as Roosevelt. I cannot discover any tendency to turn to a conservative policy," he lamented in a letter to an uncle. Prophetically, he added: "There are going to be a good many violent controversies here during the next twelve months. Especially, he seems to be embracing the spending policies of the New Deal and the making of huge loans abroad to keep up our employment in this country. I can only hope that he does not acquire the popularity of Roosevelt for election purposes."[56]

Truman sensed Taft's change of heart and felt, resentfully, that Taft had broken a sort of truce between them.[57] He was conscious of the transitoriness of his honeymoon.

"I know those boys up there very well," he told Harold Smith, intimating that the politicians in Congress would love him as long as they found it to their advantage.[58]

By June Taft was attacking Truman publicly.

An incident that foreshadowed nasty consequences for Truman occurred June 6 when the Federal Bureau of Investigation arrested six persons in connection with the discovery of classified documents in the New York offices of an obscure magazine, *Amerasia*. An offshoot of the Institute of Pacific Relations, it favored the cause of the Chinese Communists.

One of those arrested was John Stewart Service, charged with conspiracy to violate a section of the Espionage Act dealing with the unauthorized removal and possession of documents relating to national defense. Born in China of missionary parents, Service was one of the State Department's ablest experts on China. He had been part of a group of Foreign Service officers who had been assigned as political advisers to Lieutenant General Joseph W. Stilwell, commander of the China-Burma-India Theater. One of Service's responsibilities was to study and assess the Chinese Communists, who held most of north China.

American policy was one of conditional support of Generalissimo Chiang Kai-shek and the Kuomintang (the ruling National People's Party) though this backing was not a blank check and was intended to be kept flexible so that the United States could adjust to the ultimate political situation in China. To bring military pressure on the Japanese invaders and to assure future Chinese stability, however, the Roosevelt administration also favored reconciliation between the Nationalists under Chiang and the Communists under Mao Tse-tung, and eventual absorption of the Communists in a unified Chinese government.[59]

Eventually, the task of fostering reconciliation was assumed by Roosevelt's personal representative, and later ambassador, in China, Major General Patrick J. Hurley. A handsome Irishman with every color in the rainbow in his temperament, he had been born in a log cabin in what was then the Indian territory of Oklahoma, to become secretary of war under Hoover and friend of Franklin Roosevelt. Now, at sixty-two, an erratic, irascible, not to say outlandish and pathetic figure, Hurley brought to his assignment a vast ignorance of the Chinese problem and a conviction that the Nationalists were stronger than the Communists. Hence Chinese unity must be achieved through Chiang. In particular, Hurley insisted that only through Chiang would the United States furnish arms to the Communists to fight the Japanese.

John Service and other Foreign Service officers in China took a different view of things. They saw Chiang's government as corrupt, inefficient, and increasingly alienated from the people because of the failure to bring about reforms. They believed Chiang was losing support among the Chinese and was unable to fight the Japanese effectively. By contrast, as they saw it, the Communists were strong. They were sure to control at least north China after the war. They had a dedicated organization that was initiating reforms and winning the support of large numbers of Chinese. Service and his colleagues counseled that the United States should not indefinitely underwrite Chiang's politically bankrupt regime in Chungking, but should make every effort to win the friendship of the Communists, too, and not let them drift into the Soviet camp by default.[60]

Hurley demonstrated his feelings about such diplomatic reporting by upbraiding Service and threatening him with demotion.[61] Nevertheless Service and a group of other Foreign Service officers, including George A. Atcheson, Jr., charge d'affaires at the United States embassy in Chungking, drafted and signed a set of recommendations on China policy and cabled it to the State Department February 28, while Hurley was conferring in Washington. The group recommended "that the

President inform the Generalissimo in definite terms that military necessity requires that we supply and cooperate with the Communists and other suitable groups who can assist the war against Japan.'' In short, Chiang would be deprived of any veto over American policy in China.[62]

Hurley was indignant. He accused the Foreign Service officers of disloyalty. He besieged Roosevelt, Marshall, Stimson, and Stettinius, and in the end obtained the president's support of his policy of requiring Chiang's consent for any help to the Communists.[63] In the furor over the February 28 telegram Hurley forced the Roosevelt administration to reassign Service to Washington. He also got Service's colleagues sent to other posts, thus ending the reporting of America's ablest experts in China.

Service returned April 12. One month earlier, on March 11, agents of the Office of Strategic Services had made an illegal search of the *Amerasia* office at 225 Fifth Avenue because one of its articles contained, almost verbatim, classified OSS material. In their search March 11 the agents found hundreds of classified documents. These were turned over to the FBI, which then initiated surveillance of several persons, including Philip J. Jaffe, coeditor. While under surveillance, Jaffe was introduced to Service after the latter's return from China. At Stillwell's direction, Service had often briefed reporters in China. Once back in Washington, he continued providing background information to journalists, including Jaffe. In fact, he indiscreetly lent the *Amerasia* editor, for background use, his own copies of eight to ten reports he had filed from China. In April and May he saw Jaffe seven times, and, of course, the FBI knew it.[64]

Arrests were about to be made when Forrestal, learning what was afoot because a navy lieutenant was one of the suspects, urged caution lest the case embarrass the president while Hopkins was in Moscow.[65] But when Grew got wind of things and learned that the prosecution of the case was being impeded, he and Julius C. Holmes, assistant secretary of state for security, went to see Truman and told him so.

Angrily, Truman telephoned the Department of Justice and, as Holmes recalled the substance of his words, told the official who handled the call:

This is the President speaking. I don't care who has told you to stop this. You are not to do it. Go straight ahead with this and it doesn't matter who gets hurt. This has to be run down. If anybody suggests that you postpone, or anything else, you are not to do it without first personal approval from me.[66]

The suspects, including Service were arrested. Of the six, Jaffe and another man were indicted and fined. The grand jury voted unanimously not to indict Service, and the State Department cleared him and returned him to duty. This was, however, only the first of nine lives of the *Amerasia* case. All the others were to blend dismally into years of loyalty board hearings, congressional investigations, the rise of the China Lobby, recriminations over the "loss of China," and the onslaughts of Senator Joseph R. McCarthy.

7. *Atomic Bomb: The Fateful Momentum*

ON JUNE 1 TRUMAN arose with the sun and, indulging his taste for nattiness, put on one of three new seersucker suits sent him as a gift by a New Orleans cotton firm.[1] In keeping with the exorbitant pace at which he had been moving and making decisions he had a most eventful day. Somehow he even found time to do some jotting in his occasional diary and recalled a visit a few days earlier from Herbert Hoover.

"We discussed our prima donnas and wondered what makes them," he noted. "Some of my boys who came in with me are having trouble with their dignity and prerogatives. It's hell when a man gets in close association with the President. Something happens to him."[2]

Ending Hoover's long ostracism from the White House, Truman sent for him and discussed Hoover's experience in distributing relief to Europeans after the First World War, a subject that was pertinent again in the new danger of postwar starvation. Later Truman appointed him honorary chairman of the Famine Emergency Committee and in 1947 sent him on an important fact-finding mission to Germany. "He loved Harry Truman for permitting him to work and to contribute," Hoover's biographer, Gene Smith, wrote. "He told his friends Truman added ten years to his life."[3]

The two principal events before Truman that first day of June were the dispatch to Congress of a special message on "Winning the War with Japan" and a meeting with Byrnes to receive the report of the Interim Committee which the president had established in April to advise him on nuclear energy. The two matters bore upon each other. In a prophetic message Truman told Congress:

The primary task facing the nation today is to win the war in Japan—to win it completely and to win it as quickly as possible. . . . There can be no peace in the world until the military power of Japan is destroyed. . . . The strategy of the war in Europe was to have all the men that could be effectively deployed on land and sea to crush the German military machine in the shortest possible time. That is exactly what we plan to do in Japan. . . . Our military policy for the defeat of Japan calls for . . . using ships, aircraft, armor, artillery and all other material in massive concentrations. . . .

These then are our plans for bringing about the unconditional surrender of Japan. If the Japanese insist on continuing resistance beyond the point of reason, their country will suffer the same destruction as Germany. Our blows will destroy their whole modern industrial plant and organization. . . . We have the men, the materiel, the skill, the leadership, the fortitude to achieve total victory.[4]

All the elements of the great decisions of the next two months were fore-shadowed in this message.

Japan undoubtedly could have been starved out by American air and sea power eventually, but no one knew how long that would take—perhaps years; therefore the war must be won quickly. Japan was shattered; nevertheless, since the atomic bomb was still untested, an invasion on the Normandy scale was planned. Perhaps peace on terms somewhat less than unconditional surrender was possible; nevertheless, Japanese military power must be destroyed and unconditional surrender demanded. Finally, in the American military tradition, all power, including the atomic bomb—if it worked—must be brought to bear to inflict destruction and achieve total victory.

Thus quick and total victory leading to unconditional surrender and ac-complished by invasion and massed military might was the picture already in Tru-man's mind June 1. It was a picture formed through inherited strategies and weeks of talks with Marshall and others, and none of the senior advisers seriously or force-fully dissented.

The unanimous report of the Interim Committee, brought to the White House by Byrnes that first day of June, recommended: (1) The bomb should be used against Japan as soon as possible. (2) It should be used on a dual target—a military installation or war plant near houses and other buildings most susceptible to damage—so as to demonstrate the bomb's power. (3) It should be used without prior warning about the nature of the weapon.[5]

For months some of the policymakers had discussed an idea of attempting to bring about a Japanese surrender by a noncombat demonstration of the bomb before Japanese officials, if they would agree to attend, with the hope of convincing them that further resistance would be futile. For a number of reasons, however, the idea did not seem so practical then as it has appeared to many persons a generation later. In the thirty-odd years since there has been time to imagine sophisticated undertak-. ings such as demonstrating the bomb in Tokyo Bay, but the problem did not appear so simple to the men who were dealing with it in the stress of the moment.

Dr. Isidor I. Rabi of Columbia University, a Nobel laureate, who was not a member of the Interim Committee nor its scientific panel but who was knowledge-able on the subject because of his role as a periodic troubleshooter for Oppenheimer at Los Alamos, said afterward that he did not see at the time how the bomb could have been used in a demonstration for the Japanese.

"Who would they send," he asked, "and what would he report? You would have to tell him what instruments to bring, and where to stand, and what to mea-sure. Otherwise it would look like a lot of pyrotechnics.

"It would take someone who understood the theory to realize what he was seeing. It was not a trivial point. You would have to have built a model town to make a realistic demonstration. It would require a level of communications between us and the Japanese which was inconceivable in wartime.

"And while they [the Japanese] argued for weeks, or maybe months, over the meaning of the explosion, we would be honor-bound to wait for an answer. And what would President Truman say to the American people afterward? How could he explain to them that he had had a weapon to stop the war but had been afraid to use it, because it employed principles of physics that hadn't been used in wartime before?''[6]

So for various reasons the Interim Committee did not recommend a demonstration. The United States did not have atomic bombs to spare. By early August it would have only two. The nuclear device had not yet been tested in May. If a bomb was taken to a demonstration and failed to explode, the fiasco might stiffen Japanese resistance. The Japanese might expose American prisoners of war to the blast. The brilliant Dr. Oppenheimer, a member of the scientific panel advising the Interim Committee, could not think of a demonstration spectacular enough to convince the Japanese to surrender.[7] Future events did not necessarily discredit this judgment. When the attack was finally made on Hiroshima, fanatical Japanese army officers disputed its significance, opposed suggestions that peace terms be accepted, and even threw doubt on Truman's announcement that the weapon was an atomic bomb.[8]

Considering the magnitude of the subject, the Interim Committee's deliberations were superficial. Before the bomb was used the question of nuclear policy in all its aspects was never debated before Truman in the way, for example, that the Cuban missile crisis was later debated before President Kennedy. So far as is known, Truman did not explore the question outside the circle of his senior advisers, but then the secrecy of the project was inhibiting. That spring Truman's decision-making process was highly restricted.

The recommendations of the Interim Committee were only advisory. The ultimate responsibility for recommending use of the bomb to Truman rested with Stimson; and he assumed it, unhesitatingly. He recalled:

The conclusions of the committee were similar to my own, although I reached mine independently. I felt that to extract a genuine surrender from the Emperor and his military advisers, there must be administered a tremendous shock which would carry convincing proof of our power to destroy the empire. Such an effective shock would save many times the number of lives, both American and Japanese, that [than] it would cost.[9]

Truman did not challenge this recommendation nor the reasoning of the Interim Committee. He made no formal decision then. But, of course, the committee's report added to the momentum behind the bomb. Truman told Byrnes that while he was reluctant to use the weapon, he saw no way of avoiding it.[10] Thus the notion that giving the order for a nuclear attack was something he was going to have to do, like it or not, was fixed in his mind almost from the start. Nothing in the vicissitudes of the next two months changed his mind.

On that same June 1 the battle of Okinawa was at a climax, offering a dread glimpse of what an invasion of the Japanese home islands might be like and reminding Truman and his advisers what an atomic bomb might spare men under their command. Japanese soldiers were fighting to the death from caves and escarpments and even from behind old Chinese tombs. American troops were being shot while scaling cliffs to incinerate the defenders with flamethrowers.

At one point earlier in the fighting six American battleships, six cruisers, and eight destroyers joined in bombarding Japanese positions. When the naval fire ended, the holocaust was continued by twenty-seven American artillery battalions—342 pieces in all. A total of nineteen thousand shells blasted the Japanese lines, in the greatest concentration of artillery in the war in the Pacific. So well were the Japanese dug in, however, that when three American units advanced in the wake of the shells, they were repelled with heavy casualties.

Hundreds of kamikaze attacks sank or damaged scores of American warships and landing craft, spreading a particular terror through their crews. Although the plight of the Japanese soldiers became increasingly hopeless, they launched fierce counterattacks from the hills. By the time the battle ended with Okinawa in American hands the United States had suffered 45,000 casualties. The Japanese had lost 100,000 men. And Okinawa was only sixty miles long and two miles wide at the maximum.[11]

The men who would have to give the order had before them a stark image of what it would be like for American troops to grapple with the Japanese on their own soil, planning for which was proceeding. The objective of invading the home islands had been set by the Allies at a second Quebec conference in 1944.

Truman and Stimson discussed the bomb again June 6, at which time the secretary conveyed to Truman a recommendation of the Interim Committee that the bomb should not be revealed to the Soviets before it was used. Stimson also observed that he did not want the United States to get the reputation of outdoing Hitler in atrocities. On the other hand, conventional bombing was spreading such destruction in Japan, he remarked, that the atomic bomb might not seem appreciably worse and thus might lose some of its shock value. Truman laughed and said he understood what Stimson meant.[12]

Throughout those weeks Stimson had kept reflecting on the role the bomb might play in solving diplomatic problems. His diary contained references to the uniqueness of the weapon and to the royal straight flush the United States was in a position to play. In connection with settlements in Manchuria and North China, he confided to his diary that the possession of the bomb might be dominant and at another point described it as a "master card."[13] Before the end of their meeting on the sixth Truman and Stimson had considered the possibility of obtaining concessions from the Soviets in return for taking them into partnership in atomic energy. Truman mentioned some of the same areas of concession that had occurred to Stimson, including not only Manchuria but Poland, Rumania, and Yugoslavia.[14] Yet they never attempted to make any such deal with Stalin. On the other hand, their conversation and Stimson's jottings were evidence of the extent to which Truman and his advisers speculated on possession of the bomb as a means of gaining concessions from the Soviet Union. There is no evidence they ever thought of using the weapon against anyone but the Japanese.

Truman pondered the use of the atomic bomb in an epoch of commonplace carnage. Men of his generation were inured to the bombing of civilian populations. They had seen it in the First World War, in Italy's invasion of Ethiopia in 1935, and in the Spanish Civil War of 1936–38. The Germans had bombed the Poles in 1939, destroyed Rotterdam in 1940, and then turned their bombers and V-2 rockets loose on British cities. As a prologue to the Second World War the Japanese had slaughtered two or three hundred thousand Chinese civilians in Nanking.[15]

One night five weeks before Truman took office General Curtis Le May's B-29s had dropped two thousand tons of napalm bombs on Tokyo. "Huge balls of fire leaped from building to building with hurricane force, creating an incandescent tidal wave exceeding 1,800 degrees Fahrenheit." American crews in the last wave of the attack could smell burning flesh below. Some of the fliers vomited. Sixteen square miles of Tokyo were burned to the ground. The number of dead reached 125,000, although that was no novelty after the recent Anglo-American bombing of Dresden. After Tokyo, Le May's incendiary attacks turned Nagoya, Osaka, and Kobe into infernos. Another tremendous firebombing seared Tokyo May 23. Many of the more than 83,000 persons who perished died of asphyxiation as they rushed toward the Meiji Shrine for salvation.[16] It would not be surprising if by this time the moral issue had seemed a trifle shopworn to those concerned with the decision on whether to use the atomic bomb.

As the bomb neared the testing stage, nevertheless, anguish spread among many of the scientists who had worked on it and who now dreaded its implications for humanity. Like Niels Bohr, two of the leading scientists on the project, Dr. Leo Szilard, a Hungarian émigré, and Dr. James O. Franck, a German refugee and Nobel laureate, favored a system of international control of atomic energy to avert an arms race with the Soviet Union. Szilard tried to see Truman to present arguments but was directed by the White House instead to an unsatisfactory meeting with Byrnes. At the Metallurgical Laboratory in Chicago Franck chaired a committee consisting of Szilard, Glenn T. Seaborg, Eugene Rabinowitch, Donald Hughes, Joyce Stearns, and J. J. Nickson, which drew up a report that Franck took to Washington June 12. The report argued that a surprise attack on Japan might create such mistrust in Moscow as to precipitate an arms race and prejudice the case for future international control. When he got to Washington, Franck tried to give the report to Stimson, but left a copy with a subordinate when told the secretary was not available.[17]

Partly because of the Franck report, however, the question of demonstrating the bomb before using it was referred to the Interim Committee's scientific panel. For these scientists the overriding issue was the immediate saving of lives. Without attempting to assess alternative strategies, they regarded the bomb as a legitimate weapon. Before it was used, they suggested, the Allies, including the Soviets, should be notified of American progress in building an atomic bomb and the likelihood of the bomb's being used. Nevertheless their report June 16 said: "We can propose no technical demonstration likely to bring an end to the war; we see no acceptable alternative to direct military use."[18]

The secrecy surrounding the whole undertaking kept this agitation from the public and curtailed discussion of nuclear policy. Truman, too, was isolated from it. Of all the petitions, reports and statements by dissenting scientists, perhaps only one reached him, reportedly carried by Stimson. This was an emotional letter written May 24 by an engineer in the Manhattan Engineer District named O. C. Brewster. "I beg of you, sir," he addressed Truman, "not to pass this off because I happen to be an unknown, without influence or a name in the public eye." His point: "This thing must not be permitted to exist on earth." He appealed for at least a demonstration for the Japanese before the bomb was used.[19]

The Interim Committee reviewed the scientists' report, though neither then nor later did the committee listen to the dissenting scientists, nor did it pass on their views to Truman. The committee reaffirmed its original recommendation that the bomb be used in a surprise attack at the earliest opportunity. Another milestone was passed on the road to Hiroshima and Nagasaki. The committee had, however, become increasingly concerned that the sudden explosion of a secret bomb over Japan would shock the Soviets and inject new mistrust into Soviet-American relations. Reversing its earlier stand, therefore, it recommended that when the president got to Potsdam he should mention to Stalin that the United States was working on the bomb and intended to use it against Japan. Stimson agreed and conveyed the recommendation to Truman.[20]

On June 18 Truman met with his senior advisers for a decision on strategy. Leahy had informed the Joint Chiefs in advance that the president intended "to make his decisions . . . with the purpose of economizing to the maximum extent possible in the loss of American lives."[21]

Marshall opened the discussion by offering the views of the Joint Chiefs, Eisenhower, MacArthur, and Admiral Nimitz, commander of the Pacific Fleet, in favor of the invasion of the Japanese island of Kyushu November 1 as the first step toward the grand invasion of Honshu March 1. Casualties for the first thirty days were estimated at 31,000. Marshall said the invasion was the only course to take. Air power alone, he maintained, could not knock Japan out of the war. Eisenhower and Lieutenant General Ira C. Eaker, air chief of staff, supported this view, Marshall noted. He said invasion was the only way the Japanese could be forced into a feeling of utter helplessness. Originally, the navy and air force had not believed the Kyushu invasion was necessary, but had been brought around to support Marshall's view.

Truman, revealing what was on his mind, observed that the invasion would create another Okinawa closer to the heart of Japan. The Joint Chiefs agreed with him. As he understood it then, the president said, the Joint Chiefs, after weighing all alternatives, unanimously favored invasion. The chiefs confirmed this.

Truman asked Stimson for his opinion. Stimson said he agreed with the Chiefs that there was no other choice but invasion. Truman asked if invasion of Japan by white men might not cause the Japanese to close ranks. Stimson thought so. Truman told the group he would strive at Potsdam to obtain all possible assistance in the Far East from the Soviets.

Leahy objected to demanding unconditional surrender from Japan lest it make the Japanese desperate and increase casualties. Unconditional surrender was not necessary for victory, he argued. For this very reason, Truman replied, sympathetically, he had left the door open to Congress to take appropriate action with respect to unconditional surrender. He declared that he did not feel he could at that point act to change public opinion. This was not an invigorating commentary on presidential leadership. Yet unquestionably it would have strained his authority for Truman at this late date publicly to have reversed the policy of unconditional surrender, especially since he had committed himself to it before Congress April 16.

Assistant Secretary of the Army John J. McCloy finally raised the question of using the atomic bomb, but warning the emperor in advance. Since no one knew whether the weapon would work, however, the subject was not pursued.

In the end the president gave his approval to the invasion of Kyushu and said with resignation that he hoped they could avert an Okinawa from one end of Japan to another.

On June 25 a document that neither Truman nor his advisers had ever seen nor heard of came to light and was brought to Stimson with an explanation that it had been mislaid in the Roosevelt Administration. The document was an aide-mémoire that Roosevelt and Churchill had initialed secretly at Hyde Park, New York, September 18, 1944. The two leaders specifically agreed that the "suggestion that the world should be informed" about the bomb, "with a view to an international agreement regarding its control and use is not accepted."

"The matter," they said, "should continue to be regarded as of the utmost secrecy; but when a 'bomb' is finally made, it might perhaps, after mature consideration, be used against the Japanese, who should be warned that this bombardment will be repeated until they surrender."[22]

The warning was not specified as being a prior warning.

If mistrust of the Soviet Union had been that compelling and had commanded such secrecy in September of 1944, what reason was there to suppose that a new president, not elected to the office, would take a different view amid the tensions in June of 1945 or assume the political risk of reversing Roosevelt's policy? Or that Congress would have found it tolerable if he had?

8. *Truman, Stalin, Churchill*

I N CONTRAST TO Woodrow Wilson's spectacular descent on Paris for the Versailles Conference in 1918 President Truman arrived unostentatiously in Antwerp July 15 on the way to the Big Three meeting in Potsdam. He had originally informed Churchill that he could not leave Washington until the end of the fiscal year, June 30. Later he told Joseph Davies that in addition to his responsibilities for the budget he had another reason for postponing the conference until July, which was that this was the month when the atomic bomb was going to be tested in Alamogordo, New Mexico.[1] Evidently, Truman and his advisers believed that a successful test would strengthen the United States position at Potsdam.

"I have a brief case all filled up with information on past conferences and suggestions on what I'm to do and say," he had written to his mother and his sister, before departing. "Wish I didn't have to go, but I do and it can't be stopped now."[2]

He confided to Ickes, according to the latter's diary, "that he did not want to make this trip and did not believe he would accomplish anything."[3]

The president and the United States delegation sailed for Europe aboard the heavy cruiser *Augusta* from Norfolk July 7. Before retiring the first night at sea Truman noted in his diary:

I am making this trip, determined to work for and win the peace. I am giving nothing away except I will do everything I can to save starving and war-battered people but I hope we will be able to help people to help themselves. This is the only sound policy.[4]

On the crossing he studied background papers and proposals prepared by the State Department. "He rarely philosophized about the future of the world," recalled Charles Bohlen, who was aboard. "He preferred to address himself to the practicalities of the questions."[5] Truman was eager to dispose of these as quickly as possible and return to the problems accumulating at home.[6] From Antwerp he flew to Berlin in the presidential plane the *Sacred Cow* and then drove the remaining ten miles to his official residence at No. 2 Kaiserstrasse in suburban Babelsberg, a section of Potsdam, where, on the sixteenth, his first caller was Winston Churchill. It was the first time the two had ever met, although Truman had observed Churchill on several occasions in Washington.

Though self-confident, Truman seemed rather nervous at stepping upon the stage with two such overpowering figures as Churchill and Stalin.[7] Whatever his failings, Churchill's erudition, eloquence, wit and grace, his role in world affairs stretching back for decades, his inspiring leadership of the British people in their desperate days had endowed him with a grandeur such as would never emanate from Truman. A descendant of the dukes of Marlborough, Churchill exemplified yet the British Empire of its great days. He had been first lord of the admiralty when Truman was a private in the Missouri National Guard and had been colonial secretary when Truman was selling men's wear at Twelfth and Baltimore in Kansas City.

On the strength of their fame and past careers Churchill towered above Truman then. As a statesman, Truman still was an amateur next to him. Even so, changes were occurring that altered the relative status, if not the comparative endowments, of the two men. World power was ebbing from the man from Harrow and Sandhurst and flowing toward the man who had plowed the fields at Grandview. The great days of the British Empire had passed. Britain's economy was drained and her military forces overextended. It was Truman's empire on which the sun did not set now.

The two had traits in common. They were men of stamina and determination. Joie de vivre was strong in both of them, and both had an earthy humor, a sarcastic streak, and a love of conviviality. While Churchill was a person of greater presence, there was a core of dignity in Truman that could withstand any man.

Both he and the prime minister were pleased with one another. Truman particularly enjoyed listening to Churchill talk, and Churchill recalled having been captivated by Truman's "gay, precise, sparkling manner and obvious power of decision." The next day when Churchill was asked by his physician, Lord Moran, if Truman had ability, he replied, "I should think he has. At any rate he is a man of immense determination. He takes no notice of delicate ground, he just plants his foot down firmly upon it." To illustrate, Lord Moran recalled, Churchill "jumped a little off the wooden floor and brought his bare feet down with a smack."[8]

The conference had been scheduled to start that afternoon of the sixteenth, but Stalin was delayed. After the meeting with Churchill, therefore, Truman toured the ruins of Berlin. One of the stops was at the bombed-out Reichschancellery.

"It just shows what can happen when a man overreaches himself," he told reporters, righteously, and then commented to Byrnes, "I don't know whether they learned anything from it or not."[9]

When Vaughan asked him privately, however, if he wished to go inside, Truman replied, "No, I wouldn't want any of these unfortunate people to think I was gloating over them in any way."[10]

Although he did not know it at the moment, the ruin Truman beheld was but a paltry sample of that which man was now capable of spreading. For three hours earlier, as General Groves officially described the scene, a tremendous blast had shattered the desert near Alamogordo. "For a brief period there was a lighting effect within a radius of 20 miles equal to several suns in midday; a huge ball mushroomed and rose to a height of over ten thousand feet before it dimmed."[11]

Shortly after Truman returned to his residence Stimson hurried over with a top secret cable from his Washington assistant, Harrison. The message, which Stimson showed to Truman and Byrnes, read: "Operated on this morning. Diagnosis not yet complete but results seem satisfactory and already exceed expectations."[12] The atomic bomb was theoretical no longer. The culmination of this mammoth enterprise, giving the United States immeasurable power and offering hope for a quick end of the war with Japan, made it all the less likely that Truman would try to turn back the lethal tide now.

The news was a fitting backdrop for a meeting between the president and Generalissimo Joseph V. Stalin the next day, the seventeenth. The two men, who saw each other for the first time, were destined to embody one of the deepest and most dangerous political and ideological conflicts in history. It was a conflict that neither of them desired in the wake of war, certainly. Without question Truman hoped and believed it could be averted, oversimplified as his understanding of the situation undoubtedly was. The cordiality of his first meeting with the Soviet leader must have nourished his hopes that the Big Three together could achieve peace.

Stalin having arrived a day late, his call was impromptu. When his automobile pulled up to No. 2 Kaiserstrasse, there was a momentary stiffness over protocol, quickly dispelled, however, when Vaughan, now a brigadier general, bounded down the steps in a baggy uniform, pumped the generalissimo's hand and escorted him up to the house and introduced him to the president.[13]

Stalin was accompanied by Molotov, whom Truman welcomed as though their curt scene in the White House in April had never occurred. Truman told Stalin he had long looked forward to meeting him. Stalin replied that personal relationships between heads of government were important. Truman said he did not believe they would have any trouble reaching agreements at the conference.

Puffing a cigarette, Stalin was dressed in a fawn-colored uniform with red epaulets. Truman wore a double-breasted suit. Stalin, nearly five years the older, seemed tired.[14] He looked at Truman through small eyes in a pocked face with a mustache. Truman, fresh, healthy, clean-shaven, returned the gaze with his bright eyes magnified as usual by his glasses. Settling down in overstuffed chairs and speaking through interpreters, they talked at first about items on the conference agenda.[15] Stalin reminded Truman that the Yalta Conference had not settled the western boundary of Poland. There would be trouble about *that* at Potsdam, but the matter was not pursued now.

Byrnes joshed Stalin about the dictator's habit of sleeping late, but Stalin said, unhumorously, in his monotone that the war had changed that. Suddenly he denounced the Franco regime in Spain. It had been imposed on the Spaniards by the Germans and Italians, he said, and its continuance was a danger to the United Nations, since the regime would be a probable haven for Fascist remnants. Stalin thought the right thing to do would be to break off relations with Franco and give the Spaniards a chance to choose a new government.

Truman, who disliked the Franco government, agreed that the question should be studied.

The president tried to brighten things up a bit with a humorous reference to "Uncle Joe," as Stalin was alluded to by the Americans and the British; but the dictator did not seem to think it terribly funny. So Truman grew serious again. He was no diplomat, he assured his guest. He would not beat around the bush. His style would be yes-or-no. Stalin appreciated that and said he would try to be responsive.

The world had had to take many turns to bring Harry Truman and Joseph Stalin face to face as leaders of the two most powerful nations. Both had been born in rural obscurity, but little else in their careers was similar. Stalin had had a harsh youth;

prison and exile followed. Truman's boyhood had been a gentle one, colored by bourgeois dreams and ideals. Where young Stalin had turned revolutionary, Truman had gladly accepted the society into which he had been born, and he had played the game by its rules.

From his youth Stalin had been domineering, crafty, suspicious, conspiratorial, often cruel and terroristic; yet he sometimes did have in private an avuncular air and retained a peasant's interest in nature. He loved to wander in the garden of his dacha and prune twigs and enjoy the flowers and the woods.[16] In contrast to Stalin's dark traits, Truman was open, good-natured, gregarious, sensible, industrious, and conventional in morals and politics.

In his insights into men and his mastery of the tides Stalin was a giant next to Truman then, but an evil giant. Truman was a stubborn man, but Stalin was ruthless. He had a lust for power such as Truman was incapable of feeling. In diplomacy he was a master while Truman was still a novice. Murderous and deceitful, Stalin had made himself a tyrant, but one with the will to forge the Soviet Union into a strong modern nation. Despite his mistakes, the Soviet people under his leadership had performed prodigies in turning back Hitler's onslaught.

Truman had endured no such crucible. If anything, he had rather floated to the top, making scarcely an enemy or a wave on the way. Having reached the pinnacle, however, he had revealed a surprising capacity, not for commanding the tides, certainly, but for standing up to very great challenges, as he saw them. His blandness was deceptive, after all. In the case of Truman and Stalin tough fiber had grown from radically different soils.

The morning had waned at No. 2 Kaiserstrasse; and while Stalin was conversing with Byrnes, Vaughan slipped in and inquired of Truman, "Are you going to ask these guys for lunch?" A luncheon had not been arranged in advance because of the informal nature of the call.

"Can we feed them?" Truman whispered.

"Liver and bacon," Vaughan replied.

"If liver and bacon is good enough for us, it's good enough for them," Truman whispered.[17]

Interrupting Stalin's talk with Byrnes, Truman asked the generalissimo if he and Molotov would not stay for lunch. Stalin protested they couldn't.

"You could if you wanted to," Truman persisted.[18]

They did, finally. However Stalin may have found the liver and bacon, he exclaimed so much over the California wine that was served that Truman later sent him some. When he chose to indulge it, Stalin had a simple, affable side. He gave it full play at Babelsberg, and it appealed to Truman. He looked Truman in the eye, and Truman liked that, too.[19] Judging from some of Truman's later comments, he gazed back into those yellow eyes and failed to see Stalin the exterminator. He later likened him to Tom Pendergast and to William Marcy Tweed, the nineteenth-century Tammany Hall leader, suggesting that the president viewed Stalin rather as a fellow politician with whom he could bargain and hope the bargain would be kept.[20]

Subsequent conversations at Potsdam, however, seem to have given Truman conflicting thoughts. The first thing he told John Snyder when he returned home was that in one of his casual chats with Stalin he, Truman, had alluded to the alleged Soviet massacre of thousands of Polish Army officers in the Katyn Forest, near Smolensk, in 1940. As he recalled the conversation, he had asked Stalin what had happened to the officers and Stalin had replied coldly, "They went away." Truman was appalled by the answer, according to Snyder.[21]

Before the visit at Truman's residence ended on the seventeenth, Stalin told Truman that the Soviet Union would enter the war against Japan in mid-August. As Truman had said a number of times before departing the United States, that was the word he had wanted to hear at Potsdam. At least it was what he had hoped to hear before the news of the successful atomic bomb test had arrived. Whether it was such good news now was another question.

But when Stalin and Molotov departed after lunch that day, Truman merely told Vaughan that the "Russkis" had tired him out and he was going to take a nap before the first plenary meeting began at five o'clock.[22]

With the atomic bomb a reality, events at Potsdam were to proceed on two levels. One involved the bomb and the surrender of Japan. The other involved negotiations over Germany and related questions, to which Truman, Stalin, and Churchill now turned their attention.

In the political rapids into which Truman had been flung in April no current was more fraught with long-range consequences than the German issue, not only because it engaged Soviet and American policy at innumerable sensitive points but also because it came to affect the political, economic, and military future of Western Europe.

Certain steps had been agreed upon before Truman took office. Germany would be occupied by the victorious powers, each in its own zone. German war criminals would be tried and punished by the victors. The German high command would be broken up and Germany demilitarized. Future German industrial output would be regulated by the occupying powers.

Nevertheless, three years and four months after the United States had gone to war with Hitler, American policy was in flux at the time of Roosevelt's death. The various reasons for this irresolution included Roosevelt's vacillations, Big Three procrastination in deciding whether Germany should be dismembered, and an interdepartmental tug-of-war in Washington over whether Germany should receive harsh or lenient treatment. Complicating matters, the war had ended sooner than Allied planners had expected, leaving them ill-prepared for the political vacuum in Europe.[23]

Also involved in the German question—and moving to the fore at Potsdam—was the unresolved matter of reparations.

In the interdepartmental struggle in Washington, the most radical element was Secretary of the Treasury Morgenthau's harsh plan to convert Germany into a pastoral nation, without heavy industry that would enable it to wage war again.

A rival to this plan was a long-evolving State Department policy for a unified and economically rehabilitated—but disarmed—Germany. While war plants would be dismantled, German industry would be left essentially intact, providing a tolerable standard of living for the people. Though it was not contemplated that the Germans would be a major industrial power, they would in time be spared economic ruin such as had paved the way for Hitler in the past and might lead to communism in the future. They would be leniently treated and encouraged to adopt democratic reforms.

For a time the Morgenthau Plan, abetted by the War Department, made headway in the Roosevelt administration. Toward the close of Roosevelt's life, however, it began to lose out to the State Department plan, as Roosevelt came to see the necessity of maintaining substantial German industry in order that the United States would not have to subsidize the German people. Diplomatic advisers also had warned that destruction of German industry would make the Germans dependent on the Soviet Union, thereby opening Europe to Soviet domination.[24] In the end Roosevelt had indicated at Yalta that the United States would not approve indiscriminate removal of German plants to rebuild the Soviet economy.

On May 10 Truman did approve revisions of a military directive on the occupation, known as JCS 1067, which contained elements of the Morgenthau Plan. But the military found loopholes for circumventing the more punitive provisions. Furthermore support for the Morgenthau Plan in Washington vanished. Stimson quickly became influential with Truman, and the Secretary of War was vehemently opposed to the destruction of German industry for fear of chaos in Central Europe. He talked with Herbert Hoover May 13. Hoover said that after the First World War he had fought off communism by shipping food to starving Europeans, and he urged the same course now.

On May 16 Stimson warned Truman of the importance of keeping Western Europe "from being driven to revolution or Communism by famine." The revival of Europe could not be separated from the predicament of Germany, he said, and recommended that Truman shun Morgenthau's approach.[25]

The president recalled that he had never favored the Morgenthau Plan.[26] Later he agreed with Stimson that a vengeful peace should not be inflicted on Germany. Nazi war criminals should be punished, but the country should be rehabilitated.

Truman's own idea of a solution to the problems of Europe was to create a free flow of trade between the food-producing areas of Hungary, Rumania, and the Ukraine in the east and the coal-producing, industrial countries in the west. This flow, he thought, could be facilitated by linking the Rhine and the Danube with a network of canals extending from the North Sea to the Black Sea and the Mediterranean. In his view the canals and rivers should be made free waterways, and he was prepared to submit a proposal to this effect when the Potsdam Conference convened.[27]

What, then, with Truman's own preference for restoration of Germany, Stimson's advocacy, and the resumption of State Department influence after Roosevelt's death, American policy now began falling into place along the lines of the department's concept of a disarmed but revived, democratic Germany.

The economic life of Germany was bound to be affected, of course, by the nature and extent of the reparations the Germans would have to pay. Reparations had been debated at Yalta. The agreement reached was that Germany must pay in kind for the losses it had inflicted on its enemies. A figure of $20 billion (of which half would go to the Soviet Union) was to be taken by the newly established Allied Commission on Reparations as a basis for discussion in negotiating the final terms.

The Truman administration, however, resisted. Presently, arguments were heard in the government that $20 billion was probably more than Germany could afford.[28] Several factors were at work.

After Harriman and the State Department had urged the tactic of using possible loans as a lever to force Soviet cooperation, the administration began to reconsider reparations in this light, too. Since the Soviets had shown "little willingness to implement a number of the Crimean decisions," Harriman saw "no reason why we should show eagerness in expediting decisions on reparations."[29] Another major factor was the concern that excessive reparations payments would cause economic and social breakdowns in the western zones. Still a third was Truman's fear that in the end reparations would be taken out of the hide of American taxpayers.

After the First World War the United States had lent Germany money which then found its way into reparations paid by Berlin to other countries, making such reparations a burden on the United States. The Roosevelt administration had resolved that this must not happen again, and the Truman administration was equally determined about it. Economic and social chaos in Germany must be prevented. An industrial base must be provided for German stability both to avert a drain on American resources and to restrain the spread of communism. Therefore, the Soviets must not be allowed to strip the factories of West Germany.

Roosevelt had named Isador Lubin, a White House economist, as head of the United States delegation to the Reparations Commission, but Harriman, temporizing with the aim of a more satisfactory reparations agreement, had succeeded in delaying Lubin's departure to Moscow. When Truman took over he first detained Lubin in Washington and then superseded him with Edwin W. Pauley, "someone who could be as tough as Molotov," he later said, appreciatively.[30] Pauley was a conservative California oil man and Democratic fund raiser. The directive to him, approved by Truman May 18, emphasized that the German economy should be maintained intact to the extent of providing a minimum subsistence standard of living for the German people without creating an obligation for the United States to maintain this level or to finance German reparations.[31]

Pauley attacked the tentative $20 billion reparations figure as unrealistic. Backtracking from the Yalta agreement, he proposed eliminating a fixed total for reparations. Instead each claimant would be entitled to a certain percentage of what was available for reparations. By the time of Potsdam the Americans contemplated a reparations plan that would, in Pauley's words, be "more limited in scope."[32] American officials never had relished the idea of large transfers of reparations from West Germany to the Soviet zone. Neither had the British.[33]

Several things had happened that justified in American eyes a more limited reparations policy, however badly it may have set with the Soviets.

While reparations negotiations were still pending, for example, the Soviets had begun wholesale removal of German equipment from their own zone. Indeed there were reports of Soviet removals from the American zone.[34] The president said that during his Berlin tour he had seen plants whose equipment had been seized by the Soviets and loaded on flatcars.[35]

The Soviets called many of their seizures war booty, but their action affected American thinking about reparations, even though the Americans had made off with freight cars and rolling stock while they were temporarily occupying the Soviet zone.

Another bold Soviet move also caused second thoughts. Without consulting the Americans and British, the Soviets before Potsdam had turned over to Poland for Poland's administration a sizable slice of German territory within the Soviet zone, as if annexing this area to Poland. In the American view this was tantamount to creating still another occupation zone in Germany and muddied the reparations question. Partly because of these two Soviet actions, the Americans argued, the total value of German goods and products available for reparations no longer could be determined. A labyrinth awaited the Big Three.

9. *The Potsdam Conference*

W HEN THE FIRST plenary meeting opened July 17 in the Cecilienhof Palace (a country estate) Truman—the only principal who was head of government and head of state—was chosen to preside over the conference, at Stalin's suggestion.

Potsdam was intended as a preliminary conference of limited goals. Remembering the failure of Versailles, the Big Three had previously decided against trying to write peace treaties at Potsdam. These were to be drawn up later. As a vehicle for this task Truman forthwith offered a proposal for a Council of Foreign Ministers, consisting of the Big Three plus France and China. This was eventually adopted, although British and Soviet objections effectively excluded China and limited the French role.[1]

Next Truman offered a proposal on political and economic principles to guide the occupation of Germany under the previously established Allied Control Council. The proposal generally followed the Yalta agreements on the destruction of German militarism, the uprooting of Nazism, and arrest of German war criminals.

The occupying powers would impose controls to carry out reparations and other purposes. Germany, it was stated, would be treated as a single economic unit, the notion of "dismemberment" having faded after Yalta. In general these principles were approved.

The president next introduced a proposal for carrying out the Declaration on Liberated Europe that had been adopted at Yalta. The declaration was a State Department creation which Roosevelt had submitted at the Crimea conference to quiet concern at home over formation of spheres of influence in Eastern Europe.[2] Reaffirming the principles of the Atlantic Charter, it called for establishment of governments in Eastern Europe "broadly representative of all the democratic elements in the population." It was high-sounding but lacked enforcement machinery. By the time of Potsdam, however, some State Department advisers still clung to the hope that elections could free Eastern Europe from Soviet domination. The proposal which Truman introduced in an effort to salvage the Yalta pledge of democracy called for, among other things, reorganization of the governments of Rumania and Bulgaria. In due course Stalin squelched that idea. Nothing meaningful resulted from the president's effort. Any freely elected government in Eastern Europe would have been anti-Soviet, and that was something Stalin would not tolerate.

Next on Truman's list was a proposal for an interim arrangement with Italy, pending a formal treaty. Italy had declared war on Japan, and Truman said the time had come to admit the Italians to the United Nations. However, Churchill, remembering how Italy had gone to war against the allies when their cause hung in the balance, wanted more time to consider this.

Truman's style at a summit meeting, doubtless dictated in part by inexperience was entirely different from Roosevelt's, Bohlen observed. "Where Roosevelt improvised," he recalled, "Truman stuck closely to positions worked out in advance. Where Roosevelt, in his argumentations, would work in extraneous ideas, Truman was crisp and to the point."[3]

The second meeting, on the eighteenth, was dominated by discussions between Stalin and Churchill, and already Truman was growing impatient. He wrote his mother: "It is hard as presiding over the Senate. Churchill talks all the time and Stalin just grunts but you know what he means. . . . They all say I took 'em for a ride when I got down to presiding. . . ."[4]

"Winston has fallen for the President," Lord Moran wrote in his diary. "Truman's modesty and simple ways are certainly disarming. When he was on his way out, passing a piano in one of the rooms, he stopped and, pulling up a chair, played for a while."[5]

On the twentieth Truman brought up his Italian proposal, saying the Big Three should recognize Italy's ultimate contribution to the defeat of Germany. He wanted the surrender terms ended and replaced by a more moderate interim agreement. Needless to say, he desired to have Italy aligned with the West. With eastern alignments in mind, Stalin seized upon Truman's proposal as an opportunity to link the cases of Rumania, Hungary, Bulgaria, and Finland with that of Italy. The Big Three had no grounds for singling out Italy, he maintained. If they were going to improve the Italian condition, he proposed that they should do the same for that of the former German satellites.

Truman explained that he had mentioned Italy first because it had surrendered first—in 1943—and its surrender terms were the hardest of all. After Italy had been taken care of, the Big Three could take care of the others. He thought agreement could be reached on the satellites. Stalin said he favored the American proposal in principle but would extend it to the satellites. He was agreeable to having Italy on the side of the United Nations, he continued, but the same should apply to the satellites.

Truman noted that the United States planned to spend nearly $1 billion to feed Italy in the coming winter. The United States was rich, he continued, but could not forever pour its resources into aid to other nations without some return.

The way things were going, he observed, there was no prospect of making governments such as Italy's self-supporting. But unless this were done the United States could not continue indefinitely to maintain them when they should be able to help themselves. Steps ought to be taken at Potsdam to facilitate this, he said, although he had no objection to improving the situation of the satellites as well as of Italy. So he ordered the two cases referred jointly to the foreign ministers to work out terms of agreement.

But then the Americans had second thoughts overnight about linking Italy and the satellites. At the plenary meeting on July 21 the president said the two cases ought to be considered separately. Stalin, however, came right back and offered an amendment calling for restoration of diplomatic relations with the satellite countries.

"I cannot agree," Truman said. Ever since Yalta it had been American policy to postpone signing peace treaties with and withholding diplomatic recognition from the satellites as a way of compelling fulfillment of the Yalta terms, notably on free elections.

Stalin came back at Truman. If diplomatic relations with the satellites could not be considered now, he declared, then the whole question would have to be deferred, because Italy could not be dealt with independently of the satellites.

The president retorted that the United States could not recognize the governments of the Eastern European satellites. It would do so when they were properly—meaning democratically—organized and not before. In the face of the impasse the matter was laid over.

At this same meeting on July 21 the Big Three took up the vexing Polish question, involving boundaries and Polish administration of former Germany territory. It was a subject Truman handled rather emphatically.

Interestingly, the twenty-first was the day that General Groves's detailed account of the astonishing power of the explosion at Alamogordo had arrived at Potsdam by courier and had been read by Truman, Stimson, and Byrnes. Afterward Churchill surmised that Truman's forceful handling of the Polish question had been inspired by the news.[6]

Poland's western boundary, touching Germany, had been left unsettled at Yalta, even though agreement had been reached that the Curzon Line would form Poland's eastern boundary, touching the Soviet Union. The Curzon Line was a demarcation line that had been proposed after the First World War in an unsuccessful effort by Britain to mediate between the Poles and the Soviets. Since acceptance of this boundary after the Second World War gave the Soviets a large slice of old Polish territory, it was agreed at Yalta that in compensation Poland should receive "substantial accessions" of German lands to the west at Germany's expense.

Wrangling had followed over how much German territory should be given Poland.[7] Stalin had wanted to extend Poland's western frontier along the Oder River to where it joined the Western Neisse River. Roosevelt and Churchill had insisted it should stop at the Eastern Neisse. Toward the close of the war, however, Soviet forces had driven through East Prussia all the way to the Western Neisse. Then, without consulting the Western Allies, the Soviets had turned some 40,000 square miles of this territory over to Poles for administration.

Truman now challenged this decision. As agreed to at Yalta, he said, the Polish-German boundary should be decided later at a peace conference. He reminded Stalin that the occupation zones had been set previously. The Americans and British had withdrawn their troops to their assigned zones. But now, he asserted, another occupying government had been assigned a zone without consultation with them. They could not agree on reparations and other German problems, if Germany was to be divided up before the peace conference, he continued.

"I am very friendly to Poland and sympathetic with what Russia proposes regarding the western frontier," he said, "but I do not want to do it that way."

Stalin reminded Truman that Poland was to be given some German territory under the Yalta agreement.

"That is right," Truman replied, "but I am against assigning an occupation zone to Poland."

Stalin acknowledged that the precise boundary was to be left to the peace conference. He denied, however, that the Soviets had given the Poles an occupation zone of their own. In moving into the area, he explained, the Red Army had needed a local administration and the Poles were on hand to take over the task. No single German remained in the territory, Stalin noted.

"Of course not," Leahy whispered to Truman. "The Bolshies have killed all of them."[8] In fact, many had fled.

Truman told Stalin he was willing to hear opinions about the boundary. He wanted it distinctly understood, though, that the occupation zones would stand as they were. Otherwise, he made a point of saying, the question of reparations would be difficult, especially if part of Germany was gone before a reparations agreement was reached.

Stalin said the Soviet Union was not worried about the reparations issue.

Churchill said that the area now administered by the Poles was an important source of food for Germany. There was posed, therefore, a tremendous problem of feeding Germans, particularly since millions of them had been forced out of the seized lands and would become a burden on the rest of Germany.

The Germans were to blame for their troubles, Stalin commented.

"Poland is now claiming vastly more territory than she gave up," Churchill complained. "I cannot concede that such an extravagant movement of populations should occur."

He insisted that the Poles had no right to cause a catastrophe in the feeding of Germany.

"Germany has never done without the import of grain," Stalin told him. "Let the Germans buy more bread from Poland."

Churchill said he did not acknowledge that the territory in question was Polish.

It was now inhabited by Poles, who were cultivating the land and making bread, Stalin replied. The Poles could not be compelled to give bread to the Germans.

Churchill complained that the Poles were selling Sweden coal from Silesia, most of which fell under their administration, while Britain was facing a fireless winter.

"I am concerned," Truman said, "that a piece of Germany—a valuable piece—has been cut off. This must be considered a part of Germany in considering reparations and in the feeding of Germany. The Poles have no right to seize this territory now and take it out of the peace settlement. Are we going to maintain occupied zones until the peace, or are we going to give Germany away piecemeal?"

Stalin replied that because of the flight of the Germans and the Soviet labor shortage, no one was left to exploit the economy of the region but Poles. Otherwise production would be halted. He acknowledged that the Poles' demands for territory created difficulties for the Germans.

"For us all," Churchill observed, adding that he did not want to be confronted with a mass of starving Germans.

"I shall state frankly what I think," Truman said. "I cannot consent to the removal of eastern Germany from contributing to the economy of the whole of Germany."

"Are we through?" Stalin asked.

"Can't we sleep on it," Churchill suggested.

Truman announced the meeting was adjourned.

"This has been the President's best day so far," Sir Anthony Eden, the British foreign secretary, said to Churchill later.[9] But Truman recalled that he had become so impatient "I felt like blowing the roof off the palace."[10] Fortunately his temper subsided, for that night he had to attend a dinner given by Stalin and work his way through caviar, smoked fish, fresh fish, venison, chicken, duck, assorted vegetables, watermelon, vodka, and champagne. Joe Davies, a member of the United States delegation, observed an intense conversation between Truman and Stalin and later asked the president what he had said.

"Well, I was giving him an earful," Truman replied, "and I wanted to convince him that we are 'on the level' and interested in peace and a decent world, and had no purposes hostile to them; that we wanted nothing for ourselves, but security for our country, and peace with friendship and neighborliness, and that it was our joint job to do that. I 'spread it on thick,' and I think he believes me. I meant every word of it."[11]

Since arrival at Potsdam, Davies had warned Truman and commented in his own diary about a "palace intrigue" to turn the president against the Soviets. His diary of that same day, the twenty-first, noted a change in Stimson's attitude about the Soviet Union, and added:

"It was different in tone to the opinions he had expressed in Washington. The extent of the disparagement which one hears in our own delegation as to the Russians is alarming. It is not surprising that it affects even *Stimson.* The influences reach even the 'White House.' The *Pauley* Reparations Commission and *Harriman,* in fact their whole entourage, is violently critical. About the only ones here who are steady are the *President* himself, *Byrnes, Clayton* and *Dunn* [Assistant Secretaries of State William L. Clayton and James C. Dunn]. It is disheartening."[12]

On July 22 Stalin asked Truman and Churchill if they had seen a statement by the Polish Provisional Government leaders pleading for the Oder-Western Neisse boundary. Stalin suggested that the Big Three comply. Churchill refused.

Stalin argued that Germany could obtain fuel from the Ruhr and the Rhineland instead of Silesia.

The president then spoke up and said that as things now stood Poland had been assigned a zone of occupation in Germany. The Big Three could agree to this, if they chose to, he said, but he did not like the way the Poles had occupied a zone without any discussion among the powers responsible. That was his position yesterday; that was his position today, and that would be his position tomorrow, he said.

Taking note of Truman's displeasure, Stalin said that if anyone were to blame, it was not just the Poles but also circumstances and the Soviets.

That is what he had been talking about, Truman retorted.

On July 23 the question arose of revising the Montreux Convention regulating navigation between the Black Sea and the Mediterranean through the Straits of the Bosporus and the Dardanelles. The 1936 convention gave Turkey control of the Straits and authority to close them to warships of all countries when the Turks were at war or were threatened by aggression. Stalin said the situation was intolerable. Molotov circulated a paper proposing joint Soviet-Turkish control and the right of the Soviets to build bases in the Straits. The issue provided an opportunity for Truman to bring up the cherished proposal for opening the waterways of Europe, including the Rhine and the Danube rivers and the Kiel Canal, to free and unhampered navigation.

The Montreux Convention should be revised, he said. The Straits should be a free waterway open to the whole world and should be guaranteed by all the major powers. In his long study of history, the president continued, he had concluded that the wars of the last two hundred years had originated in the area extending from the Black Sea to the Baltic and from France to Russia.

Truman said it was the business of Potsdam and the subsequent peace conference to prevent future wars in Europe. To a large extent this could be accomplished, he argued, by free navigation of the Straits on the pattern of the free navigation of American rivers.

He then read a proposal calling for free and unrestricted navigation of such inland waterways as bordered on two or more nations. As a first prompt step international navigation agencies should be established for the Rhine and the Danube. The president said the United States did not want to engage in another war twenty-five years hence over the Straits or the Danube. America's goal, he continued, was an economically sound, self-supporting Europe. He wanted a Europe in which the Soviet Union, England, France, and all their neighbors would be prosperous and happy. He wanted a Europe—meaning an Eastern Europe as well as a Western—with which the United States could do business. He considered his proposal a step in that direction.

Churchill supported the president's proposal. Stalin said he wanted to study it.

The meeting on July 24 produced what Truman later called "the bitterest debate of the conference."[13] The argument began over the unsettled problem of whether to deal with Italy and the Eastern European satellites separately. Stalin was still unrelenting in favor of linking the two cases. It appeared, he said, as if Rumania, Bulgaria, Hungary, and Finland were being treated like leper colonies. They had all done less harm during the war than Italy, he argued. Since no democratic elections had been held in Italy, he went on, why such a benevolent attitude toward Italy, as contrasted with the others?

The president explained why he thought the two cases were different. The Western Allies, he told Stalin, had not been able to gain free access to the satellites or to obtain information about them, whereas everyone had free access to Italy. This was essentially a restatement of Byrnes's comment to Molotov on the twenty-second that "we would, frankly, always be suspicious of elections in countries where our representatives are not free to move about and where the press cannot report freely." Truman told Stalin that when Hungary, Rumania, and Bulgaria were so governed that free access was granted, the United States would recognize them, but not sooner.

Stalin replied that none of the satellites could hamper the movement of Allied agents or the flow of information.

But they did, Truman retorted. He said he was asking for reorganization of the satellite governments along democratic lines, as had been agreed to at Yalta; and that the United States would not recognize them until this had been done.

The satellites had democratic governments closer to the people than the Italian government was, Stalin persisted. Truman replied: "I have made it clear—we will not recognize these governments until they are reorganized."

Churchill told Stalin an iron curtain* had come down around British representatives in Rumania.

"All fairy tales," Stalin snapped.

Finally, as with many other items on which the Big Three could not agree, the question was referred to the foreign ministers. By now the bickering was really getting on Truman's nerves. He said he wanted to get the conference over in a week or ten days so he could return to Washington.

The next day, July 25, however, he opened the door a crack to an eventual compromise on the Polish controversy. In the midst of a sharp exchange between Churchill and Stalin he said he sympathized with the Poles and with Stalin in the difficulties facing them. If the Poles were to have a zone, they must be responsible to the Soviets for it. In other words, if Stalin was bent on giving part of the Soviet zone to the Poles, Truman would not object, so long as it was understood that the final boundaries should be decided at the peace conference.

"I'm doing the best I can," he told Davies afterward. "I can only be natural and direct. If it doesn't click, it can't be helped, and they can throw me out and into the ashcan."[14]

A hiatus occurred in the conference while Churchill and Clement R. Attlee, who had been attending as leader of the Labour opposition, returned to London to learn the results of recent British national elections. Announcement of returns had been delayed pending a count of the soldiers' vote. Truman fled the heat and mosquitoes of Potsdam, flying to Frankfurt to visit American troops. Either then or at some point in this period—perhaps July 20—a curious episode occurred.

In his memoirs, *Crusade in Europe,* published in 1948, Eisenhower recalled that he had been riding in a car with Truman in Germany, chatting about the future of certain of America's war leaders. Although this was not mentioned, some people were already thinking about Eisenhower as a possible presidential candidate. Recalling the discussion with Truman, the general wrote:

---

* American minutes say "iron fence" but the British minutes say "iron curtain."

I told him that I had no ambition except to retire to a quiet home and from there do what little I could to help our people understand some of the great changes the war had brought to the world. . . . I shall never forget the President's answer. Up to that time I had met him casually on only two or three occasions. I had breakfasted with him informally and had found him sincere, earnest and a most pleasant person with whom to deal. Now, in the car, he suddenly turned toward me and said: "General, there is nothing that you may want that I won't try to help you get. That definitely and specifically includes the Presidency in 1948."[15]

Truman had come to office admiring Eisenhower, even placing him in a category with Lee and Pershing. A "real man" is the way he had described the general in a letter to his mother June 16.[16] Recalling the episode in Germany, Eisenhower wrote that, astonished, he treated the remark as a jest. "Mr. President," he laughed, "I don't know who will be your opponent for the Presidency, but it will not be I."

At the moment the most astounding political news came from London. With bitter memories of Tory rule in the depression and with hopes for a higher standard of living after the war, the British people had voted the Labour party into power. Clement R. Attlee, not Winston Churchill, the Conservative, returned to Potsdam as prime minister. It was as stark a contrast as Truman's replacing Roosevelt.

For the next six years Truman and Attlee, sometimes together, sometimes separately, were to stand at the forge of vast changes in history, with Attlee presiding over the establishment of the welfare state in Britain and the granting of independence to India—the most important step in the conversion of the British Empire into the Commonwealth of Nations.

Truman was fretting to get the Potsdam Conference over with. Although Stalin failed to gain a number of his objectives at Potsdam—revision of the Montreux Convention, a Soviet naval base on the Bosporus, Soviet trusteeship over some former Italian territories in Africa, four-power control of the Ruhr, Western recognition of the satellites—the president was annoyed by the thought that the Americans were the only ones making concessions.[17] He told his mother in a letter on the thirtieth, "You never saw such pig-headed people as are the Russians. I hope I never have to hold another conference with them—but, of course, I will."*[18]

Through tough bargaining and compromise the conference was concluded in the next three days.

Reparations were the crux of the remaining negotiations. With the problem in a frightful snarl, Byrnes had proposed an arrangement under which each occupying power would take reparations from its own zone. The military commanders of the respective zones would be given autonomy over reparations.

Increasing the likelihood of a future division of Germany, this plan became the core of the American stand on reparations. The Americans finally killed the tentative $20 billion figure mentioned at Yalta. Even when the Soviets offered to settle for a lesser total to compensate for their previous removals and for Polish administration of part of Germany, the Americans rejected the idea of a specific figure.

Instead they insisted on dealing in percentages. In addition to what the Soviets

---

* No other Big Three summit conference was held during Truman's presidency.

could take from their own zone, the American plan conceded to them an outright 10 percent of the West's portion of capital equipment plus another 15 percent of it in return for food and coal from the Soviet zone.

Even so, reparations derived from removal of equipment and from shipments out of current German production were restricted, supposedly, until the German economy was in balance. Byrnes told Molotov that no reparations could be taken from the American zone until the Germans had paid for necessary imports into the zone. Otherwise American taxpayers would have to finance German reparations, he said.[19]

With Truman's backing Byrnes pushed the proposals, even though British and Soviet delegates, as well as State Department officials in Washington, feared that these would impede the treatment of Germany as a single economic unit.[20] But Truman and Byrnes, eager to minimize American obligations in Europe, moved ahead.

Byrnes put the plan over with typical Senate cloakroom tactics, tying the question of reparations to the Polish issue. In Truman's presence he told Molotov that if the Soviets would agree to the American proposal on reparations, the United States would go along with the Soviet decision to let Poland administer German territory up to the Oder–Western Neisse, though leaving formal delineation of the boundary to the German peace conference—the conference that was never to be held. Later Byrnes threw in a concession on the satellites. This acknowledged the desirability of resuming normal relations not only with Italy but with Bulgaria, Finland, Hungary, and Rumania.

On July 31 Byrnes told Molotov the United States "would agree to all three"—reparations, Polish administration, and the satellites—"or none" and that he and Truman would leave for Washington the next day. And that is the way it was, although Truman did not depart until August 2.

At the meeting on August 1 the president made a last forlorn attempt to get his free waterways proposal at least mentioned in the communiqué. Attlee was agreeable, but Stalin balked. Too much was destined for the communiqué already, he said. Furthermore, he continued, since the communiqué would not mention the Black Sea Straits, why should Truman's proposal, introduced in connection with that question, be given preferred treatment in the communiqué? The Straits question could be mentioned, Truman said. It should not be, Stalin retorted.

"Marshal Stalin," Truman said, "I have accepted a number of compromises during this conference to conform with your views, and I make a personal request now that you yield on this point."

He wanted the communiqué to note that his proposal had been referred to the Council of Foreign Ministers, he said, in order to give him the opportunity to explain his plan to Congress.

Even as Bohlen was interpreting the explanation, Stalin interjected, "Nyet!" To leave Truman in no doubt he declared in English, "No, I say no!"

Ambassador Robert Murphy saw Truman flush and heard him say, "I cannot understand that man!" Then, turning to Byrnes, the president exclaimed, "Jimmie, do you realize we have been here seventeen whole days? Why, in seventeen days you can decide anything."[21]

Amid his frustrations Truman had one good laugh at the Soviets and relished it for years. When he was elected judge of Jackson County, the custodian of the court-house was a chunky man named Fred A. Canfil. Canfil later became Truman's driver and political handyman. In the Senate, Truman used his prerogative to get him appointed United States marshal for the Western District of Missouri. Before Truman left for Germany, Canfil came to Washington on a vacation and called on him. Truman asked him how he would like to go to the Potsdam Conference.[22] Canfil thought it a suitable enterprise and wound up as an odd-job man in the presidential party. After one of the sessions Truman archly introduced him to Stalin as Marshal Canfil. Soviet officers hearing the title were awed and thereafter clicked heels for the former custodian of the Jackson County Courthouse.

Actually Canfil earned a more enduring historical footnote. Apparently when Truman was talking with him about his life as president, he remarked, "The buck stops here." Canfil had a plaque made for Truman's desk with this inscription, and the words soon became enshrined in the lore of the presidency.[23]

Toward the close of the conference Truman had written to Wallace, "We are getting some good things from it."[24] Considering that the shape of events had largely been determined before Truman took office and that he had not expected to accomplish much anyway, the results of Potsdam were tolerable in his eyes. Four-power administration of Germany began. The Council of Foreign Ministers prepared to continue the negotiations. The $20 billion reparations figure was disposed of. The way was cleared for a start on the rehabilitation of Germany. Restoration of Italy was in sight. Though battered the Grand Alliance, so-called, still breathed.

Most of the gains, however, were destined to be transitory. In large measure what the Big Three agreed to do was refer their disagreements to the Council of Foreign Ministers, itself a vehicle of futility, as things turned out. There was more shadow than substance to the final communiqué. Seeds of German division had been planted. Eventually four-power control of Germany failed, and the reparations agreement broke down. Although the Soviets had fallen short in their quest for a North African trusteeship, their very attempt had expansionist overtones to Byrnes and aroused new suspicions.[25] Finally, the Soviet grip on Eastern Europe was stronger than ever.

When the conference ended Truman said he hoped the Big Three would meet next in Washington. "May God grant this," Stalin replied.[26] In a radio broadcast from the White House August 9, Truman gave a report putting the conference in the best light. Among other things he said that Rumania, Bulgaria, and Hungary "are not to be the spheres of influence of any one power." He did not shift course immediately in reaction to Potsdam. On the contrary, he proceeded to try to live with the results. If they were disturbing in some respects, he had not given up hope of eventual accommodation with the Soviets.

10. *"Release When Ready"*

S FOR THE OTHER PHASE OF Potsdam, Harry Truman was a god of the thunderbolt now. The flash in the New Mexico sky had put in his hands the ultimate power over life. The decision to use the atomic bomb, if and when available, had not been in doubt. The reality of the bomb, however, had remained to be established in a successful test. Now that this had come about, Truman's reaction was quite human: the natural response of a harried man to good news. As favorable reports on the test flowed from Washington his confidence and enthusiasm rose visibly.[1]

Byrnes had joined Truman at the president's official residence, a yellow stucco house overlooking Griebnitz Lake in Babelsberg, a former summer resort and site of the Reich's motion picture colony, when Stimson arrived July 16 and showed them the cable from Harrison, signalling the successful test.

It was a time when Truman was under grave pressure. The war with Japan had been going on for three and a half years. While it continued, the United States would be hard put to help stabilize conditions elsewhere.

The success at Alamogordo offered a dramatic alternative.

"To avert a vast, indefinite butchery, to bring the war to an end, to give peace to the world, to lay healing hands upon its tortured peoples by a manifestation of overwhelming power at the cost of a few explosions," Churchill recalled, "seemed, after all our toils and perils, a miracle of deliverance."[2]

Some officials believed that deliverance might have been realized in another way. They held that the war might be ended by persuading Japan to accept terms short of unconditional surrender, if Tokyo were convinced that unconditional surrender did not mean abolition of the emperor's role.

On May 28 Grew had asked Truman to issue a reassuring statement on the future of the emperor that might facilitate a surrender, particularly in the aftermath of recent B-29 firebomb raids. "My mind goes along with yours," Truman said.[3] But he asked Grew to discuss the matter with the military leaders. Stimson, Marshall, and Forrestal were in favor in principle, but did not believe the time was propitious. While the fighting was raging on Okinawa, they feared that the Japanese would interpret such a statement as a sign of weakness.[4] Hence concessions might prolong the war. Grew had renewed the suggestion later, but Truman decided then to postpone a decision until Potsdam.

On July 2, before the president left for Potsdam, Stimson had met with him and given him a memorandum proposing certain steps that might yield an approximation of unconditional surrender without the necessity for invasion.

One step was the issuance of an ultimatum: surrender on reasonable terms or face complete destruction. Another was assurance that the Allies would withdraw from occupation of Japan when their reasonable objectives had been met and "as soon as there has been established a peacefully inclined government, of a character representative of the masses of the Japanese people." Stimson then added: "I personally think that if in saying this we should add that we do not exclude a constitutional monarchy under her present dynasty, it would substantially add to the chances of acceptance."[5] Overnight, however, the State Department suggested language hedging on the emperor's future.[6] Then even this vaguer version was ultimately discarded by Truman and Byrnes.

On becoming secretary of state, Byrnes—with some sense of uncertainity—had telephoned Cordell Hull before departing for Potsdam and read to the aging and ailing former secretary the pending version of Stimson's draft. In particular, Byrnes questioned offering assurances that the Japanese might choose a constitutional monarchy under the existing dynasty. Hull reinforced his doubts, admonishing him that it sounded "too much like appeasement."[7] Strong sentiment existed in the Senate and elsewhere against dealing leniently with Hirohito.[8] "Hirohito must go," was a familiar theme in much of the wartime press. Representations were made to Roosevelt that the emperor should be tried as a war criminal.

Doubts about retaining the emperor were raised within the State Department, too, and by officials as important as Assistant Secretaries Acheson and Archibald MacLeish, whose views presumably were conveyed to Potsdam.[9] They maintained that Japanese militarists had manipulated the throne in the past and might do so in the future.

When Byrnes reached Potsdam he received a cable from Hull saying that an offer then to preserve the role of the emperor might lead to serious political consequences at home—a warning likely to give pause to Truman and Byrnes. Any tampering with Roosevelt's popular unconditional surrender policy would surely hurt Truman, if it backfired. Hull said that the Japanese would oppose an offer on the imperial role. If it failed to bring about surrender, "the Japs would be encouraged while terrible repercussions would follow in the U.S." Thus Hull suggested that it would be wiser to await Soviet entry and the climax of the bombing.[10]

Stimson, whose influence on Truman did not match that of Byrnes's then, arrived in Potsdam convinced for his part that the time *was* ripe for a statement coupling a warning to Japan with assurances on preservation of the monarchy. But when he called on Byrnes July 17 he found that the secretary of state felt differently. Byrnes had replied to Hull that he agreed that the warning should be delayed and should contain no commitment about the emperor.

"Unfortunately," Stimson recalled, "during the war years high American officials had made some fairly blunt and unpleasant remarks about the Emperor, and it did not seem wise to Mr. Truman and Secretary Byrnes that the Government should reverse its field too sharply; too many people were likely to cry shame."[11]

Stimson pressed the matter no further. In fact, on the recommendation of the Joint Chiefs, he too came to advise Truman to eliminate any reference to a constitutional monarchy under the existing dynasty, though later he changed his mind again. In any event the announcement of a policy with respect to the emperor was at a critical time held in abeyance.

War Department estimates placed Japanese troop strength in the home islands at nearly two million, with slightly more than that number in China, Korea, Manchuria and Formosa. According to these estimates, the Japanese navy existed only as a harrying force against an invasion fleet and the air force had been reduced to relying mainly on suicide attacks.[12] All along, Marshall favored using the bomb to reduce American casualties, even while believing Japan should be warned about it in advance. For months he had been concerned about a shortage of combat troops.[13] Now, after the horror of Okinawa, he worried that the United States might suffer such heavy losses in the projected invasion of Kyushu November 1 that the American people would prefer a negotiated settlement to the main invasion of Honshu the following March. "One of the things that appalled me," he said later, as his remarks were recalled, "was the cost, in casualties, of an invasion that was set for November. Even an ill-equipped force can cost terrible loss to a landing party. To get to the plains would have been a very costly operation in lives. We knew that the Japanese were determined and fanatical, like the Morros, and we would have to exterminate them, almost man by man. So we thought the bomb would be a wonderful weapon as a protection and preparation for landings. But we didn't realize its value to give the Japanese such a shock that they could surrender without complete loss of face."[14] The military, in other words, had considered the bomb not a substitute for conventional warfare but a supplement. The decision on whether to use the weapon to compel Japan to surrender, Churchill wrote later, "was never an issue."[15]

Since soon after their defeat at Okinawa, the Japanese—at the wish of Emperor Hirohito—had been making diplomatic approaches to the Soviets, seeking their help, through mediation, in finding a way out of the war, unaware that Stalin had promised to declare war on *them*. Because the Americans had broken the Japanese code, they knew of the Japanese move and were able to read the messages that passed back and forth between Tokyo and Ambassador Naotake Sato in Moscow.[16]

The Combined Intelligence Committee warned July 8 that Japan might put out peace feelers to try to cause dissension among the Allies and weaken their will to fight.[17] Furthermore Tokyo repeatedly informed its ambassador in Moscow that Japan would not consent to unconditional surrender. Thus the Japanese overtures took on such an ambiguous character that the Americans never took them seriously. Stimson, Marshall, and other military advisers not only considered them vague but understood them to mean that Japan contemplated retaining important areas it had conquered.[18] The Japanese did not approach the United States about a peace settlement.

On July 18 the president and Byrnes conferred with Stalin and Molotov. Stalin gave Truman a copy of a note received from the Japanese ambassador in Moscow saying that Hirohito wished to send Prince Fumimaro Konoye as a special envoy to the Kremlin to explore the possibility of mediation. Stalin suggested that since the Soviets were going to declare war on Japan, the best course might be to ignore the note. Truman replied that that was agreeable to him, that he had no respect for Japan's good faith.[19]

His outspoken contempt for Japan's word was characteristic. In one of his talks with Churchill Truman snapped that he did not think the Japanese had any military honor left after Pearl Harbor. Then he cooled off and unburdened himself about his terrible responsibility for American lives.[20]

As the plenary meeting was breaking up July 24, Truman left his chair and, unaccompanied by his interpreter, approached Stalin and the latter's interpreter, Pavlov. The moment had arrived when he elected to act on the advice of the Interim Committee and Stimson that he mention the atomic bomb to Stalin before it was used, lest its unexpected burst create new mistrust in the Kremlin. The Interim Committee had also favored his telling Stalin about America's hopes for future talks on how to make the bomb a force for peace in the world.[21]

Truman went up to Stalin casually. As he himself described the episode a decade later, he offhandedly mentioned that the United States had a new weapon of unusually destructive force.[22] Vaughan, who was still gathering the president's papers from the conference table, could hear him. Years later he recalled that Truman spoke these approximate words to Pavlov: "Will you tell the generalissimo that we have perfected a very powerful explosive which we are going to use against the Japanese and we think it will end the war."[23]

That was all. No mention of the possibility of future collaboration in atomic energy to avert an arms race. No reference to peacetime benefits that might be shared. In fact, Truman did not say that the explosive was an atomic bomb. He was, and would remain, jealous of the invention. Certainly he was not prepared at that time to discuss with Stalin future arrangements about nuclear weapons and scientific exchange, and his brevity avoided the topic. Stalin, according to Truman, was equally brief, saying he was glad to hear the news and hoped the Americans would make good use of the weapon against Japan.

Doubtless he realized that Truman was talking about a nuclear weapon of some kind. The Soviets had begun nuclear research in 1942 and had spied on the American program.[24] No one knows whether greater candor and generosity on Truman's part at that moment would have made any real difference in shaping future nuclear policies of the United States and the Soviet Union. The exclusion practiced by Truman and by Roosevelt before him detracted from a trustful relationship with Stalin. The road to understanding between the capitalist Americans and the Communist Russians, however, was strewn with vexatious issues, of which the bomb, however important, was only one. In return for offering to share control of atomic energy, Truman would have been compelled by Congress to insist on inspection of Soviet production; and such an arrangement would have been exceedingly difficult to conclude with Stalin. Illustrative of the current attitude was a paper Stimson wrote for Truman at Potsdam, in which the secretary of war said that it was becoming clearer that "no permanently safe international relations can be established between two such fundamentally different national systems."[25]

While the success of the bomb test had heartened Truman in the parleying at Potsdam, it had also changed the minds of the United States delegation about wanting to have the Soviets in on the kill in Asia. "The news from Alamogordo," Stimson recalled, ". . . made it clear to the Americans that further diplomatic efforts to bring the Russians into the Pacific war were largely pointless.'' Truman himself suddenly lost interest in the date when the Soviets planned to march in Manchuria.[26] Marshall made the crucial point to Stimson, however, that the Soviets had their own interests in the Far East and would attack as they chose, whether the United States wished it or not.[27]

A tactic Truman and Byrnes used at this time to try to keep Stalin from entering the war immediately to seize what he wanted was to urge Chiang Kai-shek to drag out the negotiations that he and the Soviets were engaged in over the territorial, political, and commercial concession in the Far East, granted to Stalin at Yalta.[28] Under the Yalta terms the concessions were subject to Chiang's concurrence. If the negotiations were stalled, therefore, Stalin's move might be delayed. Keeping the Soviets out of Asia was an insoluble problem, however. On July 24 Truman and Churchill approved a strategy report of the Combined Chiefs of Staff that proposed, among other things, encouragement of the Soviet Union to enter the Japanese war.[29] In fact, the Soviets got anything but encouragement. When on July 29 Molotov asked that the Allies formally request the Soviets to enter, Truman backed off. Instead the Americans suggested a formula under which Soviet intervention would spring from obligation to the United Nations.[30]

As had been true since work on the bomb began, nothing occurred now to check the drift. The weapon was there waiting to be used. In Potsdam Truman was more isolated than ever from the still-worried scientists. As crews of the B-29s stood poised on Tinian in the Mariana Islands, while the cruiser *Indianapolis* steamed westward with a shipment of U-235, the momentum behind the whole enterprise was at a peak. The precise time when Truman made his final decision is impossible to define. In a larger sense, however, he had made it from the start. ''As far as I was concerned,'' General Groves wrote, ''his decision was one of noninterference—basically a decision not to upset the existing plan.''[31]

The order for the dropping of atomic bombs had been in preparation in Potsdam and the Pentagon. Dated July 24, it was addressed to General Carl A. Spaatz, Commander of the United States Strategic Air Forces. It directed that the 509th Composite Group, Twentieth Air Force, ''deliver its first special bomb as soon as weather will permit visual bombing after about 3 August 1945 on one of the targets: Hiroshima, Kokura, Niigata and Nagasaki.''* It also ordered that ''additional bombs will be delivered on the above targets as soon as made ready by the project staff.''[32]

While the order was being prepared, Truman and his advisers also were working on a proclamation calling for the surrender of Japan. With a crucial exception, the proclamation followed the lines of the ultimatum proposed to Truman by Stimson July 2.[33] Japan's militarism must be eliminated, her war-making power destroyed, and her territory occupied. Japan was to be stripped of her conquered territories.

The Japanese, however, would not be enslaved nor destroyed. War criminals would be punished, civil liberties established. Peacetime industries would be per-

---

* Kyoto had originally been on the list, but Stimson, supported by Truman, removed it because of the city's shrines. Looking also to the postwar situation in Asia, Truman and Stimson feared that a nuclear attack on Kyoto would cause the Japanese to like the Soviets better than the Americans.

mitted, access opened to raw materials. Eventually Japan could participate in world trade.

The exception from the original Stimson memorandum was any mention of a constitutional monarchy under the existing dynasty. The future role of the emperor, if any, was not alluded to. The proclamation simply said that the occupying forces would be withdrawn from Japan when Allied objectives had been accomplished "and there has been established in accordance with the freely expressed will of the Japanese people a peacefully inclined government."

The proclamation concluded: "We call upon the Government of Japan to proclaim now the unconditional surrender of all the Japanese armed forces. . . . The alternative for Japan is prompt and utter destruction." By what means was left unsaid.

The United States, Great Britain, and (by radio) China, the three allies at war with Japan, signed the proclamation without even clearing it with the Soviet leaders, who lived down the road a piece. Byrnes simply sent Molotov a copy July 26 and said the document had been given to the press for release the next morning. Molotov's interpreter called Byrnes's office and asked for a delay of two or three days. The interpreter was told it was too late—the proclamation had been released. An unhappy Molotov complained to Byrnes the next day. Byrnes replied that he and Truman had not consulted Stalin and Molotov since they were not at war with Japan and Byrnes and Truman did not wish to embarrass them.[34]

Monitored in Tokyo, the Potsdam Proclamation raised numerous doubts for Foreign Minister Shigenori Togo. As Grew and Stimson had feared, he was particularly concerned about the emperor's role. Still, believing better terms might be obtained through the hoped-for Soviet mediation, he recommended that the ultimatum be neither accepted nor rejected out-of-hand pending a Soviet answer to the Japanese overtures.[35]

The military, however, took a hard line, demanding that Prime Minister Kantaro Suzuki denounce the ultimatum. At a press conference July 28 (Tokyo time) he called it "nothing but a rehash of the Cairo Declaration." The Japanese government, he said, "does not find any important value in it." There was, he said, no recourse other than to kill the ultimatum with silence, to take a meaning of the verb he used (*mokusatsu*). Japan, he added, would "resolutely fight for the successful conclusion of this war."[36]

JAPAN OFFICIALLY TURNS DOWN ALLIED SURRENDER ULTIMATUM, read the headline in the *New York Times* July 30.

"In the face of this rejection," Stimson recalled later, "we could only proceed to demonstrate that the ultimatum had meant exactly what it said . . ."[37]

"There was no alternative now," Truman observed.[38]

With time running out, he did have another chance to stop the fatal mechanism when Stimson, now back in Washington, cabled him July 30 requesting stand-by authority to release the presidential announcement of an atomic bomb attack. This was necessary, Stimson said, because "the time schedule on Groves' project is progressing so rapidly" that it was necessary to have the statement available for use no later than August 1.[39] Truman the next day wrote his answer in longhand and gave it to his assistant naval aide, Lieutenant George M. Elsey, for transmission:

"Suggestions approved. Release when ready but not sooner than August 2. HST." According to Elsey, Truman wanted to make sure that the bomb was not dropped while he was still with Stalin in Potsdam.[40]

The Potsdam Conference ended; Truman flew to Plymouth August 2, lunched with King George VI aboard H.M.S. *Renown,* and sailed for home on the *Augusta.* On August 6 he was having lunch with some of the sailors when a message arrived: HIROSHIMA BOMBED.

His spontaneous reaction was the same as that of the eminent scientists who had witnessed the test at Alamogordo. When the device had exploded, Dr. George B. Kistiakowsky of Harvard "threw his arms around Dr. Oppenheimer and embraced him with shouts of glee. Others were equally enthusiastic." James Bryant Conant and Vannevar Bush shook men's hands in congratulations.[41] Some of those present did jigs. Dr. Ernest O. Lawrence clapped Sir James Chadwick, a British scientist, on the back.[42] "At first I was thrilled," recalled Dr. Rabi.[43]

When a captain handed the president the message about Hiroshima, Truman grasped his hand and exclaimed, "This is the greatest thing in history." It was the most ominous day in history. While sailors cheered, he left, clutching the message, and practically ran about the ship, smiling proudly and spreading the word about the first atomic bomb.[44] Mindlessly, he said he had never been happier about any announcement he had ever made.[45] The outlandish spectacle was, of course, a manifestation of tremendous release from the anxiety over the prospect of a long war in Japan.

A second message stated: FIRST REPORTS INDICATE COMPLETE SUCCESS. . . . In the wardroom the officers started to rise when the president entered, but he waved them to their seats. "We have just dropped a bomb on Japan which has more power than twenty thousand tons of TNT," he announced. "It was an overwhelming success. We won the gamble."[46] The $2 billion investment had paid off. The balance of power in the world was drastically altered.

Truman's prepared statement was released in Washington:

. . . It is an atomic bomb. It is a harnessing of the basic power of the universe. The force from which the sun draws its power has been loosed against those who brought war to the Far East. . . .
We are now prepared to obliterate more rapidly and completely every productive enterprise the Japanese have above ground in any city. We shall destroy their docks, their factories and their communications. Let there be no mistake; we shall completely destroy Japan's power to make war.[47]

"Having found [made] the bomb," Truman was to explain in a broadcast August 9, "we used it."[48] An estimated 70,000 persons had been killed and at least as many more wounded.

That same day Samuel McCrea Cavert, general secretary of the Federal Council of Churches of Christ in America, had telegraphed to him opposing further use of the weapon. Truman replied:

Nobody is more disturbed over the use of the Atomic bomb than I am but I was greatly disturbed over the unwarranted attack by the Japanese on Pearl Harbor and their murder of our prisoners of war. The only language they seem to understand is the one we have been using to bombard them. When you have to deal with a beast you have to treat him as a beast. It is most regrettable but nevertheless true.[49]

The atomic bomb was a weapon built to win the war. Its use was never seriously challenged by government or outside advisers. No other strategy seemed as effective, safe and expeditious. "It occurred to me," Truman was to remark four months later, "that a quarter of a million of the flower of our young manhood were worth a couple of Japanese cities, and I still think they were and are."[50] He never betrayed any remorse over his decision; on the contrary, he said that in the circumstances he would have done the same thing again. A later show of remorse by Oppenheimer annoyed Truman, who referred to the scientist as a "cry baby." "He came in my office five or six months ago," Truman wrote to Acheson May 3, 1946, "and spent most of his time wringing his hands and telling me they had blood on them because of the discovery of atomic energy."[51]

Truman and his advisers also heard the temptings of power. In a political struggle in which both sides counted their military assets, American leaders were sophisticated enough to know that an atomic bomb that had been used in war would give the United States a greater aura of strength in postwar negotiations than an unused bomb lying in semisecrecy in some vault. While the primary purpose of dropping the bomb was to end the fighting, the possibility that the thunderclap would shake Stalin into a more cooperative attitude did nothing to stay the decision.[52]

Also, in terms of human comprehension and feeling, the atomic bomb—after it had once been used—was different from an atomic bomb that had never been used. Less than two months after Hiroshima Truman was expressing his concern over the international situation to Harold Smith when Smith said, "Mr. President, you have an atomic bomb up your sleeve." "Yes," Truman replied, "but I am not sure it can ever be used."[53] The horror of the bomb dropped created inhibitions that were lacking when the weapon was a novelty.

The simple reason Truman made the decision to drop the bomb was to end the war quickly and save lives.

Doomsday at Hiroshima unloosed a torrent of great events around the world.

In Tokyo Foreign Minister Togo proposed acceptance of the Potsdam terms, but the military balked. "We do not yet know if the bomb was atomic," General Korechika Anami, Minister of War, said. Army leaders argued that Truman's announcement might be a ruse; scientists were dispatched to Hiroshima to investigate.[54]

At the emperor's wish, however, the government pressed the Soviets to mediate. The reply was cataclysmic. Molotov informed Ambassador Sato August 8 that the Soviet Union would consider itself at war with Japan as of the next day—almost exactly on the date Stalin had indicated to Hopkins in May.[55] Molotov informed Harriman. Harriman notified Truman. At 3 P.M. on the eighth the president summoned reporters: "I have only a simple announcement to make. I can't hold a regular press conference today; but this announcement is so important that I thought I would call you in. Russia has declared war on Japan. That is all!"[56]

After the Soviets attacked, Prime Minister Suzuki convened Japan's highest leaders and recommended acceptance of the Potsdam terms. While the subject was being discussed, the group was informed that a second atomic bomb had been dropped on Nagasaki August 9, seventy-five hours after the attack on Hiroshima.[57]

"There was no debate ever on the matter of dropping a second bomb," Groves said later. "The debate had all been on whether to use the atomic bomb as a weapon at all."

According to Groves, the suggestion about the second bomb originated with Rear Admiral William R. Purnell, a member of the Military Policy Committee, a leading group in the Manhattan project, chaired by Vannevar Bush. In December, 1944, use of the second bomb was proposed to the committee, which more or less left the matter in Groves's hands. In line with Purnell's theory, Groves agreed that two bombs—the first to demonstrate to Japan the power of the weapon, the second to prove that the Americans could make more than one—could win the war. Groves revealed his conclusions to Roosevelt, Stimson, and Marshall, and "none of them appeared to question them as being unreasonable." Later he informed Truman.[58]

On May 31 the Interim Committee recommended use of a second bomb.[59] The order to General Spaatz July 24 directed that after the first bomb had been dropped others would be used as soon as they were available. No further order was required. The target and the timing of the second attack were left to the military to decide. Actually the second raid had been scheduled for August 11, which would have allowed Japanese officials more time to react to the first one, but the date was changed to the ninth on orders of the commander on Tinian, partly because of weather forecasts.[60]

Considering the uniqueness of the weapon, the arrangement concerning a second attack—a most dubious contribution to the final outcome of the war, it developed—seems a lapse of civilian control. At Potsdam Truman had told Stimson he hoped only one bomb would be dropped, but this wish was not translated into policy.[61] The president was much too detached from the decision on Nagasaki, which resulted in the death of an additional forty thousand persons and the wounding of sixty thousand more. It was a decision that should have been reviewed by him and his senior advisers after the dropping of the first bomb.

Given their mood, of course, the result probably would have been the same. No peace offer came from Japan after Hiroshima. American officials were taking no risks and were too unfamiliar with the weapon to realize that one or even two attacks would force surrender in a matter of days. The presidential statement issued after Hiroshima still threatened invasion, as if this would be necessary to end the war.[62] Stimson prepared to take a brief vacation. Even on August 9, the day Nagasaki was bombed, Under Secretary of War Robert P. Patterson suggested that Truman's broadcast report on Potsdam that same day should contain a line that the Americans should be prepared either for early unconditional surrender by Japan "or for a long, bitter, last-ditch struggle."[63] General Arnold, commander of the air forces, said afterward that "the abrupt surrender of Japan came more or less as a surprise." Despite Truman's expressed hope at Potsdam that only one bomb would be needed, plans called for the dropping of a third bomb about August 24 and more in September, if necessary.[64]

After word of the second atomic bomb the military leaders at Suzuki's meeting still refused to accept the Potsdam Proclamation. General Anami still wanted to force the Allies to invade in hope of repulsing them in a great battle. For three hours the debate dragged on without a decision. The cabinet met in the afternoon, but the military continued to stand firm. "We must fight on to the end no matter how great the odds against us," the minister of war declared.

That evening Emperor Hirohito held an imperial conference in an underground shelter. The army still opposed unconditional surrender. Now, however, the emperor forced a decision, saying, "the time has come when we must bear the unbearable."[65]

Early on August 10 American monitors picked up a Tokyo broadcast, reporting that in accordance with the emperor's wishes Japan was ready to accept Allied terms with the understanding that the Potsdam Proclamation did not contain "any demand which prejudices the preorgatives of His Majesty as a Sovereign Ruler."[66]

Truman summoned Byrnes, Stimson, Leahy and Forrestal and asked whether the broadcast should be considered acceptance by Japan of the Potsdam terms or whether the proviso about the emperor was incompatible with unconditional surrender.[67] Stimson and Leahy favored acceptance, but Byrnes would not hear of it. At Potsdam the Allies had demanded unconditional surrender, he said, and the American people would "crucify" the president if he accepted less.[68]

Forrestal then mentioned a compromise that appealed to Truman. The secretary of the navy suggested a reply to Japan indicating a willingness to accept the broadcast, yet defining the surrender terms in a mannner consistent with the intent of the Potsdam Proclamation. In sum, accept a condition but call it unconditional surrender. Truman asked Byrnes to draft a reply along such lines.

When the meeting was resumed that afternoon Byrnes presented a proposed reply satisfactory to the president and the cabinet. As had been long favored by Marshall and the Joint Chiefs, it provided: "From the moment of surrender the authority of the Emperor and the Japanese Government to rule the state shall be subject to the Supreme Commander of the Allied Powers who will take such steps as he deems proper to effectuate the surrender terms." In accordance with the Potsdam Proclamation, the ultimate form of government would be "established by the freely expressed will of the Japanese people." At last Truman and Byrnes agreed to continuance of the emperor's role. Hence the surrender was not quite unconditional. On the other hand, the emperor's authority was to be subject to that of the Supreme Commander.

Byrnes paused in his reading of the proposal to the cabinet to say that the Supreme Commander must be an American because the administration did not wish to risk in Japan the kind of misunderstandings that had arisen over the occupation of Germany. Byrnes said the proposal had been transmitted to Britain, China, and the Soviet Union, and the British already had concurred.

Truman interposed—"most fiercely," Wallace recalled—that he did not think they would hear from the Russians but that they would go ahead without them anyway. Stimson suggested that the Soviets were interested in delay so their troops could advance as far into Manchuria as possible. Truman replied that it was in America's interest that they not push too far.[69]

Stimson and Forrestal, the two service secretaries, wanted the president as a

gesture to halt air and naval attacks on Japan, but he refused to take a chance on easing the pressure. Heavy conventional bombing raids continued to pound the Japanese to the very end. Truman did agree, however, that no other atomic bombs
should be used pending the Japanese answer to the Allied message. He told the cabinet that the thought of wiping out another hundred thousand people was too horrible. He did not like the idea of killing "all those kids."[70]

On his return from Potsdam Truman had received a telegram from the influential Senator Richard B. Russell, Jr., Democrat, of Georgia, urging harsh assault
upon Japan and recommending: "If we do not have available a sufficient number of
atomic bombs with which to finish the job immediately, let us carry on with TNT
and fire bombs until we can produce them." Truman replied August 9:

I know that Japan is a terribly cruel and uncivilized nation in warfare but I can't bring myself
to believe that, because they are beasts, we should ourselves act in that same manner.

For myself I certainly regret the necessity of wiping out whole populations because of
the "pigheadedness" of the leaders of a nation, and, for your information, I am not going to
do it unless it is absolutely necessary. It is my opinion that after the Russians enter into the
war the Japanese will very shortly fold up.

My object is to save as many American lives as possible but I also have a humane feeling
for the women and children in Japan.[71]

When the cabinet meeting August 10 ended Truman confided to Wallace that
he was having bad headaches every day. "Physical or figurative?" Wallace asked.
"Both," Truman replied. He said he had had to read a million words. Wallace
asked him if he was taking "complete vitamins." Truman said he was.[72]

Now the Soviets wanted a voice in the selection of the Supreme Commander in
Japan. Harriman told Molotov that this would give the Soviet Union a veto over the
impending selection of MacArthur and was unacceptable. Molotov suggested the
possibility of joint commanders. Squelching this idea, Harriman said that the United
States had carried the brunt of the Pacific war for nearly four years, protecting the
Soviet Union from Japan, while the Soviets had been in the war only a couple of
days. Thus the United States had earned the right to choose the Supreme Commander. Finally, the Soviets settled for a promise to be consulted about the choice.

Even though Stalin had told Hopkins in May that the Soviets expected to share
in the Japanese occupation, Harriman was following established American policy.

"The State-War-Navy Coordinating Committee had some time ago formulated
our position on the postwar control of Japan, and I had approved it," Truman
related afterward. "We wanted Japan controlled by an American commander, acting on behalf of the Allies. . . . I was determined that the Japanese occupation
should not follow in the footsteps of our German experience. I did not want divided
control or separate zones. I did not want to give the Russians any opportunity to
behave as they had in Germany and Austria. . . . I had impressed these thoughts
strongly on all our officials at Potsdam."[73]

An American reply to Japan, sent through the Swiss August 11, did not win
easy acceptance in Tokyo. Senior military leaders continued to resist, yielding in
the end only to the will of the emperor.[74]

11. Victory—and Then?

B Y AUGUST 14 THE COUNTRY WAS tingling with expectation of a victory announcement. Crowds surged through Market Street in San Francisco. Times Square was jammed. People swarmed around the White House. A conga line lurched through Lafayette Park across Pennsylvania Avenue. Late in the afternoon the Swiss notified Byrnes that Japan had accepted the Potsdam Proclamation.

At seven Truman held a press conference. He said that the Japanese reply represented full acceptance of unconditional surrender, read the text to reporters, and broke into a smile.

Pearl Harbor and Bataan had been avenged. The savage enemy was humiliated. Total victory was won, and that, as Truman knew, is what the American people demanded.[1] As later surmised, he might perhaps—as Japanese power crumbled—have obtained early surrender with few American casualties through other strategies, in which case the atomic bomb attacks were unnecessary. It was the opinion of the United States Strategic Bombing Survey, concluded in 1946, "that certainly prior to 31 December 1945, and in all probability prior to 1 November 1945, Japan could have surrendered even if the atomic bombs had not been dropped, even if Russia had not entered the war, and even if no invasion had been planned or contemplated."[2]

All this was speculation, by no means unchallengeable, based on evidence not all of which was available to Truman in August, 1945. A combination of momentum and determination in Japan might have resulted in a furious defense, if the United States had resorted to an invasion as planned. The Japanese forces of almost 2,000,000 men had plenty of ammunition. According to Samuel Eliot Morison, author of the official naval history of the war, the Japanese still had 5,350 kamikaze planes available, 7,000 more under repair or in storage, and 5,000 men in training in the Kamikaze Corps.

"The plan," Morison wrote, "was to disperse all aircraft on small grass strips in Kyushu, Shikoku and western Honshu and in underground hangars and caves and to conserve them for kamikaze crashes on the Allied amphibious forces invading the home islands. Considering the number of planes, pilots and potential targets, all within a short distance of principal airfields, it requires little imagination to depict the horrible losses that would have been inflicted on the invading forces, even before they got ashore."[3]

It is simply impossible to know what would have happened if the atomic bomb had not been used.

Having broken the news of surrender, Truman announced that draft calls would be reduced from 80,000 a month to 50,000 and declared a two-day holiday for government employees. With Mrs. Truman he walked out on the lawn facing Pennsylvania Avenue and gave the V sign to the shouting crowds. The din of automobile horns filled the summer evening. Later the president re-emerged and told the crowd, "This is the day when Fascism and police government cease in the world."[4] He telephoned Mrs. Roosevelt and said he wished the great news had been announced by her husband.[5]

In the kaleidoscope of the next several days some events flashed by almost too quickly to catch the eye, yet not too quickly to spread seeds of trouble. Such were the events involving Vietnam and Korea, which posed special problems for the victors because the two countries had been occupied by Japanese troops, whose surrender must now be taken in hand.

Vietnam, or Indochina, had been the subject of a secret interim arrangement agreed upon at Potsdam. For operational purposes an arbitrary line was drawn at the 16th parallel. Chinese Nationalist forces were to take charge north of the parallel. The British were to take charge south of it.[6] In this arrangement there was no place for complete independence for the Vietnamese and unification of their country. On the contrary, it was obvious that the British would restore Vietnam to France, an eventuality accepted by the State Department in June. The Potsdam arrangement was put into effect in General Order No. 1, approved by the president August 15, shown to the Soviet and British governments, and transmitted to MacArthur, now Supreme Allied Commander.

When the Japanese forces fighting on the Asian mainland collapsed upon the dropping of the atomic bombs, an encounter of Soviet and American interests ensued in Korea.

The American policy which Truman had inherited and to which Stalin had agreed was that Korea would, in preparation for ultimate independence, be placed under a Soviet-American-British-Chinese trusteeship.[7] This arrangement, however, did not expunge the respective interests of the United States and the Soviet Union in the area. A Korea friendly to the Soviet Union or even a divided Korea with the northern half in friendly hands would have provided the Soviets a buffer against attack from the Korean peninsula. The United States, hoping for a Korea responsive to American interests, did not want the Soviets to get control of Korean affairs. Since 1944, the State Department had recognized the importance of American participation in the administration of Korea before the establishment of trusteeship.[8]

Soviet forces advancing across Asia entered northern Korea. Against the background of the respective big-power interests, the United States decided to move in and accept the surrender of Japanese troops in the southern part of Korea. In drafting orders for MacArthur the State-War-Navy Coordinating Committee received a recommendation from Byrnes that the American forces to be dispatched to Korea should receive the surrender as far to the north as practicable. Time, distance, and the paucity of forces available to MacArthur created difficulties for the Americans in moving very far to the north ahead of Soviet troops. The military feared that if the line proposed exceeded the United States logistical capability, the Soviets might not agree to it.

During an all-night meeting of SWNCC, McCloy asked Dean Rusk, then a colonel on the War Department general staff, and Colonel Charles H. Bonesteel III to retire to an adjoining office and work out a proposal. They were instructed to reconcile the political aim of having American forces receive the Japanese surrender as far north as practicable with the limitation of available American forces.

Hours later Rusk and Bonesteel recommended that the line be drawn at the 38th parallel. Even though this was farther north than American forces realistically could be expected to reach in case the Soviets disagreed, Rusk and Bonesteel wanted the line just far enough north so that Seoul, the Korean capital, would lie within the American zone. The committee accepted the recommendation and— somewhat to Rusk's surprise, at least—so did the Soviet Union.[9]

Replacing the Japanese conquerors of Korea, the United States found itself in charge of the southern half of the country, while Soviet forces occupied the northern half.

That the 16th parallel in Vietnam and the 38th parallel in Korea would one day grow into critical political and military boundaries, two of the world's most dangerous spots, could not have been imagined by the American people in the midst of rejoicing over victory.

Meanwhile, on August 16 Stalin, reacting to General Order No. 1, sent Truman a request, the granting of which might well have had great consequences. Although no such agreement had been made previously, Stalin asked Truman for a Soviet share in the occupation of Japan proper, with the Russians stationing troops in half of the northernmost island of Hokkaido. "I should fervently hope," he said, "that my modest requests do not meet with objections." Truman answered with a flat no; all of Japan proper was to be under MacArthur. It was to remain an undivided nation. "I and my colleagues did not expect such an answer from you," Stalin replied.[10]

Most ominous was the situation developing in China. More than a million Japanese troops were on Chinese soil. In compliance with Allied orders Hirohito commanded them to surrender to Chiang Kai-shek. Chiang's troops, however, were concentrated in central and south China; the Chinese Communists were in command in the north. The Communist leaders ordered their troops to accept the surrender of the Japanese where they found them. Ambassador Hurley cabled Washington: "If the United States and the United Nations permit an armed belligerent political party in China to accept surrender of the Japanese and to acquire Japanese arms, a fratricidal war in China will thereby be made certain."[11] On August 11 Chiang commanded the Chinese Communists "to remain at their posts and to wait for further directions," but it was as futile as Canute's commanding the waves.[12]

During the war, of course, the United States had helped train and equip Chiang's air and ground forces. On September 14 Truman received T. V. Soong, Chinese foreign minister, and outlined postwar policy. The United States, he said, was prepared to assist China in developing armed forces of moderate size to maintain internal peace and to assume adequate control over liberated areas of China, including Manchuria. The military assistance, however, must not be diverted for use in civil war.[13]

As soon as the Japanese began surrendering, the United States undertook to transport Chiang's forces to the north by sea and air to accept the surrender of Japanese troops. In time between 400,000 and 500,000 Chinese troops were moved by the United States. At Chiang's request, more than 50,000 United States Marines were landed in north China to occupy cities and guard mines and railroads.[14]

While the ostensible purpose of these movements was to facilitate the repatriation of Japanese, the Americans were in reality also assisting the Nationalists against the Communists. With American help, Chiang was under less pressure to make concessions to the Chinese Communists, who nevertheless were obtaining captured Japanese arms from the Manchurians. As the Nationalist forces were transported to the northern provinces they clashed with the Communists. In the fall heavy fighting raged in an escalating civil war that would become one of the momentous conflicts of history, transforming China and altering the balance of power in the world. The former balance and the old social order in Asia had been destroyed by the war. The collapse of the European colonial system and Japan's defeat had left sparks of revolution throughout the Far East and a power vacuum filled mainly by the American military machine. Having just come through a world war, however, the American people were unprepared for the new crisis.

One truth it foreshadowed was that Asia was the political fault line that ran underneath the Truman administration. The tremors that were to be caused by revolution and civil war in China and Korea sent shock waves through American politics, impeded the progress of the Truman administration, fatefully changed the course of American foreign policy and resulted, in Korea, in what was then the third greatest war in American history.

Finally, the disturbances along this political fault line played a major part in ending a great era of power for the Democratic party and were the principal causes of the ultimate breakdown of President Truman's leadership.

II

POSTWAR UPHEAVAL

12. *The Morass of Reconversion*

OR PRESIDENT TRUMAN the postwar period did not simply arrive—it broke about his head with thunder, lightning, hail, rain, sleet, dead cats, howls, tantrums, and palpitations of panic. The storm of war had passed. But the turbulence in its wake, occasioned by the toils of simultaneously demobilizing the armed forces and reconverting the economy from wartime to peacetime production, all but capsized the Truman administration.

In August 1945 the problem was explosive because in both the Roosevelt and Truman administrations economic planners, knowing nothing about the atomic bomb, had accepted military estimates that the war with Japan would last well into 1946, at least. Thus they visualized reconversion as a process that could be dealt with gradually over many months. There had been planning, but not adequate planning.

Notorious for temporizing, Roosevelt had in any case, been preoccupied with the war. The National Resources Planning Board, to which he had looked for ideas about reconversion, was killed by conservatives in Congress. Truman likewise became absorbed in military and diplomatic problems after taking office and was absent at a time critical at home because of the Potsdam Conference. Furthermore, the extensive turnover of officials attendant upon the change in administrations hampered planning, so that a number of questions, notably that of how to handle labor disputes during reconversion, were left unsettled.

Some officials in the Roosevelt administration had favored beginning limited production of nonessential civilian goods long before the war ended, as a way of getting a start on reconversion and of diminishing inflation by easing shortages of certain goods. The military objected, however, and Roosevelt feared such a policy would have a bad psychological effect on the war effort. Thus the Truman administration had to begin the reconversion program practically from scratch, which was ironic because the Truman Committee had backed early resumption of civilian production.[1]

No one knew whether the end of the war would bring deflation and unemployment, as huge war contracts were canceled, or whether it would bring inflation, as consumers with unprecedented savings rushed into the market to compete for scarce goods. The administration had to grope forward prepared to deal with either contingency.

There was no question about what the public feared. The postwar upheaval began with near hysteria over the specter of unemployment in a generation that remembered the hard times following the First World War and was positively

haunted by memories of the depression. Some 10 million persons had still been un-
employed as recently as 1939.[2]

With war production ending and masses of troops returning, a *New York Times*
headline August 12 said, 5,000,000 EXPECTED TO LOSE ARMS JOBS. As Truman replaced a model gun on his desk with a miniature plow, the Office of War Mobilization and Reconversion reported to him August 15 that unemployment might reach 8
million by the spring of 1946.[3] Other estimates ranged as high as 18 million,
predicted by Senator Harvey M. Kilgore, Democrat, of West Virginia. "A prairie
fire unemployment crisis this week swept across the U.S. from New York to California," the *CIO News* reported in August. "Men and women thrown out of work
swarmed into U.S. Employment offices."[4]

In the first ten days of peace 1.8 million persons did lose their jobs and 640,000
filed claims for unemployment compensation, and fear of depression gained the
upper hand over fear of inflation.[5] This was a historic hoax. What was occurring,
though it was obscured by the turmoil, was a metastasis of inflation. Months before
the end of the war the Office of Price Administration (OPA) had authorized price
rises in various steel products, in pig iron, in soft coal, in certain textiles, and in
other products. Almost as soon as the war ended the prices of eggs, butter, clothes,
gasoline rose. Hedging against a depression, the administration proposed postwar
tax cuts to stimulate the economy. Yet the trend toward inflation was to prove
unrelenting and was to haunt Truman for the next three years.

At first, however, neither he nor the Federal Reserve Board nor the presidential
advisers grasped what was happening. They viewed inflation as a wartime problem
that would ease if only the line were held on prices and wages until peacetime
production could restore stability: production sufficient to end scarcities and thus
relax prices was the key. As for wages, they believed that with abnormal war
production ending, industry's scramble for workers would slacken. Hence a halt
would follow in the inflationary bidding up of wage rates.

Unprecedented inflationary pressures had been generated by the war, however.
The national debt had risen from $61 billion in 1940 to $253 billion in 1945. Government spending had grown from $9 billion in 1940 to $98 billion in 1945. Thus
danger lurked in premature relaxation of controls that had been highly effective in
stabilizing prices during the latter years of the war. The most urgent warnings
against such a course came from Chester Bowles, administrator of OPA. Arrayed
against him, however, were a host of others, liberals as well as conservatives, who
saw unemployment as a greater danger than inflation and thus demanded rapid
decontrol to restore the peacetime economy.

Another element in the nascent inflation was monetary policy, or rather the
lack of it. The Federal Reserve Board might have acted to restrain the growth of
money and credit—it might have, that is, if it, too, had thought of inflation as anything more than a temporary condition caused by the war. However, during the war
the Federal Reserve had made a commitment to the Treasury to support the prices of
government securities at predetermined levels. When hostilities ended, businesses,
financial institutions, and the public held vast amounts of government debt incurred
to finance the war. When in the course of reconversion holders sold some of these
securities, the Federal Reserve, in order to keep security prices from dropping,

would buy them under the wartime agreement. In the process it injected reserves into the banking system. Banks, therefore, were able to expand their loans and investment. "Thus in an inflation," Herbert Stein wrote, "the Federal Reserve found itself not only unable to restrain the growth of the money supply but actually forced to create new money."[6]

In July Truman had decided to send Congress a message on postwar problems, which would be in effect his first State of the Union message. Samuel I. Rosenman, a prominent New York judge, who had been special counsel and speech writer for Roosevelt and who continued in that role for a year under Truman, had flown to Potsdam and sailed home with him to begin outlining the message. Having previously listened to the conservative views of some of Truman's friends, Rosenman was pleased to discover that the president "had a very liberal point of view . . . I was agreeably surprised to hear what he . . . wanted to stress." When the *Augusta* docked at Norfolk, however, John Snyder joined the presidential party for the train trip back to Washington. Thenceforth Rosenman had no easy time drafting a liberal message.[7]

Formal yet affable, even downright jovial after a couple of drinks, Snyder was a decent man of common sense, competence, and integrity. Like Truman, he had a limited formal education, having spent a year at Vanderbilt University before joining the army in the First World War. After working in banks in Arkansas and Missouri he came to Washington in the depression as national bank receiver in the Bureau of the Comptroller of the Treasury. From there he went to the Reconstruction Finance Corporation as right-hand man to its conservative chairman, Jesse Jones, and then became director of the Defense Plants Corporation. He returned to private banking in St. Louis a couple of years later.

In the Truman administration Snyder moved up rapidly. When Vinson became Secretary of the Treasury, Snyder replaced him as director of the Office of War Mobilization and Reconversion and thus as the president's highest adviser on restoration of a peacetime economy. In the heated postwar political atmosphere Snyder's view of what was sound was typically a banker's view, though not always necessarily wrong for that. But being a man who disliked rocking the boat, he was a target for liberals' wrath. Unions disturbed him. He had an "ideological fear" of Walter P. Reuther, then moving to the forefront of American labor as vice-president of the United Automobile Workers.[8] Private initiative was Snyder's ideal. He thought Roosevelt had gone too far toward federal control of business. He frowned on deficit financing. Indeed, on many economic questions his instincts and Truman's were doubtless similar.

As president, however, Truman was forced to seek a broader consensus. He always paid close attention to influential Democrats in Congress and to his politically minded staff. He could not ignore the turn the country had taken under Roosevelt. When it was time for decision, therefore, Truman generally came down on the side of more liberal policies than his friend advised.

After Rosenman had gathered suggestions from various departments and agencies and finished his first draft of the message, Truman sought the comments of several advisers, who promptly split along liberal and conservative lines. At a series of meetings with Truman, those in favor of having him propose to carry on the New Deal included Rosenman, Charles Ross, and George Allen. A rival group, including Connelly and Vardaman and vigorously led by Snyder, held that Truman should favor a pause, a consolidation of the Roosevelt programs, a shift toward conservatism. The arguments were vehement.[9] Snyder protested that extension of the New Deal would be disastrous for the country and politically harmful to Truman. He argued with Truman privately that Truman was now president and was not bound by Roosevelt's policies.[10] Considering the victories of the New Deal and the Democrats' indebtedness to labor for its help in 1944, this was a difficult point on which to convince him.

When Japan surrendered August 14 Truman was caught high and dry without an immediate, clear policy on reconversion. With plans for a gradual transition having been incinerated by the atomic bomb, the administration was plunged into a frantic quest for a program. "Over a long week-end," wrote Craufurd D. Goodwin and R. Stanley Herren, "policies were shaped which planners had hoped could be evolved over many months."[11]

On August 16 Truman issued a statement, largely the work of William H. Davis, Director of Economic Stabilization, trying to set a middle course. Most economic controls were to be ended promptly, but those required for a smooth transition would be continued. Adopting a suggestion of Senator Vandenberg's, Truman said he would call a labor-management conference to work out a plan for the peaceful settlement of labor disputes. Until then the War Labor Board would continue. Pending the conference, labor and management would be asked to renew their wartime, no-strike, no-lockout pledges. In talks with labor leaders Truman thought he had such a pledge. Unfortunately, he either did not quite have it or the pledge was insubstantial. Finally, in the face of heavy pressure from labor, he announced that wage increases would be legalized, provided they were not used as a basis for seeking an increase in price ceilings.[12]

The reconversion policies were made formal August 18 in an executive order by the president authorizing all government agencies to "continue stabilization of the economy" as provided by law. At the same time he directed that the agencies were "to move as rapidly as possible without endangering the economy toward the removal of price, wage, production and other controls." The 1944 Democratic platform had promised no less. Indeed the feeling was common in Washington that controls soon would be superfluous, not to say undesirable, and partly for this reason many officials departed the wartime agencies after Japan's surrender, lessening their efficiency. Moreover the patriotic restraints of the war had been sundered, and all the interests were grabbing with pent-up fervor for what they could get.

Labor trouble began boiling up almost immediately, as giants like the Ford Motor Company and the Westinghouse Electric Corporation were hit by postwar strikes. During the war Congress had treated business handsomely, but not so the workers. And now termination of war production brought an end to the forty-eight-hour work week, of which eight hours had been at overtime pay. The work week reverted to the standard forty hours, reducing earnings in the process. In addition many workers were downgraded to lower-paying jobs.

"The President introduced the strike situation [at his morning staff conference] by a comment that everyone has the jitters," Assistant White House Press Secretary Eben Ayers noted in his diary September 17. The consensus of the meeting was that CIO president Philip Murray and William Green, president of the AFL, could no longer control union members, who had lived up to the no-strike pledge during the war.[13]

The time had come, the unions felt, for workers to be compensated for the sacrifices imposed by wage controls during the war and to be protected against inflation. And labor spoke with a strong voice, having been fortified during the war by the addition of several million members, bringing union strength in mid-1945 to nearly 15 million persons. Labor leaders, particularly Murray, were angry that Truman was not giving them a larger voice in reconversion policy. Murray had been close to Roosevelt and resented the cut in his ties to the White House after Roosevelt's death. One of his friends, Ed O'Connell, wrote Matt Connelly August 23:

Mr. Murray is ready to walk out. . . . Mr. Murray feels very keenly that the president is attempting to do the whole job of reconverting without so much as asking labor to kiss his royal ass, as far as taking a part in it is concerned. He turned the whole job over to the industrialists, with which the WPB is saturated.[14]

On the other hand, strikes and threats of strikes exasperated the public and business. The Truman administration was criticized for coddling labor and catering to the CIO vote.

Truman, as Murray's friend said, looked to the War Production Board to guide civilian production during reconversion. Two days after Truman's executive order on controls the WPB chairman, Julius Krug, revoked with the enthusiastic support of business 210 orders that had restricted production of household appliances. Soon to follow were controls on automobiles. Krug believed that by removing barriers to industrial expansion, more jobs would be created and a depression forestalled. Objecting to Krug's order as premature, however, William Y. Elliott of Harvard resigned as vice-chairman of the WPB.

Washington was beginning to seethe with confusion and quarrels. Despite his talk with Harold Smith in the spring about stopping interdepartmental backbiting, Truman was unable to suppress disputes within his administration over reconversion policy.

Secretary of Labor Schwellenbach feuded with William Davis and Dr. George W. Taylor, chairman of the War Labor Board, over the board's role. Schwellenbach also feuded with Davis over whether industry could afford wage rises. Henry Wallace advocated limited wage and price increases across the board. Schwellenbach wanted decisions case by case.

Secretary of Agriculture Anderson feuded with Bowles over farm subsidies and elimination of price controls on food. Bowles, who was mindful of consumers, feuded with Krug, who was sympathetic with business, over removal of production controls. Truman apparently upheld Bowles, but Krug sidled along his own way.[15] Bowles, fearing inflation, wanted to go slow on easing controls. Snyder, eager to restore free enterprise and spur business activity, considered Bowles impractical and wanted to remove controls more rapidly.

Installed as one of Snyder's top assistants, with the title of "stabilization administrator," was John Caskie Collet, an obscure Missouri judge who was an old friend of Truman's. Deputy to Collet was Professor Henry Hart of Harvard Law School. Collet was a sweet-mannered man who knew little of Washington and less about wages and prices. Hart was an expert. When other officials had presentations to make to them, they sometimes had to state their case in two forms—one that Judge Collet could understand and the other that made sense to Hart.[16]

Into the murk flashed a beacon that lifted the long-range hopes of liberals, Democrats, and labor in particular. It was a measure born of the experiences of the depression and war, called the Full Employment Bill of 1945, introduced in January by Senator James E. Murray, Democrat, of Montana, and others. The bill drew on the compensatory spending theories of John Maynard Keynes and rested broadly on the general concept of intervention by the government to improve economic conditions. One of its wellsprings was the "New Bill of Rights" proposed in a report to Roosevelt by the National Resources Planning Board in 1943, declaring that it should be government policy "to promote and maintain a high level of national production and consumption by all appropriate measures."

With the 1944 campaign approaching, Roosevelt seized on the idea, basing his State of the Union message that year on "a second Bill of Rights." That summer the Democratic platform pledged to "guarantee full employment." By fall Roosevelt was campaigning in favor of an economic Bill of Rights.

The legislation pending when Truman took office declared that Americans able to work and seeking employment had a right to full-time jobs. It would be the policy of the government to make sure that sufficient jobs were available. The president would be required to submit each year a "national production and employment budget." It would show the number of jobs required for full employment, the dollar volume of the Gross National Product necessary to provide this number of jobs, and the volume of the GNP anticipated if the economy were left to run on its own power. If the anticipated GNP fell below the level needed for full employment, the president must then submit to Congress a program providing for a wide range of measures, including federal spending on public works, if necessary, for eliminating the gap.

On September 6 Truman sent to Congress his twenty-one point message on domestic affairs.[17] "The Congress reconvenes at a time of great emergency," he said. Fully as significant, it was a time of political stalemate in the United States, and this fact overshadowed the rest of his days as president.

Any attempt to restore and extend the New Deal after the war had to take into account the decline in public support for Roosevelt's programs since early in his second term, especially since the disastrous "court-packing" bill of 1937 and Roosevelt's efforts to purge some conservative southern Democrats in the Congressional elections of 1938. Thereafter, too, a radical change had been occurring in Congress, the consequences of which Truman could not escape. In increasing numbers southern Democrats were defecting from the party ranks on issues that were objectionable to the South as well as to conservative small-town and rural America in general. On such issues, which were usually considered important in the industrial states, the southern bloc had aligned itself with Republicans, and the co-alition had brought the New Deal to a practical standstill.

As the worst of the depression subsided, the country became more conservative. Roosevelt had not been able to get a major domestic bill through Congress since 1938—seven years before Truman took office. The congressional elections of 1938 had dealt the liberals a blow, as Republicans picked up eight Senate seats and nearly doubled their strength in the House. In 1942 the Republicans, while remaining in the minority, made their biggest gains in Congress since the 1920s, increasing their seats in the Senate from 28 to 38 and in the House from 162 to 209. Convening in 1943, the Seventy-eighth Congress not only killed the National Resources Planning Board but liquidated certain other New Deal agencies and overrode Roosevelt's vetoes of tax and labor bills.

Throughout the war, as reform was sidetracked, a bitter struggle had been waged in Congress to cut appropriations for New Deal programs and agencies. Basic New Deal reforms, notably Social Security, were accepted by most people, and the existence of labor unions had become a foregone conclusion. But powerful opposition to going still further thrived in Congress and grew more formidable as the end of the war approached. Even Roosevelt's enthusiasm for the New Deal yielded to his concern for military victory.

When Roosevelt nominated Henry Wallace for secretary of commerce in January, 1945, after having deserted him in the contest for the vice-presidency, the Senate confirmed him only after a fight and after the Department of Commerce had been shorn of its control over all lending agencies. Then only two weeks before Roosevelt died his nominee for administrator of the Rural Electrification Administration, a prominent New Dealer, Aubrey W. Williams, was decisively rejected in the Senate by a coalition of southern Democrats and conservative Republicans. Even after Roosevelt had been elected to a fourth term he could not prevail against the anti-New Deal forces that still held Congress in its grip. Particularly in the House and in its committees, rural areas were heavily represented. No significant base of power remained for liberals concerned with the welfare of the cities and eager to advance social legislation.

Nevertheless Truman adopted Roosevelt's economic Bill of Rights in his September 6 message. "Let us make the attainment of those rights the essence of postwar American life," he said. Forewarned that a group of congressional liberals headed by Senator Kilgore might present their own program and thus take the issue from the president, Truman asked for more legislation than he could hope to get.[18] Drawing on lessons he had learned as a businessman in the early 1920s, he said:

We must keep in mind the experience of the period immediately after the First World War. After a lull of a few months following the Armistice of 1918, prices turned upward, scrambling for inventories started, and prices soon got completely out of hand. We found ourselves in one of the worst inflations in our history, culminating in the crash of 1920 and 1921. We must be sure this time not to repeat that bitter mistake.

The nature of his requests, however, indicated that his immediate concern was a prolonged downturn in the economy. In addition to the full employment bill these included such measures as:

Unemployment compensation—the program he had requested in May for federal grants to states to enable them to raise the maximum benefits to $25 a week for twenty-six weeks. A substantial but unspecified increase in the prevailing minimum wage of forty cents an hour, although he refrained from endorsing a pending bill, supported by liberals, to set the figure at sixty-five cents an hour. Comprehensive housing legislation. Protection and encouragement for small business. Permanent farm price supports. Grants for hospital construction. Increased public works for conservation and development of resources. Limited tax reductions in 1946. He also called for a permanent FEPC.

A generation later these vintage New Deal proposals appear undramatic, but, then, the New Deal was conservative by the Left-liberal standards of the 1970s. The New Deal had attempted little in the way of assistance specifically for the very poor, the unorganized, and the blacks. The proportion of blacks in the population was smaller then, and the trauma of the black slums was not widely understood. Furthermore the pressure for radical reform was still resistible, one safety valve being the availability of jobs for nearly everyone during and soon after the war. No one who lived through the political storms of the Roosevelt and Truman administrations, however, is likely to forget the intensity with which questions like FEPC, welfare, public works, and government controls were fought over. The struggle between liberals and conservatives was fierce. Truman's message, said Representative Chester H. Gross, Republican, of Pennsylvania, "was pretty far to the haw side. I mean to the left."[19]

Because the programs had come straight out of the New Deal, Republican members of Congress and Republican newspapers were critical. The response from southern Democrats who chaired committees that would handle the proposals was chilling. Truman's honeymoon with Congress began to sour. His proposals were, if nothing else, a symbol that a new Democratic administration proposed to continue federal controls, heavy spending, high taxes, and what appeared to many conservatives as hateful socialistic programs. Such measures as full employment, unemployment compensation, and FEPC were aggressively supported by the CIO-PAC. This made them all the more objectionable to southern Democrats who were fighting to retain their traditional dominance of the Democratic party in the face of the challenge of organized labor. Southerners had supported Truman at Chicago because they wanted to get away from the New Deal. Now *Southern Weekly* sneered that "the whole program of the CIO Political Action Committee and its allied left-wing groups, including the negro organizations, is adequately covered in this message."[20]

The unions would not stand still. Lessening the chances of a smooth reconversion, labor demanded in effect a 30 percent wage rise. The United Steel Workers of America voted September 11 to demand a $2-a-day increase. The United Automobile Workers submitted a comparable demand. At the time workers in blast furnaces and in plants producing steel products were earning on the average of $1.19 an hour or $54 a week, while those employed in the manufacture of motor vehicles and equipment were earning on the average $1.26 an hour or $55 a week.[21] The unions were acutely aware of the fact that the freeze on wages had not affected executive compensation, which in many cases had soared during the war.

At his staff meeting September 21 Truman urged his subordinates to contemplate ways of dealing with the threat of strikes. As Eben Ayers noted in his diary:

He said he must act and act quickly and said he was liable to come in some morning with a head-full of decisions and tell them all to "go to hell." He said he did not want "this job"— the Presidency—but he's got it and he's going to do it.

He spoke of how the labor leaders had come in to him and promised to do things and now they were not doing them. He asked what they wanted to do—run the country?

At the same time, the President said he did not want to go off half-cocked in acting. . . .[22]

Representative Charles A. Halleck of Indiana, chairman of the House Republican Campaign Committee, caught part of the significance of Truman's message to Congress. "This is the kick-off," he said. "This begins the campaign of '46."[23] The *Chicago Tribune* was pleased to believe the message would speed the Republicans' return to power. The next congressional elections were only fourteen months off. As the precursor of the 1948 presidential election—the first in sixteen years without Roosevelt—the approaching 1946 elections increasingly colored national politics.

13. *"Peace Is Hell"*

WHILE THEY WERE RIDING through Washington one day in November 1945, Harry Dexter White, assistant to the secretary of the treasury, told Henry Wallace that everyone could see that the administration was falling to pieces. He urged the secretary of commerce to disassociate himself from what he called the impending wreck, but Wallace loyally declined.[1] While Truman remained popular, the months following the war were a time of adversity for him.

In fact the same day as the Wallace-White conversation Harold Smith confessed to Truman his frustration that the administration was not succeeding in getting things done. He lamented that he and other subordinates were failing the president. Nothing that was being done amounted to solid achievement, Smith said, adding that somehow they all needed to get a grip on the issues.[2]

In the wake of the twenty-one-point message almost nothing went right. The labor-management conference that was supposed to convene soon after V-J Day was delayed by a dispute over agenda.[3] This postponement in turn kept the kettle boiling because the administration then deferred new wage-price policies that might satisfy labor while still keeping prices in line.

The administration was uncertain yet whether deflation or inflation was the greater danger. Strikes swept all parts of the country. Early in October Truman felt compelled to seize twenty-six struck oil producing and refining companies. On the heels of the strikes by the coal miners and New York longshoremen, great showdowns over wages impended in the automobile and steel industries. Union politics complicated the task of the administration in trying to avert strikes. The long wage freeze during the war while industry was working on "cost-plus" contracts had spread discontent through the ranks, and leaders were under pressure to show their mettle and demonstrate the value of union membership to the workers.

In the hand-to-mouth policymaking, Truman, untrained in economics, got into a cantankerous mood about the confusion over wage controls and gave Smith to understand that he was going to start "throwing things around," which he did, without accomplishing much, on September 18.[4] While William Davis, the respected director of the Office of Economic Stabilization, was attending a meeting in another part of the White House, Truman, without telling him, announced at a press conference that OES would be absorbed by Snyder's Office of War Mobilization and Reconversion, a change that had been under discussion.

"What happens to the chairman of the OES?" a reporter asked.

"The chairman of the OES? Well, he won't have anything to do," Truman replied. "John Snyder will take his job."[5]

Davis was stunned. Schwellenbach, who had a vindictive streak, had managed to get Truman on the warpath for Davis because the latter had been quoted in the newspapers as having said at a press conference that the country would have to raise the standard of living by 40 or 50 percent. In answer to a question Davis also said that wages might have to go up by that much within five years. With unions demanding a 30 percent increase while Truman was seeking to resist raises "which would imperil price ceilings," it was an inopportune moment for such remarks to appear.[6] Davis, however, was only reiterating an earlier OWMR report. Ill-informed, Truman under Schwellenbach's goading believed that Davis was assuming to set wage policy.[7] Harold Smith cautioned Truman he would have to give Schwellenbach some guidance. "I think I know what you mean," Truman replied. "I have somewhat the same problem with the Secretary of Agriculture. I begin to think that these fellows get Potomac fever."[8]

Forty-five minutes before the press conference on the eighteenth, TVA chairman Lilienthal had called on the president and found him worn, critical of the press and grumpy about some of his cabinet officers. "He repeated the remark of Wilson," Lilienthal recalled, "as to what happens to people who come to Washington: 'Some grow, some swell up.' (He put in the 'up.')"

"He is a tired man," Lilienthal added in his journal, "but a square-shouldered, plucky one. You can't help admiring him; and being struck with the extraordinary contrast with Roosevelt."

"Enjoyed talking to you," Truman said as Lilienthal was leaving. "Come back again when you haven't anything better to do."[9]

The day after Truman dismissed Davis he was shown a transcript of the Davis press conference, whereupon he wrote him an apologetic letter acknowledging a "misunderstanding." The president confessed to his staff that he had been tired and had gone off "half-cocked."[10]

Reconversion was one of those periodic adjustments that cause more bedlam, confusion, and controversy than Washington can handle tidily. Conflict among such powerful interests as agriculture, labor, big business, small business, and consumers invariably rocks the capital. The fever runs too high to be lowered by any single pill. The government itself becomes involved and has to fight its way through, laboriously. In the familiar effort to compromise, conciliate, and comprehend what was happening Truman and his various inadequate advisers made mistakes in the day-to-day hurly-burly; they made misjudgments; indeed they often made a glorious mess of things. Yet in the end they muddled through, and the country not only went on but went on to greater prosperity than it had ever experienced up to that time. The Truman years, however, were never an age of affluence such as bedazzled the country in the 1960s.

Characteristically confident that things would come out right in the end, Truman tried to please everybody and satisfied nobody. The lack of direction was obvious. "How can the people see clearly," the *Chicago Sun* asked, "if there is little vision in the White House?"

On October 18, 1945, Krock reported in the *Times* that both liberal and conservative Democrats were saying "the President is steadily losing ground in the country.'' The refreshing contrast to Roosevelt that had gratified many in the spring turned stale in the disarray of fall. Many liberals longed for the man with the cape and cigarette holder and bemoaned the fate that had turned the country over to what now seemed to them a bunch of hicks from Missouri. Increasingly, they complained that Truman advocated New Deal liberalism but catered to business and to the conservatives, who were politically stronger than the liberals. Truman reciprocated the contempt. After mingling with a number of prominent liberals at a meeting of the Roosevelt National Memorial Committee in the White House he jotted on his appointment sheet, ''Same bunch of Prima Donnas who helped drive the Boss to the grave are still riding his ghost.''[11]

Liberals were exasperated by Truman's lack of eloquence. Still under the spell of Roosevelt in his heyday, leading a frightened Congress, they now exaggerated the potential of progressive presidential rhetoric for swaying a stubborn and conservative Congress. They seem to have forgotten that in the antireformist atmosphere of the mid-1940s Roosevelt too had called for social progress, but without touching the whip to Congress or business. Truman did not lack dreams of liberalism, but they were not the same as those that brightened the sleep of the editors of the *Nation* and the *New Republic*. ''There should be a real liberal party in this country,'' he had jotted in his diary September 20, ''and I don't mean a crackpot professional liberal one.''[12] It was a subject to which he was to return.

The twenty-one-point message had committed Truman to carry forward the New Deal—he had no other political base. On the other hand he had left priorities up to Congress and made no serious efforts then to rally public support for his proposals. He did not even deliver the message in person. ''President Truman notably lacks the gift for condensed and dramatic expression that served so well his able predecessor,'' the *Detroit News* commented. Hoping to get along with Congress better than Roosevelt had in latter years, he shunned arm-twisting. Hence individual members easily went their own way. Strong leadership was lacking. ''There is a feeling at times that there is no hand at the wheel,'' said *Progressive*. Two weeks after his message the Senate Finance Committee eliminated the $25 weekly payment he had proposed for unemployment compensation. States' rights—war cry of conservatives, which was to resound in Congress during the Truman years—was the rationale of the opposition.

Hoping for better results through good-fellowship, Truman gathered up Vaughan and Snyder and headed for a two-day Democratic outing at the Jefferson Island Club, the party's hangout in the Chesapeake Bay. Addressed as ''Harry'' by some of the congressional guests, he held court in a brown leather bush jacket (he called it his ''zoot suit''), drank bourbon, played ''How Dry I Am'' on the piano, pitched horseshoes, left-handed, downed oysters, and won $52 at poker.

Not long afterward Wallace told him that some reporters believed that personal criticism of the president was imminent because of such behavior.[13] ''Well,'' Truman replied, ''you and I know how to take it, don't we?'' Yet Eben Ayers's diary of October 19 noted:

Staff delighted at Truman's announcement . . . during staff meeting that he wanted several proposed trips cancelled. Feeling of staff was that Truman was making too many unnecessary trips and that the publicity of his drinking and poker playing was doing more harm than good. Truman's decision came after Rosenman, Snyder, Ross, Connelly and Hassett [William D. Hassett, correspondence secretary] had talked to him about the problem.

The House Ways and Means Committee, dominated by rural and southern members, killed the whittled-down unemployment compensation bill when it came over from the Senate. Switching from the carrot to the stick, Truman summoned the Democratic members to the White House. On his appointment sheet beside their names September 27 he jotted: "I told 'em either I am the leader of the Dem. Party or I'm not. That the Senate had let me down. That they had no right to follow the Senate."[14] This tactic did not budge the conservatives either.

The administration asked that tax cuts be held to $5 billion. Congress reduced taxes by $5.9 billion, including repeal of the excess profits tax. Also after the Senate raised liberals' hopes by passing a modified full employment bill, Representative Carter Manasco, Democrat, of Alabama, chairman of the Committee on Expenditures in the Executive Departments, which would handle the legislation in the House, said a majority of the committee favored postponement.

One by one, the president's proposals were being rejected or delayed. Meanwhile he was increasingly worried over the epidemic of strikes. "Now let's all go home and go to work," he said at the dedication of a dam at Gilbertsville, Kentucky, October 10. "Cut out the foolishness and make this country what it ought to be."[15]

In a decision that was soon to backfire, Snyder got Truman on October 15 to remove the wartime regulation limiting the use of building materials. The step was in keeping with Snyder's eagerness to dump controls, but was also supported by liberals who hoped the building industry would provide jobs.[16] Unfortunately, housing prices soared. And instead of producing new houses that veterans could afford the materials went into more profitable ventures, like race tracks, bowling alleys, and bars.

The next day, apropos no particular incident such as the decision on building materials, Harold Smith told Lilienthal at lunch that he had just reached a conclusion about Truman. To his surprise, Smith said, he had found Truman less orderly than Roosevelt as an administrator, whereas his first impression had been that the opposite would prove true. Because of inadequate staff preparation, Smith explained, Truman had often made a mess of things, though he readily confessed to his mistakes and asked to be rescued from them. On the other hand, the budget director said that Truman was highly intelligent and acted sincerely and out of the highest motives. In noting all this in his journal later Lilienthal observed that men who have only legislative experience do not generally understand the art of administration.[17]

At a cabinet meeting October 19 Ickes warned Truman that if labor unrest continued, the Democrats would probably lose the congressional elections in 1946. He added that some corporations had made immense profits out of the war and could afford to dip into them to raise wages.[18]

With the UAW threatening a strike against the automobile industry, the Truman administration yielded on wage policy. A report of the Office of War Mobilization and Reconversion concluded that on the whole industry could, because of increased productivity and other factors, afford to raise wages 24 percent without jeopardizing either profits or the price-control program.[19] Bowles wrote Rosenman October 29: ". . . in my opinion most of the present labor-management troubles stem from a stiff-necked attitude on the part of management buttressed behind huge reserves and the present advantages of the excess profits law."[20] Various cabinet members recommended to Truman a policy of higher wages.

On October 30 the president came out in a national broadcast in favor of a reasonable rise in pay through collective bargaining. Under the policy a corporation could include the cost of higher wages in price increases but not until a six-month accounting period had demonstrated the need. Truman did not, however, go along with Philip Murray by recommending a specific percentage. With overtime pay ending, he said, wage increases were imperative "to sustain adequate purchasing power and to raise the national income."[21] Truman now assigned equal importance to the dangers of "wide unemployment" and "runaway inflation," reflecting the conflicting opinions he continued to get from his economic advisers. Still the speech did little to halt the slide toward chaos in the labor situation. "Senator Kilgore lunched with me on Tuesday," Ickes jotted in his diary November 4. "He thinks that Truman is slipping and that there is rough sledding ahead."

The National Labor-Management Conference finally convened in Washington November 5. Truman opened it with a lecture to both sides to discharge their responsibilities for averting strikes.[22] Burdened with work himself, he optimistically left it up to them to find the right procedures and completely excluded the government from the task. Many participants felt that the president must have had some plan in mind when he called the conference and that he had a share of responsibility for its success. If he had not intended to offer some leadership, they believed, he should not have called the conference.[23]

Anyhow the conference was too late. The disputes had gone too far. And, what with the CIO and the AFL at each others' throats, labor representatives could not agree on a wage policy among themselves, let alone with industry. On November 21, with the conference in midstream, Reuther called a strike of 175,000 workers at ninety-five General Motors plants in support of his union's demand for a 30 percent raise. Meanwhile Benjamin F. Fairless, president of the United States Steel Corporation, wrote Snyder asserting that the steel industry could not meet Murray's recent demand for a $2-a-day increase unless the OPA raised ceilings on steel prices.[24] Truman's mood was reflected in a memorandum to conference leaders:

The industrial crisis is obviously deepening. . . . If the conference has arrived at no conclusions which we can put into action to prevent strife, then we will be forced, in the public interest, to take steps quite independent of anything the conference has done.[25]

Still without any semblance of effective presidential leadership, the conference quit November 30, making no recommendations helpful to the situation at hand.

The country was sick of strikes, and Democrats and Republicans alike were urging Truman to get tough with the unions. On December 3, his patience exhausted, he sent Congress a special message that stunned labor. Without consulting labor leaders he asked Congress—in vain, as it turned out—to extend the principles of the Railway Labor Act to large national industries so as to head off strikes through the medium of fact-finding boards. No strikes or lockouts could occur during the thirty-day deliberations of such boards. The proposal had no teeth, however; the parties would not be bound by the recommendations of a board. Supposedly, the recommendations would sway public opinion to one side or another, creating pressure for a settlement.

Pending action by Congress, Truman said he was appointing nonstatutory fact-finding boards in the automobile strike and the impending steel strike. Meanwhile he asked automobile workers to return to the plants and asked steelworkers not to leave their jobs while the respective boards were deliberating.[26]

Business did not think the proposal went nearly far enough. Employers felt that the strikes had created a public mood favorable to clipping the wings of labor. The time had come, they believed, for revision of the Wagner Act to redress the industrial balance. And labor, having previously opposed fact-finding boards, was furious.

The UAW refused to return to work and scornfully contrasted Truman with Roosevelt. John L. Lewis called the message "an evil, vile-smelling mess." On radio Murray accused Truman of union-busting, charging that the administration had yielded "in abject cowardice."[27] On December 11 he set January 14 as the deadline for a steel strike.

Truman resented these attacks. Murray and other labor leaders, he told Wallace, had come to see him in August, favoring retention of the War Labor Board and the no-strike pledge until January 1. "Now see what Phil Murray is doing, calling me a thief!" he exclaimed. He continued to maintain in private that he had agreed to relaxation of controls late in the summer only after having received assurance from business and labor leaders, including Murray, that they would cooperate to avert strikes.[28]

On December 12, the day after Murray had ordered a steel strike, John Steelman said at a staff meeting that he had been getting calls asking why Truman did not send for the CIO president. The White House roof would fall in, Truman snapped, before he sent for him. Two days later Truman told visitors that Murray had barred himself from the White House by his union-busting charges against the president.[29] But not for long, as it turned out.

On top of everything else veterans were now in such an uproar over the housing shortage that Truman at Snyder's suggestion restored the controls on building materials that had been lifted in October.[30] He also appointed Wilson W. Wyatt, a liberal Democrat and former mayor of Louisville, as housing expediter.

Truman admitted to the cabinet December 14 that he had made a number of mistakes in removing controls too soon. He also had declined to give consistently strong support to the OPA's struggle against the special interests and rival bureaucrats to hold down prices. Bowles was one of the most talkative New Dealers, and Truman's relationship with him was not altogether comfortable. "I think I am right in saying," Bowles wrote him December 17, "that no top Administration leader has defended the OPA anti-inflation program on the floor of either house since last June."[31] Truman now assured the cabinet that he was going to support Bowles to the limit.[32] By this time the nature of the economic problem was clearer. When asked at a press conference November 29 whether he regarded deflation as any-where near as dangerous as inflation, Truman had replied, "No, I do not."[33]

The denunciation by the labor leaders was not easy for him to take eleven months before congressional elections. In any case he now shifted ground some-what and infuriated management in his effort to end the General Motors strike through his own fact-finding board.

The board met in Washington December 20. Both sides to the dispute were present. General Motors at once demanded to know whether the question of ability to pay higher wages was to be a subject of the inquiry. From the start Reuther had tailored his strategy to Truman's policy of limiting wage increases to a level at which they would not require a compensatory increase in prices. Reuther thus main-tained that General Motors could afford a 30 percent wage increase without raising prices, and he demanded that the corporation open its books to prove otherwise. Al-though the practice was not unprecedented, the demand struck General Motors as an invasion of privacy, if not an attack on capitalism itself.

Nevertheless on that December 20 as the board was assembling, Truman, against Snyder's judgment, told a press conference:

In appointing a fact-finding board . . . where one of the questions at issue is wages, it is es-sential to a fulfillment of its duty that the board have the authority, whenever it deems it nec-essary, to examine the books of the employer. That authority is essential to enable the board to determine the ability of the employer to pay an increase in wages where such ability is in question. Ability to pay is always one of the facts relevant to the issue of an increase in wages.[34]

His statement siding with Reuther was delivered to the hearing by messenger. The upshot was that the corporation withdrew from the proceedings. "General Motors has made its choice," Alfred P. Sloan, Jr., chairman, and Charles E. Wil-son, president, said in a statement December 29. "It refuses to subscribe to what it believes will ultimately become . . . the death of the American system of competi-tive enterprise. It will not participate voluntarily in what stands out crystal clear as the end of the road—a regimented economy."[35] The withdrawal did not bring down Truman's wrath. The General Motors' executives tasted none of the invective that was in store for some labor leaders who crossed him several months later.

During the autumn the full employment bill, the liberals' dream, foundered in the House Committee on Expenditures in the Executive Departments. Vinson wrote to Truman, advocating compromise.[36] He suggested, for example, that Truman agree to dropping from the bill the phrase "full employment," a red flag to conser-vatives and business groups. The term was not a practical one anyhow because of the difficulty of defining its meaning.

Vinson also suggested emphasizing in the bill that any federal action would be consistent with free enterprise and stating that no benefits would go to those persons capable of but unwilling to work.

"This appears to me to be an approach that will work," Truman scribbled on Vinson's letter. Truman and his advisers feared that unless he compromised, the

House, dominated by the conservative coalition, would not pass a bill at all. On the other hand, if even a weak bill were passed, it might be strengthened in the legislative conference called to reconcile differences in the House and Senate versions.

Fed up with Chairman Manasco and his southern colleagues, Truman told Ickes November 9 that, according to Ickes, "he wished that there might be organized a liberal party in the country so that the Southern Democrats could go where they belonged into the conservative Republican Party." Forrestal told Ickes November 24 he thought the administration was deteriorating. After having seen the president on November 26, Ickes observed: "Once again he repeated that he had not wanted to be President. He says this to me practically every time that I see him and I wish that he wouldn't. The state of mind of which this is evidence is not good for him or for the country."[37]

The secretary of interior was not alone in disapproving the humility and protestations of inadequacy in which Truman often indulged in the weeks and months following Roosevelt's death. Senator Alben W. Barkley of Kentucky, the Senate Democratic leader, felt it was not doing Truman any good as man or president to be quoted in self-deprecation. He went to him, he recalled in his memoirs, and urged him to develop and manifest a sense of confidence"—and there were others among his associates who did likewise."[38] Rayburn also protested to Truman that it was beneath presidential stature for him to keep telling people that he had not wanted the job.[39] In time Truman's attitude wore away; a man does not long remain overly humble in the presidency.

After seeing Harold Smith November 28, Ickes mused: "I gather that he feels rather sorry for Truman whom he believes, as I do, to be a straightforward honest man who wants to do his best for the country. It is just unfortunate that he has those about him who, in my opinion, are not trustworthy and who will embarrass him before he gets through, if he isn't careful."[40]

On December 5 the House Committee on Expenditures in the Executive Departments recommended a substitute employment bill that rejected some of the main features of the liberal Senate measure. The substitute eliminated a declaration of the right to work. It also rejected the commitment to federal compensatory spending on things like public works to achieve full employment—the phrase was abolished from the title of the bill. The concept of the "national production and employment budget," regarded by many as the heart of the bill, was scrapped.

Echoing the sentiments of business, the majority report held that "the way in which to achieve and maintain high levels of employment is to preserve and encourage the American system of free competitive enterprise . . . to avoid Government competition with private business."

Once the issue came to the House floor in December the administration threw its weight behind the substitute, again fearing that the House would pass only this or nothing and hoping to get a stronger measure from the conference committee. When the substitute bill was passed liberals were further disillusioned by the administration's unwillingness to stand and fight. As 1945 drew to an end, Truman wrote to the managers of the Senate-House conference committee, Manasco and Senator Robert F. Wagner of New York, asking that the committee accept the Senate bill. "In my opinion," he said, "no bill which provides substantially less than the

Senate version can efficiently accomplish the purposes intended.''[41]

Such a tactic, however, was a feeble counter to the onslaught against the Senate bill being waged by the National Association of Manufacturers, various chambers of commerce, the Committee for Constitutional Government, and their shrill allies in the House. Whether Truman could have overcome the sentiment of the House is doubtful, but he certainly could not have done so without a powerful and skillful display of leadership. And this was not forthcoming.

A problem that had been growing ever since the end of the Roosevelt administration now attained new dimensions. It was the problem of an adequate food supply.

The war had put a tremendous burden on American agriculture. While production had been expanded by a third, the increase was less than it might have been. The needs of the armed forces and of Allied peoples put a strain on supplies at the very time Americans, prosperous from war production after years of the depression, were eating better than ever in their lives—and quite determined to continue doing so.

Fear of a postwar depression was based in part on an expectation of an agricultural surplus such as had helped crush the farmers after 1929. To avert anticipated overproduction, therefore, the government in the last months of the Roosevelt administration relaxed controls so as to increase consumption. It also halted stockpiling and set limited new production goals. The miscalculation was dreadful.

By the spring of 1945 meat was disappearing from the butcher shops. Not even the Trumans could get roast beef, but friends sent them Missouri ham and turkey. Black markets were rampant: poultry was obtainable almost nowhere else. Sugar and other commodities were hard to get in the groceries. Angry shoppers were complaining to Washington. Chester Bowles told Truman that complaints and resistance to rationing were making it hard to keep the Office of Price Administration going.

Warnings of impending famine in Europe poured in. In April Rosenman had returned from a fact-finding trip, saying that democracy faced a precarious future in Europe unless Americans sent more food and coal.

Victory momentarily diverted attention from such warnings. Rather, the fear of a future farm surplus continued to trouble Secretary Anderson. Incredibly, concern about too much food obscured the danger of too little. Crop forecasts were optimistic. The food requirements of the armed services fell drastically with demobilization. Thus it seemed to Anderson that the United States would have enough to feed itself and Europe. Reflecting this optimism, Truman said in a statement September 17 that the only problem about food exports was one of finance, not of supply and availability of shipping.

As the fall wore on, however, new reports from Europe painted an alarming picture of shortages and warned of disease and starvation. On November 2 Bowles wrote Truman recommending that rations of meat, fats, and oils be cut by 10 percent to increase stocks for Europe. Truman forwarded the letter to Anderson, who had the primary authority in this field. With the interests of American farmers and consumers in mind and still hopeful about supplies, Anderson not only rejected

Bowles's suggestion but brought about the end of rationing of meat, fats, and oil. Truman did not override the decision, and the OPA dismantled its food-rationing machinery. By New Year's the situation in Europe was so bad Truman had another crisis on his hands.[42]

"Sherman was *wrong,*" he told the Gridiron Dinner in December. "I'm telling you I find peace is hell . . ."[43]

In November Truman had taken a memorable step into one of the great controversial issues of the middle years of the twentieth century—that of the proper role of the federal government in providing medical care for the general population. In 1935 Roosevelt had submitted to Congress a report of the President's Committee on Economic Security, which formed the basis of the Social Security Act passed later that year. The report approved the principle of compulsory national health insurance but made no specific recommendation concerning it. In his accompanying message Roosevelt refrained from asking enactment of health insurance, largely because the issue was so controversial he feared it would endanger the whole Social Security bill.

On November 19, 1945, for the first time a president recommended to Congress a comprehensive, prepaid medical insurance program for persons of all ages, tied to Social Security. "Everyone should have ready access to all necessary medical, hospital and related services," Truman said in a special message. For employed persons and their dependents he suggested that the program be financed by a tax of 4 percent on the first $3,600 of wages and salaries. "Needy persons and other groups" would be covered by payments from the general federal revenues. Truman asked that the plan cover doctor, hospital, nursing, laboratory, and dental services. Recipients could choose their doctors and their hospitals. Truman said the plan was not socialized medicine, because "socialized medicine means that all doctors work as employees of the government."[44]

Many of the features of his proposal had been contained in the Wagner-Murray-Dingell bill introduced in 1943. It was now revised to embody the Truman program and reintroduced.

"Let the people of our country realize," said the *Journal of the American Medical Association* December 1, 1945, "that the movement for the placing of American medicine under the control of the federal government through a system of federal compulsory sickness insurance is the first step toward a regimentation of utilities, of industries, of finance, and eventually of labor itself. This is the kind of regimentation that led to totalitarianism in Germany and the downfall of that nation."

At lunch with Ickes December 3 Rosenman said that in certain things Truman had proved much braver than Roosevelt. "For instance," Ickes recalled, "he [Rosenman] said that for a number of years Roosevelt was in favor of a bill looking to the health of people who could not afford to pay medical expenses. He kept off supporting this bill for one reason or another for a long time. Rosenman thought that surely after the last election he would get behind this bill right away. He said that Truman sent the bill up without much ado."[45]

The plight of the ill and indigent in county hospitals when he was a county commissioner responsible for their supervision evidently made an indelible impression on Truman. Some of those closest to him when he became president thought he felt more strongly about the problem of medical care for the poor and middle class than about any other domestic issue. Around the time he sent the message he was angry at physicians and hospitals over instances of lack of care of the poor.

"The President told me at that time he knew . . . that that [proposal] wasn't going to be passed," Dr. John R. Steelman, an administration official, recalled afterward, "but he wanted to scare these doctors and make them do something. So he scared the living light out of them by coming out more strongly than he ever hoped to get. He thought the doctors were getting to be pretty bad. He had instances where a baby would die on the steps of the hospital because they wouldn't take the baby in because nobody was there who could pay for him and so forth. He gathered up a lot of these individual cases, and he got a very bad impression of doctors and hospitals, and he thought he'd better give them a big scare."[46]

His message aroused continuing controversy over what was thought a radical proposal. Truman finally left office without seeing it enacted. The fight went on for years. After new efforts by John F. Kennedy and Lyndon B. Johnson, Congress enacted a program that had evolved under the name of Medicare, which covered only persons who had reached the age of sixty-five and was not the comprehensive insurance that Truman had proposed. President Johnson saluted Truman for having led the way by signing the Medicare bill in his presence at the Harry S Truman Library in Independence July 30, 1965. "We have come back here to his home," Johnson said, "to complete what he began."[47]

14. *Truman and the Military*

A<small>T THE CABINET MEETING</small> October 26, 1945, the secretaries of war and navy warned that the state of demobilization, then occurring pell-mell, was a threat to the country's strategic position. Truman agreed, saying that the process was no longer demobilization—it was disintegration of the armed forces.[1]

After V-J Day clamor for speedy demobilization, though it may have come from a minority of the people, was inordinate. Disorder simmered among troops overseas. At home wives and parents protested what seemed to them the slow pace of discharges. Congress was flooded with baby shoes, children's photographs, and even locks of hair as tokens of demand for the return of fathers. Members wilted under the heat.

Representative John E. Rankin of Mississippi told the House:

. . . if the Congress does not get busy and expedite the release of these men from the armed forces—men who are needed at home, who have jobs to go back to, who have wives and children to look after or who have crops to gather, or young men who should finish their education—you will soon be in the hottest water you have ever been in since you have been in Congress—and ought to be.[2]

As the volume of mail reached an avalanche, members of Congress, fearing reprisals at the polls, threw the burden on the administration. In response Truman said in a letter to Representative E. E. Cox of Georgia, "Members . . . are going to have to take the heat in order to keep an injustice from being done to the men who really did the fighting and to be sure we know exactly where we are going when demobilization takes place."[3]

As with postwar economic planning, plans for demobilization, approved in 1943, were complicated by the unexpectedly early end of the Japanese war. Demobilization suddenly became a global undertaking. Truman would have preferred a slower pace so that the armed forces could adjust and those discharged could more easily be assimilated in jobs.[4] He did not, however, put the prestige of his office behind any effort to change public opinion. The pressure for rapid demobilization was intensified when MacArthur announced September 17 that within six months the number of occupation troops in Japan would be reduced to no more than 200,000 because of "smooth progress."

"Obviously," noted Harold Smith after a talk with Truman on the eighteenth, "the President regarded this announcement as a political statement."[5]

"Mr. President," a reporter asked at a press conference the same day, "did you have any advance information, or know what General MacArthur said about the number of troops needed in Japan?''

"No, I didn't," he replied. "I'm glad to see that the general won't need as many as he thought. He said first 500,000, later 400,000 and now 200,000. It helps to get as many more men out of the Army as possible.''[6]

Truman followed this sarcasm, however, by joining the parade himself with a statement on the nineteenth, saying that the army's discharge rate would rise to no less than 25,000 a day by January and that more than 2 million soldiers would be returned to their homes by Christmas.[7]

Meanwhile the suspiciousness about MacArthur, which Truman had brought to the White House with him, had begun to deepen. On September 17 he had Marshall send MacArthur a message inviting him to visit the United States, after an absence of more than eight years, to be acclaimed by Congress and the people. MacArthur replied that he could not leave until conditions in Japan were more stable. On October 19 Truman directed Marshall to send a second message: "The President has asked me to inform you that he wishes you to understand that he would like you to make a trip home at such time you feel that you can safely leave your duties." Incredibly, MacArthur again declined because "of the extraordinarily dangerous" situation in Japan.[8]

"The President . . . sounded off about MacArthur," Ayers said in his diary September 18, "and said he 'was going to do something with that fellow,' who, he said, had been balling things up. He said he was tired of fooling around."

The continuing public pressure to bring men home was indeed enormous. Truman, however, still did not take the case against the debacle to the American people. To have done so with any degree of success he probably would have had to create a great scare about Soviet conduct, and he was reluctant to do it in the months following the war, while he was still hopeful of getting along with Moscow. Byrnes for his part did not want Truman to do or say anything that the Soviets could point to as justification for their own actions.[9] Furthermore rapid demobilization came to serve the policy of the administration in trimming spending in the face of inflation. Increasingly, therefore, Truman was confronted with the dilemma of espousing an ever tougher foreign policy upon a base of constantly diminishing, although still formidable, military power.

In contrast to the events of 1949 and 1950, when the Communists seized China, when the Soviets exploded a nuclear device, and when war broke out in Korea, Truman's first term was a period of retrenchment in military spending because of popular demand for demobilization, because of inflation, and because of his determination to balance the budget. Nevertheless, for the first time in its history the United States proceeded to maintain a large military establishment in the peace that followed a war. The policy and plans were laid in the Roosevelt administration and carried forward with determination by Truman. Though now the strongest power in Europe, the Soviet Union was exhausted by the war. Throughout Truman's years in office the United States held the balance of power in the world. While demobilization had made a shambles of the wartime army, the United States periodically continued the draft in peacetime, stationed sizable occupation forces in Europe and Asia, and maintained the greatest navy and air force in the world. Even so, American influence abroad was exerted chiefly through economic rather than military power. And in the background stood the American monopoly on the atomic bomb, which Byrnes at least hoped at the time would make the Soviets more compliant with United States aims, especially in settling the disputes over Poland and the neighboring satellite nations.

At the approach of the Council of Foreign Ministers' meeting in London in September the secretary of state was, Stimson recorded with exaggeration, "very much against any attempt to co-operate with Russia." The two men talked in the White House on September 4, on the eve of Byrnes's departure. Stimson noted that Byrnes looked "to having the presence of the bomb in his pocket, so to speak, as a great weapon to get through the thing"—the London conference.[10]

The question of what to do about the atomic bomb in the future confronted Truman at a time when Congress was edgy about the Soviet Union and possessive toward the secrets entailed in the bomb's design and manufacture. Since Hiroshima the country had been seething with debate. While any number of professors, scientists, and clergymen advocated sharing at least scientific information with other countries, the mood in Congress was quite different.

Some members demanded to know what the Soviets would do with the bomb, if they got it. Others could not get it through their heads why the United States should spend its talent and money and then hand foreigners the prize on a platter. Connally, chairman of the Senate Foreign Relations Committee, suggested that the United States furnish bombs to the United Nations Security Council but retain the secret of manufacture and monopolize all sources of essential materials. The ranking Republican on the committee, Vandenberg, hoped for continuing American atomic monopoly until there was "absolute free and untrammeled right of intimate inspection all around this globe."[11]

"I think," said Senator Russell, "we ought to keep the technical know-how to ourselves as long as possible."

Truman's attitude had first been revealed publicly in his broadcast report on Potsdam August 9. He said that "Great Britian, Canada and the United States, who have the secret of its production, do not intend to reveal that secret until means have been found to control the bomb so as to protect ourselves and the rest of the world from the danger of total destruction. . . . We must constitute ourselves trustees of this new force—to prevent its misuse, and to turn it into the channels of service to mankind."[12]

When Oppenheimer drafted a report noting that the scientific panel of the Interim Committee unanimously favored an international control agreement, Byrnes sent word that "for the time being his proposal about an international agreement was not practical and that he and the rest of the gang should pursue their work full force" to move on to the production of a more powerful bomb.[13]

Stimson meanwhile had come to believe that Truman should approach the Soviets to try to avert an arms race. Clearly, the United States monopoly of the atomic bomb was disturbing Soviet-American relations because the Soviets saw it as offsetting the power of the Red Army. It revived their old sense of insecurity.[14] On September 11 Stimson sent to the White House a memorandum, which he reviewed the next day with Truman, paragraph by paragraph. The memorandum said that relations with the Soviets "may be irretrievably embittered by the way in which we approach the solution of the bomb. . . . For if we fail to approach them now and merely continue to negotiate with them, having this weapon rather ostentatiously on our hip, their suspicions and their distrust of our purposes and motives will increase."

Stimson proposed that, with British assent, the United States approach the Soviet Union on entering into an arrangement "to control and limit the use of the atomic bomb. . . . Such an approach might more specifically lead to the proposal that we would stop work on the further improvement in, or manufacture of, the bomb . . . provided the Russians and the British would agree to do likewise. It might also provide that we would be willing to impound what bombs we now have . . . provided the Russians and the British would agree with us that in no event will they or we use a bomb . . . unless all three Governments agree. . . ."[15]

Truman gave Stimson the impression that he agreed with his conclusion that "we must take Russia into our confidence," though he seems not to have questioned him about various aspects and implications.[16] When the Stimson proposal was first broached to the cabinet at a luncheon September 18, Secretary of Agriculture Anderson opposed it on the ground that some 80 percent of the American people, according to a Gallup poll, wanted the United States to keep the secret of the bomb.[17] The president said that the cabinet meeting September 21—the last Stimson would attend before retiring—would be devoted exclusively to the atomic problem.

What Stimson was suggesting was a basic change in American policy. He did not offer any new control mechanism. It is uncertain, therefore, whether his approach would in the end have led to any system acceptable to both Stalin and to Congress. At every turn in this problem the issue of inspection lay like an indigestible lump.

By the time of the cabinet meeting on the twenty-first Truman was aware through talks with Marshall and Leahy that the Joint Chiefs favored retention of all secrets about the bomb. While granting that scientific principles underlying the weapon were widely known, the Chiefs held that many technical and manufacturing procedures were still secret. Pending international agreement, they maintained, sharing such secrets would hasten an arms race because of the uncertainty of the times. But they argued that during the interval of the American monopoly efforts be pressed to obtain an international agreement on restricting or outlawing use of atomic weapons. "Since this country is particularly vulnerable to attack by atomic weapons," the Joint Chiefs counseled the president, "it would appear imprudent voluntarily to place these devastating weapons in the hands of other countries at this time."[18]

"When we get down to cases," Truman had commented to Davies on the eighteenth, "is any one of the Big Powers—are we?— going to give up these locks and bolts which are necessary to protect our house . . . against possible outlaw attack . . . until experience and good judgment say that the community is sufficiently stable. . .? Clearly we are not. Nor are the Soviets. Nor is any country if it can help itself."[19]

When the cabinet met on the twenty-first to discuss the Stimson proposal, the secretary of war stressed the opinion of scientists that the secret of the bomb could not long be held exclusively.[20] He warned that the future bomb—the hydrogen bomb—would be infinitely worse than the existing one. The future of peace depended on Soviet-American collaboration, he said.

Acheson, sitting in for the absent Byrnes, supported the Stimson proposal, as did Under Secretary of the Army Robert P. Patterson. Acheson said he could not conceive of a world in which the Americans hoarded military secrets away from their allies, especially from the one ally whose cooperation was essential to peace. Vinson and Anderson spoke against the proposal because they did not believe the United States should "share the bomb," which Stimson's memorandum had not suggested, although his covering letter had loosely used the expression. If the Americans were going to share some of the secrets of atomic energy, Vinson asked, why not share all military secrets? Attorney General Tom Clark, too, was opposed, out of mistrust of the Soviets; he warned of espionage.

Truman said they were not talking about giving the secret of the bomb to the Russians, but about the best method of controlling nuclear warfare and exchanging scientific information.

Anderson reported that he had been at a meeting in Decatur, Illinois, the previous night and had asked the audience how many were in favor of giving away the secret of the bomb. He then let the cabinet in on the result of his inquiry: all were against giving away the secret. The secretary of agriculture opined that the president's prestige was precious and ought not be sacrficed by defying the peoples' will.

Forrestal fired a broadside at the Stimson proposal that would have made any admiral proud. As if pioneering European scientists had never existed, the secretary of the navy said that the knowledge that produced the bomb was the "property of the American people" and should not be given away without their assent. He reminded the cabinet that the Japanese had been America's ally in the First World War and afterward had gone back on the 1921 naval limitation agreement.

"The Russians, like the Japanese," he continued, "are essentially Oriental in their thinking, and until we have a longer record of experience with them on the validity of agreements . . . it seems doubtful that we should endeavor to buy their understanding and sympathy."

Wallace was increasingly worried about Soviet-American differences. According to most private accounts of the meeting, he advocated exchange of scientific information but not of techniques for constructing the bomb. Only a summary by Forrestal stated Wallace's position thus: "Completely, everlastingly and wholeheartedly in favor of giving it to the Russians."

What with the opposition of Vinson, Forrestal, Clark, and Anderson, cabinet resistance to the Stimson proposal was strong. Furthermore the next day the *New York Times* carried a front-page story saying that Wallace had proposed in the cabinet that the Americans, British, and Canadians "reveal the secret of the atomic bomb to Russia." Considering the foregoing summary by Forrestal, Acheson may have been right in believing, as he did, that Forrestal had leaked the story to the *Times*. In any case, the story shocked Congress. Thus Truman, though he denied the paper's account, came under all the more pressure to go slow in adopting Stimson's advice.

Numerous atomic energy bills were being introduced in Congress, and the administration had to act. On October 3 Truman sent up a special message, shaped by Acheson and Patterson and drafted by Herbert S. Marks, legal assistant to Acheson. It dealt separately with the international and domestic aspects of the problem.[21]

In the international realm Truman conceded that the essential theoretical knowledge with which the bomb had been built "is already widely known." He espoused the ideal of "international arrangements looking, if possible, to the renunciation of the use and development of the atomic bomb." He said he would initiate discussions first with the partners, Britain and Canada, and then with other nations.

"I desire to emphasize," he said, "that these discussions will not be concerned with disclosures relating to the manufacturing process leading to the production of the bomb itself."

While comment over his message was at its height Truman took off on one of his periodic capers in Missouri, amusing himself by spitting in the Mississippi River, ringing the bell of an American Legion Forty and Eight locomotive in a parade and playing Paderewski's *Minuet in G* on an upright for the ladies at a Methodist church supper. "When I played this Stalin signed the Potsdam agreement," he told them.[22] On October 7 he spoke at the Pemiscot County Fair at Caruthersville. Atomic energy, he said, "can create a world which . . . will be the happiest world that the sun has ever shone upon. . . . When the nations decide that the welfare of the world is much more important than any individual gain which they themselves can make at the expense of another nation, then we can take this discovery . . . and make this world the greatest place the sun has ever shone upon."[23]

The next day he and his buddies repaired to Tiptonville, Tennessee, across the Missouri line, to fish in Reelfoot Lake. Truman surprised the reporters accompanying him by inviting them to his lodge for some Jack Daniels and a bull session and then turning the latter into a press conference. Since the atomic bomb was the big news of the moment, a reporter asked if the Caruthersville speech meant that the secret would not be shared until the Americans had assurances that other countries would not take advantage of it.

No, Truman replied. The scientific knowledge that produced the bomb was widely held. "It is only the know-how of putting that knowledge practically to work that is our secret," he said. A reporter asked if the president's remarks would apply to letting other countries in on the know-how.

"Well, I don't think it would do any good to let them in on the know-how, because I don't think they could do it anyhow," Truman replied, reflecting a common American miscalculation of Soviet science and technology that persisted well into the Eisenhower administration. "You would have to have the industrial plant and our engineering ability to do the job, as well as the scientific knowledge, and there isn't any reason for trying to keep the scientific knowledge covered up, because all the great scientists know it in every country; but the practical know-how is our ability to do the job."

"If they catch up with us on that," he added, "they will have to do it on their own hook, just as we did."[24]

Although he had said as much before, the impact of his comments was to create the impression that he was backtracking from the spirit of the atomic energy message.

Truman's special message proposed in the domestic field an Atomic Energy Commission, an idea that had been germinating for a couple of years. Appointed by the president, the commission would control all nuclear stockpiles and plants; acquire minerals from which atomic energy is derived, and conduct all research, experimentation, and operations for the development and use of atomic energy for military, industrial, scientific, and medical purposes.

The vision of material abundance bestowed by peaceful use of the atom, incidentally, aroused Truman's concern for the effect on American character. "The President expressed considerable disquietude," Wallace noted, "that the peacetime utilization of atomic energy would so shorten the hours of labor that the people of the United States would get into mischief."[25]

The seemingly simple proposal of an Atomic Energy Commission involved Truman in a months-long, ferocious ideological and bureaucratic fight over legislation known as the May-Johnson bill. The issue was whether military or civilian authorities should have supreme control over atomic energy.[26]

Since the army had developed the atomic bomb, early planning for postwar control contemplated a continuing major role for the military. Indeed, senior War Department lawyers were recruited to draft model legislation that became the May-Johnson bill. It provided for a nine-member, part-time commission empowered to select a full-time administrator. A military man would be permitted to serve as administrator, and some members of the commission would be military men. Critics saw in this an extension into the postwar period of the dominant wartime roles of Groves and his military colleagues, a sort of permanent Manhattan Engineer District.

True, the bill did embody the proposals for domestic control of atomic energy contained in the president's message and had been seen by Truman. And some of the scientists and educators, including Bush and Conant, did support it, at least at this time. The measure, however, was roundly attacked by nuclear scientists bristling under the security regulations being enforced by the army upon research. Still Truman was unmoved.

"Does the May-Johnson bill seem satisfactory to you?" a reporter asked at a press conference October 18.

"I think it is satisfactory," he answered. "I don't know, because I haven't studied it carefully. When it comes up here for me to sign it, I will make up my mind on what I shall do with it. It is substantially in line with the suggestions in the message, I think."[27]

The bill was in trouble, however, compounded by the Senate's decision to create a Special Committee on Atomic Energy, thus diverting the issue from the Military Affairs Committee. Meanwhile a lawyer named James R. Newman, an assistant to John Snyder, became concerned about the powers the measure would confer on the AEC administrator. Newman suggested to Truman that at least the administrator should be appointed by the president. Thinking along the same lines,

Harold Smith cautioned Truman that the bill would make the commission "virtually independent of Executive control" and limit the president's power of removal of officials. The AEC, he argued, should be fully under the president's direction.

College presidents' outcries about military interference with research may have left Truman cold. He warmed up quickly, however, to a threat to presidential authority. Replying to Smith October 24, he decided against a definite commitment to the May-Johnson bill until the various criticisms had been considered.[28]

The chairman of the new Senate Atomic Energy Committee, Senator Brien McMahon, Democrat, of Connecticut, appointed Newman special counsel. With the help of the scientists Newman drafted a new bill tying the AEC closer to the executive branch and providing that the commissioners and the administrator, or general manager, be appointed by the president and removable at his pleasure.

Then in November Newman drafted a letter for Truman's signature citing deficiencies in the May-Johnson bill. Among other things the letter said: "The specific provisions in the Bill permitting either members of the Commission or the Administrator to be a member of the Armed Forces should be eliminated."[29] The letter was sent to Forrestal and to Stimson's recent successor, Secretary of War Robert Patterson. The military continued to lobby among their influential friends in Congress for the May-Johnson bill, however, and on December 4 Truman called a meeting attended by Patterson, Forrestal, and Groves, among others. After hearing their views Truman gave his. The entire AEC operation, he said, should be under civilian control.[30]

McMahon introduced a new bill vesting full control in an Atomic Energy Commission of five full-time members assisted by a general manager, all appointed by the president. In Congress, however, the issue remained deadlocked through the rest of 1945. In fact Patterson, ignoring the McMahon bill, wrote Truman, maintaining that military control over atomic energy would be essential in time of war or emergency.[31]

During the fall Prime Minister Attlee was being pressed in Parliament for a statement of policy on international control of atomic energy, such as would lessen the strain on relations with the Soviet Union. Before Truman was ready with a plan of his own he was pressed by the prime minister into the holding of an Anglo-American-Canadian conference. Attlee and Prime Minister W. L. Mackenzie King of Canada came to Washington November 10 to review the wartime nuclear partnership with Truman and American officials. Molotov had provided a timely prelude with a speech in the Kremlin November 6, saying, "We will have atomic energy and many other things."[32]

A week before the British and Canadians arrived Vannevar Bush had called on Byrnes and was startled to learn that "there was no organization for the meeting, no agenda being prepared and no American plan in form to present."[33] Typical of the confusion, Truman had endorsed international control, while Byrnes did not even want to discuss the matter until after a European peace settlement. Certainly the idea of letting the Soviets immediately in on the "know-how" was nowhere in the picture, even with the British.

"In my view," Attlee said in a memorandum, "an offer to do this now would not be likely to effect a change of attitude to world problems by the U.S.S.R. It would be regarded as a confession of weakness. The establishment of better relations should precede the exchange of technical information.''[34]

Bush had scarcely recovered from his surprise over the lack of a plan when Byrnes surprised him the more by asking him to prepare one.[35] Plunging into a weekend of work, Bush wrote a memorandum stressing the importance of conducting negotiations with the British in a way that would also facilitate step-by-step negotiation with Moscow. Thus he suggested giving foreign scientists access to basic research laboratories in all nations as a means of encouraging the Soviets to begin collaboration.

In his step-by-step plan Bush proposed that the British and Americans invite the Soviets to join with them to establish under the United Nations an organization to disseminate scientific information, including atomic fission. The second step would involve creation of a United Nations Commission of Inspection empowered to check on laboratories in any country engaging in atomic research. Until this system had been perfected, all nations would agree as a third step to stockpile materials capable of atomic fission, releasing them for peaceful purposes only.

Pending full operation of the plan, the United States would continue producing materials necessary to make bombs, but would promise not to assemble new weapons. Once the inspection system was in full operation, other nations could inspect the American stockpile of fissionable materials.

The plan was tossed into the whirl of the ill-prepared summit conference. When it emerged, the idea of joint action by the United States, Britain, and the Soviet Union was gone. Instead, contrary to Stimson's recommendation in September, Truman, Attlee, and MacKenzie King proposed that international control of atomic energy be entrusted directly to a United Nations commission. The commission would proceed by stages through scientific exchange, development of peaceful uses of atomic energy, elimination of atomic weapons, and international inspection. Each stage would have to be successfully completed before the next stage could begin.

In the many years it would take to complete the stages, the United States would retain a monopoly on its existing nuclear weapons. Hence it was unlikely that the Soviet Union would ever agree to the proposal. The Truman-Atlee-MacKenzie King talks had an air of helter-skelter statecraft. For Truman the trouble was compounded by the fact that in the scramble to produce the agreement, resentful congressional leaders were not consulted until a few minutes before Truman announced the terms at a press conference November 15.[36] ''I have never participated in anything that was so completely unorganized or so irregular,'' Bush wrote to Stimson. ''I have had experiences in the past week that would make a chapter in 'Alice in Wonderland.' ''[37]

The constant cross fire of foreign and domestic problems that fall engulfed Truman. ''The pressure here is becoming so great,'' he wrote to his mother October 13, ''I can hardly get my meals in.''[38] More problems were competing for his attention than he could deal with personally. At times he seemed worn. At a meeting with Harold Smith October 16 Smith told him that the government was having a difficult time making the transition from war to peace. Morale was low in the departments; people were tired. As a rule of thumb, Smith said, he judged how well the bureaucracy was working by the number of hours he stayed awake at night worrying. Truman replied that he was not yet lying awake nights, but he feared he was approaching that point. "I did not indicate how bad I think the situation is," Smith confided in his notes. "Actually, I believe it is worse now than at any time since I have been in Washington."[39]

That fall Washington was an utter jumble of new developments over Palestine, China, Soviet relations, steel wages, atomic energy, housing, civil rights, and military and naval policy. "The truth is," Ross wrote to Arthur Krock of the *New York Times* October 17, "that nearly all the top men in the government are trying to do too much. They don't have time for reflection. I know that I don't."[40] The White House staff was inadequate for the load. As an example of the business that all but got buried in the swirl was a message that arrived that same October 17 for the president and was referred to the State Department. It was from Ho Chi Minh and was a protest against French representation on the Far Eastern Advisory Commission soon to be convened. He sought to make the case to Truman that Vietnam was entitled to serve on the commission under the terms of the Atlantic Charter. After the message reached the State Department the chief of the Division of Southeast Asian Affairs notified the chief of the Office of Far Eastern Affairs that "SEA considers that no action should be taken on the attached telegram from Ho Chi Minh to the President."[41]

Within a span of five days Truman delivered two major speeches on military, naval, and diplomatic policy.

On October 23 he appeared before a joint session of Congress to propose a program he thoroughly believed in and would press for throughout his years in office— Universal Military Training. He once told a reporter he had been for UMT, as it was called, since 1905, the year he joined the National Guard. As a senator he had supported an unsuccessful bill to make the depression-spawned Civilian Conservation Corps permanent in the hope it could be converted into a military training program.[42] He felt an urgency about the issue now because he did not wish to see the armed forces melt away as they had been allowed to do after the First World War.[43]

Foreign to the American experience, UMT had been seized upon by military planners during the war as an idea for providing a postwar "citizen army" that could be mobilized quickly. It would be an alternative to a large standing army, which the country was thought unlikely to support. Roosevelt had favored UMT, as did Stimson, Marshall, Forrestal, Eisenhower, and other military leaders. After hearings, a House select committee on postwar military policy recommended it. Several UMT bills were pending in Congress.

As proposed by Truman along general lines recommended by the military services, all men between eighteen and twenty would be called for a year of training. All would remain civilians. Although they would receive basic military instruction, they would not be trained as professional soldiers nor during their year would they be assigned to any branch of the armed services. Their status would be that of trained citizens; ". . . if and when the Congress should declare it necessary for them to become soldiers, they could do so more quickly and efficiently," Truman said. They would constitute a large trained reserve of citizens, a component of the nation's military organization. Only by act of Congress, however, could they be conscripted into the army or navy. Those not physically or mentally qualified for combat would receive basic training in other duties required by the services in wartime.[44]

The postwar military establishment Truman favored would have had three components: (1) A comparatively small standing army, navy and Marine Corps; (2) A much strengthened National Guard and Organized Reserve for the various services; and (3) A General Reserve consisting of those who had received the year of training. This concept had been recommended to him by Marshall.[45]

"We must face the fact," Truman told Congress, "that peace must be built upon power, as well as upon good will and good deeds."

Congress was unresponsive. The pressure at the moment was all toward getting men out of the service. The atomic bomb raised doubts about the practicability of large armies in the future. Truman's proposal languished.

At the cabinet meeting October 26 Byrnes reported that the foreign ministers' conference in London had failed to reach any settlements. The bomb in Byrnes's pocket had not made the Soviets more manageable at all. The truth was that Truman and Byrnes had no grand design for using possession of the atomic bomb to coerce other nations. After hearing Byrnes out, the president cautioned members of the cabinet not to let the public know the extent to which the Soviets had tried American patience. We are going to find some way to get along with the Russians, he said.[46] Despite the frustrations of London, this was still his attitude, as indeed it was Byrnes's.[47]

The ambivalence of American policy at this time, however, was illustrated the very next day when Truman went to New York and reveled in American military power in a speech prominently displayed in all Soviet newspapers.[48] October 27 was Navy Day. In sight of throngs along the shores forty-seven fighting ships were anchored for seven miles in the Hudson River from Sixtieth Street to Spuyten Duyvil. At the Navy Yard in Brooklyn Truman dedicated the new aircraft carrier *Franklin D. Roosevelt,* after which, enjoying his first presidential visit to New York, he was greeted by a huge crowd in the Sheep Meadow in Central Park, where he spoke on foreign policy.[49] At a time of differences with the Soviet Union over the nature of the governments in Eastern Europe and the Balkans he said: "We shall refuse to recognize any government imposed upon any nation by the force of any foreign power. In some cases it may be impossible to prevent forceful imposition of such a government. But the United States will not recognize any such government." Despite demobilization, he promised continuance of great land, sea, and air power, saying: "We have learned the bitter lesson that the weakness of this great Republic invites men of ill will to shake the very foundations of civilization all over the world."

Truman also made a number of remarks that the Soviet press did not report.[50] Part of the reason for maintaining postwar military might, he said, was to enforce the peace and discharge obligations under the United Nations. Disunity among allies was a common phenomenon following wars, but the United States would strive to keep the spirit of cooperation alive. It would take time to work out current difficulties. Forbearance was needed "to understand the special problems of other nations . . . and their own legitimate urge toward security as they see it." Truman urged the people not to become disillusioned with the trials of international collaboration. He proposed a solution to the atomic problem "in partnership with all the peoples of the United Nations," further diverging from Stimson's proposal for an approach to the Soviet Union without first going through the United Nations.

One line drew a notable response from abroad. Observing that Truman had called for the "eventual return of sovereign rights and self-government to all peoples who had been deprived of them by force," Ho Chi Minh again appealed to Washington—in vain—for support of Vietnamese independence.[51]

After the program in the Sheep Meadow, Truman had lunch aboard the battleship *Missouri*. There for the first time he met Governor Thomas E. Dewey. "He took my breath away," Truman said facetiously later, "by announcing publicly that I had made a good speech on foreign affairs in Central Park and that he wholeheartedly approved it."[52]

Truman launched one of the large undertakings of his administration December 19 in a special message to Congress recommending establishment of a Department of National Defense.[53] This involved the so-called unification of the armed forces, an issue that aroused passion in Washington because it affected careers, pride, tradition, the roles of air, sea, and land power, political influence, and allocation of funds among the military services.

So difficult was the question indeed that at a cabinet luncheon on December 18 Hannegan told Truman he thought it would be a mistake to send up the message the next day, particularly because of the opposition in the Military and Naval Affairs committees. He said Truman would be inviting an unnecessary fight that he might lose at the expense of his prestige. Truman replied that he felt it was his duty to submit the message because it represented his conviction.[54]

While running for vice-president, he had written an article for *Collier's* called "Our Armed Forces *Must* Be United," drawing on the findings of the Roberts Commission inquiry into Pearl Harbor and on his own Senate investigation of duplication of costs. In the article he said he had helped draft an American Legion policy in favor of integration of the armed forces, and he recommended that the military be coordinated under a single civilian secretary with the administrative assistance of three under secretaries for ground, sea, and air forces. He favored a general staff instead of the Joint Chiefs of Staff.

In his message on the nineteenth he said:

One of the lessons which have most clearly come from the costly and dangerous experience of this war is that there must be unified direction of land, sea and air forces at home as well as in other parts of the world. . . . We did not have that kind of direction when we were attacked . . . and we certainly paid a high price for not having it.

Since 1798 the War Department and the Navy Department had been separate with no common superior except the president. When military airplanes made their appearance they were placed in the Army Signal Corps in 1907, since the corps already had jurisdiction over balloons for use in observation and communication. As these few early planes evolved into the great fighter and bomber fleets of the Second World War, the Army Air Forces still remained part of the army, though by now a virtually independent part. Meantime the navy and marines had developed extensive air arms of their own. When war came it was obvious that this whole structure contributed neither to combat effectiveness, economy nor civilian control.

In 1943, Army Chief of Staff Marshall broke with his service's tradition and proposed to the Joint Chiefs a "Single Department of War in the Post-War Period." It would consist of ground, sea, and air components and a separate service of supply. Each of these four divisions would be headed by its own civilian under secretary and military chief of staff. At the top of the whole structure would be a "chief of staff to the president," who, with the four other chiefs, would constitute a joint general staff.

The Army Air Forces supported Marshall. Understandably, they favored any plan that would insure their own identity as a separate component.

The navy was opposed. It was agreeable to some form of unification, but it insisted on being continued as an integrated service with its own air forces, even those based on shore, and its Marine Corps. It also wanted its civilian secretary to sit in the cabinet and have direct access to the president. Whereas the army advocated close unification, establishing in Washington the unity of command that had worked well in the field during the war, the navy wanted looser or "federal" coordination that would leave each service considerable autonomy.

The navy objected to unified command in Washington. It recoiled from absorption in a single department. In particular it was adamant against the "chief of staff" concept, fearing that this would lead in a number of ways to diminution of the navy, particularly to loss of some of its aviation and the marines. It even feared that the advent of the atomic bomb and the long-range bomber might create a rationale that the navy was not needed at all any more. With modern weapons the air force might take over the navy's traditional role as the nation's first line of defense. Underlying the unification controversy was the fact that technology was making such rapid and fundamental changes in the science of warfare that it was difficult to get agreement on strategy and the roles of the respective services.

After Marshall's recommendations had been aired in Congress, the navy developed proposals of its own. Forrestal had his old Wall Street friend, Ferdinand Eberstadt, former chairman of the Army-Navy Munitions Board, tackle the problem. Instead of a single department Eberstadt recommended three separate departments—war, navy, and air, all coordinated not by a secretary of defense but by committees. Instead of a new chief of staff, the Joint Chiefs of Staff, which had been created by executive order in the face of war, would become a permanent statutory body. In other words, emphasis was on coordination and cooperation rather than on unification or merger.

Another phase of the Eberstadt plan was designed to satisfy Forrestal's conviction that the greater problem was not teaming the army and navy but coordinating foreign policy and military policy. He believed new structures were needed to bridge the gap. Eberstadt proposed three new organizations: a National Security Council, chaired by the president; a Central Intelligence Agency; and a National Security Resources Board to plan for industrial mobilization.[55] A glance at the national security structure thirty-odd years later confirms the durability of much of the Eberstadt concept. After months more of infighting it was to form the basis of a compromise. Meanwhile the controversy dragged Truman into the center of interservice mistrust. On November 23 George Elsey, the assistant naval aide in the White House, wrote to Clifford:

It is being assumed publicly that the President has become a partisan of the Army against the Navy, that he has developed prejudices against the Navy which cause him to disregard naval wishes and that he will force the Navy into a single Department of Defense which will be dominated by the Army and the Air Forces.[56]

It is certainly true that the navy had felt more comfortable with Roosevelt, who had once been its assistant secretary. Navy people had been confident he would protect them when it came to unification. They had no such feeling about Truman, an army man. Nor was General Vaughan being particularly helpful to the president when he told a neighborhood audience: "During the Roosevelt Administration the White House was a Navy wardroom; we're going to fix all that."[57]

As a matter of fact while Truman felt that unification was a practical necessity, he did not feel so strongly about the particular form it took.[58]

His admiration for Marshall predisposed him in favor of the general's concept. Thus in his message of December 19 he recommended a single Department of National Defense with war, navy, and air on an equal footing. Instead of the coordinating committees recommended by Eberstadt Truman favored a secretary of national defense—a cabinet officer. The Marine Corps would continue as an integral part of the navy, and the navy would retain its sea-based aviation. Despite the navy's objections, however, the Joint Chiefs would be replaced by a chief of staff of the Department of National Defense. Also each branch of the service would have its own commander. The chief of staff, together with the three commanders, would constitute an advisory body to the president and the secretary of national defense.

By presenting the Eberstadt plan to the Senate Military Affairs Committee in October, Forrestal had got the jump on Truman. The impact of the president's message was modest. The arena of controversy shifted to Congress.

Having entered office as a war president, Truman was inevitably, and properly, in consultation with military advisers from the start. A remarkable group of military men had been brought to the forefront of American life by the war. Generals of the Army George Marshall, Dwight Eisenhower, Omar N. Bradley, Douglas MacArthur, and Henry H. Arnold, and Fleet Admirals Leahy, Ernest J. King, and Chester W. Nimitz were national heroes. Victory confirmed their reputations. Their influence had been potent and nowhere were they more celebrated than in Congress, where Truman had first been exposed to their glow. Marshall, Eisenhower, and Bradley, particularly, were men of broad vision, who did not look at the world simply through gunsights.

When Truman became president and inherited some of these renowned figures as advisers, he looked up to them and thought them sincere. As time went on he valued their advice particularly because they were not political partisans. As a former army officer, he felt at home with them and fortunate to have them around.[59] After all, the people themselves placed special trust in these men.

During the war Roosevelt had gone a long way toward giving the military a decisive role as presidential advisers. The Joint Chiefs had access to him without having to go through the secretaries of war and navy. Indeed the chiefs came to have a freer access to the White House than the secretaries. Roosevelt also had sought the advice of the Joint Chiefs on a great many questions that traditionally would have been the business of the State Department. He gave them, for example, responsibility for drawing surrender terms and occupation plans. He even involved them in the establishment of the United Nations.[60]

Although Truman had had a lifetime love of soldiering and was fascinated with the history of battles, he seemed more skeptical than Roosevelt about the wisdom of military advice in general. His years in the army and the reserves had taught him a thing or two about military foul-ups. And as the recent chairman of the Senate Special Committee to Investigate the National Defense Program and a former member of the Military Affairs and Appropriations Committees, he was not only familiar with the anatomy of the services but was well enough acquainted with the inefficiency of the military not to regard its members as all-knowing. Conferring with the budget director June 5, he had spoken critically of the armed forces, saying they had squandered billions.[61] In an interview in 1942 he had foreshadowed some of Eisenhower's concern over the "military-industrial complex" by warning that the postwar political and economic structure would be threatened if admirals and generals moved into commanding positions in industry—as they did in a number of cases.[62]

Also he was discriminating in his judgment about individual generals. One day in talking favorably with Ickes about the secretary of interior's suggestion that he name Charles P. Taft, the senator's brother, as high commissioner to the Philippines (instead he later named Paul V. McNutt ambassador to Manila after Philippine independence), Truman had expressed one reservation. According to Ickes, he "said the only question he had was whether Taft would be strong enough to keep MacArthur in line."

"Truman apparently has definite reservations about MacArthur," Ickes had noted in his diary April 29, 1945. "As a matter of fact, he has, I think, his reservations about brass hats in general." On May 6 Ickes again noted in his diary, "The President made it very clear that he did not care for MacArthur. . . ." After another talk with Truman June 9 Ickes noted: "He indulged in some pretty vigorous Missouri expletives in expressing his opinion of MacArthur."

In Truman's own personal memorandum of June 17 he had referred to the commander in chief of United States Army Forces in the Pacific as "Mr. Prima Donna, Brass Hat, Five Star MacArthur. He's worse than the Cabots and the Lodges—they at least talked with one another before they told God what to do. Mac tells God right off. It is a very great pity we have stuffed shirts like that in key positions. I don't see why in Hell Roosevelt didn't order Wainwright home* and let MacArthur be a martyr.

"Don't see how a country can produce men such as Robt. E. Lee, John J. Pershing, Eisenhower and Bradley and at the same time produce Custers, Pattons and MacArthurs."[63]

The climax of the Truman-MacArthur relationship was still nearly six years away, but the antipathy on Truman's part was already apparent. He remarked to Ickes that MacArthur would probably be a candidate for president some day.[64] The prospect of Eisenhower's becoming a presidential candidate did not disturb him, but at this point he envisioned Eisenhower as a future Democratic candidate. According to Margaret Truman, however, her father sensed that MacArthur was awaiting "a political summons from the Republican party, so he could combine a triumphal return with a nomination for the presidency."[65] In the Wisconsin primary of 1944 the general had indicated his availability as a candidate and won three delegates.

In his cable to Churchill April 16 Halifax had observed that Truman "venerates Marshall."[66] The observation was correct, and the general became a commanding figure in the Truman administration. An incorruptible man of solid bearing and distinguished air, he possessed unusual personal force, slightly camouflaged by a detached and quiet manner, soft voice, and impassive expression. Descendant of the family that had produced Chief Justice John Marshall, he had graduated from the Virginia Military Institute, not West Point. The austere soldier-statesman was a fine strategist, a superb judge of men, yet a military leader who disliked militarism. His calm in times of crisis exerted a steadying influence on Washington. As the highest army officer in the Second World War—"the true organizer of victory," Churchill said—his prestige was enormous.

Truman and Marshall had come to know each other during the Truman Committee inquiries. After Pearl Harbor, Senator Truman went to the army chief of staff and asked for a command in the field artillery on the strength of his experience in the First World War. Marshall told him bluntly that he was too old. (After the senator became president, Marshall said he still would have reached the same conclusion but would have stated it more delicately.)[67]

Even when Truman was a Democratic senator and a Democratic president sat in the White House Truman had called Marshall the greatest living American.[68] When he himself became president he took confidence in having Marshall at his side. He placed such trust in his judgment that the general said later he found it almost frightening.[69] The relationship that developed between the two was approached only by Truman's later affinity for Dean Acheson, whom he barely knew in the spring of 1945.

During the war the military had gained ascendancy over all other government departments. Military considerations influenced policy in many fields, diplomacy included. Perhaps most of the ablest men had entered the service in the war. When it was over many admirals and generals were appointed to important diplomatic and intelligence posts, and lesser officers served on innumerable government boards.

---

* From the Philippines—after the two officers had been trapped with their forces on the Corregidor by the Japanese. MacArthur was spirited away by PT boat and submarine. General Jonathan M. Wainwright remained in command and was captured.

Many of them, however, had come from civilian backgrounds to serve briefly in uniform during hostilities and were not steeped in military tradition.

Truman rather typified a prevailing attitude in a discussion March 1, 1946, with James R. Shepley of Marshall's staff. Marshall was on a mission to China, and the question arose of selecting a capable American ambassador to oversee American aims in China. Truman queried Shepley about Lieutenant General Albert C. Wedemeyer, who had been American chief of staff to Chiang Kai-shek. Yet at the moment considerable controversy was appearing in the press over military men in civilian posts, because of the recent appointments of Lieutenant General Walter Bedell Smith (retired) as United States ambassador to Moscow, succeeding Harriman, and Major General John S. Hilldring as assistant secretary of state for occupied areas.

"The President stated, however," Shepley cabled Marshall, "that he felt there were much stronger arguments in favor of appointing military men to such posts than against, since for the last few years the best talents of the nation has [*sic*] been drawn to the Army and Navy and that these men have had the best kind of practical experience in dealing with the very problems which now confront the nation."*[70]

Whenever the issue of civilian vs. military authority became clear-cut, as in the matter of control of atomic energy, Truman supported civilian supremacy once he had grasped the question. Forrestal, who served as secretary of navy and later secretary of defense in Truman's first term and who differed with him frequently, made the point forthrightly. "In the person of Harry S. Truman," he observed, "I have seen the most rocklike example of civilian control the world has ever witnessed."[71] When he thought it necessary, Truman made heavy cuts in the military budget over protests from the Pentagon. In his study of Truman as commander in chief Professor Richard S. Haynes observed that he never allowed the military to intrude upon his presidential prerogatives. He insisted on approving all but the most routine budget matters before orders were issued. "Truman did not attempt to direct the military," Haynes wrote, "but he did exercise complete supervisory control."[72]

Because of the lessons he had drawn from both world wars, Truman had come to office as a believer in preparedness, as it used to be called. He concluded from the conflicts with Germany and Japan that military power was a guarantor and foundation of peace.[73]

The large and unprecedented peacetime role of the military after the Second World War came about not against the opposition of the civilian authorities, private interests, and public opinion but in concert with all of these. It came about because the United States had decided not to withdraw behind the protection of the oceans, as it had in 1919. As Professor Stephen E. Ambrose said, the new importance of the military was caused by "a fundamental shift of revolutionary proportions in the way American political leaders—and the public—viewed the nation's relationship to the world."[74]

The collapse of America's European allies and the advent of the atomic bomb had altered the country's traditional approach to national defense. It was only to be a matter of time before no haven was left on earth. The president and the Congress,

* Nevertheless, a civilian, Dr. John Leighton Stuart, was finally chosen ambassador to China instead of Wedemeyer.

with overwhelming public support, kept the armed forces on the scale of a major national effort, with consequent influence on the economy, science, and education, as well as foreign policy.

Fear of the Soviet Union played into the hands of industries, particularly the aircraft industry, that strove to keep their military sales contracts alive after the war. The air power lobby was potent during Truman's years in office and subsequently. Its sounding board was the President's Air Policy Commission, appointed by Truman in 1947. The chairman was Thomas K. Finletter, a New York attorney and future secretary of the Air Force. The commission's report, titled *Survival in the Air Age*, endorsed practically everything the aircraft industry wanted.[75] Aided by air power advocates in Congress, the report set in motion an expansion program aimed at building the air force from fifty-five groups (an air group was roughly analogous to an army division), as budgeted by Truman, to an arbitrary seventy groups, a goal envisioned during the war.

When victorious United States forces turned to the task of occupation, army officers exerted decisive influence on American diplomacy in such vital areas as Germany and Japan. The army, navy, and air force won administration support for acquiring overseas bases. This influence was not, however, something forced upon a reluctant president. Truman and his generals and civilian military advisers were in agreement on American aims, at least until the Korean War. It was not a matter of Truman's being run by generals, as MacArthur was to discover. When it came to the question of whether to use the atomic bomb, Truman's principal advisers were, with the important exception of Marshall, civilians. The official who over the years was most influential in advising Truman to move boldly to assert American power was a civilian, Acheson. One of the first to press for development of a more powerful nuclear bomb, as has just been noted, was Byrnes.

Truman and his leading advisers were men who had matured around the time of the First World War or shortly afterward. The Great Depression, the advent of Hitler and Mussolini, the consequences of Munich, and the rise of communism conditioned their thinking. So did the fact that while the United States lapsed into isolationism in the 1920s a march of aggression led from Manchuria to Ethiopia to the Rhineland to Czechoslovakia, Poland, France, and Pearl Harbor. Truman and his policymakers were resolved that this must not happen again. They were moved by fear of another depression, fear of the emergence of a new dictator, and fear of a third world war.

In holding that the United States should offer international leadership, Truman was not simply in step with the military but was aligned with the views of formidable elements in big business, in investment houses, in banks, in the large law firms, in the universities, in the press, in labor, in Congress, and in the government bureaucracies. During the war New Deal reformers had yielded ground to corporation lawyers, investment bankers, and industrialists summoned to Washington by Roosevelt to manage war production and the armed forces. Mostly they were conservative, antiisolationist and dedicated to the ideal of American military, economic, and political leadership.

Favoring a strong internationalist policy, Truman found himself in accord not only with Harriman, Hull, and other Rooseveltian Democrats, but with influential

Republicans like Dewey, Stimson, Vandenberg, and John Foster Dulles and John McCloy, both Wall Street lawyers. Differences might arise on details, but on the main questions of a dominant American role, moral leadership, support of capitalist interests, and stopping Soviet expansion Truman stood at the heart of a broad and powerful consensus.

15. *The Trumans at Home*

THE LATE SUMMER AND THE FALL OF 1945 found the Truman family really settling down together in the White House for the first time. Part of April and May had been spent in Blair House. The president had gone west in June for the signing of the United Nations Charter. Then Mrs. Truman and Margaret visited Independence in July while he was at Potsdam. Now they were reunited, and in contrast to the aristocratic Roosevelts they imparted the flavor of small-town life to the White House. The principal possessions they had brought with them were their clothes and Margaret's piano.[1] "As far as we could we lived the way we always had," Margaret related.[2]

Seldom entertaining at private parties, they usually dined together after the president and Mrs. Truman had one bourbon old-fashioned apiece. When they did entertain publicly it was on a small scale then because of the continuing food shortages. There were exceptions, such as the state dinner for de Gaulle in August. Truman was in high spirits that night. Joining Wallace, Ickes, and Schwellenbach, he said that what he should have been in life was a piano player in a whorehouse.

"That would have been too bad because then we never would have known you," Schwellenbach said.

"Why be so high and mighty, as though you had never been in a whorehouse?" Truman cracked. Schwellenbach seemed shocked.[3] It *was* a puzzling remark for a man who had found the Folies Bergère disgusting.

At home in the evenings the three Trumans would chat, play the piano, enjoy each others' company. The last thing Mrs. Truman resembled was a baseball fan, but she was one, nevertheless, and liked to listen to the broadcasts of the Washington Senators' night games. Occasionally, she and Margaret played Ping-Pong.

Sometimes in the evening the president worked in his study with clerical help from Mrs. Truman, who had been employed in his Senate office. She was reputed to have sharp political instincts herself, but no one has ever detected her influence, if any, on specific policies of her husband. On the other hand, she did restrain his cussing in public, and sometimes she, and occasionally Margaret, would critically listen to him read a draft of a speech he was planning to deliver. Now and then he would ask his speech writers to incorporate in the final draft some new word or phraseology that Mrs. Truman had suggested.

In that first summer in the White House Mrs. Truman told Henry J. Nicholson of the Secret Service that Truman was having to prove himself and that this would have been easier to do if he had (as had every other president since Grover Cleveland) a college degree.[4]

Truman dutifully wound the clocks and checked the doors and windows at night. He slept in his own bedroom in a four-poster that never erased the memory of simpler times. "As long as I have been in the White House," he told Senator Aiken that summer, "I can't help waking at 5 A.M. and hearing the old man at the foot of the stairs calling and telling me to get out and milk the cows."[5] In addition to walking for exercise he often swam the breast stroke in the White House pool with his glasses on, worked out on the rowing machines, and did twenty-five sit-ups a day. Occasionally he interrupted his work to pitch horseshoes on the south lawn with members of his staff.

Customarily referred to by the president as "the Madame," Mrs. Truman was a plump, dignified, matronly woman with a dry wit and, in public, a rather dry expression too. She had short gray bobbed hair, dressed plainly, and at sixty, looked "exactly as a woman of her age should look," as her husband said, approvingly.[6] If, as some skeptics believed, the country needed a respite from the star role of Eleanor Roosevelt, Mrs. Truman provided it completely.

When she was asked how it felt to be the First Lady, she replied, "So-so."[7] She shunned discussion of public issues, drove her own car to go shopping, kept a sharp eye out for dust and cobwebs, superintended the family menu, periodically entertained the women's bridge club from Independence, and watched the White House budget down to the last penny. The president's salary was then $75,000 a year. Having no other income, Truman was unable to run the White House on that sum, and the Bureau of the Budget persuaded Congress to provide him another $50,000 a year for expenses.[8]

Uncharacteristically, Mrs. Truman became entangled in a controversy that first fall in the White House.

The Daughters of the American Revolution wanted to give a tea in her honor in Constitution Hall October 12. Seeing no reason not to, she accepted the invitation. Then it came to light that Hazel Scott, a black singer, one of the leading nightclub entertainers of the time and wife of Representative Adam Clayton Powell, Jr., a formidable Democratic politician and minister of the Abyssinian Baptist Church in Harlem, had sought to give a concert in Constitutional Hall, but was turned down because of her color. The rejection came from the DAR, owner of the building, because its rules stipulated that the hall could be leased to white artists only. The rule had already got the DAR into an unholy tempest with Mrs. Roosevelt in 1939 over the barring of Marian Anderson. Mrs. Roosevelt publicly resigned from the DAR.

Powell telegraphed Truman demanding action on the denial of the hall to Hazel Scott. Then the day before Mrs. Truman was to attend the tea, Powell wired her recalling Mrs. Roosevelt's action and urging Mrs. Truman not to attend. "I can assure you," he said, "that no good will be accomplished by attending and much harm will be done[.] If you believe in 100 percent Americanism, you will publicly denounce the DAR's action."[9]

Mrs. Truman wired back: ". . . may I call your attention to the fact that the invitation . . . was extended and accepted prior to the unfortunate controversy which has arisen. Personally I regret that a conflict has arisen for which I am in no wise responsible. In my opinion my acceptance of the hospitality is not related to the merits of the issue which has since arisen. I deplore any action which denies artistic talent an opportunity to express itself because of prejudice against race origin.''

The president also wrote Powell October 12 repeating his wife's lament and adding:

We have just brought to a successful conclusion a war against totalitarian countries which made racial discrimination their state policy. . . . I am sure that you will realize however the impossibility of any interference by me in the management or policy of a private enterprise such as the one in question.[10]

Mrs. Truman attended the tea. Powell called her the ''last lady.''[11] Learning of this, Truman soared into epithets against Powell. At a staff meeting October 13 he referred to him as ''that damn nigger preacher.''[12] From that day until Truman left office January 20, 1953, Representative Powell was never invited to the White House, even for the annual receptions for members of Congress.

Except for such moments, the Trumans lived a secure and comfortable home life, quite uncorrupted by the sophistication of Washington society. Under the portrait of John Tyler in the small dining room adjoining the State Dining Room, spontaneous frolics occasionally burst through the presidential decorum. As Margaret later described one remarkable scene:

''In the middle of the dessert course (watermelon), Dad flipped a watermelon seed at Mother off his thumb and she responded in kind. I joined the fray and we had a classic watermelon-seed fight at the table. In the middle of this battle one of the butlers came in to remove the plates, but retreated in short order, in a rain of melon seeds. . . . I don't remember who won, but I think it was Mother. She's pretty good at watermelon-seed fights.''[13]

As an undergraduate Margaret brought a student touch to White House life with song, movies, and slumber parties in the Lincoln bed. One of her closest friends was John Snyder's daughter, Drucie.

In modern times no occupants of the White House were as much beloved by the servants, the household staff, and the Secret Service as the Trumans, because of their thoughtfulness and lack of condescension.

''They didn't want to be a bother to anybody on the staff, they asked for very little,'' J. B. West, then assistant to the chief usher of the White House, recalled. ''They treated the staff with respect. . . . When a butler or doorman or usher would enter the room, the Trumans would introduce him to whoever happened to be sitting in the room, even if it were a King or a Prime Minister. They introduced all the staff to their visitors—something I'd never seen the Roosevelts do.''[14]

Mrs. Truman's ailing widowed mother, Mrs. Margaret Gates Wallace, lived with the family much of the time they were in the White House. She still called the president ''Mr. Truman.'' His friends resented her because they believed she never ceased to consider him beneath the Wallaces, even then when he walked in the footsteps of Washington and Lincoln.

16. *The Hurley Affair: An Omen*

THE CABINET had gathered for lunch November 27 when Truman stalked in brandishing news copy from the White House press ticker. "See what a son-of-a-bitch did to me!" he snapped. Then he proceeded to read from the news story.[1]

At 12:30 Patrick J. Hurley, back in Washington from Chungking for consultations, had telephoned the wire services and announced without word to Truman, Byrnes, or anyone else that he was resigning as ambassador to China. Also without warning he released to the press a sensational letter to the president giving the reasons for his stunning action. He said:

The professional foreign service men sided with the Chinese Communist armed party and the imperialistic bloc of nations whose policy it was to keep China divided against herself. Our professional diplomats continually advised the Communists that my efforts in preventing the collapse of the National Government did not represent the policy of the United States. These same professionals openly advised the Communist armed party to decline unification of the Chinese Communist Army with the National Army unless the Chinese Communists were given control.

Obviously referring to, among others, John Stewart Service and George Atcheson—two Foreign Service officers he had succeeded in getting reassigned from Chungking in the spring—Hurley said that, despite his recommendation that they be relieved, they were made his own supervisors or else advisers to MacArthur. "In such positions," he added, "most of them have continued to side with the Communist armed party. . . ." He charged that "a considerable section of our State Department is endeavoring to support Communism generally as well as specifically in China."[2]

For Truman this tirade was far more than a passing blow. It was an omen—an astoundingly accurate prefiguration of years of charges that would hail down on him with damaging effect from McCarthy, the China Lobby, Senator William F. Knowland of California, and other Republican conservatives in and out of Congress, including Hurley himself.

After reading the ticker copy Truman told the cabinet that Hurley had recently assured him that he would return to China. Hannegan said Hurley had called him that very morning, had spoken warmly of Truman and Byrnes, had praised the president's Navy Day speech, and had indicated he was going back to Chungking. Byrnes said Hurley had assured him he was. In fact Hurley had telephoned Byrnes that morning to discuss his travel arrangements. In talks with Byrnes and Patterson, according to Wallace's understanding, Hurley had manifested deep hatred of Service and Atcheson and had called them "Reds" who were betraying the president's policy.[3]

At his own request, Hurley had returned to Washington in September. The fighting in ensuing weeks made it clear that civil war was spreading in China. Chiang was eager for Hurley's return, and Truman and Byrnes agreed that he should go and continue his work, such as it was, of trying to reconcile the Nationalists and the Communists. Hurley had delayed his departure to keep a long-standing engagement to address a luncheon of the National Press Club scheduled for November 28.

During his weeks at home, however, Hurley had been giving some thought to resigning, partly to spare his health, partly to be with his family and make money and partly to get out in case things grew worse in China. Upon reading newspaper speculations that he might resign, he made up his mind that these were deliberate leaks from the State Department. On top of that he was outraged to discover that, as long contemplated, Service and Atcheson were being sent to Tokyo as advisers to MacArthur.

On October 13 he talked to Truman about resigning, but Truman declined to accept his resignation and urged him instead to have a physical checkup and get some rest. Byrnes then publicly announced that Hurley would return to his post. As the fall progressed, however, the Chinese situation worsened. Hurley decided to quit after all. He wrote a letter of resignation to the president, but on November 26—the day before his melodramatic exit—Byrnes talked him out of sending it and assured him of his and the president's support. Hurley then told Byrnes he would return to China after his National Press Club speech.

During the morning of the twenty-seventh he picked up a day-old newspaper and came upon a speech that Representative Hugh De Lacy, Democrat, of Washington, had delivered in the House, criticizing Hurley for having supported a "reactionary" regime in China and having purged able American diplomats. Apparently with the *Amerasia* case in mind, Hurley concluded that the speech could only have been based on confidential information, probably supplied by someone in the State Department for the purpose of undermining him. He made up his mind that despite Byrnes's assurance he would not have State Department support, and put in calls to the wire services with the news that reached Truman on his way to the cabinet luncheon.

After informing the cabinet, Truman read a wire from Pauley indicating that the Soviets had stripped factories in Manchuria and Korea of machinery. Truman complained that the Soviets and British wanted a weak and divided China and that the United States was the only large power that sought a united, democratic China. Unless the United States took a strong stand in China, he said, the Soviet Union would replace Japan as a power in the Far East. Byrnes told the cabinet that Chiang's officials had notified the State Department that the Chinese Communists were amply supplied with Soviet guns and tanks.

The tenor of such talk was a reflection of the new reporting from China. The old hands who had been scattered by Hurley were replaced by him in many cases with men of strong anti-Communist views. They reported to Washington that the

Chinese Communists were the allies of Moscow. Only nine days before the cabinet meeting Everett F. Drumwright, the new chief of the Division of Chinese Affairs in the State Department, had circulated a memorandum suggesting that the Soviet Union was helping the Chinese Communists absorb Manchuria.[4] In such a way the Soviets could control Manchuria through a puppet, as Japan had done. By the time of Hurley's departure, therefore, the idea that the Chinese Communists were agents of Moscow was in the ascendant in the State Department, naturally influencing Truman's views on the subject, which in any case were hardly well informed in those early days. In a note he had attached to his appointments sheet November 15 he had observed that Chiang's government had "fought side by side with us against our common enemy, that we have reason to believe that the so called Commies in China not only did not help us but on occasion helped the Japs."[5]

In the cabinet discussion about the resignation, Secretary of Agriculture Anderson suggested that Truman could take the play away from Hurley in the newspapers by immediately naming General Marshall as Hurley's successor. Just a week earlier Marshall had retired as army chief of staff to be succeeded by General Eisenhower. Forrestal seconded Anderson's suggestion, and the idea won favor in the cabinet.[6] Truman said he was reluctant to place new burdens on Marshall, who, with his wife, had at last retired to the tranquillity of Leesburg, Virginia. That afternoon, however, Truman telephoned him, and Marshall dutifully accepted a post as the president's special representative in China, with the rank of ambassador. Truman, Marshall, and Byrnes then applied themselves to a memorandum of instructions to the general and to a statement of policy on China, which Truman was to make public.

Meanwhile the China question was shoved deeper into domestic politics. On November 28, the day after he had set off the uproar, Hurley kept it going with his highly publicized speech before the National Press Club. He reiterated that United States policy had been subverted by Foreign Service officers. At Republican initiative a Senate investigation was started. As another omen, Senator Styles Bridges, Republican, of New Hampshire, seizing upon the theme that the Truman administration was betraying Chiang Kai-shek, urged Hurley to make a good show of it.[7] This Hurley did before the Senate Foreign Relations Committee, where he cited John Carter Vincent as well as Service, George Atcheson, and others as being members of a "pro-Communist, pro-imperialist" faction in the department. Foreshadowing the McCarthy performance, he charged at another point that United States policy in China was being crippled by Dean Acheson.

Work was begun on written instructions for Marshall and on the presidential statement, with both the State Department and the White House contributing to the latter. Leahy complained to Lieutenant Elsey, still assistant naval aide, that the department was not reliable because it put words in the president's mouth that did not convey his thoughts.

"The President is all right—he's behind Chiang," Leahy said. "But those pinkies in the State Department can't be trusted.

"The President told me the other day," he added, "that he now understands why F.D.R. didn't trust the State Department."

Truman had found, the admiral explained, that the department did not always follow instructions and that it was impossible to pin it down.[8]

Truman, Marshall, Byrnes, and Leahy conferred December 11. Marshall called attention to the possibility that unification of China might prove impossible, particularly if Chiang should refuse to make reasonable concessions. Yet if the United States abandoned Chiang, he said, the result might be a divided China and establishment of Soviet power in Manchuria, nullifying American war aims in the Far East, one of them having been the return of Manchuria to Chinese control. In that case, he asked, would he not have to support Chiang anyhow by continuing to move Nationalist troops to the north? Truman and Byrnes concurred that the United States would have to go on supporting Chiang to that extent.[9] In his early days in office, Truman was to recall, "I thought Chiang Kai-shek's Government was on the road to a real reform government in China."[10]

Marshall was to mediate, yet his government was determined that one side should prevail over the other, albeit on conciliatory terms. In receiving the final draft of his instructions at a meeting with Truman and Acheson December 14 Marshall clarified his understanding of his mission. In the event, he said, that he was unable to secure reasonable concessions from Chiang it would still be necessary for the United States, through him, to continue to back the Nationalists. Truman and Acheson confirmed this.[11]

Truman's public statement—an extension of Roosevelt's policy—was issued December 15. It made clear that the administration went on the theory that Chiang's government provided the "proper instrument" for developing a democratic nation but must be broadened to include representatives of the Communists and other substantial groups.[12]

Clearly, Washington was more hopeful of maintaining the Open Door under Chiang, with all his faults, than under the Communists. While seeking a unified Chinese government in which the Communists would participate, the United States favored a Nationalist-controlled regime that would bring about political stability favorable to American aims in the Far East and constitute a barrier against possible Soviet expansion. The public statement, however, did not allude to the secret understanding that the United States would back Chiang against the Communists even if he would not make the concessions necessary to achieve unification.

Truman advocated a meeting of all major elements in China to bring about unification, a step the Nationalists and Communists already had agreed to between themselves. The statement urged cessation of mutual hostilities. At the same time, while urging modification of China's one-party government so as to give representation to other elements, it recognized Chiang's regime as "the only legal government in China." It urged elimination of autonomous armies and their integration into a Chinese National Army. Truman said that American support of China would not extend to United States military intervention to influence the course of internal strife—a crucial decision that differentiated United States policy in China from its subsequent policy in Korea and Vietnam.

"The fact that I have asked you to go to China," Truman told Marshall in a letter accompanying his instructions, "is the clearest evidence of my very real concern with regard to the situation there."[13]

The situation was nothing less than the opening act of a drama whose climax four years hence was to spell political catastrophe for Truman.

Trouble was breaking out in Korea at the same time. American efforts to suppress communism were creating enmity between the United States occupation authorities and the people.

Under orders to occupy Korea south of the 38th parallel and to take the surrender of Japanese forces there MacArthur assigned the duty to the twenty-fourth Army Corps under Lieutenant General John R. Hodge. The Corps had fought well in the Philippines and Okinawa but had had no experience in administering civil affairs and no personnel trained for such a task. Hodge was unequipped for the assignment and was given meager guidance.

In the interval between the Japanese surrender and the arrival of Americans in Korea September 8, Korean leaders and patriots released from Japanese prisons had formed a committee to preserve order and take charge of affairs in preparation for what they supposed would be the independence of their country. It had been annexed to Japan since 1910. The group convened a national conference in Seoul, and on September 6 a People's Republic of Korea was established, claiming jurisdiction over the entire country.

Accordingly, a delegation from the People's Republic was on hand to welcome Hodge upon his arrival at Inchon. He had never heard of the People's Republic. He refused to deal with it. Instead he shocked the Koreans by announcing that the Japanese governor-general and other high-ranking Japanese officials would be retained temporarily to facilitate an orderly occupation. Although Korea was supposedly a friendly country, a 7 P.M. curfew was imposed to the resentment of the people. The Koreans recoiled at the prospect of years of trusteeship after a generation of Japanese rule.[14]

The United States had stepped into an indigenous revolutionary situation in which the Left claimed power on the strength of its resistance to Japan. Hodge's officials, however, related the Korean Left to the Soviet presence in the north.[15] Seeking a bulwark against communism, the Americans formed a Korean Advisory Council composed largely of businessmen and landlords. Its chairman had been identified with Japanese rule, and the council was distrusted by the people. In quest of stability, the American occupation became increasingly repressive. At MacArthur's request Washington approved the arming of a south Korean constabulary to combat left-wing activities.

In character with United States practice in many parts of the world, the occupation in Korea shunned the revolutionary forces for the conservative elements, who found their way into staff positions with the military government. The conservatives favored the return to Korea of the aging nationalist, Dr. Syngman Rhee. He had spent years in exile in China and the United States, where he was admired for his anticommunism, and had ties with the Korean provisional government in exile in Chungking. Hodge's political adviser from the State Department endorsed the idea of Rhee's return, and he was flown into Korea on a United States plane October 16. Under his leadership a coalition of rightist parties came into being. Before long Rhee was advocating a separate government in the south. American officials were increasingly thinking along the same lines, and occupation policies gravitated toward that end. Meanwhile anti-American feelings among the Koreans rose and the economy degenerated into chaos. Hodge warned MacArthur in December that the occupation was "drifting to the edge of a political-economic abyss."[16]

It was in the face of deepening trouble in Asia, therefore, that Marshall departed for China December 15, the day Truman's statement on China policy was released.

Around the time Marshall reached China Byrnes arrived in Moscow for another meeting of the foreign ministers. Neither of them would have had occasion to know that on December 5 Truman had commented to Harold Smith, "I would have a pretty good government, don't you think, if I had a good Labor Department and a good State Department?" In fact this was but the latest of several slighting references that Truman had made in private about Byrnes recently. A web was being spun in which the destinies of Byrnes and Marshall were soon to be caught.

17. *The Beginning of the End for Byrnes*

SOON AFTER Byrnes became secretary of state in July of 1945 Ickes remarked on a feeling in the administration that friction would develop between Byrnes and Truman. Ickes observed in his diary that in the Roosevelt administration "Jimmy showed too much of a disposition to run the whole show."[1]

Certainly by the fall of 1945 Byrnes had become an unusually independent secretary of state. In view of the history of their relationship in the Senate and at the Democratic National Convention of 1944, Byrnes no doubt thought of himself as occupying a special role under Truman. His independence would have seemed appropriate to him, owing to his seniority in the Democratic party and the authority he had exercised in managing the wartime economy under Roosevelt.

Because of the heavy diplomatic activity following the war, Byrnes traveled more extensively than any secretary of state before him. "Byrnes's personal style," Bohlen recalled, "was to operate as a loner, keeping matters restricted to a small circle of advisers. . . . Moreover, he was not in daily, intimate consultation with the President, as Hopkins had been with Roosevelt and subsequent national-security advisers have been with other Presidents. Byrnes was his own man and demanded the freedom to operate that way."[2]

While Byrnes had been bitter over losing the vice-presidential nomination, he gave no sign of blaming Truman. In the beginning the two appeared friendly, and they worked hard together, particularly at Potsdam. When Byrnes was in London in September Harold Smith asked Truman if he had heard a quip that was going around: The State Department fiddles while Byrnes roams. Truman had heard it, but the two men had a good chuckle anyhow.[3] As the fall progressed, however, Truman's chuckle disappeared. Talking with Wallace on November 16 about appointments to the Export-Import Bank, he said, according to Wallace, that "Jimmie Byrnes had given him the devil of a time because of certain State Department attitudes." "The way he said this," Wallace observed, "indicated to me that the situation between the President and Jimmie is not all that happy."[4] Truman also expressed displeasure about the State Department to Harold Smith and said he might have to jack up the department from top to bottom.[5] There is no evidence that Truman ever complained to Byrnes about his independent ways, and the secretary evidently considered his conduct acceptable to the president.

That fall Truman was beginning to feel the heat of anti-Soviet sentiment developing in Congress and in the administration itself because of Soviet conduct in Poland and Eastern Europe and in negotiations, such as the foreign ministers meeting in London. On Byrnes's return from that meeting he appeared before the Senate

Foreign Relations Committee and was complimented on his refusal to compromise with Molotov. Indeed, according to the *New York Times,* the senators did not question whether Byrnes's "tough line was right but whether it was tough enough and whether it was his intention to 'be tough' or only to 'act tough.' "

While Byrnes was publicly advocating firmness toward the Soviets, he was still seeking avenues of compromise and conciliation. In the process he stepped on a trap door in his relations with Truman by taking it upon himself to launch a new meeting of the foreign ministers in Moscow in mid-December of 1945.

Trouble was brewing for him even before he packed his bags. At one of the White House conferences on China policy in preparation for Marshall's departure for the Far East, Admiral Leahy was rankled at Byrnes's stress on settling the Chinese civil war by encouraging Chiang Kai-shek to bring the Communists into the government. "Today for the first time," Leahy wrote in his diary November 28, "I sense a feeling that Secretary Byrnes is not immune to the communisticly [*sic*] inclined advisors in his Department."[6]

Leahy, who had been the highest-ranking American military officer in the Second World War, was an influential figure in Washington. A forceful man with pince-nez and a scowl that masked a considerable charm, he had gone from the United States Naval Academy to the Spanish-American War and from there up the ladder to chief of naval operations, Governor of Puerto Rico, ambassador to Vichy France, Chairman of the Joint Chiefs of Staff and chairman of the Combined (British and American) Chiefs of Staff. Simultaneously, he occupied the unique role of chief of staff to the commander in chief under Roosevelt and Truman. Enjoying the trust of both presidents, Leahy was not a policymaking official but an articulate, informed, prestigious man in places where policy was made. He was nationalistic, patriotic, dedicated to American power, indignant at Soviet intransigence, and hostile to communism. He was to have further comment on Byrnes after the Moscow conference began.

Meanwhile as Byrnes was still preparing to depart, Truman revealed his distrust of the secretary of state when he took Joseph Davies aside during a weekend cruise down the Potomac on the presidential yacht *Williamsburg* and asked Davies to talk to Byrnes about what Byrnes was going to do in Moscow. Truman said that he was fond of Byrnes but that Byrnes was a "conniver." The president observed that he would have to do some conniving himself to keep the ship of state steady. Davies later observed in his journal:

It was clear that someone had been needling him again—at Byrnes. I fear Jim has not kept his lines of communication with the Commander in Chief sufficiently active. I did the best I could to reassure the President and to fortify Jim. But it was clear that it couldn't be done. He had been poisoned and his mind was "sot" [set?]—Jim is through—and it is a great pity.[7]

Boding more difficulty, Byrnes got himself, and eventually Truman, into a bad spot with leading senators over an approach to the Soviet Union on atomic energy. Just before leaving for Moscow the secretary met with a delegation from Capitol Hill. He mentioned that he intended to suggest an exchange of scientific information with the Soviets. He was talking in terms of the Truman-Attlee-Mackenzie King agreement about eventual international control of atomic energy under the United

Nations in stages, the first stage being the dissemination of scientific information. In the new mood of Congress, however, the senators were suspicious. "We are opposed," Vandenberg noted in his diary that day, "to giving any of the atomic secrets away unless and until the Soviets are prepared to be 'policed' by UNO. . . . We consider an 'exchange' of scientists and scientific information as sheer appeasement because Russia has nothing to 'exchange'."[8] It was all right to talk about stages, Vandenberg indicated later, if each stage itself required adequate security arrangements: the point was security, not stages.

After Byrnes left Washington, Vandenberg and his colleagues asked to see Truman and gave him an uncomfortable time because Truman was still far from being well informed on the atomic question. He assured the senators that no information about the bomb would be disclosed while Byrnes was in Moscow nor at any time until inspection and safeguards had been agreed to.

When the Moscow conference began, Byrnes kept Truman in the dark about what was happening. After the first session Harriman offered to draft a telegraphic report to the president unless Byrnes preferred to do so. Byrnes said he was not going to send any telegrams. It was customary, Harriman replied. Byrnes persisted. "The President has given me complete authority," he said. "I can't trust the White House to prevent leaks."[9] Also communications out of Moscow presented difficulties for Byrnes. Meanwhile Truman was telling his staff he was tired of learning about foreign policy through the newspapers.[10]

The one message Byrnes did send Truman, on Christmas Eve, was not (as Truman complained in his memoirs) "what I considered a proper account by a Cabinet member to the President. It was more like one partner in a business telling the other that his business trip was progressing well and not to worry."[11]

During this time anti-Soviet feeling in the United States was being fanned by grave Soviet-American differences boiling up in Iran, and this was another subject that evoked Truman's displeasure over the Moscow conference.

In the war British and Soviet forces had entered Iran to prevent a possible German thrust against the oil fields. When Lend-Lease began the United States established a command there to distribute supplies to Iran and to supervise transshipments to the Soviet Union.

A great deal else was going on too. In their occupation of the northern Iranian province of Azerbaijan, contiguous to the Soviet Union, Soviet forces interfered with the Iranian government and armed the Communist-led Tudah party, which favored separation of the province from Iran. As Soviet political activities intensified, fears grew that the Kremlin would transform Azerbaijan into an autonomous state under Soviet control. Increasingly, the Iranian government looked to the United States for support against Moscow.

The Americans had their own fish to fry. As were the Soviets, the Standard-Vacuum Company and Sinclair Oil, along with the British Shell Company, were negotiating with Iran for oil concessions. The State Department supported their efforts, as American interest in Middle East oil reserves rose during the war. Moreover the United States wanted no great power established on the Persian Gulf opposite the major American petroleum development in Saudi Arabia.

At the Teheran Conference in 1943 Roosevelt, Churchill, and Stalin had signed a declaration reaffirming the territorial integrity of Iran. Ostensibly, this gave the United States cause for involvement in the trouble now arising over Soviet activities. Stalin based his case on a 1921 treaty with Iran, permitting the Soviets to send troops to Iran if circumstances warranted.

By the time Truman took office, Soviet troops had closed Azerbaijan to all other foreigners and were stirring up disaffected tribes. After Germany surrendered, Iran asked its allies to withdraw their forces within six months, in accordance with a 1942 agreement. The Americans and British began withdrawals. At the London conference of foreign ministers in September an understanding was reached that all foreign forces would be withdrawn six months after the Japanese surrender. Hence, March 2, 1946, became a crucial date.

While United States officials discussed expansion of American economic interests in Iran, Washington grew concerned that Moscow was trying to extend Soviet influence to the Persian Gulf.[12]

With the movement for autonomy growing in Azerbaijan, incidents multiplied. When the Iranian government dispatched troops to quell uprisings in Azerbaijan, the Red Army blocked the road. Iran asked for American support. On November 24 the United States protested that the Soviets had no right to restrict the Iranian army and suggested that all Allied troops be withdrawn by January 1. Molotov replied that events in Azerbaijan were a local movement for democratic rights and declined to reconsider the troop withdrawal schedule. In Moscow Byrnes tried to exact a promise from Stalin that his troops would be removed by March 2, but Stalin balked.

"Another outrage, if I ever saw one," was Truman's reaction.[13]

Byrnes had gone to Moscow hoping to get on with the peace treaties, only to come up once more against the Soviet hammer lock on Eastern Europe. The best he could win from Stalin was a concession of some minor opposition posts in the governments of Bulgaria and Rumania rather along the lines of the Polish settlement. The concession, disappointing to Truman, was not enough to weaken the Soviet grip on Eastern Europe. But it was a token that would enable Byrnes to justify eventual extension of diplomatic recognition to and treaties with Bulgaria and Rumania. In return he made a token concession to Stalin in the Far East whereby the Soviet Union and other allies could consult with and advise MacArthur on occupation measures in Japan through an Allied Council. MacArthur's authority in Japan, however, remained as unchallenged as Stalin's in Eastern Europe.

John Snyder later recalled that while Byrnes was in Moscow Leahy kept saying around the White House that the secretary was not being firm, that he was practicing appeasement that would not lead to peace. Leahy complained that Byrnes was horse-trading in Moscow without Truman's complete knowledge.[14] Byrnes's worst tactical mistake came when he assented to the release of the conference communiqué without having first sent a copy to Truman. Truman was incensed that the agreements on Rumania and Bulgaria had been reached without his approval. The communiqué also disclosed a decision by the three powers to propose creation of a United Nations Atomic Energy Commission and listed its goals, including exchange of scientific information. Reading more into it than was intended, Vandenberg again descended on Truman and pressured him into new assurances that no information would be shared with the Soviets without proper safeguards.[15] It was all exasperating for Truman and galling to Leahy, who wrote in his diary December 26 that Byrnes "has made concessions to expediency that are destructive of the President's announced intention to adhere strictly to his policies that are righteous. . . . . It appears now that Russia has been granted every demand that wrecked the London conference."

When Leahy saw the communiqué in the newspapers December 28 he observed in his diary that it "appears to me from the view of America an appeasement document which gives to the Soviet everything they want and preserves to America nothing."

On his return from London in September Byrnes had made a national radio broadcast reporting on the foreign ministers' meeting there. Departing Moscow now in blithe ignorance of Truman's new mood, he telegraphed the president, asking that Ross arrange for time on all the major networks for a Byrnes report on the Moscow conference December 30. Awaiting him on his return December 29 was this telegram from Truman, who was cruising on the Potomac aboard the *Williamsburg:*

Happy to hear of your safe arrival. Suggest you come down today or tomorrow to report on your mission. . . . We can then discuss among other things the advisability of a broadcast by you. . . .[16]

Truman had told his staff that he wanted to see Byrnes on the *Williamsburg,* "if he has to swim," according to Steelman.[17] It fell to Acheson to have to inform the secretary of state of the president's displeasure and to have to allude to the dubious etiquette of requesting broadcast time before reporting to Truman. Weary from the long trip and loath to journey on to Quantico, Virginia, where the presidential yacht was anchored, Byrnes was "disbelieving, impatient and irritated," Acheson recalled.[18]

From that point on the story is bizarre and elusive, the more so because a vessel like the *Williamsburg* is so compartmentalized that it is difficult to observe all that is happening at any one time.

Byrnes in his memoirs recalled the meeting with Truman as having been cordial. He said the president expressed pleasure at his report of progress in Moscow.[19]

Truman, who tended to exaggerate such recollections, said in *his* memoirs: "We went into my stateroom . . . and I closed the door behind us. I told him that I did not like the way in which I had been left in the dark about the Moscow conference. I told him that, as President, I intended to know what progress we were making and what we were doing in foreign negotiations. I said that it was shocking that a communiqué should be issued in Washington announcing a foreign-policy development of major importance that I had never heard of. I said I would not tolerate a repetition of such conduct."

After reading some documents on the conference left by the secretary, Truman said he had concluded that Byrnes "had taken it upon himself to move the foreign policy of the United States in a direction to which I could not, and would not, agree."[20]

The witnesses were like blind men describing the elephant, each imagining the whole from the part that he knew. Thus Clifford told Jonathan Daniels that Leahy gently needled Byrnes for slighting the president.[21] Snyder recalled that Leahy gave Byrnes a dressing down on Truman's behalf. Vaughan agreed, recalling that, with Truman absent, "Leahy gave Byrnes a hell of a chewing out," leaving Byrnes "in a huff"—hardly a peculiar reaction for a secretary of state in the circumstances, if true. Rosenman remembered having heard raised voices while Truman, Leahy, and Byrnes were in the president's cabin. Steelman recalled that Byrnes "got the trimming of his life." At dinner, Steelman said, Leahy challenged Byrnes on some of the things that had happened in Moscow, soliciting the secretary of state's version and then quoting from reports to refute him.[22]

This cacophony, of course, was unheard outside the inner circle. When Truman was asked at his press conference January 8 about the Moscow communiqué, he put aside his pique with Byrnes and said, "Well, I was satisfied with the communiqué and satisfied with the accomplishments of the Foreign Ministers' Conference in Moscow, and I think it will have constructive results."[23] He had, incidentally, approved of Byrnes's making a broadcast report December 30.

Then, after a lapse of more than six years, a most bewildering development came to light. In 1952 a book called *Mr. President* appeared under the authorship of Truman's friend, William Hillman, a journalist, who had been given access to some presidential diaries and correspondence. In the material was a letter in longhand from Truman to "Hon. Jas. F. Byrnes, Secretary of State," dated January 5, 1946. That was at the height of Truman's pique, six days after the *Williamsburg* imbroglio and three days before the president publicly expressed satisfaction with the Moscow communiqué. In an accompanying memorandum Truman said he read the letter to Byrnes on the fifth.

Beginning, "My dear Jim," the letter said that Truman wanted to continue delegating authority to members of the cabinet but that "I do not intend to turn over the complete authority of the President nor to forego the President's prerogative to make the final decision." Although he complained about the lack of communication from Moscow, he expressed confidence in Byrnes, but said he would not agree to recognition of the Rumanian and Bulgarian governments "unless they are radically changed." In words that betrayed a feverish view of Soviet intentions and that were quite in keeping with the tone of reports from the State Department's Office of Near Eastern and African Affairs, he said: "There isn't a doubt in my mind that Russia intends an invasion of Turkey and the seizure of the Black Sea Straits to the Mediterranean. . . .

"Unless Russia is faced with an iron fist and strong language," he warned, "another war is in the making. . . .

"Only one language," he added, "do they understand—'How many divisions have you?' . . .

"I do not think we should play compromise any longer . . .

"I'm tired of babying the Soviets."[24]

"Byrnes accepted my decision," Truman later recalled in his memoirs. "He did not ask to be relieved or express a desire to quit."[25]

"Of course, Byrnes said in his memoirs, "such a letter was never sent to me, nor read to me. Had this occurred, with my deep conviction that there must be complete accord between the President and his Secretary of State, I would have resigned immediately. My first knowledge of the 'memorandum-letter' came with its appearance in the Hillman book.''[26]

A note written by Hillman while he was working on *Mr. President* turned up in material opened by the Harry S. Truman Library in 1976, and it supports Byrnes's statement.

Quoting Truman, Hillman noted that the president had let the date of January 5, 1946, on the letter stand ''because that is the day he wrote the whole thing out in long hand for the purpose of helping him review his thoughts on the subject and at the same time have a clear personal handwritten copy for his private file.'' Actually, Hillman explained, Truman said he had read the ''communication'' to Byrnes late in December, presumably on the *Williamsburg*. The ''communication'' supposedly was in character with the letter, although no copy of it has come to light. But Truman's letter as published was not written until several days after his discussion with Byrnes.[27]

In another respect the Hillman note gives the letter a new importance. Instead of being one of Truman's periodic outbursts, it was obviously a calm, deliberate attempt by him to define his thoughts. He wrote it at a time when he was feeling political pressure at home, springing from public anger at Soviet conduct. Not only was he being harassed by Vandenberg about keeping atomic secrets from the Soviets, but on December 5, 1945, a committee of the Republican leaders of both houses of Congress had issued a statement deploring the ''desertion'' of the principle of self-determination for the satellite states of Eastern Europe. It was against this sort of criticism that Truman read the Moscow communiqué. Indeed he wrote in the letter, ''We should refuse to recognize Rumania and Bulgaria until they comply with our requirements.'' As if in line with the opinions he was hearing from Leahy, he indicated a belief in the letter that an uncompromising stand was the way to deal with the Soviet Union.

In an interesting sequence of events Truman had been talking to Ickes on January 4, the day before he wrote his letter. Byrnes's name had come up. ''The President said he loved him like a brother,'' Ickes noted in his diary that day, ''but that Byrnes was too disposed to compromise matters.''

Throughout Byrnes's tenure as secretary of state no basic difference on policy between himself and Truman had been discernible. But now matters of personality and emphasis on policy were coming between them. They continued to work together for some months, but, as John Snyder, who probably knew the president's moods as well as anyone did, said later, the Truman-Byrnes relationship deteriorated after the *Williamsburg* affair.[28] It may have been symptomatic that when a reporter started to ask Truman at a press conference a few weeks later whether he supported State Department policy on Latin America, the president cut him off with the rejoinder, ''The State Department doesn't have a policy unless I support it.''[29]

The significance of what was happening had been reflected in the mood of Congress, in the rigidity of Vandenberg's position on exchange of nuclear information with the Soviets, in Leahy's rumblings about ''appeasement.'' It was reflected in the declining public trust in the Soviet Union, as measured in American opinion polls. It was reflected in a decision by Forrestal to commission a report on the relationship between communism and Soviet foreign policy.[30]

It was reflected, too, in the comment which the executive assistant to the secretary of war, William S. Gaud, made to Henry Wallace: that we ought to "kick the Russians in the balls." It was reflected in Joseph Alsop's likening of the Soviet Union to Germany on the same occasion.[31] It was reflected in the increasingly tough attitude in Washington toward the conflict in Iran. It was reflected in Truman's dissatisfaction with the results of the Moscow conference and in his angry comment that he was "tired of babying the Soviets."

In sum, as 1946 arrived, the Truman administration was moving in a powerful national current across the line of conciliation and concession. Nothing was left of the "Grand Alliance." The policy of trying to compromise was ending. The United States and the Soviet Union were becoming hostile rivals instead of allies.

18. 1946: A Disastrous Year Begins

"MY grandmother used to say that a green Christmas made a fat graveyard," Truman remarked during the banter that preceded his last press conference of 1945.[1] Unfortunately for the undertakers, the weather was such that the president threw snowballs on the White House lawn before leaving for the holidays on a rough, probably dangerous flight to Kansas City. All scheduled flights at Washington National Airport had been grounded because of poor visibility. Before departing he signed a proclamation pardoning all former convicts—1,118 of them qualified—who had served honorably in the war for at least one year. Truman celebrated Christmas at Independence, eating turkey, greeting carolers, and giving his ninety-three-old mother "the usual sort of thing a fellow buys."[2]

Throughout America the first Christmas after the war was gay, carefree, and lavish despite shortages. Money and liquor flowed as never before. During the holidays people flocked to the movies to see *The Lost Weekend*. Radios serenaded the land with "It's Been a Long, Long Time" and "It Might As Well Be Spring." Among the big Christmas books were Betty MacDonald's *The Egg and I* and Sinclair Lewis's *Cass Timberlane*. *State of the Union* was the leading play on Broadway.

When the festivities were over at last Truman returned to deal with a state of the Union that was muddled and volatile. Nearly every major industry in the country was plagued by strikes or threats of strikes. Before the year was out a record 4.6 million workers would stop work, at a cost of 116 million man-days of work.[3] In all nearly five thousand strikes were called, albeit with a remarkable absence of violence.

In political terms 1946 was to be a bad year for Truman almost to the very end.

With his twenty-one-point program still stalled, he began the New Year with his own atonal version of a fireside chat on radio January 3. A sense of worry permeated it. "Unless we can soon meet the need of obtaining full production and full employment at home," he said, "we shall face serious consequences. . . . As industrial strife has increased, with automobile workers out on strike, and with steel workers, electrical workers and packinghouse workers scheduling strikes very soon, I have been deeply concerned about the future." His concern over inflation too was growing: "The inflationary pressures now at work can bring an inflation and a crash that will be much more serious than 1920."

With a foretaste of the tactic that would reach its peak in the 1948 campaign, he blamed Congress for placing obstacles in the path of coping with reconversion. In what the press billed as a fighting speech, he adopted the technique of reviewing his legislative requests, citing particular Congressional committees that were withholding action and appealing to the people to put pressure on their respective senators and representatives. "The members of Congress," he said, "are now at home. . . . I urge you to tell [them] your own views concerning the grave problems facing the country."[4]

Senator Taft replied in a broadcast the next night. Despite their earlier cordiality, Taft was now one of Truman's severest critics. Recently he had said of him, "He hasn't got the background or education to analyze complex economic problems for himself, and so he takes what is handed down to him by the bureaus, which are full of New Dealers."[5] In his broadcast Taft attacked some of the president's proposals as "Communist"—the charge was already a right-wing reflex. The senator's run-of-the-mill political comments all too often fell sadly below his intelligence, integrity, patriotism, dedication, and decency.

"If I had picked a man to answer the speech, so it would do the most good," Truman wrote his sister, "I would have picked Taft to do it. He only added fuel to the fire I had already started."[6] It was scarcely what politicians call a prairie fire, however. Truman lacked Roosevelt's ability to evoke response. Congressional and White House mail was light, and Robert Sherwood, after witnessing the reaction of a crowd in the Beverly Hills Hotel during the broadcast, wrote Rosenman January 5:

It may be that even now Mr. Truman can go over the heads of the Congress and appeal successfully to the people, but I'm greatly inclined to doubt it. It is difficult to find anyone who is strongly opposed to Mr. Truman, but even more difficult to find anyone who is violently for him. Those most antipathetic are those who were the most ardent and militant supporters of F.D.R. and the New Deal. The feeling seems to be that Mr. Truman is content merely to put liberal policies on the record and leave them there.[7]

"The trouble is he just can't get a speech across," Ickes noted in his diary the same day.

Another part of the picture was that the American people were simply not hungry for new political reforms that winter. The enthusiasm that had propelled Roosevelt's early New Deal measures did not exist after the war. A sense of this void permeated unused handwritten notes Truman had made for the speech, in which he poured out anguish over the people's lack of support for his policies. "But you are lying down on me now," he wrote. "You are leaving me the burden without the cooperation. A superman cannot successfully meet world problems in this age without the help of his people . . . I am asking particularly that labor stop now it's [*sic*] new rich, power crazy demands. I am asking management to meet the situation halfway. . . . Labor is following exactly the same path that arrogant industry followed in the 1920's."[8]

If Truman did not get action in Congress, he got it everywhere else. Internal quarrels broke out in the administration, notably a long-developing collision between Ickes and Pauley. The epidemic of strikes had reached a point where it was hard to walk through parts of midtown Manhattan, for example, without getting entangled in a picket line. Neither could one send a telegram in New York, as Western Union employees went on strike, snarling the city's commercial and financial affairs. Next came a nationwide strike against the Western Electric Company. Then Truman was forced to seize 134 struck meat-packing plants. After that he seized ninety-one tugboats in New York harbor to keep a tug strike from strangling the island city.

Reacting to an announcement of a slowdown in demobilization January 4, thousands of American troops demonstrated in Manila January 7 and booed the secretary of war. The next day Truman issued a statement explaining that "the critical need for troops overseas has begun to slow down the Army's rate of demobilization." The rising international tensions were having their effect. The president said, ". . . we must devote all necessary strength to building a firm foundation for the future peace of the world. The future of our country is now as much at stake as it was in the days of the war."[9] Nevertheless other demonstrations erupted in Calcutta, Guam, Frankfurt, Paris, Le Havre, Vienna, London, Yokohama, Tokyo, Seoul, and Honolulu, and even at Andrews Air Force Base outside Washington.

When the White House press conference January 8 ended, Drew Pearson, a columnist and operator, remained behind to give Truman a stack of petitions from soldiers demanding to come home. In his column Pearson had made himself a spokesman for the disgruntled soldiers and the sheets of signatures he wanted to give Truman were headed by a political warning, "No Boats, No Votes."[10] Truman indignantly refused Pearson's offering. He said it would be improper for him to accept the petitions.[11]

That was by no means all he said. Pearson had picked quite the wrong day to face Truman, for in his weekly Sunday night radio show the columnist had criticized Mrs. Truman and Margaret for having returned from the holidays in Independence in a private railroad car when accommodations were scarce. Actually, they had returned in a stateroom and had waited their turn in line in the diner. Furthermore they had paid their own fares.

The criticism of his wife and daughter enraged Truman, and he did something rare for him. He jabbed his forefinger into Pearson's abdomen. Henry Nicholson, the Secret Service man standing behind the president, noticed that Pearson turned pale. As Nicholson recalled, Truman said, "God damn you, call me what you want—thief, robber—but the next time you tell a falsehood about my wife I will punch you right in the nose, and don't think I wouldn't."

"I am sorry, Mr. President," Pearson apologized, according to Nicholson.

"Why don't you tell the truth?" Truman demanded. "Ninety-nine percent of your statements are falsehoods."

Before Pearson could reply, Truman snapped, "That's all" and departed.[12] Pearson confessed afterward that he had taken the item from some newspaper without checking it.[13] At a cabinet meeting later that same day Truman was still denouncing him as a liar.

Truman said at the staff meeting that day that the demonstrations in Manila were "plain mutiny," though he acknowledged he did not have all the facts.

His conclusion was much more extreme than MacArthur's. Assessing the Manila demonstrations in a report that reached Eisenhower and that Eisenhower subsequently sent to Truman, MacArthur said that the discontent had been caused primarily by "acute homesickness aggravated by the termination of hostilities.

These men are good men who have performed magnificently under campaign conditions and inherently are not challenging discipline or authority.''[14]

When the president's fact-finding board in the General Motors strike reported its recommendations, Truman expressed hope January 10 that "the parties will follow the recommendations and bring about a speedy end to this most costly conflict."[15] The board had recommended to Truman's satisfaction an hourly pay rise of 19½ cents, a compromise between the union's demand and the company's offer. No increase in price was recommended. Reuther agreed to accept, but General Motors refused to, and the strike continued.

Because of its critical effect on the economy and reconversion, the impending steel strike was more worrisome. Truman had appointed a fact-finding board in this dispute, too, and won a postponement of the United Steel Workers' strike deadline to January 21. After receiving the board's recommendations and calling both parties to the dispute to the White House, the president recommended an 18½ cents an hour increase without intending that it should become a pattern for all industries. "Each industry and each individual case should be worked out on its own merits," he wrote.[16] On January 18 Philip Murray accepted the proposal. To Truman's embarrassment, United States Steel rejected it. Thereupon he slapped the corporation on the wrist with a statement saying, "I urge the United States Steel Corporation on the ground of the public interest, as well as good business, to accept this settlement."[17]

United States Steel and the rest of the industry were not hung up over payment of a couple of more cents an hour. Rather they were playing a tough game to make the government yield on control of prices, if wages were to rise. On January 19 Representative John E. Lyle, Jr., of Texas, fearing a complete economic breakdown, wrote Truman to urge that he seize the steel plants.

Truman was weighing seizure, but listened to the almost frantic pleas against it by Snyder, who was mindful of the troubles Roosevelt had got into by seizing Montgomery Ward in 1944 and was opposed to having government take over coal mines or any other private enterprise. One afternoon, as Truman swam in the White House pool, Snyder sat by the side the whole time, peppering him with arguments.[18] In the end Truman concluded that the storm that would have greeted his seizure of United States Steel was not a prospect to be relished in the midst of his other difficulties. The steelworkers struck January 21.

Fearing a business slump, the steel industry had been seeking a price rise since the end of the war, but almost until the eve of the strike Bowles had tried to hold the line. Finally he yielded and offered an increase of $2.50 a ton. The industry rejected this. The government offered $4. This too was rejected.

Bowles dug in his heels against a higher offer. The advice he gave Truman was that if the government further relaxed the line on steel prices, it could no longer hold the line on rents and on prices of farm products and other goods. The day after the strike began, however, the United Press reported that 1,650,000 persons were out of work in current labor disputes at a cost in wages of $13.5 million a day. The situation had become intolerable for Truman. After a world war it was inevitable that prices were going to rise sometime, and he and Snyder simply took the matter out of Bowles's hands.

They did not tell him so in advance. He began to hear rumors nevertheless that the steel industry had rejected $4 a ton in the belief that Snyder would come round to offer more. About to leave on a vacation, Bowles wrote Truman January 24: "That a major industry can obtain a concession by pressure tactics is bad enough, but I believe the Government simply cannot stand the common knowledge that an industry's blunt rejection of the first concession will extract a better one." Completely out of step with Truman and Snyder, he said the situation had drifted so far that seizure of the steel mills seemed essential.[19]

Bowles's suspicion about prices was well founded. From the outset Snyder had been determined that price ceilings that threatened to retard reconversion must be adjusted by the OPA. Business leaders were putting increasing pressure on him. Now, with the war over for six months, he was convinced that Bowles was trying to hold too tight a rein on prices, impeding a return to a free market. He commissioned a group of "top cost accountants" from outside the government to make an independent analysis for him. The group's finding was, he recalled, that without a substantial increase in prices the companies, as they were maintaining, could not meet an 18½ cents an hour wage increase.

"I laid this before the President," Snyder recalled, "and said this looks like the fair thing and how to get it done. We need the steel."[20] Forced to choose between holding the line on prices and assuring increased production, Snyder elected the latter because he viewed increased production as the way to solve the postwar economic problems. Truman agreed.

So while Bowles was away playing golf with his wife, Truman and Snyder called in the big operatives—Byrnes, Vinson, Baruch—who knew how to talk with steel magnates without getting all tangled up in liberal New Deal rhetoric.[21] And just as Bowles and his wife were beginning to "unwind" in the South, as he recalled, he turned on a radio before dinner and heard the news that Snyder had overruled the OPA and agreed to the industry's demand for a sizable increase in the price of steel—$5 a ton, as it developed.[22] Bowles caught the night train back to Washington. But the next day he and Snyder talked past each other, and the president—"who seemed harassed and tired," according to Bowles—said he had to support Snyder. The upward trend of prices continued.

Angrily, Bowles resigned as director of OPA. "Would you, if the President should ask you to, agree to become Director of Economic Stabilization?" Byrnes asked him. At first unwilling, Bowles finally assented.[23] Truman reestablished the Office of Economic Stabilization to accommodate Bowles and appointed Paul A. Porter, a Washington attorney, as the new director of OPA.

"I have been thinking every week," Truman remarked to some Civil Service officials February 9, "that perhaps next week will not be quite so hectic as the week just past, but the coming week is always just a little more hectic . . . there is always a crisis just around the corner and I have to do something about it."[24]

"Good people are leaving the Government," he wrote Baruch February 15, "and those who remain are cutting each others' throats."[25]

Truman tried to dismiss the higher price of steel as merely "a bulge in the old line." Baruch warned him at a meeting in the White House that wages and prices generally would be driven up by an inflationary settlement in the steel strike. Truman argued in reply that the "bulge" could be held. "There's no holding it," Baruch insisted. "Ain't I the boss?" Truman asked. Later Baruch sent him a note saying, "There is only one way to avoid inflation and that is not to let it start. . . . No one has ever yet been able to control inflation. If it can be controlled upon the new plateau to which you are going, it will be the first time in history."[26]

In truth the wartime stabilization program was tottering. For the third time since the end of hostilities Truman on February 14 issued a new wage-price policy. Like the others, it permitted wage increases, while continuing wage controls. Reflecting the decision to permit a rise in the price of steel, the new policy also authorized price increases in any industry that might experience hardship because of higher wages. And there would be no requirement to await the results of a six-month accounting period as theretofore.[27]

The steel strike ended February 15 with wages rising by 18½ cents an hour and the price of steel by $5 a ton.

The General Motors strike continued. However, the fact that the steelworkers had settled for 18½ cents—a figure approximating settlements in certain other large strikes—cut the ground out from under the automobile workers and their higher demands. Reuther tried to get help from Truman. At first he sent a widely publicized telegram saying the union's fight was Truman's fight and "demands your immediate and militant support."[28] By then Truman was swamped with the steel negotiations.

Finally Reuther tried to reach him through Bowles.[29] The way Schwellenbach reported it to Truman at the cabinet meeting March 8, Reuther was making it difficult to get a settlement in the General Motors strike and was trying to compel the president to use his prestige to back up his demands. The secretary of labor declared that Reuther was able to start strikes but had not demonstrated ability to settle them. He alleged that Reuther (still the union's vice-president) was using the strike to further his own ambition to be president of the UAW—a post to which he was soon to be elected. This presentation got Truman up on his high horse. He said that he would not allow his office to be used in any such manner. He concluded that he would not bypass the secretary of labor, even though he said Reuther had made a number of attempts to have him do so.[30]

After 113 days the General Motors strike ended March 13 with the union accepting 18½ cents an hour, though Reuther maintained that other benefits brought the total to the 19½ cents that Truman's fact-finding board had recommended two months earlier. Like prices, wages were on the rise.

Truman's combined State of the Union and budget messages in January, 1946, continued to identify him with a social and economic program that included housing legislation, medical care, grants for hospital construction, aid to small business, conservation, an increased minimum wage, permanent farm price supports, modernization of Social Security, development of the St. Lawrence Seaway, and a permanent Fair Employment Practices Commission. He became the first president to endorse statehood for Alaska as well as for Hawaii.[31]

He also recommended federal assistance to the states for "more nearly equal opportunities for a good education," although he had no great personal enthusiasm for it. Discussing the matter with Harold Smith January 4, he questioned to what extent buildings and equipment contributed to the effectiveness of education. Stonewall Jackson, he said, had sat on the War Department steps until someone gave him an appointment to West Point, and Lincoln educated himself. If youngsters wanted to learn, they could do so under any conditions, he ventured. Furthermore he questioned the practicality of schooling. He cited a niece and nephew as typical high school graduates who could not write a decent letter nor look up words in a dictionary.

While he was on the subject, he said that the schools were not doing much about what he called the general moral lapse, either. "Of course, we can't blame the schools—the trouble really is at home," he observed, "but certainly the schools are not helping much in this respect." But on the issue of federal aid to the states he said he guessed he would have to go along with the current.

His plan for Universal Military Training would have educational advantages, he noted. He explained that he did not intend to allow the army to run a conventional training program. His idea, he said, was to democratize the services and overthrow the West Point and Annapolis cliques. Officers could be recruited from among the civilians trained under UMT.[32]

In the message he renewed his support of the so-called full employment legislation, again asking the Senate-House conference committee to approve the more liberal Senate bill. This appeal also failed. The fact that the anticipated serious unemployment had not materialized strengthened the hands of opponents of the Senate version.

The compromise measure that was finally enacted by Congress and signed by Truman February 20 as the Employment Act of 1946 disappointed many liberals and labor leaders because it followed the lines of the conservative House bill. Yet if Truman had vetoed the compromise bill, he probably could not have got another in its stead.[33]

So Congress had passed an Employment Act, but not a Full Employment Act. "Taken together the affirmative and negative actions reveal the central agreement upon which all postwar economic policy has been based," Herbert Stein has written. "To keep unemployment low is accepted as a national goal of very high priority, but full employment is not accepted as an absolute goal overriding all others."[34]

The Employment Act was a landmark in the Truman administration. While the act did not specifically authorize federal expenditures to create jobs, it declared that "it is the continuing policy and responsibility of the Federal Government to use all practical means . . . functions and resources" to foster "maximum employment, production and purchasing power." Even without specific new authority, the government already had great economic power to apply through taxing and spending. For the first time the government was directed by law to use such power to prevent serious unemployment.

"It is a commitment by the government to the people," Truman said on signing the bill, "a commitment to take any and all of the measures necessary for a healthy economy."[35]

As the heavy unemployment in the very different circumstances of the mid-1970s demonstrated, the measure was far from a panacea.

The act established the President's Council of Economic Advisers to assess the economic outlook and weigh the impact of government programs on the economy. Largely on the recommendation of Charles Ross, Truman appointed Dr. Edwin G. Nourse, vice-president of the Brookings Institution, chairman of the council, after Representative A. S. Mike Monroney of Oklahoma had declined the post.[36] As the two other members, Truman named Leon H. Keyserling, a Harvard Law School graduate, New Dealer, and general counsel of the National Housing Agency; and Dr. John D. Clark, a conservative, former vice-president of the Standard Oil Company of Indiana and dean of the School of Business Administration at the University of Nebraska. Of these, the one who was destined to carry the most weight, with respect not only to the economics but also the politics of the Truman administration, was Keyserling, an advocate of economic growth. At least until the Korean war the council itself did not carry much weight with Truman.[37]

Soon after Congress convened in the winter of 1946, controversy resumed on the question of civilian as opposed to military control of atomic energy. By the close of 1945 Truman had come round to the position that—contrary to the May-Johnson bill—the projected Atomic Energy Commission should be under civilian control.

In a letter to Forrestal and Patterson January 26 he put an end to official military support for the bill, informing the secretaries of war and navy that henceforth they were to adhere strictly to his policy that the AEC should be exclusively composed of civilians.

On February 2 he wrote to Senator McMahon, in effect endorsing his bill.[38] The road ahead in Congress, however, was difficult. Exclusion of the military from atomic energy control did not warm the hearts of the conservative majority as it did the hearts of the liberals and scientists. Then at a critical moment in mid-February sensational news broke in Ottawa, throwing the debate over the McMahon bill into turmoil.

A cipher clerk in the Soviet embassy there, named Igor Gouzenko, had seized incriminating documents in the building and turned them over to Canadian authorities. A royal commission disclosed in an interim report that "a network of undercover agents" had been organized in Canada the previous August by "the staff of the Soviet Embassy at Ottawa under direct instructions from Moscow." The man in charge was Colonel Nicolai Zabotin, the Soviet military attaché. The aim of the ring was to get secret information about the atomic bomb, uranium, radar, electronic shells used by the United States Navy, and the disposition of American, Canadian, and Brazilian troops. A number of Canadians were immediately arrested, some of them employees of the National Research Council, which was Canada's atomic energy agency.

Shortly afterward Dr. Alan Nunn May, a British scientist and an underground Communist, who had worked on the atomic project in the Montreal laboratory of the National Research Council, was arraigned in London. He was convicted of having given secret information as well as samples of uranium 235 to a Soviet agent, who forwarded the material to Moscow. May had visited some of the American laboratories, and certain of the information he passed to the Soviets concerned the American project.

The affair created a hullabaloo in Washington and in the American press. Representative Rankin announced that the House Committee on Un-American Activities was "trailing" Communist spies in the United States. Drew Pearson said in a broadcast that atomic secrets were being smuggled to the Soviet Union from Seattle. Byrnes felt compelled to deny that any American secrets had been leaked. Actually, Prime Minister Mackenzie King had confided the discovery of the espionage to Truman September 30. Truman took the disclosure in stride, assuming that the Soviets were working on a bomb but hoping that by the time they perfected one an international control agreement would have been instituted and nuclear weapons outlawed.[39] The rest of the country did not take the headlines with such equanimity in February, however. As debate on the McMahon bill continued, the revelation decisively strengthened the hands of conservatives who were insisting that the military have a role in atomic energy.

The need for wheat abroad grew desperate as the world food crisis worsened in the depth of winter. On January 4 Attlee warned Truman by cable that famine threatened Europe and Asia. The next day Byrnes wrote the president pressing him to mobilize government agencies "to export during this critical period every bushel of wheat we can."[40] The difficulty was that the domestic wheat supply was falling drastically below expectations. Meat rationing had been ended. Eager to forget the wartime sacrifices, Americans were ravenous for steaks. Thus an unprecedented amount of grain was being fed to livestock.

On February 6 Truman ordered the use of wheat in the direct production of liquor and beer discontinued. He raised the wheat flour extraction rate, a consequence of which, he explained, would be that "consumers may not be able to get exactly the kind of bread that many prefer." Also: "We will not have as large a selection of meats, cheese, evaporated milk, ice cream, margarine and salad dressing as we may like."[41]

In reality the program did not solve the shortage because, among other things, of the continuing high consumption of grain by livestock and chickens.

Budget Director Smith had been talking to Truman about what he called the administrative chaos in the government.

"Mr. President," Smith told him, "there are some serious administrative difficulties today which are accumulative. While you yourself are an orderly person, there is disorder all around you, and it is becoming worse. . . . For one thing, you need good, continuous, organized staff work, and you are not getting it."

"I know it," Truman replied, "and the situation is pretty serious."

"Not more than three or four weeks ago," Smith continued, "top people in Agriculture were making speeches which indicated their worry about a possible food surplus in this country. Now you are issuing a statement about black bread. Of course, the international picture was not taken into consideration, but I doubt that a food surplus would have existed even for this country alone."

"At any rate, if that sort of thing continues, Mr. President, the people of the country will think that the Administration has gone completely crazy. It was entirely possible to know precisely the situation months ago rather than weeks ago. The only excuse for not knowing is the lack of careful putting together of all the pieces."

Smith said he did not know who did what around the White House.

Truman did not hide his distress. Smith assured him it was not entirely the fault of his administration. Some of the difficulties had been inherited from the Roosevelt administration. Others were inherent in the structure of the government.

The president seemed aware that he was in trouble and that more was coming. But even granting that it was an unusually difficult period, he was baffled as to why things were going so badly for him.

When Smith saw him again February 28 Truman was inundated with problems and was having a frantic time with the navy budget, because the postwar role of the navy had not come into focus. Truman was irritated by pressure Forrestal was putting on him. The navy, he told Smith, had a complex about him. Admiral Nimitz, then chief of naval operations, Truman said, had recently declared at the British embassy that he was against UMT and would fight military unification to the end.

"Nimitz does not know that I know he said it," Truman added, "but I think it is pretty bad business for an admiral in his position."

Truman told Smith he was swamped with work and was reading perhaps as much as thirty thousand words of memorandums every night. Smith said the president should not be doing this, that somehow they ought to get the White House organized so that he would not be burdened with such detail.

"The President," Smith noted, "expressed various notes of despair about the avalanche of things that were piling up on him. While I did not express despair, I came away . . . with my own despair, accentuated because of the President's inability to use staff as yet."[42]

As more troops returned and the national unity inspired by the war eroded, racial disturbances grew. In December Mrs. Roosevelt had written Truman complaining about ill treatment of certain Japanese-Americans in the West. Truman replied December 21, saying, "This disgraceful conduct almost makes you believe that a lot of our Americans have a streak of Nazi in them." He wrote Attorney General Clark and asked: "Isn't there some way we can shame these people into doing the right thing by these loyal American-Japanese. I'll listen to any suggestion you may have to make on the subject." The president was particularly sensitive to mistreatment of Japanese-American servicemen and their families.

The problem, as Clark told the president in reply, was that the alleged crimes lay within the jurisdiction of the states. Thereupon Truman accepted Clark's advice and requested the attorney general to investigate the complaints of violence or discrimination and take appropriate action. Where the federal government did not have jurisdiction he asked that the results of the investigation be turned over to the states. He directed that the Department of Justice assist the states in prosecution or any other courses of action.[43]

The civil rights issue was pressing on Truman from many directions.

He had become president at a time not only when the South was rearing up against extending the reforms of the New Deal but when blacks, too, were becoming more articulate, determined, and effective. Their wartime migration to the North had given them new political muscle. More blacks had jobs now. The educational level among them was rising. Their service in the armed forces had given them a new claim to fair treatment. During the war the Supreme Court had handed down critical decisions according blacks the right to accommodations in Pullmans and the right to vote in southern primaries. The black press took strong stands against some of Truman's conservative appointments, notably that of Byrnes. Blacks were far better organized than before. Membership in the NAACP, for example, had increased sevenfold during the war.[44] Blacks had seen the effectiveness of direct pressure, particularly in the case of forcing Roosevelt to establish the FEPC. Moreover racial discrimination at home became glaringly out of place for a nation that had just committed itself to the international cause of human rights by ratifying the United Nations Charter.

Once more the issue of the permanent FEPC came to the fore almost as soon as Congress reconvened in January in a bill brought up by Senator Dennis Chavez, Democrat, of New Mexico. Southern senators promptly launched a filibuster against it and for three weeks occupied the Senate with attacks on the CIO and questions about the desirability of the affiliation of blacks with the Democratic party.[45]

This time, in contrast to his intervention the previous June, Truman washed his hands of the bill.[46] An attempt at cloture failed. For all practical purposes that was the end of any hope for a permanent FEPC, and, with its funds cut off, the wartime FEPC was doomed to close shop June 30.

In this period, too, Truman began to experience the early ripples of a tide—not a Red tide but an anti-Red tide, as it were—that was destined to dampen and at times soak his administration. A hunt for Communists in government was on in earnest. For some time Whittaker Chambers and Elizabeth T. Bentley had been informing the Federal Bureau of Investigation in secret that Communist espionage activities had occurred in the government. They cited names of persons involved. Chambers, a senior editor of *Time,* who had been a Communist engaged in espionage activities in the 1930s, and Miss Bentley, who was a Vassar College graduate who also had joined the Communist party in the thirties and taken part in espionage, were two figures who were to dominate the headlines later in the Truman administration. Augmenting their disclosures was information supplied the FBI by the Soviet defector, Gouzenko, who had exposed the Ottawa spy ring.

On November 8, 1945, J. Edgar Hoover had sent Truman a letter saying that "information has been recently developed from a highly confidential source indicating that a number of persons employed by the Government . . . have been furnishing data and information to persons outside the Federal Government, who are in turn transmitting this information to espionage agents of the Soviet Government."[47]

Of those cited, the person of most immediate concern to Truman was Harry Dexter White, assistant to Secretary of the Treasury Vinson, who had held the same post under Secretary Morgenthau. A brilliant expert in the field of international finance, White had been, as Morgenthau's right-hand man, an architect of the International Monetary Fund and the World Bank—soon to be attacked, as John Kenneth

Galbraith has noted, as the very symbols of capitalist imperialism.[48] White had, however, been under electronic surveillance by the FBI. There was a suspicion, of whatever merit, that he had been the true author of the Morgenthau Plan, put up to it by friends or agents of the Soviet Union in the Kremlin's interest of seeing Germany reduced to a pastoral state.[49]

When Vinson succeeded Morgenthau, Vinson, too, became involved in international finance problems and relied heavily on White. In time he recommended to Truman that White be named as United States executive director of the International Monetary Fund. Despite Hoover's letter, Truman on January 23, 1946, sent to the Senate the nomination of White, the man who two months earlier had urged Wallace to desert the administration.

Piecing the story together from the recollections of persons then in the government, what appears to have happened is that Truman looked to Vinson for advice and Vinson did not attach great importance to Hoover's letter. Neither then did Truman. After all, the letter did not specify what acts White had committed. It even left open the question of whether he had known that information he had supplied was being fed, allegedly, into "the Soviet espionage system."

Truman had come to office, incidentally, with some reservations about the FBI, which he expressed to Budget Director Harold Smith during 1945. On May 4, for instance, he criticized the amounts of money being spent in South America by army and navy intelligence and by the FBI, whose jurisdiction during the war was not confined to the United States. Truman told Smith he was "very much against building up a Gestapo." On May 11 he indicated strong disapproval of certain FBI methods, particularly snooping on the sex lives of bureaucrats and members of Congress. Again on July 6 he questioned whether the presence of the FBI in South America was good for inter-American relations. And on September 5 he said he intended to limit the jurisdiction of the FBI to the United States, a step he subsequently was to take.[50]

In any case consideration of White's nomination went ahead in the Senate. Meanwhile on February 4 the FBI repeated its warning in another letter delivered to Truman. This time copies were sent also to certain other high officials, including Byrnes. More worried about the possible consequences of the White nomination than either Truman or Vinson had been, the secretary of state flagged Truman down on it in a memorandum February 5 and then went to the White House February 6 to press his admonition. Truman was now concerned but discovered that the Senate had that afternoon confirmed White. Byrnes suggested that Truman ask some senator to move for reconsideration, but Truman thought poorly of this approach. Byrnes then recommended that Truman withhold the presidential commission from White. Truman said that this would be out of order. Finally, Byrnes recommended that Truman send for White and confront him with Hoover's letter. That was the last Byrnes ever heard of the matter.[51] In due time, White assumed his new duties. He resigned after a year, receiving a courteous note from Truman. He was named publicly by Chambers in testimony in 1948 and died of a heart attack soon afterward.

The bizarre climax to this episode did not occur until the Eisenhower Administration. Nearly a year after Truman had left office Attorney General Herbert Brownell, Jr., looking for opportunities to discredit Democrats, appeared before the Executive Club of Chicago on November 6, 1953, and with Eisenhower's knowledge made an unexpected attack on Truman. The former president, he said, knowingly had promoted a "Russian spy" in the person of White and left the Senate in ignorance of Hoover's letter while White's nomination was pending. A great political uproar followed. On November 10 Representative Harold H. Velde, Republican, of Illinois, chairman of the House Un-American Activities Committee, issued a subpoena for Truman, which was served on him at the Waldorf Towers during a visit to New York. The action was without precedent. Truman refused to comply with the subpoena and appear before the committee. Even though he was then a private citizen, he demurred on the ground that the subpoena violated the constitutional principle of separation of powers between the legislative and executive branches. Restrained by cooler Republican heads, Velde did not move to cite Truman for contempt. Truman attacked Brownell as a liar in a nationwide radio and television broadcast from Kansas City. It took no subpoena to produce Brownell and Hoover before the Senate Internal Security Subcommittee, where they testified that Truman's decision to promote White had hindered an FBI investigation into White's alleged connection with Soviet espionage.

By the close of 1945 Truman had found office space in the White House—"the taxpayers' house," as he sometimes called it—cramped and decided to build a southerly extension of the West Wing. This is an adjunct to the White House proper, housing the offices of the president and senior staff members as well as the press room. Congress was asked to appropriate $1,650,000 for the addition, which would have included an auditorium for press conferences and other presidential meetings. The mere idea of tampering with White House grounds, however, brought traditionalists to their feet. The American Institute of Architects objected to the plans.

"These architects, Mr. President, feel that the White House should be the President's home," a reporter noted at a press conference January 15.

"Well, I feel that way too," he replied. "But this has no connection whatever with the White House. This is an addition to the offices of the President."

"That is what they are opposed to," the reporter said. "They think—"

"They don't want the President to have any offices to work in," he retorted. "It's just something to talk about."[52]

Soon, however, the talk had reached such a pitch that Truman no longer could brush it off.

At his press conference January 24 the president said, defensively: "I want to clarify the situation, if possible, and then if some of our good friends want to come down and chain themselves to a bush or a shrub out here, that will be entirely satisfactory, just as the ladies did when they were building the Jefferson Memorial. Some ladies chained themselves to some of the Japanese cherry trees, you remember."

The president said that the Fine Arts Commission had approved his plans, prepared by Lorenzo S. Winslow, the White House architect.

"This additional office space is absolutely essential to the President," he said.

"I don't want to have to do what Dolley Madison was supposed to have done. They say she used to hang her washing in the East Room on rainy days."

"That was Abigail Adams," a reporter said.

"Dolley Madison too," Truman replied. "So they say. That is just the story around here."[53]

The end of the story on Truman's dream of new office space was that the Senate Appropriations Committee rescinded the appropriation, ostensibly "to preserve the general architectural scheme." "They've never done that to a President since I've been here," said Howell G. Crim, the chief usher of the White House since 1933. After learning of the committee's vote, Truman beckoned Crim and his assistant, J. B. West, to a window overlooking the south lawn, the Ellipse, the Washington Monument, and the Jefferson Memorial. West detected a gleam in his eye as Truman viewed the panorama.

"I'd like to be able to take better advantage of that view," Truman said. "It would be far more correct, in an architectural sense, to have a balcony up here on the second floor."

The president got out some sketches of a balcony above the south portico.

"Is there any precedent for this?" he inquired.

"Mr. Coolidge put on a new roof and a third floor," Crim recalled, "but they got a special Congressional appropriation."

"Can we get this out of our own budget?" Truman asked. Crim thought so. A smile flashed over the president's face.

"I'm going to preserve the general architectural scheme of the White House any damn way I want to!" he said.[54]

Very, very secretly he began to make plans.

19. *Ickes Quits*

A
S HAVE ALL PRESIDENTS, Truman made good appointments and poor ones, although some of his poor ones did have a distinctive, bizarre quality. As always, good appointments were rather taken for granted, while poor ones often caused ridicule or controversy, some of it raucous.

In the winter of 1946 Truman managed to make his troubles worse with a succession of inept choices. He began stirring dissatisfaction by nominating to important posts two friends—George Allen to be a director of the Reconstruction Finance Corporation and Jake Vardaman to be a member of the Board of Governors of the Federal Reserve System.

Allen had appeared on the White House scene in the Roosevelt administration. He was competent but widely regarded as a backslapper who used friendship with important politicians for business advantage. When Roosevelt wanted someone to keep an eye on Truman in the 1944 campaign Allen was assigned to the latter's staff, and that is where Truman came to know him and like him for his jovial manner.

On becoming president, he gave him an unsalaried job studying liquidation of war agencies and used him as a confidant, political handyman, and sometime emissary to Congress. While Allen was never a senior adviser, he was close enough to Truman to be influential. Vice-president of the Home Insurance Company and director of a score of corporations, he was a great self-promoter. The Senate confirmed him only after a skirmish in which Taft questioned his right to serve while continuing to draw salaries and own stock in other corporations that might do business with the RFC.

Vardaman, it will be recalled, had been selected by Truman as his first naval aide, partly because Truman was sour on regular navy brass. Once on the job, however, Commodore Vardaman became brassier than the superintendent of the Naval Academy. Sometimes when Truman changed his mind about an associate he promoted him out of sight instead of dismissing him. "I don't like to dismiss people any better than my predecessor did," he had once remarked to Ickes.[1]

As Margaret Truman has described this particular case: "One of the Truman prima donnas who eventually got the ax was Jake Vardaman. . . . In the White House Mr. Vardaman proceeded to stick his nose into almost every office and tell them how it should be run. Then he made the blunder of all blunders. He descended upon Mother's side of the White House and started telling *them* how to do the job. That was the end of Mr. Vardaman as naval aide. Dad elevated him to the Federal Reserve Board, and he repaid him for this kindness by voting against every Truman policy for the next seven years." So much for the doctrine of independent judgment on the part of Federal Reserve governors. Miss Truman added: "He also went around Washington spreading the nasty story that he was kicked out of the White House because he did not drink or play cards."[2]

Vardaman's competence for his new high post was challenged vehemently in the Senate, but the nomination got through.

He and Rosenman left the White House at about the same time, Rosenman to practice law in New York, and their departures opened the way for Clark Clifford's rise to high influence on the White House staff in 1946. While still assistant naval aide he was already helping Rosenman, who needed a hand from a lawyer, speech writer, and someone adept at pulling things together, as Clifford was. With Vardaman gone, Clifford became the naval aide. When Rosenman left, Truman said he was not going to appoint another "Special Counsel," a title which Roosevelt had created for Rosenman.[3] Rosenman's functions remained to be performed, however, and naturally fell to Clifford. Within a few months Truman changed his mind and gave him the title of "Special Counsel to the President." The job was essentially political. Clifford did not give the president formal legal opinions. In accordance with tradition Truman continued to receive legal advice concerning executive orders, legal papers, and the like from the assistant solicitor general of the United States—a post held during most of the Truman administration by George T. Washington, a collateral descendant of the first president.

Moving up in the shuffle also was another young assistant naval aide, George Elsey, who worked with Clifford. Elsey had graduated from Princeton in 1939 and had received an M.A. in American history from Harvard in 1940. He joined the navy and later in the war was assigned, as a lieutenant, to the White House map room. Now, along with Clifford, his duties were expanded, and he was to become one of the ablest, most important members of the White House staff throughout the Truman administration.

The appointment that let the hornets loose was Truman's selection of Edwin Pauley in January as under secretary of the navy. Pauley had big hands, big shoulders, big jaw, and a squint; and all seemed appropriate features for a hard-boiled but able speculator, oil producer, real estate developer, leader of the right-wing California Democrats, and aggressive political fund raiser. His fund raising had put the Democrats in his debt, and he became their national finance chairman during Roosevelt's time. Under pressure Roosevelt agreed to appoint him assistant secretary of the navy. Behind the scenes Eleanor Roosevelt fought the appointment.[4] In any case Roosevelt died before he got around to doing anything about it. Then sometime before February 1946, according to Truman, Forrestal came to him and said that Under Secretary of the Navy Bard intended to resign before long, and Forrestal recommended Pauley as a successor.[5]

Pauley, it will be recalled, had worked to get the vice-presidential nomination for Truman. Truman liked him, admired his capacity to bend other men to his will and wanted him in the administration. Having seen Pauley's toughness in action, especially in the reparations negotiations with the Soviets, Truman felt he was a man who could knock the admirals' heads together and get things in order at the

Pentagon. Looking ahead to the unification of the armed forces, he was at least thinking of Pauley as the future secretary of defense. His vision of Pauley's strength in the Pentagon might not have been mistaken. Furthermore he was aware of Roosevelt's intentions of appointing him assistant secretary of the navy and undoubtedly felt under some obligation about it. He could have named him to almost any other post in the government without a backfire. Truman's miscalculation came on Pauley's singular vulnerability for high office in the navy.

Mrs. Roosevelt had taken her stand because "I was very much opposed to having Mr. Pauley in any position where oil could be involved." It was this issue that brought the collision between Ickes and Pauley and that got the Senate's back up over the nomination. With Teapot Dome still fresh in memory, it became a sensitive question whether a California oilman ought to be in a position of authority with respect to the Navy's large oil reserves.

Then seventy-one, Ickes was popularly known as the "Old Curmudgeon" and relished the reputation. Samuel Johnson thought the word *curmudgeon* may have come from *coeur méchant,* or wicked heart. In Ickes's case it denoted an older, cantankerous politician with a talent for invective. "The old man" or "old man Ickes," as Truman referred to him, had been a reporter, lawyer, Bull Moose leader in Illinois, and reformer before becoming one of Franklin Roosevelt's most famous cabinet officers. He was a belligerent department head, but widely regarded as an excellent public servant.

On the train returning from Roosevelt's funeral Ickes had gone to Truman's car to pay his respects. Truman was napping, however, and Ickes fell to talking with Pauley. Pauley, he later recalled, "had the hardihood to turn to me and ask me what I proposed to do about offshore oil," in which the Department of the Interior had an interest. Ickes replied that the question was one for the courts and observed that "no administrative officer would be doing his duty if he decided that the Government had no right, title or interest when it might have." Pauley replied that it has been the policy of the Department of the Interior to regard the tidelands as belonging to California.

"I could just about ruin him," Ickes confided to his diary at the time, "by relating the pressures that he has tried to exert on me with respect to offshore oil in California so that he might be able to collect large sums of money from the oil interests for Democratic campaign expenses."[6]

On May 29, 1945, the Department of Justice filed a suit in the United States District Court in Los Angeles to determine whether the federal government or California owned the mineral deposits in the tidelands. In noting this in his diary, Ickes said: "Pauley has interests there and he has been moving heaven and earth to protect them. . . . The permits that Pauley and others have run [derive] from the State of California." Truman told Ickes he had approved the filing of the suit despite Pauley's interests and assured Ickes that Pauley was an honest man. Truman then made some curious remarks, as Ickes later recalled:

During our talk, I don't remember how it came in, President Truman expressed the hope that I would not blast him, telling me that if I ever had any criticism to make he hoped that I would come in and talk to him to his face. I told him that I would. He said something about liking me better than I realized. . . . He also said that he didn't think that I could hurt him and I told him that I didn't want to try.[7]

In a notable decision, spurred by his concern over the war's drain on domestic petroleum reserves, Truman on September 28, 1945, formally asserted federal jurisdiction over the natural resources of the continental shelf.[8] Months of litigation impended, however, and Ickes continued to fret about Pauley and oil. In his diary October 20 he noted that Pauley had made representations to oilmen on the West Coast that no federal suit would be filed if they contributed to the Democratic National Committee.

Meanwhile Ickes's relations with Truman went along satisfactorily and he was willing to give the president his due. After a luncheon with Harold Smith toward the end of 1945 Ickes noted: "He spoke highly of the President's personal courage and willingness to do the right thing. I am in accord with him on these points. My own feeling is that Truman's difficulties go back to the fact that he feels that out of personal loyalty he has to make appointments that are not for the good of the country."[9]

Then Forrestal came to lunch January 9, 1946, and gave Ickes to understand that Pauley would be named under secretary of the navy, some months after which Forrestal would resign and Pauley would become secretary. He inquired if Ickes would fight the nomination.

"I told him," Ickes recorded in his diary January 12, 1946, "that I would not on my own initiative; that I owed it to the President not to oppose one of his nominations. I added, however, that if the Senate Committee should call me and ask me questions I would answer the question truthfully, adding that my answers to certain questions would not do Pauley any good. . . ."

Ickes was puzzled as to how Pauley's nomination could strengthen the administration politically. "Where he has helped in the past has been in the raising of money but he could not very well hold up the oil companies on the West Coast for money as Secretary of the Navy. . . ." he noted in his diary on the twelfth.

The president sent up the nomination January 18. It was immediately opposed by Senator Raymond E. Willis, Republican, of Indiana, second-ranking minority member of the Senate Naval Affairs Committee, to which the nomination was referred. In sum he charged that, as under secretary, Pauley would have a conflict of interest over naval oil reserves. This signaled a partisan attack, and at the request of Senator Charles W. Tobey, Republican, of New Hampshire, Ickes was called as a witness before the committee.

On January 30, two days before he was to appear, Ickes had a meeting with Truman. Truman told him he needed him and wanted him to remain in the cabinet. Ickes replied that he did not intend to initiate any attack on Pauley nor leak any unfavorable information. If asked, however, he said, he would have to answer questions honestly.

Ickes was to testify February 1 after attending a cabinet meeting. As the meeting was breaking up, he slipped over to Truman and showed him the committee's telegram summoning him.

Truman, as Ickes noted in his diary February 3, "told me that of course I must tell the truth but he hoped that I would be as gentle with Pauley as possible. I told him that this was my intention."[10]

When Ickes arrived at the hearing, Tobey was ready for him, primed with information from Edwin A. Harris of the *St. Louis Post-Dispatch,* who had written a series on tidelands oil and Pauley's activities.

Did Pauley, Tobey asked, ever tell Ickes that the filing of a government suit to claim the tidelands was bad politics and might cost several hundred thousand dollars in campaign contributions?

"Yes," Ickes replied.

Pauley, who was in the room, followed Ickes to the witness stand and testified that he never had accepted "contingent" contributions. On the occasion in question, he said, he had gone to see Ickes to get a personal campaign contribution.

Along with similar testimony by Norman Littell, former assistant attorney general, Ickes's appearance had put the fat in the fire, and the Republicans were hungrily sniffing the aroma. At the same time Pauley's contradiction of Ickes's testimony set war drums pounding in the ears of the Old Curmudgeon. Through Harris of the *Post-Dispatch* he reminded Tobey that he had certain entries in his diary and that if he were summoned to return to the hearings with these notes, he would, of course, feel obliged to read them. He also told Harris, as he noted in his diary February 3, that if Tobey asked sharper questions, they would produce a stronger case. With this morsel in hand Harris went to Tobey's apartment. The upshot was that Ickes was summoned to reappear before the committee February 5 and bring all pertinent documents he might have bearing on the case.

He did, and, with Pauley sitting directly behind him, he revealed the whole business of Pauley's waylaying him over tidelands oil on the way back from Roosevelt's funeral. As the *New York Times* reported, he pictured Pauley as intriguing in high circles, dangling before the Democrats a gift of $300,000 from oilmen if he could be assured that the tidelands suit would be abandoned.

This imbued the nomination with an aura of scandal and put the Naval Affairs Committee in an impossible position. Returning to his office, Ickes tried to get an appointment with Truman, but his secretary hit a stone wall.

Obviously alluding to Teapot Dome, the *Times* said in an editorial February 7, "There has been an unceasing fight through the years to defend from private exploitation the oil reserves that the Navy needs. . . . We believe Mr. Pauley's oil interests disqualify him for a post in the Navy Department."

Truman praised Pauley at a press conference held the same day. Then—from Ickes's point of view—came a fatal exchange:

"Mr. President, you don't consider that this situation involves anything at all, any change in your relations with Mr. Ickes?"

"I don't think so. Mr. Ickes can very well be mistaken the same as the rest of us."[11]

"The President clearly lined up with Pauley and of course this meant that he was in opposition to me," Ickes wrote in his diary. "He said, among other things, that I had not cleared with him before appearing before the Senate Committee on Naval Affairs and that I 'could be mistaken as well as anyone else.' "

When Ickes got home that evening his wife, Jane, said to him, simply, "Well, he puts it up to you, doesn't he?"

The next morning Ickes told her he had no recourse but to resign, and she agreed. Over the weekend he worked on his letter, then submitted it for comment to his friend, Thomas Corcoran, and sent it to Truman February 13.[12] Ickes said he did not care to "commit perjury for the sake of the party" and asked Truman what he had meant in urging him to be "gentle" in his testimony. On national radio Ickes said, "I could no longer, much as I regret it, retain my self-respect and stay in the Cabinet of President Truman."

The mention of perjury angered Truman, who maintained that Ickes had told him personally that Pauley was a good man. In an unpublished memorandum to Charles Ross, Truman said: ". . . I told Ickes to tell the truth and be as kind to Mr. Pauley as he could be. In his statement to the press yesterday he said he had been asked by me to commit perjury. This is not true. He was told by me to tell the truth."[13]

Truman not only accepted Ickes's resignation but in his letter added a line: "I also consider that this terminates all your other governmental activites." Stung, Ickes wrote him a second letter, saying, "I assure you that I have no secret design, having resigned as Secretary of the Interior, to hold on to any other office under your jurisdiction."

With his political instinct for the jugular, Ickes at one point in his running commentaries said, "I am against government by crony," nourishing an expression that clung to the Truman administration. In the parlance of much of the press other presidents had friends; Truman had cronies.

"Mr. President," a reporter asked at the White House press conference February 15, "were you speaking in a Pickwickian sense when you asked Mr. Ickes to tell the truth about Mr. Pauley?"

"I never speak in a Pickwickian sense," he replied.

"Would you regard it, sir—would you regard Mr. Ickes's statement as an attempt to impugn your integrity?"

"Well, I don't think he would dare do that," Truman said.

"Will you withdraw Mr. Pauley's nomination, Mr. President?"

"I will not."

"Do you expect Mr. Pauley may ask that it be withdrawn?"

"I don't expect he will."

"Will you be embarrassed if he does withdraw it?"

"I don't think I will be embarrassed by it."

"Do you expect Mr. Pauley to be confirmed, Mr. President?"

"Yes, I do. Mr. Pauley is a good man."[14]

When asked about the president's remark that Ickes would not dare impugn his integrity, Ickes retorted that Truman was "neither an absolute monarch nor a descendant of a putative Sun Goddess."

Growing demands that Pauley withdraw were rejected by Truman.

"Does that mean, Mr. President, that Mr. Pauley will have your full support if he wants to stay in and fight for confirmation?" he was asked at a press conference February 21.

"That is my policy," Truman answered. "And when I get behind a man, I usually stay behind him."[15]

But it was clear the Senate would not confirm the nomination. The way the impasse was resolved was that a majority of the Naval Affairs Committee affirmed Pauley's personal integrity, then he asked Truman to withdraw the nomination, and finally Truman assented and wrote Pauley a glowing public letter, March 13, praising his integrity and deploring the tactics used against him.[16]

In departing, Ickes left one interesting thought behind.

"Will you work against Harry Truman politically?" he was asked at his final press conference.

"I might work for him in 1948," he answered. "I can think of worse contingencies."[17]

Meanwhile Truman gave Senator Tobey a piece of his mind. On behalf of poultrymen in New Hampshire the senator had telegraphed the president an appeal to order more grain set aside for them. "This is a Macedonian cry," he said, to which Truman replied in a letter May 29:

. . . it seems to me that you have been making Macedonian cries or yells ever since I have been in the White House. . . . Your unwarranted attacks on Mr. Pauley almost ruined a good public servant. Between you and Mr. Ickes you have made it exceedingly difficult for me to get good men to fill the necessary places in the Government. You are still continuing your Macedonian cries, and I hope you will get a lot of pleasure out of them.

If it came to a choice between chickens in New England and human beings in Europe, Truman added, he would help feed the latter.[18]

The White House did not let Ickes out of its sight altogether. On December 4, 1946, Vaughan telephoned J. Edgar Hoover to inquire whether he had any information in his files linking the former secretary of the interior with any gas company interested in acquiring the Big Inch Pipeline. This was a pipeline from Texas to Pennsylvania built by the government during the second World War and later sold to the Texas Eastern Transmission Corporation. Hoover found no link directly involving Ickes. However, he informed Vaughan by letter that Ickes was "very friendly with Mr. Thomas G. Corcoran," on whom the FBI was spying, it will be recalled. And Corcoran "reportedly is in the process of organizing a gas company for the purpose of submitting bids for the procurement of the Big Inch Pipe Line." Also "during the initial stages of this company's formation Mr. Ickes was proposed for consideration as a director."[19]

Ickes's departure brought lamentations from the liberals. "One has the feeling," the *New York Post* commented, "that a poorer and poorer cast is dealing desperately with a bigger and bigger story." Truman tried to offset liberal discontent by sending Forrestal to ask William Douglas if he would resign from the Supreme Court and take Ickes's place. In urging this course upon Truman, Forrestal had written him: "And if Bill went in, he would be loyal to you."[20] However, if Ickes's own previous observations are correct, they raise some doubts about this. A couple of months after Truman became president, Douglas, according to Ickes, warned him that Truman would want to get rid of him and urged him to force Truman to fire him rather than resign. "In the meantime," Ickes noted, "he thinks I ought to document everything possible so that I would be able to make out a case against Truman. With all due respect I don't agree with this point of view."[21]

In any event Douglas declined the offer, and Truman chose as Ickes's successor Julius Krug, former chairman of the War Production Board and a protege of Baruch's who stood as high in the esteem of the business community as Ickes and Douglas did with the liberals. The president had known him since the days of the Truman Committee and considered him, as did many others, an able administrator. With Ickes gone, Wallace was the last of the New Dealers in Truman's cabinet. "The President said he had always had the highest regard for me and still had the highest regard," Wallace recalled after the cabinet adjourned February 15. "He thought that we understood each other and he hoped that I would not resign like Ickes."[22]

20. *Sharp Turn toward the Cold War*

"WHAT IS RUSSIA UP TO NOW?' It is, of course, the supreme conundrum of our time," Vandenberg said in the Senate February 27. Reporting on the United Nations General Assembly meeting in London, which he had attended as an American delegate, Vandenberg told applauding senators that United States foreign policy must match that of the Soviet Union in candor and firmness.

The next night, addressing a dinner of the Overseas Press Club at the Waldorf-Astoria in New York, Byrnes said that the United States "cannot allow aggression to be accomplished by coercion or pressure or by subterfuge such as political infiltration." In what was dubbed the "Second Vandenberg Concerto" Byrnes noted that the United Nations Charter bound all members, large and small, not to use force or threat of force except in defense of the principles of the Charter.

"We will not and cannot stand aloof if force or the threat of force is used contrary to the purposes and principles of the Charter," he said.

"Jim, I've read it and like it," Truman had noted in returning a copy of the speech sent in advance to the White House.[1]

"Taken together," the *New York Times* commented in an editorial March 1, "these two speeches must be considered as ushering in a new orientation of America's international relations."

More precisely, the shift away from conciliation and compromise with the Soviets that had materialized around the time of the Moscow conference, and Byrnes's subsequent encounter with Truman, was now visibly gaining momentum.

With a proposed loan to Britain the United States set out to strengthen the economy of Western Europe. Kremlin rhetoric and reports from the United States embassy in Moscow sounded new alarms in Washington about Stalin's intentions. The image of a permanently divided Europe was fastened on the American mind. Far more forthrightly than in the case of Poland, the United States challenged the Soviet course in Iran, drawing the line for the first major conflict in the United Nations Security Council. Soviet pressure on Iran, Greece, and Turkey was seen in Washington as an attempt by Stalin to extend his control beyond the area of immediate Soviet security needs.

In one of the milestones of postwar foreign policy Truman asked Congress January 30 to approve a $3.75 billion loan to Great Britain. Some weeks before, Wallace had cautioned him that when the United States came to make a loan to Britain, it also should make a comparable one to the Soviet Union in order to appear evenhanded in its foreign relations.[2] But Truman made no mention of the Soviets in his special message.[3] The end of Lend-Lease had left the British in dire shape financially. They were in debt and had used up their foreign resources and reserves in waging war. After Potsdam Truman had sent William L. Clayton, under secretary of state for economic affairs, to study the situation in London. He recommended that some emergency assistance be extended, after which a British delegation, including Lord Keynes, came to Washington to negotiate with an American group that included Clayton and Vinson.

The British wanted a grant or interest-free loan of at least $5 billion. Clayton inclined to $4 billion at low interest, but Vinson resented Keynes and took a narrower view and, of course, was the most influential of the group with Truman. Finally, the American negotiators agreed upon $3.5 billion as a fair minimum and $4 billion as a maximum. Truman compromised at $3.75 billion at 2 percent interest and stuck to it despite British disappointment.[4] Not only did this sum prove inadequate, but the Americans drove a hard bargain to boot, forcing upon the British a number of trade concessions including, after one year, removal of all restrictions on the free exchange of sterling, thereby ending the imperial preference system that had been a barrier to trade between countries of the sterling area and the United States. "We loaded the British loan negotiations with all the conditions the traffic would bear," Clayton was pleased to write Baruch.[5] Even so the agreement had a difficult passage through Congress.

Before its submission to Congress Byrnes gave a dinner for a group of leading senators. Vandenberg predicted that the Senate would approve the loan. He ventured, however, that the Senate would not vote for a loan to the Soviet Union.[6] Nor was it asked to do so.

Periodic discussion of a loan for postwar reconstruction had been going on between Soviet and American officials since early 1943. Three months before Truman became president, Harriman had been approached in Moscow about a $6 billion loan. In Washington Morgenthau had proposed a loan of $10 billion. Roosevelt held back, however, to seek political concessions from the Soviets in return for the money.

When Truman took office Harriman was favorable to a loan but as a lever to influence Soviet policy. Byrnes consigned the Morgenthau proposal to the "Forgotten File."[7] Members of the House Select Committee on Postwar Economic Policy and Planning visited Moscow and talked with Stalin. On return to Washington the committee expressed willingness to approve a Soviet loan but only after the Soviets had agreed to open their records to a degree that would have been intolerable to the Kremlin.[8] The Truman administration obtained approval of Congress to lend the Soviets up to 1 billion through the Export-Import Bank of Washington. The Soviets applied, but did not press the matter. The State Department favored withholding credits from Moscow until the Soviets gave assurances that their economic policies "are in general accord with our announced international economic policies."[9] For the time being that is where the matter rested.

Meeting with Harriman January 23, 1946, Stalin asked whether Washington would meet Moscow halfway, if the Soviet government raised the question of a loan. Harriman temporized, but told Stalin that the differences between the two countries created problems.[10] Indeed the American attitude had hardened to such a point in the winter of 1945–46 that, as Vandenberg indicated, Truman might not

have been able to win congressional approval for a Soviet loan, even if he had
wished to.

The great wrench in Soviet-American relations continued. On February 9
Stalin announced a new five-year plan to increase production to guarantee the
country "against all kinds of eventualities." Indicating a hardening in the Soviet attitude, too, he flaunted the might of the Red Army. He foresaw no possibility of a
peaceful international order because capitalism, monopoly, and imperialism, he
said, were in command outside the Soviet Union.

Byrnes and Acheson were disturbed.[11] Justice Douglas told Forrestal the
speech was tantamount to "the declaration of World War III."[12] Walter Lippmann,
the columnist, wrote, "Now that Stalin has [decided] to make military power his
first objective, we are forced to make a corresponding decision." William C. Bullitt, former United States ambassador to Moscow, carried the warning to Henry
Wallace, but to no avail. "I told him," Wallace wrote in his diary February 12,
"that I thought this [Stalin's speech] was accounted for in some measure by the fact
that it was obvious to Stalin that our military was getting ready for war with Russia;
that they were setting up bases all the way from Greenland, Iceland, northern
Canada and Alaska to Okinawa with Russia in mind. I said that Stalin obviously
knew what these bases meant and also knew the attitude of many of our people
through our press. We were challenging him and his speech was taking up the
challenge."

Nine days after Stalin's speech the story of Soviet atomic espionage broke in
Ottawa. It not only affected the debate on the atomic energy bill in the Senate but
played into the hands of those everywhere who were advocating a hard line toward
Moscow. For in this affair were contained the most insidious ingredients of the agitation surrounding the developing Cold War: profound fear of the atomic bomb
combined with a sense of vulnerability through espionage. Under the glare of
headlines Truman no longer took the casual attitude he had adopted in September
when Mackenzie King had informed him of the spy ring. Leahy in his diary of February 20, 1946, noted reports of "insulting treatment" of American officials in
Yugoslavia and Bulgaria and asserted: "The President expressed to me sharp disapproval of the recent attitude of appeasement toward the Soviet and said he is convinced of the necessity of taking a strong attitude without delay."[13]

"Mr. President," a reporter said at a press conference the next day, "several
months ago you said . . . that you didn't share the unholy fear of Russia that was
manifested by some people, and that sometime you would comment at length on
that. I wonder if you could comment now in view of the current revelations about
the atomic secrets."

"No comment," Truman said.[14]

On February 22 a cable arrived at the State Department from George F. Kennan, the American chargé d'affaires in Moscow, that crystallized the changing attitude of the administration. A scholar, Kennan had first been attached to the embassy
in Moscow in the 1930s and found Stalinism a horror. Returning to the embassy late
in the war, he had recoiled from Soviet policy, particularly in Eastern Europe and
Germany, and regarded many of the American hopes and plans for collaboration

with Stalin a pipe dream. In the face of the bewildering events of early 1946 Washington had cabled him for an explanation of Soviet behavior.

The Soviets, Kennan replied, still harped on encirclement by capitalism, "with which in the long run there can be no permanent peaceful coexistence." Thus "everything must be done to advance relative strength of USSR as factor in international society." Kennan made a point that was a blow to hopes for negotiating with Moscow: the Soviet party line had little to do with conditions outside the country. Rather it arose "mainly from basic inner-Russian necessities which existed before recent war and exist today." Beneath the Kremlin's "neurotic" view of world affairs lay "the traditional and instinctive Russian sense of insecurity." Soviet leaders "are driven by necessities of their own past and present position to put forward a dogma which pictures the outside world as evil, hostile and menacing." Hence the justification for increased military and police power.

Kennan predicted Soviet efforts to enlarge their power, at first restricted to nearby points such as Iran and Turkey. Later, however, efforts might extend to acquiring a port on the Persian Gulf or a base at Gibraltar. Still later might come indirect efforts to undermine the "political and strategic potential of major Western powers." In the same way "violent efforts will be made to weaken power and influence of Western powers over colonial, backward, or dependent peoples."

In words avidly read in the highest circles in Washington, Kennan summarized:

. . . we have here a political force committed fanatically to the belief that with the US there can be no permanent modus vivendi, that it is desirable and necessary that the internal harmony of our society be disrupted, our traditional way of life be destroyed, the international authority of our state be broken, if Soviet power is to be secure. This political force has complete power of disposition over energies of one of the world's greatest peoples and resources of the world's richest national territory.

Encouragingly, he said that Soviet power usually backed off "when strong resistance is encountered at any point."[15]

Kennan afterward acknowledged that the result of the telegram "was nothing less than sensational."[16] Truman was among those who read it, but it was Harriman who unsuspectingly touched off a chain reaction by sending a copy to Forrestal, who responded like Paul Revere to the lanterns in the Old North Church.[17] According to Walter Millis, editor of *The Forrestal Diaries,* Kennan's analysis was "exactly the kind of job for which Forrestal had looked vainly elsewhere in the government."[18] The secretary of the navy, Kennan recalled, had the "long telegram," as it has become known to history, reproduced and "evidently made it required reading for hundreds, if not thousands, of higher officers in the armed services." Years later Kennan ruefully likened the message to "one of those primers put out by alarmed congressional committees or by the Daughters of the American Revolution . . . to arouse the citizenry to the dangers of the Communist conspiracy."[19] It aroused Washington indeed and set a pattern then and for years to come for official American thinking about the Soviet problem. The containment concept, however, did not then nor at any time in Truman's first term lead, as Alexander L. George and Richard Smoke say, to any systematic strategy or theory linking military planning to foreign policy objectives. Each crisis was dealt with as it came along.[20]

Two days after the Kennan dispatch Robert Murphy, political adviser to General Lucius D. Clay, military governor of the United States zone in Germany, cabled Washington February 24, warning that Moscow might be preparing to seek a unified Germany under Soviet auspices.[21] His message arrived at a time when Washington was becoming increasingly uneasy about Soviet intentions in Germany, much the most sensitive of all areas of conflict.

Next came Vandenberg's speech in the Senate on the twenty-seventh, insisting that "the U.S. must speak as plainly upon all occasions as Russia does"—in so many words reiterating Republican demands that the Truman administration must stop "appeasement" of the Soviet Union. Recalling the General Assembly meeting in London, Vandenberg praised the performance of every leader who came to mind except Byrnes. His conspicuous omission of the secretary's name was regarded as a gesture of criticism for what Vandenberg had privately called Byrnes's "loitering around Munich."[22] Only someone in Vandenberg's current state of mind could have thought Byrnes softheaded about the Soviets. Molotov was not likely to have formed such an opinion. In any case Vandenberg's implied criticism had come twenty-four hours too soon.

The speech that Byrnes had prepared for the Overseas Press Club dinner the following night, to Truman's liking, gave a new tone to the administration's policy toward the Soviet Union. Yielding to weeks of pressure from Truman, Leahy, Republican leaders, and critical newspapers and columnists for a harder stance, Byrnes said that the United States could not ignore "a unilateral gnawing away at the status quo." No country, he declared, had the right to keep its troops in the territories of other sovereign states without their consent. Apparently referring to the actions of the Soviets in removing Japanese machinery from Manchuria, as they had removed industrial equipment from Germany and Eastern Europe, he said that no power had authority to help itself to enemy property in liberated countries before a reparations settlement had been agreed to by all the Allies. The United States would defend the United Nations Charter and would not stand aloof from the use or threatened use of force, Byrnes said.

Earlier that same day Forrestal had asked Byrnes if he would assent to the dispatch of a navy task force to the Mediterranean to encourage Turkey, which was alarmed by Soviet pressure, and Greece, which was threatened with armed conflict between the government and the Communist-led opposition.[23] From Potsdam onward, problems of Greece and Turkey gradually built up pressure on Truman, and this pressure intensified through the remainder of 1946, creating a situation that resulted in one of the great landmarks of postwar United States foreign policy—the Truman Doctrine of 1947.

Ever since the war Stalin, in the tradition of the Czars, had been probing in the Mediterranean area. While Stalin had failed at Potsdam to win Allied support for a Soviet share in control of the Black Sea Straits—the agreement was simply on a need to revise the Montreux Convention—he maintained pressure on Turkey. The United States threw its weight against a Soviet claim that control of the Straits was a matter of concern only to the Black Sea Powers. It opposed Moscow's efforts to organize a joint Soviet-Turkish defense of the Straits. Meanwhile State Department reports from the Middle East repeatedly warned that the Soviets intended to take control of Turkey itself, which made their conduct in Iran seem doubly menacing as a possible flanking operation. Truman continued to be convinced of the danger.[24] "I am of the opinion," he had written to Byrnes the previous October 13, "if some means isn't found to prevent it, Russia will undoubtedly take steps by direct action to obtain control of the Black Sea straits."[25]

Forrestal's idea of a show of the flag in support of Greece and Turkey came at a time when the Truman administration already had decided on the gesture of sending home the ashes of the dead Turkish ambassador to Washington on the battleship *Missouri*. Byrnes was pleased with the idea of a task force accompanying the *Missouri*, and Truman approved. Then naval operational problems intervened. It was only to be a matter of months, however, before the proposal materialized on a more formidable scale.[26]

Back in October Franc L. McCluer, president of Westminster College in Fulton, Missouri, had read in the newspapers that Winston Churchill planned to visit the United States in the winter of 1946. This was a matter of special interest to McCluer because the college had a fund for bringing famous speakers to the campus. But how to capture the most famous of all? First he drafted a letter of invitation. Then he went to Washington to consult an old Westminster classmate, Harry Vaughan. Vaughan spirited him into the office of the president, another Missouri acquaintance.[27] Truman read McCluer's letter, approvingly, and penned on the bottom: "This is a wonderful school in my home state. Hope you can do it. I'll introduce you. Best regards. Harry S Truman." Accepting November 8, Churchill observed in a letter that speaking "under your aegis . . . might possibly be advantageous from several points of view."[28] As casually as all this, one of the celebrated events of the gathering Cold War was set in motion.

On the afternoon of March 4 Truman, Churchill, their assistants, and a company of correspondents departed Washington by special train for Fulton. The train had scarcely reached the Maryland state line when Truman asked, "What do you have to do to get a drink on this thing?" Vaughan rang for a waiter, and the president and Churchill settled back at ease.

"When I was a young subaltern in the South African War," Churchill said, eyeing his glass, "the water was not fit to drink. To make it palatable we had to put a bit of whiskey in it. By diligent effort I learned to like it." At a stop along the way Truman put on an engineer's cap and gloves and a red bandanna, climbed into the cab of the diesel locomotive, and sat at the throttle for twenty-five miles. Later he and his poker-playing staff got Churchill into a modest game. In one hand of stud Truman and Churchill were the last in. The final card gave the president a pair of fives showing and the former prime minister a jack high. "Mr. President," Churchill asked, "do two knaves beat your fives?" "If you have 'em they do," Truman replied. Churchill turned over a jack in the hole.[29]

Churchill had arrived in Miami Beach for a vacation in January. On January 29 he wrote Truman: "I need a talk with you a good while before our Fulton date. I have a Message to deliver to your country and to the world and I think it very likely that we shall be in full agreement about it. Under your auspices anything I say will command some attention and there is an opportunity for doing some good to this bewildered, baffled and breathless world.'' Truman replied February 2 that he was headed for a Florida vacation himself and would be happy to talk with Churchill about his speech.[30] While in Florida the former prime minister outlined to Truman, Byrnes, and Leahy what he intended to say at Fulton.

Before the train left Washington March 4 Byrnes had read the text and had given Truman a résumé of its contents. At first Truman decided not to read the text in advance in order to be in the clear when anticipated charges came from Moscow that the British and the Americans were ''ganging up'' on the Soviets. As the train sped through the night toward Missouri, copies were widely distributed to the reporters aboard. Truman changed his mind and read the text, remarking, according to Churchill, that ''it was admirable and would do nothing but good though it would make a stir.'' At the same time Churchill also cabled London, noting a hardening attitude in Truman and Byrnes and applauding the dispatch of the battleship *Missouri* to the Mediterranean.[31]

In the state of Missouri the next day a round of ceremonies preceded the speeches, and when Churchill finally retired to don a scarlet robe, Truman was solicitous for him. ''Harry,'' he said to Vaughan, ''you had better get Mr. Churchill a drink before we go into the gymnasium.'' Fulton was a dry town and Vaughan had trouble finding a pint, but he carried out Truman's instructions just in time. ''General, I'm glad to see you,'' said Churchill, who was about to send shock waves around the world. ''I didn't know whether I was in Fulton, Missouri, or Fulton, Sahara.''[32]

''I know,'' Truman said, introducing the former prime minister to the audience, ''that he will have something constructive to say to the world.''

''From Stettin in the Baltic to Trieste in the Adriatic,'' Churchill rumbled, ''an Iron Curtain has descended across the Continent. Behind that line lie all the capitals of the ancient states of central and eastern Europe. Warsaw, Berlin, Prague, Vienna, Budapest, Belgrade, Bucharest, and Sofia, all these famous cities and their populations around them lie in what I might call the Soviet sphere, and are all subject, in one form or another, not only to Soviet influence but to a very high and in some cases increasing measure of control from Moscow.''

The heart of the speech was a call for a ''fraternal association of the English-speaking peoples,'' stated in terms that made it appear he was proposing a military alliance between the British Empire and the United States to check Soviet expansionism. Churchill did not believe the Soviets wanted war:

What they desire is the fruits of war and the indefinite expansion of their power and doctrines. . . . From what I have seen of our Russian friends and allies during the war, I am convinced that there is nothing they admire so much as strength, and there is nothing for which they have less respect than for weakness, especially military weakness.

Truman was right in predicting a stir. It was all the greater because by escorting Churchill, introducing him, and applauding his speech, the president invited the interpretation that he endorsed the prime minister's remarks, although he wrote to his mother a week later saying that he was not yet ready to do so.[33]

Obviously, however, he was ready to have Stalin hear some strong words of warning about where Soviet conduct might be leading. Privately, administration

leaders were pleased that Churchill had said some things they believed needed saying, although Truman found it prudent to take refuge from the initial reaction of
shock and criticism, particularly from liberals concerned that an Anglo-American
alliance would frustrate the United Nations.

"Mr. President," a reporter asked at a press conference March 8, "your presence on the stage at Fulton . . . has led to some speculation that you endorse the
principles of Mr. Churchill's speech. Would you comment on that?"

"I didn't know what would be in Mr. Churchill's speech," he replied. "This
is a country of free speech. Mr. Churchill had a perfect right to say what he
pleased."[34]

In an interview with *Pravda* March 13 Stalin called it "a dangerous act
calculated to sow the seeds of discord among the Allied Governments. . . . Mr.
Churchill is now in the position of a firebrand of war. And Mr. Churchill is not alone
here."

When reporters asked Truman the next day about Stalin's charges, he declined
to comment, although he said he did not think the situation was as dangerous as
some believed.[35]

Truman seemed to turn hot and cold in his assessment of the degree of danger
involved. Receiving Harriman at a somewhat earlier date to ask him to accept the
post of ambassador to the Court of St. James's, which he did, Truman said, "There
is a very dangerous situation developing in Iran. The Russians are refusing to take
their troops out . . . and this may lead to war."[36]

While Churchill's speech was ahead of American opinion, American opinion
gradually caught up with it as tensions with the Soviet Union increased. "Iron Curtain" became a fixture in American thought and idiom.

One of the intriguing episodes at the time of the trip to Fulton occurred before
Truman ever boarded the train. On that afternoon of March 4 the *Washington
Evening Star* appeared on the streets with its lead story under the headline
GEN. MARSHALL REPORTED SLATED FOR BYRNES JOB. What made the story all the
more engrossing was that it was written by Constantine Brown, a conservative columnist, known to be close to Admiral Leahy. Attributing his information to well informed diplomatic quarters, Brown wrote:

It is an open secret that while Mr. Truman backed Secretary Byrnes on the question of the
agreements signed in Moscow last December, he was not particularly happy about
them. . . .
    According to some of President Truman's close friends, he is determined to put into ef-
fect a new policy which would end all criticism within the United States and abroad that we
are continuing a policy of appeasement.

The story said Byrnes had already acknowledged to Truman that he ought to
resign.

When the train reached St. Louis March 5 Truman told reporters the article did
not contain a word of truth, and the State Department issued a denial that Byrnes
had discussed resignation with Truman. Marshall, of course, was still on his China

mission. After Truman returned to Washington a reporter again asked him about the story. "It's news to me," he replied.[37] Nevertheless speculation continued so that at his next press conference, on the fourteenth he volunteered an opening statement: "I want to make it strong and emphatic, as there still seem to be rumors about that there has been a rift between the Secretary of State and myself, that there is no such rift, never has been one and never will be, I hope." He said that "somebody just wants to tell a big lie."[38]

A month later, on April 16, Brynes, citing a health problem involving myocardial damage, privately submitted his written resignation to Truman, effective July 1. On April 26 Eisenhower, about to leave on a tour of Far Eastern bases, was invited to an unpublicized meeting with the president aboard the *Williamsburg* and was asked by Truman to sound out Marshall on his willingness to accept the post of secretary of state because Byrnes had "stomach trouble."[39] On May 2 Truman remarked to Harold Smith that Byrnes, who had returned to Paris April 23 for a meeting of the foreign ministers, had cried on his shoulder, long distance, the day before. Truman said he did not have any shoulder to cry on.[40] On May 9 Eisenhower met Marshall in Shanghai, and Marshall consented to become secretary of state at the president's pleasure. The public, of course, knew none of this.

What was the meaning of it? While there may have been no "rift" over policy that spring between Truman and Byrnes, as the latter horse-traded in Europe with Molotov and British Foreign Secretary Ernest Bevin over the peace treaties and the German question, a deterioration of the Truman-Byrnes relationship had begun at Christmastime, as Snyder said. Truman's remark to Smith certainly manifested no warmth for Byrnes. Furthermore Truman time and again had expressed to his associates dissatisfaction with the administration of the State Department, nor was he alone in his criticism. Numerous people in Washington shared the view that with Byrnes in Europe most of the time the department was not being managed well. All in all the time seems to have come when Truman was not comfortable with his old and admired Senate friend.

With the difficulties with Truman over the Moscow conference still fresh in mind, Byrnes too may have felt it was time to get out. Anticipating his return to the diplomatic haggling in Europe, he had a physical examination April 12 at the Naval Hospital in Bethesda, Maryland. An electrocardiograph, according to the hospital report, evidenced "added myocardial damage." The report said that "the patient was advised to refrain from excesses of physical exertion and mental strain."[41]

Acheson in his memoirs rather makes light of this "heart murmur" and says that Byrnes submitted his resignation as a hedge against the possibility of another falling out with Truman.[42] On the other hand, the respected Benjamin V. Cohen, counselor of the State Department under Byrnes, recalled that Byrnes was worried about his condition and that, as Byrnes said in his letter to Truman, "The only way I can comply with the advice of the Doctors is to resign."[43] According to Cohen, Byrnes, and Truman talked about prospective successors. Marshall's name came up, and Byrnes expressed his approval.[44] In setting July 1 as the date for his resignation he was allowing time for the Council of Foreign Ministers and the Paris Peace Conference to do their work. But delays occurred, and Byrnes continued in office through 1946.

Meanwhile in Iran the situation went from bad to worse.

When Byrnes had seen Stalin in December, the secretary had warned that unless Stalin gave assurances on troop withdrawals Iran would take its case to the United Nations. However unfortunate for American-Soviet relations, Byrnes said, "we would have to support Iran vigorously."[45] With no assurances forthcoming, Iran filed a complaint in the Security Council January 19, charging Soviet interference in its internal affairs and calling for a United Nations investigation. The Soviets not only denied the charge, but quietly assured the Americans that they would negotiate with Iran. They suggested that the Security Council merely issue a statement endorsing negotiations and asking to be kept informed. The United States was no longer playing the game that way. Firmness against extension of Soviet influence was in the ascendant. The United States introduced a resolution to retain the Iranian complaint on the agenda, with the council to be kept informed by the two sides of the progress of the talks.

Thus the stage was set when March 2— the appointed day for withdrawal of all Soviet troops—arrived. Instead of complying, Moscow announced that while some troops would be removed, others would remain in the north until the situation had been "elucidated." Truman and Byrnes conferred March 4 before the president left for Fulton. Evidently they regarded Soviet tactics as offensive in character without allowing for the possibility that Stalin's actions may have been essentially defensive, aimed at strengthening Soviet security in a neighboring country where the United States already was supplanting British influence.

On March 5 the State Department sent a note to Moscow alleging violation of the Teheran Declaration and saying that the United States "cannot remain indifferent." The note called for immediate withdrawal of all Soviet forces.

That same day, however, the American vice-consul at Tabriz cabled word of Soviet troop movements, reporting to Washington that some five hundred trucks with ammunition and supplies and twenty tanks were being deployed toward Teheran. More startling, two cavalry regiments with artillery, he said, were moving toward the Turkish border.[46] News of Red Army troop movements hit the American headlines, and on March 17 Kennan cabled his opinion that the Soviets would intimidate Iran into installing a regime that would meet their demands.[47] Iran asked that the issue be placed on the Security Council agenda for the meeting in New York March 25. The Soviets insisted on a postponement, but Truman and Byrnes were unwilling.[48]

After a farewell meeting March 23 with Walter Bedell Smith, who was departing for Moscow as the new American ambassador, Truman jotted on his appointment sheet, "Told him to tell Stalin I had always held him to be a man to keep his word. Troop[s] in Iran after Mar 2 upset that theory. Also told him to urge Stalin to come to U.S.A."[49] Iran obviously left Truman in doubt that the Soviets could be trusted to keep their commitments.

In fact by March 25 a Soviet-Iranian settlement was in progress, and as the Security Council met that day Tass announced that barring unforeseen developments, all Soviet troops would be withdrawn within six weeks. In reply to a cabled inquiry from the United Press Stalin confirmed that an agreement had been reached. Nevertheless Soviet troops were still in Iran. Washington was suspicious about the agreement. And the Truman administration was now determined to use the United Nations to bring pressure to halt further Soviet expansion, as it was viewed. In a meeting with former Assistant Secretary of State Adolf A. Berle on the fifteenth Truman had said, according to Berle, that while the Russians did not want to risk a world war, "they would carry on local aggression unless world opinion stopped them. He hoped to do this through the United Nations . . ."[50]

With the American press widely praising what was perceived as stout support of the United Nations, Byrnes dramatized the importance of the Iranian issue by going to New York and sitting on the Security Council in place of Stettinius. In those days the United Nations, still in search of a permanent headquarters, held its meetings at Hunter College in the Bronx. A new age was dawning: the Security Council sessions were carried on television.

On the third day, March 27, the proceedings took a turn that astounded many Americans and created a new wave of popular suspicion about the Soviets. The Soviet representative on the Council, Andrei A. Gromyko, a bleak-looking man who had come to personify his country in the United States that winter, moved to postpone the Iranian question until April 10. The vote went against him, overwhelmingly. He poked his finger in the air, seeking recognition.

"For reasons which I explained clearly enough in our meeting of yesterday and in today's meeting, Mr. Chairman," he said, speaking in Russian, "I, as representative of the Soviet Union, am not able to participate further in the discussions of the Security Council because my proposal has not been accepted by the Council, nor am I able to be present at the meeting of the Council. I am, therefore, leaving the meeting."[51]

When the translation was completed, Gromyko gathered up his papers from the crescent-shaped table, removed his horn-rimmed glasses and walked slowly from the chamber followed by his advisers and, bringing up the rear, a Soviet general. It was still the heyday of American idealism about the United Nations, and Gromyko's exit was a shock, something that set the Soviets apart from the rest of the world. Although the act was a parliamentary maneuver, it gave the impression of the Soviets' turning their back on the United Nations, even threatening it. In other words, a *New York Times* editorial said the next day, "Russia has served notice on the United Nations Organization that unless she gets her way she will paralyze it even at the risk of wrecking it."

Actually the steam was escaping from the Iranian issue. The prospect of a grave international crisis only months after the end of a devastating war was a great deal for the Soviets to contemplate. Within weeks their troops were withdrawn. Azerbaijan ultimately remained part of Iran.

At a time when the Truman administration was groping for a way to make Soviet power back down the outcome encouraged officials to believe that firm resistance—perhaps containment, if anyone had yet thought of the word—was indeed the right course. It seems to have gone unnoticed that Iranian tenacity and diplomatic skills had been major factors in that country's deliverance.[52]

Even as the Iranian crisis had been heating up, the State Department had reopened the question of a $1 billion loan to the Soviet Union, probably hoping, among other things, for concessions from Moscow. While negotiations were getting started, Henry Wallace sent Truman a memorandum March 14, urging "a new approach along economic and trade lines" as a means of improving relations with the Soviets. He wanted to go beyond the immediate matter of a $1 billion loan:

We know that much of the recent Soviet behavior which has caused us concern has been the result of their dire economic needs and of their disturbed sense of security. The events of the past few months have thrown the Soviets back on their pre-1939 fears of "capitalist encirclement" and to their erroneous belief that the Western World, including the U.S.A., is invariably and unanimously hostile.

I think we can disabuse the Soviet mind and strengthen the faith of the Soviets in our sincere devotion to the cause of peace by proving to them that we want to trade with them and to cement our economic relations with them.

Wallace concluded by recommending that Truman send an economic mission to Moscow. Truman ignored the suggestion.[53]

As the loan negoatiations progressed, the United States pressed for a new international economic environment, and for Soviet membership in the World Bank and the International Monetary Fund, which went against the grain in Moscow. Agreement on terms of the loan became impossible. Then in May the Export-Import Bank made what seemed a politically astute loan of $650 million to France to counter Communist influence on the eve of French elections. In the aftermath of the Iranian crisis and new tensions in Germany it would have been awkward for the administration to ask Congress to replenish this money to cover a loan to the Soviets, particularly while the loan to Britain was still being debated. What with one thing and another, therefore, the prospect of a Soviet loan finally evaporated.[54]

In the broader view, two economic systems based on different ideologies were functioning in Europe in the postwar period. The gap became too great to forge ties between them.

Under the wave of developments from December through April, generally speaking, the Truman administration abandoned the idea of making important concessions to the Soviet Union. The domestic political climate destined an end to "appeasement." Although Truman had come to the presidency with no more than the ordinary degree of American suspicion and disapproval of the Soviet Union, a year of rising conflict had left him indignant, mistrustful, and contentious. Such hope as may have been entertained in the closing months of the war that American possession of the atomic bomb would make the Soviets more compliant had proved false.

Truman was steeped in accounts of Soviet intransigence in London and Moscow. He had read tens of thousands of words of reports from American representatives on Allied Control Commissions and from other agencies, depicting Soviet transgressions in Eastern Europe, the Balkans, and Iran. Military and diplomatic reports reaching him in the winter of 1946 presented a picture of a Soviet Union that was powerful, ruthless, and deceitful.[55] When the Council of Foreign Ministers met in Paris late in the spring to arrange for the peace conference an uncompromising Molotov vilified the United States.

A corner was turned in Soviet-American relations that winter and spring. The interaction of events in the United States and the Soviet Union was leading to an increasingly divided world, totally at variance with the dreams and expectations born of the Second World War.

21. *Building on Sand: The Baruch Plan*

W HAT A LIFE!'' Truman said aloud to himself as he stood by his desk waiting for reporters to crowd in for a press conference.[1] The spring of 1946
was another extravagantly complicated period for the Truman administration, another time of dense convergence of domestic and foreign problems. As if
in reflection of his difficulties, the president held up a copy of *Collier's* with an
article called ''Truman's Troubled Year'' to show to callers one day.[2]

Although strikes against United States Steel and General Motors had been
settled, new labor disputes were posing an even greater menace to reconversion. On
March 1 the Brotherhood of Locomotive Engineers and the Brotherhood of Railroad
Trainmen voted a national railroad strike. It was set for March 11, but then held in
abeyance when Truman appointed a fact-finding board. On March 12 the United
Mine Workers Union submitted demands for a new contract with the soft coal mine
operators. As the deadline for a coal strike neared, negotiations between the two
sides were deadlocked.

A long fight over price controls, stretching back into the Roosevelt administration, was also approaching a climax. Even while the war with Japan was still in
progress opposition had developed in Congress to extending the life of the Office of
Price Administration beyond June 30, 1945. Representative Clare E. Hoffman,
Republican, of Michigan, reflected the feelings of many people when he said, ''I'm
sick and tired of OPA.'' Ration coupons, rent control, and price ceilings, along with
the black market, had aroused great hostility to the agency charged with holding the
line against inflation. The business community hated it for its inflexibility, restrictions on profits, and plethora of forms and regulations. Many consumers with savings accumulated during the war complained that price ceilings were causing scarcity of goods they were eager to buy, even if at inflated prices.

Congress did finally vote a year's continuance of the OPA in June 1945, but
then after the war ended two months later the agency was beset by ever greater controversy. The OPA was a stamping ground for liberals, who regarded it as the
defense line between stability and inflation. Conservatives detested it as regimentation in peacetime, a ''socialistic'' obstacle to a free economy. The ending of controls, they argued, would stimulate production and fill the stores with goods, thus
bringing lower prices. By December 1945, Taft was leading the attack, accusing the
OPA of ignoring the needs of small business and of being more interested in curbing
profits than prices.

Although Truman had not given the OPA anything like the kind of support that
Bowles and his fellow liberals had considered important in the fight against infla-

tion, he asked Congress in his 1946 State of the Union message to act promptly to extend the OPA for another full year beyond the expiration date of June 30, 1946. Inflation, he said,

is our greatest immediate domestic problem. . . . Prices throughout the entire economy have been pressing hard against the price ceilings. The prices of real estate . . . are rising rapidly.[3]

Alluding to a problem that would become more and more troublesome, he noted that manufacturers were holding back goods from the market in anticipation of higher prices following removal of controls. The use of this tactic by cattle producers later on was destined to raise severe political problems for the administration.

Truman also reluctantly sided with Bowles against Clinton Anderson and recommended continuance of wartime food subsidies. This was a system under which certain retail food prices were rolled back and producers and processors compensated by government payments. Farmers opposed such subsidies because they felt the system left them at the mercy of Congress and accustomed consumers to artificially low food prices. But unless subsidies were continued, Truman said,

we may find the cost-of-living index for food increased by more than 8 per cent, which in turn would result in more than a 3 per cent increase in the cost of living.[4]

When hearings began in both houses on his request for a one-year extension of the OPA, business groups all over the country met and showered Congress with resolutions calling for an end to controls. Bankers and corporate officials paraded in opposition before the Banking and Currency committees. The United States Chamber of Commerce and the National Association of Manufacturers helped marshal propaganda against extension. Trade organizations testified in support of amendments exempting the products of their members from further price controls. A no less fervent campaign for extension of the OPA was waged by labor, consumer groups, teachers, and civic organizations. A "March of the Housewives" descended on Capitol Hill in April, with women buttonholing legislators to demand continued price protection.

The raucous fight over the OPA, the *New York Times* reported, was reminiscent of the height of pacifist agitation in Washington before Pearl Harbor.

With every passing day it became clearer that Truman would have a political mess on his hands when Congress began trying to accommodate the conflicting interests in enacting legislation early in the summer. Indeed it was a rather large assumption on Truman's part, and on the part of the liberals, that in the United States of America wartime price controls could be extended intact for a second year beyond the end of the war.

While relations with the Soviet Union grew more troubled, demobilization of the armed forces continued, although, for that matter, so did demobilization of the Red Army, although less precipitately. Truman was unable, and unwilling to try. substantially to slow demobilization of American forces; and Stalin needed his soldiers for the farms and factories.[5]

Being unable to check the drain of the wartime forces, Truman was compelled to seek new manpower to meet America's global military commitments. In related matters he also had to deal with the abiding conflict over unification of the armed services, in which the navy remained at the core of the controversy, as well as with a fight over the pending navy budget, which was not directly connected with the unification issue.

To cope with the military manpower shortage he resorted to the distasteful course of continuing the draft in peacetime. In his State of the Union message he said that unless the number of enlistments was adequate he would have to ask Congress to extend the Selective Service Act, due to expire May 16.[6] The number proved inadequate, and he sent up his request, explaining the alternatives in an Army Day speech in Chicago April 6: "Either we shall have to keep our men in foreign lands who, by reason of long service, are justly entitled to come home to their families; or we shall turn our backs upon the enemy before victory is finally assured."[7] Urged by Eisenhower and others as well, Congress extended Selective Service until March 31, 1947. Even though the reduction in military manpower worried the State Department, the United States maintained its strategic superiority through naval and air power; and to strengthen the nuclear arsenal Truman approved atomic bomb tests in the Bikini atoll in the Pacific in July, 1946.

The problem of the navy budget was a particularly troublesome task, the difficulties turning on complex questions of the navy's new role and size and on the larger issue of how much military spending should be reduced in the restoration of a peacetime economy. Truman cut back on all ship construction that was less than 50 percent completed. As a dispute raged in February over navy manpower, he instructed Budget Director Smith to ignore the admirals and hold the line on spending. In vain Forrestal argued with him to reinstate five heavy cruisers.[8] Then, after wrangling over figures with Forrestal and others for hours, Truman discovered that the navy was lobbying on Capitol Hill for $6.5 billion when he had recommended $4.5 billion.

On March 20 Truman angrily told Budget Director Smith that the situation was the worst he had ever encountered, more difficult even than the Ickes-Pauley row. He indicated that he felt offended and believed discipline had been breached. He had told Forrestal so, he said; and added that he would veto any appropriation bill that contained such sums as the navy was asking. In a not very positive way he talked about the possibility of his firing the chief of naval operations, a hero of the Pacific war, Admiral Nimitz—an act which, if done, would have provided the most ornate imaginable companion piece to the later dismissal of General MacArthur.[9] In the end Congress voted essentially the amount Truman had recommended.

Then the problem of the navy's place in a unified defense system began coming to a head. With Truman's approval, the Thomas-Hill-Austin bill was introduced in the Senate in April. Among other things it provided for a single Defense Department, headed by a single secretary, and a single chief of staff, each a feature of Truman's message of December 19. Forrestal told him the new bill was "completely unworkable."[10]

After interminable wrangles all parties set foot on the road to accommodation, long though it was to prove. At new congressional hearings the navy and marines made such a strong stand against the Thomas-Hill-Austin bill that it was unlikely that Congress would force the measure down their throats. In the White House Clark Clifford recognized this, and began to question the proposal for a chief of staff.[11] He talked with Truman about it, and Truman called a meeting of both sides May 13.

He opened the discussion by saying he was not prejudiced toward either service; his goal was a balanced system of defense. He called on Leahy, and the admiral ventured that compromise was possible if the "chief of staff" concept—a dangerous one, he said—were eliminated.

Then the logjam began to break. In a complete turnabout, Truman agreed there was a danger that a chief of staff might arrogate too much power to himself and become a "man on horseback," an opinion widely held in Congress. He said he had finally made up his mind against such a system. This was a decisive victory for Forrestal, confirmed when Truman next called on the secretary of war.

Patterson had been staunchly for the army's plan. He said he still felt that a single department with a single secretary and a single chief of staff would assure the greatest efficiency. Following Truman's lead, however, he said he was not ready to "jump into the ditch and die for the idea" of a chief of staff.[12]

Subsequent meetings between the army and navy produced further agreements, but not on a single Department of Defense. The navy resisted. Truman, however, notified Congress that he stood by his position in favor of such a department.

The president and his secretary of the navy were in a deep conflict. Forrestal called on Truman June 19 and told him he had a hard time overcoming his own misgivings about a single secretary of defense. As he recalled in his diary that day: "I told the President that the Navy had very sincere misgivings and apprehensions about the 'mass play-steam roller' tactics of the Army."

Truman said he intended to see to it that such tactics did not succeed.

Then Forrestal frankly raised the question of whether he could remain in the Truman administration.

"I told the President," he said in his diary, "that my general view of Cabinet members' responsibilities in supporting and securing orderly government was this: that he [*sic*] support policies of his President up to the point where he encounters sincere and *major* disagreement. That he should then ask to withdraw from the Cabinet.

"I remarked parenthetically that I didn't take myself overseriously in this whole matter and that I had no illusions that my resignation, if it occurred, would have had any earth-shaking consequences. I said I was simply trying to avoid following in the footsteps of Mr. Ickes!"[13]

Forrestal's resignation would have been rather earthshaking. In the sultry atmosphere of the debates in Congress it would have threatened to snarl unification legislation. In the midst of the angry controversies that were already swirling over labor troubles in the coal mines and the railroads, as well as over the extension of OPA, the exit of the man who had led the navy through its greatest days would have strained the Truman administration.

Obviously Truman had no intention of letting Forrestal go. While the two were in conflict, they were not in irreconcilable conflict. Forrestal had supported Truman on a strong postwar military establishment and had endorsed Universal Military Training and extension of the draft. Moreover, as Professor Demetrios Caraley, an authority on unification, has noted, Truman could not have rammed unification through Congress or compelled the high uniformed navy officers to like it. He needed Forrestal to persuade Congress and the navy in favor of a form of unification acceptable to the president. Forrestal had a stake, too. He believed some form of unification was inevitable, and he wanted to keep the navy intact.

Rather than rid himself of a subordinate who opposed him in certain areas Truman went through patient negotiations with Forrestal. In an exchange of letters in June he brought the secretary around reluctantly to agreement on a single secretary of defense. In doing so Truman included a number of concessions, allowing the navy to keep certain land-based aviation and agreeing that under the secretary of defense the navy would retain its integrity and that the three services would retain a good deal of autonomy.

In Tokyo MacArthur told Stuart Symington he was amazed at Truman's leniency with Forrestal and Admiral Nimitz. In words full of irony for MacArthur's own future, he said that all Truman would have to do to halt the "sabotage against the Commander-in-Chief" would be to fire one high-ranking official.[14] Forrestal assessed Truman's attitude differently. "To be fair to him," he wrote to General Thomas B. Holcomb, a retired marine officer, "he has exhibited a most extraordinary degree of patience and tolerance and understanding, in addition to which he has acquired a good deal more fundamental knowledge of the Navy. . . . If it had been anyone else but Mr. Truman I think I would have been fired long ago."[15]

Much detail remained to be worked out, and Truman asked that the legislation be held over until Congress returned in 1947.

The American response to cries from abroad for food had fallen short during the winter despite the measures Truman had initiated. Such factors as limited wartime farm production resulting from fear of a surplus, resistance to shorter rations after the war, and consumption of grain by livestock to satisfy a meat-hungry population continued to affect Americans' capacity to help others.

After Attlee's appeal to Truman in January the British prime minister cabled the president again a month later, enumerating sacrifices which the food crisis was calling forth from Britons and asking for still further American help.[16] Thereupon Truman appointed the Famine Emergency Committee, with Herbert Hoover as honorary chairman. The committee was charged by Truman with making plans for "an aggressive voluntary program on the part of private citizens to reduce food consumption in this country."[17]

"Most Americans are eating too much," Truman told a press conference April 17. Replying to a suggestion that Americans voluntarily confine themselves one day each week to a diet similar in caloric content to that of hungry nations in Europe, he said the sacrifice should be made two days a week. "We throw too much away," he observed. "There is enough wasted every day in this country to feed all the starving peoples [during the crisis]."

A reporter then steered Truman to the subject of Herbert H. Lehman, former

Democratic governor of New York, who, upon his recent resignation as director general of the United Nations Relief and Rehabilitation Administration, had criticized the American effort to provide food. Lehman had called for a return to rationing, characterized Hoover and Anderson as shortsighted for opposing it and, on April 16, had accused the government of "faulty planning and unrealistic measures."

"I think Mr. Lehman is very much mistaken," Truman told the reporter.[18] Later he complained to Harold Smith, to quote Smith's undoubtedly bowdlerized version, that Lehman had "sat on his fanny" for years, had botched UNRAA, and was obviously campaigning for the United States Senate nomination in New York. (He won it, but lost to the Republicans in November.)

Publicly, Truman's rationale for not returning to rationing—and no doubt he had a point—was that it would have taken three months to restore it and that that would have been too late for meeting the current crisis.[19] Politically, it would have been most unpopular. A more pertinent question was whether the United States should have ended rationing so quickly while rationing was being continued in other nations with food surpluses.

While Hoover was surveying conditions abroad, Truman appealed to the people on radio April 19 to tighten their belts. "Millions will surely die unless we eat less," he said. "Again I strongly urge all Americans to save bread and to conserve oil and fats."[20]

With rising enthusiasm the Famine Emergency Committee asked Americans to eat 25 percent less wheat, then 50 percent less wheat and 20 percent less fat; and then published thirty-nine ways to conserve food. In the nature of such campaigns, however, Truman's voluntary approach accomplished little. On the contrary, even more wheat was fed to livestock to produce steaks. After six weeks the committee's efforts had fallen so pathetically short of goals that it called for new measures by the government to get grain off the farm at a time when world demand was putting heavy pressure on prices.

The administration acted. On April 19 it announced a bonus of thirty cents a bushel for wheat delivered to it by May 25 and a similar bonus for the first 1.3 billion tons of corn offered before May 11. The results of this program, too, were disappointing. Then, with inevitable inflationary effect, Washington capitulated to the farmers' demands for a twenty-five-cent rise in the ceiling price on corn and a fifteen-cent rise in the ceiling on wheat. The combination of these higher ceilings and the wheat bonus sent the grain flowing to the ships instead of to the cattle and hogs.[21] European agriculture recovered. The emergency gradually receded. In the year ended June 30, 1946, the United States performed the feat of shipping one-sixth of its food supply abroad. "It is no exaggeration to say," wrote the historian, Allen J. Matusow, an expert on the subject, "that American relief shipments in 1945–46 were the salvation of Europe."[22]

Of all the problems being worked on behind the scenes that winter and spring of 1946, doubtless the most difficult was that of international control of atomic energy. As early as January 16 David Lilienthal, the TVA chairman, had noted in his journal:

Saw Acheson . . .

He talked frankly and in detail: Those charged with foreign policy—the Secretary of State [Byrnes] and the President—did not have either the facts nor an understanding of what was involved in the atomic energy issue. . . . Commitments, on paper and in communiques, have been made and are being made . . . without a knowledge of what the hell it is about—literally![23]

In such statements as his Navy Day speech and the joint declaration with Attlee in the fall Truman had committed himself to the goal of international control. In January the United Nations General Assembly had established the United Nations Commission on Atomic Energy to study the problem. The commission was scheduled to hold its first meeting in New York June 14, which gave the Truman administration barely five months in which to prepare a policy. A United States representative, still to be chosen, would sit on the commission. To make policy studies to guide that delegate, Byrnes appointed an elite committee, headed by Under Secretary Acheson. In turn the latter in need of technical advice created a board of consultants under Lilienthal. For weeks the two groups worked on a study that became known as the Acheson-Lilienthal Report, though it was largely the creation of Dr. J. Robert Oppenheimer, wartime director of the Los Alamos laboratory and a member of Lilienthal's board of consultants.[24]

Members of the committee realized that if the plan were to get anywhere it would be necessary to assume the good faith of the Soviet Union. Nevertheless the report was prepared under the shadow of the Ottawa spy ring disclosure and the known hostility in Congress to premature disclosure of American atomic secrets. The committee had been told by Vannevar Bush, one of the Acheson group, that the Soviets had a large army and the United States a relatively small one now and that an early end of the American monopoly on the atomic bomb could give the Soviets a preponderance of power.[25] Above all, the gulf of mistrust between the United States and the Soviet Union was already so deep that neither side was likely to jeopardize its security to take the steps that might be needed to entice the other into an international control agreement.

Still the Acheson-Lilienthal Report proposed an ingenious—and in the American view a generous—plan for international control and one that minimized international inspection and did not depend upon sanctions or punishment for violation. According to Acheson, his committee concluded "that provisions for either 'swift and sure,' or 'condign' punishment for violation of the treaty were very dangerous words that added nothing to a treaty and were almost certain to wreck any possibility of Russian acceptance."[26] But the plan was designed to come into effect in stages. It would have required disclosure of certain Soviet secrets. It would have barred the Soviets from working on a bomb.

The report proposed an international Atomic Development Authority, under the United Nations, that would take over ownership or lease of raw materials needed for atomic energy, operate plants that processed materials for weapons, direct research, and license nuclear activities. All dangerous work would be carried on by the ADA. Thus no individual nation could lawfully make atomic bombs, and that would apply to the Soviet Union. Pending fruition of international control, however, the United States could retain its stockpile. A survey would be made of raw materials, which would involve foreign penetration of the Soviet Union. Also among its facilities the ADA would have plants on Soviet soil, and that too would require freedom of access as a check on possible violations. Realistically, therefore, the plan had little chance of winning Soviet support. The next link in the chain of events diminished even this chance.

When Acheson submitted the report to Byrnes, the secretary told him that he was recommending to Truman the nomination of Bernard Baruch as United States representative to the United Nations Atomic Energy Commission and that Baruch would translate the Acheson-Lilienthal Report into a workable plan. Futilely, Acheson protested the choice. When Lilienthal learned of the decision, he wrote, "I was quite sick." What was needed, he said, was a person "whom the Russians would feel isn't out simply to put them in a hole, not really caring about international cooperation."[27]

In Acheson's and Lilienthal's opinion, shared by others, Baruch was a poseur who had, since the Wilson administration, cultivated an exaggerated reputation as a presidential adviser, using such publicity artifices as making his "office" on a park bench across from the White House.* They regarded him as vain and shallow, a man who had cleverly made a fortune in the stock market and just as cleverly built political influence by contributing to the campaigns of both Democratic and Republican candidates for the House and Senate. On the other hand, the press (especially in New York) and conservatives in Congress (Vandenberg, notably) considered Baruch charming, wise, and sound in the most conventional sense, a patriot, elder statesman, sturdy oak. Such, certainly, was the image the public had of this stately-looking, white-haired man of seventy-five with pince-nez and a hearing aid. Moreover friends as shrewd as Marshall, Forrestal, and Robert Lovett seemed to value his advice.

Born in South Carolina, he had, upon acquiring his fortune, purchased as his "Garden of Eden" a 12,000-acre estate on his native soil, called Hobcaw Barony. He became a friend of South Carolina's rising young political star, Jimmie Byrnes. In 1942 when Byrnes became director of war mobilization, he appointed Baruch, who had been chairman of the War Industries Board in the First World War, special adviser.

Now, with an eye to winning support in the Senate for the Acheson-Lilienthal plan Byrnes recommended him for the atomic energy post. Truman also saw political advantages in the appointment. Baruch's exalted reputation would inspire public confidence in the policy proposed by the administration in the United Nations. Moreover the Senate was still debating the McMahon bill on domestic atomic energy control, and Truman felt Baruch's prestige among the Senators might dispel some of the opposition.[28] Problems developed, however, after Acheson explained his report to the Joint Congressional Committee on Atomic Energy in executive session, and the details were leaked to the press, creating the impression that the report was the ultimate American plan. Thus Baruch feared that he would be merely a

---

* To this day a historic marker designates the bench in Lafayette Park as the "Bernard Baruch Bench of Inspiration."

"messenger boy" and not the big cheese who would draw up the historic proposal.[29]

Truman humored him and assured him that the Acheson-Lilienthal Report was merely a working paper. Byrnes was then enlisted in the task of repairing Baruch's ego. In a coaxing letter April 29 to "Dear B. M." (addressing him by his first two initials) the secretary noted that the president determines policy. "However, as a practical matter, I know that the President will ask for my views . . . and I, in turn, will ask for your views." Byrnes believed too that Truman would allow Baruch the honor of unveiling the final American plan.[30]

This Baruch did June 14 at the high-water mark of American dilettantism about the United Nations. Fashionable women descended on Hunter College in the Bronx as if it were opening night at the Metropolitan Opera, and heard in awe Mr. Baruch's introductory line (composed by Herbert Bayard Swope, then a member of the New York State Racing Commission): "We are here to make a choice between the quick and the dead."[31]

The Baruch Plan adopted the concept of the Atomic Development Authority contained in the Acheson-Lilienthal Report. However, two critical new points were added. Baruch favored appropriate punishment for any nation that violated the control agreement. With the Soviet Union in mind, he also proposed that no member could veto such punishment. Whereas the Acheson-Lilienthal Report sought only to establish control of atomic energy to prevent clandestine production, leaving it to other nations to act in self-protection in case of a violation by one nation, the Baruch Plan included methods for invoking sanctions against a violator. Acheson was opposed. He feared that the Soviets would perceive this as an attempt by the United States to turn the United Nations into an alliance against Moscow.[32]

Baruch was adamant. According to Lilienthal, he told Truman that unless the ban on a veto remained, he would resign.[33] In the final analysis, Baruch argued at a meeting with Truman June 7, the only penalty that could be invoked against a nation having violated the control agreement was war. Truman agreed, Baruch recalled. Truman went on to cite the example of the Manchurian crisis of 1931–32 when, as secretary of state, Stimson informed Japan that the United States would not recognize any development that impaired American treaty rights or the Open Door policy. If the other nations had stood behind the so-called Stimson Doctrine, Truman suggested, the Second World War would not have occurred. He signed his approval of the Baruch Plan.[34]

Baruch's proposal chilled the Soviets, who were developing their own bomb. It defies the imagination to think who could have fashioned a plan that would have been acceptable to the Seventy-ninth Congress and Joseph Stalin. Baruch cemented the impasse fairly well, however, with the vulnerable proposals for sanctions and suspension of the veto. The issue was debated in the United Nations Atomic Energy Commission for months, fruitlessly. The American press played up the angle that the United States was offering to give up its atomic bombs and reveal its nuclear technology upon adoption of the international controls proposed by Baruch. To Americans, including their president, this seemed a noble and plausible way to avert a nuclear war, and the Soviets won no good will in the United States for their contrary view.

The McMahon bill for domestic control of atomic energy fared better, finally. The shock occasioned by the Ottawa spy ring did, it is true, alter the thinking of many persons about total exclusion of the military from atomic energy matters. Although he favored civilian control, Vandenberg in particlar came to believe that the army should have power of review on military aspects of atomic energy. He introduced an amendment to the bill creating a Military Liaison Committee to advise the civilian Atomic Energy Commission. In case of disagreement the liaison committee could appeal to the president, who would have the final word.* The amendment passed, but the principle of civilian control remained intact. The work of many hands, notably McMahon's, the Atomic Energy Act of 1946 was a creditable landmark in the Truman administration.

* As of March 1977, no such appeal had been made.

22. *One Way to Handle a Rail Strike*

FOR THE AMERICAN PEOPLE AND, of course, for the president the labor disputes that came to a head in April in the coal mines and on the railroads were exasperating in the extreme because of their direct effect on the daily life of the country. Because in the end he let his exasperation get the better of him, the situation held undreamed-of pitfalls for Truman.

Negotiations having failed, 400,000 soft-coal miners went on strike April 1. Since coal was then America's major source of energy, steel production tumbled; automobile production slowed; thousands of workers were laid off; railroad service, already facing a complete shutdown by the engineers and trainmen, was ordered cut; and wartime dimouts were reintroduced in twenty-two states to conserve dwindling supplies of coal. Even the White House lights were dimmed; one morning the president's office was so dark Truman suggested he might have to move his desk to the lawn. New Jersey declared a state of emergency.

On April 10 the White House announced the recommendations of the fact-finding board Truman had appointed in March to try to avert a railroad strike. The board proposed a wage increase of 16 cents an hour; this was 2½ cents less than the new pattern, but the drop was offset by suggested changes in working rules, which would have augmented the workers' pay. Eighteen of the railroad unions accepted. But on April 25 the two operating unions—the Brotherhood of Locomotive Engineers under Alvanley Johnston and the Brotherhood of Railroad Trainmen under Alexander F. Whitney—rejected the offer. They set May 18 as the new date for a rail strike.

Because of the cumulative effect of the coal strike, the Office of Defense Transportation ordered an embargo on freight shipments, except food, fuel, and essential items, and a 25 percent cut in passenger service on coal-burning trains, effective May 15. Then after another attempt to settle the coal strike failed the reduction in service was extended to 50 percent.

United States Steel curtailed its operations, and on May 4 Truman released an OWMR report calling the coal strike a "national disaster." Although the strike was then in its thirty-fourth day, the people, the report said, "have barely begun to feel the impact." The Railway Express Agency embargoed shipment of all except essential commodities as of May 10. On May 8 the Civilian Production Administration issued orders on conservation of coal that affected consumption of electricity and gas in the East. The Association of American Railroads reported that about two thousand passenger trains would be discontinued by the end of the week.

In the coal negotiations Lewis had not been willing to settle for 18½ cents an hour. The crux of the dispute was that he also insisted upon—and the operators rejected—a royalty of 10 cents on each ton of coal mined, the proceeds to go into a miners' welfare and pension fund. A reporter asked Truman May 9 about his opinion of the royalty.

"I haven't gone into that phase of the situation," he replied, "but I think the Wagner Labor Relations Act provides against that very thing."

"What does Truman know about the legality of anything?" Lewis was reported to have said.[1]

With the public resentful over the proliferation of strikes in general and, in particular, over the longtime belligerency of John L. Lewis in his battles for a better lot for the coal miners, Congress was in a mood to curb labor "abuses" and redress what was widely considered the prolabor bias of the Wagner Act.

After Truman had asked Congress in December to legislate a cooling-off period and fact-finding procedures, conservatives on the House Rules Committee substituted a much stronger antistrike bill introduced by Representative Francis H. Case, Republican, of South Dakota. Providing for a thirty-day cooling-off period before strikes could begin, the measure permitted injunctions against certain union activities. Previously injunctions had been restricted by the Norris-LaGuardia Act. Furthermore the Case bill made unions and management liable to suits for breach of labor contracts and prohibited organized boycotts to force employers to come to terms in bargaining or jurisdictional disputes.

Labor and the liberals opposed the bill. So did the administration, although Truman had written to Wallace in February that unions had become adult with legal recognition and ought to assume responsibility accordingly.[2] Nevertheless the House passed the Case bill February 7 and sent it to the Senate, where the Education and Labor Committee softened some of the provisions. Now when the bill reached the Senate floor in the midst of the coal and rail disputes, however, stronger amendments were voted.

As General Motors and Chrysler announced shutdowns and the use of electricity in Chicago was ordered cut by 50 percent, Truman called both sides in the coal strike to the White House May 10 and demanded a settlement by May 15. With a familiar tactic, however, Lewis had beaten him to the draw by ordering the miners back to work May 13 for a twelve-day truce, at the same time lowering his demand for a royalty from 10 cents to 7 cents a ton. The operators rejected this figure, too. In a letter on the thirteenth to Charles Sawyer, former United States ambassador to Belgium, Truman said:

It is difficult for me to understand why the necessity for two such men as Molotov and John Lewis on earth at the same time as principal contenders for top rating as walking images of Satan. Of course, I have to deal with both of them and either one would be a load, but two of them are almost beyond belief when it comes to getting things done.[3]

On May 15 Truman turned his attention to the rail dispute. He set aside the recommendations of the fact-finding board and offered the brotherhoods 18½ cents an hour, with rules changes postponed for a year. The unions took the offer under consideration.

The next day the president was back in the middle of the coal strike, conferring with Lewis and Charles O'Neill, representing the mine operators. Before noon he called in reporters and said: "They told me that after further consultation with their committees last night they had come to the conclusion that the negotiations . . . had completely broken down and that further negotiations would be useless. I therefore proposed arbitration. I asked them to consider this proposal carefully and report back to me with their decision at 5:30 o'clock this afternoon."[4]

At that hour both sides rejected his proposal, notifying him that the coal negotiations had collapsed.

And now the May 18 deadline for the railroad strike bore down upon him.

"If they don't settle this strike before the deadline," Truman was asked at his press conference May 16, "do you plan to seize them?"

"Certainly."[5]

On May 17 he called both sides to that dispute to the White House. The union leaders, Johnston and Whitney, told him the negotiations were deadlocked. Thereupon in their presence Truman signed an executive order directing the Office of Defense Transportation to seize and operate the railroads at 4 P.M. on the eighteenth. He also appealed to the railroad workers to remain on the job when the government took over. He asked, too, that negotiations continue, but Whitney and Johnston boarded a train for Cleveland, headquarters of the two brotherhoods.

On May 18, one hour before government seizure was to take effect, Truman telephoned Whitney and Johnston. He told them he was confident that further progress could be made by negotiation and asked them to delay the strike five days—until May 23. Evidently taking this as a hint that a higher offer would be forthcoming, Whitney and Johnston called Truman back at 3:34 P.M. and agreed to the postponement. They said they would return to Washington the next day to resume negotiations. Seven minutes before the government was to take possession, Truman called a press conference and announced the agreement to delay.[6]

Then back to the coal strike. On May 21, with Lewis's truce nearing an end, with negotiations still stalled and the country starved for coal, Truman ordered Secretary of the Interior Krug to seize the mines.

Then to the railroad dispute. While Truman was dealing with the coal situation on the twenty first, John Steelman, his labor troubleshooter in the White House, was meeting with the brotherhoods and the railroads. Finally, the White House issued a statement: "No conclusive results were achieved today toward averting a rail strike now set for 4 P.M. Thursday [May 23]." Tempers were flaring all over Washington. Things had come to such a pass that in the Senate debate on the Case bill that day the usually courtly Senator Harry F. Byrd, Democrat of Virginia, referred to Senator Claude R. Pepper, Democrat of Florida, as a skunk.

On May 22 the Brotherhood of Railroad Trainmen and the Brotherhood of Railroad Engineers rejected the 18½ cents an hour offer Truman had made on the fifteenth, although the other rail unions accepted. The brotherhoods called the offer less favorable than the recommendation of the fact-finding board. Johnston and Whitney checked out of their hotel and again headed for Union Station to return to Cleveland. Before they boarded the train Steelman reached them and told them the president wanted them to remain in Washington. The White House got the hotel to give them back their rooms.

The country was almost in a state of siege over the impending railroad strike. When May 23 dawned the Post Office Department prepared a partial embargo on mail. The banking of blast furnaces began in Pittsburgh. City commuters were warned to quit work early and go home before the trains stopped at four o'clock. In the face of the worst transportation crisis in American history, exasperation overflowed. "The Administration itself has played a weak and spineless role in this affair," cried the *New York Times*. "President Truman allowed the decision of his fact-finding board to be rejected without throwing his support behind the decision, without even making a clear public statement pointing out what rejection would mean."

The White House desperately kept the two sides negotiating around the cabinet table during the day, but to no avail. Johnston and Whitney wrote a curt note to the president of the United States, simply addressing him as "Sir" and telling him that his offer was still inadequate. The recommended rules changes, deferred in his May 15 proposal, were the most critical issue, they said, adding that 18½ cents an hour would amount to only a 12 percent increase in pay. The two union presidents lectured Truman: "We have told you many times that the present agitation among the men . . . is extremely serious and that their demands could not be abandoned or disregarded, and, therefore, your offer is unacceptable."[7]

As four o'clock approached, trains moved only to terminal points and then were abandoned by their crews. Despite the warnings, thousands of commuters at Grand Central and Pennsylvania Station in New York and at other terminals around the country had arrived too late for transportation home. Other thousands of passengers on through trains were stranded throughout the United States. Ignoring the appeal that Truman had made when he seized the railroads May 17, the engineers and trainmen refused to work for the government. A quarter of a million of them walked off the job that afternoon. On top of that, 164,000 soft-coal miners were refusing to work in the coal mines that had been seized by the government. The Associated Press reported a total of 960,000 persons idled by strikes.

Harry Truman went off the rails.

The long, rough road of reconversion had jolted his political prestige badly. Now simultaneous disastrous strikes had raised questions about his ability to govern. He was bursting with resentment against the unions.

In one year he had seized the coal mines twice; he had seized the railroads; he had seized 134 meat-packing plants; he had seized ninety-one tugboats; he had seized the facilities of twenty-six oil producing and refining companies; he had seized the Great Lakes Towing Company. And all he had on his hands now was disaster. He had grappled with huge strikes against General Motors and United States Steel. He had proposed labor legislation only to see Congress ignore it. However unrealistically, he had felt double-crossed by Murray and other labor leaders that there should have been any strikes at all after he had agreed to relax wage controls. He was in a rage about Johnston and Whitney, although they had supported him in his senatorial campaign in 1940 and had backed him for the vice-presidential nomination. Long after the railroad strike he told Jonathan Daniels that early in the negotiations he had admonished the two leaders, "If you think I'm going to sit here and let you tie up this country, you're crazy as hell."[8]

"Truman thought Whitney and Johnston were completely intransigent," Clark Clifford recalled.[9]

Truman balked at strikes against the government. "I don't think it is legal or ever will be," he had said at his press conference May 2. "Whenever [strikes against the government are legal] the government will cease to exist."[10]

On May 24 the railroads were almost totally shut down. Truman had an idea: if the men who operate the trains refuse to work, draft them into the army and order them to duty on the locomotives, coaches, and cabooses. If someone else suggested this idea to him, the evidence has not survived.[11] He met with the cabinet at 10 A.M. and discussed the crisis in preparation for two messages he was planning to deliver. The first was a broadcast to the American people that same night. The other was a special message he would read to a joint session of Congress at 4 P.M. the next day. Attorney General Clark sent Truman a memorandum saying:

Any language that might leave the inference that the Draft Act or any Constitutional or other statutory powers of the President, or any threat to individual liberty, or to draft persons or groups, should not be used. The Draft Act does not permit the induction of occupational groups and it is doubtful whether constitutional powers of the President would include the right to draft individuals for national purposes.[12]

Secretary of War Patterson suggested in a memorandum that Truman call the walkout a strike against the government and declare that unless union members had returned to work by 4 P.M. May 25 the army would operate the trains.[13]

Meanwhile Truman plunged ahead with a longhand speech draft of his own, which stands, surely, as one of the astonishing documents in the history of the presidency. He began by saying that he would, under his constitutional powers, declare a national emergency and "call for volunteers to support the Constitution." The nature and purpose of the volunteers became clearer when, after a paean to American military and industrial feats in the war, he continued:

At home those of us who had the country's welfare at heart worked day and night. But some people worked neither day nor night and some tried to sabotage the war effort entirely. No one knows that better than I. John Lewis called two strikes in War Time to satisfy his ego. Two strikes which were worse than bullets in the back to our soldiers. The rail workers did exactly the same thing. They all were receiving from four to forty times what the man who was facing the enemy fire on the front was receiving. The effete union leaders receive from five to ten times the net salary of your president.

Now these same union leaders on V.J. day told your president that they would cooperate 100% with him to reconvert to peace time production. They all lied to him.

First came the threatened Automobile strike. Your President asked for legislation to cool off and consider the situation. A weak-kneed Congress didn't have the intestinal fortitude to pass the bill.

Mr. Murray and his Communist friends had a conniption fit and Congress had labor jitters. Nothing happened.

Then came the electrical workers strike, the steel strike the coal strike and now the rail tie up. Every single one of the strikers and their demagog leaders have been living in luxury, working when they pleased. . . .

I am tired of government's being flouted, vilified and now I want you men who are my comrades in arms you men who fought the battles to save the nation just as I did twenty-five years ago to come along with me and eliminate the Lewises, the Whitneys the Johnstons, the Communist Bridges* and the Russian Senators and Representatives and really make this a government of by and for the people. I think no more of the Wall Street crowd than I do of Lewis and Whitney.

Lets give the country back to the people. Lets put transportation and production back to work, hang a few traitors make our own country safe for democracy, tell Russia where to get off and make the United Nations work. Come on boys lets do the job.[14]

This frontier diatribe could be interpreted (as indeed it has been by some critics since the document was disclosed in 1966) as a hysterical and rightist presidential call to war veterans to form vigilante mobs against union leaders and supposed Communists.[15] No doubt at the height of his anger at the unions Truman derived ferocious satisfaction from writing it. Once he had let off steam, however, he allowed Clifford, Ross, and Rosenman (who had come from New York to assist Truman in the crisis) to sit down quietly and prepare a speech free from hysteria. Even so it was a tough talk.

When Truman went on radio at 10 P.M. on the twenty-fourth he tore into Johnston and Whitney for having rejected an "eminently fair" wage offer and placed their own interest above that of the country's, inflicting cruel hardships at home and abroad. Continuing:

I am a friend of labor. You men of labor who are familiar with my record in the United States Senate know that I have been a consistent advocate of the rights of labor and of the improvement of labor's position. I have opposed and will continue to oppose unfair restrictions upon the activities of labor organizations and upon the right of employees to organize and bargain collectively. . . .

[But] this is no contest between labor and management. This is a contest between a small group of men and their government.[16]

In line with Patterson's memorandum he announced that unless enough workers had returned to operate the trains by 4 P.M. the next day, the twenty-fifth, he would turn the task over to the army. Nothing was said in the speech about drafting the strikers. The decision had been made, however. Assistant Solicitor General George T. Washington, Tom Clark, George Allen, and Charles S. Murphy of the Office of Legislative Counsel in the Senate worked much of the night on legislation to be introduced in Congress the next day to authorize a draft.[17] The element of bluff, of frightening the brotherhoods into ending the strike by the mere mention of a draft, was surely a large part of Truman's tactic.

Saturday, May 25, was an uproarious day in Washington. It was, for one thing, the day when Lewis's truce in the coal strike came to an end. He and Krug, who was operating the mines for the government, could not agree on terms for extending the truce. The miners who were still working quit in the absence of a contract.

Overshadowing this, of course, was the continuing paralysis of the railroads. In midmorning Ross announced that Truman had ordered the government to stop mediating. Meanwhile Johnston and Whitney sent Truman a letter deploring the im-

---

* Harry R. Bridges, president of the International Longshoreman's Association and West Coast director of the CIO, who was accused of having been a Communist.

pression his broadcast had conveyed that the strikers would not work for the government. The brotherhoods, according to the two leaders, were willing to negotiate a temporary agreement for the duration of federal operation of the railroads, if Truman would approve a wage increase of 18½ cents an hour or $1.48 a day, with certain provisions for rules changes.[18] If the seeds of a settlement were here, they fell on barren ground, for Truman was thrusting ahead, single-mindedly, with his message to be delivered to Congress at four o'clock. He did not even read the letter.

As the message took shape, with Truman doing a lot of the writing, Rosenman among others thought he was going too far, but Truman insisted that it be "hardhitting."[19] Meanwhile, despite Ross's announcement about the end of mediation, Steelman went to see Whitney and Johnston at their suite in the Statler Hotel.[20] At three o'clock he called the White House with the news that a settlement might be reached by the time the president was to begin addressing Congress at four o'clock. Truman was not in his office at the moment, but Ross, Clifford and some of the others hastened to draft an alternate first page of the speech for Truman to read if the strike were settled. At 3:30, ten minutes before Truman was due to depart for the Capitol, the White House called Steelman at the Statler to check on the situation, but could not reach him. Five minutes later he called Connelly back and reported no settlement yet. The call was switched around to different members of the staff, and finally Clifford got on the line and asked Steelman, if a settlement were reached in time, to call him at the office of Leslie Biffle, secretary of the Senate, so word could be conveyed to Truman at the Capitol. The president was now five minutes late in leaving, and Ross and Clifford had to rush to catch his car.

With the president on his way, with the country in a near state of siege and with antiunion sentiment boiling in Congress, Whitney and Johnston were under geological pressure to end the strike. At about the time Truman reached Rayburn's office at 3:55 they told Steelman they would settle on Truman's terms—18½ cents an hour. Steelman, however, was unwilling to notify the president on the basis of an oral agreement. He insisted that it be put in writing, typed and signed.[21] While Johnston and Whitney were writing out their terms Truman entered the House chamber at 4:03, unsmiling, to receive a hero's welcome. The joint session gave him his greatest ovation since becoming president. At about this same moment Clifford went to an anteroom off the House floor and called Steelman, but could not reach him. Whitney and Johnston did not have a stenographer with them. When the agreement was drafted, therefore, they and Steelman took an elevator downstairs to the hotel manager's office to get the document typed. Clifford called the telephone supervisor at the Statler to enlist her help in finding Steelman. He waited in the anteroom for Steelman to call.

Meanwhile Truman had begun to speak and was holding Congress rapt with a stark description of the strike and an attack on the "obstinate arrogance" of Whitney and Johnston.[22] He asked for emergency legislation empowering the president to deal with strikes in "those few" industries in which an emergency could affect the national economy.

The terms proposed were stiff. When the government had seized such an industry and the employees refused a presidential request to remain at work or return to work, the government could proceed against the leader of the union by injunction, perhaps the device most hated and feared by labor. The injunctive proceedings could be brought against the union leader to forbid him to encourage or incite his members to leave work or refuse to return to work. He would be subject to contempt proceedings for failure to obey any court order that might be issued. Moreover, workers who without good cause persisted in striking against the government could be deprived of their seniority rights. Truman also proposed criminal penalties against union leaders and employers who violated the provisions of the act.

As Truman was explaining the terms, Clifford's telephone rang. Steelman was calling.

"We have reached an understanding!" he said. "The strike is broken! The men are going back!"[23]

Clifford scribbled this down on red paper and handed it to Biffle. Biffle hurried to the House chamber just as Truman was delivering his climactic passage: "As a part of this temporary emergency legislation, I request the Congress immediately to authorize the President to draft into the Armed Forces of the United States all workers who are on strike against their government." Congress applauded. When the lines had been spoken, Biffle stepped up to the rostrum and handed Truman Clifford's note.

"Word has just been received," Truman told Congress, "that the railroad strike has been settled, on terms proposed by the President!"

Congress was ecstatic and let the world know it with whoops and cheers. Having already read three quarters of his speech, Truman went ahead and finished it, asking for early action by Congress.

Both houses of Congress turned to the question immediately. In the debate in the House, Representative William J. Green, Jr., Democrat, of Pennsylvania, observed: "President Roosevelt went all through this war without requesting any legislation as drastic as this." Left-wing Democrats, like De Lacy of Washington, attacked the bill on the grounds that it nullified the provisions of the Norris-LaGuardia act and raised the threat of military action against labor. A more interesting phenomenon was the way in which moderate Republicans were galvanized by the strike. Typifying their viewpoint was Representative Sherman Adams of New Hampshire, who was destined to be a power in the conservative Eisenhower administration and who told the House:

It is unfortunate that the results of this paralysis demands such prompt and vigorous action by the President and the Congress. It is to be regretted that conditions are so desperate that the legislation now before this body must be thus so hastily considered and enacted. However, the conditions confronting the country have left the President no alternative nor do they leave us here any choice but to accept his recommendations promptly and vigorously.[24]

After having debated for less than two hours, the House passed the bill, 306 to 13.

In the Senate, meanwhile, Alben Barkley, the Democratic floor leader, asked for the unanimous consent required for consideration of the bill, intending that it be voted on that night without first being referred to a committee.

"I object," Taft said.

That was, in effect, the end of Truman's proposal to draft strikers.

In a brief discussion that followed Taft argued that the bill no longer was essential since the strikers had agreed to return to work. Furthermore Senator Sheridan Downey, Democrat, of California, having looked at the fine print, said that the bill also would permit the drafting of corporation executives who might be found responsible for work stoppages in an essential industry seized by the government.

"I think," he said, "we should pause to ask how this law will be regarded in the nation—a law so harsh and stern that in the hands of a bad President it might become an instrument of tyranny. Oh, yes, I know that President Truman is one of the kindest and most patient of men. But that does not allay my fears."

"It seems to me," Taft said, "that it violates every principle of American jurisprudence."

"I venture with all kindliness to predict, Mr. President," said Pepper, "that the President of the United States has been imposed upon by his counselors and that he will live to see the day when he will regret that he made to this Congress the recommendation for the passage of this measure."

The galleries applauded. Then, with Taft having sidetracked the Truman legislation, the Senate proceeded to pass, 49 to 29, the Case bill—opposed by the administration—which had by now been toughened by new amendments. Among other things, the bill prohibited establishment of health and welfare funds paid for by employers but administered by unions and extended the cooling-off period before a strike to sixty days.

The next day, May 26, 1,170 representatives of CIO unions met in New York and, stung by Truman's message, cheered an attack on him as "the No. 1 strikebreaker of the American bankers and railroads." The union members pledged vengeance at the polls. On May 27 the American Labor Party, then a power in New York State, telegraphed Truman:

Unless you make a concerted effort to undo the damage to labor by your anti-labor address to the Congress the American Labor Party must consider withdrawing support from the Democratic Party candidates.

At Truman's direction Connelly wired back:

He feels that the public welfare of all the people comes before any desire on his part for party support. His position in the rail emergency or any similar one will be exactly the same. The President is not easily intimidated.[25]

Liberals were in shock. Sidney Hillman, near death, publicly attacked Truman for the first time. Ickes was heard from, charging that Truman had "opened the door for the striking down of much social legislation enacted under Roosevelt." Helen Fuller, writing in the *Nation,* said that Truman had "killed any chance of his being elected President in 1948" in the opinion of labor and liberal leaders. David Dubinsky, president of the International Ladies Garment Workers Union, called for a labor-based third party.[26] On May 27 Mrs. Roosevelt wrote Truman a motherly letter:

. . . I hope you realize that there must not be any slip, because of the difficulties of our peace-time situation, into a military way of thinking. . . . I have seen my husband receive much advice from his military advisers and succumb to it every now and then, but the people as a whole do not like it. . . . I hope now that your anxiety is somewhat lessened, you will not insist upon a peace time draft into the army of strikers. That seems to me a dangerous precedent.[27]

Truman admired Eleanor Roosevelt for her achievements, but considered her, as Tom Clark recalled, "something of a gadabout." Or, as Truman remarked to Harold Smith two days after Mrs. Roosevelt's letter, she was a great woman, but she did aggravate him at times.[28]

In Washington A. F. Whitney was quoted as having said that the Brotherhood of Railroad Trainmen would use the entire $47 million in its treasury (he later insisted that he had mentioned a figure of only $2.5 million) to defeat Truman, if he should seek reelection. He accused the president of a "double-cross" and afterward revealed that he had hired an investigator to scrutinize "Pendergast politics" for information to be used against Truman.

Whitney possessed no monopoly on investigations. Several days later J. Edgar Hoover had some things to tell Truman about Whitney. In a letter delivered by special messenger to General Vaughan, Hoover said:

I wanted to inform the President and you of the following information which indicates that Mr. A. F. Whitney, national head of the Brotherhood of Trainmen in Cleveland, is contributing $500 to fight the President's proposed labor legislation and that in this regard Mr. Whitney is utilizing the services of a member of the Communist Party.

There followed, in Hoover's characteristic cloak-and-dagger style, an account of how, in collaboration with rail union officers, a Communist party official in Buffalo, Leo Levison, had prepared a newspaper advertisement apparently hostile to Truman's labor policies. Hoover also related how Levison, prior to publication, had read the advertisement to Whitney and Johnston over the telephone from the Communist party headquarters in Buffalo. The two union officials approved the advertising copy, according to Hoover; and Whitney was so enthusiastic he promised to send Levison $500 for the cost of the advertisement and for a proposed radio broadcast attacking Truman's labor policy. But then Hoover spoiled his own story by adding: "According to the reliable and confidential source there is no indication that either Mr. Whitney or Mr. Johnston were aware of the fact that Leo Levison is a Communist Party member."[29]

At the cabinet luncheon May 27 Truman was sardonic about the senators who had spoken against his bill. Pepper, he said was an opportunist whose only motive was publicity. Downey was a synthetic liberal—only a week earlier, Truman said, he had got in touch with the White House to demand vigorous action on the strikes. Talk turned to Truman's proposal for the draft of strikers.

"Well, if the Senate changes it on him, he doesn't need to feel too badly," Wallace said, and could tell by Truman's grin that he would not have felt badly at all.[30]

The Senate eventually removed the draft provision, 70 to 13, through an amendment offered by Senator Robert F. Wagner, Democrat, of New York, sponsor of the Wagner Act. A much-amended version of Truman's legislation finally was passed, 61 to 20, and sent to the House where interest in it had vanished. The bill never went to conference and died with the end of the session.

Truman had one avenue still open to him to avert a complete rupture with labor. That was a veto of the Case bill. The White House was deluged with messages sent to influence his decision. The chairman of the board of the National Association of Manufacturers and the presidents of General Electric, the United States Chamber of Commerce, and the Southern States Industrial Council bombarded him with appeals to sign the bill. The National Grange and the American Farm Bureau echoed the call. Philip Murray and Sidney Hillman and local union leaders from around the country appealed desperately for a veto. The presidential advisers were divided. Wallace, Clark, Krug, and Schwellenbach were opposed to the bill. Snyder urged that it be approved on its merits.[31] On June 11 Truman vetoed it, incorporating in his message some suggestions from Wallace.[32] In a tone entirely different from that of his address to Congress May 25 he said that the Case bill would not contribute to prevention of strikes.[33] The House sustained his veto by a margin of five votes. In a friendly letter to Hillman about the veto Truman said:

It has been the policy of some labor leaders to throw bricks and bark at their best friend at every opportunity. I have never seen any of them come forward to defend the President when he is right which has been, in my opinion, most of the time.[34]

While the veto had been upheld, the closeness of the vote encouraged Taft and opened the door to the thunderous debate on the Taft-Hartley bill in the next session.

The brouhaha over the railroad strike overshadowed the difficulties the administration had in settling the coal strike, which had resumed with the end of Lewis's truce May 25. It was not until the twenty-ninth that Lewis signed a contract in the White House, and then on terms highly satisfactory to his union. In addition to 18½ cents an hour, the miners won $100 in vacation pay, a guaranteed work week of five nine-hour days with overtime pay after the seventh hour, and enforcement of a revised Federal Mine Safety Code. Above all, it won a welfare and retirement fund to be financed by a royalty of 5 cents on every ton of coal mined, adding a new element to the future of collective bargaining in the United States. In time health care became a feature of union contracts in many industries.

A week later anthracite miners received almost identical terms. Two weeks after that the price of soft coal rose 40½ cents a ton, anthracite 91 cents a ton.[35] The cost of living was going up and up.

But at last Truman had John L. Lewis off his back. Or so it seemed. Within months the agreement was to blow sky-high and so—with surprising results—was Truman.

23. *The Firing of Henry Wallace*

———

B Y MIDSUMMER OF 1946 major differences among the Great Powers growing out of the war had turned into enduring conflicts. Truman said at a meeting with Clifford and others July 12 that he was tired of being pushed around by the Russians, "here a little, there a little," and that it was time to stand up to the Kremlin.[1] While he and his senior advisers did not think war with the Soviet Union was in prospect nor were they preparing for war, ambivalent talk was being heard in Washington about just such a possibility. Felix Belair of the *New York Times* told Wallace that at a gathering aboard the *Williamsburg* Truman had assured some reporters, as Wallace recorded in his diary June 25, the United States could lick the Russians.

In talking with Wallace July 23, however, Truman said he was prepared to be patient with the Russians because he felt they had come a long way in a mere twenty-five years. He hoped that before too many more years had passed the Soviet Union would be a genuine democracy. Yet within an hour Wallace was surprised to hear Truman at a cabinet luncheon agreeing with barbed comments Byrnes was aiming at the Soviets. "I suspect," Wallace noted in his diary, "there has never been a President who could move two different directions with less time intervening than Truman. He feels completely sincere and earnest at all times and is not disturbed in the slightest by the different directions in which his mind can go almost simultaneously."[2]

Discouragement was growing over the outlook for international control of atomic energy. On June 19, five days after Baruch had submitted his plan, Gromyko proposed a different approach. He advocated an international convention prohibiting production and use of atomic weapons. All existing bombs would have to be scrapped within three months after the convention took effect. This would have meant abandonment of control by stages. Thus, the Gromyko proposal was an unlikely one in American eyes. Yet on June 24 *Pravda* denounced the Baruch Plan as a scheme to perpetuate the American monopoly. "I am of the opinion," Truman wrote Baruch July 10, "that we should not under any circumstances throw away our gun until we are sure the rest of the world can't arm against us."[3]

No one in Washington was more worried over this deadlock than Henry Agard Wallace. He deeply feared that a third world war would result from America's hardening stance toward the Soviet Union, a trend he suspected was due in no small part to Truman's efforts to appease the powerful Republican minority in Congress. Without anyone's realizing it, Wallace's concerns were setting the stage for a major crisis in the administration.

Internationally known, Wallace was one of the oddest yet best-intentioned public officials the United States has ever produced. An Iowan, son of the secretary of agriculture under Harding and Coolidge, he began his career as editor of *Wallace's Farmer,* a family-owned periodical. As a plant geneticist he developed several strains of hybrid corn. A Republican turned Democrat, he was himself an able secretary of agriculture under Franklin Roosevelt before being elected vice-president in 1940. He was a reformer who had a way of startling the country, as when he said, half facetiously, in 1942, "The object of this war is to make sure that everybody in the world has the privilege of drinking a quart of milk a day." Such of his statements as, "The century on which we are entering can be and must be the century of the common man" gave him the aura of a prophet.

Tousle-haired, blue-eyed, and rumpled, he was shy, solitary, ascetic, introverted, humanitarian, righteous, erratic, naive, evangelical, and fascinated with occultism and oriental religions. As secretary of agriculture he had supported the work of Dr. Nicholas Roerich, a White Russian artist, who studied Oriental mysticism in Central Asia. In writing to Roerich, Wallace sometimes addressed him as "Dear Guru." Publication of some of these letters in the newspapers aroused considerable skepticism of Wallace's competence for high office. Quite apart from this, he was an inept politician.

In the summer of 1946, however, he was the leading figure among the liberals. His beliefs in human brotherhood strengthened his desire for good relations with the Soviets. The century of the common man, as he visualized it, would have been impossible without them. Churchill's "Iron Curtain" speech shocked him. He recognized the problems posed for Stalin by American anticommunism, the arrogance of military power in Washington, and the hardening American policy. Wallace perceived that Soviet policy was partly motivated by a sense of insecurity. On the other hand, his experience in diplomacy was limited. He was short of practical solutions, which were what Truman needed. Often utopian, he seemed to have little grasp of the difficulties that the Soviets themselves were throwing in the path of better relations and of the evils of Stalin's dictatorship.

Wallace wrote a long letter outlining his concerns over foreign policy, which had been brought to a head by the impasse over atomic energy control. With results that were to prove explosive, he handed Truman the letter during their meeting July 23.[4]

The letter suggested that the Bikini atomic bomb tests, the American acquisition of foreign bases, and a decision to build long-range bombers might well look menacing in Soviet eyes. Wallace criticized the Baruch Plan for control in stages, asking: "Would we have been enthusiastic if the Russians had a monopoly of atomic energy and offered to share the information with us at some indefinite time in the future at their discretion if we agreed now not to try to make the bomb and give them information on our secret resources of uranium and thorium?"

Wallace said "there is a school of military thinking" that "advocates a 'preventive war,' an attack on Russia *now* before Russia has atomic bombs."

He concluded by appealing to Truman for "a shift in some of our thinking about international matters."

The effect upon Truman was quite the opposite of what Wallace had intended.

Instead of arousing Truman's skepticism about American policy, it made him suspicious of Wallace. Showing the letter to Clifford the next morning, Truman said, "It looks as though Henry is going to pull an Ickes." Clifford reached the same conclusion, suspecting that Wallace was preparing to release the letter for publication as a step toward an open break with Truman. When the letter was shown to Elsey, he disagreed. "I do *not* believe," he wrote in a note, "that the letter in any way means that Wallace is thinking of 'taking a walk.' It is a serious, sober, and very earnest plea by an intellectual for a program in which he sincerely believes."[5]

On August 8 Truman acknowledged Wallace's letter but without inviting further discussion. Meanwhile Elsey told Clifford the White House should "indoctrinate" Wallace on some of the facts of life about the Soviet Union.[6] The remark bore upon a project of some renown in the history of the Truman administration—a review of Soviet-American relations, on which Elsey was then working. Even before receiving the Wallace letter July 23 Truman, concerned about Soviet trustworthiness, had asked Clifford for an account of Soviet violations of agreements with the United States, and Clifford had turned the spadework over to Elsey, his assistant. Elsey, however, decided to go well beyond Truman's request for a list of Soviet violations and to explore the reasons for and consequences of Soviet policy. He solicited the views of Byrnes, Patterson, and other senior advisers and pored through pertinent documents, including Kennan's "long telegram." Clifford made some changes in Elsey's first draft; Kennan wrote a critique of the second.

Titled "American Relations with the Soviet Union" the top secret report reflected at the outset Kennan's convictions about Soviet expansionism.[7] Moscow, the report said, continued either to violate the Teheran, Yalta, and Potsdam agreements or interpret them to suit its own aims. To enhance Soviet power, Stalin was preparing for a clash "by many means." In order to keep the Red Army in control of Eastern Europe, he was delaying peace settlements. The Soviets wished to install a friendly government in Greece, make Turkey a puppet state, and acquire Middle East oil fields. Moscow was supporting Communists in China and resisting unification of Korea except under a pro-Communist government.

The Kremlin, the report continued, was making "harsh and strident propaganda attacks upon the United States" to justify to the Soviet people the hardships of maintaining large military forces and to insure support for aggressive Soviet actions against the United States. "Development of atomic weapons, guided missiles, materials for biological warfare, a strategic air force, submarines of great cruising range, naval mines, and mine craft . . . are extending the effective range of Soviet military power well into areas which the United States regards as vital to its security." The Red Army was being mechanized. Soviet airfields "are being developed in Eastern Siberia from which strategic air forces could attack the North American continent." The Kremlin was "actively directing espionage and subversive movements in the United States." Under Soviet policy war might come at any time.

What, then, must be done?

The United States must seek to prevent further Soviet aggression and, above all, must keep Western Europe, the Middle East, China, and Japan outside the Soviet sphere. On September 17, in addressing State Department employees, Kennan said that the preponderance of world opinion on the side of the United States gave Americans an edge that "should enable us, if our policies are wise and nonprovocative, to contain [the Soviets] both militarily and politically for a long time to come." This was Kennan's first recorded use of "contain," soon to be followed by "containment."[8]

In the same tenor the Clifford-Elsey report said that the United States must maintain the necessary military power "to restrain the Soviet Union and to confine Soviet influence to its present area." Indeed the United States "must be prepared to wage atomic war and biological warfare," thus creating a "deterrent" to Soviet aggression. Compromise and concession were viewed by the Soviets as signs of weakness.

Practically foreshadowing aid to Greece and Turkey under the Truman Doctrine as well as the wider assistance of the Marshall Plan the report said:

In addition to maintaining our own strength the United States should support and assist all democratic countries which are in any way menaced or endangered by the U.S.S.R. Providing military support in case of attack is a last resort; a more effective barrier to Communism is strong economic support. Trade agreements, loans and technical assistance missions strengthen our ties with friendly nations. . . . The United States can do much to ensure that economic opportunities, personal freedom and social equality are made possible in countries outside the Soviet sphere by generous financial assistance.

Such was the state of mind of the Truman administration at the end of the summer of 1946. "I think the general tone is excellent and I have no fault to find with it," Kennan began his critique of the second draft.[9]

Still the report, submitted in early September, did not summon the country to a war footing. Nor was it designed for impact on Truman. By this time he was well rehearsed on the information and viewpoints it contained and did not expect the worst. "There is too much loose talk about the Russian situation," he wrote to his friend, the former vice-president, John Nance Garner, September 21. "We are not going to have any shooting trouble with them but they are tough bargainers and always ask for the whole earth, expecting maybe to get an acre."[10] As for the report, Elsey hoped rather that it would be enlightening to other members of the administration, particularly Wallace. Clifford got Truman to agree that when the report was finished a copy would go to the secretary of commerce. But when Truman saw the document he said it was too explosive to distribute.[11] Furthermore the Wallace situation was about to take a most drastic turn.

Wallace had a long-standing invitation to address a rally in Madison Square Garden in New York September 12, called to oppose Dewey's reelection as governor in November. The meeting was sponsored by the National Citizens Political Action Committee and the Independent Citizens Committee of the Arts, Sciences, and Professions. C. B. Baldwin, executive vice-president of the NCPAC, had first suggested to Wallace that he discuss Republican obstructionism in Congress, and Wallace had a speech drafted in that vein. Meanwhile, however, one of his assistants had slipped Baldwin a copy of Wallace's July 23 letter to Truman advocating a shift in thinking about Soviet-American relations. Baldwin thereupon urged that

Wallace concentrate on foreign policy in his speech. With disastrous consequences, he assented, assigning the task of writing a draft to two aides.[12]

While they were going about it Byrnes delivered a celebrated speech in Stuttgart, Germany, a part of which was critical of Soviet policy. When, therefore, Wallace went to the White House September 10 to have his speech, titled "The Way to Peace," cleared by Truman it was at a time when the United States was again making a show of toughness toward the Soviet Union. According to Richard J. Walton, a Wallace biographer, Wallace took the speech to Truman for clearance because he did not believe the State Department would clear it.[13]

Ordinarily, a secretary of commerce does not make a major address on foreign policy, especially when the secretary of state is in the middle of critical negotiations abroad. The Wallace speech was poor administration to begin with. He was something of a special case, however. He had been vice-president and accustomed to considerable latitude. He was the last remaining New Dealer in the cabinet (and the only cabinet holdover from the Roosevelt administration except Forrestal), and Truman humored him. Furthermore Wallace was being billed as a leading Democratic speaker in the developing congressional election campaign, and the New York rally was a political affair. Any help that Wallace could attract from liberal voters was welcome to Truman.

Moreover Wallace's prepared speech was consistent with Truman's foreign policy on many points: approval of the British loan, the necessity for an American foreign policy independent of British and Soviet policies, support of the United Nations, the need for international control of atomic weapons, and the desirability of greater foreign trade in general and the open door to Eastern Europe and China in particular.

Truman, who was never quite comfortable with Wallace, was busy with other things at the time. The White House was again in the middle of a major labor dispute, this one a nationwide shipping strike. Also the shortage of meat was becoming a harassment for the administration. Still Truman sat and listened as Wallace ran through his speech, page by page. Frequently, according to Wallace, the president would interpose such comments as, "That's right," and, "Yes, that is what I believe." He did not suggest any change. If Wallace's account, which rings true, is correct—though it is much different from Truman's subsequent four-sentence version[14]—the president, either through preoccupation with other matters or simply through lack of insight as to how others might read the speech, allowed Wallace to consider it cleared. When Wallace returned to the Department of Commerce he told his executive assistant, Bernard L. Gladieux, that he was not sure Truman had grasped the implications of what he was going to say.[15]

Copies were released to the press late in the morning of September 12, hours before Wallace was to speak. Reporters caught the news in it—contrary to the secretary of state's course, peace could not be achieved by a "Get tough with Russia" policy.

"The tougher we get," Wallace's text read, "the tougher the Russians will get. . . . We must not let our Russian policy be guided or influenced by those inside or outside the United States who want war with Russia."

Ignoring Byrnes's opposition to a Soviet sphere of influence in Eastern Europe,

Wallace said that the United States should recognize "that we have no more business in the *political* affairs of Eastern Europe than Russia has in the *political* affairs of Latin America, western Europe, and the United States . . . whether we like it or not the Russians will try to socialize their sphere of influence just as we try to democratize our sphere of influence." As Acheson was to observe, Wallace spoke "in the manner of all critics of United States policy in Europe over the next twenty years."[16] Adroitly handled, however, the embarrassment to the government might yet have been limited because Wallace was not speaking until that evening, and Truman had a press conference scheduled for 4 P.M.

Sometime before then, according to Elsey's understanding, Leahy had been told of the contents of Wallace's speech by a newspaperman. The admiral, reportedly, advised Truman that any speech by Wallace dealing with the Soviet Union should be cleared by the State Department.[17] If so, Truman did not act upon advice that might have spared him excruciating embarrassment. He met reporters on schedule and promptly fell into a trap that lurked in this passage of Wallace's text: "I am neither anti-British nor pro-British—neither anti-Russian nor pro-Russian. And just two days ago, when President Truman read these words, he said they represented the policy of his administration."

"Does that apply just to that paragraph or to the whole speech?" a reporter asked.

Without watching where he was stepping, Truman replied, "I approved the whole speech."

Then:

Q. Mr. President, do you regard Wallace's speech a departure from Byrnes's policy—
The President. I do not.
Q. —toward Russia?
The President. They are exactly in line.[18]

As soon as the President had endorsed Wallace's speech, James Reston reported in his story to the *New York Times* that day, foreign correspondents in Washington began filing copy abroad to their papers—to be read by Byrnes, Vandenberg, Connally, and others in Paris—reporting that the United States was shifting toward a softer policy toward the Soviet Union.

The State Department was slow catching up with the text. It was not until nearly six o'clock that a group of high officials gathered gloomily around Clayton, who was acting secretary of state with Byrnes and Acheson out of town. Under Secretary of the Navy John L. Sullivan asked Clayton if he had protested to the White House. When Clayton said he had not, Sullivan suggested that he call the White House and try to stop Wallace or at least get him to delete the passage about Truman's having declared that Wallace's words represented the policy of the administration. Clayton put in a call for various presidential assistants and finally got Charles Ross in the press office and told him that Byrnes would feel that the ground had been cut from under him. Then Sullivan got on the phone and told Ross that if the speech were delivered as written, Truman would have to repudiate either Wallace or Byrnes. Despite this and subsequent calls to the press office, however, the two secretaries were unable to get definitive action from Ross, who seemed to think it was too late.[19] Truman was at a stag dinner at Clifford's house.

At the Garden that night the effect of Wallace's words was magnified by a blistering attack on Truman's foreign policy by Wallace's fellow speaker, Senator Pepper, who asked, "What do you expect in a foreign policy which really meets the approval of Senator Vandenberg and John Foster Dulles?"

Pressures began building at once. The next day Taft said that by approving Wallace's speech Truman not only had betrayed Byrnes but was making a bid for left-wing support in the campaign. The embarrassed White House staff tried to spread the word that a misunderstanding had occurred. In Paris an angry Byrnes laid low while the rest of his delegation fended off queries from other diplomats about a possible change in American policy. On September 14 Connally and Vandenberg issued statements in Paris supporting Byrnes's policies, Vandenberg saying, "We can only co-operate with one Secretary of State at a time." That same afternoon Truman made a lame effort to still the controversy. Calling reporters to his office he read a statement, saying that his answer at the press conference before Wallace's speech "did not convey the thought that I had intended it to convey." Rather:

It was my intention to express the thought that I approved the right of the Secretary of Commerce to deliver the speech. I did not intend to indicate that I approved the speech as constituting a statement of the foreign policy. . . .

There has been no change in the established foreign policy of our Government.[20]

A quiet weekend followed, and if the chain reaction could have been contained there, the incident might have blown over. On Monday, September 16, however, two fresh disasters struck. First, Wallace told reporters, "I stand on my New York speech." This news grated on Byrnes in Paris.

Then, learning that Drew Pearson had obtained a copy of Wallace's July 23 letter to Truman, Charles Ross—without the president's approval—told Wallace to make the letter public so that Pearson would not have an exclusive story.

The avalanche of newspaper stories about the letter set off a new wave of outrage. Editorials, of course, excoriated Truman for his handling of the whole affair. Forrestal and Patterson were angered at Wallace's statement in the letter that a school of thought among the military advocated preventive war. The White House issued the secretaries' joint denial. In New York that night Forrestal made a speech lavishly praising Byrnes. Baruch was enraged over the airing of Wallace's criticism of the Baruch Plan in the July 23 letter. On September 18 Baruch, who had an appointment at the White House, read Truman something of a lecture and vaguely threatened to resign. Truman urged him not to rush into any such step. He was going to see Wallace in a few minutes, he said, and ventured that Baruch would be satisfied with the outcome of that meeting.[21]

Writing his mother and sister before Wallace arrived, he observed that the trouble "grows worse as we go along. I think he'll quit today and I won't shed any tears. Never was there such a mess and it is partly my making. But when I make a mistake it is a good one."[22] Wallace did not quit, however. The only detailed account of what happened in the ensuing meeting, which was to last for two hours and twenty minutes, is contained in his diary for that day, although Truman's diary has a few things to say on the subject, too.

According to Wallace, Truman complained that the controversy was causing him more sleepless nights than at any time since the Chicago convention.[23]

"Peace is going to be an issue in the campaign," Wallace countered. "The people are afraid that the 'Get tough with Russia' policy is leading us to war. You yourself, as Harry Truman, really believe in my speech."

"But Jimmie Byrnes says I am pulling the rug out from under him," Truman replied. "I must ask you not to make any more speeches touching on foreign policy. We must present a united front abroad."

Wallace said he had a speech scheduled in Providence. He read to Truman a long passage from it, including the line, "I do not agree with our present bipartisan, Republican-dominated foreign policy." Wallace asked if he could make the speech with a disclaimer that it did not represent the views of the president or the administration. Truman said no, Wallace must stop talking about foreign affairs.

Wallace told Truman that he, the president, was viewing the situation too negatively. Speeches on foreign policy would arouse people's emotions and get out the vote to elect a Democratic Congress. Truman said he thought the Republicans would win control of Congress in the elections.

Wallace quoted Associate Justice Hugo L. Black and others as having admonished him that Truman's foreign policy was leading to war. Truman denied that it was a policy of getting tough with the Russians. He said he would see to it that no war occurred. He was not an imperialist, he reminded Wallace.

"I know you are not an imperialist," Wallace said, "but what about Admiral Halsey's jingoistic statement?"

Evidently this referred to Fleet Admiral William F. Halsey, Jr.'s, comment on a charge on the Moscow radio that American warships were in the Mediterranean to exert pressure against Soviet claims to the Dardanelles. "It's nobody's damn business where we go" Halsey said August 28. "We will go anywhere we please."[24]

Truman assured Wallace he had called Halsey to task for this and also the head of the Veterans of Foreign Wars for warmongering over the recent downing of two army transport planes by Yugoslavia. He had also, he said, tried to persuade Roy Howard to tone down the anti-Soviet line in the Scripps-Howard newspapers.

As soon as the peace treaties were signed, Truman said, he was going to ask Congress for a loan to the Soviet Union similar to the British loan.

"Without political strings attached to it?" Wallace asked. When Truman replied affirmatively, Wallace said, "Do you think for a moment you can get a loan of this sort through Congress? I don't think you know your Congress. It will take a lot of effort during the next six weeks to elect the kind of Congress that will put through a Russian loan."

Wallace said he was "dumbfounded" when Truman persisted in thinking he could get a loan approved. Truman said Americans could not be tough with the Russians because they did not have the military equipment with which to be tough. With demobilization, he said, the country had only one fully equipped division.

Because reporters were waiting to interview Wallace on his departure, Ross was summoned to help prepare a statement. Wallace then drafted one, saying that after a friendly discussion Truman and he had concluded that Wallace should make no public comments or speeches until the Paris conference was ended. Thereafter Wallace would feel free "to express himself in such ways as he feels to be wise and in conformity with the peace objective which he feels to be the supreme issue in this campaign and in 1948." Ross objected. He wanted Wallace to stick to domestic issues. Wallace demurred. He said he had switched from the Republican party to the Democratic party after the First World War on the basis of foreign policy, and he could not campaign without getting into foreign issues.

Finally, it was agreed that Wallace would say: "The President and the Secretary of Commerce had a most detailed and friendly discussion, after which the Secretary reached the conclusion he would make no public statements or speeches until after the Foreign Ministers' Conference in Paris is concluded." And that is what he proceeded to tell reporters with a smile. When a reporter asked him if he was remaining in the cabinet, he replied, "Yes, I am." Upon seeing his assistant, Gladieux, he remarked about how sincere Truman had been.

Wallace might not have felt like smiling if he had known that in his own diary the next day Truman would say, "I am not so sure he is as fundamentally sound intellectually as I had thought. He advised me that I should be far to the 'left' when Congress was not in session and that I should move to the right when Congress is . . . in session." Truman called Wallace "a pacifist 100 per cent" and added:

He wants us to disband our armed forces, give Russia our atomic secrets and trust a bunch of adventurers in the Kremlin Politbureau. I do not understand a "dreamer" like that. The German-American Bund under Fritz Kuhn was not half so dangerous. The Reds, phonies and "parlor pinks" seem to be banded together and are becoming a national danger.

I am afraid they are a sabotage front for Uncle Joe Stalin. They can see no wrong in Russia's four and one-half million armed force, in Russia's loot of Poland, Austria, Hungary, Rumania, Manchuria. They can see no wrong in Russia's living off the occupied countries to support the military occupation.

But when we help our friends in China who fought on our side it is terrible. When Russia loots the industrial plant of those same friends it is all right. When Russia occupies Persia for oil that is heavenly although Persia was Russia's ally in the terrible German War.[25]

When Byrnes read in Paris on the eighteenth that Wallace had agreed to refrain from comment only until after the peace conference, he cabled Truman saying that his own position had been undermined. Unless Wallace was ordered to stop criticizing foreign policy while he was a member of the cabinet, the secretary of state added, "I must ask you to accept my resignation immediately."[26]

Unable to get Byrnes on the telephone, Truman set up a teletype conference with him the next day. After receiving Byrnes's warning against espousal of a foreign policy that was in reality the policy of a faction of the Democratic party, the president assured him: "No speeches by anyone will be approved unless they are in accord with the foreign policy as it now stands." "Your statement makes me feel good," Byrnes replied.[27]

Before the day was out, however, Truman's temper gave way. He burned with anger at Wallace for having created a situation over which he himself had stumbled. He was especially irate ("I was never so exasperated since Chicago," he was to write his mother and sister) that Wallace had told his associates, and *they* had told reporters, some of the things Truman and Wallace had discussed on the eighteenth.[28]

His patience exhausted, Truman dashed off an unelevated but not profane letter to the secretary of commerce demanding his resignation. Wallace received it when he arrived for work early September 20. Instead of embarrassing Truman by giving the letter to some reporter, Wallace, the victim now of rather shabby treatment considering that the president had cleared his speech, called Truman and asked if he did not want the letter back. Truman said he did and dispatched Clifford to retrieve it.[29] At 9:30 A.M. Truman telephoned Wallace and formally requested his resignation. Wallace submitted it:

Dear Harry:
    As you requested, here is my resignation. I shall continue to fight for peace. I am sure that you approve and will join me in that great endeavor.

Respectfully yours,
H. A. Wallace[30]

"He was so nice about it I almost backed out," Truman wrote his mother and sister.[31] But an hour later, in a seemingly good mood, he called reporters to his office and read a statement announcing his action with "regret." He said:

It had become clear that between his views on foreign policy and those of my administration . . . there was a fundamental conflict. We could not permit this conflict to jeopardize our position in relation to other countries.[32]

The situation had simply gone too far for Truman to tolerate. He could not risk a resignation by Byrnes in the circumstances. It doubtless would have cost the administration the backing of Vandenberg. Republican support of foreign policy would have been jeopardized, and Wallace's continuance in the cabinet then would have exposed Truman to partisan charges that he was "soft" on communism—a more menacing prospect in the approaching campaign than the liberals' ire over the dismissal of Wallace.

Hence the firm foreign policy stood, its chief critic banished. Truman summoned Harriman home from the embassy in London to be secretary of commerce. "It has been the habit of the Commerce Department under Wallace," Truman wrote his friend, Mayor Roger T. Sermon of Independence, several weeks later, "to appoint somebody that is decidedly unfriendly to me. I don't know what Harriman's program will be but I hope it will reverse that situation."[33] Be that as it might, Wallace had passed out of Truman's administration, becoming the editor of the *New Republic,* but by no means out of Truman's life.

"I thought the President and you would be interested in knowing," J. Edgar Hoover wrote on September 25 to George Allen at the Reconstruction Finance Corporation, "that national figures affiliated with the Communist Party and its front activities have expressed an opinion that the resignation of Mr. Wallace is a good move for them as it opens the issue of war with Byrnes and peace with Wallace."[34]

24. *The Beefsteak Election of 1946*

H AD ENOUGH?'' The 1946 Republican campaign slogan, credited to a Boston advertising agency, hit the bull's-eye.

As in all congressional elections, local sentiment decided the outcome of various races, but from coast to coast the campaign took place under a pall of disgust with the Truman administration. After years of wartime controls voters were rebellious. The worsening meat shortage, in particular, created a state of national exasperation.

Reconversion, demobilization, and the wrench of changing policy toward the Soviet Union had exacted a heavy toll from Truman. Also he was suffering the consequences of his failure to deal with some of these enormous problems with greater finesse. In little more than a year his popularity, as measured by the Gallup Poll, had plunged from 87 percent to 32 percent. In dealing with the the clash of interests after the war Truman had incurred the disapproval of groups that the Democratic party relied on for support in elections.

In the letter to his mother and sister September 20, informing them, ''Well, I had to fire Henry today,'' he mentioned that ''the crackpots are having conniption fits'' over Wallace's ouster.[1] That was the reaction of the liberals in a nutshell. The Wallace dismissal split the Democrats seriously at that time.

Dr. Frank Kingdon, chairman, and C. B. Baldwin, executive vice-chairman, of the NCPAC, Wallace's cohost at Madison Square Garden, issued a joint statement on his removal, saying, ''It underscores the extent Truman has drifted from the policies and programs of Franklin D. Roosevelt.'' Jack Kroll, who had succeeded to the directorship of the CIO-PAC after Hillman's death in July, said, ''Clear-thinking Americans who abhor the thought of another world conflict will join Mr. Wallace in the fight for world peace.'' ''The New Deal as a driving force,'' commented the *Chicago Sun,* ''is dead within the Truman administration.''

Labor was disenchanted, apathetic. Daniel J. Tobin, president of the International Brotherhood of Teamsters, wrote in a summer issue of the union's magazine that Truman and the Democratic leaders had lost the confidence of labor.

In the South, Truman's problems were deepening. Numerous measures he had supported with the approval of many urban voters in the North aroused the opposite sentiment in the South. Southerners like Manasco had taken the lead in weakening the full employment bill. Southerners had been in the forefront of the fight for the Case labor bill and urged Truman to sign it. When he vetoed it, they were resentful. Southern business interests had fought extension of the OPA partly because of price controls on cotton.

Offshore oil was another issue that drove a wedge between Truman and the South. Oil found off the coasts of Texas, Louisiana, Mississippi, and Florida was becoming a substantial source of revenue for some southern states.[2] As will be recalled, however, Truman issued a proclamation in September, 1945, asserting federal jurisdiction and control over offshore oil, a violation of states' rights in southern eyes. Under the impetus of the South and California, Congress approved a joint resolution to nullify the proclamation and vest title to the oil in the respective states. On August 1, 1946, Truman vetoed the resolution on the grounds that the issues should be decided in the Supreme Court,[3] which was then reviewing it.*

As sectional bitterness grew, a Jefferson-Jackson Day dinner was held in Little Rock, after which Governor Ben Laney of Arkansas announced that the proceeds would be withheld from the Democratic National Committee out of dissatisfaction with the national party leadership. "The day is coming," warned Representative Charles E. McKenzie of Louisiana, "when the administration is going to have to listen to us or get no support from us."[4]

Over and above the South's disappointment with Truman on the FEPC, the president and the southerners were steadily parting company on a host of economic and political issues. In contrast to many discontented liberals in the North, southerners viewed Truman as a president who was determined to continue the New Deal. The South perceived that Truman had replaced Roosevelt's advisers but not his policies.

In the low state of Truman's prestige Taft wrote Dewey: "If Truman wanted to elect a Republican Congress, he could not be doing a better job." People made fun of the president or, worse still, patronized him. Martha Taft, the senator's wife, supposedly coined the quip, "To err is Truman."[5] Republicans never had more fun with slogans: "Harry Truman for Governor," "Two Families in Every Garage."

Things about Truman that were to appeal to a later generation of Americans caused millions of his contemporaries to look down on him in the summer and fall of 1946. The poker games and bourbon, the Missouri capers, the talk about his cussing in the companionship of old buddies, the utter lack of affectation and pose, the homespun manner, the twang on radio simply did not seem quite up to the presidency, as many voters with memories of Woodrow Wilson and long familiarity with Franklin Roosevelt regarded it. The homey style, combined with the undeniable confusion and blunders of his first year and a half in office, made Truman seem out of place in the White House to many people. And as stories of the Pendergast machine were revived and Truman's background reconsidered, he came to suffer the image of the "little man," as the saying went.

Truman endured the scorn and ridicule, the editorial broadsides and cutting cartoons, unflinchingly. To all appearances he went about his job as buoyantly as if things had never been going better. In some ways they were indeed going well. The fear of depression that had swept the country only a year earlier was forgotten. Apart from the serious shortages of meat and housing, the economy was booming in

* In 1947 and in 1950 the Supreme Court ruled that the federal government had paramount rights to the submerged lands.

the fall of 1946. Full employment had arrived in fact.[6] The eighth report of the OWMR, dated October 1, declared that out of a labor force of 60 million, 58 million Americans had jobs. Farm income, business profits, and dollar volume of industrial production all stood at new peaks, as did the income of individuals and consumer spending. People were again buying washing machines, radios, electric irons, and other appliances. Production curves were ascending. And substantial as inflation had been, it had never been a runaway inflation, although prices were still rising. "All this adds up to a splendid achievement," Truman said at his press conference October 3.[7]

The government had canceled war contracts promptly after the Japanese surrender. With dispatch, government-owned machinery had been removed from factories. Industrial facilities were reconverted to peacetime production at a surprising pace. Although delays of one kind and another persisted into 1946, the physical aspect of reconversion had been practically completed by the end of 1945.[8]

In the campaign, however, the general prosperity could not offset the effect of particular annoyances and doubts—the kinds that Representative John M. Vorys, Republican, of Ohio, alluded to in a speech. "Got enough meat?" he asked. "Got enough houses? Got enough OPA? . . . Got enough inflation? . . . Got enough debt? . . . Got enough strikes? . . . Got enough Communism?"[9]

Communism.

"The word 'Communism' was whooped about like an Indian war cry," wrote Tris Coffin, a journalist. "One [Republican] campaign leaflet, entitled *Prophets of Planned Chaos,* showed an idiotic donkey staring into a crystal ball and wearing a turban with a hammer and sickle on it. [Republican] Headquarters was piled high with records on 'the Communist threat' to send out in the field. They were very popular. . . . Communism was the battle cry in Catholic areas."[10]

Taft said in a campaign speech that the Democrats "at Teheran, at Yalta, at Potsdam, and at Moscow pursued a policy of appeasing Russia, a policy which has sacrificed throughout Eastern Europe and Asia the freedom of many nations and millions of people." Truman, he continued, wanted Communist support in the elections and a Congress "dominated by a policy of appeasing the Russians abroad and of fostering Communism at home." The senator depicted the Democratic party as being "so divided between Communism and Americanism that its foreign policy can only be futile and contradictory."[11]

In California Richard Milhous Nixon, launching the first political campaign of his career in a race for the seat in the House of Representatives held by Jerry Voorhis, a Democrat, denounced high officials "who front for un-American elements, wittingly or otherwise, by advocating increasing Federal controls over the lives of the people."[12] In New York Representative John Taber, Republican, said the country was imperiled by Communist infiltration of the government, the universities, and even the army. In Oklahoma Representative George B. Schwabe, Republican, warned of the "imminent danger of Communism." In Nebraska a Republican senator, Hugh A. Butler, accused the Democrats of having failed to remove Communists from labor unions.[13]

The anti-Red tide was rolling in ever faster on Truman—not that he was without his own prejudices against "parlor pinks" and "Reds" and (after the Ottawa espionage affair) his own concern about internal security. The tide had been gathering force for years.

As highlighted by the notorious "Red Scare" of 1919 and 1920, fear of Communist activity in the United States had disturbed Americans since the start of the Bolshevik dictatorship under Lenin. Congress and the Department of Justice conducted periodic investigations until the mid-1930s, after which, partly perhaps because of the rise of totalitarianism in Europe, congressional action quickened.

In May 1938, the House of Representatives created a special committee to investigate "un-American activities" under the chairmanship of Representative Martin Dies, Jr., Democrat, of Texas, a zealot against Communists, real and imagined. "Stalin baited his hook with a 'progressive' worm," he wrote, "and the New Deal suckers swallowed the bait, hook, line and sinker."[14] During the war the committee focused increasingly on suspected "subversives" who had obtained jobs in the enlargement of the federal bureaucracy caused by the New Deal and the war. An expanding bureaucracy under a liberal Democratic administration was bound to have attracted persons who had participated in social reform and antifascist movements, in which the American Communist party also was active. To the consternation of the Roosevelt administration, such persons readily became objects of suspicion to such stalwarts on the committee as Dies and Representative J. Parnell Thomas, Republican, of New Jersey; and the administration found itself charged with harboring subversives.

The onset of the war brought certain legitimate concerns about espionage, sabotage, and subversion.

In 1938 Congress passed the Foreign Agents Registration Act, requiring agents of foreign governments to register with the attorney general. In 1939 Congress inserted a provision in the Hatch Act making it unlawful for any federal employee "to have membership in any political party or organization which advocates the overthrow of our constitutional form of government . . ." The act provided for immediate dismissal of such employees.

In 1940 Congress authorized summary dismissal of civil service employees of the War and the Navy departments whose removal was deemed "warranted by the demands of national security." Aiming at the Communist party, Congress the same year voted to require the registration of every organization dedicated to the overthrow of the government by force or threats of force.

Also in 1940 Congress passed the Smith Act, making it unlawful for anyone to be or to become a member of or affiliate with any society, group, or assembly that teaches, advocates, or encourages the overthrow or destruction of the United States government by force or violence. In 1940 also Congress added to practically all appropriations bills a provision barring the use of funds to pay salaries to "any person who advocates, or who is a member of an organization that advocates," the forceful overthrow of the government. Indeed it was made a criminal offense for any such person to accept government employment. In 1943 Roosevelt set up an interdepartmental committee to recommend standards for screening government employees and getting rid of those considered undesirable. The committee obtained from Attorney General Biddle a list of allegedly subversive organizations, membership in which might be thought a basis for questioning an employee's loyalty.

During the Roosevelt administration, therefore, the country already was deeply enmeshed in the difficult question of how to reconcile the demands of internal security with the freedoms guaranteed by the Constitution.

The sensitivity of the Roosevelt administration to charges about subversives in the government was not lost on the Republicans. For years they had butted their heads into a stone wall attacking New Deal measures. As time went on, however, they could see the advantage of going beyond ineffective cries of socialism and linking Roosevelt's reforms as well as his allies, such as the CIO-PAC, with communism. In the 1944 presidential campaign Dewey found the issue irresistible. Typically, he accused the New Dealers of trying to smother discussion of their alliance with American Communists, of "insinuating that Americans must love Communism or offend our fighting ally, Russia."

"I do not now propose to be silent," he said, "when the New Deal through Mr. Roosevelt's political lieutenant Hillman strikes up a cynical alliance with Browder's * Communists."[15]

Democrats were by no means free of the virus. Communist support of Wallace for renomination as vice-president hurt him at Chicago.

Roosevelt's election to a fourth term did not in the least slow the momentum of anticommunism. Against his wishes, the House in January 1945 voted with strong American Legion support to give the Committee on Un-American Activities permanent status; theretofore it had been a special, not a standing committee. Truman rapidly inherited the nettles of the Communist issue because of, among other things, the *Amerasia* case, the Ottawa spy ring, Soviet conduct in Eastern Europe, and the charges flung about by Patrick Hurley. The shape of things to come grew clearer in the spring and summer of 1946. In the annual appropriation bill for the State Department, where suspicion centered early because of the *Amerasia* case, Congress included a rider sponsored by Senator Pat McCarran, Democrat, of Nevada, giving the secretary of state power, "in his absolute discretion," to dismiss any employee "whenever he shall deem such termination necessary or advisable in the interests of the United States." Such a person would have no right to be informed of the reasons for his dismissal nor the right to submit affidavits to show why he should be reinstated.

From the Department of Justice Truman had been getting pressure to authorize wiretapping and bugging against persons thought to be a threat to national security, and he went along with it. On July 17, 1946, he received a memorandum from Tom Clark reminding him that in 1940 Roosevelt had authorized the use of electronic surveillance in cases where "grave matters involving defense of the nation" were involved. The authority for Roosevelt's action was confirmed by an opinion of his assistant solicitor general who advised the then attorney general that electronic surveillance could be conducted where national security was concerned.

In Clark's memorandum to Truman the attorney general recommended that the

---

* Earl R. Browder was general secretary of the Communist party of the United States.

1940 directive "be continued in force" because of the "increase in subversive activities." Truman signed his concurrence. He intended simply to extend Roosevelt's policy. He was apparently unaware at the time that, technically, he was expanding the scope because Clark's memorandum had omitted a clause contained in Roosevelt's authorization, asking that such investigations be limited "insofar as possible to aliens."[16]

Meanwhile in the large cities Catholic organizations were conducting almost feverish campaigns against communism. Writing in the November issue of *Cosmopolitan,* Francis Cardinal Spellman, archbishop of New York—"the political leader of Catholic anti-Communism in America"[17]—said, "Every Communist is a potential enemy of the U.S. and only the bat-blind can fail to be aware of the Communist invasion of our country."

The United States Chamber of Commerce also was waging a heavy campaign, managed by its Committee on Socialism and Communism, whose chairman was Francis P. Matthews. A future secretary of the navy in the Truman administration, Matthews was an Omaha business executive, banker, and prominent Catholic layman, who had been designated "Secret Papal Chamberlain with Cape and Sword" by Pope Pius XII. Matthews hired as a writer of a projected anti-Communist report the Reverend John F. Cronin, assistant director of the Social Action Department of the National Catholic Welfare Conference. Father Cronin was an intimate of J. Edgar Hoover's, who sometimes gave him access to FBI files. The priest became, beginning in 1947, an unofficial adviser and behind-the-scenes speech writer for Richard Nixon—a role he continued to play until the 1960 presidential campaign. Cronin warned Matthews in the spring of 1946 that it was likely "that Soviet armies may be on the march in but a few weeks," and completed his report in September. Appearing under Matthews's by-line, it was entitled "Communist Infiltration in the United States," and the Chamber's first printing of it ran to four hundred thousand copies.[18]

J. Edgar Hoover contributed his share to the pressure on the administration. Addressing the American Legion convention in San Francisco September 30, he warned that at least 100,000 Communists were at large in the country—in "some newspapers, magazines, books, radio and the screen . . . some churches, schools, colleges and even fraternal orders."[19]

The House Post Office and Civil Service Committee ordered an investigation of current methods of ascertaining the loyalty of government employees. The subcommittee that conducted the investigation found that the "only way to afford complete protection to our Government is to require all persons who apply for positions to be thoroughly investigated and fingerprinted" before being hired. Critical of current methods, the report recommended that the president appoint a six-member commission to study the problem.

The recommendation did not go far enough for the Republicans, however. A minority report by the ranking Republican, Representative Edward H. Rees, of Kansas, demanded "an immediate and thorough housecleaning of all those of doubtful loyalty."[20] The call was reechoed in various ways by Republicans during the campaign. Truman's attempted accommodation, with lamentable results, was not long forthcoming.

The ultimate blow to Democratic hopes in 1946 was the shortage of meat. "This is going to be a damn *beefsteak* election," Rayburn said.[21]

The issue evolved from a fight over price controls as the OPA was about to expire June 30. Truman had asked for a simple extension of the price control act. Instead Congress passed a bill late in June under which the OPA would be extended for a year, but its authority restricted. Furthermore amendments offered by the Republican leaders, Taft and Senator Kenneth S. Wherry of Nebraska, would have insured higher prices on many items by allowing price ceilings to reflect cost increases.

Truman's advisers were divided as to whether he should sign the bill or veto it and cut the country adrift from price controls for the first time since 1942. He sided with his liberal advisers, notably Wallace, and vetoed the measure in the hope that public opinion would force Congress to pass a stronger law. After a wrangle Congress passed a new OPA extension bill that was at best somewhat tougher, which Truman signed "with reluctance." The bill contained one provision that Truman was to seize upon in a desperate attempt to shift the blame for the meat shortage during the campaign. This provision was that controls on livestock could not be reimposed until August 20.

Livestock growers, therefore, had practically the whole summer in which to rush their animals to market and reap ever higher prices. When controls were restored, the growers resented the end of their bonanza and took it upon themselves to try to destroy controls for good. In the manner of the steel executives who forced the government to yield on the price of steel in return for settling a strike and of the farmers who forced the government to raise ceiling prices on corn and wheat in return for marketing foodstuffs for Europe, the livestock growers in effect went on strike and kept most of their cattle on the farm.[22]

As a national meat famine spread in the fall, worried Democrats pleaded with Truman to remove controls. The signs of political disaster multiplied. Lines of customers stretched for blocks at stores that still had some meat. Other stores closed for lack of it. The New York City Council adopted a resolution asking Truman to seize all available meat and distribute it fairly. Horse meat was being sold for human consumption in Newark, and a laboratory in Columbus reported that its rabbits were being stolen for food. Packinghouse employees were laid off; shoe factories closed for lack of leather. Hair pulling and face scratching broke out among a queue of customers in New York. Price control was now as hopeless as Prohibition, Representative Clifford P. Case of New Jersey wrote Truman.[23]

The effect of the shortage was to turn the public against controls at the very time Truman was posing as a defender of controls. When controls were off in July and August, meat was available. When controls were restored in September, meat disappeared. To most people, therefore, it appeared that the way to get meat, albeit at higher prices, was to scrap controls. On October 8 Representative Herman P. Kopplemann and three other Democratic members of the Connecticut delegation in the House wrote Truman:

The only thing people will talk about is meat. No matter what group we address, no matter on what subject, invariably people will fire at us "why doesn't Washington do something about meat."

Party workers canvassing the voters are being told by Democrats "No meat—no votes."

The situation is growing desperate. It can snowball into a sure defeat. Immediate action on your part can save the day for the entire ticket because the rank and file of the voters in Connecticut are still Democratic.[24]

All four signers were to lose their seats on Election Day.

On October 14 Truman capitulated. Sounding strained and tired and, inevitably, conveying the impression of vacillating leadership, he announced in a broadcast from the White House: "There is only one remedy left—that is to lift controls on meat. Accordingly, the secretary of agriculture and the price administrator are removing all price controls on livestock and food and feed products therefrom—tomorrow."

He struck at the provision in the second price control act exempting livestock until August 20, and charged that the real blame "lies at the door of the reckless group of selfish men who, in the hope of gaining political advantage, have encouraged sellers to gamble on the destruction of price control. . . . This same group hated Franklin D. Roosevelt and everything he stood for."[25]

"After a close analysis," he wrote Bowles, "there wasn't much I could do, except what was done."[26]

In this early period of his presidency at least, the elemental economic struggles reflected in strikes and conflict over controls occasionally swept Truman to the point of despair. His anger and frustration at the clash of economic interests and the resultant political turmoil drove him in the privacy of his room or office to exorbitant rhetoric, like the speech draft during the railroad strike, in which he wildly proposed to "hang a few traitors." The pressures leading up to the removal of price controls brought him to the brink of hopelessness again. Pen in hand, he put the American people on the witness stand, as it were, and drafted—though never delivered—a speech indicting them for greed, selfishness, loss of ideals and thirst for power:

You've deserted your president for a mess of pottage[,] a piece of beef—a side of bacon. My fellow citizens *you* are the government. . . . If you the people insist on following Mammon instead of Almighty God—your President can't stop you all by himself. He can only lead you to peace and happiness with your concent [*sic*] and your willing cooperation.

You've decided that the Office of Price Administration should be a goat and a whipping boy. You've decided not to support Price Control although price control has saved your bonds[,] your insurance policies, your rent—in fact has kept our economic structure sound and solvent.

I can no longer enforce a law you won't support. . . . You've gone over to the powers of selfishness and greed.

Therefore I am releasing the controls on meat and will proceed to release all other controls. . . .

Tell 'em what will happen and quit[.][27]

Quit? Characteristically after such blowoffs of steam, Truman would be back early the next morning in his office in the Big White Jail, as he called it, resilient, cheerful and full of common sense, his rhetoric relegated to the files. On this particular occasion he probably never even remembered that for a long time he himself had been less than a fanatic about controls.

While his decision of October 14 did not denote the end of all controls, it hastened the country toward the end of wage as well as price controls because of the interaction of the economy.

Livestock returned to the market. Prices rose. But Truman's action was too late to turn the political tide, and he had better judgment than to try to campaign himself. Some recordings of his speeches were broadcast, but much more prominence was given to recordings of Roosevelt's voice.

As if Truman did not have troubles enough, John L. Lewis declared one week after the "meat speech" that the government had broken the contract so laboriously negotiated in May with the soft-coal miners. The next day, October 22, he hinted at another coal strike November 1, four days before the election. An extraordinary showdown between Truman and Lewis was now indeed set in motion. The crisis was eased past election day, however, when Attorney General Clark held on October 29 that Lewis was within his legal rights in requesting reopening of negotiations.[28]

On November 5 the voters went to the polls to elect the Eightieth Congress, Truman casting his ballot in Independence. The results were staggering for the Democrats. Their large majorities on Capitol Hill were wiped out. In a landslide, the Republicans won control of both houses for the first time since 1928. Republicans would control the new House of Representatives, 246 to 188,* and the new Senate, 51 to 45. As a sample of some of the new Republican faces, the Twelfth District of California elected the thirty-three-year-old Nixon. Wisconsin sent as its freshman Senator Joseph R. McCarthy.

With results that were to be felt in Congress throughout Truman's remaining years in office and beyond, liberals and prolabor members were defeated in large numbers and replaced by conservative and antiunion candidates. (One of the exceptions occurred in the Eleventh District of Massachusetts, which elected as its freshman representative twenty-nine-year-old John Fitzgerald Kennedy, his complexion still yellowish from Atabrine taken to prevent malaria in the South Pacific.) Democrats lost heavily in large states like New York, California, Pennsylvania, Michigan, and Illinois and did poorly in border states. The returns dimmed the glory that had been the Roosevelt era and complicated the task of holding the New Deal coalition together. Inescapably, they were a reflection on President Truman's leadership.

Stoical but not surprised at the outcome of the election, having predicted a Republican victory to Wallace in September, Truman returned by train to Washington. There in lone sartorial excellence to welcome him at Union Station was the under secretary of state, Dean Acheson. Truman insisted on taking Acheson back to the White House with him. Acheson's loyalty was growing on the president. The bond that had developed as the two had worked together during Byrnes's absences was to become stronger in their dealings with other great international problems that lay just ahead.

Despite Roosevelt's victory in 1944, the Republicans had been gaining strength since 1938, and the triumph in 1946 was generally read as a portent of the

---

* The American Labor party held one seat—that of Vito Marcantonio of New York.

presidential election of 1948. Dewey's reelection as governor of New York on November 5 by a plurality of 680,000 votes brightened the picture that much more for the Republican party. Thenceforth Truman was regarded increasingly as a caretaker, serving out his one and only term.

25. *Showdown with John L. Lewis*

W HILE THE PRESS WAS full of speculations that the election had ended the New Deal, had introduced another Republican era, and had pointed to a return of "constitutional government," the spirit inside 1600 Pennsylvania Avenue was quite different. "Nobody here in the White House is downhearted," Ross wrote to his sister November 13. "The consensus is that President Truman is now a free man and can write a fine record in the coming two years."[1]

Mrs. Roosevelt wrote to Truman suggesting that he might not have as much trouble with a Republican Congress as with the kind of Congress the Democrats had offered. Truman saw her point. "I think we will be in a position," he replied, "to get more things done for the welfare of the country, or at least to make a record of things recommended for the welfare of the country, than we would have been had we been responsible for a Democratic Congress which was not loyal to the party."[2]

The same day he wrote to Sherman Minton, an old friend in the Senate, now a federal judge: "I don't expect to knuckle under to the Republicans." Furthermore: "Between you and me I don't expect this Congress to be any worse than the one I had to deal with for the last two years."[3]

Obviously, Truman was disposed to end his defensiveness and take the initiative. And his postwar foul weather—the nasty mixture of ill luck, ill preparation, inexperience, incompetence, and the dislocations of the war—had finally cleared.

Meat was back on the counters. Except for John L. Lewis's hovering threat, the great wave of strikes had finally passed. General Motors and United States Steel were prospering. The trains were running. The clamor over Ickes and Wallace had subsided. Housing remained tight, but other shortages were disappearing. The Gross National Product was soaring. Above all, the tempestuous reconversion period with its despised controls had come to an end at last. If the president did not act on removing the remaining controls, the new Congress would. On November 9, less than a month after he had lifted price controls on livestock and food during the campaign, Truman ordered termination of all controls on wages and salaries and on prices, except in the case of rent, sugar, and rice.

At just this moment when the waves were subsiding, however, Lewis began to blow upon the waters again. His renewed threat of a coal strike on the threshold of winter provided Truman his first opportunity after the election to go on the offensive, and Truman grabbed it.

An eventual battle between Truman and Lewis had been a likelihood from the start. Truman had come from the Senate, where Lewis and his coal strikes, especially during the war, were condemned. Senator Truman had said in a letter to Margaret that Lewis was a "racketeer."[4] "Once [at a hearing of the Truman Committee] I had to give John L. Lewis a real dressing-down," he told Jonathan Daniels.[5] In 1940 Lewis had fallen out of step with the Democratic party by refusing to support Roosevelt for a third term. And after Truman entered the White House he felt that Lewis was browbeating the administration.[6] The thought that anyone would dare try to intimidate the president of the United States, as Truman believed to be the case with Lewis, was enough to bring Truman into the ring.

For his part Lewis did not hide his contempt for Truman. "Let Truman dig coal with his bayonets," he scoffed when the administration seized the mines the previous spring.[7] Lewis was a coarse, shaggy lion of a man, ferocious on behalf of those who spent their hard lives in dark and dangerous shafts underground for wages of $58.98 a week that November.[8] Under huge, menacing eyebrows and a white mane, Lewis had cold eyes, matched by a sullen mouth, made to say, as he once said to Fiorello H. LaGuardia during a labor dispute in New York, "We don't take any stuff off the president of the United States and we're not taking any off you, Mr. Mayor." Defiant of public opinion, defiant of Franklin Roosevelt, defiant of Harry Truman, his coal strikes year after year had made Lewis a pariah, excoriated in Congress and the press, as hated by many Americans as he was loved by the miners. Now, therefore, his second threat within a six-month period of 1946 to shut down the mines made a showdown likely.

The trouble began when Lewis in October accused the government of breaking by "unilateral misinterpretations" the contract under which the government had been operating the mines since the seizure during the spring strike.[9] He declared that the agreement between himself and Secretary of the Interior Krug was dead and asked for a new contract taking into account changes that had occurred in government wage policy since May. That was when he made the oblique threat to strike November 1. After the administration had maneuvered the problem beyond election day Krug told Truman in a memorandum that a new contract would be seen by the country "as another surrender to Lewis" and another stimulus to inflation.[10] Attorney General Clark had advised Krug that a strike would violate the existing contract. Krug suggested to Truman that Lewis would be in an untenable position with the public if he struck against the government. Truman, therefore, should be prepared to exploit the weak ground on which Lewis stood, even at the risk of a strike.

With Truman's approval Krug proposed to Lewis that the union and the coal mine operators negotiate a new contract that would end government seizure. Lewis refused, saying that the mine owners had no status under the Krug-Lewis agreement. Krug then refused to reopen the agreement.[11] Truman issued a statement November 15 calling Krug's policies "eminently fair." The government, he said, could not replace the mine owners in negotiating new wages. He asked the United Mine Workers to reconsider.[12]

Lewis remained silent, and there began all over again the dreary spectacle of a nation girding for a coal strike. Krug froze all bituminous coal supplies, and this action was followed by the familiar routine of orders from the Office of Defense Transportation for a 25 percent cut in the mileage of coal-burning passenger trains and an announcement by the War Department that it was preparing to guard the mines. Steel production was reduced; workers were laid off. New dimouts were ordered. Lights that flooded the dome of the Capitol were turned off. *Déjà vu* did not just afflict the country—it possessed it. As Krug had foreseen, the public found Lewis's position intolerable. Walter Lippmann called it a "brazen mockery of a contract." The *New York World-Telegram* said Lewis was "a power-drunk autocrat." The *St. Louis Post-Dispatch* branded him "a selfish demagogue." The country was menaced by a "labor dictatorship," cried Senator Byrd.

With the strike deadline approaching, Truman returned home late on November 16 from the White House Photographers Association dinner and conferred into the early hours of the morning with Krug, Clark, and John R. Steelman, then director of OWMR. Truman's decision was to wage—as he said in his diary—"a fight to the finish."[13] Then he went off to the sunshine of the navy submarine base at Key West, Florida, his first of many sojourns there during the next several years. Attired in a short-sleeved pink shirt, tan slacks, and white sulky cap, he boarded the captured German submarine U-2513 for a cruise and dived to a depth of 440 feet, a preposterous place for a president to be at any time.

Eagerly the White House staff described the labor dispute to the press, and so the press widely reported it, as a great test of whether John L. Lewis or the president of the United States was superior. Hence, if Lewis should lose, Truman would stand alone in the ring with glove upraised.

The conflict, in short, was being treated in the White House, particularly by Clifford—who, with Krug and Clark, had taken the lead in advising Truman on an aggressive course—as a rare opportunity to refurbish Truman's image. With whatever justification, Steelman afterward maintained that the strike could have been averted had it not been for this tactic. According to Steelman, he went secretly at Truman's direction first to Lewis, who suggested orally that an agreement on a forty-four-hour work week would be a "way out," and then to the operators, who concurred. Steelman said that he reported this to Truman and that Truman agreed to a forty-four-hour compromise. Steelman reported the President's position to both sides. "But Clifford and Clark and Krug," Steelman said, "seemingly persuaded [*sic*] we should not deal with Lewis, should 'have a showdown.' " Steelman believed that Truman, perhaps out of forgetfulness about the approach to Lewis, double-crossed the miners' leader. "Clifford thought it would be a great opportunity," Steelman said, "if the President got into an open fight with Lewis and licked him. He regarded it as a good political build-up and would strengthen Mr. Truman because a lot of people were against Lewis."[14]

Lewis repeatedly tried to reach Truman by telephone at Key West and later at the White House, but Truman refused to accept his calls.[15]

The administration's strategy was to take Lewis to court. A temporary order was obtained from Judge T. Alan Goldsborough in the United States District Court for the District of Columbia, directing Lewis to cancel his plans for a strike on the grounds that he was violating the Smith-Connally Act. This prohibited strikes against government-seized facilities. On November 20, however, a silent Lewis permitted the strike to begin under his familiar rule, "No contract, no work."

In Key West Truman instructed the Department of Justice to press for a contempt citation. Goldsborough held that the antiinjunction provision of the Norris-

LaGuardia Act did not prevent the government from enjoining a union in order to prevent "a public calamity." He ordered Lewis to stand trial. In court December 3 Lewis "respectfully" refused to obey Goldsborough's order. He could not "acquiesce in what must be described as an ugly recrudescence of 'government by injunction.' " The next day Goldsborough fined the United Mine Workers $3.5 million and Lewis personally $10,000 for civil and criminal contempt.

Criminal contempt proceedings against Lewis were dropped at the request of the government, acting in the belief that the jailing of the miners' leader would not have halted the strike. The effects of the coal shortage were spreading, however. Truman, back from Key West, prepared to broadcast an appeal to the strikers when Lewis called off the strike December 7 because the Supreme Court was going to review "the Administration 'yellow-dog' injunction."

Tom Clark and some members of the White House staff gathered in the president's office for a brief party. Recalling how he had rebuffed all efforts to persuade him to talk with Lewis in the last two weeks, Truman said that the White House was open to any citizen with legitimate business, but he would not confer with Lewis—that "son of a bitch." After the case had been disposed of by the Supreme Court, he continued, he might have Lewis in as far as the door to his office. Then he might have two of the biggest Secret Service men on the beat boot Lewis out.[16]

(The following March the court upheld, 7 to 2, the conviction of Lewis and the UMW for contempt but reduced the $3.5 million fine to $700,000 on condition that Lewis withdraw the notice of termination of the Krug-Lewis agreement. He complied.)

Thus in one of the celebrated conflicts in American labor history Truman, relying on the power of the courts, triumphed over John L. Lewis. The time came in fact when Tom Clark excitedly introduced the president in Dallas as the man "who stopped Joe Louis." "Tom, you gave me too much credit," Truman responded. "It wasn't Joe Louis I stopped—it was John. I haven't quite *that* much muscle."[17]

Scorned a few months earlier, Truman was now lionized by editorial writers and cartoonists. "Harry S. Truman stood fast, where Franklin D. Roosevelt had met [Lewis] half way," said *Newsweek*. "The mild-looking, often indecisive man from Missouri was stubborn in his determination that no man, not even John L. Lewis, could push the United States of America around." Clark Clifford's instincts had been flawless. Chest out, Truman wrote his mother and sister December 9: "Well, John L. had to fold up. He couldn't take the gaff. No bully can. Now I have the auto workers, steel workers and RR men to look forward to. They'll get the same treatment if they act the same way."[18] Truman's standing in the Gallup poll rose.

Truman also reacted to the recent campaign in other ways.

The returns had demonstrated again the potency of anti-Communist feeling in the country. It had proved the readiness of Republican candidates to play on fears of Communist infiltration of the federal government. Finally, the Republican victory posed for Truman the threat that the new Republican majority of Congress would take the initiative on this problem and investigate "subversion" in Washington as a means of showing the voters in 1948 that Roosevelt and Truman had been lax.

Truman had been coming under increasing pressure to try to neutralize Communist infiltration as an issue. The disclosures made to the FBI by Chambers and Bentley had stirred J. Edgar Hoover, and his vibrations had set Tom Clark, his friend and nominal superior, humming. For months Clark, seconded by members of the United States Civil Service Commission, had been urging Truman to adopt the recommendation of the House Post Office and Civil Service subcommittee and appoint a six-member commission to study the problem of loyalty among federal employees.

Rather than lean against the wind, Truman on November 25 created the President's Temporary Commission on Employee Loyalty. The chairman, recommended by Hoover, was A. Devitt Vanech, special assistant to the attorney general.[19] The other five were high officials of the Civil Service Commission and the State, Treasury, War, and Navy departments. Truman instructed the commission to examine the procedures for investigating government employees and applicants for federal jobs. He bade it inquire into the removal or disqualification of any disloyal or subversive persons; to recommend improvement in loyalty investigation procedures; to define standards of loyalty for the protection of the government; and to recommend standards of fair hearings of accused persons. The commission would make its report three months later, with results that were to be felt almost until recent times.

The election debacle also had suggested that black voters, having switched to the Democratic party under the New Deal, were starting to drift back to their historic Republican moorings. Naturally, this exerted pressure on Truman for some new action—pressure that was greatly intensified by the racial troubles that had been occurring in the Deep South throughout 1946.

Blacks were demanding to vote in Southern primaries on the basis of the 1944 Supreme Court decision in *Smith* v. *Allwright,* outlawing their exclusion from the Texas Democratic primary. States were resisting. Black veterans were returning, seeking jobs. The Ku Klux Klan was taking to the road at night, burning crosses. In Columbia, Tennessee, in February, an altercation between a white radio repairman and a black woman and her son had led to shooting. Four policemen were wounded. The Highway Patrol and State Guard arrested more than seventy blacks. A black neighborhood was looted and vandalized in an ostensible search for weapons. Two blacks were killed in jail.

The violence and hatred caused outrage in the North. Malcolm Ross, chairman of the FEPC, then in the final months of its existence, recommended to Truman that he institute an inquiry into community tensions.[20] Truman's administrative assistant, David K. Niles, wrote Attorney General Clark that it must be made manifest "that the federal government is doing all it can in order to protect civil rights."[21] Although Clark exhibited a narrow view on civil liberties when it came to dealing with the supposed Communist menace and the rights of suspected government employees, he was not a racist. On the civil rights question he was notably liberal for a Texan of those days.

With impetus from Walter White, executive secretary of the NAACP, the National Committee for Justice in Columbia, Tennessee, was established with Eleanor Roosevelt and Dr. Channing H. Tobias, director of the Phelps-Stokes Fund, as cochairmen. Clark directed the United States attorney on the scene to investigate the violence, and FBI agents were dispatched. A federal grand jury refused to find that a violation of civil rights had occurred and returned no indictment.

Meanwhile one of the most lurid white supremacists, Senator Theodore G. Bilbo, Democrat, of Mississippi, made a campaign speech in Laurel calling on every "red-blooded Anglo-Saxon man in Mississippi to resort to any means to keep hundreds of Negroes from the polls in the July 2 primary." For emphasis he added: "And if you don't know what that means, you are just not up on your persuasive measures."

In this spirit a horrible crime was committed in Aiken, South Carolina. With their clubs policemen blinded Sergeant Isaac Woodard, Jr., a black, only three hours after he had been separated from the army. R. R. Wright, Sr., former president of the Georgia State College, wrote an impassioned letter to Truman saying, "To 'gouge out the eyesight' of a man who had used his eyes to safeguard the freedom of our country is surely a disgrace unheard of in any other country in the world." Truman handed the letter to Niles, who futilely promised Wright the government would do all it could to bring the guilty to justice.[22]

Scene of the next horrors was Georgia just after Eugene Talmadge had won the Democratic gubernatorial nomination in a primary, having promised, "No Negro will vote in Georgia for the next four years." In Taylor County, Macio Snipes, the only black to have voted in his district, was killed in his front yard by four white men. Worse yet, in Walton County a white gang shot and killed two blacks, Roger Malcolm and George Dorsey, who were accompanied by their wives. Then, when one of the wives recognized a member of the gang, the two women were murdered.[23]

In this intolerable situation black women picketed the White House for several days with signs reading, "Speak! Speak! Mr. President!" Dr. Max Yergan, president of the National Negro Congress, led a thousand persons from Union Station to the White House, after which he criticized Truman for not condemning perpetrators of violence. Fifteen thousand marched to the Lincoln Memorial demanding, among other things, the outlawing of the Klan, and an equally large number held a protest meeting in New York. Black newspaper publishers appealed to Truman to demand enactment of an antilynching bill by Congress. Clark announced he would recommend such legislation in the next session of Congress. In his press conference August 1 Truman indicated his approval.[24]

Writing to Charles G. Bolte, chairman of the American Veterans Committee, August 28, he said: "Discrimination, like a disease, must be attacked wherever it appears. This applies to the opportunity to vote, to hold and retain a job, and to secure adequate shelter and medical care no less than to gain an education compatible with the needs and ability of the individual."[25]

Representatives of more than forty religious, professional, labor, veterans', and civil rights organizations met under the auspices of the NAACP and the American Council on Race Relations to form the National Emergency Committee Against Mob Violence. As this committee moved to mobilize public opinion, Truman conferred September 19 with its leaders, who petitioned him to take several measures, including calling Congress into special session to pass an antilynching bill. The recent fate of the FEPC and the successful Senate filibuster against anti-poll tax legislation could not have encouraged Truman to believe that a special session would be anything but a gesture.

He seemed horrified at the fresh recital of violence offered by his callers. When White described the blinding of Sergeant Woodard, Truman rose and said, "My God. I had no idea it was as terrible as that. We've got to do something." He added that "everybody seems to believe that the President by himself can do anything he wishes on such matters as this, but the President is helpless unless he is backed by public opinion." Before the meeting he and Niles had discussed the possibility of establishing a commission to study mob violence and civil rights, an idea that had been in the air since the race riots of 1943. Niles proposed it at the meeting. White said that Congress might not approve. Under pressure to take the initiative on civil rights regardless of Congress, Truman said he would create the body by executive order.[26] The next day he wrote to Tom Clark, expressing his alarm over the racial situation and suggested that a commission to propose remedies should be "something similar to the Wickersham Commission on Prohibition." he added:

I know you have been looking into the Tennessee and Georgia lynchings, and also been investigating the one in Louisiana, but I think it is going to take something more than the handling of each individual case after it happens—it is going to require the inauguration of some sort of policy to prevent such happenings.[27]

Much in favor of the idea, Clark had an executive order drawn to create a committee.

Meanwhile in another session, which produced more heat than light, Truman received a delegation from the American Crusade to End Lynching, headed by the outspoken left-wing singer, Paul Robeson. One of the group nettled Truman at the outset by suggesting that American lynchings were like the Nuremberg trials that had led to the hanging of German war criminals. The United States could deal with internal affairs, Truman said, without reference to events abroad. Then Robeson rankled him by suggesting that it would be time for foreign powers to intervene in the United States unless mob violence was halted. Truman replied in effect that he would deal with American problems without foreign interference. Niles ended the meeting as quickly as possible.[28]

On December 5 Truman signed the order for the President's Committee on Civil Rights, with Charles E. Wilson, president of General Electric, as chairman. The liberally tinged, distinguished membership, black and white, drawn from different parts of the country, included college presidents, bishops, lawyers, business executives, and labor leaders. The committee was instructed to study not merely mob violence but the whole problem of civil rights. Hardly unmindful of the South's attitude, Truman had taken an irrevocable step forward in the troubled history of race relations in the United States. It would be ten months before the committee would report. The effect would be profound.

26. The Unraveling of the Old Order

D URING 1946 events were occurring in China, Korea, Germany, Greece, Turkey, the Middle East, and Indochina, the outcome of which was to have a great bearing on the alignment of nations in the second half of the twentieth century.

When General Marshall at the start of the year got down to business in China as the president's special representative and mediator he found unbridled mistrust between the Nationalists and the Communists after years of internal strife. Each side still hoped to win control of the country. Chiang's regime was unwilling to admit the Communists to the government until they gave up their armed forces. The Communists, however, feared to make such a sacrifice without guarantees of their status in the government. Still a truce was arranged January 10 and a National Assembly was called for May to adopt a constitution. A plan for integration of the two opposing armies was agreed to.[1] Encouraged, Truman wrote to Representative De Lacy February 15:

I have received another communication from General Marshall and, if things continue going as favorably as they are going now, I believe we can have all our forces out of China before the year is out. . . . . I hope we will come out with a unified China and a good friend in the Far East for the United States.[2]

Nevertheless the attempted reconciliation soon commenced to unravel in fighting for control of Manchuria.

In accordance with a Sino-Soviet treaty of August 14, 1945, Soviet forces began withdrawing from Manchuria in the winter of 1946. Chinese Communists moved into areas the Soviets were abandoning. Violent conflicts broke out as the Nationalist troops tried to extend their control into these regions and displace the Chinese Communists. In the disturbed atmosphere, the impending National Assembly was postponed indefinitely.

On April 14 the Soviets withdrew from Changchun, capital of Manchuria. The next day the Chinese Communists attacked and quickly occupied the city in violation of the truce. At the same time Nationalist belligerency was growing. Chiang's political and military advisers were urging a policy of force they were not powerful enough to carry out, Marshall cabled Truman from Nanking May 6, adding:

"In brief, we are now at an impasse. . . . The outlook is not promising and the only alternative to a compromise arrangement is, in my opinion, utter chaos in North China, to which the fighting will inevitably spread."

Marshall summarized the problem: the Communists feared "that the stalwarts of the Government Party do not mean to go through with genuine coalition govern-ment'' and the Nationalists feared that the Soviet Union was influencing or assisting the Chinese Communists' military operations in Manchuria.[3]

On May 23 the Nationalist forces not only recaptured Changchun but, despite Marshall's appeal for a cessation of offensive operations, moved north toward Har-bin. By this time the Nationalists were confident they could win by force in Man-churia, and their interest in compromising with the Communists was fading.

Even so, another truce was arranged June 7. Chiang's armies, however, con-tinued to exploit their position near Changchun, and the Communists began an of-fensive in Shantung Province. Marshall mediated between Chiang and the Commu-nist general, Chou En-lai, for days. Chiang's demands invariably went further than Chou En-lai would accept. The desire of the Nationalist generals to settle matters by force kept the situation explosive. The Communists complained that American aid to Chiang was contributing to civil war. Ostensibly to appear impartial Marshall had military assistance suspended.

"The situation is extremely critical," he cabled Truman June 17. It had been aggravated, the general explained, by the Nationalists' policy of force and by their belief that the Communists could be quickly crushed, which Marshall viewed as a miscalculation.[4]

In July hostilities spread in north China. Political negotiations failed. On the twenty-second Marshall cabled Truman that he feared the heavy fighting "was heading directly into uncontrollable civil war."[5] Marshall warned Chiang that the Nationalist troops were dangerously overextended in the north. Chiang, however, would end the fighting only on his terms. In August the Chinese Communist Party issued a general mobilization order.

On August 10 Truman wrote to Chiang, hinting that the United States might re-examine its China policy. Reflecting Marshall, he said that "recent developments have forced me to the conclusion that the selfish interests of extremist elements, both in the Kuomintang and the Communist Party, are obstructing the aspirations of the people of China." Unless the Chinese moved promptly toward a settlement, he said, American opinion was unlikely to "continue in its generous attitude towards your nation."[6]

Earlier Truman had told Wallace he had never met Chiang but had met Ma-dame Chiang and did not like her. He said that, like any other dictatorship, the Kuomintang was untrustworthy on civil liberties.[7]

Truman's letter was a waste of time. A week later Marshall informed him that Chiang was bent on achieving a settlement by force. The Communists reached the same conclusion, according to Marshall, and were striking heavy military blows to protect their positions. Again Marshall urged Chiang to halt the fighting, but in-formed Truman in mid-September that the generalissimo was adamant in believing that only Nationalist military success could bring the Communists to terms.

Late in September Marshall told a representative of Chou En-lai's that unless the Communists ceased their propaganda challenging his own integrity he would withdraw as a mediator. Then on October 1 he sent a memorandum to Chiang deploring the tactics of both sides and said that unless they got together he would recommend to Truman the termination of his mission.[8]

Marshall was particularly disturbed over a Nationalist advance on Kalgan, an important city northwest of Peiping, which was held by the Communists and which Chiang had assured Marshall he would leave alone. Chou En-lai had told Marshall that unless the advance was halted the Communists would conclude that Chiang's regime had abandoned the idea of a peaceful settlement. Chiang would not call a halt, however, and Marshall cabled Truman suggesting that the president notify Chiang that Marshall could not continue as mediator in the circumstances. "I believe," Marshall said, "that this is the only way to halt this military campaign and dispel the evident belief of the Government generals that they can drag us along while they carry through an actual campaign of force."[9]

Chiang got wind of Marshall's suggestion and quickly proposed a truce over Kalgan. Marshall withdrew the recommendation for his recall only to have the mistrustful Communists reject the truce. The Nationalists then captured Kalgan October 10. The same day they announced resumption of conscription, which had been suspended after the Japanese surrender.

On November 16 Chou En-lai called on Marshall in Nanking and said he was returning to the Communist headquarters in Yenan. While voicing his respect for Marshall, he said, "The Chinese problem is too complicated and the changes are tremendous."[10]

In a glimpse of great trouble that lay ahead at home the State Department informed Marshall December 11 that extreme right-wing sentiment was demanding "all-out support of Chiang."[11]

With Marshall's mission a year old and obviously in its final stage, Truman on December 18 issued a statement which warned that the Chinese conflict constituted "a threat to world stability and peace." He concluded by reiterating a crucial point of his December 1945 statement: "We are pledged not to interfere in the internal affairs of China."[12] The close of 1946 brought an end of American efforts to foster coalition government in China. The Truman administration did not interfere in China's internal affairs in the sense of underwriting Chiang's military and economic policies or dispatching forces. It did, under heavy Republican pressure, continue to furnish limited economic and military aid to Chiang's regime. In the forthcoming debacle this assistance was neither effectual in rescuing Chiang nor successful in appeasing the Republicans.

As always, the situation in Korea went badly in 1946. At the foreign ministers' meeting in Moscow at the end of December 1945, Byrnes, Molotov, and Bevin had agreed to the formation of a Joint Commission representing the Soviet and American commands in Korea to establish a single provisional Korean government. After a five-year, four-power trusteeship this government would gain independence.[13]

The two commands, however, disputed which Koreans should be consulted by the commission. The Soviets insisted on excluding groups on the right and the Americans on excluding many organizations on the left. In bitterness the Soviet-American talks in Korea deadlocked, leaving an indefinite division between the Soviet-occupied north Korea and the American-occupied south Korea. On June 22 Edwin Pauley, on a reparations mission that took him to both areas, wrote Truman: "Frankly I am greatly concerned with our position in Korea. . . . While Korea is a small country, and in terms of our total military strength is a small responsibility, it is an ideological battleground upon which our entire success in Asia may depend.'' Pauley recommended that the Soviet Union should be compelled to comply with the Byrnes-Molotov-Bevin agreement. Also the United States should institute a campaign of propaganda, education, and technical assistance.

Pauley's recommendations were incorporated in a revised policy on Korea then being prepared in Washington. Replying to Pauley July 16 in a letter drafted by Acheson, Truman said,

While I agree that we should continue our efforts to persuade the Soviet Union to comply . . . I believe that the most effective way to meet the situation in Korea is to intensify and persevere in our present efforts to build up a self-governing and democratic Korea, neither subservient to nor menacing any power.

American policy, Truman said, would be to create a legislative assembly and to hold elections for local and provincial offices. ''Obviously,'' Truman said, ''we cannot set up a separate government for south Korea.'' That was to come later, after things had grown still worse. Truman said that the United States would give the South Koreans economic and technical assistance, adding,

Our commitments for the establishment of an independent Korea require that we stay in Korea long enough to see the job through and that we have adequate personnel and sufficient funds to do a good job. . . . I am, therefore, requesting the agencies concerned to see that the means are found to assure that General Hodge has the men and funds he needs to attain our objectives.[14]

''Our future, I think,'' he said in a talk July 17, ''lies in the Pacific, from a foreign trade standpoint, if we can get peace in the Pacific—and I think we will eventually get it.''[15]

In Europe the goal set at Potsdam of a common economic policy for Germany was going by the boards, hastening the drift toward division of the German nation.

At Yalta, France had been given a zone of occupation in Germany and a seat on the Allied Control Council. Nevertheless the French had not been invited to Potsdam. Thus they were not bound by the decisions made by the Big Three. While the French government had accepted the Potsdam agreement in general, it notified the other three powers of its opposition to a unified Germany. France feared revival of the old Germany or a new Germany dominated by the Soviets. And as a member of the Control Council, France could—and did—veto proposals for a central German transport administration, central operation of postal service, power grids, financial institutions, and similar vehicles for reviving central German management. Thus effective administration of Germany under four-power auspices was frustrated from the start and a new pressure for partition brought into play, since each zone increasingly ran its own affairs in its own way.

Seeds of the eventual partition of Germany had been carried on the wind for a considerable time. The original wartime decision to create separate zones of occupation provided matrices for a Germany different from what it had been before 1940. The heightened authority of the zonal commanders contributed to setting the zones apart. The American plan approved at Potsdam under which each of the occupying powers would take reparations from its own zone, with the respective military commanders given final authority over reparations, weakened the treatment of Germany as a single economic unit. Now French intransigence toward central administration intensified the independence of each zone. The Soviets went their own way in their zone.

Postwar change, of course, did not occur all at once but evolved through innumerable developments, including conflicts over reparations, that sharpened Soviet-American differences. The cost of managing the German economy soared as the winter of 1945–46 arrived and disease and hunger spread. With a mounting burden on their own taxpayers, the Americans and British had to move food and supplies into the western zones.

Byrnes feared that, as things were going, the occupation program agreed to at Potsdam would bring chaos, not just to the western zones of Germany but to all of Western Europe. Despairing of collaboration with the Soviets and worried that the hard-pressed British would develop their own economic program in their zone, Byrnes decided on a course of making West Germany economically self-sufficient. Increased output of German coal and steel could help rebuild Western Europe as a whole, diminishing the danger of communism in the process. On July 11, 1946, in Paris, therefore, the secretary of state offered to join the economy of the American zone with that of any other. The proposal led to the merging of the economies of the American and British zones in what was called "Bizonia"—a development that was to provide a basis for an eventual West German government.

On September 6, 1946, Byrnes made his speech in Stuttgart, intended to win the allegiance of the German people. Challenging both Soviet and French aims in Germany, he advocated a provisional German government and an increase not only in German self-rule but in the German standard of living. He opposed separation of the Ruhr and the Rhineland from Germany. Finally, without objection from Truman, he said that United States forces would remain in the occupation of Germany indefinitely, which became another important factor in the eventual division of the German nation.

Having no background in German affairs, Truman entrusted German policy largely to Byrnes, while assigning the conduct of the occupation to the army and, through it, to General Lucius D. Clay as the United States military governor of Germany. While relations between Truman and Byrnes lacked the mutual confidence necessary to endure, the two continued to work together despite the recent strains over the Moscow conference and the episode on the *Williamsburg*. Truman and Byrnes communicated through personal conversation and cables. They would discuss problems during the secretary's periodic stays in Washington. Then, on returning to Europe, Byrnes would proceed within the framework of what he thought acceptable to Truman.[16] Byrnes remained nevertheless a very independent diplomat, running much of the country's foreign policy, as Bohlen recalled, "from within his head."[17]

While the evolution of postwar Germany was one of the great events of that epoch and United States policy for Germany was a cardinal responsibility of the president, the issues in Germany did not divide the American people as did questions of Asian policy. Thus Germany, despite crises ahead, never became the personal or political burden for Truman that China and Korea were to become.

On August 7 the Soviet Union had jolted Washington with a new demand upon Turkey for joint Soviet-Turkish defense of the Black Sea Straits. With Byrnes in Paris, Acheson went to Truman; and Truman agreed that the secretaries of war, state, and navy should recommend an American response.[18] On August 15 Acheson, Patterson, Forrestal, and high army and navy officers called on the president and handed him a memorandum, saying, in part,

In our opinion, the primary objective of the Soviet Union is to obtain control of Turkey. . . . If the Soviet Union succeeds in its objectives . . . it will be extremely difficult, if not impossible, to prevent the Soviet Union from obtaining control over Greece and over the whole Near and Middle East.

Hence, the memorandum said, establishment of Soviet bases in the Dardanelles or the introduction of Soviet armed forces into Turkey on some other pretext would cut off "from the Western world" Greece, Turkey, and the whole region from the Mediterranean to India. This version of what came to be called the domino theory added:

When the Soviet Union has once obtained full mastery of this territory, which is strategically important from the view of resources, including oil . . . it will be in a much stronger position to obtain its objectives in India and China.

In our judgment that best hope of preserving peace is that the conviction should be carried to the U.S.S.R., Turkey and all other powers that in case the United Nations is unsuccessful in stopping Soviet aggression the United States would not hesitate to join other nations in meeting armed aggression by the force of American arms.[19]

Truman approved such a policy and said he was prepared to pursue it "to the end." The United States, he said, might as well find out then as five or ten years hence whether the Soviet Union was bent upon conquest of the world.[20]

In concrete terms he also approved the dispatch to the Mediterranean of a naval task force—harbinger of the Sixth Fleet—headed by the new supercarrier *Franklin D. Roosevelt.* On August 19 Acheson handed the Soviet chargé d'affaires a note saying, "It is the firm opinion of this Government that Turkey should continue to be primarily responsible for the defense of the Straits."[21]

During the fall reports persisted that for economic reasons Britain would have to pull its troops out of Greece and cut its military aid to Turkey. On September 24 Byrnes cabled Under Secretary of State Clayton from Paris that it was "of the highest importance" for the United States to assist Greece and Turkey.[22] A subsequent study by the Office of Near Eastern and African Affairs concluded that "Greece and Turkey form the sole obstacle to Soviet domination of the Eastern Mediterranean which is an economic and strategic area of vital importance. . . . We cannot afford to stand idly by in the face of maneuvers and machinations which evidence an intention on the part of the Soviet Union to expand its power."[23]

On October 15 Acheson cabled Lincoln MacVeigh, United States ambassador in Athens, saying that "we are prepared to take suitable measures to support territorial and political integrity of Greece."[24] On November 8 Acheson informed Edwin C. Wilson, the ambassador in Turkey: "In case the Turks should ask the British for arms . . . which the latter are not able to furnish but which we are in a position to provide, we might be prepared to furnish such supplies to Great Britain for delivery to the Turks."[25]

The ingredients of the Truman Doctrine were rapidly being assembled.

In the United Nations a long stalemate had settled over the gulf between the Baruch Plan, with its stage-by-stage control, and the Gromyko proposal for prompt scrapping of nuclear weapons. Then stalemate yielded to failure. On October 29 Soviet Foreign Minister Molotov attacked Baruch and the Baruch Plan in the General Assembly. He not only urged immediate adoption of Gromyko's proposal for scrapping all atomic bombs, but introduced a resolution calling on the Security Council to sponsor general reduction of all armaments. In fact Baruch had from the outset of his endeavors favored the idea of general disarmament. Byrnes was opposed, however; and Truman objected that it would distract attention from the immediate problem of atomic energy control.[26]

Despite Molotov, the United States pressed for action on the Baruch Plan. Before the year ended the United Nations Atomic Energy Commission by a vote of 10 to 0, the Soviet Union and Poland abstaining, approved a control program conforming almost exactly with Baruch's and sent it to the Security Council—and, thanks to Soviet opposition, oblivion. Meanwhile the United States monopoly on the bomb continued to cloud Soviet-American relations.

As 1946 drew to an end, the situation in Indochina took a grave turn, profoundly affecting the perspective of the Truman administration on events in that part of the world. At the time of Roosevelt's death, it will be recalled, French forces were trickling back into Indochina without American protest. The State Department assented to French sovereignty. Standing aloof, Washington hoped that the French would come to satisfactory terms with Ho Chi Minh.

During 1946, however, the United States became increasingly uneasy about Ho in light of the deterioration in Soviet-American relations and the futility of the Marshall mission, raising the specter of Communist control of China. The spread of communism wherever it might occur was bad news in Washington; and as early as January 30, 1946, the State Department inquired of American officials how "Communist" the Viet Minh was.[27]

As tension grew between the French, bent on reestablishing colonial rule, and the Viet Minh, intent on the independence of Vietnam, American interest in the aims of Ho's guerrillas intensified. On September 9, Acting Secretary of State Clayton telegraphed Charles S. Reed, American consul general in Saigon: "Keep Dept informed indications subservience to Party line by Ho and other leaders, relative strength Communist and non-Communist elements Viet Nam, and contacts with Communists other countries."[28]

On November 29 the United States Ambassador in Paris, Jefferson Caffery, cabled Byrnes: "The French are very concerned over developments in Indochina. A high Foreign Ministry official said they are particularly worried because they have

August 18, 1944: Following the 1944 Democratic National Convention Roosevelt and Truman meet for breakfast at the White House to map their election campaign.

Truman sworn in soon after Roosevelt's death on April 12, 1945.

President Truman waits in Washington for train bearing body of FDR from Warm Springs, Georgia. James F. Byrnes, left, Henry Wallace, right.

At the United Nations organization conference in San Francisco June 16, 1945, President Truman, in passing, shook hands on the dais with Alger Hiss, who was secretary-general of the conference.

Above: July 31, 1945: The "Big Three" at Potsdam pose for a formal photograph seated in a garden near the meeting place. Left to right: Winston Churchill, Truman, and Joseph Stalin.

Left: Secretary of War Henry L. Stimson at the Potsdam Conference in July 1945. Stimson was responsible to the president for the development of the atomic bomb, as the decision on dropping it on Hiroshima neared.

Sec War

Reply to your 41011
suggestions approved
Release when ready
but not sooner than
August 2.

HST

Reproduced here for the first time, this handwritten note from the Potsdam Conference was President Truman's last-known personal message concerning the atomic bomb before the weapon was dropped on Hiroshima August 6, 1945. From Washington Secretary of War Henry L. Stimson had cabled Truman, requesting standby authority to release the presidential announcement of the attack after the bomb had been dropped. In his message number 41011, Stimson had said things were moving so rapidly the statement must be ready for use no later than August 1. Truman wrote out his answer.

Truman announces surrender of Japan, August 14, 1945.

President Truman and Secretary of the Treasury John W. Snyder. *A banker, Snyder was probably Truman's closest personal friend and his leading adviser on economic reconversion after the war.*

March 4, 1946: Churchill, Admiral William D. Leahy, Clark M. Clifford, Harry H. Vaughan, and President Truman at Fulton, Missouri. Mr. Churchill gave his "Iron Curtain" speech.

On the facing page, above: The president propounds the Truman Doctrine to a joint session of Congress, Senator Arthur W. Vandenberg and Speaker Joseph W. Martin, Jr. on the dais.

Below: President Truman gives a send-off to United States delegates to the inter-American conference at Bogotá in the summer of 1947. With Truman, from left to right, are Ambassador Warren R. Austin, Secretary of State George C. Marshall, and Senator Arthur W. Vandenberg.

On the facing page, above: Edward Jacobson, Truman's old friend and partner in the renowned Kansas City haberdashery of Truman & Jacobson, which failed in the 1920-21 recession, leaves the White House June 26, 1946, after urging Truman to support a Jewish homeland in Palestine. A Jew, though not a Zionist, Jacobson became a mediary between the president and Chaim Weizmann, head of the World Zionist Organization. In May 1948, Jacobson was briefly a quasi ambassador of the new state of Israel to the White House.

Below: At the start of the 1948 campaign Truman and Dewey meet at dedication of Idlewild International Airport on Long Island. Grover Whalen on left.

June 1948: Reunion of the Thirty-fifth Division with President Truman in Omaha, Nebraska, during his first cross-country political swing.

President Truman, at the extreme right, addressing a crowd in Richmond, Indiana, in a typical scene in his 1948 whistle-stop campaign. The audience seated on boxcars was a familiar sight in scores of towns across the country.

November 8, 1948: Harry S Truman with Bernard F. Dickmann, holding the Chicago Tribune issue bearing the headline "Dewey Defeats Truman." They are in the St. Louis, Missouri, train station.

On the facing page, above: President Truman talks with Under Secretary of State Dean Acheson and Secretary of State George C. Marshall.

Below: George M. Elsey, a young Harvard- and Princeton-trained historian, who rose from the post of assistant White House naval aide to become one of President Truman's most important administrative assistants and speech writers.

With reporters in tow, President Truman takes a walk in Independence, accompanied as usual by Secret Service agent Henry J. Nicholson, who over the years became something of a confidant of Truman's.

Above: The White House, as it appeared in summer, spring, and fall before the construction of the Truman balcony.

Below: The White House with the Truman balcony, built in 1948. The balcony did away with the need for awnings.

'positive proof that Ho Chi Minh is in direct contact with Moscow and is receiving advice and instructions from the Soviets.' ''[29] On this same day the French reported the recapture of Haiphong airfield in fighting that had broken out between their forces and the guerrillas.

Thirty years of war had begun in Indochina.

On December 5 Acheson, cabling a summary of State Department thinking to Abbot Low Moffat, chief of the Division of Southeast Asian Affairs, who was visiting Saigon, said:

Keep in mind Ho's clear record as agent international communism, absence evidence recantation Moscow affiliations, confused political situation France and support Ho receiving French Communist Party. Least desirable eventuality would be establishment Communist-dominated, Moscow-oriented state Indochina in view Dept.[30]

Moffat replied in this vein: "The Vietnam Government is in control of a small Communist group possibily in indirect touch with Moscow and direct touch with Yenan [Chinese Communist headquarters]."[31] In a memorandum to Acheson December 23 John Carter Vincent, director of the Office of Far Eastern Affairs, said:

Although the French in Indochina have made far-reaching paper-concessions to the Vietnamese desire for autonomy, French actions on the scene have been directed toward whittling down the powers and the territorial extent of the Vietnam "free state." This process the Vietnamese have continued to resist. . . . The French themselves admit that they lack the military strength to reconquer the country. . . . Given the present elements in the situation, guerrilla warfare may continue indefinitely.[32]

On December 23 Acheson conferred with the French ambassador, Henri Bonnet, and expressed "deep concern" over the outbreak of war. The United States was not prepared to intervene at that point, but Acheson said it was "ready and willing to do anything which it might consider helpful in the circumstances."[33] The aloofness of the Truman administration toward Indochina had ended.

III

COLD WAR

27. 1947: The Eightieth Congress Convenes

QUIET FELL OVER the joint session of Congress January 6 as a committee trooped out to escort President Truman to the rostrum to deliver his State of the Union message.

Republicans on one side, Democrats on the other, the six women and five hundred and twenty-five men—two of them black—sat in rows, looking generally industrious, important, responsible, high-minded, and—however deceptively in certain cases—sober. Who would have dreamed that day that before eighteen months had passed Mr. Truman would call this assemblage the good-for-nothing, do-nothing Eightieth Congress?

Who were these gray heads and bald heads and even sandy-colored heads, these wearers of watch chains and bifocals, these hearts of gold, silver, and tin who constituted—or so Truman was to allege—the worst Congress in history, or at least the worst since the days of Representative Thaddeus Stevens of Pennsylvania, chairman of the Joint Committee on Reconstruction and one of the House managers in the Senate trial of the impeached President Andrew Johnson?

Taken at random, the members of the Eightieth Congress included three future presidents of the United States—John Kennedy, Richard Nixon, and Lyndon B. Johnson; one future vice-president—Senator Alben Barkley of Kentucky; and a future secretary of state—Representative Christian A. Herter of Massachusetts.

The membership included about the last batch of men the country has seen who looked like senators of old. Senator Clyde R. Hoey of North Carolina never appeared on the floor in anything but gray trousers and a gray swallow-tailed coat, with a red rose in the lapel. When Senator Millard E. Tydings of Maryland reached the climax of a speech he could spread his arms wide enough to shelter six medium-built senators of either party. Senator Tom Connally, reared on a Texas farm, affected broad-brimmed black hats, full-cut black coats, gold studs, and black bow tie, and let his silvery locks curl down over his stiff white collar. To one observer at the Capitol, Connally was the only man in the Senate who could don a Roman toga and not look like a fat man in a nightgown.

Nearby sat Kenneth Wherry of Pawnee City, Nebraska, the Senate Republican whip. When, after a career as a farmer, merchant, lawyer, automobile salesman, auctioneer, county-fair promoter, and embalmer licensed in four states, Wherry was leaving for Washington, his father said, "Ken, remember to keep your big mouth shut." "Seldom," wrote Paul F. Healy in the *Saturday Evening Post*, "was parental advice so spectacularly ignored." Day after day, it seemed, Wherry flooded the Senate with malapropisms and uncontrolled metaphors, including one in which he accused Truman of "sugar-coating his red ink." Wherry once referred to the military leaders as the "Chief Joints of Staff" and on another occasion spoke of Southeast Asia as "Indigo China."

On the rostrum awaiting the president's arrival were two of the most likable men in Washington, the new Speaker of the House, Joseph W. Martin, Jr., and the president *pro tem* of the Senate, Arthur Vandenberg.

A native of North Attleboro, Massachusetts, the Speaker was the Martin of Roosevelt's famous "Martin, Barton, and Fish" speech in the 1940 campaign, in which he castigated the Republican isolationists to the cadence of "Wynken, Blynken, and Nod." At the age of twelve Joe had marched in a torchlight parade for William McKinley in 1896, and he wished McKinley were still in the White House. He thought Calvin Coolidge had been an excellent president for his time, revered Douglas MacArthur, and worshipped at the altar of party regularity. Perennial permanent chairman of Republican National Conventions—and sometimes considered a dark horse himself—he had pounded the gavel at Philadelphia in 1940 when the galleries were chanting, "We Want Willkie." "Well, if you'll be quiet long enough," Martin shouted, "maybe you'll get him."

Vandenberg, son of a harness maker, was a jovial, round-faced, heavy-set, cigar-smoking former editor of the *Grand Rapids Herald,* author of short stories and composer of a popular ballad to a reigning movie queen, Bebe Daniels, entitled, "Bebe, Bebe, Bebe—Be Mine." He was credited with having furnished the Republicans' 1920 campaign slogan, "With Harding at the Helm, We Can Sleep Nights." When asked if "Back to Normalcy" was his creation too, he thought a moment and said, "Normalcy—that sounds like one of my words." "It surely did," wrote Richard H. Rovere, whose researches into Vandenberg's "compulsive" tinkering with words yielded such other phrases as "our merific inheritances," "marcescent monarchy," and "nautical nimbus."[1] Vandenberg became a senator on March 31, 1928, and a statesman on January 10, 1945, when he delivered a speech on the Senate floor renouncing isolationism in favor of internationalism. Roosevelt went to Yalta with fifty copies of the speech, which had the effect of weakening Republican isolationism in the Senate. With great relish and at minimum cost Vandenberg, now chairman of the Senate Foreign Relations Committee, found himself a celebrated international figure on Capitol Hill. This was to be sure a matter of high importance to Truman, because as the leading Republican spokesman on foreign policy Vandenberg was an effective agent for enlisting indispensable Republican support in the Senate for the president's programs for Europe, although not for Asia and Latin America. Those areas lay outside the realm of bipartisan foreign policy, so-called. The State Department treated Vandenberg as if he were a foreign dignitary. In the Senate, Vandenberg was the Republican leader in foreign affairs and Taft in domestic. Truman remarked privately that Vandenberg was afraid of Taft—the two, Truman said, were "just like two roosters" squaring off.[2]

On the Democratic side of the aisle that day sat the spidery Representative John Rankin of Mississippi, with wild gray hair and a malevolent look. He considered everyone to the left of, and including, Harold J. Laski, then chairman of the British Labour party, a vicious Communist bent on destroying Christianity in the United States. A Shakespearean scholar by repute, Rankin thrived on shrill bigotry. On the

House floor he once referred to Representative Celler as "the Jewish gentleman from New York" and in the next breath said that the Daughters of the American Revolution—"the finest band of Christian ladies in the world"—was "one of the greatest organizations over which the flag ever floated."

Across the aisle with the Republicans sat big, lumbering, phlegmatic William Knowland of California, son of the proprietors of the *Oakland Tribune* and a senator by appointment of Governor Earl Warren, acting to fill the vacancy left by the death of Hiram Johnson. In January 1946, Knowland made his first trip to the Far East as a member of a two-man subcommittee. He met Chiang Kai-shek, who told him the Soviet Union threatened to expand in Asia. He also met General MacArthur, who told him the Soviet Union threatened to expand in Asia. Impressed, Knowland returned to the Senate and brooded over the Soviet threat to expand in Asia.

Men who knew their minds sat in the Eightieth Congress.

Representative Clare Hoffman of Michigan had his jackets made without pockets because he once lost an important paper he had been carrying. Senator John H. Overton of Louisiana would not countenance daylight saving time. Anyone having business with him in summers had to adjust his appointments accordingly, as Overton hung on his door a notice, "This Office Runs on God's Time." Sensitive to other issues as well, he once shouted, "Don't shake your gory locks at me," to Taft, who was semibald. Senator Forrest C. Donnell, a prim and bespectacled Missouri Republican, treated detail the way a Vatican council might treat dogma. He drove points of order into the ground like tent pegs, carried a dictionary almost wherever he went, and was so circumspect in his correspondence that before closing a letter with "Mrs. Donnell and I send our warmest regards," he was apt to telephone his wife to make sure she *did* send her warmest regards.

Representative Clarence Cannon, from Missouri,—even though he was sixty-seven, scholarly, and the author of *Cannon's Precedents* and *Cannon's Procedure,*—settled arguments on more occasions than one by springing up and punching another member in the face. No less emphatic, but safer to be around, was Senator William Langer of North Dakota, an inveterate table-pounder, who was once so possessed by an issue that he split the top of his desk in the Senate with his fist.

The most piercing voice in the chamber, especially when challenging liberal policy, was that of Representative John Taber, Yale '02, a Republican from Auburn, New York, and, as chairman of the House Appropriations Committee, a budget-cutter par excellence. One day in a debate on a labor measure he roared with such power that he restored the hearing in a deaf ear of Representative Leonard W. Schuetz of Illinois, who had been afflicted since birth. Schuetz thanked Taber.[3]

Among the senators sat sixty-nine-year-old Carl Hayden, who had represented Arizona in Congress ever since it had become a state in 1912. Legend had it that once when he was plodding to an elevator in the Capitol he inadvertently stepped into a telephone booth and said, "Up."

The Eightieth Congress was peculiarly the preserve of powerful southerners, powerful conservatives, and powerful old men. Legislators ranging in age from sixty-eight to eighty-three were either the Republican chairmen or the ranking Democratic minority members of the House Banking and Currency Committee, the House Ways and Means Committee, the House Rules Committee, the House

Foreign Affairs Committee, the Senate Appropriations Committee, the Senate Judiciary Committee, the Senate Finance Committee, and the Senate Agriculture and Forestry Committee.

Except for the modified Employment Act of 1946, the Seventy-ninth Congress had squelched practically every piece of social and economic legislation Truman had requested. The outlook for domestic programs in the Eightieth Congress was, if possible, dimmer. Many of the remaining New Dealers in Congress had been swept out by the November elections. As prosperity quelled the appetite for reform, conservatives marched onto Capitol Hill believing the future was theirs.

The metallic voice of Robert Alphonso Taft called the shots on domestic issues for the Republican majority of the Senate. The Ohioan, Truman's sharpest critic, won the chairmanship of the Senate Republican Policy Committee. Determined on legislation to curb the power of unions, he then shunted aside the more liberal Senator Aiken, a Vermont Republican, and took the chairmanship of the Committee on Labor and Public Welfare himself. Otherwise he would have preferred to chair the Finance Committee to lead a fight to cut taxes, but he solved that problem by throwing the chairmanship to Senator Eugene D. Milliken of Colorado, who was more conservative than he.

Southern Democrats who for years had been powers on the main Senate committees—Russell, McKellar, Byrd, George, and James O. Eastland of Mississippi—were natural allies of Taft, not Truman. The coalition of conservative Republicans and southern Democrats had a stronger grip than ever.

The House Republican hierarchy—Joe Martin; and Representatives Charles A. Halleck of Indiana; Leslie C. Arends of Illinois; Clarence J. Brown of Ohio; Taber; Harold Knutson of Minnesota, chairman of the Ways and Means Committee; Jesse P. Wolcott of Michigan, chairman of the Banking and Currency Committee; and Leo E. Allen of Illinois, chairman of the Rules Committee—had all risen to power chanting the same refrain over and over again.

Its lines, in no particular order—they were interchangeable—were: "arrogant individualism of Franklin Delano Roosevelt . . . un-American . . . unconstitutional dictatorship . . . NRA . . . AAA . . . lavish spending . . . socialistic experiments . . . New Deal spoilers and wasters . . . never known the necessity of meeting a payroll . . . New Deal pump-primers . . . planned economy . . . reman the citadels of liberty . . . America is in peril . . . Valley Forge."[4]

Overlooking the unusual circumstances that had produced the landslide, many Republicans assumed they had a mandate to turn back the New Deal, particularly in respect to favoritism to labor, and to curb the power of the executive branch. It was in this spirit that they launched the Eightieth Congress, the prelude to the 1948 presidential election.

"The main issue of the election," Taft said in a broadcast on the eve of the new session, "was the restoration of freedom and the elimination or reduction of constantly increasing interference with family life and with business by autocratic government bureaus and autocratic labor leaders."

Taft and Martin both supported a tax cut. Promising to use a "sledge hammer" on the budget, Taber predicted that the Republicans could save the taxpayers $9 billion, and Knutson proposed a flat 20 percent reduction in taxes to "stop the New

Deal practice of using tax laws to punish its enemies and promote social innovations." Taft forecast a revival of the Case labor bill, which Truman had vetoed the previous June. Other Republicans wanted to go further than Case and abolish the closed shop and limit industry-wide bargaining.[5]

Truman moved off to a conciliatory start with the Eightieth Congress. "Let us have the will and the patience to do this job together," he said in a State of the Union message containing a minimum of political challenge and controversy.[6] He had already removed one Republican target when he ended wage and price controls. Then Elsey passed along from the bureaucracy a suggestion that Truman proclaim the end of hostilities of the Second World War (but not of the states of emergency declared by Roosevelt nor of the state of war). Even so, ending hostilities—a legal technicality—would terminate a host of government powers and cut the ground from under those Republicans who were prepared to challenge their continuance. "Swell, says H.S.T. Grand idea & wants to do it," Elsey noted.[7] Truman issued the unexpected proclamation December 31. In his State of the Union message he also revealed that he would submit for the fiscal year starting July 1 a budget showing a small surplus.

For the fiscal year 1948 the budget estimated expenditure of $37.5 billion, including $11.2 billion for national defense. In conferences with the new director of the budget, James E. Webb, Truman had said he anticipated a time a few years hence when the federal budget would level off at $25 billion, with $6 billion or $7 billion for defense. Webb reminded him that fixed charges already were running close to $25 billion, even without defense. "If we could achieve a budget in a few years of $30 billion to $35 billion," Webb said, "that would be about as much as we could hope for." [8] In a few years the United States was fighting a war in Korea, shattering dreams of a $30 billion federal budget.

Because the Republican majority—so strongly representative of business interests, farming, and the small towns—was pointed toward legislation to restrict unions, Truman's proposals on labor attracted the most attention in his State of the Union message. With 1948 on the horizon he abandoned talk about drafting strikers and fighting John L. Lewis to a finish. Rather he admonished against a "punitive" bill. Also, because of the virtual crusade in progress against Lewis, he added: "We must not, in order to punish a few labor leaders, pass vindictive laws which will restrict the proper rights of the rank and file of labor." Management, he observed, shared the responsibility for the postwar strikes.

He recommended certain reforms. He asked for a ban on strikes caused by intralabor disputes over which union had jurisdiction in a particular case. He requested a ban on secondary boycotts by unions against companies in furtherance of unjustifiable objectives. He proposed binding arbitration in disputes over interpretation of existing agreements. At the suggestion of Tom Clark, he also asked that Congress provide for appointment of a Temporary Joint Commission to study labor-management relations.[9] Such measures, of course, fell far short of what the Republicans had in mind. Neither did they make much sense to Clifford and Elsey, who drafted the message.[10] Truman was temporizing with the labor problem, awaiting the Republican initiative.

Requests he made in other areas in his State of the Union message included a call for comprehensive housing legislation. The Truman administration had had a difficult time of it with housing. With the arrival of 1947, housing was still shockingly inadequate. In February 1946, weeks after Wilson Wyatt had become Housing Expediter, he had persuaded Truman to adopt a Veterans Emergency Housing Program with a two-year goal of 2.7 million housing starts, of which 850,000 were to be prefabricated houses.[11] The program contemplated, among other things, Reconstruction Finance Corporation loans to the prefabricated housing industry, which was then just getting started. The program also required strict allocation of materials. Legislation became necessary, but, of course, the request for allocations encountered the juggernaut of conservative demands in mid-1946 for an end of controls. The building industry wanted to build expensive houses, not inexpensive ones for veterans. Finally, however, Congress passed a modified bill, and for a time Wyatt's program moved along fairly well.

The obstacles were great, however.

Wyatt found the construction industry a rabbit warren surrounded by a maze of local building codes and union regulations. Getting such an industry to spring into a huge building program was a nightmare, especially when the National Association of Home Builders and the National Association of Real Estate Boards were battling any direct government role in housing. Plumbers, electricians, and other skilled workers were often hard to find, as some of them were still getting out of the service. The multitude of strikes intensified the shortages of all kinds of building materials, even nails.

Trying frantically to make up for lost time in the fall of 1946 Wyatt got into quarrels within the administration. Angrily he went to the White House in October to denounce the Reconstruction Finance Corporation for not lending money to the prefabricated housing industry, on which his plans depended heavily. But then Truman ended price controls, which were essential to Wyatt's program. The two men soon found themselves on a collision course. Wyatt wanted reestablishment of controls. Sobered by the November election, Truman knew well enough how such a program would be received in the new Congress. Wyatt, the most prominent liberal left in the administration, resigned. Completely outdated, the Veterans Emergency Housing Program soon died.[12] The thing that saved the day was the GI Bill of Rights, enacted during the war, which enabled veterans to go into the private housing market and make purchases through guaranteed low-interest loans.

Looking to the future, Truman asked Congress in his State of the Union message to enact a housing measure along the lines of the Taft-Ellender-Wagner bill, one of the controversial pieces of legislation of the period. A notable aspect of it was that it represented a commitment to public housing by Taft in the face of overwhelming conservative disapproval. Fiercely contested in the Seventy-ninth Congress, the bill had been passed by the Senate but, despite Truman's appeals, died in the House Banking and Currency Committee. Among other things it set a goal of 1.25 million new housing units a year for ten years, slum clearance with federal grants, and low-interest loans for building 500,000 public housing units within four years. Despite his new appeal, however, Truman had a long wait ahead for major housing legislation.

An aspect of the problem that troubled him was the equation between poor housing and juvenile delinquency. Under the heading "Homes & Juvenile Delinquency" he had written a note several months earlier saying that "bad boys and unruly girls" were becoming a serious problem. "There is nothing fundamentally wrong with the young people," he observed. "When the facts are examined it will be found that in a great many cases it is mamma and papa who are delinquent and not the children."

"The greatest and most important job in all the world is mother's job," he added. "She makes the character and influences the career of the next generation more than any other person. When mother has to pass on the raising of the children to the State or any other institution then delinquency increases."[13]

While the president was off to a temperate start with the conservative Congress, the political and economic storms of 1945 and 1946 had caused a ferment among liberals that was beginning to harden into new patterns that would have an important bearing on Truman's prospects for reelection in 1948.

Throughout the New Deal years Roosevelt had been a magnet for the liberals. When war came and the United States and the Soviet Union were allied, the divisive Communist issue was bridged by a popular front against fascism. Liberals, progressives, Communists, and fellow travelers were striving toward the same end. Suddenly, however, Roosevelt's death robbed the liberals of their unifying leader. And the postwar conflict between Washington and Moscow rent the popular front. When Wallace attacked United States foreign policy in Madison Square Garden he put a dynamite charge under liberal unity, and when Truman fired him he set it off. After the blast some liberals fell in line behind Wallace and his call for a friendly shift in policy toward the Soviets. Others supported Truman's show of firmness and strength.

At the approach of the 1946 elections the two organizations that had sponsored Wallace's speech at Madison Square Garden—the National Citizens Political Action Committee and the Independent Citizens Committee of the Arts, Sciences, and Professions—had, together with the CIO, already joined in calling a Conference of Progressives. It met in Chicago shortly after Wallace had been dismissed. The prominent liberals assembled adopted a resolution urging "a swift return to the progressive global thinking of Franklin Roosevelt." The resolution called upon the United States, not the Soviet Union, to "exert every effort" to recapture the wartime trust. As had Wallace, it criticized the Baruch Plan and accepted spheres of influence abroad. Although Wallace was not present, a separate resolution was adopted praising him and asking him to "carry on in your fight for the fullest, freest discussion of that basic problem of our day—international co-operation."[14]

A committee was appointed to continue the work of organization. Nevertheless the liberal split widened along two divergent lines. One line was traveled by the Chicago conference groups, who favored continuance of the popular front, including Communists. The other line was traveled by the Union for Democratic Action, a small organization that had boycotted the Chicago conference. Headed by James Loeb, Jr., and the Reverend Reinhold Niebuhr and boasting Eleanor Roosevelt as a patron, the UDA disagreed with Wallace's foreign policy and barred Communists and fellow travelers from its ranks. A haven for those who opposed Communist penetration of American liberalism, it was attempting a large-scale expansion of its own.

During that fall of 1946 the National Citizens Political Action Committee and the Independent Citizens Committee of the Arts, Sciences, and Professions merged. Significantly, the CIO did not join the merger. Nevertheless the combined groups, along with some lesser state and local organizations, met in New York in December and formed the Progressive Citizens of America. The reception given Henry Wallace upon his appearance left no doubt as to who its hero was. Moreover its "Program for Political Action" denounced the Democrats for having alledgedly abandoned the Roosevelt tradition and declared, "We cannot, therefore, rule out the possibility of a new political party, whose fidelity to our goals can be relied on." [15] A breeze was coming up from the left, blowing in the direction of the nomination of Henry Wallace for president on a third-party ticket.

The UDA was moving also. Mrs. Roosevelt made overtures on its behalf to Philip Murray, the CIO president, who had attended the Chicago conference but was not disposed to being taken into camp by Communists. He moved steadily away from the Chicago conference groups, a serious blow to them because of the importance of CIO money and numbers. Another circumstance that lent impetus to the move to expand the UDA was the Republican landslide in November. Plainly, the Democrats had been hurt by the Communist issue, and many saw the need for a new liberal organization that excluded Communists.

With Loeb and Niebuhr taking the initiative, a celebrated group of liberals met in Washington January 3, three days before the State of the Union message. The gathering included newspaper writers and publishers; labor leaders; famous old New Dealers; Washington lawyers like Joseph L. Rauh, Jr., David Ginsburg, and James H. Rowe, Jr.; and scholars and politicians like John Kenneth Galbraith, Arthur M. Schlesinger, Jr., Franklin D. Roosevelt, Jr., Mayor Hubert H. Humphrey of Minneapolis, and Richardson Dilworth of Philadelphia. The star of the cast was Mrs. Roosevelt.

The group voted to form the Americans for Democratic Action. Mrs. Roosevelt delivered the keynote speech. She said the United States should steer a democratic course between fascist and Communist totalitarianism and gave the ADA its first contribution—$100. [16] Wilson Wyatt became national chairman. Gradually the Americans for Democratic Action and the Truman administration moved to parallel courses, but the way to warm relations between the ADA and Truman personally was to prove a bumpy one.

Ten days after the State of the Union message Truman announced "complete agreement" on one of the major issues before him. On January 16 he received a letter from Forrestal and Patterson stating their agreement on a proposed form of unification of the armed forces. The same day Truman made public his reply expressing approval of the legislation they recommended. [17]

The unification controversy had been an exhausting one. Truman had begun in 1945 by espousing General Marshall's concept of a single Department of National Defense in which the army, navy and an air force would have equal status. A secretary of national defense would head the department. The highest uniformed officer would be a chief of staff, who would be in supreme command of all the forces. The navy had reacted against tight unification, preferring a "federal" coordination of largely autonomous services. In particular it was adamant against the idea of a single chief of staff.

When legislation embodying Truman's proposals was introduced in the spring of 1946, the navy opposed it. Under navy pressure Truman dropped his plan for a chief of staff. The navy still opposed a single Department of Defense, but Truman would not yield on this point. In letters to Forrestal and Patterson June 15, 1946, he insisted on a single department, while placating the navy in regard to the functions of the Marine Corps. Forrestal reluctantly assented.

Fundamental differences remained unresolved, however, and Truman deferred legislation until the 1947 session of Congress.

The two main questions still at issue then involved the authority of the prospective secretary of defense and the respective roles and missions of the three services.

In the fall of 1946 the Pentagon elite, particularly the Wall Street crowd of Forrestal, Patterson, McCloy, and a recent Pentagon alumnus, the former secretary of war for air, Robert A. Lovett, worked out a final compromise. The army, navy, and air force would be autonomous. The new secretary of defense would have no general nor specific responsibility with respect to administration of the three departments. Neither would he have control over them nor the right to interfere in their affairs. Oblivious to the terrible consequences that awaited him as a result of the limitation on the secretary of defense's authority, Forrestal had carried the day with his concept of the secretary as a coordinator.

As the necessary legislation was prepared for submission to Congress, it was clear how much the months of bureaucratic struggle had wrenched the plan out of the shape originally envisioned by Truman. In a note to Clifford, Elsey complained:

—President's intention was merger.
—We are not getting merger. . . .
—We have three services, headed nominally by a "Secretary" with no staff, no tools, no control. . . .[18]

Hence notable changes in the Washington landscape were in the offing and not simply because of a proposed new Department of the Air Force at the Pentagon. Also to be established, as originally proposed in the Eberstadt plan, were the National Security Council and the Central Intelligence Agency, a venture that was to draw Truman into decisions beyond anything, surely, that he had ever imagined.

28. *China Mission Fails;*
Marshall Secretary of State

CIVIL WAR IN China had gone so far that Marshall had written Truman December 28, 1946, suggesting that the United States end its futile efforts at mediation and withdraw the marines from Tientsin and Peiping. "At the same time," he said, "I think I should be recalled."[1] A recent communication from the Communists had convinced him that they wanted to terminate not only American mediation but all further attempts at a negotiated peace.[2]

Truman's concurrence in Marshall's recommendation was conveyed to the general January 3 by Byrnes, who had returned to Washington from a meeting of the Council of Foreign Ministers in New York, where work had been completed on peace treaties with Italy, Rumania, Bulgaria, Hungary, and Finland. Byrnes cabled Marshall that Truman "would appreciate it if . . . you would return for consultation on China and other matters."

In the interest of coordination, the general's liaison officer at the State Department, Colonel Marshall S. Carter, showed Truman Byrnes's telegram. Truman instructed him to send Marshall another message that same day, urging him to return promptly. "Mr. Truman's concern," Carter explained, "is connected with the last two words of Mr. Byrnes's message, and the project that the President has previously discussed with you."[3]

The last two words of Byrnes's message were "other matters," although Byrnes evidently did not realize their significance at the time of the cable. The words referred to Truman's earlier query to Marshall as to whether he would agree to become secretary of state at some point. As will be recalled, Truman the previous April had delegated Eisenhower to put the question to Marshall in China. Marshall had said yes. "I knew all that time whom I wanted for the job," Truman related later.[4]

Marshall cabled Carter January 4: "I think I fully understand the matter to be discussed. My answer is affirmative if that continues to be his desire. My personal reaction is something else."[5]

"He has a free hand over there [at the State Department]," Truman told reporters after the appointment had been announced.[6]

So the end of the Truman-Byrnes relationship as president and secretary of state was at hand. How did Byrnes feel? Ostensibly because of his health, he had submitted his resignation the previous April, but had stayed on to see negotiations over treaties with the satellite nations through to a conclusion. As time passed, his concern over his health diminished. Then in September he was elated at the dramatic manner in which Truman had finally sided with him against Wallace. It seemed to Byrnes that the firing of Wallace was proof that the president and the secretary of state were in harmony on foreign policy. He even mentioned to Vandenberg in Paris that he might now have to continue as secretary as an obligation to Truman.[7]

After the terms of the treaties had been settled in New York, Byrnes thought it proper to remind Truman of his resignation, which left the president the option of accepting or rejecting it. In a cordial but subtle way Truman spoke of reasons why Byrnes should remain, but he did not reject the resignation.[8] Several days later he told Byrnes he was going to nominate Marshall, who was sixty-six—and weary. At the time of Byrnes's letter in the spring, it will be recalled, Truman had mentioned Marshall as a possible successor and Byrnes's reaction had been favorable. Now, however, his associates sensed that he was somewhat shaken to learn that Truman already had taken practically irreversible steps to bring Marshall to the State Department. But Truman and Byrnes seemed to part as friends. In fact, considerable time would elapse before they began exchanging blows in public, but over domestic issues, not foreign policy.

Truman's selection of Marshall was a superlative political stroke. Despite the recent failure of an impossible mission, Marshall's character and reputation were unblemished in the public eye. Such was his stature yet that the president of Harvard, Dr. Conant, was soon to suggest he was the only other American in history who could be compared with George Washington.[9] Being highly regarded as a soldier and statesman positioned absolutely above politics, Marshall's appearance greatly enhanced the prestige of the Truman administration after its recent decline. The fact that Marshall had accepted another arduous post against his inclination said something about his regard for Truman as a man and as a president.

Marshall's standing with Congress was unique. The Senate unanimously confirmed his nomination the same day Truman submitted it. Whatever the Republican majority might have in store for Truman on domestic policy, it was not disposed to slight or ignore the testimony of George Marshall on foreign affairs. Truman's devotion to him remained incurable. After Marshall's name on his appointment list February 18 he noted: "The more I see and talk to him, the more certain I am he's the great one of the age. I am surely lucky to have his friendship and support."[10]

It was widely accepted then and has been subsequently that Marshall's arrival as secretary brought vigor, clarity, and heightened morale to the State Department. No one has argued the point more forcefully than Dean Acheson, who agreed to remain as under secretary for another six months. Marshall took office at a time of accelerating difficulties abroad, especially in Germany. He relied to a great extent on State Department professionals, who had a deep distrust of the Soviet Union. Twenty months of ever-diverging Soviet and American policies had passed since V-E Day, and compromise was at low tide.

The title of "Under Secretary" inadequately describes the role Acheson played in the last sixteen months of the Byrnes regime and was to play in his forthcoming six months under Marshall.

With the secretary of state—Byrnes or Marshall—making the rounds of conferences in London, Paris, Moscow, and the United Nations, Acheson was acting secretary much of the time, dealing directly with Truman and the cabinet and exerting his own potent influence on the principal decisions of foreign policy. A man of intellect, wit, snobbery, arrogance, high style and charm, he was a gifted lawyer, skilled advocate, formidable negotiator, and strong administrator. Tall and straight, he had flashing dark eyes, the eyebrows of a grandee, and the mustache of a guardsman, which he had grown in the summer of 1911 while working as a supervisor's assistant on a railroad in Canada between the time he left preparatory school and entered college.

In contrast with Truman, he was a prize bloom from the garden that had long produced the American elite, having attended Groton, Yale (where Harriman, two classes ahead of him, was his rowing coach), and Harvard Law School and having studied under Felix Frankfurter, clerked for Associate Justice Louis D. Brandeis in the United States Supreme Court, and joined the preeminent Washington law firm of Covington & Burling. A protégé of Frankfurter's, he was appointed by Roosevelt as under secretary of the treasury early in the New Deal, but soon was forced out over disagreement with the president's gold purchase plan.

Acheson was the son of an English-born father and a Canadian-born mother. At the time of his birth in Middletown, Connecticut, on April 11, 1893, his father was rector of an Episcopal church and later became the Episcopal bishop of Connecticut. Acheson was reared in an upper-middle-class environment imbued with esteem for the British Empire and the stable world order of the nineteenth century. He responded to the rise of Hitler by advocating American rearmament and solidarity with the European Allies. He and Benjamin Cohen were among those who devised a legal basis on which Roosevelt transferred obsolete destroyers to Great Britain in return for bases. Grateful, Roosevelt got Hull to appoint Acheson assistant secretary of state for economic affairs. He represented the United States in setting up a number of the postwar international economic organizations, in the course of which he acquired a fair amount of experience in negotiating with the Soviets. When the Senate was passing on his nomination as under secretary in 1946 the right-wing Republican Wherry charged that Acheson had "blighted the name" of General MacArthur in a recent comment noting that the American occupation of Japan functioned under policies made in Washington. Wherry's words were only a trickle; the flood from the Republican right came later. Acheson brought to his influential post a conviction that the moral, economic, and military power of the United States was fundamental to peace and, as he told the Associated Harvard Clubs of Boston that August, to achieving recovery in other countries "along lines which are essential to our own system."[11]

Now, after nearly twenty months in office and with some bad times behind him, Truman was showing new confidence. Not only had his stature with the public improved over the leashing of John L. Lewis, but the White House staff was being materially strengthened, and some of the earlier controversial figures around the fringes had disappeared. George Allen retired to private life. Vardaman vanished behind the marble of the Federal Reserve. The prestigious Averell Harriman was quietly conducting the once contentious office of Henry Wallace in the Department of Commerce. James E. Webb, a North Carolina attorney and former vice-president of the Sperry Gyroscope Corporation, had come to the directorship of the Bureau of the Budget from the Treasury on Snyder's recommendation.

The replacement of Harold Smith by Webb turned out to be a godsend for the White House. Smith had jealously insisted that only he and one or two of his senior assistants in the Bureau of the Budget should be permitted access to the president. Thus his staff worked separately from the White House staff, which was overwhelmed and starved for talent. Webb not only put the Bureau of the Budget staff so completely at the disposal of the White House staff that the two organizations became almost indistinguishable except on political questions, where he drew the line for Bureau participation; but he also recruited able young men, some of them recently out of uniform, including Richard Neustadt, David H. Stowe, and David Bell, who later became President Kennedy's budget director. This new infusion of talent helped straighten out the muddles that Truman had lived with ever since taking office.

Substantial changes occurred in the White House, involving particularly Steelman, Clifford, Elsey, and Charles Murphy.

A large, genial, ingratiating man, Dr. John R. Steelman had been a professor of sociology and economics at the old Alabama College in Montevallo during the New Deal. When Secretary of Labor Perkins delivered a commencement address there, she met him, was impressed by his knowledge of labor affairs, and offered him a job. In time he became director of the United States Conciliation Service and then left the government at the end of the Roosevelt period. After Truman took office and found his secretary of labor, Schwellenbach, unable to cope with strikes, he brought Steelman into the White House to help. Steelman's responsibilities multiplied. He took over the Office of War Mobilization and Reconversion, for example, after Snyder became secretary of the treasury.

In December, 1946, Truman gave Steelman a permanent appointment as "Assistant to the President." Without public announcement, this title became in time "*The* Assistant to the President." The reason was never altogether clear, but several elements obviously went into Truman's decision. The decision to abolish the OWMR of which Steelman was director, made it necessary to find another adequate position for him. Truman was groping for a better organization. Being an able mediator, Steelman was sometimes assigned by the president to resolve quarrels between departments and agencies and even jurisdictional disputes between cabinet officers. Truman even asked him to chair certain cabinet committees. Nevertheless the appearance of the *The* in his title became a source of heightened tension between him and Clark Clifford, whose title was "Special Counsel to the President," whose prestige had soared as a result of the victory over Lewis, and who scarcely considered himself subordinate to anyone else on the White House staff.

In fact, he was not. Steelman's title did not carry the kind of authority that the same title came to carry with the next man who held it—Sherman Adams, "*The* Assistant to President Eisenhower." Adams was indisputably the White House chief of staff. Steelman was not. Unlike Eisenhower after him, Truman did not have a staff hierarchy, although, of course, some members became more influential than others. Members of Eisenhower's staff reported to Adams. Members of Truman's staff—the senior ones, at least—reported to Truman. Steelman's title was not meaningless, however. A tide of paper work flowed across his desk, as he did much of the task of coordinating the business of the White House with the rest of the executive branch. As the years passed, his fields widened. Generally, Steelman handled the normal daily flow of White House business, whereas Clifford dealt with large special problems and speech writing.

However, since Steelman's authority and Clifford's were not fixed in a hierarchy, an inevitable rivalry occurred as to which of them was going to be the larger power in the White House. As Steelman's comments on Clifford's role in the coal strike indicate, differences had developed between them even before Steelman became "The Assistant to the President." Afterward competition set in over handling assignments from Truman. "Steelman mad at C.M.C.[Clark M. Clifford] for carrying this ball . . . ,"[12] Elsey noted in connection with preparation of a presidential message on the signing of the Housing and Rent Control Act June 30, 1947.

The rivalry between them never really came to a head. One man was more influential than the other, or vice versa, depending on the matter at hand, although in 1947 and 1948 Clifford had the reputation of being the big wheel in the White House. This, along with his suave manner and his attractiveness to reporters and hence his entrée to publicity, vexed the older members of the "Missouri Gang," who tended to regard him as an interloper who was, they believed, getting the lion's share of the credit. Certainly no one on the staff could match Clifford's flair and social glamor. He was bright, clever, pragmatic, cool, and—possibly excepting Hoyt Vandenberg, the air force general and the senator's nephew—the handsomest man in public life in Washington at the time, with a smile that would have put Hamlet at ease. Although his "golden hair" was much remarked upon, it was not nearly so golden as his voice. With elegance he could talk his way through situations as thick as walls, being the kind of lawyer who excels at getting practical things done. In the course of it he brought a bedside manner to the starkest political situations and had an attaché case full of tricks, not the least of which was that he always tried to be the last member of the staff to see Truman at the end of each day so that he could give the final word of advice.

Relations between Clifford and Snyder also were uneasy. Snyder was less than impressed by Clifford's style, and Clifford was less than impressed by Snyder's political acumen. Snyder had fought Rosenman over the liberal cast of Truman's twenty-one-point message to Congress in 1945, and as Rosenman's successor Clifford had stepped into the continuing conflicts over the Truman program. Paradoxically, Clifford's personal relationship with Truman was never comparable to Snyder's, yet Clifford's counsel was more in line with Truman's political instincts at the time, and thus Clifford was on the winning side, so to speak.

Meanwhile behind the scenes two other men—Elsey and Charles Murphy— were moving up as major but publicly obscure figures in the Truman administration, not only for the moment but for the duration, which was not to be the case with Clifford, as he returned to law practice early in Truman's second term.

Soon to advance from assistant naval aide to civilian assistant to Clifford, the youthful Elsey was a foresighted, self-contained individual who tackled problems with balance and incisiveness and who did, among other things, put his own stamp on presidential statements and documents. His commentaries on material submitted to Truman for inclusion in speeches and messages read like the judgments of a good editor. At random:

"Keyserling's Housing statement totally unsatisfactory . . . wallows around for another paragraph of big but meaningless words." "State [Department] material very vague. Requires *much* work." "I do not believe that Pres should explicitly state anything about his relations with Congress. Not dignified, too binding. Let it be said in less formal fashion. Also, in a sense it is an admission of weakening of Pres's authority. It is true that it has been weakened, but don't admit it." "Can you speed up Steelman's efforts?" "Tell CMC not to yield on issues—if it is to be shortened—I can shorten it without dropping out points. Don't drop out strong points to leave in the pretty words."

"God damn it, C.M.C. keeps stalling." "Essential to have Pres. make another Housing pronouncement. This is the perfect occasion." "CMC and I annoyed that the Drama & Significance of our original idea has been completely lost by State Dept. leaks. We wanted Truman to take the lead in headlines etc. by calling this conference."* "The speech must be 'inspirational', which it is not now."

Elsey and Clifford even took it upon themselves to rewrite a draft by Marshall. "It just didn't measure up to standard," Elsey noted.[13]

Murphy was a droll North Carolinian, educated at Duke University and Duke Law School, who joined the Office of Legislative Counsel to the Senate at about the time Truman became a senator. In January, 1947, Truman brought him to the White House as an administrative assistant concerned chiefly with helping to put together legislative proposals and, occasionally, shepherding them on Capitol Hill. The practice of having members of the White House staff whose regular assignment was liaison with Congress began later with the Eisenhower administration, although Truman made an approach to it in his second term. In his first term he had no such assistant at all, except that Murphy performed the duty off and on. Truman used the telephone a great deal himself to untangle knots on Capitol Hill. In contrast to Clifford, Murphy was self-effacing and inconspicuous. A meticulous man with detail, he naturally understood Congress and the history of the legislation of that period, and in addition he turned out to be a good speech writer and a deft political operator. In time he was to become Truman's chief political lieutenant in the White House.

Early in January a partisan group met for the first of many Monday night dinners at the old Wardman Park Hotel† residence of Oscar Ewing, who was then acting Democratic national chairman because Hannegan was ill. The group, whose membership was expanded to include others of similar persuasion from time to time, included Clifford, Assistant Secretary of Agriculture Charles F. Brannan, Assistant Secretary of the Interior C. Girard Davidson, Assistant Secretary of Labor David A. Morse, and Leon Keyserling of the President's Council of Economic Advisers.

* Inter-American Conference at Rio de Janeiro, August–September 1947.
† Later the Sheraton Park.

The group's distinctive characteristic was that it consisted of officials to the Truman administration and the Democratic National Committee who believed that in order to win in 1948 Truman must sponsor a liberal program. Ewing, soon to be appointed administrator of the Federal Security Agency (forerunner of the Department of Health, Education, and Welfare), had conceived the idea of a liberal advisory group at the time of Truman's unpopularity and the Democratic defeat of 1946. The purpose was not only to try to counter the influence of Snyder and other conservatives around Truman but to suggest positive action that the president might take on various issues so as to create an appeal to those blocs of voters who had supported Roosevelt.

Truman knew what was afoot but he never attended any of the dinners nor had the group to the White House for talks, although he did business with the individual members frequently. The method the group used rather was liaison through Clifford, allowing him at his discretion to draw upon what was said and proposed at the dinners when counseling with Truman on bills, messages, and speeches. It was by this means that the group hoped to encourage a liberal Truman program. Unquestionably the dinners were important to the participants. To what extent they influenced Truman, except possibly in matters of tactics, is problematical.

By the winter of 1947 his course had been largely set by his votes in the senate since 1935 and by his own recommendations to Congress as president. While he had at times talked a more liberal game than he had played, his record nevertheless had by this time taken him far down the road as champion of New Deal programs. With a conservative band of Republicans in control of Congress, bent on turning the party's 1948 presidential campaign into an attack on the New Deal, it is doubtful whether he had any practical alternative to a liberal course, or needed a committee to tell him which way to go. Undeniably, however, a number of actions he was to take did correspond with positions recommended by the liberal group.

The first serious trouble between the Truman administration and the Republican conservatives in Congress materialized February 8, when Senator Styles Bridges, chairman of the Senate Appropriations Committee, opposed Truman's nomination of David Lilienthal, the TVA chairman, as chairman of the new United States Atomic Energy Commission created by the McMahon act. Bridges, an arch-conservative and zealous anti-Communist, charged that Lilienthal was "an extreme Left-winger" who was "sympathetic toward Russia, which is Communist-controlled." In the 1946 elections, Bridges said, the voters had rejected the brand of "extreme New Dealism" espoused by Lilienthal.

A graduate of De Pauw University and Harvard Law School and a protégé of Felix Frankfurter's, Lilienthal had begun his career in the early 1920s practicing law in Chicago with Donald R. Richberg, who became one of the early New Dealers. In 1923 Lilienthal was appointed to the Wisconsin Public Service Commission and ten years later was named by Roosevelt as one of the three directors of the TVA. He became chairman in 1941. His years with TVA were studded with battles with competing private interests, which made him a conspicuous target for Republican conservatives. Between his work at the TVA and his contribution to the Acheson-Lilienthal Report he was a logical choice for the AEC post.

When the nomination had first come before the Eightieth Congress, it was challenged, as Truman had anticipated, by Lilienthal's old, vindictive foe, McKellar. At the same time he was taking on Lilienthal again, McKellar also opposed the nomination of Gordon R. Clapp, general manager of the TVA, to succeed Lilienthal as chairman. McKellar based his opposition to Clapp on charges that twenty-two "well-known Communists" were or had been employed there—an allegation that reflected on Lilienthal too.

McKellar's renewed attack on Lilienthal had undertones of anti-Semitism. Lilienthal was a Jew. McKellar also questioned his loyalty because his parents had been born in a part of Austria-Hungary that had subsequently become part of Czechoslovakia and because Czechoslovakia had come under Soviet influence. McKellar's tactics were not surprising, however, and his opposition alone did not jeopardize Lilienthal's nomination. But the rise of Republican opposition loomed menacingly because it resurrected, along with the Communist issue, the once bitterly debated question of military control over atomic energy and the issue of public versus private power.

Bridges, whom Lilienthal considered a "spokesman for the lowest of the private utility crowd,"[14] objected that Lilienthal had "directed the TVA, a social experiment, which is a wide departure from the American system of private ownership of property." On February 10 Wherry echoed the charges by Bridges, but, worse still, word spread that Taft would oppose the nomination. The afternoon edition of the old conservative *Washington Times-Herald* that day carried a banner headline, LILIENTHAL BRANDED APPEASER OF RUSSIA. Depressed, Lilienthal called Clifford and said that if Truman felt that standing by the nomination would embarrass him or damage his relations with the new Congress, Lilienthal would ask that his name be withdrawn. Clifford already had discussed the situation with Truman. He told Lilienthal there was only one thing Truman wanted to know: would Lilienthal see the fight through? Clifford reported, Lilienthal recalled, "that the President had said to him and asked that he say to me that he was in this fight to a finish; that he was in it if it took 150 years with all the effort and energy he had; that if they wanted to make an issue of this matter, he would carry the issue to the country."[15]

On February 21 Taft attacked Lilienthal as not only a "typical power-hungry bureaucrat" but as being "too 'soft' on issues connected with Communism and Soviet Russia."

On February 28 the Senate Public Works Committee voted not to recommend confirmation of Clapp.

"Mr. Clapp is a career public servant and a good one," Truman said at his press conference that afternoon, "and he contributed as much as anybody else to the success of TVA. And I think that he is perfectly fitted for the job, and I shall stand behind him to the finish, just as I am doing with Mr. Lilienthal."[16]

Regardless of McKellar's plea that he would regard Clapp's confirmation as a slap in his own face, the Senate voted for it despite the Public Works Committee. The fight over Lilienthal, however, grew increasingly nasty and hung in the balance for weeks.

Conservative Republicans maintained that Lilienthal was what nowadays would be called an elitist, seeking a position in which he would make vital decisions that ordinary people could not make. Senator John W. Bricker of Ohio warned that it was the last chance for the Senate to take the Atomic Energy Commission out of the hands of leftists. According to Taft, Lilienthal was a radical being considered for an important post at the very time when the electorate had repudiated radicalism. When Senator Homer E. Capehart of Indiana suggested that the continuing Soviet pressure on Greece and Turkey justified turning control of atomic energy back to the army, Taft agreed. McMahon and the Democratic liberals were appalled that Lilienthal's nomination might be used as a wedge for reopening this question.

None too soon, the tide was turned by another Republican, Vandenberg. Marshall, among others, had appealed for his help, and at a critical moment the chairman of the Foreign Relations Committee rose in the Senate, deprecated the charges of communism against Lilienthal, and urged his confirmation.[17] This was a fatal setback for the opposition. Lilienthal was confirmed. "Mr. Taft has succeeded in making a real fool of himself as have several so-called leading Republicans," Truman wrote his mother and sister. "I am of the opinion that the country has had enough of their pinhead antics."[18] Nevertheless the episode was a foretaste of the reception that the Eightieth Congress would accord liberals and liberal causes in the field of domestic affairs.

29. *Crisis in Europe*

THE WEATHER FORECAST for London for January 6 was "Cold or very cold."[1]

At daybreak snow began falling on the city. By afternoon children were tobogganing in the parks. At dusk a patch of snow topped the dome of St. Paul's Cathedral. Heavy snow was reported in the North of England and the Midlands. In Scotland roads were snowbound. Train service became disrupted throughout the country.

The next day falling snow painted pretty scenes in Richmond, Hyde Park, and Hampstead. Storms pelted the Lake District. The Glasgow Express was two and a half hours late arriving in London. The supply of gas was reduced by 25 percent in Birmingham. Worst of all, coal deliveries were hard-hit everywhere.

On January 14 gales and fog disrupted shipping in the English Channel. Snow fell on the Continent. Around Berlin shipments of coal were immobilized by frozen canals and rivers. Electric power was reduced in Dusseldorf. In the second winter after the war Germans were reported despondent from the cold.

Meanwhile the British government issued a White Paper January 20 acknowledging the "extremely serious" position of the country's economy. Not only were British debts accumulating abroad, but inflation in the United States was seriously reducing the purchasing power of the British loan. Clearly, Britain would be forced to lessen its commitments abroad and reduce its armed forces. The underlying problem was that the economies of Britain and Western Europe were still unable to rally from the destruction and disruption of the war, and the worst winter weather in memory was bringing paralysis on top of breakdown.

Over the weekend of January 25–26 wild winds and heavy snow wreaked disaster on Britain. On the twenty-fifth the snow was nine inches deep in West Malling, Kent. Long lines of lorries were abandoned. Most of the country was covered with a white blanket. Rural lanes disappeared in snow up to the hedge tops. Towns were isolated. In one area of Kent a hundred miles of roads were blocked by drifts. Arctic weather howled over the Straits of Dover, scattering ships. Bread was carried on foot to the isolated village of Bradhurst in Kent. As fresh snow fell on London, water pipes burst all over the city. Frost choked Big Ben.

Rationing of gas for houses was instituted in Paris. Floating ice hampered shipping on the Rhine. In Berlin it was announced that nineteen thousand persons had been treated for frostbite since December 1.

On February 3 the British embassy in Athens announced, not surprisingly, that half of the British forces that had been stationed in Greece since 1944, propping up a right-wing regime, would be withdrawn as soon as possible.

The weather in Britain was relentless. At some places in Lincolnshire February 5 only the tops of utility poles could be seen above the snowdrifts. Paralyzed transport caused the closing of factories, throwing hundreds of thousands of people out of work. In Birmingham alone sixty thousand were affected by the closing of the Austin Motor Company.

On February 7 Emanuel Shinwell, minister of fuel and power, announced a plan for cutting off electric power from industrial users in London and in most of the manufacturing areas of England and Wales. An "economic Dunkirk," cried Raymond Blackburn, Socialist M.P. from King's Norton.

On February 9 it was announced in Berlin that since December 1 forty persons had died from the cold in the German capital and sixty-eight had perished in Hamburg. Large towns in Holland were short of food because of the cold, and thaws caused floods in Italy. The winter's hardships helped Communists make notable gains in Italy and France.[2]

With electricity cut, candles and hurricane lamps alone kept London offices, restaurants, and shops going. BBC canceled television programs for the duration. Papers were read in the London City Council by flashlight. Nearly exhausted, Ernest Bevin lumbered into the candlelighted office of Arthur Creech-Jones, colonial secretary, while delicate talks on the Palestine problem were being conducted with such high officials of the Jewish Agency as David Ben-Gurion and Moshe Shertok. Candles were not really needed, Bevin observed, since Israe*lites* were on hand. Ben-Gurion and Shertok were only mildly amused.[3] Royal Air Force planes dropped food for snowbound villages near Leek. Thousands of sheep were buried under the snow throughout the country. On February 10 Attlee told Commons that nearly forty thousand railroad cars loaded with coal were immovable in the Northeast of England alone.

At a time when the British economy desperately needed to export more goods, British industry was all but disabled.

"We face an emergency of the utmost gravity," the prime minister said.

The snowfall continued.

The implications of the emergency, which had by this time thrown millions of people out of work, were sinking in on both sides of the Atlantic. United States foreign policy "will inevitably be affected," the *New York Herald Tribune* observed. Writing in the same newspaper, Walter Lippmann noted the relationship of the difficulties in the British Isles to Britain's overseas commitments and cautioned that the crisis could "shake the world and make our position highly vulnerable and precariously isolated." Anne O'Hare McCormick commented in the *New York Times:* "The extent to which democratic government survives on [the] Continent depends on how far this country is willing to help it survive.". On February 13 Truman offered to divert to British ports American colliers at sea bound for the Continent, but Attlee declined, thankfully, saying that "the need for coal in Europe is no less pressing."

The emergency caused by the weather had distracted attention from a deeper problem. British production, including production of coal, had been diminishing for years. With the end of the imperial role in India, Burma, Egypt, and Palestine already being written in the pages of the swiftly moving events of 1947, Britain's standing as a great power was in decline.

Meanwhile American officials were worried by successes of Communist-dominated guerrillas in Greece. On January 8 Ambassador Walter Bedell Smith had cabled from Moscow, warning of persistent Soviet ambitions in Turkey and saying, "Turkey has little hope of independent survival unless it is assured of solid long term American and British support."[4] Mark F. Ethridge, publisher of the *Louisville Courier-Journal* and United States representative on a United Nations commission to investigate Greek border incidents, cabled Marshall from Athens February 17 that with good reason the "SOVIETS FEEL THAT GREECE IS RIPE PLUM READY TO FALL INTO THEIR HANDS."[5]

On behalf of Paul Porter,* then head of an American Economic Mission to Greece, Ethridge, and himself, Ambassador MacVeigh in Athens cabled Marshall February 20 that to regard Greek collapse "as anything but imminent would be highly unsafe." The message recommended that the United States should make plain to everyone, including the Soviet Union, that its policy was "not to permit foreign encroachment, either from without or within, on independence and integrity of Greece."[6]

It was a momentous time. On February 20 also Attlee announced in Commons the impending end of British rule in India. The government, he said, intended to transfer power "into responsible Indian hands" by June 1948.

Friday, February 21, dawned with heavy snow falling over most of England.

In London a White Paper surveying the economy for 1947 was issued. Revealing an adverse balance of payments of £450 million in 1946, the paper was, the *Times* of London said, "the most disturbing statement ever made by a British government."

In Washington that afternoon the secretary to the British Ambassador, Lord Inverchapel, telephoned Secretary Marshall's office requesting an immediate appointment to deliver "a blue piece of paper"—diplomatic parlance for an important formal message. Marshall had left town for the weekend. Having ascertained from the ambassador that the message pertained to Greece, Acheson arranged to have it delivered by Herbert M. Sichel, first secretary of the British embassy, to Loy W. Henderson, director of the Office of Near Eastern and African Affairs.[7] Actually, Sichel handed Henderson two aide-mémoire.

One said, in part:

His Majesty's Government have already strained their resources to the utmost to help Greece and have granted . . . assistance up to 31st March, 1947. . . . The United States Government will readily understand that His Majesty's Government, in view of their own situation, find it impossible to grant further financial assistance to Greece.

The core of the other was:

In their existing financial situation His Majesty's Government could not, as the United States will readily appreciate, contemplate themselves making any further credits available to Turkey.[8]

* Paul Porter, economist, not Paul Porter, Washington lobbyist and lawyer who had headed OPA.

Even before Marshall had left town that morning and prior to the call from the British embassy, Acheson had given him a memorandum he had received from Henderson and edited. Reflecting the warnings from Porter, Ethridge, and Mac-Veigh, it said: "Unless urgent and immediate support is given to Greece, it seems probable that the Greek Government will be overthrown and a totalitarian regime of the extreme left will come into power." To head off this situation that "might eventually result in the loss of the whole Near and Middle East and northern Africa" the memorandum recommended not only that the administration ask Congress for a loan to Greece but that it reverse its standing policy and assist Greece with military equipment. As he was departing his office Marshall ordered that work be started on drafting necessary legislation.[9]

Late that day Acheson notified Truman and Marshall by telephone of the British notes. In a sense the shocked reaction in Washington was incongruous. For months the State Department had been made aware by the British that they were having difficulties supporting their commitments in the Middle East. The department knew that while the British Foreign Office was insisting that resources should be stretched to hold the position in Greece, the British Treasury maintained that such a course was impossible. When the snow and the coal shortage descended on Britain the Treasury prevailed.[10] Nevertheless, the sudden appearance of the notes February 21 seems to have startled American officials and filled them with a sense that an historic turning point was at hand.[11]

In its notes the British government voiced hope that the United States would assume the burden in Greece and Turkey. It estimated that Greece would need between $240 million and $280 million in foreign exchange currently and more in the future. It reported that Turkey was the stronger of the two but was still unable to finance the modernization and maintenance of forces needed in the face of Soviet pressure.

The administration, however, had no funds for Greece and Turkey. If Truman wished to help them, he would have to get the money from the Eightieth Congress, which as yet knew nothing of the two notes and whose Republican majority in the House had just pushed through a resolution recommending a $6 billion cut in Truman's budget despite warnings by Marshall, Eisenhower, and Forrestal.*

Furthermore it was obvious that the Greek situation was but a small part of the threat to American postwar aims posed on a vast scale by the collapse of the British Empire and faltering economic recovery in Britain and Western Europe. To meet these drastic conditions a huge outlay of money would be required, and for this too Truman would have to go to Congress.

After a weekend of State Department discussions of the issue raised in the British notes Acheson told Marshall in a memorandum: "This puts up the most major decision with which we have been faced since the war."[13]

* Later the Senate recommended a $4.5 billion cut. The two goals never were reconciled. The actual expenditures for the year turned out to be close to the original presidential estimates.[12]

30. *The Truman Doctrine and the Marshall Plan*

RETURNING TO Washington after the weekend, Marshall went to the White House February 24 to discuss the situation in Greece and Turkey with Truman. Before a cabinet luncheon, the secretary of state told Forrestal about the British notes. He said, in effect, that Great Britain was abdicating its dominant position in the Middle East and that the United States would have to assume the British role there.[1]

Events moved swiftly. On February 26 Marshall gave Truman a memorandum saying that he, Patterson, and Forrestal believed that the collapse of Greece would threaten American security and that "we should take immediate steps to extend all possible aid to Greece and, on a lesser scale, to Turkey."[2] Truman agreed in principle.[3] He was "very convinced," Steelman recalled, "that there was only one way to deal with the Communists and that was to let them know straight from the shoulder where he stood." His purpose, Steelman added, was to convince Stalin that "we mean business."[4]

While the circumstances were dramatic to the participants and while Truman's decision to act was indeed a far-reaching one, he had not made a revolutionary change in policy.[5]

Almost precisely a year had passed since the arrival of Kennan's "long telegram" from Moscow on the hazards the Kremlin posed for the United States. During that year Truman had resisted further concessions to the Soviet Union. He had taken a strong line toward Soviet penetration in Iran. He had dispatched a naval force to the Mediterranean to discourage Soviet designs on the Dardanelles. He had supported Baruch's plan on international control of atomic energy. He had accepted Byrnes's decision resulting in the economic merger of the American and British zones in Germany. He had backed Byrnes in his stubborn negotiations on the Eastern European peace treaties. He had fired Wallace for denouncing the firm American policy. He had approved economic aid to south Korea. He had received the Clifford-Elsey report recommending that the United States keep Western Europe and the Middle East outside the Soviet sphere of influence.

To take over from Britain the task of strengthening Turkey and trying to insure that Greece not succumb to a Communist regime that would transmit Soviet influence to the Eastern Mediterranean was an act of continuity. A Greek-Turkish aid program was but a next step—albeit a spectacular one—in an established direction, wherever that direction might be leading.

Two concepts grew side by side. One was the Greek-Turkish aid program, which came to be called the Truman Doctrine partly because of the sweeping terms in which the president broached it to Congress. It sprang from the basic United States policy of opposing Soviet expansionism—of preventing possible Soviet domination of Europe through the ascendancy of Communist parties linked to the Kremlin. The other was the massive economic aid to Europe, including West Germany, which became known—in honor of the secretary of state—as the Marshall Plan, although the word *plan* gives a misleading impression of its rambling evolution from the jungle of problems that called it forth.

In its simplest terms the Marshall Plan was, on a grander scale, a sequel to the assistance which had been extended through the United Nations Relief and Rehabilitation Administration and the British loan but which had failed to revive Europe from war. As the plan developed, it was many other things, too. These ranged from a program to stimulate trade and thus preserve prosperity in America to a design for rescuing Western European civilization, containing communism, and—according to a recent study by the historian, John Gimbel—restoring Germany in an economic and political framework that was acceptable to the rest of Western Europe and to the Congress of the United States.[6]

The Truman Doctrine sprang to life just before the Marshall Plan, because of the urgency of Greece's plight.

On February 27 Truman called a meeting with the Congressional leaders. As yet they knew nothing of the British notes on Greece and Turkey. Truman invited them to the White House not to seek their advice on what to do but to inform them that he had decided to aid the two countries and to ask their help in getting legislation passed promptly. He turned the floor over to Marshall, who dwelt on the Soviet menace in the Middle East. He explained the need for appropriations to keep the Greek economy from collapsing and for military equipment to help the Greek government suppress Communist-led guerrillas. In the event of civil war, he said, Greece might emerge as a Communist state under Soviet control. Turkey then would be surrounded.

"Soviet domination might thus extend over the entire Middle East to the borders of India," Marshall continued. "The effect of this upon Hungary, Austria, Italy and France cannot be overestimated. It is not alarmist to say that we are faced with the first crisis of a series which might extend Soviet domination to Europe, the Middle East and Asia."

The choice for the United States, he concluded, lay between "acting with energy or losing by default."[7]

Acheson was disappointed. His chief, he thought, had been too low-powered to convince the Republican leaders. Of all the crises that had come along, this one was Acheson's favorite. Having nourished it for days, as he was to recall, he was full of fervor over the possible consequences of the fall of Greece and Turkey. Obtaining the floor, he took the essence of Marshall's message and made it glow with high voltage.[8] Not a Republican sat in that room but knew before Acheson's crisp phrases had died away that not since ancient times had such a situation prevailed; that not since Rome and Carthage had such a polarization of power existed; and that American security and freedom would hang by a thread if the Soviet Union succeeded in extending its sway over two thirds of the surface of the globe and three quarters of the population of the world.

Vandenberg looked grave. When he found his voice he said he had been impressed, even shaken.[9] "Mr. President," he declared, "if you will say that to the Congress and the country, I will support you and I believe that most of its members will do the same."[10] None of the leaders present demurred. Until the subject of this meeting began appearing in the press the public had no awareness of the dire discourse. It had, on the contrary, many other less weighty matters on its mind. The purport of Vandenberg's advice was that Truman must move smartly to frighten the people and an economy-minded Congress out of their apathy if the administration wished to put over such an unusual program.[11] What this boiled down to was requesting funds with which to assume the British role in Greece and Turkey as a way of meeting a challenge by the Soviet Union.

Vandenberg had pointed out to Truman, if that were necessary, a possible opening in the face of an impasse in Congress. The opposition to big spending on foreign aid had been growing since the end of the war. It had taken six months to get the British loan through Congress. One of the tactics that helped put it across finally was the argument, made by Vandenberg himself, that the loan would be an instrument for stopping communism. Their victory in November, 1946, had confirmed the Republicans' belief that the voters wanted economy in government. With many Republicans the only issue that took precedence over economy was halting communism. One way to win their votes for a foreign aid bill, then, was rather obvious. A call to action was more than a legislative tactic with Truman, however. He believed the time to act had come.

He decided to address Congress in person. The speech was drafted in the first instance in the State Department, under Acheson's direction, with the idea that it should be bold in character, global in breadth. The sweeping concept that guided officials of the State, War, and Navy departments who had a hand in the task was that the United States would hold the line against communism, back democracies everywhere, and assist non-Communist governments until they could defend themselves. Acheson's only word of caution was that the message should not be belligerent nor provocative.[12] Since Marshall had to depart March 5 for a meeting of the Council of Foreign Ministers in Moscow he left Acheson in charge of drawing up the Greek-Turkish program for the president. As under Byrnes, therefore, Acheson continued to work intimately with Truman on major matters, their collaboration ever strengthening the bond between them.

After Truman had approved the Greek-Turkish aid program in principle a subcommittee of the State-War-Navy Coordinating Committee was set up to deal with public information about it—with propaganda, in short. The result of its work was a paper called "Public Information Program on United States Aid to Greece." It contained a passage to the effect that the policy of the United States was to give support to free peoples—no geographic limitations were mentioned—who were attempting to resist subjugation by armed minorities or outside forces. At Acheson's insistence, this passage was transferred almost word for word into the first working draft of Truman's speech.[13] Carried through all subsequent drafts in only slightly altered form, it remained the core of Truman's message, the hub around which controversy still swirls, having reached a crescendo during the debate over the Vietnam war in the 1960s and 1970s.

On March 4, at a speech-drafting conference presided over by Acheson, the wording was changed to read that it *must* be the policy of the United States to support free peoples.[14]

When a departmental draft finally was ready for consideration by the White House a copy was shown to Kennan. Because of the prestige he had achieved in the government over the "long telegram," he had been recalled from Moscow and temporarily assigned as a lecturer at the National War College in Washington. When he saw the draft he remonstrated with Acheson and others, mainly for the same reason that a generation of critics was to object. Although Kennan thought the United States should help Greece, particularly, he felt that the sentence which declared American policy to be the support of free peoples who resisted subjugation by armed minorities or outside pressures went too far. He felt that it placed aid to Greece in a universal context that could lead to unlimited commitments around the world. He believed the language should have been limited to the specific circumstances of Greece and Turkey. His objection came too late to change matters.[15]

Marshall's feelings about the final State Department draft are in some question. Acheson said it was sent to him in Paris while he was on the way to Moscow, and he approved it. Bohlen, who was with Marshall, recalled that the two of them thought the rhetoric too flamboyantly anti-Communist. Marshall, according to Bohlen, sent back word to this effect but was informed that the president and his advisers believed Congress would not approve the program without emphasis on the Communist danger.[16]

In any case when the draft was submitted to the White House for Clifford and Elsey to work into a speech that suited Truman's style, Elsey immediately recoiled in the manner of Kennan. In a memorandum to Clifford March 7 he said:

There has been no overt action in the immediate past by the U.S.S.R. which serves as an adequate pretext for "All-out" speech. The situation in Greece is relatively "abstract"; there have been other instances—Iran, for example—where the occasion more adequately justified such a speech and there will be other occasions—I fear—in the future.[17]

Clifford understood the problem differently. The speech, he informed Elsey, was to be "the opening gun in a campaign to bring people up to [the] realization that the war isn't over by any means."[18] It was being written in other words as much for its effect at home, selling a costly program, as for its impact abroad.

As the text neared final form, preliminary work also began without public announcement on what was to become the Marshall Plan. Some authorities trace the origin of massive foreign aid to talks between Truman and Acheson on the Greek-Turkish program in late February or early March of 1947. On March 5, Acheson wrote to Patterson that during the talks frequent reference had been made to the fact that Greece and Turkey were only "part of a much larger problem growing out of the change in Great Britain's strength and other circumstances. . . . I believe it important and urgent that study be given by our most competent officers to situations elsewhere in the world which may require analogous financial, technical and military aid on our part.''[19]

Acheson informed Patterson that he had asked Assistant Secretary of State Hilldring, as chairman of the State-War-Navy Coordinating Committee, to start such a study. SWNCC set up an *ad hoc* committee that tackled the subject immediately. The same day Clayton, the under secretary of state for economic affairs, sent Acheson a memorandum urging that $5 billion be appropriated to help the war-torn, non-Communist countries. ''The United States must take world leadership and quickly,'' he said, ''to avert world disaster.''[20]

Meanwhile Truman laid the Greek-Turkish aid program before the cabinet. According to Forrestal, he said that the situation was the most serious that had ever confronted a president.[21]

Clifford recalled afterward that the tone of emergency in the speech was adopted not merely to meet Vandenberg's strategy for getting the program through Congress but also ''because we wanted to send a signal to Stalin.''[22]

The cabinet approved the program. Some members suggested that Truman enlist Baruch's support before it was announced, but he declined, saying: ''I'm just *not* going to do it. I am not going to spend hours and hours on that old goat, come what may. If you take his advice, then you have him on your hands for hours and hours, and it is *his* policy.''[23]

On March 12 Truman appeared before a joint session of Congress. The collectively written speech he delivered was certainly the most controversial of his presidency and remains probably the most enduringly controversial speech that has been made by a president in the twentieth century.

He began by saying that the gravity of the world situation affected American security. Without discussing the dimensions of the situation, he said he would present only one aspect of it at the moment—the plight of Greece and Turkey.

The Greek government, Truman revealed, had made a formal appeal to the United States for assistance, along with a request for the assignment of American administrators, economists, and technicians to insure that aid given would be used effectively. The mission would include members of the American military. Because the Greek army was ill-equipped, Truman explained, it needed supplies and equipment in order to restore the authority of the Greek government. Although the United States had theretofore sent abroad missions including the military, the mission to Greece was the forerunner of the many postwar military assistance agreements that were to be entered into by Washington in the postwar period.[24]

The United States must supply the assistance, Truman said, because no other country could. He said that the administration had considered how the United Nations might assist, but could see no way. In truth the consideration devoted to this question was cursory.[25] Unquestionably the United Nations was not in a position to provide large-scale relief. Nevertheless the Truman administration was moving outside the United Nations framework and abandoning the principle of collective security in pursuit of its goals—a development that shocked many Americans. Many people did not comprehend as yet that unanimity among the victorious big powers was the premise on which the United Nations had been organized. When the big powers were in conflict, the United Nations could not act effectively.

Truman said that the Greek government had conducted its affairs in an air of chaos and extremism; that it had made mistakes, and that the United States condemned extremism of the left and right. In fact the Greek government was proroyalist and reactionary. Its repressions had driven dissenters into the hills to fight as guerrillas. There were a number of such resistance groups, the most important being the Communist-led Popular Army of Liberation (ELAS). Indeed, civil war was being waged in Greece. The guerrilla forces were receiving arms and ammunition from Yugoslavia, Bulgaria, and Albania—on instructions from Moscow, General Markos Vafiades, a Greek guerrilla leader, said.[26] Truman declared that the United States did not condone what the Greek government had done. What he went on to say, nevertheless, added up to the conclusion that the United States was not going to step aside from an area where it felt its vital interests were involved because it disapproved of a government with which it dealt.

A primary aim of American policy, he explained, was to bring about conditions "in which we and other nations will be able to work out a way of life free from coercion." Germany and Japan, he continued, had tried to impose their way of life on other nations, and that was a fundamental reason why the United States had fought them. Without mentioning the Soviet Union by name he then, in effect, equated it in this respect with Germany and Japan, saying:

We shall not realize our objectives . . unless we are willing to help free peoples to maintain their free institutions and their national integrity against aggressive movements that seek to impose upon them totalitarian regimes. This is no more than a frank recognition that totalitarian regimes imposed upon free peoples, by direct or indirect aggression, undermine the foundations of international peace and hence the security of the United States.

The peoples of a number of countries of the world have recently had totalitarian regimes forced upon them against their will. The Government of the United States has made frequent protests against coercion and intimidation, in violation of the Yalta agreement, in Poland, Rumania and Bulgaria.

He called for demarcation between democracy and a way of life that "relies upon terror and oppression, a controlled press and radio, fixed elections, and the suppression of personal freedoms."

Such rhetoric—"He put this nation squarely on the line against certain ideologies," Senator George was to observe[27]—combined with a proposed program that was patently aimed at checking Soviet influence, fed anti-Communist sentiment in the United States, inflating the issue in the political life of the country. The more the issue was inflated the more it became an attraction for hotheads and demagogues, some of whom, ironically, were to learn how to use it against Truman and Acheson themselves as well as against the Democratic party.

Truman then came in his speech to the intensely controversial core:

I believe that it must be the policy of the United States to support free peoples who are resisting attempted subjugation by armed minorities or by outside pressures.

This was the epitome of containment, although not the beginning of it. Containment had been the aim of United States policy for a year, even though the

United States had no true global strategy of containment and even though the word had not yet received popular currency.*

The aura of Truman's words was to envelop United States foreign policy for years. To be sure, the Truman Doctrine did not bind Truman's successors. Its application was limited. The Truman administration made no attempt, for example, to rescue China from subjugation by an armed minority. But the vaunted concept of helping "free peoples" beset by armed minorities (meaning Communists) or outside pressure (meaning from the Soviet Union and later Red China) influenced future American actions all the way down the line, probably to Vietnam. By dramatically drawing a distinction between ideologies, as Senator George said, the Truman Doctrine lent a rigidity to foreign policy that for a generation inhibited a turn from the Cold War.

While the United States possessed preponderant air and sea power and of course the atomic bomb, Truman clearly was not planning military action to contain the Soviet Union or communism, although the new program was largely military and was stated in stern language. Since 1945, however, the armed forces had declined in number from 12 million to 1.5 million, and in the second quarter of 1947 the rate of military spending was $10.3 billion a year compared with $90.9 billion annually in January, 1945. In his State of the Union message in January, 1947, Truman, still hoping for enactment of Universal Military Training, did not ask for renewal of the draft. In his speech on Greek-Turkish aid he indicated that changes in the status quo through coercion and infiltration were to be resisted by political means and the overwhelming resources of the United States. In fact, in the early postwar years the main vehicle of American influence abroad was not military but economic, and, though Congress had to be coaxed, there was a consensus that included military and civilian leaders on the application of economic power.

Truman asked Congress to approve $300 million for Greece and $100 million for Turkey and to authorize the dispatch of selective military personnel and military equipment to those countries. If the United States failed to provide leadership for free peoples, he said, "we may endanger the peace of the world."

Worn out, Truman flew to Key West. "This terrible decision I had to make," he said to Margaret in a letter March 13, 1947, "had been over my head for about six weeks." He had known at Potsdam, he told her, "that there is no difference in totalitarian or police states, call them what you will, Nazi, Fascist, Communist or Argentine Republics," and added:

The attempt of Lenin, Trotsky, Stalin, et. al., to fool the world and the American Crackpots Association, represented by Jos. Davies, Henry Wallace, Claude Pepper and the actors and artists in immoral Greenwich Village, is just like Hitler's and Mussolini's so-called socialist states.

Your Pop had to tell the world just that in polite language.[28]

---

* This resulted from an article in the July 1947 issue of *Foreign Affairs,* entitled "The Sources of Soviet Conduct," written by George Kennan under the soon-to-be-exposed pseudonym of "X." Somewhat in the familiar vein of his "long telegram," the article urged a "patient but firm and vigilant containment of Russian expansive tendencies." Although Kennan later protested that he had meant political containment, the article was popularly interpreted as a doctrine of military containment of the Soviet Union around the world.

The fact that the president had appeared before Congress and requested a program as necessary in a crisis made it hard for Congress to rebuff him before the world. Difficult as voting "aye" might be for the old isolationists, the issue trapped them between the devil and the deep. As Representative Carl Vinson of Georgia told Forrestal on the telephone the day after the speech, "They don't like Russia, they don't like the Communists, but still they don't want to do anything to stop it. But they are all put on the spot now, and they all have to come clean."[29] On such a basic, anti-Soviet foreign policy question many Republicans were indistinguishable from Democrats. Being helpful, Vandenberg worked to disarm the critics. To calm those who complained about the open-ended language of Truman's proposal he said, "I do not view it as a universal pattern but rather as a selective pattern to fit a given circumstance."[30] To assuage concern about bypassing the United Nations, Vandenberg and Connally put through meaningless amendments paying obeisance to the U.N. It was only to be a matter of time before Congress approved the program.

Acheson assured the Senate Foreign Relations Committee March 24 that Greek-Turkish aid would not set a pattern for future requests for American assistance. Future requests, he said, would be weighed singly to determine whether a country "really needs assistance, whether its request is consistent with American foreign policy, whether the request . . . is sincere and whether assistance by the United States would be effective in meeting the problems of that country."[31] Acheson was reducing to size a speech he had done the most to inflate.

Nothing said in all the discussions illuminated the attitude high in the Truman administration at that time better than an exchange between Acheson and Senator H. Alexander Smith of New Jersey at a hearing of the Foreign Relations Committee in executive session April 1, 1947. Smith inquired whether the aid program "will press Russia to really sit down with us and settle some of these differences."

"Are we thinking," he asked, "in terms of sitting down with the Russian officials, even the President with Stalin, at some kind of a party and saying, 'Here, let's get this straightened out?' Is that in our policy?"

"Senator," Acheson replied, drawing on some experience in negotiations with the Soviets, "I think it is a mistake to believe that you can, at any time, sit down with the Russians and solve questions. I do not think that is the way our problems are going to be worked out with the Russians. I think they will have to be worked out over a long period of time and by always indicating to the Russians that we are quite aware of what our own interests are and that we are quite firm about them and quite prepared to take necessary action. Then I think solutions will become possible."

"You are not planning any early participation for the settlement of the issues?" Smith asked.

"You cannot sit down with them," Acheson answered.[32]

On May 7 Truman wrote Mrs. Roosevelt in answer to a letter she had sent him questioning the "taking over [of] Mr. Churchill's policies in the Near East, in the name of democracy" and asking whether it was not more important, as a way of combating communism, to pursue progressive policies at home. Truman said he agreed with her on the latter point, adding,

We simply must not fall into political division, economic recession, or social stagnation; there must be social progress at home. I shall continue to point out to the country what seem to me the measures most suited to accomplish this purpose. . . .

Nor does it seem to me that we can overlook the fact that as much as the world needs a progressive America, the American way of life cannot survive unless other peoples who want to adopt that pattern of life throughout the world can do so without fear and in the hope of success. If this is to be possible we cannot allow the forces of disintegration to go unchecked.[33]

After Congress had passed and Truman had, on May 22, signed the Greek-Turkish aid bill, the program went forward that summer.

Tentative work progressed that spring on the plan that was, upon Truman's insistence, to bear Marshall's name. Truman wanted to honor Marshall, who was a vital force behind the plan, though not its sole author. The president had a practical motive also. As he told Clifford, a Republican Congress in an election year would be drawn more easily to a program named for General Marshall than to the same one named for Truman.[34] On April 21 the SWNCC study committee appointed at Acheson's direction submitted an interim report—one that revealed the cast of official thinking about the problem of aid to Europe. Promoting American security and the national interest was, inevitably, a paramount objective.

It is important to maintain in friendly hands areas which contain or protect sources of metals, oil and other national resources, which contain strategic objectives, or areas strategically located, which contain a substantial industrial potential, which possess manpower and organized military forces in important quantities, or which for political or psychological reasons enable the U. S. to exert a greater influence for world stability, security and peace.

It is desirable that military collaboration between the U.S. and foreign nations important to U.S. security be continued.[35]

Examining the prospects for the American economy against the backdrop of devastation abroad, the report noted that in 1947 the United States would export $7.5 billion of goods and services more than it imported. Most of this balance would be financed by the United States government. However, existing policies called for a rapid diminution of such financing during late 1948 and 1949. At the same time the ability of foreign purchasers to pay for American goods with gold and dollars would diminish as their gold and dollar reserves were drawn upon.

"The conclusion is inescapable," the report said, "that under present programs and policies the world will not be able to continue to buy United States exports at the 1946–1947 rate beyond another 12–18 months."

Noting that the President's Council of Economic Advisers had indicated that "a slight business recession may be anticipated sometime within the next twelve months," the committee added:

A substantial decline in the United States export surplus would have a depressing effect on business activity and employment . . . if the export decline happened to coincide with weakness in the domestic economy, prices and employment might be most serious.[36]

Massive foreign aid, in other words, might be a tonic for the domestic economy.

Marshall's experiences in Moscow gave new impetus to American policy. The draft of a German peace treaty was the main question before the foreign ministers. By the afternoon of April 15 the discussions had reached dead end. That night Marshall called on Stalin and said he was depressed by the impasse. As a result of the afternoon session, Marshall continued, he had concluded that there was no desire in Moscow for a German treaty and that he would so inform Truman.[37]

Stalin, working on a doodle of a wolf's head in red ink, was remarkably bland. He did not view the situation as being so tragic, he said. The Moscow conference was, after all, only an opening skirmish on the treaty, and experience had shown that compromise was possible in the end, Stalin argued. If he had meant to reassure Marshall, he did the opposite. Marshall suspected that Stalin viewed drift and crisis as auspicious for Soviet purposes.[38]

At the same time Marshall and Bevin, at the latter's urging, agreed in Moscow that the industrial output in their zones should be increased to prevent economic breakdown there and to help make West Germany self-sufficient and halt the drain on American and British resources.[39] En route home Marshall stopped at Tempelhof airport in Berlin for a conference with General Clay. He asked him to proceed vigorously with the economic development of Bizonia.[40]

In Washington the secretary of state gave Truman a pessimistic account of the Moscow conference, heightening Truman's feeling that time was of the essence in reviving Europe's economy.[41] The situation in Moscow came as no surprise to Truman, however. In contrast to Byrnes's practice in the Soviet capital sixteen months earlier, Marshall had sent Truman a report on practically every session. On April 28 Marshall made a somber broadcast about the problems of a settlement in "the vital center of Europe—Germany and Austria—an area of large and skilled population, of great resources and industrial plants." While Marshall did not spell it out, the fear that this vital center of Europe might somehow be combined with the Soviet Union to form a hostile and overpowering bloc lay close to the heart of the Truman administration's policymaking.[42] Marshall warned:

The recovery of Europe has been far slower than had been expected. Disintegrating forces are becoming evident. The patient is sinking while the doctors deliberate. . . . Whatever action is possible . . . must be taken without delay.

The next day he recalled Kennan from the National War College and told him to form a Policy Planning Staff in the State Department and tackle the European problem immediately. "Avoid trivia," Marshall ordered.[43] In a memorandum May 16, Kennan advanced the view that American aid should be used to foster some form of regional political association of Western European countries. Most American assistance would be in the form of outright grants, not loans, which could not be repaid anyhow. The focus of effort would be on Western Europe but the door should be left open for Eastern European nations to participate if they promised to do so constructively.[44] Then on May 23 the Policy Planning Staff submitted its report, written by Kennan. From it the Marshall Plan largely evolved.

The report proposed both short-range and long-term remedies.[45] For the short term a crash program to increase European coal production was recommended. Because of Germany's great coal deposits, a limited German economic recovery was necessary. But in the long term Germany's recovery would have to be coordinated with the revival of Europe. While German recovery was essential to the success of the Marshall Plan, the defeated enemy must not be treated better than the rest of Europe.[46] In the long term the United States would provide economic assistance to put Europe back on its feet, but the initiative must come from Europeans. The enterprise must be a large, coordinated venture among European nations. Request for aid must come from them, acting jointly. The program "must give promise of doing the whole job."

Although the Communists were exploiting the European crisis, the Kennan report saw not communism but war damage and dislocation as its cause. Designed to avoid the anti-Communist, unlimited, quasi-military line of the Truman Doctrine, which was causing an unfavorable reaction, the report proposed rather that the new program be directed not at combating communism as such but at restoring Europe.

The concept of large-scale United States assistance for the recovery of Europe was broached by the secretary of state in the commencement address at Harvard June 5, 1947.[47] Marshall spoke in broad terms because he had no detailed plan in hand yet. The short-range goal of increasing coal production had been set in motion, but the long-term program for European restoration remained to be hammered out in the months ahead.

The Kennan report had noted the possibility that the Soviet Union might refuse to join the plan and might even force its Eastern European satellites to decline. At a later meeting, Kennan recalled, he recommended to Marshall that the United States "play it straight" as far as the Soviets were concerned. "If they responded favorably, we would test their good faith by insisting that they contribute constructively to the program as well as profiting from it. If they were unwilling to do this, we would simply let them exclude themselves. But we would not ourselves draw a line of division through Europe."[48] Marshall, too, was emphatic that it would be a mistake for the United States to expose itself to blame for having divided Europe by excluding the Soviets from the plan.

Administration officials recognized that extending it to include Eastern Europe and the Soviet Union might entail staggering costs and raise a political obstacle at home because of anti-Soviet sentiment in Congress. In talks with Acheson, Marshall said he would have to take a calculated risk on these questions.[49]

At Harvard he declared that the plan was not directed at any country or ideology.

"Any government that is willing to assist in the task of recovery," he said, "will find full co-operation, I am sure, on the part of the United States government. Any government which maneuvers to block the recovery of other countries cannot expect help from us."

Without limiting the definition of Europe or mentioning any particular countries, Marshall said merely that the program should be agreed to "by a number, if not all European nations." Personally he hoped that the Soviet Union and the satellites would participate—on American terms, to be sure—and said at a subsequent press conference that they were specifically included. Benjamin Cohen, counselor to the State Department, privately assured the Polish ambassador in Washington on this score, and Clayton publicly urged the Soviets to participate.[50]

The Marshall Plan, like the Baruch Plan, however, contained conditions almost certain to be unacceptable to the Soviet Union. The American concept of a joint program among European nations implied international planning and hence an exchange of information. This would have exposed the Soviet economy to Western scrutiny and would have involved linking certain Soviet decisions on internal policy with an outside program. Also it would have meant the merging of the Soviet economy to some extent with a multilateral trading group and the opening of Eastern Europe to American enterprise. *Pravda* charged that the Marshall Plan threatened interference in the internal affairs of other countries.

Nevertheless Molotov and a delegation from Moscow did go to Paris at the end of June for a three-power conference called by the British and French to take advantage of Marshall's offer. On grounds of unwarranted interference, Molotov rejected an integrated economic plan for the whole of Europe. Instead, he proposed that each nation prepare a list of its needs, whereupon the lists would be gathered and presented to the United States with a joint request for assistance. His proposal defeated, Molotov and his colleagues walked out.

Britain and France responded by calling a conference of all European nations interested in joining the Marshall Plan. Moscow promptly announced regrets for Poland, Yugoslavia, and Rumania. Desperate for American aid, Czechoslovakia decided to send a delegation. Meanwhile, however, the Czechs had a delegation in Moscow to negotiate a trade agreement, and they asked Stalin about their participation in the Marshall Plan. As Polish Foreign Minister Jan Masaryk recalled the occasion, Stalin replied that the Marshall Plan was an attempt "to form a Western bloc and to isolate the Soviet Union," and added:

"We look upon this matter as a question of principle, on which our friendship with Czechoslovakia depends. . . . All the Slavic states have refused. . . . That is why, in our opinion, you ought to reverse your decision."

Masaryk suggested a graceful Czech withdrawal from Paris as soon as possible.

"If you take part in the conference," Stalin said, "you will prove by that act that you allow yourselves to be used as a tool against the Soviet Union."[51]

The Czech delegation was recalled. Nevertheless sixteen nations—Britain, France, Italy, Austria, Belgium, Denmark, Greece, Iceland, Ireland, Luxembourg, the Netherlands, Norway, Portugal, Sweden, Switzerland, and Turkey—met. They formed the Committee for European Economic Cooperation, which worked for the rest of the summer defining goals and preparing estimates.

Instead of all Europe's being united in participation of the Marshall Plan, the division of Europe between East and West now approached its most acute stage.

Ironically, in view of the many constructive aspects of the plan, a situation was developing that was fraught with greater tension than ever. On August 20 high State Department officials met with leading Pentagon officials to acquaint the latter with State's views. The discussion was led by the new under secretary of state, Robert Lovett, who had recently succeeded Acheson. Acheson, it will be recalled, had promised Marshall he would remain only for six more months. After leaving, he did not return to the government again in Truman's first term. Lovett told the meeting that the world was definitely split in two. The United States, therefore, must consider Europe west of the Iron Curtain as an entity, he said, and furnish aid to those sections whose economy could be revived quickly. Again he stressed the concept of Western Europe as contrasted with the individual countries in that region. The three western zones of Germany—American, British, and French—should be regarded, Lovett declared, not as part of Germany but as part of Western Europe.

Charles Bohlen, the new counselor of the State Department, having been named to succeed Benjamin Cohen, who retired, said that a major political showdown between what he called the Soviet and the non-Soviet world impended.

"There is," he continued, speaking from a memorandum, "virtually no chance of any of the problems existing between those worlds being settled until that crisis comes to a head. . . . From present indications this crisis will mature considerably earlier than has been expected. It is not a matter of several years in the future. It is more likely a question of months. . . . it will obviously contain in it the very real danger of outbreak of hostilities."[52]

31. *The Misguided Loyalty Program*

As MATTERS came to a head over Greece and Turkey in February 1947, the President's Temporary Commission on Employee Loyalty, appointed after the November elections, submitted its recommendations for preventing government employment of allegedly disloyal persons. The report laid the groundwork for a decision that troubled Truman and certainly produced some deplorable results for a constitutional democracy.

Measures designed to bar disloyal persons from employment in the United States Government were not new. In 1942 the Civil Service Commission had issued a war regulation disqualifying any applicant for federal employment if the commission entertained "a reasonable doubt as to his loyalty."[1] Anti-Communist zealots in Congress kept the heat on, however, and in 1943 Roosevelt promulgated Executive Order 9300, establishing in the Department of Justice a committee of five government officials. Its function was to study the problem of subversion, to advise the Department of Justice on handling it, to receive FBI reports on accused employees and follow up on actions taken in the various departments and agencies as a result of these reports.[2]

Legally, this committee was still in existence in February 1947, but its activities had about petered out.

In creating the temporary commission in November, 1946, Truman had asked it to consider whether existing procedures adequately protected the government. After holding hearings in rather hasty fashion the commission found the procedures "ineffective." In its report to Truman February 20 it said that recent events had demonstrated the presence of disloyal persons in the government and that this constituted "a problem of such importance that it must be dealt with vigorously and effectively."

The temporary commission confessed that it did not know how far-reaching the threat was. Attorney General Clark informed the members in a memorandum that the number of disloyal employees "has not yet reached serious proportions." But this was not the crucial point, he argued, explaining, "I do not believe that the gravity of the problem should be weighed in the light of numbers, but rather from the viewpoint of the serious threat which even one disloyal person constitutes to the security of the government of the United States."[3] One forest ranger? One receptionist in the American Battle Monuments Commission?

Truman evidently accepted Clark's hypothesis, however, for he afterward told Jack Redding, publicity director of the Democratic National Committee, as Redding recalled his remark, "I believe the issue has been blown up out of proportion to the actual number of possible disloyal persons we may have. But the fact is that one disloyal person is too many."[4]

J. Edgar Hoover also sent a memorandum to the temporary commission warning that subversive or disloyal persons might influence the formulation and execution of domestic or foreign policy in a way that "might favor the foreign country of their ideological choice." Or they might spread anti-American propaganda among their fellow employees or recruit them into subversive organizations.[5]

Existing procedures did lack uniformity. The commission favored a new loyalty program with greater uniformity and so recommended to Truman.

In the winter of 1946–47 he was scarcely overcome by the Communist menace at home. In a letter to former Governor George H. Earle of Pennsylvania February 28 he said:

People are very much wrought up about the Communist "bugaboo" but I am of the opinion that the country is perfectly safe so far as Communism is concerned—we have far too many sane people. Our Government is made for the welfare of the people and I don't believe there will ever come a time when anyone will really want to overturn it.[6]

The reason for not going beyond American traditions and due process of law in peacetime to question the loyalty of all government employees could not have been stated more succinctly.

In the circumstances, nevertheless, Truman accepted the findings of the temporary commission, with some modifications. That Soviet espionage posed a problem for responsible government officials was clear. The report of the Canadian royal commission on the Ottawa atomic spy ring had particularly disturbed Washington in describing how Soviet espionage agents had lured into their service Canadian officials having a susceptibility to Communist ideology and had snared others having such traits as homosexuality that made them vulnerable to blackmail. It was anything but clear, however, how a program to inquire into the loyalty of two million civilian government employees could catch the kind of spy who had operated out of Ottawa or Los Alamos. As for sabotage the problem had not amounted to a hill of beans even at the height of the war.

In the political tempests of 1946 Truman had appointed the temporary commission to deflect the heat of the Communist issue, and its proposals offered him a shield against the ongoing agitation. Catholic spokesmen and the United States Chamber of Commerce continued beating the drums. In assuming control of the Eightieth Congress, Republicans made clear their determination to end, as Speaker Martin put it, "boring from within by subversionists high up in the government."[7] Threats of investigations of the Federal Housing Authority and the State Department were heard at the Capitol. The attack on Lilienthal was further evidence of the attitude of many leading Republicans.

Evidently, Truman was particularly concerned about the House Committee on Un-American Activities and its rabid new chairman, J. Parnell Thomas. Later Clifford J. Durr, a member of the Federal Communications Commission, recalled Truman's having told him he had created the Temporary Commission on Employee Loyalty "to take the ball away from Parnell Thomas."[8] Furthermore, having appointed the commission in November, he was in effect committed to a new loyalty program. The commission's concerns were sure to have become known; and if Truman had rejected them, Congress probably could not have been restrained from acting on its own.

With the Greek-Turkish aid program already before a critical Congress and the much more grandiose Marshall Plan in preparation, Truman had his own priorities. Getting these unprecedented measures through a Congress controlled by the Republicans was not an easy prospect. Obviously, it would not have been helpful to Truman to resist communism in Europe, at great cost to American taxpayers, while appearing to be "soft" on communism at home. The loyalty program would help absolve him from this sin. With the presidential election twenty months away, the question of who was tougher on communism than the other fellow was already a vital issue.

On March 21, nine days after he had delivered the overblown speech to Congress about the Soviet challenge in Greece and Turkey, Truman promulgated— and the press trumpeted—Executive Order 9835, "Prescribing Procedures for the Administration of an Employee Loyalty Program in the Executive Branch of the Government."[9] Coincidental as the timing doubtless was, the succession of these exciting actions fanned "the Communist bugaboo," which was relentlessly leading the country into an unwholesome time.

Truman's order superseded Roosevelt's Executive Order 9300. Roosevelt had acted under the emergency of war. Truman, on the other hand, had taken an unprecedented step in peacetime by setting up a program to afford the country, as his order declared, "maximum protection . . . against infiltration of disloyal persons into the ranks of its employees." Clark's thesis that even one disloyal or subversive person in the government threatened democratic processes was embodied in the order.

The order required a loyalty investigation of every person entering civilian employment in the federal government and made department and agency heads personally responsible for programs to assure that disloyal persons already on the job were not retained.

Investigators were required to consult such sources of information as FBI files, military and naval intelligence files and, of all things, the files of the House Committee on Un-American Activities, as well as those of local law enforcement agencies. Whenever information derogating a person's loyalty was revealed, a so-called full field investigation was to be conducted.

Being responsible for the loyalty of his employees, each department and agency head was to appoint one or more loyalty boards to hear loyalty cases and recommend their disposition.

An employee accused of disloyalty would be entitled to an administrative hearing before a loyalty board in his department. If he wished, he could be accompanied by counsel and could testify and present evidence through witnesses and affidavits. Nothing was said, however, about a right to be confronted by persons who made accusations against him. Investigators in the various departments could refuse to disclose names of confidential informants, if that were thought essential for the operations of the program.

If a person's removal was recommended by a loyalty board, he could appeal to the responsible authorities in the department. The decision of the departmental authorities could be appealed to a Loyalty Review Board to be established in the Civil Service Commission. The review board's findings, however, were to be advisory and not binding on department and agency heads.

In consonance with the executive order, the Loyalty Review Board would make the rules necessary to run the loyalty program and would coordinate policies of the various departments. It would maintain an informative central master index covering all persons on whom loyalty investigations had been made since September 1, 1939. All departments were directed to furnish appropriate information for the index.

Also the Loyalty Review Board would receive the attorney general's current list of subversive organizations.

With the onset of the war Attorney General Biddle had compiled a list of organizations, some of them allegedly Communist front groups, furnished him periodically by the FBI. Against it he would check the names of questionable employees in the Department of Justice. As the existence of the "Attorney General's List," as it was usually called, became known, other departments and agencies also would sometimes make use of it in the same manner. Although the list was maintained informally and although membership in one of the subversive organizations was not a cause for dismissal, Biddle's list was a point of reference in the case of anyone suspected of being a security risk. Membership in a listed organization could be a factor consisdered in disposition of the case. Or it could be a cause for investigation of an employee. In short, to be a member of one of the organizations on the list raised a question about an employee.[10]

Under the Truman program the attorney general's list of subversive organizations maintained by Tom Clark received much wider and more formal application. Furthermore, whereas the Biddle list was private, the Loyalty Review Board late in 1947 published Clark's list, thereby opening to doubt and calumny all the organizations listed, including such institutions as the National Negro Congress, the Ohio School of Social Sciences, the Samuel Adams School in Boston, and the Walt Whitman School of Social Sciences in Newark.

The standard for banning employment set forth in Truman's order "shall be that, on all the evidence, reasonable grounds exist for belief that the person involved is disloyal to the Government of the United States." Activities and associations that might be considered in reaching a determination of disloyalty would include—along with sabotage, espionage, treason, sedition, and knowingly consorting with spies—advocacy of revolution or force to alter the American form of government, intentional unauthorized disclosure of official secrets, or membership in (or "sympathetic association with") any organization on the attorney general's list, which at that time numbered eighty-two. However, membership in or sympathetic association with any of them did not automatically disqualify an employee. In practice, of course, it did not help in the least.

All civilian employees of the government, however near or far from high national security concerns, were to be listed with the FBI for a check of their names against its records (and fingerprint file). Any derogatory information unearthed would require an investigation of the person involved. The submission of the names of all employees expanded the wartime procedure, under which investigation of incumbent employees was undertaken only upon the request of the agency that employed them and about whom their superiors had doubts as to loyalty.

The new program also retained the right of summary dismissal of employees in sensitive jobs.

Uniformed members of the army, navy, and Coast Guard were not included in the program. For them the Articles of War and the Articles for the Government of the Navy set the standards for loyalty.

The loyalty boards were an innovation of the Truman program; no such bodies had existed under the Roosevelt orders.

While the signing of the executive order establishing the program had occasioned no great controversy within the government, the next step, involving the role of the FBI, brought an internal squall down around Truman. His order had left unclear which agency, the FBI or the Civil Service Commission, would conduct full field investigations in certain cases. Reluctant to add to FBI powers, already swollen by wartime directives, he sent George Elsey to consult Harry B. Mitchell, president of the Civil Service Commission, and Frances Perkins, the former secretary of labor, who was now a member of the commission, as to whether it could handle the investigations.[11] J. Edgar Hoover threatened in memorandums to Tom Clark "to withdraw from this field of investigation rather than to engage in a tug of war with the Civil Service Commission."[12]

The FBI claimed that the Hatch Act of 1939 gave it responsibility for investigating all persons employed by the government. Since the FBI already had investigated many of those then on the job, Truman agreed that it made sense for the FBI to continue such work, and the United States Civil Service Commission assented. Then over the objection of the Civil Service Commission, the FBI insisted upon its duty also to investigate those whose hiring had been certified by the commission subject to the commission's investigation—a large number of persons. The Bureau of the Budget sided with the FBI, whereupon Harry Mitchell and Mrs. Perkins took the issue to Truman. What the proposal meant, they told him in a letter April 25, 1947, was that practically all loyalty investigations were to be made by the FBI. They added:

The members of the Loyalty Commission were strongly opposed to investigations by the FBI on the basis that whatever unfavorable reaction there was against the Executive order would be much stronger if the FBI made these investigations, than if the Civil Service Commission made them. If we understood you correctly in our conference with you, that also was your opinion.[13]

Truman asked for an opinion from Budget Director Webb. Webb upheld the FBI because of the Hatch Act and because of a Roosevelt directive making the FBI preeminent in matters of espionage and sabotage. Furthermore, Webb said, the FBI had developed the facilities for such investigations. Tom Clark supported this position in a memorandum to the president May 1.[14] Truman's mood, however, had become cantankerous.

"Pres feels very strongly anti FBI & sides positively with Mitchell & Perkins,'' Elsey noted May 2. ''Wants to be sure & hold FBI down, afraid of 'Gestapo.'

"Pres came in twice to CMC's [Clark M. Clifford's] office on 1st May to express these views."[15]

The kettle boiled for several days, but the logic of the FBI's vastly superior facilities and historic role was inescapable. At the urging of Clifford, Webb, and Tom Clark, Truman finally sided with the Bureau of the Budget and the FBI. He notified Mitchell May 9 that the FBI would conduct all loyalty investigations ''of persons who are now or may hereafter be placed on the pay rolls of the Federal Government.'' Investigation of persons before a decision about hiring them would continue to be the function of the Civil Service Commission.[16]

Some administration officials feared that when the appropriations bill for the program reached Congress there would be objections that the FBI had not been given the last function, also. Clifford reported this to Truman in a memorandum, but said he thought the concern was a molehill, not a mountain. On the bottom of the memorandum Truman jotted:

"Clark: you have properly diagnosed the case. But J. Edgar will in all probability get this backward looking Congress to give him what he wants. It's dangerous. H.S.T."[17]

Truman's guess about Congress proved right. His budget request of $16 million for the Civil Service Commission and $8.7 million for the FBI to conduct loyalty investigations was revised by Congress to allocate $7.4 million for the FBI and only $3 million for the Civil Service Commission. The issue was finally resolved to the FBI's satisfaction when Truman issued a statement saying that there were to be no exceptions to the rule that the FBI would make all loyalty investigations.[18]

In retrospect Truman lamented that he and his advisers had not realized that once a person had been cleared by a loyalty board his name was not included on the general card file kept on employee loyalty matters. Hence every time a cleared employee transferred to another job in the government he was subjected to a new investigation. As Truman remarked ruefully in his memoirs, ''This is not in the tradition of fair play and justice.''[19]

Criticism of the program then and thereafter went far beyond the narrow point mentioned by Truman. Indeed, less than a month after the order had been promulgated Philip Murray wrote to him asking that it be repealed unless it could be made to comply with due process. Murray cited the absence of a definition of disloyalty in the executive order, a flaw that was to lead to confusion. He objected that the order did not guarantee an accused person the opportunity to confront his accusers and cross-examine witnesses. Murray's letter raised the essential question, as important now as then. Are there to be democracy and constitutional freedoms at all times? Or in times of danger, real or imagined, must free expression and constitutional procedures be modified, thus subtly changing the system while trying to preserve it?

"The Order," Truman replied, "was carefully drawn with the idea in view that the Civil Rights of no one would be infringed upon and its administration will be carried out in that spirit."[20]

He strove to keep that promise and to make sure, though not always successfully, that individual records were not misused.[21]

Nevertheless a basic fault of the program, which continued in effect throughout Truman's tenure and then was made even more drastic in some respects by President Eisenhower, was that it placed a perceived need for national security ahead of the traditional rights of individuals. As John Lord O'Brian, senior attorney at Covington & Burling, former assistant to the attorney general in the Hoover administration and a leading critic of the loyalty program, said, it established in effect something like a new system of preventive law applicable to the field of ideas and essentially different from traditional American procedures.[22]

The departmental loyalty boards and the Loyalty Review Board were not judicial but administrative bodies, and for the first time administrative officials and agencies were authorized to inquire into and pass judgment on personal beliefs, associations, and opinions of a private citizen employed or seeking employment in the government. The fact that it was considered necessary to hold a hearing showed that there was "derogatory" information serious enough to require an answer. Thus the individual became the accused with no presumption of innocence to protect him. Persons were adjudged untrustworthy not because of overt wrongful acts but because of their ideas, because of motives attributed to them, or because of suspicion as to their future conduct. Established in American jurisprudence thereby was a doctrine of imputing guilt because of association. No provision was made for judicial review. The size of the program made it an administrative monstrosity.

With the program in effect, O'Brian noted, antiintellectual movements grew and, paradoxically, citizens experienced less security and more mistrust and anxiety than before it had been established.

Certainly, the public accepted the program, however. Indeed, Truman's move to eliminate disloyal persons from the government, his dramatic stand on Greece and Turkey, his appointment of Marshall as secretary of state, and the fact that in March the Supreme Court upheld the contempt citation and fine against John L. Lewis helped prolong the rise in Truman's popularity that had begun late in 1946.

In April the Gallup Poll indicated that 60 percent of the voters approved of his performance. Truman's recovery from the fiascos of 1946 impressed Republican leaders. He was moving with a surer step and without some of the antics of the past. Fewer stories appeared in the newspapers about his poker games and bourbon. "The old days of government by crony are gone . . ." *Time* reported April 7, 1947. It was still widely believed that he could not be reelected, but he was looking more formidable than many would have imagined. Taking heart, the North Dakota Democratic Committee endorsed a Truman-Eleanor Roosevelt ticket in 1948.

Of more immediate concern to Truman than the thought of running with Mrs. Roosevelt was a major political showdown between himself and Congress over labor legislation.

32. *Taft-Hartley: Truman on the Offensive*

IN THE HOSTILE ATMOSPHERE TOWARD labor that had enveloped the convening of the Eightieth Congress, seventeen labor bills had been introduced in the House on the opening day. Despite Truman's plea in his State of the Union message against punitive labor legislation, the ensuing weeks had brought a total of more than a hundred labor bills into the hoppers of the Senate Labor and Public Welfare Committee, headed by Taft, and the House Committee on Labor and Education, chaired by Representative Fred A. Hartley, Jr., Republican, of New Jersey.

Finally emerging from these committees was legislation, which, if enacted, would supplant the Wagner Act, a keystone of the New Deal, and would be aimed at redressing the advantage that that measure was alleged to have given labor at the expense of business.

Goaded by public resentment against strikes, against John L. Lewis, against reports of Communist penetration of unions, against high prices, the Republican assault upon New Deal labor policy got off to a hot start April 17.

The House passed overwhelmingly—and with "exultant shouts," the *New York Times* reported—the Hartley bill, rich in the red meat for which the National Association of Manufacturers had been hungering for twelve years.

In 1935, on the strength of an opposite swing of the pendulum—on the strength of a conviction that business had become too powerful in relation to labor—the Wagner Act had been passed, placing the federal government in the position of encouraging the organization of labor. The act guaranteed workers the right to join unions, to bargain collectively, and to strike. It created the National Labor Relations Board, with power to conduct elections to determine whether a union should be certified as representing employees in a plant or office. Employers were forbidden to interfere with, restrain, or coerce employees in their rights to organize and bargain. Employers were forbidden to discourage union membership through discrimination in hiring or promoting. They were forbidden to refuse to bargain collectively.

Now by a margin of nearly 3 to 1, swelled by the support of conservative southern Democrats, the Hartley bill soared through the House on the wings of a new sentiment that labor had become too powerful in relation to business and to government—that it was time to swing the pendulum the other way, toward a better balance. The bill's provisions, however, could hardly have been exceeded in fantasies of the directors of the United States Chamber of Commerce. Along with more basic reforms, for example, pension plans, group insurance, and hospitalization would be outlawed as subjects for collective bargaining. Illegal also would be mass picketing and most industry-wide bargaining. Unions would be brought under the antitrust laws. Employers would not be permitted to contribute to welfare funds that were in any way administered by a union.

Following the House vote, the Senate took up a bill introduced by Taft. During the hearings, his and Hartley's committees had maintained a loose relationship. Hartley was shrewd enough to know that if his bill got a reputation for being too harsh, as it did, then Taft, by eliminating some of the more extreme provisions, could still produce a strong bill—yet one that had, by contrast, a reputation for being fair and mild, and hence a good chance of enactment. Hartley had elected to throw in all the red meat he could find so that he would have in the end, he said, "something to concede and still get an adequate bill."[1]

The Taft bill eliminated such excessive features of the Hartley bill as the ban on mass picketing. Discarded also were prohibitions on industry-wide bargaining and restrictions on welfare and pension plans. Many of the basic provisions of the Hartley bill were retained, however, and other strong provisions were added as amendments on the Senate floor. Nevertheless Hartley's tactic was successful, as the press depicted the Taft bill as fair and mild in comparison with the House measure.

The Senate passed it, also by a margin of nearly 3 to 1. The differences between the two measures were reconciled in a conference committee, and the final bill was passed by both houses and sent to Truman June 9, 1947.

The Taft-Hartley bill was a formidable piece of legislation. Union hiring halls and the closed shop—a shop in which membership in a particular union was a prerequisite for being hired—were prohibited. However, collective bargaining agreements were allowed to include union-shop provisions requiring employees to join a union, provided a majority of them voted in favor of a union-shop clause in a special NLRB election, and provided also that the union shop was not forbidden by state law. In effect, this provision permitted states to pass "right-to-work" laws outlawing union-shop agreements, as many of them did.

A number of unfair labor practices, as well as unfair business practices, were specified. The United States Conciliation Service in the Department of Labor was abolished and replaced by an independent agency, the Federal Mediation and Conciliation Service. Unions were made liable for suits in federal courts for violation of contract. They were required to make annual financial reports to the Department of Labor and to their members. Unions and corporations were forbidden to contribute in federal elections. Union officials were required annually to sign an affidavit that they were not Communists, or their unions would forfeit their rights under the act. When, in the president's opinion, a national emergency was threatened by a strike, he was empowered to appoint a fact-finding board. Upon receiving its report the president could ask the attorney general to seek a federal court injunction to prevent the strike, or a lockout. Once the court had granted an injunction, a cooling-off period totaling eighty days would come into effect to delay a shutdown.

Notwithstanding any existing provisions of the Norris-LaGuardia act, injunctions also were permitted to stop unfair labor practices, if sought by the NLRB or its general counsel. Welfare funds in most cases would have to be administered jointly by union and employer. Secondary boycotts and jurisdictional strikes were banned.

Nevertheless the Taft-Hartley bill retained the framework of the Wagner act, under which a union seeking to be recognized as representative of a particular group of employees could ask the NLRB to conduct a certification election. Workers retained the right to join unions, to bargain collectively and to strike. The NLRB still had the power, upon complaint that business had committed an unfair practice against labor, to order it stopped and to enforce the order through the federal courts. Now, however, the NLRB had the same power to protect business against an unfair practice by labor.

The dust-dry terms of this legislation, a bundle of technicalities and legalistic language that few people understood well, let loose a landslide of prolonged controversy. Taft-Hartley became a touchstone. The bill materialized as a dividing line between liberal and conservative, New Dealer and anti-New Dealer, friend of labor and foe of labor, defender of business and critic of business. The hordes of lobbyists on both sides who had worked like beavers at the Capitol while the legislation was evolving now swarmed to Truman's doorstep as he considered what action to take. While the legislation had been moving through Congress Truman had not lifted a finger to influence its terms, although administration officials had criticized the bill in hearings.

To labor, the bill symbolized repression and an attack by its enemies, and labor reacted accordingly.

The presidential press office reported that the volume of mail was the greatest ever received in the White House on any issue. Five days after the bill had been passed, 460,000 postcards, 140,000 letters, and 20,000 telegrams were received—overwhelmingly in favor of a veto. Eventually the number of communications exceeded 750,000.

The AFL alone spent nearly $1 million on newspaper and radio advertising and mass meetings. In the hottest lobbying campaign in its half-century history the organization assessed each member fifteen cents to help raise the fund.[2] Both the AFL and the CIO marshaled tens of thousands of people for their respective parades in New York and rallies in Madison Square Garden. According to *Time,* an AFL and CIO "veto caravan" of a hundred automobiles crossed the country from California to Washington.[3] The mayors of New York and Detroit proclaimed municipal "Veto" days. Eleanor Roosevelt, Henry Wallace, and Harold Ickes denounced the bill. Franklin D. Roosevelt, Jr., called it "class legislation in the worst sense." The Communists branded it a sellout to the reactionaries, but the Catholic bishops, speaking through the National Catholic Welfare Conference, warned that the bill might play into the Communists' hands.

While Truman received divided counsel from his advisers, a poll of Democratic national committeemen showed that 103 favored a veto, 66 favored approval of the bill, and 4 suggested that Truman allow the bill to become law without his signature.

When Congress convened at noon Friday, June 20—the deadline for presidential action—no information had come from the White House regarding Truman's decision, although a veto was generally expected. No doubt Truman had genuine objections to the bill, fearing that it would prove unworkable, even though he acknowledged that some kind of labor reform was due. "We have got to have a certain restriction on the union element, because if we don't, we go haywire," he had told a group of broadcasters in January. "You take the underdog and put him on top, and he is just as bad on top, and sometimes a little worse."[4] According to Steelman, however, Truman felt that the country had long been in too much of an emotional state over labor and that no law could overcome that condition. It would be better, he believed, to wait until the postwar passion over strikes had subsided and then attempt reform in a calmer atmosphere.[5]

The problem for Truman, however, was primarily political. If he approved the bill one year after his proposal for drafting rail strikers and seventeen months before the 1948 election, his standing with labor would have been destroyed. An unbearable strain would have been placed on the alliance between labor and the Democratic party. If he vetoed the bill, his previous sins in the eyes of labor would be absolved. At the same time he might counteract certain liberal support still building for a possible third party under Wallace. Moreover it was evident from the voting on the bill in both houses that Congress probably would override a veto. What did Truman have to lose, therefore, by vetoing it and winning labor's acclaim, if the bill was going to become law anyhow?

In the excitement over a fight, long lines of spectators waited to get into the visitors' galleries of both houses. The crowded House of Representatives was tense when a few minutes after noon the reading clerk broke the seal on the envelope containing the message. Simultaneously copies were distributed to members, whose eyes fell upon the opening line: "I return herewith, without my approval, H.R. 3020, the 'Labor Management Relations Act, 1947.' "[6]

As the clerk droned on, reading Truman's string of technical objections, Hartley followed the text, red-faced. Some Republicans occasionally let out snorts of laughter. After the generalities—"It contains seeds of discord which would plague this nation for years to come"—Truman dealt with the individual provisions at length and with exaggeration, considering the use to which he was to put the Taft-Hartley act in the next five years.

Thus, he said, the bill would create an unworkable administrative structure. It would enable employers to engage in endless litigation, draining the resources of unions. It would complicate the collective bargaining process for employers by permitting—sometimes requiring—the splitting up of stable patterns of representation. Perhaps his most prescient criticism was that difficult labor-management problems would be hard to solve by oversimplified legal devices.

"This bill would go far toward weakening our trade union movement," Truman declared at the climax. When the reading was over Charles Halleck, the Republican leader, said nothing more remained to be debated and called for a vote. The House then voted to override the veto, 331 to 83, with 106 Democrats, including Lyndon Johnson, opposing Truman. Only 71 Democrats, John F. Kennedy among them, supported the president.

Taft meanwhile told reporters that Truman's message resembled a memorandum Lee Pressman, counsel to the CIO, had prepared in opposition to the bill.

The Senate began debating at 2:30 P.M., and Democratic opponents of Taft-Hartley soon had a filibuster going in hopes that labor pressure might yet turn the tide. The filibuster was led by Senator Glen H. Taylor, Democrat, of Idaho, who had got himself elected to the Senate in 1944 by going about the state, singing, cowboy style—to the tune of "Home On The Range"—"Oh, Give Me a Home by the Capitol Dome." Sipping milk and munching on cough drops, Taylor rambled on for hours about how he had been forced to eat jackrabbits to survive the depression and how Taft-Harley would impoverish the workingman.[7]

While the talk went on through the night in the crowded, brightly lighted Capitol, Truman made a national radio broadcast from the White House at ten o'clock. "I vetoed this bill," he explained, "because I am convinced it is a bad bill. It is bad for labor, bad for management, and bad for the country." Then he turned on the political faucet. Taft-Hartley was "a shocking piece of legislation." It was "unfair to the working people" and "deliberately designed to weaken labor unions."[8]

After Truman had finished speaking, Taft went on the air from the Capitol and accused him of "complete misrepresentation." Dawn Saturday found the Senate still debating, diverted from Taft-Hartley by a long discussion as to whether it would be more or less deferential to Christianity to keep the debate going through Sunday. Finally, at 6:52 P.M. Saturday, the Senate recessed until Monday, June 23, agreeing to vote then at 3 P.M.

Before the final vote was taken, Alben Barkley, the Democratic leader, read a letter from Truman saying that in "a critical period in our history" enactment of Taft-Hartley could "adversely affect our national unity."[9] The letter was futile. The Senate overrode the veto, 68 to 25.

Considering its prosaic history in the years ahead, as strong unions grew stronger, the Taft-Hartley bill thus became law in a burst of emotion that was to spill over into the 1948 presidential election.

"One thing Taft-Hartley did accomplish," A. H. Raskin wrote in the *New York Times* on the twenty-fifth anniversary of the passage of the bill. "It got unions into politics on a year-round basis. The old Congress of Industrial Organizations, child of the New Deal, did not need the new law as a spur. But it was resolved to get Taft-Hartley repealed that moved the American Federation of Labor far beyond the old Samuel Gompers concept of cranking up to 'reward your friends and punish your enemies' at election time."[10]

From this resolve sprang the political activities that were to make the AFL and the CIO powerful lobbies and principal sources of political funds and manpower, usually in support of the Democrats. Harry Truman in 1948 was to be the first beneficiary of the new labor politicking.

Indicative of the changed mood of labor was a statement soon after the veto by Walter J. Munro, Washington spokesman for the Brotherhood of Railroad Trainmen. Less than a year after A. F. Whitney, the brotherhood's president, had promised to open its treasury to defeat Truman in 1948, Munro said: "It is indicated that our Brotherhood will throw all its resources behind President Truman and his Administration in an effort to elect a Congress which will back the President's liberal program."[11] The previous night Whitney himself had said in Pittsburgh that Truman's veto of Taft-Hartley "vindicated him in the eyes of labor."

At the same time Truman won the applause of old critics among the New Deal crowd and the liberals. The *Nation* said he had given American liberalism "the fighting chance that it seemed to have lost with the death of Roosevelt." "Mr.

Truman," James A. Wechsler wrote in *Progressive,* "has reached the crucial fork in the road and turned unmistakably to the left."[12]

Such encouragements, however, were not convincing enough to dispel doubts, even among some of those who were applauding, that in 1948 Truman could defeat a resurgent Republican party led by Dewey or Taft.

33. *CIA*

AS HEARINGS NEARED AN END that summer on the National Security Act of 1947, questions were raised in Congress whether the proposed Central Intelligence Agency might inject police state methods into American society.

Theretofore discussion of the bill, recommended by Truman in February to carry out the form of unification of the armed forces agreed upon after long controversy, centered largely on the new defense structure. Because of Forrestal's concern for coordination of diplomatic and military policies, however, the measures provided for other things, too, including a Central Intelligence Agency.

As chairman of the Joint Research and Development Board, Vannevar Bush was asked whether the CIA might "become a Gestapo or anything of that sort?" He replied reassuringly that the CIA was not concerned with intelligence on internal affairs. "We already have . . . the FBI in this country concerned with internal matters," he explained.[1]

Congress was uneasy about the problem of creating for the first time in American history a large peacetime intelligence establishment. Anxiety over importing the evils of secret police in Europe kept showing up in the hearings. Representative Clarence Brown of Ohio asked whether the proposed CIA "might possibly affect the rights and privileges of the people of the United States."

"No, sir," replied General Hoyt Vandenberg, director of central intelligence under an interim arrangement. "I do not think there is anything in the bill, since it is all foreign intelligence, that can possibly affect any of the privileges of the people of the United States."

Forrestal also sought to quiet fears that the CIA might harbor dangers for a democracy.

"The purposes of the Central Intelligence [Agency]," he testified, "are limited definitely to purposes outside of this country, except the collation of information gathered by other government agencies."[2]

"Collation" was a clue to understanding what it was that was being asked of Congress. The CIA was to be an organization for centrally gathering and coordinating information. The CIA was to collect, evaluate, estimate.

Yet, as the public has since learned, the CIA engaged over the years in a variety of domestic activities, many of them completely out of character with the functions considered by Congress in 1947. As David Wise, a leading authority on the subject, has noted, the agency secretly funded academic centers. It subsidized business, labor, church, and student groups through a maze of foundations. It established a Domestic Operations Division a block from the White House in the 1960s. During the Watergate episode the CIA outfitted burglars on a White House mission; prepared two psychological profiles on Daniel Ellsberg, the former government official who had given the Pentagon Papers to the *New York Times;* and cooperated briefly with President Nixon's attempt to divert the FBI from investigating the break-in at the Democratic National Committee headquarters in the Watergate.[3]

The bill did not explicitly authorize the CIA to engage in covert political or paramilitary operations abroad, either. The thrust of the testimony at the hearings was that CIA activities were to be related to intelligence.[4] Secret political operations were not mentioned in the legislation.

Again, however, it was only a matter of time before the CIA was supporting Chinese Nationalist troops who had fled to Burma; was assisting the campaign against Huk guerrillas in the Philippines; was organizing a coup to overthrow Premier Mohammed Mossadegh in Iran; was plotting the downfall of a Communist-dominated regime in Guatemala; was training a brigade of Cuban exiles that later invaded the Bay of Pigs; was maintaining an airline, Air America; was supporting a 30,000-man army in Laos; was working with generals who conducted the coup against, and later assassinated, President Ngo Dinh Diem of South Vietnam; was scheming to block the election of the leftist Salvador Allende Gossens in Chile; was plotting the assassination of Fidel Castro in Cuba and Patrice Lumumba in the Congo (Zaire). And this is only part of the list of covert operations that were undertaken by the CIA in the first three decades of its existence.

How did this seeming miscarriage of congressional intent come about? To answer the question, in which Truman was involved, it is necessary to go back to the beginning.

When, despite a number of warnings, Pearl Harbor was surprised by the Japanese attack, it was obvious that the country's old-fashioned, decentralized intelligence system, which could not pick out the "significant sounds" from the background noises, was disastrously inadequate.[5] Roosevelt had met the need for coordinated intelligence in part by creating the wartime Office of Strategic Services under Major General William J. Donovan. Eventually Donovan prepared for Roosevelt a plan for a permanent central intelligence organization, but the Joint Chiefs of Staff sidetracked it.[6] Hence no adequate peacetime centralized intelligence agency existed when Truman took office, confronting global disorders and rivalry with the Soviet Union. In the extensive government reorganization he initiated after V-J Day Truman disbanded the OSS, which had not been designed as a peacetime instrument, transferring some of its agents to army intelligence and others to the State Department.

Acting on a recommendation from Byrnes, supported by the Bureau of the Budget, that an intelligence agency should be responsible to the secretary of state, Truman asked Byrnes to take the lead in developing for presidential consideration a coordinated intelligence program. The undertaking, however, soon ran into trouble. Congress, eager for economy and suspicious of professional intelligence, cut State Department funds for intelligence work. Within the department, moreover, the geographic divisions—particularly the offices of Near Eastern and African Affairs and

American Republic Affairs—opposed intelligence work done by a group not under their control. The armed services also wanted to handle intelligence thought essential to their responsibilities.

Byrnes yielded to these objections and forsook his own recommendations.[7] Instead he proposed to Truman a compromise plan that had its origins in the navy. It provided for the formation of a National Intelligence Authority, which was to make policy, and a Central Intelligence Group, which was to assist in carrying it out. In addition to collecting, evaluating and disseminating intelligence, the CIG was to perform "such other functions and duties related to intelligence affecting the national security as the President and the National Intelligence Authority may from time to time direct."[8] By executive order January 22, 1946, Truman established these agencies.[9] The National Intelligence Authority was the forerunner of the National Security Council, and the Central Intelligence Group was the precursor of the Central Intelligence Agency. Under the 1946 makeshift plan supervision of intelligence was placed in the Executive Office of the President.

The CIG was in fact an interdepartmental body, the stepchild of the departments of State, War, and Navy. Ironically, in view of the later CIA sprawl, Truman's original intention was not to create a large new agency.[10] After several months of experience, however, CIG officials maintained that the organization could not function effectively as a stepchild of three departments. It would be preferable, they said, to have an organization established by statute so that it could operate as an integrated agency with its own personnel.

Marshall warned Truman against this approach. No doubt concerned about preserving the influence of the State Department, he sent Truman a memorandum February 7, 1947, saying that the Foreign Service was the only agency in the government that collected intelligence from around the world. In peace time, he said, "we should be very slow to subject the collection and evaluation of this foreign intelligence to other establishments." "The powers of the proposed agency," he cautioned, "seem almost unlimited and need clarification."[11]

Nevertheless Truman submitted to Congress a proposed draft of the National Security Act February 26, including provision for a Central Intelligence Agency. In accompanying letters to the Speaker and the president *pro tem,* he dwelt on unification of the armed forces and did not even mention the CIA, let alone "dirty tricks," as the covert political and paramilitary operations of later days came to be called.[12]

Some of the CIA provisions evolved from the experiences of the wartime intelligence agencies and the CIG.[13] The directives governing these early operations had deliberately allowed flexibility to enable the agencies to cope with unforeseen problems, and such flexibility became a heritage of the CIA through the 1947 act. It was this flexibility, or vagueness, that opened the door to adventures at home and abroad that were not foreseen by Congress at the time. Nor, surely, by Truman.

Truman's draft was bare of any details on the duties of the proposed CIA. The House decided, however, that these should be specified. It accomplished this simply by picking up the language of Truman's 1946 directive establishing the CIG and, without essential change, applying it to the CIA. Most of the terms thus adopted in the new legislation were unexceptional. The CIA was to advise the National Security Council on government intelligence activities. It was to correlate and evaluate intelligence. To avoid the danger alluded to in talk about a gestapo, provision was made that the CIA "shall have no police, subpoena, law-enforcement powers, or internal security functions." Two other descriptions of functions transferred from the old CIG, however, were to provide the flexibility, so-called, that opened broad vistas for the CIA in future years.

One of these was the authority to perform "such other functions and duties related to intelligence affecting the national security" as the National Security Council might from time to time direct. The other was the authority for the CIA to take responsibility for "protecting intelligence sources and methods" from unauthorized disclosure. These abstract, open-ended provisions became part of the National Security Act of 1947 and eventually were interpreted in the executive branch as justification for activities that would have astounded Truman and many members of the Eightieth Congress who had voted to insert the clauses.

The clause authorizing the CIA to perform other duties and functions related to intelligence was the vehicle through which the CIA, under National Security Council directives, engaged in covert operations.[14] Yet in its massive study of the CIA in 1975–76 the Senate Select Committee on Intelligence Activities, chaired by Senator Frank Church, Democrat, of Idaho, concluded: "There is no substantial evidence that Congress intended by the passage of the National Security Act of 1947 to authorize covert action by the CIA or that Congress even anticipated that the CIA would engage in such activities."[15] Confronted nevertheless with ambiguity in the legislative history, the committee also said that Congress did not intend to prohibit covert actions by the CIA.[16]

The authority contained in the act for the CIA to assume responsibility for protecting intelligence sources and methods became the avenue for all sorts of domestic activities, including wiretapping, undertaken in the name of counterintelligence. The CIA interpreted this provision, according to the Church Committee, "to authorize investigation of domestic groups whose activities, including demonstrations, have potential, however remote, for creating threats to CIA installations, recruiters or contractors."[17]

In its study twenty-nine years after the legislation was passed the Church Committee found that because the National Security Act that Truman had submitted in 1947 was preoccupied with military unification, it failed to define the policy and purpose of the American intelligence establishment. The act constituted "a vague and open-ended statement of authority for the President through the National Security Council." It did not provide "an adequate charter for the Central Intelligence Agency"—one that would insure "effective accountability, management control and legislative and executive oversight." The act failed "to establish clear and specific limits on the operation of America's intelligence organizations which will help ensure the protection of the rights and liberties of Americans under the Constitution and the preservation of America's honor and reputation abroad."[18]

Thus while the National Security Act did enable the United States to develop a large, modern, often impressive intelligence service, it also opened the door to abuses that were to startle the country upon their disclosure a generation later. These abuses did not come about automatically. When, as will be seen, the Cold War reached a seemingly alarming stage some months later, the National Security Council authorized covert operations. In doing so, it ushered in a new phase in which the CIA no longer was content to report and analyze events abroad but was to try also to influence them in behalf of American interests.

Even in 1947 Truman yielded to Cold War pressures to approve a program, not directly involving the CIA, that was at a minimum an invasion of privacy in peacetime, undertaken on grounds of national security.

During the war the government had persuaded three international telegraph companies—RCA Global, ITT World Communications, and Western Union International—to make some of their international traffic available for inspection by military intelligence. In the beginning the purpose was to reveal messages involving foreign targets of American intelligence. As time passed, however, the government also began to look at telegrams sent by, and to, certain American citizens about whom it had suspicions.

In 1947 the secretary of defense sought to renew this arrangement, which went under the code name "Shamrock." Meeting with representatives of three companies, Forrestal assured them that if they continued the cooperation with the government, they would suffer no criminal liability nor public exposure, at least while the Truman administration was in power. Their participation, he said, was in the highest interests of national security.

Forrestal said that the arrangement had the approval of Truman and Attorney General Clark. He also volunteered the information that legislation making clear that such activity by the companies was permissible would be considered by Congress at the next session, but no such legislation was ever introduced.

In 1949 the companies sought renewed assurances from Forrestal's successor, Secretary of Defense Louis A. Johnson, and again were told that Truman and Clark had been consulted and had given their approval.

"Shamrock" was handled at various times by the Army Security Agency, the Armed Forces Security Agency, and the National Security Agency created by Truman in 1952. So secret was this project for scanning hundreds of thousands of communications during the twenty-seven years "Shamrock" existed that it appears that no president other than Truman ever knew about it. "Shamrock" was terminated by Secretary of Defense James R. Schlesinger May 15, 1975. Senator Church said that the program apparently violated the Communications Act of 1934 and the Fourth Amendment.[19]

With regard to unification of the armed services, which was the main purpose of the National Security Act, the legislation reflected compromises worked out over many months, notably in deference to the navy's insistence on coordination rather than merger. Nothing radical was done. On the contrary, the 1947 act was evolutionary. It went perhaps as far as it was possible to go at that time against the grain of military tradition, but did not go far enough to produce an efficient defense organization and had to be drastically redone in 1949.

Forrestal's fight against giving the proposed new secretary of defense administrative control over the services had frustrated Truman's desire to have the secretary preside over a new unified Department of Defense. As the bill finally passed, a Department of Defense was not created at all. That was to come in new legislation in 1949. Instead the secretary was put in the weak position of presiding over a nebulous new entity called the National Military Establishment.

The army, navy, and new Department of the Air Force remained executive departments with their own secretaries. The three departments retained all their powers and duties except for the vague responsibilities conferred on the secretary of defense, who was essentially a coordinator but who represented the three services in the cabinet. His duties included setting common policy, exercising general direction, eliminating duplication of supplies, and supervising budget estimates. He was, however, the principal assistant to the president on national security. Though inadequate, the act was an important step toward the national security structure that has existed to the present time.

It was passed July 25, 1947. Truman was caught in unusual and sad circumstances while waiting to sign it July 26. Early in the day he had received word that his ninety-four-year-old mother was in critical condition in Grandview as a result of the fracture of her right hip, which she had suffered in a fall in February. During the spring Truman had visited her four times, once for a stay of twelve days. Now he decided to return, but deferred his departure long enough for an important meeting with Forrestal.

He told him that he had asked Patterson, who had just resigned as secretary of war, to become the first secretary of defense, but that, being pressed for money, Patterson felt he had to resume law practice. Thereupon Truman offered the post to Forrestal, the man who had done the most to make it a hollow one. Forrestal accepted.[20] In a prophecy that was to come tragically close to the mark for him, he wrote Robert Sherwood soon afterward, "This office will probably be the greatest cemetery for dead cats in history."[21] With Patterson out of the picture, Forrestal—because of his ability, seniority, and experience in the unification negotiations—was a logical candidate for the office. Furthermore Truman believed that giving Forrestal a taste of administering an act that the secretary had done so much to shape would soon make him an advocate of reshaping it more in line with what the president had wanted in the first place.[22] It proved a shrewd judgment. Meanwhile John Sullivan, under secretary of the navy, replaced Forrestal as secretary of the navy. Under Secretary of War Kenneth C. Royall succeeded Patterson, with the revised title of "Secretary of the Army." Stuart Symington became the first secretary of the air force.

When Truman's meeting with Forrestal ended he left for National Airport. Before the old presidential plane, the *Sacred Cow,* took off, a copy of the National Security Act was rushed to him and he signed it on the plane. The trip began at 12:30 P.M. As the plane was passing over Cincinnati, the pilot received a message from Missouri, which he gave to Matt Connelly, who passed it to the president's personal physician, Brigadier General Wallace H. Graham. Graham handed it to the president. His mother was dead. "Well, now she won't have to suffer any more," Truman said.[23]

Throughout the remainder of 1947 the international situation deteriorated.

Melancholy news came from Poland October 5. Four years after Stalin had dissolved the Comintern (Communist International) to relieve his wartime allies of fear of world revolution a successor organization, the Cominform (Communist Information Bureau), was established at a secret conference in Silesia. Solidifying Stalin's grip on Eastern Europe, the Cominform consisted of the Communist parties of the Soviet Union, Yugoslavia, France, Italy, Poland, Bulgaria, Czechoslovakia, Hungary, and Rumania. Undoubtedly it was founded in reaction to the Marshall Plan.[24] Like their American counterparts, the Soviet leaders saw the world divided in two. "The Truman-Marshall Plan," on October 5 manifesto by the Cominform said, "is only a farce, a European branch of the general world plan of political expansion being realized by the United States of America."[25]

In these same weeks General Clay and Ambassador Walter Bedell Smith, each on a visit to Washington, made portentous statements at a meeting of the National Security Council, chaired by Truman. Reviewing Soviet-American differences over Germany, both warned that the United States must be prepared for some Soviet action to force the Americans out of Berlin. They said that such an action must be resisted.[26]

The five-months-old NSC met December 17, 1947, and made a critical decision. The council, an instrument of the president, launched the CIA on the path of covert action.

The National Security Act did not, it will be recalled, authorize such action. It did empower the CIA to perform "such other functions and duties related to intelligence affecting the national security" as the National Security Council might from time to time direct. Relying on this provision, the council that day promulgated NSC-4-A. It authorized Rear Admiral Roscoe H. Hillenkoetter, then director of central intelligence, the first head of the CIA, to conduct covert psychological operations in cooperation with the State Department and the national military establishment.[27] Amateurish in comparison with what was to follow, the CIA's first venture into covert operations included acquisition of a radio transmitter for broadcasting behind the Iron Curtain, establishment of a secret plant in Germany for printing propaganda and assembly of a fleet of balloons for dropping leaflets in Eastern Europe. Six months later, when the international situation was even more tense, the National Security Council was to expand the range of covert operations, vastly.

34. *Palestine*

IN THAT FALL OF 1947 Truman was deeply involved in and much perturbed by a problem that had been with him since his earliest days in the White House and was now approaching a climax attended by a great deal of passion at home and abroad. It was an issue that posed singular difficulty for a president in terms of humaneness, conscience, diplomacy, strategy, intrigue, oil, domestic politics, prejudice, and personal pressure. It was the question of creating a Jewish state in Palestine against the implacable hostility of the Arabs and the resolute opposition of the British, who held a League of Nations mandate on the territory.

Eight days after he had been sworn in as president in 1945, Truman first received Rabbi Stephen S. Wise of New York, cochairman of the American Zionist Emergency Council, who came to plead the cause of a Jewish national home in Palestine, a land where Jews and Arabs lived side by side under the British mandate.

By the time of Roosevelt's death the problem of where to settle Europeans, especially Jews, who had been uprooted by Hitler's aggressions was growing critical. The enormity of Hitler's atrocities against Jews was just coming into focus. Political pressure over the Palestine issue in the United States was rising. The 1944 Democratic and Republican platforms had called for the opening of Palestine to unrestricted Jewish immigration and land ownership.

As a senator, Truman, along with a majority of members of Congress, had endorsed the Zionist goal. When the right time came, Truman declared, he would be willing to aid the Zionist cause.[1] In his memoirs he said he believed that Great Britain had an obligation to honor the Balfour Declaration of 1917, viewing favorably the establishment of a Jewish homeland in Palestine.

Before seeing Wise April 20, 1945, Truman received a memorandum from Secretary of State Stettinius cautioning him that Zionist leaders would try to exact an early commitment from him. Because the United States had vital interests in the area, Stettinius said, the subject should be handled carefully.[2] Truman assured Wise that he sympathized with the plight of Jewish refugees. He said he would carry out Roosevelt's policy.[3] To a Zionist this must not have sounded particularly encouraging. Roosevelt had for complex reasons continually shrunk from doing anything about Palestine.

On May 1, 1945, Acting Secretary of State Grew sent Truman a memorandum, reminding him that "although President Roosevelt at times gave expressions to views sympathetic to certain Zionist aims, he also gave assurances to the Arabs which they regard as definite commitments on our part." Roosevelt had authorized the State Department to tell them that "in the view of this Government there should be no decision altering the basic situation in Palestine without full consultation with both Arabs and Jews.'' Grew quoted Roosevelt as having said that a Jewish state in Palestine ''could be established and maintained only by military force.''[4] On June 16 Truman read a memorandum from Grew saying,

Our basic attitude on Palestine is that it is one of the problems which should come up for settlement after the war through the United Nations Organization, and that in any event no decision regarding it should be taken without full consultation with both Arabs and Jews.

''Suggestion OK. HST,'' Truman noted.[5]

Mahmud Fahmy el-Nokrashy, prime minister of Egypt, wrote him, lamenting Hitler's persecutions but saying that the Arabs would resist establishment of a Jewish state ''at all costs.'' In the tenor of Roosevelt's correspondence, Truman replied noncommittally that the United States would make no decisions affecting the situation without full consultation with both sides.[6]

He decided to let the problem lie until he could discuss it with Churchill. The pressure upon him in support of the Jewish cause, however, did not abate. Almost from the moment Truman turned to this question and for years thereafter Jewish leaders, tormented by the ravages of Hitlerism, made an extraordinary effort in alliance with their political friends to influence the president's policy on Palestine. Before Truman met with Wise he received a letter urging a favorable hearing for the rabbi from Senator Robert F. Wagner, Democrat, of New York, where Jewish political strength was most heavily concentrated. In ensuing weeks individual letters pleading the Jewish cause arrived from governors, members of Congress, and Jewish spokesmen.[7] Dr. Israel Goldstein, Louis Lipsky, and Henry Monsky, cochairmen of the Interim Committee of the American Jewish Conference, wrote to Truman asking him to use his influence with the British to have Palestine opened to massive Jewish immigration.[8]

At the Potsdam conference that summer he sent the British prime minister a memorandum urging the British to lift the restrictions they had imposed in 1939 on Jewish immigration. At that point, however, Attlee succeeded Churchill and was not prepared to discuss the issue.[9] By the time Truman returned to Washington the European refugee problem was pressing, and he was asked about Palestine at a press conference.

''We want to let as many of the Jews into Palestine as it is possible. . . ,'' he said. ''Then the matter will have to be worked out diplomatically with the British and the Arabs, so that if a state can be set up there, they may be able to set it up on a peaceful basis. I have no desire to send 500,000 American soldiers there to make peace in Palestine.''[10]

Leahy had told Truman that, based on talks with King Ibn Saud of Saudi Arabia after Yalta, Roosevelt's understanding was that the king would go to war to prevent large Jewish immigration and that Roosevelt did not intend to commit American forces against the Arabs.[11] In March 1945, Saudi Arabia, Egypt, Syria, and Lebanon had signed a pledge to take united action to protect the Arab position in Palestine and Trans-Jordan.

After Potsdam the State Department again tried to steer Truman away from any course that would offend the Arabs. The department counseled him that no government should advocate a policy of mass immigration unless it was prepared to help facilitate it. If immigration was to be the answer, it should be the responsibility of Great Britain, which held a League of Nations mandate over Palestine.

Truman did not consider this advice adequate to the problem posed by the plight of the displaced Jews in Europe, nor, presumably, to the politically sensitive situation being created by the pressure of American Jews. The State Department, he suspected, was more concerned about Arab reaction than about Jewish suffering.[12] He turned his attention, therefore, to a report sent him by Dean Earl G. Harrison of the University of Pennsylvania Law School, former United States Commissioner of Immigration and Naturalization, who had recently surveyed the situation in Europe for the administration. Giving a poignant account of European Jews, Harrison supported a petition by the Jewish Agency for Palestine for 100,000 additional immigration certificates.[13]

Against the advice of the State Department, Truman seized on this proposal. Since Byrnes was departing in September 1945 for the London meeting of the Council of Foreign Ministers, the president gave him a personal letter to Attlee, recommending the Jewish Agency plan.

The British replied that any violent change in the face of Arab opposition "would probably cause serious disturbances throughout the Middle East, involving a large military commitment, and would arouse widespread anxiety in India." Playing for time, they proposed a study by an Anglo-American Committee of Inquiry. Cautiously hopeful, Truman assented.[14] He was concentrating on the short-range problem of succor for Hitler's victims. The long-range issue of the future of Palestine he vaguely left to the United Nations in line with the State Department's view, but he resented Zionist pressure on him to commit the United States to the creation of a Jewish state.

Pressure continued nevertheless. On October 15 Truman wrote Dean Virginia C. Gildersleeve of Barnard College:

The Jewish and Arab situation in the Near East is a most difficult one and has caused us more difficulty than most any other problem in the European Theater. . . .[15]

The Zionists were complaining that the Anglo-American Committee of Inquiry was a British trap and would lead to endless delays on a Palestine settlement. "Having only a Hobson's choice," Representative Emmanuel Celler wrote, discontentedly, to Truman November 15, "American Jewry must bow down to the inevitable and accept your decision concerning the . . . Committee of Inquiry." The New York Democrat was chairman of the House Judiciary Committee and the foremost Jewish spokesman in Congress. The same day Rabbi Wise and the cochairman of the American Zionist Emergency Council, Rabbi Abba Hillel Silver, wired Truman, "It was with the deepest regret that we learned of the acceptance of our government of the British proposal. . . . What is needed above all are immediate concrete measures." On November 12 a thousand Orthodox rabbis met in Washington and sent a delegation to see Truman. The callers had to settle for leaving a petition asking him to facilitate a Jewish national homeland within the "Biblical boundaries" of Palestine.[16]

A glimpse of Truman's attitude in the fall of 1945 was contained in a letter he wrote November 24 to Senator Joseph H. Ball of Minnesota but never mailed. Ball had written him about a resolution adopted by a Minneapolis Jewish group urging faster action on establishing a Jewish state. Truman said:

I told the Jews that if they were willing to furnish me with five hundred thousand men to carry on a war with the Arabs, we could do what they are suggesting in the Resolution—otherwise we will have to negotiate awhile.

It is a very explosive situation we are facing, and naturally I regret it very much but I don't think that you, or any of the other Senators, would be inclined to send a half dozen Divisions to Palestine to maintain a Jewish State.

What I am trying to do is to make the whole world safe for the Jews. Therefore, I don't feel like going to war for Palestine.[17]

Toward the close of 1945 Truman met with a dynamic Zionist with whom he was to become deeply involved. He was Dr. Chaim Weizmann, then president of the Jewish Agency for Palestine and of the World Zionist Organization. The meeting was cordial. Writing Truman December 12 to thank him for a sympathetic hearing Weizmann, too, lamented the resort to the Committee of Inquiry and said:

Mr. President, six million Jews have perished. No people has suffered such devastating loss in proportion to its size in modern history. The remnants can still be saved. . . . I can see in the gloom which still enshrouds a great part of the world no glimmer of light for hundreds of thousands of my people except the hope of bringing them as quickly as possible to Palestine.[18]

As the Anglo-American Committee of Inquiry pursued its task in early 1946, the tension in Palestine between the Jews and the British and between the Jews and the Arabs rose relentlessly. The stream of Jewish immigrants, legal and illegal, that had been flowing into Palestine ever since Hitler's accession continued. "The Jewish community in Palestine had come of age during the war," Walter Laqueur, the historian, writes. "It was now to all intents and purposes a state within a state, with its own schools and public services, even an army of its own."[19] Strengthening the already formidable Jewish presence—some six hundred thousand persons at the end of the war—Haganah, the illegal Jewish army, formed alliances with two Jewish terrorist groups, Irgun Zvai Leumi and the Stern gang.[20] Violence spread. A wave of burning, stoning, and dynamiting was climaxed July 22, 1946, when the Irgun bombed the King David Hotel in Jerusalem, site of a British army headquarters, killing ninety-one persons. In their own way the Jews already were fighting to establish a state, and the future of the Middle East hung in the balance.

With Byrnes abroad much of the time Truman relied to a considerable extent on the loyal help of Acheson, who did not share the president's views on the desirability of immigration. In line with State Department tradition Acheson feared that transporting Jews in great numbers from Europe would bring trouble. And to establish a Jewish state large enough to receive a million or more immigrants, he feared, would create such a problem as to imperil American interests in the Middle East.[21]

The administration official who at this time probably kept after Truman most persistently on furthering the Zionist cause was a White House assistant who was little known to the public and who indeed cultivated an air of mystery about himself.

He was David K. Niles, born Neyhus, son of Russian Jewish immigrants and reared in a poor section of North Boston. During the First World War he got a job in the information office of the Department of Labor in Washington. Then he became associate director of the Ford Hall Forum in Boston, where he met Robert M. LaFollette. When LaFollette ran for president on the Progressive Party ticket in 1924, Niles directed his speakers' bureau.

After crusading unsuccessfully to save Nicola Sacco and Bartolomeo Vanzetti from execution for murder, he became, in the 1928 presidential campaign, director of the National Committee of Independent Voters for Al Smith. There he met Roosevelt and Hopkins. Four years later he became an early New Dealer and eventually was appointed an administrative assistant to President Roosevelt, specializing in the problems of minorities.[22] Truman, who liked Niles very much, retained him in the same capacity, in which, inevitably, he became involved in Truman's dealings with American Jews over Palestine. Niles not only was dedicated to the Zionist cause, but was in close touch with leading members of the Executive of the Jewish Agency. Doubtless exaggerating, Truman once told Oscar Ewing that Niles was so emotional on the subject that he would break into tears over a discussion of Palestine.[23] Because of his strategic position, Jewish leaders kept Niles abreast of developments known to them. He in turn sought to keep the case for Zionism before Truman.

When, for example, Myron C. Taylor, the president's personal representative to the Vatican, who had a background in the refugee problem, wrote Truman warning of the possible dangers of Zionist aims, Niles promptly countered with a memorandum taking issue with Taylor. Whereas Taylor had cautioned about Ibn Saud's likely reaction, Niles reminded Truman "that President Roosevelt said to some of us privately he could do anything that needed to be done with Ibn Saud with a few million dollars." And whereas Taylor warned of possible Arab aggression against Western interests, Niles said: "I am also inclined to think that 100,000 Jews would be of great assistance in that area as the Jews of Palestine were during the second World War. . . . The Allies got no help from the Arabs at all but considerable help from the Jews in Palestine."[24]

The report of the Committee of Inquiry was published April 30, 1946, and caused a storm. Spreading wrath in London and among the Arabs, it recommended immediate admission of 100,000 European Jews into Palestine. It rejected nevertheless the idea of a Jewish state. Rather it recommended that government in Palestine should be based on the principles that (1) Jew should not dominate Arab nor Arab Jew, (2) the state should be neither Jewish nor Arab, and (3) it should protect the interests of all the holy places of the Christian, Moslem, and Jewish faiths. It also recommended that Britain's mandate continue pending a United Nations trusteeship.

To the consternation of Attlee and Bevin, Truman hailed the recommendation on immigration while reserving judgment on the long-range questions.[25] In the postwar upheaval Britain was having trouble maintaining its friendly relations with the Arabs and its historic role in the Middle East, focusing on protection of the Suez Canal and access to oil. The ferment over creation of a Jewish state magnified Britain's difficulties and, as seen in London, threatened Middle Eastern stability. In

Bevin's eyes the Jews were not a nation and hence did not need a state of their own.[26]

Attlee told the House of Commons that Britain would not carry out the recommendations unilaterally. In any case, he said, nothing would be done to admit any of the 100,000 immigrants until the "illegal armies" in Palestine were disarmed. British authority in the mandate was menaced by the rising wave of terrorism. The bitterness of the dispute was illuminated by a remark by Bevin at the annual Labour Party Conference: "Regarding the agitation in the United States, and particularly in New York, for 100,000 Jews to be put into Palestine, I hope it will not be misunderstood in America if I say, with the purest of motives, that that was because they did not want too many of them in New York."[27]

At this point in the drama an interesting actor with a fascinating role made his first appearance on the scene. He was Edward Jacobson, born on the East Side of Manhattan in 1891, the son of immigrants from Russian Lithuania, who reared their children in the Orthodox Jewish tradition. The father was a shoemaker. At the turn of the century the Jacobsons moved to Leavenworth, Kansas; and then to Kansas City, where young Eddie, a stock boy for a dry goods firm, met Harry Truman, a $60-a-month clerk at the Union National Bank.[28] When the war came the two of them landed at Camp Doniphan. Appointed regimental canteen officer, Truman had Jacobson detailed as his assistant. After the war Jacobson suggested that they resume their partnership, an idea that led to the establishment of Truman and Jacobson, haberdashers.[29] After the firm failed in the recession of 1921 Jacobson drifted back into the same business and was now prospering with his own store in Kansas City. The friendship continued throughout Truman's political career.

Jacobson did not belong to any Zionist organization, but he shared the dream of a national homeland and wanted to be helpful in the cause. On June 10, 1946, he wrote Truman and asked if he might bring to the White House his friend, Rabbi Arthur J. Lelyveld, executive director of the Committee on Unity for Palestine of the Zionist Organization of America. Truman met with them and Charles Kaplan, vice-president of the Shirtcraft Corporation, of which Jacobson had once been a representative, on June 26. Lelyveld was gratified by Truman's attitude on Palestine.[30] As they were leaving, Jacobson told reporters, "Kaplan sells shirts, I sell furnishings, and the rabbi sells notions." Jacobson was to return to the scene many times, eventually as the quasi ambassador of the new state of Israel.

Truman solicited the views of the Joint Chiefs of Saff on the Palestine problem. They responded, unequivocally, that the United States should commit no armed forces to carry out the recommendations of the Committee of Inquiry. No action should be taken that would cause trouble in Palestine beyond the capabilities of British troops to control. This was a time, it must be remembered, when the United States was still worried over Soviet activity in Iran. American officials were touchy about any developments that might offer Moscow a pretext for wider penetration in the Middle East.

The Chiefs warned that, if antagonized by Western policy in Palestine, the Arabs might make common cause with Moscow. Thus the Soviet Union might replace the United States as a power in the Middle East, with serious consequences for control of the oil there. Since the United States had vital security interests in the area, the Chiefs concluded, no action should be taken that would reorient the Middle East away from the West.[31]

Political pressure from the opposite direction continued nevertheless. Representative Celler repeatedly asked the White House to arrange for the entire New York delegation in Congress to call on Truman. Tired of such visits, Truman was evasive. On June 19, 1946, Celler called again and warned a secretary that if Truman did not grant the appointment, members of the delegation might tell the press that the administration was refusing to see them. Niles tried to persuade Truman, but with no success.

Celler irritably wrote Matt Connelly June 25 saying he was "startled" at Truman's attitude and added: "It certainly will give political ammunition to the upstate Republicans who wanted to attend and you remember that New York faces a very critical election. Frankly, it is my opinion that it is bad politics for the President not to meet with them—even if it is on the Palestine question.

"If I do not hear from you by return mail, I shall take it that the 'jig is up' and I shall have to tell the members regretfully that the appointment could not be arranged."[32]

Under such goading the White House staff prevailed on Truman to see the New York delegation which he did with a show of annoyance, constantly ruffling papers and commenting that he wished that people would call on him about the country's problems, not their own.[33] His irritation was not unique. According to Samuel Rosenman, Roosevelt also resented similar pressures and became reluctant to receive Jewish representatives.[34]

Attlee's criticism of America's lack of help on the proposed immigration and an appeal to Truman for financial assistance from the American members of the Executive of the Jewish Agency brought results. Truman offered to finance the transportation of European Jews to Palestine.[35]

In response to further appeals from Attlee for talks, he appointed a cabinet committee composed of the secretaries of state, war, and treasury, or their alternates, with negotiating authority. The alternates, headed by former Assistant Secretary of State Henry F. Grady, were flown to London in the president's plane to meet with a British group under Herbert Morrison, lord president of His Majesty's council. American members of the Executive of the Jewish Agency for Palestine (Wise, Silver, Dr. Nahum Goldmann, and Louis Lipsky) wrote Truman July 8 suggesting that Grady and his colleagues be instructed to press for immediate immigration without reference to the other proposals in the report of the Committee of Inquiry.[36]

The American and British negotiators, however, came forward with the so-called Morrison-Grady Plan. A British concept, it proposed a Palestine federation. Palestine would be divided into four areas: Arab and Jewish provinces, a district of Jerusalem, and a district of the Negev. The central government would be British, although the Arab and Jewish provinces would be empowered to manage their domestic affairs. In the first year 100,000 Jewish refugees could immigrate, but thereafter a British high commissioner would be authorized to regulate immigration. However, consummation of the plan would depend in part upon acceptance by Arabs and

Jews, and that gave the Arabs an initial veto over immigration.

Acheson later defended the plan as containing seeds of possible compromise and said that Truman at first contemplated accepting it in modified form. According to Wallace, Truman considered it fair.[37]

The public reaction, however, was horrendous. Taft attacked the plan, as protests reverberated through Congress. From Paris Rabbi Wise cabled Truman his dismay. From the White Elephant Hotel on Nantucket Island Herbert Lehman sent a letter asking Truman to oppose the plan "in the name of humanity."[38] Former American members of the Anglo-American Committee of Inquiry called the new plan a betrayal of the Jews. One of them, James G. McDonald, went to the White House with New York's two Democratic senators, Wagner and James M. Mead, to protest. By this time Truman was so angry at the pressure that he refused to allow McDonald to read a one-page memorandum.[39]

"I am not a New Yorker," Truman snapped, as the story was recounted to Wallace. "All these people are pleading for a special interest. I am an American."

This remark drew an expression of indignation from McDonald, and Truman retreated somewhat.[40] On July 31, 1946, he wrote McDonald, apologetically: "I hope I wasn't too hard on you. It has been a most difficult problem and I have about come to the conclusion that there is no solution, but we will keep trying."[41]

Wallace telephoned Truman and said that in the Taft attack he could see the hand of Rabbi Silver.[42] Truman despised Rabbi Silver. A year hence he was to write to Niles: "We could have settled this Palestine thing if U.S. politics had been kept out of it. Terror and Silver are the contributing causes of *some*, if not all, of our troubles."[43] A resident of Cleveland, the militant rabbi had been credited with influencing Taft in favor of unrestricted Jewish immigration leading to creation of a Jewish homeland. Silver also had worked with Taft on the pro-Zionist plank in the 1944 Republican platform.[44]

At a cabinet meeting July 30, 1946, Wallace warned Truman that the Morrison-Grady Plan was "loaded with political dynamite." Feeling harassed, Truman was angry at the Jews—"put out" with them, as Wallace recalled his words. According to Wallace, Truman snapped, "Jesus Christ couldn't please them when he was here on earth, so how could anyone expect that I would have any luck?" Wallace further recalled that "Truman said he had no use for them and didn't care what happened to them."

"You must remember that it is easy for them to get into quite a state of mind," Wallace told Truman, "because nearly all of the Jews in this country have relatives in Europe, and they know that about 5 million out of 6 million Jews have been killed and that no other people have suffered in this way."

Forrestal said that if another war occurred, the United States would need oil from Saudi Arabia.

Truman replied that he wanted to handle the problem not in the light of oil but of justice.[45]

Paul E. Fitzpatrick, chairman of the New York State Democratic Committee, wired him: "If this plan goes into effect it would be useless for the Democrats to nominate a state ticket for the election this fall."[46]

In the end political heat was too strong. Truman summoned the Grady group home and notified Attlee August 7 that he could not approve the plan because it was politically unsupportable.[47]

With the approach of the 1946 Congressional elections and Dewey's race in New York, Jews were questioning the effectiveness of Truman's performance. A year had passed since he had first proposed admission of 100,000 immigrants, yet it had not come about. In frustration Truman wrote to the Bronx Democratic leader, Ed Flynn:

Of course, the British control Palestine and there is no way of getting One Hundred Thousand Jews in there unless they want them in.

I have done my best to get them in but I don't believe there is any possible way of pleasing our Jewish friends.[48]

On October 9 Eliahu Epstein (later Elath), Washington representative of the Jewish Agency for Palestine, wrote to Dr. Goldmann, a member of the Executive, saying that the dissension over the Morrison-Grady Plan had put Truman in a mood to wash his hands of Palestine but that Wise had talked to him again and persuaded him to persevere. "The last, but not least factor in the situation," Epstein added, "was the activity of the Republican candidates in the forthcoming elections, and especially in New York, who overtly showed their determination to make the Palestine issue one of the focal points of attack on Truman and the Democratic administration."[49]

Bartley C. Crum, a Republican San Francisco attorney, who had been a member of the Committee of Inquiry, saw Democratic National Chairman Hannegan October 1 and gave him a letter arguing the political advantage of a pro-Zionist statement by the president. The same day Hannegan passed the letter on to Truman with a note of his own, concluding, "I hope that you will give this consideration."[50] The State Department already had offered contradictory counsel. Under Secretary Clayton had cautioned Truman in a letter September 12 that Wise and other Jewish leaders would press for a presidential declaration supporting a Jewish state. Clayton said that it would "merely be encouraging them to make fresh demands and to apply pressures in the future." In the end, however, Truman's feelings and the political pressures generated by the competition for Jewish votes and Jewish money prevailed.

With Niles evidently playing a major role, Truman had a statement prepared for issuance on Yom Kippur, October 4, 1946, a month before Election Day. On October 3, Bevin, who had been holding talks with the Jews and the Arabs, was notified in Paris by Attlee that the statement was coming. Believing that another presidential appeal for one hundred thousand Jewish immigrants would undermine his talks, Bevin begged Byrnes, who also was in Paris, to get Truman to withhold his statement. Byrnes declined, however, saying that if Truman did not speak out, Dewey would.[51] In fact on October 6, while campaigning for reelection as governor, Dewey said at a Jewish dinner in New York, "It must be an immigration of not one hundred thousand but of several hundreds of thousands."[52]

In Paris in August the Executive of the Jewish Agency had adopted a resolution expressing its willingness to negotiate on the basis of a viable Jewish state in an adequate area of Palestine—meaning partition—rather than of the whole of mandatory Palestine. Dr. Goldmann had then returned to Washington to negotiate accordingly.[53] In his Yom Kippur statement Truman cited the Jewish Agency's proposals and said: "To such a solution our Government could give its support."[54] Thus for the first time he publicly lent his backing to the creation of a "viable" Jewish state in Palestine, the most pro-Zionist statement ever made by a president. It established American policy in favor of partition of Palestine, an alternative that had been discussed off and on over the years.

The day after Truman's statement appeared the chairman of the Senate Finance Committee, Walter George, wrote to him, warning that "Congress will not support a course calling for the further expenditure of American money and/or the use of American troops in the Palestine area."

"I sincerely wish," Truman replied, "that every member of the Congress could visit the displaced persons camps in Germany and Austria and see just what is happening to Five Hundred Thousand human beings through no fault of their own."[55]

As reflected in his correspondence, however, his feelings on the Palestine problem oscillated between such high-mindedness and despair and bitterness. For on October 22 he wrote to Ed Pauley, calling the situation insoluble. Not only were the British muddying the waters, he complained, "but the Jews themselves are making it almost impossible to do anything for them." Reiterating his familiar observation about underdogs becoming arrogant once they get on top, he added: "I am going to spend the rest of my time here at this place working for the best interest of the whole country and let the chips fall where they may."[56]

Typifying Arab reaction to the Yom Kippur statement, Ibn Saud wrote Truman October 15: "I was . . . astonished at the latest announcement issued in your name in support of the Jews in Palestine and its demand that floodgates of immigration be opened in such a way as to alter the basic situation in Palestine in contradiction to previous promises." In a reply made public by the White House October 28 Truman said that the American people had supported the concept of a Jewish home in Palestine since the First World War. "It is only natural, therefore," he continued, "that this Government should favor at this time the entry into Palestine of considerable numbers of displaced Jews in Europe, not only that they may find shelter there, but also that they may contribute their talents and energies to the upbuilding of the Jewish National Home." He denied that this policy broke a promise since consultation with both sides had been going on during the year.[57]

Epstein's earlier noted letter to Goldmann offered fascinating insights into the access the Jewish Agency had—or thought it had—to well-placed officials in the Truman administration. In accordance with Goldmann's instructions, for example, Epstein had sought a presidential statement concerning partition of Palestine. Epstein and an associate had prepared a draft and had presented it to "our friend"— undoubtedly David Niles in the White House—but nothing had come of the effort at that time. Epstein again got in touch "with our friend." The "friend" then performed "an important service" in connection with Truman's Yom Kippur statement. The Crum letter to Hannegan urging a pro-Zionist statement was, according to Epstein's account, "inspired by our friend and even written in his office."

The credit for the statement, Epstein wrote, "must go again primarily to our friend who at this time, as in the past, has shown determination and great courage in attempting to overcome all kinds of tangible and intangible difficulties in order to accomplish the matter at hand. He consulted me frequently during the critical days preceding the statement and has shown an admirable spirit of understanding and co-operation." After the statement had been published, however, Epstein "found it necessary to express frankly to our friend disappointment over some parts of it."

On October 14, 1946, Senator George again wrote to Truman, expressing concern that the United States was becoming too much involved in the Palestine issue. He said, "I fear it would be a serious error for the United States to assume the responsibility of England in Palestine."

Truman replied:

Of course, I have no intention of attempting to assume the British responsibility in Palestine—my only interest is to find some proper way to take care of these displaced persons, not only because they should be taken care of and are in a pitiful plight, but because it is to our own financial interest to have them taken care of because we are feeding most of them.[58]

The intensifying controversy made Byrnes so uneasy that he summoned William A. Eddy, United States Minister to Saudi Arabia, and three other American diplomats in the Middle East home to tell Truman directly of the decline in United States influence among the Arabs. For months Arab leaders had been writing Truman citing what seemed to them their own moral and legal case involving such matters as possession of land in the region. "The natural rights of the Arabs therein go back thousands of years," Ibn Saud had said. After Truman had listened to the testimony of the four American diplomats, however, he replied, as Eddy recalled his words: "I'm sorry, gentlemen, but I have to answer to hundreds of thousands who are anxious for the success of Zionism; I do not have hundreds of thousands of Arabs among my constituents."[59]

The turn of the year brought no relief. By all signs "1947 is going to be a bad year in Palestine and the Middle East, with increasing violence and grave danger to our interests in that area," Dean Acheson wrote in a "secret" memorandum that February to Loy Henderson in the Office of Near Eastern and African Affairs.[60] Writing to a friend ten days later, Truman said, "I wish we could find a solution—we have been trying to find one ever since July 1945 but we seem no nearer to the solution now than then. I regret it very much." [61]

Since 1947 began, Jewish armed resistance to British authorities had led to increased terroristic bombing, machine gun attacks, and use of homemade flame-throwers. On March 2 after numerous British fatalities martial law was declared in Tel Aviv and part of Jerusalem. As time passed, strife only intensified. The most dramatic incident was the British boarding of the Jewish refugee ship *Exodus 1947*, a tragic spectacle in which three Jews were killed, a hundred wounded, and most of the rest dragooned back to Germany.

In the latter part of 1946 British Foreign Minister Bevin had explored avenues to a settlement with Zionist leaders without reaching a solution. The British then called both sides in Palestine to a conference in London in January, although the

Jews and Arabs refused to meet directly. Meanwhile on January 24, 1947, in reply to a letter from Ibn Saud, Truman wrote the king to give assurances that the United States neither wished to prejudice Arab rights nor would endorse a solution that would permit a majority to discriminate against a minority in a partitioned Palestine. Truman said:

I am convinced . . . that the responsible Jewish groups and leaders interested in developing the Jewish National Home in Palestine have no intention of expelling now or at a later date the indigenous inhabitants of that country or of using Palestine as a base for aggression against neighboring Arab States.[62]

In a message sent to Secretary Marshall February 9, however, Bevin said that partition could be imposed only by bayonets. He was determined, he added, "that the British Troops who fought for freedom in the late war shall not now be used to impose a policy by force in Palestine." [63]

The climax of the London conference was Bevin's proposal of a modified version of the Morrison-Grady Plan. Jews and Arabs rejected it. On February 18, 1947, Bevin announced in Parliament that the whole problem would be referred to the United Nations. The next day, speaking at a Labor Party caucus, he blamed the failure of the London conference on the pressure American Jews had put on Truman. And on February 25 he aired his frustration with a vengeance by going before a cheering House of Commons and accusing Truman of having brought about the impasse by playing politics with the Palestine issue at home.[64]

Pounding a table, the British foreign minister, who reminded Truman, unfavorably, of John L. Lewis, said Britain might have arranged for increased Jewish immigration in 1945 if the Americans had not insisted on immediate admittance of one hundred thousand. He then related the story of how he had tried to get Byrnes to head off Truman's Yom Kippur statement only to be rebuffed on the grounds that if Truman did not speak out, Dewey would.

"I really must point out," Bevin told Commons, "that in international affairs I cannot settle things if my problem is made the subject of local elections. I hope I am not saying anything to cause bad feeling in the United States, but I feel so intense about this. . . .

"The statement was issued, however, and the whole thing was spoiled."

"This was wishful thinking," wrote Herbert Feis in accord with the views of other historians that Bevin never had been as close as he suggested to an agreement with the Jews.[65] Bevin also misjudged Truman in hoping that his words would not cause bad feelings across the Atlantic. By his own subsequent testimony Truman was outraged and regarded Bevin's speech a personal, undiplomatic, and "almost hostile" affront to himself.[66]

The General Assembly, the U.N. body to which the British chose to refer the Palestine question, was not scheduled to meet again in regular session until September. To avert dangerous delay it was decided, therefore, that the Assembly would be called into its first special session in New York April 28, 1947. The main business of the session was to create a United Nations special committee to study the Palestine question and make recommendations to the General Assembly in September.

The most surprising development was the position of the Soviet Union. Before the Second World War the Soviets had been anti-Zionist and pro-Arab. After the war Soviet policy had been to oppose partition and favor a unified, binational Arab-Jewish state in Palestine, the existence of which, supposedly, would be cause for British departure from the area. Probably with this same aim of diminishing Western influence and advancing their own interests in the Eastern Mediterranean, the Soviets changed course in the General Assembly. On May 14, after reiterating his preference for a binational state, Andrei Gromyko said that if such a solution proved unrealizable, it would be necessary to consider partition.[67] This was a crucial development for the Zionist cause. Surprisingly, in light of subsequent Soviet support of the Arabs against Israel, it had the effect, too, of making the Soviet Union seem a rival of the United States for the friendship of the Palestine Jews, a matter that weighed upon Truman as events unfolded.

On May 13 Truman had written to Niles: ''I surely wish God Almighty would give the Children of Israel an Isaiah, the Christians a St. Paul and the Sons of Ishmael a peep at the Golden Rule. Maybe he will decide to do that.'' [68]

Setting the stage for decision at the regular session of the General Assembly, starting in mid-September 1947, the United Nations Special Committee on Palestine issued its report at the end of August. It recommended unanimously that the British mandate be terminated and that a form of independence be granted to Palestine under United Nations auspices.

A majority of UNSCOP proposed that Palestine be partitioned into a Jewish state and an Arab state within an economic union. Jerusalem would be held under a United Nations trusteeship.

The Jews, of course, supported partition. The Arabs opposed it. Partition was espoused by the White House, which was bombarded with mail and appeals from members of Congress on its behalf. In the State Department it was resolutely opposed by Loy Henderson and the Office of Near Eastern and African Affairs.

Bane of the Zionists, Henderson was then a medium-built, conservatively attired, fifty-five-year-old lawyer and Foreign Service officer, who was a native of Arkansas but who had acquired an air slightly resembling that of a Boston Brahmin. He had seen a great deal of service in Eastern Europe, the Soviet Union and the Middle East. A man of strong convictions, he had a reputation of being pro-Arab and anti-Soviet. He viewed partition as a medium for Soviet penetration of the Middle East, as a barrier to continued American friendship with the oil-rich Arabs, as a violation of the principle of self-determination in Palestine, as an unworkable policy that would destabilize the Eastern Mediterranean region, and as one that could be implemented only by force.

At a meeting of the United States delegation to the General Assembly September 15, Marshall was reluctant to take a definitive stand on partition at the opening session lest it drive the Arabs into the arms of the Soviets. He had in mind the maneuvering in the General Assembly.[69] But the record makes it clear that Marshall, who had no long experience in the diplomacy of the Middle East, was attentive to the opinions of Henderson and other State Department professionals, who feared a permanent alignment between the Soviets and the Arabs. Marshall was especially concerned that United States troops would have to be used to enforce partition. In line with the president's wishes, however, the secretary of state told the General Assembly September 17 that the United States gave great weight to the majority proposal for partition.

Arab leaders met with Ambassador George Wadsworth of the United States delegation in New York October 3 and said that six Arab states were considering bartering with the Soviet Union for support on the Palestine issue. Dr. Fadhil Jamali of Iraq said overtures had been received from the Soviets. He made the point that while the Arabs were reluctant to link themselves with the Soviet Union, the issue was so important to them that they were ready to make a deal on votes unless the United States helped to block creation of a Jewish state. He said the deal would not denote a permanent Arab orientation toward the Soviet Union.[70] The mere mention of such a possible development, of course, struck at American concerns about future influence of Moscow in the Middle East.

On October 9 a statement supporting partition was reviewed by Truman, who, while approving it, told Lovett that he wanted the United States delegation to understand two things clearly.

One involved financial aid to Palestine. The United States, Truman said, would contribute its share only under the auspices of the United Nations. No direct American economic assistance should be expected.

The other consideration was that the United States was not going to assume on its own the long-standing British responsibility for maintaining order in Palestine. Any contribution that the United States might make toward preserving order would be in keeping with its obligation to the United Nations and as part of a United Nations police force.[71]

During these weeks the domestic political aspects of the Palestine question kept intruding. Pro-Zionist mail deluged the White House. Truman was particularly angered by one letter he read accusing him of "preferring fascist and Arab elements to the democracy-loving Jewish people of Palestine." He turned it over to David Niles with a note saying, "It is such drivels [*sic*] as this that makes Anti-Semites. I thought maybe you had best answer it because I might tell him what's good for him."[72]

In a letter to Mrs. Roosevelt August 23, 1947, he warned that excesses by American Zionists would turn the country against their cause. He added:

I fear very much that the Jews are like all underdogs. When they get on top they are just as intolerant and as cruel as the people were to them when they were underneath. I regret this situation very much because my sympathy has always been on their side.[73]

At a cabinet luncheon September 4, 1947, the retiring Democratic national chairman, Postmaster General Hannegan, said that large Jewish campaign contributions would be influenced by Truman's policy on Palestine. Forrestal replied that Truman's Yom Kippur statement during the 1946 campaign had not prevented the Dewey landslide in New York. At another cabinet luncheon October 6, 1947, Hannegan reported that many Jews who had contributed heavily to Roosevelt's campaign in 1944 were pressing for assurances that the administration would support the Jewish position in Palestine. Truman replied that if the Jews would keep quiet, he thought everything would turn out satisfactorily. But if they tried to force the administration to go beyond the UNSCOP report, he warned, prospects of a settlement might be wrecked.[74]

During the summer Niles had cautioned Truman in a memorandum that two diplomats who were in line to be advisers to the United States delegation—Henderson and Wadsworth—were widely regarded as "unsympathetic to the Jewish viewpoint [and] much resentment will be engendered when their appointment is announced." Advising Truman that at least one of the several advisers should be an indvividual "in whom you, members of the United States Delegation and American Jewry have complete confidence," he recommended appointment of General John Hilldring, who was retiring as assistant secretary of state for occupied areas.[75] Hilldring's handling of the problem of displaced persons in Europe had commended him to the Zionists. Truman named him as an alternate delegate.

American support for partition was announced October 11, 1947, by Ambassador Herschel V. Johnson, United States deputy representative on the Security Council. The Zionists were elated. When, however, one of their sympathizers, Senator Pepper, wrote to Truman October 17, commending him on the decision, his letter found the President in an indignant mood. Truman replied:

I received about thirty-five thousand pieces of mail and propaganda from the Jews in this country while this matter was pending. I put it all in a pile and struck a match to it—I never looked at a single one of the letters because I felt the United Nations Committee was acting in a judicial capacity and should not be interfered with.[76]

Indignation sometimes led Truman into fantasizing actions he felt like taking but did not, and these remarks seem to have been such an occasion. Inquiry among several surviving members of the Truman staff who would have been in the best position to have known about a presidential bonfire of unwanted mail were negative. "I don't remember that incident at all," Truman's personal secretary, Rose Conway, said. Vaughan said: "I never saw anything burned in the eight years I was there. We had no place for doing anything like that." "No papers were burned," Steelman agreed.[77]

In announcing United States support for the UNSCOP majority report in favor of partition, Ambassador Johnson said that some territorial changes should be made in the recommendations in an attempt to make it workable.

Infuriating to the Arabs, the report had assigned most of the Negev, the desert comprising the lower half of the region, to the prospective Jewish state. A State Department position paper of September 30, 1947, however, had recommended that the Negev should be included in the Arab state since the area was "useful only for seasonal grazing purposes." The paper said that the area was inhabited by some sixty thousand Arabs and contained no Jewish settlements.[78] The United States delegation met in New York October 23 and decided to recommend a change in the majority report to transfer virtually all of the Negev to the prospective Arab state.[79] This decision, as it happened, snared Truman in a preposterous mix-up, from which he nevertheless emerged with a great deal of credit from the Zionists.

The Jewish Agency refused to surrender its claim to the Negev, but the United States delegation reaffirmed its stand. And in a message to the delegation November 12 Marshall strongly concurred. In fairness, he said, the Negev was historically

Arab. Being barren, the area had little chance of large-scale development. Furthermore, he concluded, any chance of developing a part of Palestine on the Red Sea as a port was open to question.[80]

The General Assembly had created subcommittees to deal with different aspects of the Palestine question, and the Negev issue was due to come up in Subcommittee No. 1 on the afternoon of November 19. Unbeknown to the delegation, Chaim Weizmann decided to carry the fight against the American position to higher ground. Through Niles and the new British ambassador in Washington, Lord Inverchapel, Weizmann, a British national, arranged a secret meeting with Truman at noon on the same November 19.

The president gave him a friendly reception. Weizmann was a chemist and lost no time spreading before Truman a vision of what the Jews would do to make the desert bloom with desalted brackish water. In his eloquence he said almost exactly the opposite of what Marshall had told the delegation. As maps were laid on the president's desk, Weizmann recounted the successful experiments the Jews already had conducted on desalination in Palestine and told how they were producing carrots, bananas, and potatoes in places where not a blade of grass had grown for thousands of years. Truman, the erstwhile farmer, had an imagination that responded to such a vision. Unless the Jews had access to the waters of the Gulf of Aqaba, however, Weizmann said, the desert would remain a desert. Furthermore, he continued, if the gulf were dredged, it could accommodate sizable ships and thus provide the Jewish state with an outlet to the seas, particularly vital if Egypt were to become hostile and close the Suez Canal to Jewish shipping. The Gulf of Aqaba is an arm of the Red Sea. Again Weizmann was contradicting Marshall, whose message to the delegation Truman would not have seen.

So the meeting between the president of the United States and the future first president of Israel went off famously. Weizmann was elated at Truman's attitude and even more so at his promise to get in touch with the delegation at once.[81]

At 1 P.M., about the time Weizmann was happily leaving the White House, however, Acting Secretary of State Lovett sent a message from the State Department to the delegation with final instructions not to yield to demands of the Jewish Agency but to vote for transfer of the lower Negev to the Arabs.[82]

At 3 P.M., just as Herschel Johnson was to enter the meeting of Subcommittee No. 1, the president called the delegation, and all plans fell apart. In those days, before the permanent United Nations headquarters had been built in Manhattan, its committees met in the remodeled plant of the Sperry Gyroscope Company at Lake Success on Long Island. The place was cluttered and disorganized, a perfect setting for what followed.

How were things going? Truman asked General Hilldring.

Hilldring replied by telling him of Lovett's instructions and saying that he was not too happy about them.

Truman said he agreed with Weizmann's views. Without issuing direct instructions, he made it plain to Hilldring, or so the general thought, that he wished Johnson to go along with the majority report giving the Negev to the Jews. Nothing should be done to "upset the apple cart," Truman admonished.

Caught between the president's wishes, favoring the Jews, and the acting secretary of state's instructions favoring the Arabs—just as the subcommittee was about to meet—Hilldring and Johnson frantically decided that the United States would take no position at all on the Negev at the moment. Meanwhile telephones were ringing around the government. Hilldring put in an urgent call to Bohlen in Washington to tell him what had happened. From Lake Success Dean Rusk, director of the Office of Special Political Affairs, telephoned Robert M. McClintock, his assistant, at the State Department to say that there had not been enough of a discussion between Truman and Hilldring for the president to have got a clear idea of the nature of the issue.

Lovett got through to Truman on the telephone around six o'clock. Truman said he had not in the least sought to change Lovett's instructions. He merely had been concerned, he said, lest the United States stand out as a useless minority on the question.[83]

Nevertheless Lovett subsequently canceled his instructions and told Johnson and Hilldring to act independently but not to allow the United States to be placed in the position of lone dissenter on the Negev issue or to sacrifice any gains that may have been made with the Arabs, if this could be avoided.[84]

The upshot was that on November 22 Johnson withdrew his proposal to award the Negev to the Arabs. By way of compensation, however, he introduced a resolution, which carried, providing that Beersheba and a strip of land along the border with Egypt be assigned to the Arab state—a compromise previously suggested by the Jewish Agency. So, as probably would have happened anyway, Subcommittee No. 1 awarded the Negev to the Jews. In his autobiography published in 1949, Weizmann gave Truman the credit. Aware that Truman had called Lake Success, Weizmann wrote, "Obviously the President had been as good as his word, and a few short hours after I had seen him had given the necessary instructions to the American delegation."[85]

Tension, conflict, and political pressures ran high in New York, Washington and around the world at the approach of the final vote in the General Assembly.

"Without doubt," King Ibn Saud wrote Truman, "the results of this decision will lead to a deathblow to American interests in the Arab countries and will disillusion the Arab's confidence in the friendship, justice, and fairness of the United States."

He pleaded for last-minute American reconsideration to prevent bloodshed in the Middle East.

Noting that the United States had been heavily influenced by the majority vote in UNSCOP, Truman replied,

The United States decision was not based on any desire to be unfriendly to the Arabs, and should not be construed as an unfriendly act, any more than the decision taken in this respect by other members of the United Nations.[86]

Representative Bloom of New York, ranking minority member of the House Foreign Affairs Committee, said that he approached representatives of several countries, including the Philippines, Haiti, and Liberia, "and in most instances I was successful in obtaining their support and in one or two cases their abstention rather

than casting a negative vote.''[87]

During the closing debate Ambassador Carlos P. Romulo, delegate of the Philippine republic, indicated that his government would oppose partition. A United States "representative"—evidently Clark Clifford—thereupon told Joaquin M. Elizalde, the Philippine ambassador to Washington, that such a vote would impair United States-Philippines relations. Ten United States senators cabled President Manuel Roxas of the Philippines, putting pressure on him, he later complained, to reverse his decision on Palestine. In distress, because of the effect such an action would have on the Mohammedan population of the islands, he instructed Romulo—lest the Philippines' relations with the United States suffer—to vote for partition, which Romulo did.[88] Indeed, according to Loy Henderson, Romulo's vote also had been solicited by two justices of the United States Supreme Court, Felix Frankfurter and Frank Murphy.[89]

When Lovett learned of the pressure on Roxas and reported it to the President, Truman replied, "It seems to me that if our Delegation to the United Nations is to be interfered with by members of the United States Senate and by pressure groups in this country we will be helping the United Nations down the road to failure.'' Then Truman had something to tell Lovett:

I have a report from Haiti, in which it is stated that our Consul in Haiti* approached the President of that country and suggested to him that for his own good he should order the vote of his country changed, claiming that he had instructions from me to make such a statement to the President of Haiti. As you very well know, I refused to make any statements to any country on the subject of its vote in the United Nations.

It is perfectly apparent that pressure groups will succeed in putting the United Nations out of business if this sort of thing is continued and I am very anxious that it be stopped.[90]

Meeting with Lovett November 24, Truman gave instructions that the United States delegation was not to use threats or improper pressure to influence other delegations to vote for partition. Lovett immediately passed the order on.[91] Evidently, however, many transactions went on that Truman probably was unaware of. Niles was maneuvering behind the scenes in New York. According to Herbert Feis, he told Herschel Johnson to use every kind of persuasion and inducement to win votes for partition, which, if true, was an outright countermand of the president's instructions.[92] Niles also got some Greek-American businessmen to cable an appeal to the government in Athens to support partition (which it did not do).[93]

In curious contrast to Truman's instructions to Lovett against exerting pressure and to his letter to Lovett about American diplomatic intervention in Haiti were some notes later found among Truman's papers. Undated and unsigned, although apparently in Charles Ross's handwriting, the notes were attached to a memorandum November 20, 1947, referring to the cabinet meeting November 11, eighteen days before the final vote in the General Assembly. They said:

Palestine votes look a little better.

1. We have been in touch with *Liberian* minister to try to get the Government's instructions changed to support us.

* Robert H. McBride, a London-born, Princeton-educated Foreign Service officer.

2. I think we have *Haiti.*

3. We may get *Philippines* out of *No* into abstention or, with luck, yes.

4. *Cuba* still won't play.

5. *Greece* is uncertain but has the excuse of the Balkan Commission vote trade with Moslems.[94]

This is not the language of aloofness.

On November 27 Celler telegraphed Truman that he had been spending considerable time at Lake Success and feared that partition might fail by one or two votes. He asked that the United States delegation be allowed to put pressure on recalcitrants like Haiti, China, Ecuador, Liberia, Honduras, Paraguay, and especially Greece, "which is immeasurably indebted to us" (because of the Truman Doctrine). In fact, Celler said, it might be necessary to have Lovett put pressure on Greece.[95]

Fearful of a Jewish boycott of his firm's products, Harvey S. Firestone, Jr., of the Firestone Tire & Rubber Company, which had a concession in Liberia, brought pressure on the president of that country, William Tubman. Liberia voted for partition.[96] Intrigue was rife.

Former Ambassador William Bullitt, was a leading advocate of American aid to China. According to an official memorandum by George Kennan, Baruch admonished Bullitt to tell his Chinese friends that unless China voted for partition the Chinese would not get a penny of American assistance. Bullitt passed this warning on to Dr. V. K. Wellington Koo, the Chinese ambassador in Washington. China, however, decided to abstain from voting. Koo explained to Bullitt that the large Moslem element among the Chinese necessitated such a course.[97]

On November 25 Matt Connelly had informed Truman in a memorandum that Lovett had called to say "that our case is being seriously impeded by high pressure being exerted by Jewish agencies. There have been indications of bribes and threats by these groups." The memorandum added:

In the case of Liberia, certain groups have informed the Liberian delegation that if they do not go along, the Stettinius pact with Liberia will be cancelled.* In the case of Nicaragua, the delegate was told by some of these groups that if he went along these groups would see to it that they were recognized by the United States.[98]

Two days later, curiously, Weizmann wrote to Truman from the Plaza Hotel in New York to say that he had been disturbed by "unwarranted rumors" going around "which do us injustice and possible damage." He denied that his representatives had "gone beyond the limits of legitimate and moderate persuasion."[99]

On Thanksgiving Weizmann's right-hand man, Dr. Nahum Goldmann, called on Adolf A. Berle, former assistant secretary of state, and solicited his help in bringing Haiti around. Berle cabled President Dumarais Estimé, and was assured by return cable that the desired instructions were on the way to the Haitian delegation.[100]

Connelly's mention to Truman of bribes was echoed in a memorandum from

---

* Evidently a reference to the former secretary of state's venture in 1947, organizing a company linking the Liberian government with American capital to develop Liberian natural resources, with part of the stock going to the Liberian Educational Foundation. Harvey Firestone gave Liberia $250,000 for an institute for tropical medicine.

Llewellyn E. Thompson, Jr., chief of the Division of Eastern European Affairs in the State Department, to Loy Henderson. Reporting on a conversation with Guillermo Belt, the Cuban ambassador, Thompson said:

Mr. Belt . . . stated that one Latin American delegate had changed his vote to support partition in return for $75,000 in cash and that another Latin American delegate, I believe the Costa Rican, had refused a forty thousand dollar offer but that subsequently had been ordered by his Government to support partition. It was Mr. Belt's belief that some member of the delegate's government had accepted the bribe.[101]

Meanwhile the Arabs were not idle. Greece in the end voted against partition in a secret deal with the Moslem states. In return for the Greek vote the Moslems agreed to support Greece in all future matters of interest to Athens arising before any United Nations organ.[102]

Nevertheless on November 29 the General Assembly, by slightly more than the required two-thirds majority, voted to recommend partition, 33 to 13, with 10 abstentions. The extent to which skulduggery offstage had affected the outcome was unclear. Obviously, Jewish tactics, whatever they were in total, did not jeopardize the outcome as much as some had feared. Without doubt the vote was due in large part to the rare circumstance of the Americans' and Soviets' siding together on an important question, which already had commanded majority support in UNSCOP, and to the revulsion throughout the world against Hitler's genocide. Arab talk about a deal with the Soviets had fizzled.

Overnight violence erupted in the Middle East as the Arab populations rejected the idea of partition. In time the British announced they would turn Palestine over to the United Nations at 6 P.M., May 14, 1948 (Washington time). As the weeks passed, conflict between the Jews and the Arabs spread. With the Arabs unwilling to accept the United Nations recommendation, who was going to stop the conflict and bring about partition in an orderly fashion? Partition did not automatically and peacefully occur because of a vote in the General Assembly. Legally, the General Assembly resolution was a recommendation to the members and did not have the force of legislation.[103] In the growing chaos it soon became an urgent question whether partition could be consummated without the use of force by outside powers. The British announced in effect, however, that they would not take responsibility for carrying out the plan.

At a cabinet luncheon December 1 Forrestal said that the situation was fraught with danger for the United States. Truman replied that there was a limitation on the American role, that he had repeatedly said that United States armed forces would not be used to enforce peace in Palestine. Forrestal did not see how this could be avoided if the United Nations were to ask the United States to contribute its share of an international force—a possibility that Truman had acknowledged in his instructions to Lovett October 9.[104] But as one of the Big Five on the Security Council, the Soviet Union might also be asked to send troops to the Middle East. American policymakers, however, regarded direct Soviet participation in administration, policing, or military operations in Palestine as tantamount to a Soviet lodgment in the Middle East and, therefore, a threat to the security of the United States. The worst of the Palestine problem was still ahead of Truman.

35. *The Historic Civil Rights Report*

AS IMMENSE AS THE developments in foreign relations were, none of them in the fall of 1947 held such deep implications for the future of American society as the occasion, on October 29, when the President's Commission on Civil Rights handed Truman the report on which it had worked for nine months. The report was a point of departure for the modern era of race relations in the United States—a political bombshell that catapulted the civil rights question to the forefront as never before in the twentieth century, led to a split in the Democratic Party in 1948, and "served for a generation as the basic statement of most of the goals of civil-rights advocates."[1]

Where President Truman was concerned, the Palestine issue and the civil rights question were similar in a sense. In both cases Truman had, if not a consuming conviction, an attitude of decency and fairness that accorded with the courses offering the greatest political advantages—in the first instance, support of the Jewish cause, despite personal annoyance over political pressure; and, in the second instance, advocacy of equal treatment for blacks. What was humane, in other words, was also good politics, although risky politics in some ways.

In the case of Palestine, Truman sympathized with the victims of Hitler and believed that the Balfour Declaration had promised the Jews a homeland. His resentments sprang from the determination of the Jews to achieve their goal at a faster pace and under conditions that American policymakers thought incompatible with United States security. But for Truman to favor an eventual homeland, as he did, and to move, however haltingly, in that direction also meant to stake a claim to vitally important Jewish votes in the large states.

Likewise, on the civil rights issue, Truman—while not favoring integration as it was visualized a generation later—believed that blacks were being discriminated against and were entitled to education, welfare, jobs, and ballots. He believed also that continued injustices to them would invite trouble. Increasingly he accepted the need for more federal action. And to advocate correction of abuses was to insure black votes in the large cities of the North and West.

Such were the possible pitfalls in both issues, however, that Truman went backward and forward and moved ahead finally only under strong political pressures. The risk in Palestine, apart from loss of Arab friendship, lay in possible developments that would bring about Soviet intervention in the Middle East or the embroilment of American troops there, or both. The risk in civil rights was that a strong program recommended by Truman would cost him the support of the southern states in 1948. No Democrat since the Reconstruction had ever been elected president without the support of the Solid South.

Truman had appointed the distinguished civil rights committee in December 1946, in the face of appalling violence in the South earlier that year and after the Democratic defeat in the 1946 elections, in which signs appeared that blacks might be drifting back to the Republican party after years of supporting the New Deal. He had launched the committee on its task at a White House ceremony January 15, 1947, saying that progress on race relations had not come fast enough. He warned:

This country could very easily be faced with a situation similar to the one with which it was faced in 1922. That date was impressed on my mind because in 1922 I was running for my first elective office—county judge of Jackson County—and there was an organization in that county that met on hills and burned crosses and worked behind sheets. There is a tendency in this country for that situation to develop again unless we do something tangible to prevent it.

He said that he did not think the federal government should be allowed to exercise unlimited powers in the states but that he wanted to know exactly how far the attorney general could go in upholding constitutional rights, "which I think the Federal government has a right to protect."

"It's a big job," he told the committee. "Go to it!"[2]

For Truman the first part of 1947 was a time of mixed effects on minorities. In his economic message to Congress he again called for a permanent FEPC, but he did little afterward to urge Congress to pass this or other civil rights measures. On January 22 the three Trumans went to the National Theater for a revival of Sigmund Romberg's *Blossom Time*. The Congress of Racial Equality had posted a picket line in front of the entrance to protest the exclusion of blacks from the theater. The president and his family crossed the line, perhaps unaware of it because of the crowd. Members of CORE were enraged. "First time I heard of it," Truman said when asked about the criticism at his press conference January 23. "I didn't know it was being picketed. . . . I wanted to see that [musical] for twenty years, so I went down there and saw it."[3]

On the other hand he accepted an invitation to join Mrs. Roosevelt and Senator Wayne Morse of Oregon as a speaker at the closing session of the thirty-eighth annual convention of the NAACP at the Lincoln Memorial June 29, 1947. Although Niles had suggested that only the final paragraph of the speech be devoted to civil rights, Truman had other ideas.[4] It was a time when he was riding a wave of popularity with liberals over the Taft-Hartley veto. He was eager to mend the frayed Democratic coalition. He asked Walter White of the NAACP to suggest points he ought to cover. Two members of the staff of the Committee on Civil Rights, Milton Stewart and Robert K. Carr of Dartmouth College, helped write the speech.[5] It was an unusual statement for a president to make at that time. Speaking before ten thousand persons and to a world-wide radio audience, Truman, first president ever to address the NAACP, said:[6]

We cannot be content with a civil liberties program which emphasizes only the need of protection against the possibility of tyranny by the government. . . .

We must keep moving forward with new concepts of civil rights. . . . The extension of civil rights today means not protection of the people *against* the government, but protection of the people *by* the government.

We must make the Federal government a friendly, vigilant defender of the rights and equalities of all Americans. And again I mean all Americans.

As drafted, the speech said that "each man must have equality of opportunity." With a pencil Truman changed this to read that each man must "be guaranteed" equality of opportunity.[7]

He then alluded to another consideration that was bringing pressure on him when he said that "the support of desperate populations of battle-ravaged countries must be won for the free way of life. We must have them as allies in our continuing struggle for the peaceful solution of the world's problems." With the United Nations as an especially convenient forum, the Soviets were drumming into the consciousness of the underdeveloped countries the plight of blacks in the United States, so that, as Truman indicated, the civil rights issue was suddenly a significant factor in the cold war.

"For these compelling reasons," he said, "we can no longer afford the luxury of a leisurely attack upon prejudice and discrimination."

"I said what I did," Truman told White after the speech, "because I mean every word of it—and I am going to prove that I do mean it."[8]

Thirty years later it is difficult to evoke the state of race relations in America as it existed on the day the Committee on Civil Rights gave Truman its report. With the Detroit race riots of 1943 only four years behind, it was an age of Jim Crow, white supremacy, states' rights, "we don't serve colored here," "separate but equal" but unequal, "Nigras," "niggers," "boy," "white only," a revived Ku Klux Klan, indifference, patronization, police brutality, Gerald L. K. Smith, malign neglect. Thus the sweep of recommendations in the book-length report to the president, titled *To Secure These Rights,* was startling.

The committee proposed strengthening the legal machinery for protecting civil rights in a number of ways. It recommended that the Civil Rights Section of the Department of Justice be made a full division of the department (this has been done) and be enlarged to include regional offices to facilitate investigation of civil right violations, even where no complaints were filed. The committee recommended establishment of a permanent Commission on Civil Rights in the Executive Office of the President and corresponding and cooperating commissions in the states. (The United States Commission on Civil Rights was created as an independent agency by the Civil Rights Act of 1957.) A number of changes in the law were proposed to strengthen the safety of persons. Among the proposals were a statute to curb police brutality and an antilynching law. (Lynching declined, and no Federal antilynching legislation was ever enacted. Nor was anyone ever able to draft a feasible federal law to deal with police brutality.)

To strengthen the rights and privileges of citizenship the committee proposed, among other things, an end to poll taxes. (The Nineteenth Amendment to the Constitution, barring a poll tax in Federal elections, was proposed by Congress in 1962; ratification was completed January 23, 1964.) Recommended also was a statute to protect the right of qualified persons to participate in federal primaries and elections against interference by public officials and private persons. (The Civil Rights Act of 1964 outlawed unequal application of voting registration requirements, as between whites and blacks; prohibited denial of the right to vote because of immaterial errors or omissions by applicants; made a sixth-grade education, if in English, a rebuttable presumption of literacy; and gave the attorney general authority to enter into agreements with state or local authorities that their literacy tests are fairly administered and need not be given in writing.) The committee recommended a constitutional amendment giving residents of the District of Columbia the right to vote in presidential elections. (The Twenty-third Amendment, conveying this right, was approved by Congress in 1960; ratification was completed March 29, 1961.) Recommended also was home rule for the District, with its predominantly black population. (Home rule was won in 1974.)

To enhance the right of equality of opportunity the committee recommended, generally, the elimination of segregation. It recommended also that as a condition for federal grants-in-aid and other federal assistance to public and private agencies Congress must require the absence of discrimination and segregation. (On a wide scale these conditions were written into the Civil Rights Act of 1964.) Along the same line the committee recommended enactment of a fair employment practices bill, prohibiting discrimination in private employment. (Fair employment practices were embodied in the Civil Rights Act of 1964.) The committee also recommended state laws forbidding discrimination in health services. (The 1964 act authorized the Department of Justice to bring suits to secure desegregation of state or locally owned public health facilities.) The committee recommended state laws defining fair educational practice laws for public and private schools and colleges, prohibiting discrimination in the admission and treatment of students. (The 1964 act authorized the attorney general to file suit for the desegregation of public schools and colleges if such an action would materially further desegregation.)

In regard to housing the committee recommended renewed attack through the courts on racially restrictive covenants. (According to Tom Clark, Truman suggested to him that this recommendation be carried out.[9] On December 5, 1947, the Department of Justice set an important precedent by intervening in the Supreme Court in *Shelley* v. *Kraemer,* arguing that housing covenants, restricting the sale of properties to whites, perpetuated "an artificial quarantine of minority groups," and should, therefore, be nullified. On May 8, 1948, the court held that restrictive housing covenants were unenforceable.)

The foregoing recommendations and others in the report were not all original, but taken together they constituted the body of civil rights issues that were to be fought over in the next two decades. Many of the proposed reforms, as has been noted, were years in coming to pass and then only as a result of a complex interplay of events that could not have been foreseen in 1947. But Truman was president at a time when the first streaks of a new day in American democracy were glimmering.

When the commission handed him the report, it initiated a new phase of an historic struggle, and this was quickly perceived by the contending political forces.

Black spokesmen and the black press were jubilant. Civil rights leaders recognized that their cause had been given new impetus. The effect on the South, on the other hand, was radical. "I really believe that you have ruined the Democratic party in the South," John B. McDaniel, chairman of the Democratic Committee of Danville, Virginia, telegraphed Truman October 31. The Reverend A. C. Shuler sent a telegram from Florida, saying: "If that report is carried out you won't be elected dogcatcher in 1948. The South today is the South of 1861 regarding things that your committee had under consideration." Charles H. Doggett of North Carolina wrote: "Your recent stand and utterances on the Negro question will no doubt cause many thousands of Negroes to vote for you, but this stand of yours will cost you hundreds of thousands of white votes."[10]

Truman's long decline in standing in the South as a result of his support of New Deal programs and his veto of the Case and the Taft-Hartley bills had been serious but never serious enough to activate periodic threats by some southern factions to bolt the Democratic party. The South clung to its traditional ties to the party and enjoyed powerful leverage in Congress as a result of them. Southerners had still hoped to use their influence to modify liberal tendencies within the party. Now the civil rights report raised, as never before, a threat to the southern way of life. The idea of a Truman candidacy in 1948, backed by a platform upholding the spirit of *To Secure These Rights,* was more than many southerners could tolerate. Suddenly talk of a bolt was no longer merely rhetorical.

Truman thus was caught in new tension. On the right, leading contenders for the Republican nomination—Dewey, Taft, former Governor Harold E. Stassen of Minnesota, and Governor Earl Warren of California—declined to respond to telegrams from the *Norfolk Journal and Guide,* soliciting their comments on the civil rights report.[11] On the left, Henry Wallace, back from a European trip that had turned into a case of international barnstorming against Truman's foreign policy, was making speeches around the country as if in preparation for running on a third-party ticket. His appeal to black sentiment was evident in his refusal to appear before segregated audiences in the South.[12] Truman, therefore, moved cautiously at first in discussing his own intentions about the recommendations contained in the report. Asked at his press conference November 6, 1947, whether he was going to submit the report to Congress, he replied that it could be used as a basis for part of his 1948 State of the Union message.

> *Q.:* In other words you will use it as a part of your message?
> *A.:* I didn't say that. I said it could be used as a foundation for part of the message— some of it maybe. I haven't read it carefully yet.[13]

Truman wanted the support of white southerners. He wanted the black vote. The dilemma of reconciling these objectives was discussed in the White House for weeks. Meanwhile the likelihood grew that Wallace would run as an independent and would lure black voters. Despite the clamor in the South, Truman on December 9 instructed Clark Clifford to confer with Attorney General Clark on recommendations for a civil rights program to be submitted to Congress early in 1948.[14] Whether anyone in the administration fully realized it at the time, events were taking shape that would bring about a realignment of American politics caused by the shattering end of the Solid South.

36. *Wallace Declares*

THE SCHISM OVER civil rights was only one of many events, including the emergence of Wallace as a threat to the Democratic party, that made 1947 and 1948 landmarks in American political history.

Although no record of it exists, a most extraordinary transaction also seems to have occurred between Truman and Eisenhower—a sequel to Truman's offer to Eisenhower in Germany in 1945 to support him for the Democratic presidential nomination in 1948. Such close friends of Truman's as John Snyder do not discourage the speculation that Truman in 1947 again offered to step aside for Eisenhower.[1] Rosenman said Truman had confided to him that "in 1947 or 1948" he had offered to support Eisenhower.[2] Steelman said, "My memory is that he told Ike he would back him. I am sure he told him so. President Truman did not want to run in 1948."[3]

Eisenhower's true confidant was his brother, Dr. Milton S. Eisenhower, then president of Kansas State College and later president of Johns Hopkins University. According to Dr. Eisenhower, General Eisenhower understood on the basis of whatever communication he may have had with Truman on the subject in 1947 that the president was willing to support him for the Democratic nomination the next year.[4]

Not having sought the presidency in the first place, Truman evidently was not consumed in 1947 with a desire to run again.

Contemporary observation sustains later recollections. Recording in his diary of November 12, 1947, a conversation with Truman, Forrestal noted: "He said as far as he himself was concerned he would be delighted not to run again if it were not for a sense of duty which compelled him to do so. He said there was little satisfaction outside the reward of service in the presidency—that his 'baby,' as he called her, Margaret, was limited—had her entire life conditioned by the fact of being the daughter of the President. . . . There is no question in my judgement as to the complete sincerity of the President that the only thing that holds him to this grinding job is a sense of obligation to the country and, secondarily, to his party."[5]

In 1948 it was a different matter. Stung by the contempt and criticism of Republicans, pro-Eisenhower Democrats, southerners, and much of the press, Truman was angry and wanted to run and win to spite his enemies. As far as an Eisenhower candidacy at that time was concerned the general was not yet ready to enter politics and told Truman so.[6] If he had accepted Truman's offer, the Democratic party might have remained in power at least until 1957, with incalculable effects upon politics for a generation. Instead Eisenhower decided to accept the presidency of Columbia University. By that time, Forrestal had indicated in his diary of November 12, Truman was impatient to replace Eisenhower as army chief of staff with General Omar Bradley, who had been serving as head of the Veterans Administration.

The final weeks of 1947 were filled with political developments. Because of the unabating trouble in Europe, Truman called a special session of Congress to convene November 17. But instead of limiting his request to interim foreign aid, he put the Republican majority on the spot by proposing also an extensive antiinflation program. If the political implications were obvious, it was also a fact that throughout 1947 Truman, under the prodding of the Council of Economic Advisers, had been alarmed about rising prices. On April 7, 1947, the council had warned him that inflation posed a threat to prosperity and suggested efforts to restrict installment credit and to urge business executives to cut prices.[7] Truman sounded the theme of voluntary price reduction in press conferences that spring. The responsibility rested on business leaders, he told reporters April 10. "They want free enterprise," he said. "They have got it. Now let's see if they will make it work."[8]

In June he had got into a spat with Taft. The senator blamed the administration for keeping up prices at home by creating shortages resulting from shipment of goods abroad for foreign aid. To abandon foreign aid because it caused problems for the economy, Truman retorted in a statement he read at his press conference June 5, 1947, would have been comparable to abandoning the war aims because they entailed economic dislocation.

Taft's philosophy, Truman said, was that "high demand justified or necessitated high prices." His own philosophy he stated this way: "The higher and more stable the demand, the more opportunities there are to sell goods—and with assured high volume operations there is less and less justification for wide margins of profit per unit." Since high demand assured a general level of high profits, the prices of many individual items could be cut.[9] Truman's worry that high prices would cause hard times was plain.

He said in his June 5 statement that appeals for voluntary price cuts had already yielded substantial results. Yet when he went before the special session November 17 he declared that inflation was dangerous, and worsening. Not only were Americans being hurt, Truman said, but "inflation threatens our entire program of foreign aid."[10]

Truman had received divided counsel on remedies. Snyder and Harriman were against a strong program of controls. The Council of Economic Advisers, however, recommended that the "full armory of control measures" should be examined. The council suggested a broad program with the emphasis on fiscal and monetary policy and stand-by controls.[11] The economic advisers were heartily seconded by the political advisers. The latter sensed that the people wanted action against inflation and reasoned that one year before the election Truman would benefit even if—or particularly if—the Republicans, as was probable, refused to give him all he might request.

Chester Bowles, no longer in the administration but eyeing the Democratic nomination for governor of Connecticut, had caught the spirit in a letter to Truman November 5. "If we can load the blame for all that has happened and all that is likely to happen squarely on their shoulders," he said, "I believe we will be richer by five or six million votes in 1948."[12]

The advice of the Council of Economic Advisers prevailed. Moreover the proposals Truman recommended to the joint session were to remain the basis of his wage-price policy for several years to come. The approach consisted of three kinds of measures. One was to relieve monetary pressures, such as excessive use of credit. The second was to channel scarce goods to the most essential uses. The third was authorization of direct controls on particular high prices.

"This is the end of economic freedom," Taft countered on radio.

Specifically, Truman's measures included restoration of consumer credit controls and restraint on lending by banks. Rationing would be authorized on products that affected the cost of living and that also were in short supply. Price ceilings would be allowed on such products, along with wage controls necessary to maintain the price ceilings. Allocation and inventory control of scarce commodities affecting the cost of living would be permitted. Rent control would be strenthened. The government would be given power to regulate speculative trading on commodity exchanges.

Truman also recommended: (1) extension of export controls, (2) authority to allocate transportation facilities, and (3) authorization for the Department of Agriculture to expand its domestic conservation program and to advance measures for increasing food production abroad. What was notable about these last three minor proposals was that they were the only parts of the antiinflation program that Congress was to pass.

During the hearings Snyder got into a dispute with Marriner Eccles, head of the Federal Reserve, opposing an antiinflation plan Eccles had devised—with unfortunate consequences for Eccles, as it turned out. The Eccles plan would have required member banks to maintain a special reserve as a way of restraining credit. The administration sided with Snyder.[13] While quarreling went on in Congress, the president struck a pose as an inflation fighter with a program he said would keep prices in line, even though he knew it never would be passed in its entirety.

When Congress finally passed only minor sections of his antiinflation program, Truman signed the joint resolution with a show of reluctance. In an accompanying statement on the eve of the election year he voiced "deep disappointment that the Congress has seen fit to take such feeble steps toward control of inflation."[14]

As was typical during the Truman administration, Congress, while rejecting the president's domestic legislation in a conservative dudgeon, went grumblingly along with the essentials of his program for European assistance out of fear of Soviet dominance.

Truman requested interim aid of $597 million for Austria, France, and Italy as a "vital prelude" to the Marshall Plan. In contrast to its handling of the antiinflation program—and, incidentally, the Truman Doctrine, in which case the president had suddenly called in Congressional leaders and informed them what he was going to do—the administration had laid the groundwork well for interim aid and the Marshall Plan.

As usual in such matters, Senator Vandenberg was a catalyst. After Marshall's speech at Harvard in June the chairman of the Foreign Relations Committee suggested that Truman appoint a bipartisan council to study the feasibility and desirability of the proposed plan. He let the White House know that he would not cooperate until this had been done.[15] Accordingly, Truman named a Committee on Foreign Aid, headed by Harriman and containing an array of important figures from both parties in banking, labor, education, and business. Furthermore, Truman directed the Council of Economic Advisers to assess whether the economy could bear the burden of heavy foreign aid. He also created a committee under Secretary of the Interior Krug to make a similar study with respect to natural resources.

In the fall these groups issued impressive and reassuring reports. Thus the Council of Economic Advisers reported that if the country acted to curb wastefulness and inflation, it could support a $22.3 billion foreign aid program over the next four years. This total was almost identical to the sum that had recently been recommended by the sixteen-nation Committee of European Economic Cooperation in its summer-long study following Molotov's walkout at Paris.

The prestigious Harriman committee reported that the United States had a "vital interest—humanitarian, economic, strategic, and political—in helping" Europe in the face of "open ideological war" by the Soviet Union. It recommended appropriation of between $12.7 billion to $17.2 billion for Europe in the ensuing four years.

Congress made only one conspicuous change in the interim aid program. As a step in the developing Republican effort to give greater help to Chiang Kai-shek, it appropriated $18 million in Chinese aid, which Truman had not requested. The appropriation voted for Europe was $522 million.[16]

With Soviet-American relations worsening, Marshall told the cabinet November 7, 1947, according to Forrestal, that the "objective of our policy from this point on would be the restoration of balance of power in both Europe and Asia."[17] The deterioration conditioned Congress to favor foreign aid, and the mood was strengthened that fall by sour news from the fifth meeting of the Council of Foreign Ministers in London.

Speaking in Chicago on the eve of his departure, Marshall had said that the ongoing difference between the United States and the Soviet Union over Germany sprang from a "direct clash between the national interests." As will be recalled, the deadlock over a German peace treaty reached by the foreign ministers in Moscow the preceding April had left Marshall pessimistic about a German settlement and led him to instruct Clay to hasten the economic development of Bizonia. Now the angry sessions in London turned the impasse to stone, made 1947 the point of no return in the Cold War, and provided impetus toward critical new steps by the United States and its Western European allies, which were to include introduction of a new West German currency, strengthening of West German political institutions, and ultimately creation of a West German state. With no further hope for East-West collaboration on the government of Germany, the London meeting adjourned without setting a date for reconvening. It was to be the last time the Council of Foreign Ministers met during Truman's first term. On his return to Washington Marshall said in a broadcast that until the political vacuum on the Continent left by the war had been filled through restoration of the European community, "it does not appear possible that paper agreements can assure a lasting peace."

In furtherance of the major effort by the United States to restore Europe, Truman sent Congress a special message on the Marshall Plan December 19. In a proposal unique in history in its magnitude, he recommended apropriation of $17 billion for European recovery in the period from April 1, 1948, to June 30, 1952. The total approximated the maximum figure in the Harriman committee report. The cooperative undertaking by the United States and a group of European nations, Truman said, "is proof that free men can effectively join together to defend their free institutions against totalitarian pressures and to promote better standards of life for all their peoples."[18]

On December 29 Henry Wallace met in Chicago with officials of the Progressive Citizens of America. This was the group whose components had sponsored the Madison Square Garden rally at which Wallace criticized Truman's foreign policy and whose formation in December, 1946, had provided a vehicle for remnants of the popular front to oppose Truman's firm stance against the Soviet Union. After the Chicago meeting Wallace was to make a national radio broadcast, the subject of which was no great secret.

In the fifteen months since Truman had fired him as secretary of commerce, Wallace had kept up a broadside of criticism of the administration as editor of the *New Republic* and as a public speaker. As when he had been in the government, his theme was better relations with the Soviets. He abominated the Truman Doctrine and attracted crowds in Europe and the United States as he assailed Truman for attempting a "global Monroe Doctrine" and for having abandoned Roosevelt's supposedly peaceful policies in favor of Churchill's warlike aims. As the months passed, he poured out what was tantamount to the whole left-wing litany of grievances against Truman, and became an obvious challenger for the presidency. His followers strove in several western states to line up delegates to the forthcoming Democratic National Convention and anticipated powerful backing in New York from the American Labor Party.

Meanwhile, however, Truman had been gaining ground with liberals because of such policies as the Marshall Plan and the veto of the Taft-Hartley bill. Even Senator Pepper, who had shared the platform at Madison Square with Wallace, had announced his support of Truman. Labor moved behind the president. The Amalgamated Clothing Workers of America, the largest single constituency of the American Labor Party, indicated its support, too. Liberals in and out of Congress, the latter including the Americans for Democratic Action, endorsed the Marshall Plan. Many of Wallace's old friends, Eleanor Roosevelt among them, signed the ADA statement.

At first Wallace had commended the Marshall Plan as an improvement on the Truman Doctrine. Then when Molotov walked out at Paris Wallace reconsidered. Finally he saw the Marshall Plan as a vehicle for divisiveness and political and economic domination.

Isolated, therefore, he had increasingly to look to the Left for support. Apprehension was strong among most liberals that entrance of a third party might throw the election to the Republicans. Early in December Senator J. Howard McGrath of

Rhode Island, who had recently succeeded Hannegan as Democratic national chairman, said that the Democrats welcomed Wallace's support. Wallace replied, however, that he could not back Truman unless Truman ceased advocating Universal Military Training. Some of his friends warned Wallace that the Communists would try to manipulate his movement, but with utter unrealism he talked about winning 12 million votes.[19] In fact Americans by the million were disgusted with Wallace for having gone abroad to denounce his country's foreign policy.

On December 16, 1947, the executive committee of the PCA endorsed the idea of a third party and urged Wallace to run. Despite warnings by his family and some old friends, Wallace allowed himself to be carried along by his temperament, emotions, and convictions toward his broadcast on the nineteenth. Surrounded by naive and in some cases self-seeking advisers, he was poorly informed about the realities of the conflicts in which the United States found itself. His conception of what the Communists were doing not only in Eastern Europe but in gaining power in the PCA itself was murky. He feared that Truman was leading the country toward war with the Soviet Union. His faith in the ideals for which the country fought the Second World War was still strong, and he was right in thinking that these ideals had been damaged by events of the past two years.[20] Quixotically, therefore, he went on radio and declared that he would run for president as an independent candidate.

The speech epitomized his months of oratory. He pledged "a positive peace program of abundance and security, not scarcity and war." He called the Democrats a party of "war and depression"; as for the Republicans, "there is no hope."

"There is no real fight," he insisted, "between a Truman and a Republican."

The time had come for "a new party to fight these war-makers." Of his own movement he said:

"We have assembled a Gideon's army—small in number, powerful in conviction, ready for action."[21]

Of the speech Truman privately observed, "it was certainly an education in misrepresentation and the garbling of facts." In a misjudgment, surely, of a man and his cause he told his staff that Wallace was motivated by anger, hatred, and revenge and had forgotten the helpful things Truman had done for him.[22]

Five weeks after Wallace spoke, on January 27, 1948, J. Edgar Hoover notified Truman through a letter to General Vaughan:

A reliable and confidential source advised that he received the following information from a member of the National Committee of the Communist Party, USA:

He stated that the National Secretariat of the Party held a special meeting the day after Henry Wallace announced that he would run for President. . . . According to him, the Secretariat decided to take immediate steps to organize national groups in the United States behind the Wallace movement. He advised that the National Groups Commission of the Communist Party was asked to contact the leaders of organizations with whom the Commission is in contact for the purpose of "starting the ball rolling." Every District Organizer of the Communist Party throughout the United States was reportedly informed of this decision and asked to contact national group organizers for the same purpose.[23]

As a matter of fact nothing could better have demonstrated the impotence of the Communist party and the American Left than the fate of the Wallace movement.

IV

1948

37. *A Stormy Beginning*

T HE CRITICAL YEAR BEGAN in gusts of controversy. Indeed one of the last nights of December had witnessed an episode that was to put many liberals in a bad mood, a state that was to prove chronic with them during the first half of 1948.

Tommy Corcoran, the old New Dealer, who was still under FBI "technical surveillance," and Stanley Gewirtz, executive assistant to the chairman of the Civil Aeronautics Board, were sitting alone together in the apartment of still another renowned New Dealer, James M. Landis, awaiting the expected good news of a meeting Landis had had with Truman. Former law clerk to Justice Brandeis, former dean of Harvard Law School, an important figure in the Roosevelt administration, a drafter of the Securities and Exchange Act of 1934, and later a member of the Securities and Exchange Commission under the chairmanship of Joseph P. Kennedy, Landis had been appointed by Truman as chairman of the Civil Aeronautics Board in 1946 for the term expiring at the end of 1947. As his term neared its close, Landis had been assured by Speaker Rayburn and Senator Barkley that he would be reappointed and was pleased, therefore, to be called to the White House late in December.

While Corcoran and Gewirtz were waiting on the night in question, Landis, who drank too much, entered, unsteadily. According to Gewirtz, he related the following story of his meeting with Truman:

Truman began by congratulating him on having done a "hell of a job" at the CAB. But, he added, he had bad news—he was not going to reappoint him. Had he displeased the president? Landis asked. No, Truman replied. But when he became president he was told by former Democratic National Chairman James A. Farley that there would be occasions on which he would have to be a son of a bitch. This was one of them.

"When a President of the United States calls himself a son of a bitch," concluded Landis, according to Gewirtz, "what else is there to do but pick up your hat and leave, and I picked up my hat and left."[1]

As chairman of the CAB Landis had insisted on strict regulation. By favoring more competition by nonscheduled airlines on main routes, he frightened the big airlines to which such routes had been assigned. He sought more innovation in the industry; and managed to offend not only the politically influential carriers, but officials in the State Department and in the Department of Commerce, where the CAB was lodged. In particular, Landis's views clashed with those of Juan Trippe, president of Pan American World Airways, a potent figure in those days. Trippe was a

passionate advocate of the idea that the United States should choose one airline—
Pan American—as the instrument for furthering its various interests abroad, giving
the airline a virtual monopoly on overseas routes. Landis was opposed.

When Truman dropped him, Landis spread the word, believed by many liberals, that he had been banished on demand of the airlines because of his efforts to
block their monopolies and to require better safety measures. One of his friends,
who was antagonistic to Truman, said that Landis had been dropped because Pan
American had threatened to withhold campaign contributions from the Democrats
otherwise.

None of these accusations was ever translated into formal charges, much less
proved. No doubt the airlines, especially Pan American, wanted Landis removed.
Truman never explained his decision. Afterward an explanation offered by his subordinates who had been close to the situation was that the war had left the airlines in
financial and operational disarray and that under Landis the CAB did not pull things
together satisfactorily.

For twelve years, Marriner Eccles, a New Deal stalwart, had held the prestigious post of chairman of the Board of Governors of the Federal Reserve System.
The first effective champion in the Roosevelt administration of deliberate deficit
spending and the use of government to bring about greater purchasing power
through public works, Eccles had helped draft the Banking Act of 1935.[2] Roosevelt
had appointed him to the Federal Reserve Board in 1934 and two years later named
him chairman for a term ending February 1, 1948.

Nine days before the expiration Eccles received a call from Dr. Steelman asking him to come to the White House. Because he was busy, Eccles asked if the next
day would do.

"All right," Steelman replied, "but don't make it any later than that."

After a few pleasantries in their meeting on January 23, Steelman came to the
point.

"The President has given me a very unpleasant assignment," he said, as
Eccles recalled his words. "I am to inform you that he is not going to redesignate
you as chairman of the Board of Governors. But he told me to be sure you understand that he wants you to stay a member of the board."

Eccles was shocked. Before Christmas he had had a cordial meeting with
Truman. Eccles expressed regret about the publicity over his differences with Snyder. He was referring to his own proposal at the recent session of Congress for a
special reserve requirement for member banks as a way of restraining credit. Seemingly untroubled, Truman offered no hint that he would appoint a new chairman. Incredulous at Steelman's message, Eccles asked to see Truman again. This meeting
on January 24 was an ordeal for both of them, according to Eccles. Truman, he
recalled, said he would make him vice-chairman of the board.

"What is behind this change?" Eccles asked.

Truman did not explain.[3] Presently, he announced the appointment of Thomas
B. McCabe, president of the Scott Paper Company and a director of the Federal
Reserve Bank of Philadelphia, as the new chairman. McCabe had been in Washing-
ton during the war as a Lend-Lease official, had entertained at the Wardman Park,

was well acquainted with members of the Senate and House banking committees and had met Truman, who was impressed with him. Eccles remained a member of the board, but Truman never got around to designating him as vice-chairman.

Later Steelman offered an explanation of the Eccles demotion, recalling that he had sat in on the discussions of the case with Truman and had himself favored demotion of Eccles. "Eccles was squeezing when we needed expansion," Steelman said.[4] When inflation struck after the First World War the national directors of the Federal Reserve Bank met in a mahogany-paneled room in New York and adopted a resolution to curb inflation by the classical means of deflating the currency.[5] Among the worst to suffer as a result were farmers in the Midwest, and because of bad times in Missouri and Kansas, Harry Truman and Eddie Jacobson went out of business. Once in the White House, Truman was determined that no such "wringing out," to apply the term he used in his memoirs, was going to occur in his administration.[6]

As Steelman recalled the Eccles case, the administration not only was uneasy about the specter of tight money but also felt that Eccles was too close to the bankers and not cooperative enough with the White House. "He and Snyder didn't get along," Steelman said. "It was partly personality." In a letter to the author he added: "He [Truman] & I, and others, felt the Fed. (1) was not enough public interest oriented—rather more banker interest—and (2) that, in general, the Fed. had too much power, that it should be cut down just a notch etc. . . . I recall being surprised when he [Eccles] accepted the offer to remain as a member."[7] In May Truman told his staff he had wanted Eccles to learn "who's boss."[8]

In the midst of these jolts Harold Stassen, then a serious contender for the Republican presidential nomination, appeared before a Senate subcommittee and made more trouble for Truman. He charged that eleven government "insiders" had made $4 million since the war in transactions in the commodity markets. Among them he cited Ed Pauley and Truman's personal physician on the White House staff, General Wallace Graham. The incident foreshadowed the kinds of disclosures and allegations of corruption that were to plague Truman in his second term, and the timing was not in the least helpful to him now with the election approaching.

In his broadcast October 5, 1947, asking people to conserve food to help Europe,—the first event at the White House to be televised—he had criticized "gambling in grain" and said it was a cause of high food prices. Grain prices, he said, "should not be subject to the greed of speculators who gamble on what may lie ahead in our commodity markets."[9] A wave of grain speculation in September had caused not only these remarks by the president but repercussion in Congress, stimulated the more when Secretary of Agriculture Anderson said in Chicago October 9: "I can call names—some of them public figures—who are speculating in large quantities of grain."

Styles Bridges, chairman of the Senate Appropriations Committee, smelled a problem for Truman in all of this, and a subcommittee investigated. It remained for Stassen, however, in a speech in Doylestown, Pennsylvania, to cite Pauley, then special assistant to Secretary of the Army Royall, as an insider who had profiteered. Congress then passed a joint resolution requiring the Commodity Exchange Authority to publish the names of market speculators. Truman signed the joint resolution

December 19, and ten days later the name of his friend and physician, General Graham, showed up on a list of speculators.

A handsome and personable officer, who had been wounded in Normandy, General Graham was the son of the Truman family's doctor in Missouri. Serving in Germany, he had joined Truman's party at Potsdam and remained on duty at the White House as the president's personal physician throughout the Truman administration. The information released December 29 indicated that with capital of at least $22,500 he had speculated in wheat in mid-September to the extent of 50,000 bushels. Graham issued a statement saying that his speculation in wheat futures was unwitting since he had left the handling of his account, consisting of modest savings and a few common stocks, to his broker, Bache and Company, of New York. On October 7, two days after Truman's criticism of grain speculation, he said, he had asked Bache if he had any holdings in commodities. When the answer was yes, he said, he ordered that the commodities be sold. Bache publicly denied this. According to Charles Ross, Graham told Truman about his speculations December 18, the day before the president signed the joint resolution requiring publication of the lists.

"Mr. President," a reporter asked Truman at his press conference December 31, "do you consider that Dr. Graham did anything wrong in his speculation?"

"I don't think he did," he replied.[10]

Before the subcommittee January 11 Pauley testified that in three years of commodity speculation he had made $932,703.10. The next day he denied that inside information had played any part in his successes. Stassen already had said that Pauley's "sense of right and wrong is not fully developed" and had demanded that Truman dismiss him. Before Truman could be asked about his testimony, Pauley announced that he would resign.

Graham was called to testify January 13 and under questioning admitted that his statement that he had ordered his holdings sold October 7 was not true. The account was not closed until December 18, the day he told Truman about his investment and the day before Truman signed the joint resolution. Graham said that he had made a net profit of $6,165.25 on a $5,700 investment in commodity transactions, but had lost $11,012.26 on the sale of stock.

The New Year had scarcely begun when some right-thinking people were treated to a shock of another sort—an announcement of plans for what soon became known—and still is—as the "Truman balcony."

Two years earlier, it will be recalled, the idea of a balcony outside his second-floor study had occurred to Truman after Congress had blocked his plan to build an extension of the west wing. While he had mentioned the balcony at the time to Howell Crim, the chief usher, and his assistant, J. B. West, Truman had otherwise kept his thoughts secret until Charles Ross made the announcement. Again there was the same outcry from traditionalists and architects, amplified this time by Republicans who joined in the fun, seeing the controversial balcony as a bonus in an election year.

Ross said that construction would begin forthwith on the forty-foot eliptical balcony, which would rest entirely within the six pillars on the south portico and which Ross, in those days before airconditioning, described as "a porch which will

give the family outside breathing space with a degree of privacy not now possible."
The plans had been drawn by William Adams Delano, a New York architect who
had been in charge of extensive alteration of the White House during the Coolidge
administration.

Three days after Ross's announcement Gilmore D. Clarke, a prominent landscape architect and chairman of the Commission of Fine Arts, declared that Truman
had proceeded with the plans despite unanimous disapproval by the commission. Its
authority, however, was only advisory.

"As the first citizen he is not following an exemplary course," the Washington
Evening Star said of Truman in an editorial January 6. The *Star* rejoiced at least that
his travels had never taken him past the Taj Mahal or the Old Moulmein Pagoda,
where, in one place or the other, the paper suggested, he might have received an
even more outrageous inspiration. Critics overlooked a principal argument of Truman's. This was that the balcony would eliminate the need for the old first-floor
awnings, which used to project from between the pillars of the south portico,
thereby, in the president's opinion, disfiguring the White House.

A Charleston architect likened Truman's desire for a balcony, however, to that
of Mussolini, who used to address the Fascists in Rome from the balcony of the
Palazzo Venezia. The *Washington Post* accused Truman of "meddling with a structure that does not belong to him," and the *New York Herald Tribune* reminded him
that he was "only a tenant."

"Well, they don't know the facts, or they wouldn't be that way," Truman said
at a press conference. "And you can't explain it to them because they don't want to
know." The introduction of a cooking stove and gaslight had also caused an uproar
in their day, he said. Furthermore: "Mrs. Fillmore put the first bathtub in the White
House, but they almost lynched her for doing it."*[11]

At a later press conference he said that his reason for building the balcony had
been misunderstood. "They thought it was a selfish reason I had," he explained.
"But that portico on the porch was designed by Thomas Jefferson . . . it was intended to have a balcony."[12] "A man with my kind of work doesn't have time for
sitting on verandas and porches," he told John Hersey during a series of interviews
for the *New Yorker* in 1951. "I put that on there for architectural reasons. . . . It
was to make the building look right."

For a while the balcony was the biggest tourist attraction in town. "It looks
real good from this distance," one visitor told a guide. "As a matter of fact you can
hardly notice it."[13] The $20 bills had to be redesigned to include the balcony in the
engraving of the White House, but that was a small inconvenience for the pleasures
presidents and their families have enjoyed ever since. Even Nixon, after taking up
residence, said that Truman had done the right thing in building the balcony.

State of the Union messages in election years invariably cause dissension, and
Truman that January went before a joint session of Congress intending to stir political controversy, to appeal to different groups of voters, and to shape the Democratic

---

* According to P. J. Wingate, writing in the *Washington Post* of January 4, 1977 (p. A-13), the
story that Millard Fillmore installed the first bathtub in the White House was a hoax perpetrated by
H. L. Mencken. No one knows when the first White House bathtub was installed, Wingate said.

platform the following summer.[14]

Borrowing from the title of the civil rights report, he said that his first goal was "to secure fully the essential human rights of our citizens." Furthermore, he announced, he would soon send Congress a special message on the subject.

Piling request upon request, he recommended comprehensive health insurance, extension and increase in unemployment compensation, old age benefits, and survivors' benefits. He asked for federal assistance to education and to housing, public and private, extension of rent control, and continuance of the school lunch program. For the western states, which loomed large in his thoughts throughout 1948, he wanted dams, water, conservation, and reclamation. For the farmers he wanted continuance of price supports and crop insurance and rural electrification. For labor he wanted the minimum wage of forty cents an hour increased to seventy-five cents an hour.

With the speech nearly at an end the fare was already too rich for conservative Republicans and southern Democrats, but the *pièce de résistance* was yet to come. Truman had twice in 1947 vetoed Republican bills to cut taxes, and the vetoes had prevailed. In an election year, however, Congress was bound to cut taxes, especially with a large budgetary surplus in prospect. A veto would not stand. It was perfectly evident around the White House that if somebody was going to get credit for lower taxes in 1948, it might as well be the Democrats. Enlarging, therefore, upon a recommendation made to him by the Council of Economic Advisers and pressed by Clifford, Truman proposed in a sheer political gesture that each taxpayer in the country and each of his dependents should be given a cost-of-living tax credit of $40 (double the figure recommended by the council).[15] Thus the income tax of a man with a wife and two children, for example, would be reduced by $160.

"It is estimated," Truman said, "that such a tax credit would reduce federal revenue by $3.2 billion. This reduction should be made up by increasing the tax on corporate profits in an amount that will produce this sum—with appropriate adjustment for small corporations. . . . It gives relief to those who need it most without cutting the total tax revenue of the Government."

Republicans could not find words adequate to such impudence. "He has," Taft exclaimed, "raised all the ghosts of the old New Deal with new trappings that Tugwell and Harry Hopkins never thought of."

The thunderclap came three weeks later when Truman on February 2 sent up a "Special Message to the Congress on Civil Rights," something no other president had ever done.[16] The program went beyond any proposed by Roosevelt, and opened a fissure in the political landscape that Truman had not foreseen. He said in his message:

The Federal Government has a clear duty to see that Constitutional guarantees of individual liberties and of equal protection under the laws are not denied or abridged anywhere in our Union. That duty is shared by all three branches of the Government, but it can be fulfilled only if the Congress enacts modern, comprehensive civil rights laws, adequate to the needs of the day and demonstrating our continuing faith in the free way of life.

He asked for enactment at the current session of an antilynching law, an antipoll tax law, a permanent Fair Employment Practices Commission, a permanent

Commission on Civil Rights, and a Joint Congressional Committee on Civil Rights for a continuing study of legislation.

The constitutional right to vote, he said, was still subject to interference. Some individuals were prevented from voting by intimidation. Some groups were barred by outmoded practices prevailing in certain states or communities—meaning the South, particularly. In quest of stronger statutory protection he recommended legislation forbidding interference by public officers or private persons with the right of qualified citizens to participate in primary, special, and general elections in which federal officers were to be chosen. He said the legislation should be extended to elections for state officers also insofar as interference with the right to vote resulted from racial discrimination.

He requested Congress to prohibit discrimination and segregation on interstate trains, planes, and buses, but then, the Supreme Court already had led the way on that issue. Otherwise Truman did not directly attack segregation, ignoring the recommendations in *To Secure These Rights* that elimination of racial segregation be a condition for grants-in-aid and other forms of federal assistance to public or private agencies. Although he asked for home rule for the District of Columbia, he recommended that the people themselves be given the opportunity to "deal with the inequalities arising from segregation."

Finally, he alluded to proposed action in areas where the executive branch had been laggard, namely, in eliminating discrimination in the civil service and the armed forces and in the provision of federal services and facilities. "I shall shortly issue an Executive Order," he said, "containing a comprehensive restatement of Federal non-discrimination policy, together with appropriate measures to insure compliance. I have instructed the Secretary of Defense to take steps to have the remaining instances of discrimination in the armed services eliminated as rapidly as possible."[17]

While more moderate and less comprehensive than the recommendations in *To Secure These Rights,* the message was a strong one in the circumstances and was intended to be so in order to counterbalance Wallace's appeal to blacks. Furthermore, it accorded with Truman's mood at the moment. Most black spokesmen applauded the message. Certainly, the program was ahead of public opinion in February of 1948. The effect of what amounted to an appeal to the conscience of Congress and white Americans—"a noble deed," the *Chicago Sun-Times* called it—was to make it more difficult than ever for the country to turn back on civil rights. Delays and evasions would abound, but a tide was rising. Nowhere was this better understood and more feared than in the South. Although Clifford had admonished him that the message might cause the biggest explosion in Congress in modern times, Truman seems to have anticipated a more indifferent reception. In a diary entry the morning he submitted the message to Congress he noted: "They, no doubt, will receive it as coldly as they did the State of the Union Message. But it needs to be said."[18]

In parts of the South it was received with white heat. Even before the message had been sent, Governor Fielding L. Wright of Mississippi, attacking the recommendations of the Committee on Civil Rights, had demanded a break with the Democratic party if its leaders continued to support legislation "aimed to wreck the South and our institutions."[19] Truman's message touched off such an outburst of comment on Capitol Hill from members from Mississippi, Alabama, Louisiana, South Carolina, and Georgia as often exceeded the standards of what was printable in the newspapers of those days. Comments that were quoted in the press accused Truman of "kissing the feet of minorities" and "stabbing the South in the back." Senator Connally, Truman's loyal ally on foreign policy, told a Jefferson-Jackson Day dinner in Raleigh that the message was "a lynching of the Constitution." "We will not take it lying down," he said. In the kind of jibe that had the effect of raising Truman in the estimation of northern blacks, Representative Cox of Georgia declared that "Harlem is wielding more influence with the administration than the entire white South."

Typifying the resentment against Truman personally, Representative John Bell Williams, Democrat, of Mississippi, said: "If it were not for Southern Democrats, Henry Wallace would be in the White House today instead of Harry Truman. Southern Democrats have always been the best friends that President Truman or the Democratic Party ever had. May I say . . . that it is a mighty poor way for him to evince his gratitude."

The White House had drafted a bill embodying Truman's proposals and sent it to Barkley to introduce in the Senate. After sampling southern reaction and weighing the danger of a filibuster that would snag other important legislation, the Senate Democratic leader put the bill on ice without any loud objection from the White House.

The Southern Governors' Conference met in Wakulla Springs, Florida, February 7. Governor Wright proposed that the governors notify Democratic party leaders that "we no longer will tolerate the repeated campaigns" for civil rights legislation. He recommended holding a "Southern Conference of true Democrats" in Jackson, Mississippi, March 1 to "formulate plans for activity and adopt a course of action." Instead, the governors voted for a forty-day cooling-off period during which a committee in defense of white supremacy, headed by Governor Thurmond, would weigh the situation and interrogate the Democratic national chairman about Truman's policies.[20]

So formidable was the pressure that rumors circulated that Truman desired a compromise. "There will be absolutely no retreat on any point," Ross said at a daily White House briefing. "The whole story is without foundation and fact." On the basis of Ross's statement Eastland of Mississippi rose in the Senate February 9 and called on the South to revolt against the national party leaders. He said that the election could be thrown into the House of Representatives and a southerner elected president if the South would nominate its own candidate. The same day Representative Oren Harris, Democrat, of Arkansas, wrote to Truman, saying that compromise by the South on the civil rights program was impossible. "We cannot agree," Harris said, "to relinquish our violent opposition to proposals for Anti-lynch, Anti-poll tax laws and the establishment of FEPC."[21]

Four thousand Democrats assembled in Jackson February 12 and endorsed Wright's call at Wakulla Springs for a conference there of "all true white Jeffersonian Democrats" to act against the national party.

Commenting on the southern reaction, Truman told his staff it might be a good thing if the civil rights issue were eventually to split the Democratic party in the

South, causing a new realignment between liberals and conservatives. But he still did not foresee in February a southern bolt in 1948. He remarked in a personal letter to the Speaker of the Alabama House of Representatives that the southerners had to let off some steam, but "I am sure that none of them have any intention of leaving the Democratic Party—it has always been their Party and I don't see how they can afford to leave it."[22]

February 19 was the hundredth anniversary of the Democratic National Committee, and in commemoration Jefferson-Jackson Day dinners were held in cities around the country. The centerpiece was the dinner at the Mayflower Hotel in Washington where Truman spoke over a national radio hookup. With the party racked by bitterness over his program, the celebration could scarcely have come at a worse time. In Richmond Senator Byrd made a speech saying that some parts of the program would open the way to dictatorship. In Little Rock, Arkansas, half of the eight hundred and fifty guests at the dinner walked out when Truman's voice came over the radio. The most memorable scene was at the Mayflower. A table with eleven settings, positioned directly in front of the speakers' stand, remained empty, a silent symbol of the gathering southern revolt. The table had been reserved by the wife of Senator Olin D. Johnston, Democrat, of South Carolina. Mrs. Johnston and her guests boycotted the dinner when it became known that some blacks would attend and would not be segregated.

Truman took no notice. The theme he struck that night was one that would ring through his political speeches for the next nine months. Jefferson, Jackson, Wilson, and Roosevelt had led the Democratic party on behalf of the people against exploitation by the commercial interests. In 1948 the issue was drawn again. Truman was the one who carried the fight now.

The people will again decide whether they want the forces of positive, progressive liberalism to continue in office, or whether . . . they want to entrust their government to those forces of conservatism which believe in the benefit of the few at the expense of the many.[23]

Concentrating on economic issues, Truman did not mention civil rights, but the controversy was not stilled. On February 20 fifty-two southern Democratic congressmen held a caucus under the chairmanship of Representative William M. Colmer of Mississippi and adopted a resolution warning against inclusion of the civil rights program in the forthcoming Democratic platform. And on February 23 the committee of southern governors called on Democratic National Chairman McGrath. Thurmond belabored him on the administration's attitude on civil rights and asked if he would use his influence to have Truman withhold his program. While trying to keep the southerners in line, McGrath declined the request. His only offer was to try to seek an accommodation in the platform, possibly through repetition of the harmless civil rights plank of 1944. Clearly, the governors of the Deep South were not going to determine national Democratic policy. "The present leadership of the Democratic Party will soon realize," Thurmond said, menacingly, after the meeting, "that the South is no longer 'in the bag.' "[24]

Governor William M. Tuck of Virginia asked the legislature to pass a law under which Virginians would vote for presidential electors who would be required to support whatever candidates a state party convention designated. E. H. Crump, the Tennessee Democratic leader, announced his opposition to Truman's candidacy. The South Carolina Democratic Committee did likewise. The Mississippi Democratic Committee voted to withdraw from the Democratic National Convention in July unless it promised to reject "anti-Southern" laws.

At the other end of the political spectrum the Americans for Democratic Action met in Philadelphia in February and refrained from endorsing Truman. Reports were that the liberal organization might support someone else.

Truman moved quickly to head off the entry of other candidates. McGrath and officials of the Democratic National Committee met with him March 8. Afterward McGrath surprised reporters by announcing: "The President has authorized me to say that if nominated by the Democratic National Convention, he will accept and run."

McGrath himself brought up the civil rights issue.

"I talked to the President with respect to his civil rights message," he said. "The President's position remains unchanged since he delivered that message."[25]

Thus was Truman's candidacy launched at a time when the Democratic party was in disarray in North and South. Southern Democrats in at least four states were in near rebellion. Liberals in the big cities were disgruntled. Roosevelt's winning coalition was being courted by Wallace. The Republican Congress was in a fighting mood. *Time* concluded that "only a political miracle or extraordinary stupidity on the part of the Republicans can save the Democratic party, after 16 years in power, from a debacle in November."[26] For the moment, however, attention was diverted from politics by dramatic events abroad.

38. *Czechoslovakia and the Berlin Blockade*

ARCH 17, 1948, was one of the somber days in Washington in the postwar years. The Communists had seized the government of Czechoslovakia, which had historic ties with the United States, and Truman was to address a joint session of Congress on the crisis. It was the beginning of one of the most trying periods of his presidency thus far.

Czechoslovakia was suddenly gone. Scandinavia seemed threatened. Four-power rule of Germany was crumbling. In a development without precedent in peacetime the United States was groping toward a military alliance with Western Europe. The realization was dawning on the administration that in China the Communists might soon conquer Chiang Kai-shek's Nationalist forces. The National Security Council was increasingly concerned lest the United States get trapped in a war in Korea. The fighting was escalating in Palestine. Pressures from abroad led to radical changes in CIA functions. Above all, an attempt by the Soviet Union to force the Allies out of Berlin, or at least to exclude Allied influence from the Soviet zone, created a fear of war that lasted for months, at times overshadowing the presidential election campaign.

Appearing before Congress on the seventeenth, Truman said, "Rapid changes are taking place in Europe which affect our foreign policy and our national security." He asked that Congress restore the draft. He renewed his plea for Universal Military Training. He urged swift passage of the Economic Cooperation Act of 1948, embodying the Marshall Plan, now officially called the European Recovery Program. Truman accused the Soviet Union and its agents of having "destroyed the independence and democratic character of a whole series of nations in Eastern and Central Europe. It is this ruthless course of action, and the clear design to extend it to the remaining free nations of Europe, that have brought about the critical situation in Europe today."[1]

After the First World War Woodrow Wilson had played an important part in the birth of the Czechoslovakian republic. Its first president, Thomas G. Masaryk, had, upon his death, been succeeded by Eduard Beneš, who was still president in 1948, although his regime had had Communist officials forced upon it by Moscow after the Second World War. Then elections were held in 1946, resulting in a coalition government in which the Communists were the most numerous single faction. Klement Gottwald, one of them, became prime minister. Jan G. Masaryk, American-educated son of the late first president and a liberal belonging to no party, was appointed foreign minister. Vaclav Nosek, a Communist, was named minister of interior with control over the police.

Equilibrium between Communists and non-Communists prevailed for a time. In 1947, however, agitation developed as a result of cold war pressures. Tension was heightened by the approach of new Czech elections, scheduled for May 1948. Then a government crisis occurred in February 1948. When Nosek began substituting Communists for non-Communists in the police force, twelve non-Communists resigned from the cabinet.

Gottwald demanded of Beneš that he appoint a new cabinet containing no anti-Communist members. Beneš, who was in poor health and lacked Western support, temporized, whereupon all Communist organizations in the country were mobilized. Many persons were arrested. Soviet Deputy Foreign Minister Valerian A. Zorin arrived in Prague on the eve of the cabinet showdown, ostensibly to supervise distribution of Soviet wheat. The Red Army was never far away. On the other hand there was no direct evidence of Soviet interference.[2]

Despite the sentimental American-Czechoslovakian relationship in the past, Washington's practical concern was that an unchallenged Communist seizure of Czechoslovakia would encourage Communist action in Western Europe, especially in Italy where elections were scheduled for April 18.[3]

On February 25 Beneš, who was to die, a broken man, within seven months, capitulated to Gottwald. The Czech government passed under Communist domination, although Jan Masaryk remained foreign minister.

An intense reaction swept the United States. The popular view was that a democracy-loving, friendly nation had been swallowed by the Communists in a coup d'état staged by the Kremlin. The plight of Beneš evoked sympathy. News reports of men crying in the streets of Prague recalled Hitler's conquests. Indeed in a telegram to Marshall February 26 Laurence A. Steinhardt, United States ambassador in Prague, reported that the Czech Communists had "browbeaten and exercised a degree of duress on President Beneš strikingly similar to methods employed by Hitler in dealing with heads of state."[4]

The analogy between Stalin and Hitler lodged itself at the heart of American decision making. A National Security Council document, NSC-7, dated March 30, 1948, said: "Today Stalin has come close to achieving what Hitler attempted in vain. The Soviet world extends from the Elbe River and the Adriatic on the west to Manchuria on the east, and embraces one fifth of the land surface of the world."[5]

The news broke February 27 that Stalin had invited Finland to sign a mutual assistance pact. "Now she's[the Soviet Union] after Finland and the Scandinavian Peninsula," Truman wrote in a speech draft. "We cannot sit idly by and see totalitarianism spread to the whole of Europe. . . . We must meet the challenge if civilization is to survive. We represent the moral God fearing peoples of the world. We must save the world from Atheism and totalitarianism. Only our strength will save the world."[6]

"Mr. President," Truman was asked at a press conference in Key West March 1 while returning from a visit to the Virgin Islands, "Czechoslovakia and perhaps Finland seem to be going down the drain in the classic style. Do you think the time may have come for the western powers to form a military alliance?"

"I cannot comment on that at this time," he replied.[7]

In fact, a decision was taking shape amidst the apprehension, particularly in

Paris, but shared in London and Washington, that economic aid no longer was enough to provide security.

Worried over the failure of the London foreign ministers' conference in December 1947 to reach agreement on Germany, Ernest Bevin had broached to Marshall in London the idea of "some western democratic system comprising the Americans, ourselves, France, Italy, etc., and of course the Dominions" to stop "further Communist inroads." Marshall, who had been taking an increasingly activist stance against the Soviet Union, agreed "there was no choice in the matter." On January 13 Lord Inverchapel informed him that Bevin had in mind prompt formation of a Western Union, based upon a treaty among Britain, France, and the Benelux countries (Belgium, the Netherlands, and Luxembourg.). Thus would be created, the British ambassador said, a solid core in Western Europe, around which a larger system could develop. Accompanying Inverchapel's letter to Marshall was a memorandum from Bevin, envisioning the United States, Scandinavia, Italy, Greece, possibly Portugal, and as soon as circumstances permitted, Germany and Spain as members of the new system.

John D. Hickerson, director of the Office of European Affairs in the State Department, advised Marshall that for the United States the most practical system would be a regional defense pact under Article 51 of the United Nations Charter, on the model of the Inter-American Treaty of Reciprocal Assistance, signed at Rio de Janeiro September 2, 1947. On January 20 Marshall wrote to Inverchapel: "The initiative which he [Bevin] is taking in this matter will be warmly applauded in the United States." With far-reaching consequences, a conference of representatives of Britain, France, and the Benelux countries was scheduled to be held in March in Brussels.[8]

A meeting of ambassadors of the United States, Britain, France, and the Benelux countries had also convened in London in February to weigh the German situation. With their deep fear of a reunited and rearmed Germany, or of a rearmed Western Germany aligned with the United States and other Western powers, the Soviets protested that the meeting violated the Potsdam agreement on four-power control of Germany. Nevertheless on March 6 the ambassadors announced agreement in principle on three steps fiercely opposed by Moscow: economic integration of the American, British, and French zones (Trizonia instead of Bizonia); West German participation in the European Recovery Program; and formation of a West German government.

In the meantime the Allied Control Council for Germany was rapidly going to pieces in the harsh conflict over these questions and over the long-pending proposal of the Western powers to issue a new currency in Germany. For some weeks also Soviet inspectors had been periodically interrupting Allied military train service to Berlin.

In a handwritten note March 5, attached to a memorandum from Marshall, Truman jotted: "Will Russia move first? Who pulls the trigger? Then where do we go?"[9]

Inadvertently, General Clay contributed that same day to the feverish mood in Washington. Having been asked recently by army intelligence for something that would help the military persuade Congress on the need for enlarged appropriations, he sent a cable outside the normal command channels, and relating to no particular change in Soviet strategy, in which he expressed a feeling nevertheless that war "may come with dramatic suddenness."[10]

It was into this atmosphere that news came screaming out of Prague March 10 that Jan Masaryk had been found dead—a suicide or a victim of assassination—on the ground below his apartment in the foreign ministry. No witness to those times in the United States can forget the despair, the rage, and—justified or not—the loathing, for Communists behind the Iron Curtain that welled up around the headlines and radio bulletins.

The Pentagon advised Clay and MacArthur "to survey carefully your current emergency plans and insure that such implementing instructions as might be required to expedite placing these plans into effect are prepared."[11]

The Joint Chiefs of Staff were meeting with Forrestal at the Key West submarine base. They recommended that Selective Service be restored. They also proposed that the president should seek a supplemental appropriation from Congress to bring American military strength more nearly into line with demands that might be made upon it. These recommendations were sent to Truman at once. When Forrestal returned to Washington Truman told him that he already had decided to address a joint session and to go all-out for Selective Service and UMT.[12]

At a staff meeting March 16 the president declared that the country would be "sunk" if Congress did not act in the face of Soviet expansion and the spread of communism. He revealed that Marshall feared that he, Truman, would "pull the trigger" by his action. But Truman said that if a war was to occur, it was better that the people and Congress should be warned in advance than that it should burst upon them unexpectedly, as in 1941.[13]

"What Truman wanted to do in asking for the draft," Budget Director Webb recalled, "was to give the Soviets a signal that although we had cut down on military spending, we were ready to go back up again."[14] Beyond this, the available military manpower appeared very tight to those responsible in view of the existing potential for crises in Europe, the Middle East, and Korea.

March 17 was a milestone. In Brussels, Britain, France, Belgium, the Netherlands, and Luxembourg signed a fifty-year collective defense treaty.

In Washington, in his speech to Congress, Truman hailed the Brussels Pact, saying: "This development deserves our full support. I am confident that the United States will, by appropriate means, extend to the free nations the support which the situation requires."

Speaking that night at a dinner of the Society of the Friendly Sons of St. Patrick at the Hotel Astor in New York, Truman not only renewed his call to action but castigated Henry Wallace, who had said that the Czech Communists had seized power to protect themselves from a right-wing coup encouraged by Ambassador Steinhardt.

"I do not want and I will not accept the political support of Henry Wallace and his Communists," Truman told a cheering audience in a passage he had interpolated. "If joining them or permitting them to join me is the price of victory, I recommend defeat. These are days of high prices for everything, but any price for Wallace and his Communists is too much for me to pay. I'm not buying."[15]

Wallace was not a Communist, and Truman did not say he was. Yet in his comment on Czechoslovakia Wallace could hardly have said anything more pleasing to the Communists. In battling the Progressive party candidate Truman adopted the obvious political strategy of treating the Wallace movement as a Communist pawn. It was so logical that from the day Wallace announced his candidacy the tactic of Democratic leaders generally was to characterize it as one supported entirely by left-wingers and Communists. Wallace's own tactics were rough enough that he had no reason to expect that the campaign would be a picnic. When, in February, the president had grave problems on his hands in the Middle East, Wallace campaigned in a special election in a Jewish district in the Bronx, telling the voters that Truman "still talks Jewish but acts Arab."[16]

On the whole Congress was responsive to Truman's March 17 appeal. While continuing to balk at Universal Military Training, it restored Selective Service, making men between the ages of nineteen and twenty-five liable to be drafted for twenty-one months. It approved the European Recovery Program. When it came to actual appropriations Congress reduced administration requests and voted $4 billion for the Marshall Plan countries for the first twelve months. It also voted more than $2 billion in other foreign aid.

Following Masaryk's death, a momentary lull descended on Europe. Not so in China and Korea. In China the Communists had cut off Chiang Kai-shek's garrisons in Manchuria.[17] At the suggestion of the State Department Truman sent a message to Congress asking for $570 million to bolster Chiang's "rapidly deteriorating economy"—and to satisfy Republican critics.[18] Then Marshall appeared before an executive session of the Foreign Relations and Foreign Affairs Committees and painted a dark picture.

"We must be prepared," he said, "to face the possibility that the present Chinese government may not be successful in maintaining itself against the Communist forces or other opposition that may arise in China." Evidently, he continued, Chiang could not smash the Communists unless the United States underwrote the Nationalist military effort and the Nationalist economy. "The U.S.," Marshall declared, "would have to be prepared virtually to take over the Chinese government." American financial aid, in his opinion, could not remedy the Nationalist government's lack of self-discipline and inspiration.

Reflecting one of the cardinal decisions of the Truman administration, Marshall said that for the United States to tie up large forces and resources in China would play into Soviet hands, presumably by leaving Europe vulnerable, or even lead to war. He concluded:

. . . the costs of an all-out effort to see Communist forces resisted and destroyed in China would . . . be impossible to estimate. But the magnitude of the task and the probable costs thereof would clearly be out of all proportion to the results to be achieved.[19]

Acting on Truman's request, while reducing it, Congress appropriated $400 million for China, of which Chiang could spend $125 million for military supplies. At a meeting June 7 Marshall said that simply providing military equipment would not defeat the Communists. The United States, he noted, already had sent Chiang large quantities of arms under previous programs, but the arms and the divisions handling them had been misused by the Nationalist leadership.[20]

In September, 1947, the United States had referred the question of Korean independence to the United Nations General Assembly. The resolution called for election throughout Korea, under the observation of a United Nations commission, of a Korean National Assembly, which would then establish a national government. Thereupon the new Korean regime would arrange with the United States and the Soviet Union for withdrawal of their troops. Over Soviet opposition and warnings of "grave consequences" the General Assembly voted to hold elections throughout Korea. This undertaking was set in motion in the winter of 1948. The Ukraine, however, refused to perform as a member of the United Nations Temporary Commission. To test this Soviet boycott the commission invited the Soviet commander in North Korea to cooperate. On January 23 the Soviets refused to allow the commission to enter the Communist zone to supervise elections there.

The General Assembly being in recess, the commission sought the counsel of the Interim Committee of the General Assembly (the "Little Assembly") as to whether elections should be held. The United States representative, Dr. Philip C. Jessup, proposed that the commission should hold elections which meant holding them in the United States zone only, with the understanding that the Korean national assembly, when elected, ought not constitute the final or complete form of the government, but should endeavor to consult Koreans in other parts of the country to determine the form of government that all the Korean people wished to establish. The "Little Assembly" adopted this proposal, and the commission accepted the recommendation. Koreans in the United States zone went to the polls May 10 and gave Syngman Rhee's anti-Communist party a majority of seats in the national assembly.

Thereafter a provisional government for the Republic of Korea came into being, with Rhee as its head. In North Korea the Soviet-sponsored People's Committee already had proclaimed a People's Republic and declared that Seoul would eventually be its capital. On April 2 the National Security Council promulgated NSC-8, stating that the United States' objective was a settlement that would enable the Americans to end their military occupation "as soon as possible with the minimum of bad effect," although without abandoning the South Korean government or tolerating Soviet control over all of Korea.

"The extension of Soviet control over all of Korea would," NSC-8 said, "enhance the political and strategic position of the Soviet Union with respect to both China and Japan and adversely affect the position of the U.S. in those areas and throughout the Far East."

The policy was, therefore, for the United States, in preparation for withdrawal, to complete plans for expanding, training, and equipping the South Korean constabulary for protection against aggression from the north. The Korean relief program was to be completed.

"Every effort should be made to create conditions for the withdrawal of the occupation forces by 31 December 1948," NSC-8 said, and warned:

The U.S. should not become so irrevocably involved in the Korean situation that any action taken by a faction in Korea or by any other power in Korea could be considered a *casus belli* for the U.S.[21]

In the absence of a satisfactory solution to the problem of Communist domination, however, the occupation continued.

On March 11 the British delivered to the State Department an aide-mémoire saying that Norway feared a Soviet demand for a mutual assistance pact, that Norway was determined to refuse, and that Norway wanted to know what help it might receive from the Allies if it were attacked. According to the aide-mémoire, Bevin thought the Soviet demand likely and feared that the Soviet sphere of influence would be extended to the Atlantic. "He considers," the aide-mémoire said, "that the most effective course would be to take very early steps, before Norway goes under, to conclude under Article 51 of the Charter of the United Nations a regional Atlantic Approaches Pact of Mutual Assistance, in which all the countries directly threatened by a Russian move to the Atlantic could participate . . ." The very next day Marshall wrote Inverchapel:

Please inform Mr. Bevin that . . . we are prepared to proceed at once in the joint discussions on the establishment of an Atlantic security system.[22]

By late March serious trouble was breaking out in Germany. While it was triggered by immediate developments, such as currency reform and the holding of the Allied conference on German problems in London that spring, the true cause lay in the whole complex of issues that had drawn the two sides apart since Potsdam. The trouble was a culmination of the mutual distrust and conflict of aims in Germany that had been rising through years of controversies over reparations, control of the Ruhr, levels of industry, and occupation policies generally. The Western powers still aimed at a degree of German prosperity that would relieve their own taxpayers of the burdens of occupation. This goal, however, continued to elude them in the spring of 1948, and they resolved, as one course of action, to seek improvement through currency reform.

When the Allied Control Council met March 20 Marshal Vasily D. Sokolovsky, the Soviet representative, demanded that the Western members reveal all agreements concerning Germany which their ambassadors had reached at the recent London sessions. They replied that the actions had been recommendations to the respective governments and that no formal directives had been received on which a report could be made. Thereupon Sokolovsky declared the London actions illegal and the Control Council machinery disrupted. He pronounced the meeting adjourned, and the Soviet delegation departed.[23] This marked the absolute end of four-power government of Germany—the Allied Control Council never met again.

The Soviet authorities notified Clay that effective April 1 all Americans, military and civilian, passing through the Soviet zone by highway or by rail en route to Berlin would have to be checked by Soviet guards for their identity and affiliation. Except in the case of American military personnel and American citizens employed by government agencies, the baggage of passengers on American trains or motor vehicles would be subject to inspection. Military freight trains would have to be cleared by Soviet officials.

Clay submitted to Washington for approval a letter rejecting the order as an infringement of United States occupation rights. He granted the right of the Soviets to check the identification of passengers travelling by motor vehicle but not their belongings. He denied their right to check army passenger and freight trains. He agreed that train commandants would furnish lists of passengers and cargo manifests. But he declared that "we cannot permit our military trains to be entered by the representatives of other powers . . . and our train commandants have been instructed accordingly."

He asked Washington for authority to order train commandants to resist by force if necessary any attempt by Soviet personnel to board army trains. Clay interpreted the blockade as a Soviet effort to drive the Americans out of Berlin and hence, as a practical matter, out of Europe.

In a transatlantic teleconference March 31 Secretary of the Army Royall cautioned Clay that shooting might lead to war. Hence, he said, thought was being given to Truman's sending a note to Stalin alleging Soviet violation of agreements. Then even if no reply had been received, trains would resume normal operations after twenty-four hours. Another suggestion, Royall said, was that the trains should move but that shooting must be prohibited. He asked Clay's reaction to these two suggestions.

"Any weakness on our part," Clay replied, "will lose us prestige important now. If Soviets mean war, we will only defer the next provocation for a few days. For that reason I don't think either [suggestion] realistic. I do not believe this means war, but any failure to meet this squarely will cause great trouble."

High Pentagon and State Department officials took Clay's proposals to the White House where Truman approved a positive but, it was hoped, an unprovocative course.

"If our action now should provoke war," General Omar Bradley told Clay in a subsequent teleconference, "we must be sure that the fault is not ours."

Bradley said that the president had authorized Clay to send his letter of rejection with only minor changes. Clay also was authorized to move trains as he saw fit. He was not authorized, however, to increase the normal number of guards on the trains nor to change the types of arms they had been carrying.

"Furthermore," Bradley said, "it is important that our guards not fire unless fired upon."

At midnight April 1 three American trains entered the Soviet zone. Soviet guards signaled them to a stop. On one of the trains the commandant apparently lost his nerve and permitted Soviet guards to board. This train was allowed to pass through to Berlin. Soviet guards sought to board the other two trains also. The two commandants barred them. The Soviet guards did not try to board forcibly. No shooting occurred. Traffic control at that point was in Soviet hands, however; and the two trains, their commandants unauthorized to try to force their way through, were stalled. The same thing happened to British trains.

For the time being, therefore, Clay had the American trains backed out of the Soviet zone and canceled rail schedules. With American ingenuity and on his own initiative he put into operation instead a small-scale airlift to carry food in Air Force transports from Wiesbaden to Tempelhof Airport in the United States sector of Berlin.[24]

Days of strain followed. The Truman administration was caught in the awkward position of not having in writing a guarantee of American rights of access to Berlin over highways, railroads, and canals. Truman blamed Eisenhower.[25] Eleven days after the president's message to Stalin about access rights June 14, 1945, Marshall as army chief of staff had advised Eisenhower in Europe to make the necessary arrangements with Soviet commanders.[26] Discussions went on sporadically and oral assurances were given by Soviet officials, but the United States never got what it wanted in writing.

Clay blamed himself, according to Truman.[27] On the other hand Truman, busy as he was, had not followed the matter up in 1945 when the Soviets let it drift. Nor had he pressed for written guarantees at Potsdam. In mid-1945 few had expected serious troubles with the Soviets in matters of this kind.

On April 5 a Soviet fighter, attempting to harass a British transport plane, collided with it over Gatow Airport in the British sector of Berlin. All fourteen persons aboard the transport, including two Americans, were killed, as was the pilot of the fighter. British and American authorities ordered fighter escorts thenceforth for all their unarmed planes in the air corridors.[28] Sokolovsky apologized and said no harassment had been intended, though the Soviets later turned around and blamed the British for the accident.

After ten days without further serious trouble tension eased.

"You will understand, of course," Clay cautioned Bradley in a teleconference April 10, "that our separate currency reform in near future followed by partial German government in Frankfurt will develop the real crisis. Present show probably designed by Soviets to scare us away from these moves."[29]

In Washington the move toward alliance was progressing. The foreign policy of the United States was shifting toward a distinctly military character in a series of deliberate steps, partly caused by pressure from the British and French. On April 13 a far-reaching policy paper, NSC-9, was circulated, declaring that national security required more than the Marshall Plan. What was needed was deterrence of the Soviet Union "from attempting further aggression by confronting it with concrete evidence of determination to resist and with increasing organized force."

NSC-9 recommended that the United States approach the members of the Brussels Pact about concluding a collective defense agreement for "the North Atlantic Area." If they were agreeable, a further approach should then be made to Norway, Sweden, Denmark, Iceland, and, if the Italian elections were favorable, Italy. (They were favorable; the Communists lost.) When circumstances permitted, West Germany, Austria, Spain, and other countries were to be invited to join the alliance. The paper suggested the treaty should embody the principle that an attack upon one country be considered an attack upon all.

NSC-9 noted that, because it was an election year, Congress would not be in session long enough to consider American membership in the proposed alliance in 1948. But preliminary steps could be taken. The document suggested a resolution declaring it to be the sense of the Senate that United States policy should favor regional and collective arrangements under Article 51 of the United Nations Charter, which the Brussels Pact was. United States policy also should manifest a willingness to associate with such arrangements.[30]

To obtain a show of bipartisan support for the new policy the administration wanted the resolution introduced by a Republican. Vandenberg agreed to do it, and he and Lovett drafted Senate Resolution 239—the "Vandenberg Resolution." However vague, it pointed the way toward a United States military alliance with Western Europe and was the forerunner of unprecedented American participation in the North Atlantic Treaty Organization in 1949. With little debate the Senate adopted the resolution, 64 to 4.

Explaining the reasons behind the new developments in United States policy, Truman told editors of business and trade papers April 23 that the "Russians have a peculiar psychological approach."

"It is oriental, so I am told," he said, evidently reflecting the opinion Forrestal had expressed in 1945 when the question of collaborating with the Soviets on international control of atomic energy was under discussion. "Their idea is that force counts for everything." Truman continued:

So it became perfectly evident that if we expected to make agreements with that eastern-minded people known as the Russians, we must have the ability to implement those agreements on our side, if we expect them to be kept . . . .

I know that we can get peace in the world if we are in a position to enforce that peace . . . .

So I am asking for what amounts fundamentally to a police force [Universal Military Training] . . . which will keep peace in the world . . . .[31]

The impact of the alarming events abroad led to a drastic change in the use of the CIA, a change that was to haunt the country in later years. In the face of the continuing crises, the Truman administration in May and June of 1948 took a long step from the December authorization of covert psychological operations by the CIA to covert political operations. As director of the Policy Planning Staff in the State Department George Kennan advocated an American capability for covert political action, which at the time implied direct intervention in elections in foreign countries. Specifically, he recommended that his staff have a small directorate for overt and covert political warfare. The body, visualized as a contingency force for limited operations, would be known as the Special Studies Group. It would be under State Department control but not formally associated with the department. Rather it would operate elsewhere with concealed funds and concealed personnel.

Kennan has since recalled that "we were alarmed by the inroads of the Russian influence in Western Europe beyond the point where Russian troops had reached."

We felt that the Communists were using the very extensive funds that they then had in hand to gain control of key elements of life in France and Italy, particularly the publishing companies, the press, the labor unions, student organizations . . . and all sort of organizations of that sort . . . and use them as front organizations.

His proposal reflected the prevailing attitude in Washington in the late 1940s that if the Soviet Union played the game a certain way, the United States must play it that way too or suffer the consequences.

So persuasive was Kennan's idea that on June 18 the National Security Council went far beyond it and promulgated NSC 10/2. Instead of creating a small separate group under State Department control, NSC 10/2 established within the CIA an Office of Special Projects, later renamed the Office of Policy Coordination.[32] The directive authorized a dramatic increase in the range of covert operations directed against the Soviet Union, including political warfare, economic warfare and paramilitary activities. Where this was to lead President Truman could not have dreamed.

On June 18 also the Western Powers notified the Soviet Union that in their zones, though not initially in Berlin, the reichsmark would be replaced by a new deutsche mark June 20. Lacking public confidence, the reichsmark had become practically worthless.[33] Marshal Sokolovsky told the Western commanders that the new currency was illegal and would complete the division of Germany. In retaliation the Soviets on June 23 introduced new currency of their own into all sectors of Berlin. Viewing this as a challenge to *their* rights in the German capital, the Allies introduced the deutsche mark into the Western sectors of Berlin the next day. Thereupon the Soviets imposed that day a dramatic blockade of rail, highway, and water routes to Berlin. Excluding air transport with its separate status, they cut all modes of supply to Berlin, not just concentrating on Allied military traffic, as previously.

The blockade was a stark challenge to Truman. To leave those Germans who lived in the Allied sectors of Berlin at the mercy of the Soviets for food and fuel would jeopardize the loyalty of the West German people to the United States. To withdraw from the beleaguered capital would cast doubt on the dependability of the United States as a military ally at the very moment the North Atlantic Treaty Organization was in the throes of birth. To rely on an airlift to supply indefinitely a city of more than 2 million persons was a gamble. To use force against the Soviets on the ground might cause war.

Truman reacted cautiously and quietly—and firmly. He refused to withdraw. He supported expansion of the airlift. He sought a diplomatic rather than a military solution.

Ambassador Murphy recommended in a telegram to Marshall from Berlin June 26 that the United States, Britain, and France demonstrate their determination to take any measures necessary to open the surface routes to Berlin. Clay recommended retaliation against Moscow by closing American ports and the Panama Canal to Soviet ships. In conference with his advisers Truman rejected this suggestion as ineffective and self-defeating.[34]

Then on June 28 Marshall notified the London embassy that Truman had approved a policy for consideration by the cabinet. Point No. 1, Marshall said, was: "We stay in Berlin." A second major point, rejecting Murphy's proposal to open the land routes by force if necessary, was: "We will supply the city by air as a beleaguered garrison." A third point: "Subject to final checking by the Secretary and the President we will further increase US air strength in Europe."[35] Truman that same day approved, upon the urging of Clay, the dispatch to Germany of two squadrons of B-29s, the type of planes that had dropped atomic bombs on Japan.

The act was a gesture. The B-29s ordered to Germany, as was the case with two other squadrons later sent to Britain, were not modified for atomic bombs.[36] But that was a secret, and if anyone in the Kremlin chose to think they were, that was his business.

These historic events in the spring and summer of 1948 occurred in the midst of tempestuous presidential election-year political developments in the United States. High among these was the controversy that now flamed around the climax of the Palestine issue.

39. *Truman and the State of Israel*

THE JOY AMONG THE Jews over the recent General Assembly vote recommending partition of Palestine into a Jewish state and an Arab state was still vibrant in December of 1947 when, unbeknown to the public, chilling judgments began to temper American policy. The assembly's decision was barely two weeks old when the heavy fighting in the Middle East raised fresh doubts in Washington about the feasibility of partition. Even before the vote Loy Henderson had recommended, and Marshall had approved, an embargo on the export of American arms to the Middle East.[1] The policy, which did not restrain Britain from continuing to sell arms to the Arabs, although the British limited such sales, was announced December 5—to the Zionists' dismay.

Twelve days later someone in the State Department drafted a secret report recommending alternative courses in the Middle East. One of these was that the United States "should immediately announce that we have become convinced that the partition of Palestine is impossible of implementation" and that the problem should be returned to a special session of the General Assembly. At that session the United States should propose "a middle-of-the-road solution" and try to win support for it from Jews and Arabs. "If this should prove impossible," the draft said, "we should propose a UN trusteeship for Palestine pending agreement by the Arab and Jewish communities."[2] Favored by Henderson in his influential role as director of the Office of Near Eastern and African Affairs, trusteeship was an idea that had been simmering in the State Department for months.[3]

While a trusteeship was in operation, of course, there would not be a separate Jewish state and a separate Arab state. In effect, Palestine would be a ward of the United Nations instead of the League of Nations. The effect of such an official proposal on the Jews, if made known, would have been anguishing in the midst of their emotional state over the long struggle for partition and over the precarious situation prevailing in the Middle East.

Another secret report at the end of 1947 from Robert B. Macatee, the American consul general in Jerusalem, told of Arab preparations for war. As the crux of the dilemma Macatee noted that the United Nations had not announced who was going to enforce partition when the British withdrew in May. "We feel," he cabled, "that if the UN expects to be able to partition Palestine without forces to help maintain order and to enforce partition, its thinking is most unrealistic and its efforts will be in vain."[4] The British refusal to take any part in carrying out partition had put a new light on the problem for all concerned.

Meanwhile early in 1948 the Arab League tentatively decided to deny American companies oil pipeline rights until Washington changed its policy.[5] The League announced January 15 that the armies of its members—Egypt, Lebanon, Iraq, Saudi Arabia, Syria, Trans-Jordan, and Yemen—would occupy all of Palestine as soon as the British withdrew. The same day the Jewish Agency told the United Nations Commission on Palestine that either an international police force would have to impose partition or the Jews would have to be allowed to import arms and organize their own militia. The United Nations had no armed force, however. And London refused to allow the Jews to organize and train a militia while British forces were still present, although the forces of Irgun Zvai Leumi and the Stern Gang were increasingly effective.

Further impetus toward reconsideration of American policy occurred when Kennan's Policy Planning Staff circulated on January 19 a position paper based on a new look at the situation in the Middle East. According to the "top secret" document, the United States had voted for partition in the belief that a workable plan could be devised that would receive international support so long as the Arabs and Jews cooperated. Now, with the Arabs refusing to cooperate, this was a doubtful proposition.

"Therefore, one of the major premises on which we originally supported partition has proved invalid," the paper said. Without outside help, it continued, a Jewish state could not survive. For the United States to intervene with force on behalf of the Jewish state, the paper warned, would be regarded by the Arabs as a virtual declaration of war. Animosity toward Americans in the Moslem countries would, according to the paper, jeopardize important oil and pipeline concessions, air base rights, and trade. Enforcing partition would open the door to Soviet military and political penetration. Peace and security would be affected throughout the Eastern Mediterranean region. Furthermore anti-Jewish sentiment would be aroused around the world.

"In the United States," the paper predicted, "the position of the Jews would be gravely undermined as it became evident to the public that in supporting a Jewish state . . . we were in fact supporting the extreme objectives of political Zionism to the detriment of overall U.S. security."

The Policy Planning Staff recommended that the issue, now lodged in the United Nations Security Council, be returned to the General Assembly with a recommendation that that body investigate the alternative of trusteeship. Finally: "We should take no further initiative in implementing or aiding partition."[6]

An important aspect of the Palestine crisis was that it came at a time of growing tension in Berlin, Czechoslovakia, and other trouble spots and aroused concern in Washington as to whether the United States had the military resources to meet its global responsibilities if conflicts erupted. The discrepancy between manpower and obligations was discussed at a meeting of the National Security Council February 12. A question was raised whether some American ground units might have to be sent to Greece. Someone recalled a recent letter from the Joint Chiefs, saying that a dispatch of any sizable force to Greece would necessitate partial mobilization. This was five weeks before Truman finally asked Congress to restore the draft because of events in Czechoslovakia. Surveying the world situation in light of the total available armed forces, Marshall said that the United States was playing with fire while having nothing with which to put it out.[7]

Closer to the nerve, however, was the question before the Truman administration of whether establishment of a Jewish homeland in Palestine under the circumstances was really in the interests of the United States.

A school within the Department of State and the Pentagon, the views of which were more or less reflected by Forrestal, Marshall, Lovett, and Henderson, believed that war in the Middle East and loss of Arab friendship would be too high a price to pay for a Jewish state. Forrestal particularly advanced the view that American military reserves might be completely drained in the dispatch of forces to the Middle East as part of a United Nations contingent to enforce partition.[8] The opposing viewpoint, reflected by Truman's advisers, was that a Jewish homeland might be secured instead by lifting the arms embargo so that the Jews could get the weapons to defend their own state, perhaps aided by some United Nations action to deter other Arab nations from invading Palestine.[9] Truman was plainly worried by the argument that troops would be needed, and he insisted that American troops would not be sent to Palestine, except possibly as a part of a United Nations force.[10]

The approaching end of the British mandate, along with the continued fighting, brought the Palestine crisis ever closer to a climax. As the tension grew, State Department thinking, still withheld from the public, became increasingly weighted in favor of a change in United States policy from support of partition to advocacy of trusteeship. This shift was to have utterly explosive consequences, causing, among other things, a flash flood of internal controversy in the Truman administration over the question of the State Department's loyalty to Truman. A critical question, therefore, was what the president knew about the proposed shift, for which he bore the ultimate responsibility, and whether, or to what extent, he actually approved it before it was announced to the United Nations.

An apparent summary of the January 19 Policy Planning Staff's paper was in the White House by mid-February—at least it turned up, dated February 17, 1948, among Clifford's papers. This summary contained the suggestion that as an alternative to partition it might be necessary to consider another solution, such as trusteeship.[11]

Moreover, George Wadsworth, who had been serving as political adviser to the American delegation at the United Nations, was going to Iraq as ambassador and, before leaving, called on Truman February 4. Not only did the two of them discuss Palestine, but Wadsworth had submitted in advance a memorandum, which Truman told him he had read. The memorandum said that no solution to the Palestine problem could be found until the General Assembly's recommendation on partition was changed. The best course would be trusteeship, the paper added, saying: "Earliest possible establishment of such a trusteeship seems vital to prevent the present situation from further, perhaps irreparably, degenerating toward chaos."[12]

Without reference to this particular point, Truman told Wadsworth that he and the State Department saw eye-to-eye on Palestine and that he was keeping in close touch with Secretary Marshall and Under Secretary Lovett. Wadsworth said that to the diplomats dealing with the problem partition seemed unworkable. Truman ended the conversation by saying that he felt he could go along with what the State Department might recommend.[13]

The State Department's written communication to Truman on the issue was a long message sent him aboard the *Williamsburg* February 21 while he was cruising among the Virgin Islands. The first part of the message concerned a speech to be delivered in the United Nations Security Council February 24 by Ambassador Warren R. Austin. The head of the mission in New York, Austin was a portly former Republican senator from Vermont, who had been one of Truman's good friends in the Senate. The president had nominated him as United States representative to the United Nations in 1946 when Stettinius had resigned. Essentially, Austin's proposed speech was to enunciate the American interpretation of the legal situation in the Security Council. It was that the council was empowered to deal with any internal or external threat to the peace in Palestine, but was not empowered to enforce a recommendation by the General Assembly. In short, the council did not have the power to enforce partition—a debatable proposition but one not challenged by Truman.

The second part of the message to the *Williamsburg*—the more critical one in the end—dealt with matters that were not to be mentioned by Austin on the twenty-fourth but were submitted for Truman's "consideration and approval in relation to the further development of the problem." The message stated in unmistakable language that if, in the face of Arab intransigence, the Security Council was unable to develop an alternative to partition, the issue should be referred to a special session of the General Assembly.

"The Department of State considers," the message said, "that it would then be clear that Palestine is not yet ready for self-government and that some form of United Nations trusteeship for an additional period of time will be necessary."[14]

Whether Truman fully understood the implications, he must have known by this time, or should have known, that the State Department was moving toward a switch from partition to trusteeship. The State Department message had solicited his views, and on February 22 he cabled Marshall:

Your working draft of recommended basic position for Security Council discussion Tuesday received. I approve in principle this basic position. I want to make it clear, however, that nothing should be presented to Security Council that could be interpreted as a recession on our part from the position we took in the General Assembly. Send final draft of Austin's remarks for my consideration.[15]

The State Department then sent the president a text of Austin's speech and assured Truman it was not a recession from the position taken by the United Nations in the General Assembly.[16] After Austin spoke on the twenty-fourth, others were not so sure about this. James Reston of the *New York Times* reported from the United Nations that doubts had been raised among some delegations as to "whether the partition policy will really be enforced."[17] At the State Department's suggestion, Truman issued a public statement approving the speech.[18]

One further step occurred before the blowup that was coming. According to Lovett, he and Marshall conferred with Truman on the morning of March 8. Lovett said he told Truman that on March 5 the United States had met with failure in the

Security Council on a resolution Austin had introduced calling for acceptance of the General Assembly's recommendation on partition. "I said," Lovett recalled, "that we would have to have an alternative and that was the trusteeship proposal contained in the latter part of the draft statement. The president said we were to go through and attempt to get approval of the [General Assembly] resolution but if we did not get it we could take the alternative step. *That was prefectly clear.* He said it to General Marshall and to me. . . . *There was a definite clearance there.*"[19]

Supporting Lovett's account is a telegram that Marshall sent to Austin in New York at once—at noon that same March 8, saying that Truman had approved the policy of referring the Palestine issue to the General Assembly with consideration to be given to trusteeship.[20] Indeed Clifford two months later made a handwritten note: "Marshall to Austin March 8. President has approved draft statement."[21] "The suggestion that the mandate be continued as a trusteeship under the U.N.," Truman said in his memoirs, "was not a bad idea at the time."[22]

Within the State Department, then, preparations went forward for announcement of the new American position. A bizarre chain of events followed.

Jewish pressure on Truman had begun to mount again early in the presidential election year as partition failed to materialize, although the Jews were completely unaware that the United States government was moving toward abandonment of partition, at least temporaily. The new pressure got under Truman's skin. "Individuals and groups asked me," he recalled, "usually in rather quarrelsome and emotional ways, to stop the Arabs, to keep the British from supporting the Arabs, to furnish American soldiers, to do this, that, and the other." Finally he became so much annoyed that he refused to see any Zionist leaders.[23]

In the bright days following the General Assembly vote on partition Chaim Weizmann had departed for London on the way to Palestine. As anxiety rekindled among American Jewish leaders, however, he was importuned to return and, once back in New York, sought another appointment with Truman. Matt Connelly replied to Weizmann by letter February 12 that such a meeting was "out of the question."[24]

Thus matters stood on February 20, 1948, when Eddie Jacobson was awakened in the middle of the night at his home in Kansas City by a telephone call from New York from Frank Goldman, president of B'nai B'rith.[25] Goldman was in despair over Truman's isolation. None of the friendly politicians, not even Ed Flynn, Goldman said, could budge him. Goldman told Jacobson that Truman was about to depart for a vacation in the Virgin Islands and at Key West. He asked Jacobson if he would charter a plane at once—in the darkness of night—to try to catch the president at the White House and beg him to see Weizmann. The timing was impractical. Truman was on his way south while Jacobson was still in Kansas City. Jacobson wired Matt Connelly for an appointment. Truman replied from Key West in a letter February 27, explaining to his friend that Weizmann could not tell him, the president, anything he did not already know:

The Jews are so emotional, and the Arabs are so difficult to talk with that it is almost impossible to get anything done. The British have, of course, been exceedingly noncooperative. . . . The Zionists, of course, have expected a big stick approach on our part, and naturally have been disappointed when we can't do that.

As if reflecting the State Department view on the infeasibility of partition, Truman added: "I have about come to the conclusion that the situation is not solvable as presently set up."[26]

When Truman's vacation ended Jacobson flew to Washington and went to the White House March 13 without having an appointment. Connelly received him and, as usual, arranged for him to see Truman. Connelly adjured him, however, not to mention Palestine. Jacobson demurred.

Entering the Oval Room, he was pleased to see Truman tanned from his days in the sun, and the two men began their talk, as customary, by exchanging news about their families. Then Jacobson mentioned Palestine to Truman.

"He immediately became tense in appearance, abrupt in speech, and very bitter in the words he was throwing my way," Jacobson recalled in his account of the episode. "In all the years of our friendship he never talked to me in this manner or anything approaching it."

Truman told Jacobson he did not want to discuss Palestine or the Jews or the Arabs or the British. He was satisfied, he said, to let the issue take its course at the United Nations.

Jacobson would not yield. He reminded Truman of the admiration the president had expressed for Weizmann. Jacobson said that Weizmann was old and ill and had made a long trip to the United States to see the president. Truman's indignation had not subsided, however.

"He replied how disrespectful and how mean certain Jewish leaders had been to him," Jacobson recalled. Truman named them, but Jacobson omitted the names from his account of the meeting.

"I suddenly found myself thinking," Jacobson recalled, "that my dear friend, the President of the United States, was at that moment as close to being an anti-Semite as a man could possibly be, and I was shocked that some of our own Jewish leaders should be responsible for Mr. Truman's attitude."

Jacobson remembered that he could not mollify Truman "because, after all, he had been slandered and libeled by some of the leaders of my own people whom he had tried to help while he was in the Senate and from the moment he stepped into the White House." Truman's words and attitude added up, Jacobson felt, to a rejection of his request for a meeting with Weizmann; and he was, he recalled, crushed. In his despair he noticed, as he had on previous occasions, the model of an equestrian statue of Andrew Jackson on a table at the west side of the room. Jacobson suddenly found himself pointing to the statue and telling Truman that just as Truman had a hero in Andrew Jackson so, too, did Eddie Jacobson have a hero in Chaim Weizmann.

"Now," he went on, "you refuse to see him because you were insulted by some of our American Jewish leaders, even though you know that Weizmann had absolutely nothing to do with these insults and would be the last man to be a party to them. It doesn't sound like you, Harry, because I thought you could take this stuff they have been handing out to you."

Jacobson noticed that Truman had begun drumming on the desk. Truman swung around in his swivel chair and gazed out on the Rose Garden. Suddenly, he whirled back and looked Jacobson in the eye.

"You win, you bald-headed son of a bitch," he said. "I will see him."

Truman arranged the appointment but insisted it be kept secret. This was not an unusual procedure in such circumstances. In this case, however, it was to make difficult problems worse than they needed to be, because the State Department, moving according to its own schedule, was unaware that the president was about to discuss Palestine policy with Weizmann.[27] On March 16, according to Clifford's previously mentioned handwritten notes, Marshall had instructed Austin to make a statement on the new American policy in the Security Council "as soon as possible as Austin believes appropriate."

On March 18 Weizmann was spirited into the White House to see the president. That was, to keep things in perspective, the day after Truman had appeared before the joint session of Congress in the Czechoslovakian crisis and asked for Universal Military Training and resumption of the draft because events in Europe were, he had said, affecting the national security. Truman gave Weizmann a friendly reception and together they reviewed the Middle Eastern situation. According to his wife's memoirs, Weizmann particularly pleaded for the lifting of the American arms embargo and for continued support of partition. The memoirs of both Mrs. Weizmann and Truman indicate that the Zionist leader departed with a sense of understanding between Truman and himself.[28]

Twenty-four hours later, on Friday, March 19, Austin was recognized in the Security Council and set off a fire storm. Because war loomed upon the departure of the British, he asked the council to instruct the Palestine Commission to suspend its efforts to implement the partition plan. He recommended that the council call a special session of the General Assembly to reconsider the whole problem. Meanwhile, he proposed, a temporary trusteeship for Palestine should be established under the United Nations Trusteeship Council.[29]

The Jews were devastated. Rabbi Silver told the Security Council that Austin's proposal was "a shocking reversal," "a fatal capitulation" to Arab threats. Any change in the partition plan, he said, "will have to be imposed upon the Jewish community of Palestine by force." In Jerusalem David Ben-Gurion as chairman of the Executive of the Jewish Agency said: "It is we who will decide the fate of Palestine. We cannot agree to any sort of trusteeship, permanent or temporary—the Jewish state exists because we defend it." Jews flooded the White House with angry letters and telegrams. In some places Jewish war veterans paraded. Worshipers gathering in synagogues around the country Saturday, March 20, were overwhelmed by a sense of misfortune. As Weizmann was to say, it appeared that independence had been granted in the fall only to be withdrawn in the spring. Representative Celler called Austin's speech an "under-handed turnabout." It was apparent, the *New York Times* said in an editorial, that the White House was "utterly at sea."

Mrs. Weizmann wrote in her diary, "Chaim is nonplussed and indignant."[30] Publicly he remained silent, though he eventually expressed his opposition to trusteeship. In Kansas City Eddie Jacobson was dazed when someone telephoned him the news.

"Almost immediately," he recounted, "calls and wires started coming in from all over America, all telling me what a terrible traitor my friend, Harry Truman, turned out to be and how he betrayed the Jewish people and how he had violated his promise. . . . There wasn't one human being in Kansas City or anywhere else during those terrible days who expressed faith and confidence in the word of the President of the United States."[31]

By all reports Truman was astounded at the timing of Austin's speech and mortified at the seemingly false position he was in with Dr. Weizmann. According to Clifford, Truman said, "I assured Chaim Weizmann that we were for partition and would stick to it. He must think I am a plain liar."[32] Heatedly, Truman put pen to paper that Friday, scribbling on his calendar:

The State Dept. pulled the rug from under me today. I didn't expect that would happen. In Key West or en route there from St. Croix I approved the speech and statement of policy by Sen. Austin to U.N. meeting. This morning I find that the State Dept. has reversed my Palestine policy. The first I know about it is what I see in the papers! Isn't that hell! I am now in the position of a liar and a doublecrosser. I've never felt so in my life.

There are people on the third and fourth levels of the State Dept. who have always wanted to cut my throat. They've succeeded in doing so. Marshall's in California and Lovett's in Florida.[33]

On the face of it the explanation for the confusion was contained in Clifford's handwritten notes:

5. Marshall & Lovett left no word that President was to be informed when Austin was to speak.
6. Text of Austin's speech was not submitted to President for his approval.
(a) It was the same substance as the draft previously submitted to President.

Samuel Rosenman called on Truman on Saturday, the twentieth, and found him angry and agitated. Truman asked Rosenman if he knew where "the little doctor" was. He bade Rosenman find Weizmann and assure him that Truman had not known that Austin was going to speak when he did and that Truman was still for partition. Rosenman delivered the message to Weizmann at the Shoreham Hotel.[34]

Truman summoned Clifford and instructed him to call Marshall and Lovett, who were out of town, to ascertain what had happened.

"When Clifford called me," Lovett remembered, "he took the line that the President said he had never approved the so-called 'Mandate Speech' of Austin's." Thereupon Lovett drew up a private statement detailing the history of his, Marshall's, and the State Department's communications and discussions with Truman on the trusteeship question.[35]

In Los Angeles that Saturday Marshall called a press conference and said: "The course of action . . . which was proposed . . . by Ambassador Austin appeared to me, after the most careful consideration, to be the wisest course to follow. I recommended it to the Presdent, and he approved my recommendation."[36]

At the White House staff meeting that Saturday morning, the twentieth, Truman gloomily said that he had telephoned Austin and that Austin said he had spoken on instruction from the State Department.[37]

"The President said," Eben Ayers noted in his diary that day, "he had told Secretary Marshall and Undersecretary Lovett that he was not going to change our position and he did not believe they knew anything of it [the Austin speech]. . . . The President commented something about feeling 'blue'. . . . Clifford said he did not agree with the President that Marshall knew nothing of it. He said that, although he was speculating when he said this, he believed they had had such action in mind. The President said he did not believe Marshall knew of it or would have done it without talking with him.''

After the staff meeting Matt Connelly confided to some of his colleagues, according to Ayers, "that the President had approved some agreement, during the Caribbean trip, setting forth the new policy"—a reference to the State Department message sent to Truman aboard the *Williamsburg* February 21 and Truman's favorable reply.

At Truman's direction Clifford called to the White House that afternoon some leading State Department officials to ascertain what had happened. Among them were Charles Bohlen, then counselor of the department, Dean Rusk, then director of the Office of United Nations Affairs, and General Marshall Carter, special assistant to the secretary of state. "The P [Truman] had told us to get the facts," Ross, who was present, noted afterward. "Clifford was the chief inquisitor."[38] "Clark said, 'Who authorized this? Heads will roll,' " Bohlen recalled. The session collapsed, he added, when the State Department officials convinced Clifford that Austin had acted in accordance with the secretary of state's instructions.[39] This squared with Ross's written recollection also.

By Monday, March 22, Truman was cooling down. In a memorandum to Bohlen that day George Marshall said:

In my discussion of Palestine with the President today, he said that the reason he was so much exercised in the matter was the fact that Austin made his statement without the President having been advised that he was going to make it at that particular time. He had agreed to the statement but said that if he had known when it was going to be made he could have taken certain measures to have avoided the political blast of the press.[40]

At his press conference March 25 Truman read a statement intended to calm the controversy. He said that despite American support for it, partition could not be carried out peacefully in the circumstances. "We could not," he explained, "undertake to impose this solution on the people of Palestine by the use of American troops, both on [United Nations] Charter grounds and as a matter of national policy." Endeavoring to reassure Weizmann and the Jews, he said that trusteeship "is not proposed as a substitute for the partition plan but as an effort to fill the vacuum soon to be created by the termination of the mandate. . . . Trusteeship does not prejudice the character of the final settlement."[41]

Truman nevertheless completely supported Austin's speech. How, then, is the uproar of the preceding days to be explained?

Canny as he usually was in such matters, Truman seems not to have foreseen the elemental nature of the Jewish response to a proposal for trusteeship. Since the American plan was secret until March 19, there had been no advance public discussion or Jewish comment that would have foreshadowed the character of the reaction. It was a time when Truman was living under a waterfall of great events from Czechoslovakia to the approaching crisis over Berlin, and many problems were competing for his attention. The record contains no evidence that any of his advisers raised a warning that the Jews might explode with wrath over trusteeship. Lending credence to the hypothesis that Truman did not anticipate the consequences of the new policy was his complaint in his memoirs that the State Department should have known when it recommended trusteeship to him "that the Jews would read this proposal as a complete abandonment of the partition plan on which they so heavily counted."[42] The implication is that Truman did not know. As his press conference statement March 25 underscored, he believed, rightly or wrongly, that trusteeship would not replace partition for long but would merely postpone it until a settlement had been reached. In those terms it probably did not strike him in advance as a serious abandonment of Jewish interests, even though elements in the State Department were as strongly as ever opposed to the creation of a Jewish state.

A question persists as to whether Truman grasped that once trusteeship had been voted, the action would have superseded the General Assembly's resolution on partition of November 29, 1947, and that the political struggle for a Jewish state would have to have been waged all over again in the future, perhaps under circumstances less favorable to the Jews as the immediate horror of Hitlerism receded. It was because Truman may not have understood the full significance of his policy, or because the State Department did not make it clear to him, that Jews have justified the political pressure that the president so deeply resented. In this sense, as they see it, they were saving him from a step he did not intend to take.

At the time of his meeting with Weizmann March 18 Truman continued to think of his ultimate policy as partition, which may be why he never alluded to trusteeship with his caller, if he had thought about trusteeship at all. In his memoirs he reiterated his conviction that Weizmann understood his long-term goal.

The juxtaposition of events and the gap in communications combined to blow the affair sky-high. The State Department did not know that Truman was talking to Weizmann on the eighteenth, and Truman did not know that Austin was going to address the Security Council on the nineteenth. According to Ross, Truman assumed that the alternative of trusteeship would not be proposed by the United States until a vote had been taken in the Security Council, dramatizing, in Ross's words, "the impossibility of putting over the partition plan."[43]

Bits and pieces of the State Department's written and oral communication with Truman were such that they could indeed have left this impression.[44] Furthermore, in his message to Marshall from the *Williamsburg* February 22 Truman had stipulated that "nothing should be presented to the Security Council that could be interpreted as a recession on our part from the position we took in the General Assembly." Truman was referring to Austin's speech of February 24, but still the State Department took liberties with the spirit of his instructions.

Caught off base by the harsh Jewish reaction to Austin's speech, Truman had vented his ire against the State Department in his diary March 19 in a typical one of his passing outbursts. "What caused all the trouble?" Ross wrote in his previously mentioned notes. "The cause lay in the fact that no final check had been made with the P. before Austin spoke. . . . No pronouncement of the momentous nature of Austin's should have been made without prior consultation with the P. or someone of his staff." Yet the fact that the State Department did not send him an advance copy of the speech seems not to have been a breach of custom. "Actually," wrote the American diplomat, Dr. Philip C. Jessup, in examining these events later, "it was not usual to ask the President to approve speeches to be made at the United Nations once the general line of policy had been cleared with him."[45] Could Truman promptly and publicly have reversed Austin, if he had wished to? Unthinkable, Ross noted: it would have made Truman appear vacillating and ignorant of what had been going on and "could only have been accomplished with wholesale repudiation of the State Department."

"What a dilemma!" Ross lamented.

In 1976 Clark Clifford came close to implying that the State Department had been disloyal to Truman. Addressing the annual meeting of the American Historical Association in Washington, Clifford charged that the department had tried to "sabotage" Truman's efforts on behalf of a Jewish state and said that Austin's speech had been a "de facto reversal of the President's policy," known in advance to Marshall and Lovett.[46]

As the historical record stands, it is clear that Truman knew that the State Department contemplated a switch from partition to trusteeship. It appears that intentionally or unintentionally he gave Marshall and Lovett to understand that Austin could go ahead with the speech that Truman had approved in principle in the Virgin Islands. It is a fact that neither before nor after the speech did Truman put his foot down on the change in policy. The resulting embarrassment may have been due as much to misunderstanding and confusion on the part of Truman and Marshall as to bureaucratic "obstructionism," to use Clifford's word in 1976.[47] Plainly, Truman, to whom personal loyalty in politics was one of the most exalted of human virtues, did not suspect Marshall and Lovett of disloyalty and insubordination on the Palestine issue. If he had, it is inconceivable that later in the even more treacherous waters of the Korean War he would have appointed Marshall, and, on Marshall's retirement, Lovett as secretary of defense.

Events swept toward a greater drama. On April 12 the General Zionist Council in Tel Aviv declared: "We have decided, relying on the authority of the Zionist movement and the support of the entire Jewish people, that upon termination of the mandatory regime there shall be an end of foreign rule in Palestine, and that the governing body of the Jewish state shall come into being."[48] Furthermore, in the spread of the fighting Jewish troops continually got the better of Arab forces, making it appear increasingly plausible that the Jews could defend their own state. Under American leadership, it is true, the United Nations persisted in its search for a political solution. One by one, however, the various proposals fell by the wayside.

The Security Council adopted a resolution calling for a cease-fire and truce and created a Truce Commission to supervise a halt in the fighting. Nevertheless the fighting raged on. The Jews would not accept a truce so long as, they charged, Arab troops from Syria, Lebanon, Trans-Jordan, and Iraq were in Palestine.[49] The Jews feared that the Arabs would use a truce to strengthen their military position. On the other hand, as Macatee, the United States consul general in Jerusalem, notified Marshall March 22, the Arabs were determined to continue to fight "until Zionism [is] eradicated."[50]

The Security Council called a special session of the General Assembly, which convened April 16 and at which the United States continued to press for trusteeship. But the Jews rejected trusteeship as a barrier to statehood. The Arabs opposed it lest trusteeship prove a subterfuge for partition.[51] And most members shied away because they could not see how trusteeship could be enforced.[52]

As May 14 and the end of the mandate drew nearer the United States proposed a ten-day extension of the British mandate as an emergency measure. The British refused to consider it out of fear that such a first step might lead to indefinite extension.[53]

The options, therefore, were running out. Meanwhile great pressure was building on Truman to recognize the new state that the Jews were preparing to proclaim May 14.

On May 4 Dr. Jessup of the United States delegation to the General Assembly sent Rusk a telegram, saying that the Soviet Union might recognize the Jewish state upon its establishment. Possibly, he suggested, this could provide Moscow with a legal basis "for invoking article 51 of the charter and providing assistance to the Jewish state to fend off 'aggression.' "[54] Such a move might in turn give the Soviets their dreaded foothold in the Middle East. In the ensuing days the idea that the Soviets might rush in and be the first to recognize the Jewish state became a bugbear, particularly in the White House, lending urgency to plans for American action. This was, it will be recalled, a time when the first Berlin blockade had already been imposed by the Soviets, and Washington was nervous about the possible outbreak of war in Europe.

On that same May 4 Clifford penciled the following notes:

1. Recognition is consistent with U.S. policy from the beginning.
2. A separate Jewish state is inevitable. It will be set up shortly.
3. As far as Russia is concerned we would do better to indicate recognition.
4. We must recognize inevitably. Why not now [?]. . . .[55]

Democratic leaders were urging recognition as a way to appeal to Jewish voters and perhaps head off disaster in the presidential election. Clifford was both a source and a conduit of this pressure. Sensitive to Jewish demands, he not only argued the case for recognition on his own but on behalf of others of like mind, including Sam Rosenman, Democratic politicians, and Max Lowenthal, an occasional outside adviser to Truman. Assisting Clifford, David Niles worked on drafts of statements Truman might make in connection with recognition.

Then forty-one and new to fame, Clifford suddenly found himself the adversary of the renowned General Marshall, sixty-seven, rich in power and public esteem and occupying a unique place in the affections of the president. Marshall did not believe the time had come for the establishment of a Jewish state and said so bluntly May 8 to Moshe Shertok of the Jewish Agency, who, as Moshe Sharrett, would be foreign minister of the new state. Recalling the conversation, Marshall said:

"I . . . stressed that it was extremely dangerous to base long-range policy on temporary military success. There was no doubt but that the Jewish army had gained such temporary success but there was no assurance whatever that in the long-range the tide might not turn against them. I told Mr. Shertok that they were taking a gamble. If the tide did turn adversely and they came running to us for help they should be placed clearly on notice now that there was no warrant to expect help from the United States, which had warned them of the grave risk they were running.[56]

In a long-distance call May 11, however, Rusk gave Jessup a clearer picture of how the wind was blowing in Washington. In the White House, he said, it was believed that, despite the activities in the General Assembly, the definitive events were occurring in Palestine.

"It is not according to plan," Rusk continued, "but nevertheless there is a community in existence over there, running its own affairs. Now that community apparently is going to get an open shot at establishing itself. We have told them that if they get in trouble don't come to us for help in a military sense. Nevertheless I don't think the boss [Truman] will ever put himself in a position of opposing that effort when it might be that the U.S. opposition would be the only thing that would prevent it from succeeding."[57]

Forty-eight hours before the British mandate was to expire Truman called a strategy conference. It was in the opening round of statements in this meeting May 12 that Marshall told of his warning to Shertok four days earlier.

Truman gave Clifford the floor, having instructed him before the meeting to argue the case for recognition.[58] Marshall, however, bristled at Clifford's mere presence, since it was obvious that the special counsel to the president was motivated to a large extent by political considerations in an issue that the secretary of state regarded as a purely international affair under his jurisdiction.

Clifford began by discounting the likelihood of a last-minute truce and said that partition was coming into effect in fact. He urged Truman to get the jump on the Soviet Union by granting recognition first. Recognition was consistent with United States policy, he said. According to Marshall's account of the meeting, Clifford said that the act of prompt recognition "would have the distinct value of restoring the President's position for support of the partition of Palestine." In other words the act of recognition would, in Clifford's opinion, restore Truman's standing with the Jews to where it had been before Austin's March 19 bombshell. To make certain of beating the Soviets to the draw Clifford advocated that Truman announce his intention to recognize the next day, May 13, twenty-four hours before the state was due to come into existence.

Making a note of Clifford's recollections of the meeting, George Elsey, who had not been present, later wrote that Marshall had "glared" at Clifford, that the general's reaction was "violent"—an exaggeration, according to Lovett.[59]

It was Lovett who first rebutted Clifford. Referring to Clifford's discount of a last-minute truce, the under secretary of state noted that the issue was still legally before the Security Council and that the United States was a member of the Truce Commission. The United States, he continued, could not unilaterally discharge the Security Council of the issue. Any such attempt, he said, would be most unbecoming in light of the American efforts to promote a truce.

Raising a point that bore directly on uproarious scenes ahead, Lovett observed that the special session of the General Assembly had been called at the request of the

United States and was still considering the question of the future government of Palestine. On this ground alone he opposed premature recognition. He alleged that the idea was a transparent attempt to win Jewish votes. He ventured that it would lose more votes than it would win.

"Finally," Lovett said, according to Marshall's account of the meeting, "to recognize the Jewish State prematurely would be buying a pig in a poke. How did we know what kind of Jewish State would be set up? At this stage Mr. Lovett read excerpts from a file of intelligence telegrams and reports regarding Soviet activity in sending Jews and Communist agents from Black Sea areas to Palestine."

State Department officials often argued that a Jewish state might become a Communist lair.

Lovett saw no cause for urgency in granting United States recognition ahead of Soviet recognition.

The meeting then came to a startling climax. General Marshall, a man who was considered by Truman and by other of his distinguished contemporaries to be perhaps the greatest American of the twentieth century, a man who undoubtedly could have been president of the United States himself, if he had wished, delivered his opinion.

"I remarked to the President," he recalled, "that, speaking objectively, I could not help but think that the suggestions made by Mr. Clifford were wrong. I thought that to adopt these suggestions would have precisely the opposite effect from that intended by Mr. Clifford. The transparent dodge to win a few votes would not in fact achieve this purpose. The great dignity of the office of the President would be seriously diminished. The counsel offered by Mr. Clifford was based on domestic political considerations, while the problem that confronted us was international.

"I said bluntly that if the President were to follow Mr. Clifford's advice and if in the elections I were to vote, I would vote against the President."

Harry Truman had never had to swallow harder medicine than that. Yet the respectful relationship between him and Marshall was strained, not broken. Marshall did not challenge the president's right to grant diplomatic recognition.

As the meeting ended, Marshall and Lovett told Truman that upon termination of the mandate they would take another look at the Palestine situation in light of existing facts. Truman said he was aware of the difficulties and dangers in the situation, to say nothing of the political risks involved for him.

The next day, May 13, he did not announce in advance at his press conference, as Clifford had recommended, that he intended to recognize the new state. Marshall and Lovett had killed that suggestion, as Clifford conceded.[60] When a reporter inquired of Truman's intentions, Truman replied, "I will cross that bridge when I get to it."[61]

In fact by then he was well on his way across. Behind the scenes the climax unfolded. David Ginsberg, a well-connected Washington lawyer, who was advising the Jewish Agency, telephoned Weizmann in New York on the afternoon of the thirteenth and counseled him to write a personal appeal to the president for recognition and rush it to Washington by messenger on an overnight train.[62]

Lovett sent Clifford a copy of an opinion by Ernest A. Gross, legal adviser to the State Department, holding that while there would be no legal bar to recognition, the United States "probably should not recognize the existence of any new state" while the General Assembly was in special session.[63] This was the same point Lovett had emphasized at the White House meeting. Its importance lay in this fact: while working for a truce, the United States delegation in New York had stressed to other delegations that no action of a political character should be taken that would, during the deliberations, alter the status quo or prejudice the claims of Arabs or Jews. "This position of ours," Jessup has written, "was generally understood to apply primarily to the establishment of a Jewish state. . . . We had persuaded other delegations of the correctness of our position and induced them to come forward and carry a large share of the burden of the argument. Thus they had become publicly identified with our position." The American delegation did not believe "that the United States would actively promote the establishment of a Jewish state while the special session was still wrestling with the problem of finding an overall solution," Jessup said.[64]

On the morning of May 14, last day of the mandate, Weizmann's appeal was delivered to the White House.

I deeply hope that the United States . . . will promptly recognize the Provisional Government of the new Jewish State. The world, I think, would regard it as especially appropriate that the greatest living democracy should be the first to welcome the newest into the family of nations.[65]

Clifford had lunch with Lovett at the F Street Club and told him that Truman was, in Lovett's words, "under unbearable pressure to recognize the Jewish State promptly." Lovett again urged against what he called indecent haste, lest the United States sacrifice the good effect "of many years of hard work in the Middle East with the Arabs." At least, he said, Ambassador Austin and the United States delegation in New York, as well as leading Allied governments, should be notified that recognition was coming. Could not the president wait a day or so in the interest of orderly procedure? Clifford replied that Truman could not risk having the news of recognition leaked in advance.[66]

Lovett returned to his office. Clifford worked feverishly. Among other things, he made arrangements with Eliahu Epstein, as "Agent of the Provisional Government of Israel," to send Truman a formal request for recognition. Epstein, who as Eliahu Elath would in 1949 be the first Washington ambassador of the new state, dispatched a letter. It notified Truman that the state of Israel had just been proclaimed as an independent republic within the borders approved by the General Assembly resolution on partition. The Act of Independence would become effective at one minute after 6 P.M. in Washington. "I have," Epstein said, "been authorized by the provisional government of the new state to tender this message and to express the hope that your government will recognize and will welcome Israel into the community of nations."[67]

Telephone calls were flashing back and forth between the White House and the State Department. No longer in doubt as to what was going to happen, Lovett called Clifford at 5:30 and told him that the General Assembly was in session attempting at American instigation to find a political solution. Lovett said that the session would be over by around 10 P.M. and asked if the announcement, to which he now expressed no opposition, could be delayed until after adjournment. Clifford agreed to consult Truman, but said that time was critical and he did not believe the president would wait.

"My protests against the precipitate action and warnings as to consequences with the Arab world," Lovett was to recall three days later, "appear to have been outweighed by considerations unknown to me, but I can only conclude that the President's political advisers, having failed last Wednesday afternoon [at the May 12 meeting] to make the President a father of the new state, have determined at least to make him the mid-wife."[68]

At 5:45 Clifford telephoned Rusk and said the President would announce recognition shortly after six o'clock. Clifford asked Rusk to notify Austin.

"But this cuts across what our delegation has been trying to accomplish in the General Assembly," Rusk protested.

"Nevertheless," Clifford replied, "this is what the President wishes you to do."[69]

The General Assembly was meeting in Flushing Meadow, Queens, in what had been the New York City Building at the New York World's Fair 1939–40–41. Rusk telephoned from Washington and had Austin called from the floor. Rusk's message appalled the head of the United States mission, obviously. Instead of returning to the Assembly floor to notify Dr. Jessup and Ambassador Francis B. Sayre, who were taking part in the proceedings, Austin got in his limousine and went home, leaving his associates totally unprepared for the storm that was about to break. "My guess is," Rusk surmised afterward, "that he thought that it was better for the General Assembly to know very clearly that this was the act of the President in Washington and that the United States Delegation had not been playing a double game with the other Delegations."[70]

At about 6:15, as a vote was coming up on trusteeship for Jerusalem, a rumor, seemingly bizarre enough to make delegates laugh, spread through the General Assembly chamber, the *New York Times* reported. When the rumor reached Jessup and Sayre, they laughed, too. The rumor was that President Truman had just recognized Israel. No such thing could have happened, the two American diplomats agreed, because they, as the United States delegates, had not been informed. Nevertheless John C. Ross, an alternate member of the delegation, hurried over to them to report that other delegations were asking for comment on a bulletin about recognition on the news tickers. With the chamber now astir, Dr. Alberto Gonzales Fernandez of Colombia formally asked the United States delegation for a report. Sayre went to the podium and said, apologetically, that "for the time being," he had no information to impart.

Ambassador Belt of Cuba, angry because he had, three hours earlier, helped the United States get the trusteeship resolution through committee, said he was surprised that the United States delegation did not know what was going on. The Soviet and Polish delegations knew, he said, adding that it was now pointless to vote on the trusteeship resolution.

Frantically, Jessup sent for the news ticker copy and learned what had happened.[71] At 6:11 Charles Ross had announced at the White House:

This Government has been informed that a Jewish state has been proclaimed in Palestine, and recognition has been requested by the provisional government thereof.

The United States recognizes the provisional government as the *de facto* authority of the new State of Israel.[72]

De jure recognition was not granted for the technical reason that the new government was provisional. Nevertheless *de facto* recognition was full and unconditional recognition.

The General Assembly was by now in pandemonium, in the midst of which Ambassador Belt made known his intention of rising to announce that Cuba would withdraw from the United Nations rather than sit in an organization in which a leading member was guilty of duplicity. Porter McKeever, press officer of the United States delegation, physically restrained the Cuban ambassador from going to the podium. He did so, Rusk later revealed, by sitting in Belt's lap.[73]

Andrei Gromyko charged that America's "unprincipled conduct" had put the United Nations in a "ludicrous situation." Mahmoud Bey Fawzi of Egypt asserted that the General Assembly session had been a "fake." "For four weeks," cried Dr. Charles Malik of Lebanon, "we were dupes and the whole thing was a show and a game."

In Washington Marshall got wind of what was happening. Sensing the mortification of Austin, Jessup, Sayre, and the other American diplomats, he telephoned Dean Rusk. "Rusk," he ordered, "get up to New York and prevent the U.S. delegation from resigning *en masse.*"[74]

Rusk got to New York as fast as he could and was relieved to find that the delegates were not quitting.

Eleanor Roosevelt, who had not been on the Assembly floor that evening, wrote to Marshall two days later, saying that the "way in which the recognition of Palestine came about has created complete consternation in the United Nations." "Several of the representatives of other governments have been to talk with me since," she said, "and have stated quite frankly that they do not see how they could ever follow the United States' lead because the United States changed so often without any consultation."

Marshall replied: "We were aware here of the unfortunate effect on our situation with the United Nations, which is much to be regretted. More than this, I am not free to say." [75]

In a letter to the Historical Office of the State Department June 13, 1974, recalling the episode, Rusk wrote:

I cannot vouch for this, but there was a story later that some of Secretary Marshall's friends had told him that he ought to resign because of this incident. He was reported to have replied, "No, gentlemen, you do not accept a post of this sort and then resign when the man who has the Constitutional authority to make a decision makes one. You may resign at any time for any other reason, but not that one.[76]

Certainly, the quotation has the aura of Marshall, but it is hard to believe that the rumor had much substance. Marshall's biographer, Forrest C. Pogue, has found no evidence to support it, and the two associates who were closest to the secretary of state in 1948—Robert Lovett and Marshall Carter—never heard of the story until

Rusk's letter was made public in 1976.

On May 15, 1948, Arab armies invaded Israel. The first Arab-Israeli war had begun.

Weizmann called Eddie Jacobson to a meeting in his hotel in New York May 16. Since the new state did not yet have an ambassador in Washington, Weizmann asked Jacobson to see Truman and bring up such questions as the lifting of the arms embargo and the granting of a loan to Israel. Before Jacobson left New York for Washington on the seventeenth Weizmann received word of his election as Israel's first president. He requested Jacobson, therefore, to present his formal greetings to President Truman. When Jacobson arrived at the White House, Truman welcomed his old business partner as the ambassador of Israel. "What a thrill it was!" Jacobson recalled. Speaking on Weizmann's behalf, he asked Truman to do what he could to encourage the Export-Import Bank to lend Israel $100 million. He also pleaded that the arms embargo was hurting the new state. Truman made no specific promises, but he offered to do all he could to help Israel.[77]

So, with the granting of diplomatic recognition, one phase of the American-Israeli relationship had been accomplished and, with Truman's offer of assistance, another unending phase was born. Commitment to the existence of Israel and support in the form of money and arms gradually became a fixture of United States foreign policy. Truman did not bring Israel into being. The Jews did that. But his decisions then and later began what eventually became a special relationship between the two countries.

However halting and disjointed some of Truman's actions were as the Palestine crisis approached a climax, it is hard to see how he could have taken a basically different course through 1948. The Second World War had left Palestine as an unavoidable problem on the White House doorstep. All the alternatives for reaching some other kind of settlement, whether through mass Jewish immigration, partition, federation, trusteeship, or extension of the British mandate, fell by the wayside. By dint of history, of immigration, legal and otherwise, and of their own efforts to build and defend a community, the Jews had a destiny in Palestine that was beyond Truman's power to change, even if he had wished to, which was not the case. According to Samuel Rosenman, Truman's familiarity with the Old Testament had given him a sense of appropriateness about the Jewish return to Palestine. In the United States, moreover, the Jews had achieved an influence that a president, whatever his momentary annoyances, could neither banish nor ignore. Never was there an issue in which foreign policy and domestic politics were so thoroughly intertwined.

At a private meeting with Marshall February 19, 1948, Truman had assured him, in the secretary of state's words, that "whatever course we considered the right one we could disregard all political factors." On April 30 Truman conferred with Rusk and said, as Rusk recalled, "that he did not wish to approach the matter from the point of view of personal political considerations but wanted to get the matter settled."[78] While accepting the goal of a Jewish homeland, Truman wanted to move in a way that was consistent with what he and his advisers believed to be the security of the United States.

Yet as the proposed devices of settlement collapsed and a vacuum developed in Palestine, the resolution of the issue came down to a Jewish proclamation and defense of Israel. This ending offered Truman a dramatic chance to assist in the establishment of a Jewish homeland and, in the process, to appeal in his own seemingly desperate political straits to Jewish voters. The Republicans had ever been alert to the issue. Dewey, with his particular constituency, had already displayed in the 1946 campaign a willingness to outbid Truman for Jewish votes. Correctly gauging the extent of Marshall's loyalty, Truman therefore lunged at the political opportunity, ignoring in the bedlam such niceties as the momentary situation in the General Assembly.

Finally, however, above the maneuvers and strategies, above the pressures and irritations loomed the visage of Adolf Hitler. Three years after the full disclosures about the gas furnaces it is inconceivable that any president of the United States in office in May 1948 would have done essentially other than that which Truman did.

40. *The Liberals versus Truman*

W HEN THE Jews turned on Truman after the proposal to shelve partition of Palestine in favor of trusteeship in March, his candidacy seemed hopeless and, to many, preposterous. The Democratic extreme left—the Wallace following—was gone. Part of the South was going. Many New Deal liberals were looking for an exit. And now another important element of the Roosevelt coalition—the Jewish vote—was in rebellion.

"As you no doubt know," Senator Francis J. Myers, Democrat, of Pennsylvania, wrote to Truman, "there has been a veritable uproar in this country over the American position in the United Nations on Palestine. . . . A few Democratic party leaders in my state, in the lower political levels, have resigned in protest and have stated categorically that they can no longer support our party because of what was 'done' in the Palestine case. Many Pennsylvanians of Jewish extraction seem to be as bitter against you and the party over this incident as some of our brethren from the South profess to be."[1]

A Gallup poll taken in March indicated that Truman would lose the election to either Dewey or Stassen or Vandenberg or MacArthur. The March 13 issue of the *Nation* appeared with an article, "Must It Be Truman?" An April issue of the *New Republic* carried a front-page editorial by Michael Straight, the publisher, saying that Truman should retire.

A week after Ambassador Austin's blockbuster in the General Assembly two of President Roosevelt's sons, Franklin, Jr., and Elliott, issued separate statements urging the Democrats to draft Eisenhower. They did so despite that fact that Eisenhower, alerted by the Pentagon after the White House had got wind of what was afoot, had telephoned Franklin earlier that same day. Eisenhower told him that it was a dangerous time to give the impression abroad that the president's leadership was being weakened. He also insisted that he himself would not be a candidate.[2] Meanwhile a third Roosevelt son, James, California state Democratic chairman and national committeeman, worked behind the scenes for an Eisenhower draft. "Eleanor herself called several times to discuss it," recalled Hubert H. Humphrey, then mayor of Minneapolis, who announced his support of Eisenhower or Douglas.[3] Walter Reuther and David Dubinsky told James Loeb that Truman's nomination would be a disaster for the Democratic party and the Liberal cause.[4] According to Arthur J. Goldberg, then counsel to the CIO, Philip Murray, maneuvered behind the scenes for Eisenhower's nomination.[5]

Former Secretary of the Interior Ickes had his moment of revenge. Writing to Truman March 27, he asked him to retire and added:

You have the choice of retiring voluntarily and with dignity, or of being driven out of office by a disillusioned and indignant citizenry. Have you ever seen the ice on a pond suddenly break in every conceivable direction under the rays of the warming spring sun? That is what has happened to the Democratic Party under you, except that your party has not responded to bright sunshine. It has broken up spontaneously.[6]

The Liberal party in New York withdrew its support from Truman and called for an Eisenhower draft. So did Senator Pepper. Senator John C. Stennis, Democrat, of Mississippi, also fell in line. Truman was affronted. Having himself offered Eisenhower the nomination only to have it rejected, he thought the party should now rally around him.

"There is speculation," the *New York Times* reported March 28, "that he would fail to win the Democratic nomination for President."[7] Many Democratic aspirants to other offices feared that Truman's name at the head of the ticket would drag them to defeat. Chester Bowles, seeking the Democratic nomination for governor of Connecticut, made a splash of publicity by urging on a national radio broadcast that Truman yield to Eisenhower, after which he sent Truman a lofty letter of explanation. "Dear Chester," Truman replied. "I'm sorry to say I hadn't noticed any statement of yours in the press but I have been expecting it. Everybody, of course, has a right to his viewpoint and a right to express it."[8]

J. Edgar Hoover knew what was going on. He sent a messenger to Vaughan with a letter containing information "from a highly confidential and reliable source which I thought would be of interest to the President and you." The source had reported on a conversation between Bowles and Tilford Dudley, assistant director of the CIO-PAC. Dudley, naturally, had been in touch with Philip Murray. Dudley told Bowles that Murray wanted the Americans for Democratic Action to cooperate in an Eisenhower draft movement. Bowles assured Dudley, according to Hoover's source, that this would be a splendid arrangement because if "we're going to try to remove him [Truman], we'd better get all the help we can."

Dudley explained that Murray did not want the CIO to become too much involved in the intrigue at first for the sake of its own image. It would be better for men like Bowles and Dudley to get the movement going; then organized labor could help at a propitious moment. Bowles agreed, according to the report, but said that labor leaders like Murray and Reuther should speak out, at least as individuals.

"It was further pointed out by Bowles," Hoover reported, "that if Philip Murray, Walter Reuther and Jack Kroll [national PAC director] would come out against President Truman, stating that it was impossible to get support for him but they desired to stick with the Democratic Party, this alone would almost be enough to kill President Truman's chances."[9]

The day after the election Truman telephoned Murray in Pittsburgh to thank him for his help in the campaign. Murray cried.[10]

When Eisenhower's name had been entered in the New Hampshire Republican primary by a group of admirers in January, he had it withdrawn and categorically declined to be a candidate. With the Democratic boom in progress he issued a statement saying that "under no conceivable circumstances" would he accept a draft. Instead of taking this declaration at face value and seeking out a willing candidate of some stature to challenge Truman, the panicky Democratic foes of the president did him the greatest possible service by plunging all the more energetically up the blind alley after the hero of Normandy, thereby insuring that when the convention opened the only opposition of note to Truman would be a phantom.

Meanwhile Truman was winning delegates in state Democratic primaries and caucuses and assuring himself of control of the convention not only through these delegates but through the Democratic National Committee and powerful congressional allies, including Rayburn, Barkley, Senator Scott Lucas of Illinois, and Senator Myers of Pennsylvania.

Less than two weeks after Eisenhower's rejection of a draft the national board of Americans for Democratic Action held a special meeting and advocated an open Democratic convention, saying that "this Nation has the right to call upon men like Dwight D. Eisenhower and William O. Douglas if the people so choose."

"The ADA actions particularly made Mr. Truman apoplectic," Clifford recalled. "He felt he had consistently followed the policies of FDR, and here were the liberals after Ike. He concluded that the liberals didn't give a damn about ideals. They were more interested in winning an election."[11]

The irony of it was that as the convention approached Truman grew increasingly liberal, yet the liberals increasingly shied away from him because they did not think he had the stature to vanquish the Republicans in November.

When a Jackson Day dinner was held in Los Angeles April 12 James Roosevelt drew applause by mentioning Eisenhower. When his turn on the rostrum came, Howard McGrath tried to get support for Truman by recalling his record. "Can you ask for more than this in leadership?" the Democratic national chairman asked. "Yes," many in the audience shouted.

Emil Rieve, president of the CIO Textile Workers Union, and James B. Carey, secretary-treasurer of the CIO, came out for Eisenhower. Many assumed, rightly, that the latter was reflecting Murray's views.

Writing to James W. Gerard, an old-time Democrat and former ambassador to Germany, Truman observed:

General Eisenhower, I am sure, is not a candidate for President and I don't think he would be a candidate on the Democratic ticket anyway—his whole family are Republicans and I know them all.[12]

"The main difficulty with the Democrats and with my friends," he also wrote to an acquaintance in Missouri, "is that they seem to have an inferiority complex and there isn't any reason for such a situation. The last three years have been about as difficult a period as the country has ever been through. We have sixty million people at work and it seems to me that the world situation is slowly and gradually straightening out."[13]

Truman was also having trouble with the blacks. It was over discrimination in the armed forces, and the trouble grew so serious that some black leaders threatened a campaign of civil disobedience. The esteemed A. Philip Randolph personally warned the president that blacks might refuse to serve in uniform.

The predicament came about as a result of Truman's request to Congress for Universal Military Training and revival of Selective Service. On the one hand this put Southern members in a position to vote against these proposals unless Truman played down civil rights. On the other hand it gave militant blacks a fresh opportunity to press for equal treatment in the armed services.

Truman was vulnerable to the black agitation. The President's Advisory Commission on Military Training had recommended that segregation should be banned in any universal training program submitted to Congress. The bill, however, contained no such provision. The President's Commission on Civil Rights had branded discrimination in the armed forces especially repugnant. Thus, as will be recalled, when Truman submitted his civil rights message in February he promised that he would soon issue an executive order to eliminate discrimination in the civil service and the armed forces. As the danger of a Southern revolt from the Democratic party developed, preparation of such an order lagged.

Philip Randolph and other black leaders called on Truman March 22 to ask that an antisegregation provision be incorporated in the Selective Service legislation. Truman seemed jolted when Randolph told him that around the country he had found blacks who did not want to bear arms in defense of democracy abroad unless they found democracy at home. Truman said he was doing the best he could.

Randolph took a graver stand before the Senate Armed Services Committee. Blacks, he said, would refuse to serve if the new draft law did not prohibit segregation. "I personally pledge myself," he stated, "to openly counsel, aid and abet youth, both white and Negro, to quarantine any Jim Crow conscription system." Did this mean, Senator Morse asked, that Randolph would counsel disobedience to the draft if the United States was at war? "Yes," Randolph replied. That would be treason, Morse observed. "I would be willing," Randolph said, "to face that . . . on the theory . . . that we are serving a higher law than the law which applies to the act of treason."

When the Selective Service renewal legislation was passed without a ban on segregation, Randolph launched the League for Non-Violent Disobedience Against Military Segregation. Its objective was to persuade Truman to issue an executive order eliminating segregation in the armed forces before the new draft law became effective August 16. Otherwise, Randolph told him in a letter, the League would urge whites and Negroes to refuse to register under Selective Service. Unless Truman acted, he added, "Negro youth will have no alternative but to resist a law, the inevitable consequences of which would be to expose them to un-American brutality so familiar during the last war."[14]

With the political campaign approaching and a crisis already at hand in Europe, this put Truman in a corner. He had less than two months to work his way out of it.

While the charade of the Eisenhower draft continued, the issues that were to become the staples of Truman's campaign were being forged in conflicts between the president and the Republican-run Eightieth Congress. His assault on the Republican party from the railroad tracks of America in the fall drew its substance largely from a series of congressional actions and presidential responses in the spring, as well as, to be sure, from the conflict over the Taft-Hartley Act in the 1947 session.

In the spring of 1948 the Republicans, with considerable Democratic support, sidetracked Truman's proposed $40 "cost-of-living" credit for each taxpayer and dependent and passed their own tax bill. It raised the exemption for each taxpayer and dependent from $500 to $600 and permitted couples filing joint returns to split their incomes. These and other changes, it was estimated, would reduce taxes by $4.8 billion. Truman vetoed the bill as being inflationary and reckless in the face of the critical situation abroad. The same day Congress overrode his veto. In Truman's campaign speeches the measure became "the rich man's tax bill"—it "was not passed for the benefit of the common everyday man."[15]

On three occasions in the spring Congress became involved in Social Security questions that provided Truman with ammunition in the fall.

Congress passed a Republican bill excluding from Social Security—at least until other arrangements were made—certain news venders, on the ground that they were independent contractors, not employees covered by existing Social Security regulations. Truman vetoed the bill, warning that removal of persons from the protection of Social Security threatened the integrity of the system. Congress overrode the veto.

The Treasury Department announced it would start collecting Social Security taxes from hundreds of thousands of door-to-door salesmen, insurance agents, truck and taxicab drivers, pieceworkers, and others previously considered independent contractors but now, as a result of recent Supreme Court decisions, held to be employees and thus eligible for Social Security benefits. Republicans felt that in such case these persons should be covered by special legislation. Congress passed a Republican measure countermanding the Treasury's decision and classifying the hundreds of thousands as independent contractors after all, thus excluding them from Social Security. Truman vetoed the bill, saying Social Security should be expanded, not contracted. Congress overrode his veto the same day.

In May he sent up a special message on Social Security, proposing, in language not intended to be concealed from voters, liberalization of payments and other benefits. He said that old age benefits were "seriously inadequate," having been adjusted last in 1939.[16] Republicans accused him of politics and shelved his message.

In Truman's campaign rhetoric these actions translated into: "The Republican Eightieth Congress actually passed a law not to extend Social Security but to take Social Security away from hundreds of thousands of workers. That's the way they kept their promises. I vetoed the measure. Ninety-eight percent of the Republicans in Congress voted to override my veto."[17]

By 1948 controversy surged around the question of whether the Tennessee Valley Authority should be allowed to expand its generating capacity to cope with the dramatic increase in postwar electric power consumption. Advocates of public power clamored for such a policy. Private industry and conservatives were scandalized at this "socialistic" proposal for government competition with private industry. Truman brought the controversy to a boil by siding with the public power advocates and asking Congress to provide $4 million to start building a steam generating plant at New Johnsonville, Tennessee.

Liberals in Congress lined up with Truman, but bearing down on the hearings were conservative and business forces led by the chambers of commerce and the

National Association of Electrical Companies. The House Appropriations Committee under John Taber eliminated Truman's request. The way the voters heard it from Truman in the fall the Republicans "really messed up our national power policy" and invited a threat of a power shortage. "They even refused funds for the Tennessee Valley Authority to build a steamplant to help furnish power needed for our work on atomic energy."[18]

Congress passed the Reed-Bulwinkle bill authorizing common carriers to agree among themselves on rates and fares, subject to approval by the Interstate Commerce Commission, without being subject to antitrust prosecution. The bill would have killed two pending antitrust suits against railroads. Truman vetoed it, holding that the legislation was monopolistic and gave private groups substantial control over the transportation industry with "serious potential harm to the public."[19] Congress overrode his veto. The moral drawn by Truman in the campaign was the influence of the railroad lobby on the Republicans.

Truman wrote to Speaker Martin asking that the House pass legislation for federal aid to elementary and secondary schools. In his budget message in January the president had included an item of $300 million for the purpose, and the Senate had acted favorably. With the House procrastinating, Truman warned Martin that the postwar baby boom was hastening the day when existing schoolrooms would be swamped.[20] It was all politics, Joe Martin told reporters. The question never got beyond the House Committee on Labor and Education.

In a typical Truman campaign speech this came out: "They refused to provide aid to education. In several messages I suggested that . . . the education of the grades is in a condition that is going to cause us serious trouble in the next generation if we don't do something about it. Teachers are overworked—they are underpaid. There are not adequate facilities, and there are teachers who are teaching as many as fifty-five to seventy-five pupils."[21]

Truman urged enactment of the Taft-Ellender-Wagner housing bill. The House Rules Committee voted not to report it. The echo from the rear platform of the Truman train: "It is almost a crime against the public."[22]

Truman asked Congress for legislation permitting the immigration of war refugees of all faiths. Congress passed the Displaced Persons Act, but included a cutoff date that apparently excluded a number of Jewish and Catholic refugees. The way Truman put it to campaign audiences: "This display of intolerance aroused such a storm of protest from all fair-minded people that I thought the Republicans might be glad of a chance to correct the injustice they had done to the good people of those faiths. I gave them that chance. Did they use it? They did not."[23]

Believing that the people were fed up with the New Deal, the Republicans voted with gusto to pass conservative measures and override Truman's vetoes. They were not through yet, either. A bill perhaps packed with more political dynamite than any of the others—one providing for a new charter for the Commodity Credit Corporation—was still inching through committees toward a final vote. Outside the committee rooms no one seemed to be paying any attention to it.

The gloom over the Democratic party that spring did not daunt Truman. The harsh opposition by the Republican Congress was no more than he had expected, and the legislation he had most wanted—enactment of the Marshall Plan, a great landmark of modern history—had been obtained skillfully. Two events in April held particular political promise. One was the disclosure that Truman would go to California in June to deliver the commencement address at the University of California at Berkeley. The other was his appearance at the convention of the American Society of Newspaper Editors in Washington, involving an experiment that was to succeed, famously.

Dr. James F. Bender of the National Institute of Human Relations had stated the opinion that Thomas Dewey's vocabulary and diction constituted "the most perfect type of American English."[24] Moreover Dewey was endowed with a baritone so rich that as a young man he had considered a career as an opera singer. The opposite was true of Truman. The moment he started to read a speech his voice went flat. His delivery was monotonous. With his thick glasses, he had trouble returning to a line once he had raised his eyes to look at the audience. Bright lights often bothered him. His diction must have horrified Dr. Bender. He had a tendency to say "hr-ever" for *however,* "freign" for *foreign,* and "b'lieve" for *believe. World* sometimes sounded like "war." *Small* and *all* were nasal. He could chew *individual* to bits and referred to the country as the *"Yoo-*nited States."

Nevertheless, in his early campaigns in Missouri he had spoken effectively without texts. And his staff observed that in talking extemporaneously to small groups in the White House his wit, colloquialisms, and flourishes had been captivating. With the campaign in mind, therefore, someone in the White House suggested that he should experiment with an impromptu talk before larger audiences in public. He agreed, and the appearance before the editors was chosen as the occasion.

He first read an after-dinner speech about inflation. When this bore was over, he told the editors he was going to talk to them off the record about Soviet-American relations. As was to be the case with his whistle-stop speeches, he had before him notes and outlines, prepared by Charles Murphy in this instance, to refer to or even, if necessary, to read. He chatted about Potsdam and Stalin, remarking, "I like old Joe—not a bad guy when you get a chance to talk face-to-face." The Soviets "have a different code of morals from ours—if they have any. They are materialists. They do not believe in a moral code as we understand it."[25] Thrilled at coming to Washington and getting the inside dope from the president himself, the editors practically gave Truman an ovation, thereby guaranteeing that he would adopt a style of campaigning that two thirds of them would denounce on their editorial pages.

A clue to Truman's mood as the national conventions approached resounded in his speech at the Young Democrats Dinner at the Mayflower May 14, four hours after recognizing Israel. Condemning the "calamity howlers," he said: "I want to say to you that for the next four years there will be a Democrat in the White House, and you are looking at him."[26]

41. *A President Comes Out Fighting*

ROLLING ACROSS Ohio on the fine morning of June 4 was a seventeen-car train about to become a symbol of the most colorful and astonishing political campaign in modern American history. After an overnight run from Washington the California-bound Presidential Special was approaching its first stop in Crestline, Ohio. Everywhere the passengers—reporters, photographers, Secret Service agents, Army Signal Corps operators in the communications car, and White House assistants—were astir, and the end car, the "Ferdinand Magellan," was bustling with last-minute preparations.

Specially built for the president of the United States during the Roosevelt administration at a cost to the government of one dollar, the Ferdinand Magellan was a model of comfort and safety. The undercarriage had a shield to protect passengers, one in particular, from any bomb that might be placed on the tracks. The green-tinted windows were bulletproof. In the dining area stood a table large enough for twelve settings. There were five staterooms, among them the president's private quarters, the amenities of which included a shower. Toward the rear of the car was a living area, walls paneled with limed oak. A green carpet bore a sofa and several overstuffed chairs. Viewed from the outside the most striking feature of the car was a canopied rear platform adorned with the presidential seal. Attached to the back railing was a lectern from which stemmed a microphone connected with loudspeakers overhead.

The train stopped on an embankment leading into Crestline. A crowd of about a thousand persons swarmed around the rear platform. Television sets were a rarity then, and spectators peered for a sight of their visitor, whom most of them had seen only in newsreels in motion picture theaters and who was being endlessly portrayed in editorials, political columns, and cartoons as a miscast and bungling little politician who could not do much that was right in the White House but who would not be there much longer, fortunately. The door of the Ferdinand Magellan opened, and the visitor stepped through the blue velvet curtain, a good-looking man with a wide, friendly grin lighting a face remarkably unlined in his sixty-fifth year. Poised, square-shouldered, and trim in a summer suit, he expressed his thanks in a neighborly way to those who had come to greet him.

"You know how intriguing it is, and helpful it is," he said, "for the president to get away from the White House and get to see the people as they are. The president, you know, is virtually in jail. He goes from his study to his office and from his office to his study, and he has to have guards there all the time. . . . when you get out and see people and find out what people are thinking about, you can do a better job as President of the United States."[1]

After recalling with a chuckle that he was on a "non-partisan, bipartisan trip," he put in a word for former Governor Frank J. Lausche, who was running for a new term in Ohio. Then he was off to Fort Wayne, Indiana, where he told another similar crowd how all his life he had been an admirer of Mad Anthony Wayne.

When, in midafternoon, the train pulled into a railroad yard in Gary surrounded by factories and filled with a large crowd of workers, Truman suddenly changed tone. Bluntly, he attacked the Eightieth Congress for rejecting economic controls that he had proposed. Blaming it for the rising cost of living, he said:

This Eightieth Congress has not seen fit to take any action. They have decided that the National Association of Manufacturers and the . . . Chamber of Commerce of the United States . . . know all about prices and price controls.

He asked the workers to vote for a new Congress, one "that will work in the interests of the common people and not in the interests of the men who have all the money."[2]

While the airplane had by 1948 become the principal means of travel by the president and other politicians, the campaign train still appealed to Truman. In traditional style, his favorite candidates of the past had stumped the country by rail, and Roosevelt had made effective use of the train on trips camouflaged as nonpolitical inspection tours of federal projects. The idea of a similar trip by Truman had been flickering in the White House for months and began to take form after the University of California had sounded out Washington on the president's delivering the commencement address.[3] An honorary degree was to be thrown in for good measure, and Truman, traveling at government expense because the trip had been declared nonpartisan, was on his way.

Fun and embarrassment awaited in Omaha. The fun was the reunion of the Thirty-fifth Division. In a parade Truman, doffing his hat right and left, marched for several blocks with his old outfit, Battery D, 129th Field Artillery, alongside the battery's barber, Frank Spina. When Truman dropped out of line at the reviewing stand, "Omaha Joe" Whisman, in cowboy garb, riding a horse, gave the Secret Service a novel scare by lassoing the president. Fortunately, the rope was not tied to the saddle. The embarrassment came that evening when he went to Ak-sar-ben (*Nebraska* spelled backward) Coliseum on the outskirts of town to deliver a farm speech. The hall held ten thousand seats. Perhaps one thousand persons showed up, and only the hardiest could do anything but cringe for him when Truman walked out on the stage into the vast emptiness. The excrutiating moment seemed the perfect symbol of a hopeless campaign.

The best available information was that the public had believed that the meeting was restricted to the Thirty-fifth Division and stayed away. But so did the veterans, who had seen Truman that afternoon and sought other diversions at night. In sum, the effort to get out a crowd had been botched. Truman realized this the moment he approached the hall and saw the sparsely filled parking lots. Ed McKim, his former sergeant in Battery D, now an Omaha businessman, had been in charge of arrangements and was riding with Truman when he, too, spotted trouble and apologized.

"Eddie," Truman said, as McKim recalled his words, "I don't give a damn whether there's nobody there but you and me. I am making a speech on the radio to the farmers. They won't be there—they'll be at home listening to that radio. They're the ones I am going to talk to."[4]

With that resolve Truman strode on stage as if before a standing-room-only audience and gave radio listeners an earful of denunciation of Congressional delay on the farm bill. Outside the minds of the farmers, however, the largely vacant hall preempted public attention. It became the big joke of the day and was one of the many incidents that helped fix the enduring opinion among experts and laity alike that Truman's campaign was a pathetic waste of time. Recalling Ak-sar-ben long afterward, Truman told McKim, "That was one of the best things that happened to me in my whole campaign. It made a martyr out of me."[5]

The farther west Truman traveled the taller the corn grew—in field and rhetoric. At Pocatello, Idaho he referred obliquely to the years of effort by his opponents to link him with the misdeeds of the Pendergast machine.

I am coming out here so you can look at me and hear what I have to say and then make up your own mind as to whether you believe some of the things that have been said about your president.

I have been in politics a long time, and it makes no difference what they say about you, if it isn't so. If they can prove it on you, you are in a bad fix indeed. They never have been able to prove it on me.[6]

He relaxed overnight at Sun Valley where, just before the presidential party departed by motorcade for Idaho Falls June 8, the makings of another celebrated embarrassment for Truman took shape. Carey, Idaho, lay along the day's route, and before breakfast the mayor of the town telephoned Charles Ross to invite Truman to speak at the dedication of an airport. Ross and some reporters had closed the bar at Sun Valley the night before, and the press secretary had awakened with such a hangover as made the thought of talking with the mayor of Carey, Idaho, forbidding. Ross told a Secret Service agent to take down the details. The agent, probably in not much better shape than Ross, got them wrong in some respects, after which he passed on to General Vaughan the request that the president speak and the circumstances as he had recorded them. Vaughan asked if the man to whom the airport was being dedicated had been killed in the war. That was the agent's understanding.

When Truman finally arrived at Carey, it seemed appropriate, therefore, to find a uniformed honor guard on hand. "I am honored," the president said, "to dedicate this airport and present this wreath to the parents of the brave boy who died fighting for his country—" A gasp from the crowd interrupted him. Someone, apparently the mother, cried out that it was not a boy, it was a girl. Frantically, Truman responded, "Well, I am even more honored to dedicate this airport to a young woman who bravely gave her life for our country." It was all a disaster. The field was named Wilma Coates Airport in memory of a sixteen-year-old girl who had been killed in a plane crash nearby, some said as a result of her boy friend's stunting. Her parents were upset. Truman was upset. He apologized and they responded graciously. But, of course, on the heels of Ak-sar-ben the news of the incident made it seem another absurdity of the Truman campaign.

Truman rode in silence the rest of the way to Idaho Falls where the train was waiting. He had in mind a speech to deliver in town on the merits of municipally owned power plants. In the main square a crowd was on hand. The motorcade stopped, and he made the speech and headed for the railroad station. When he arrived he discovered a larger gathering behind the Ferdinand Magellan, a meeting which the local committee had billed as the event of the day, taking the White House staff by surprise and catching Truman completely unprepared. He climbed up on the rear platform, rattled off some inane sentences and told members of his staff he would see them when the train departed.

"He called the meeting, I am sure," Charles Murphy recalled, "for the purpose of dressing the staff down, but when the time came for him to do that, he couldn't quite manage to scold us."[7]

Instead he parceled out specific assignments for future stops. Truman, as far as is known, never raised his voice to his staff.

That night the embarrassments were eased by a noisy welcome in Butte, Montana, from a crowd huge in proportion to the size of the city and one whose enthusiasm moved Truman to a good lambasting of the Eightieth Congress. "If this Congress goes away without passing an agricultural bill, without passing a housing bill, without doing something about prices," he said, "this Congress has not done anything for the country. . . . I am out here to tell you the truth, which you haven't been getting."[8]

The next day he was a real firecracker. When the train stopped in Spokane, Senator Warren G. Magnuson, Democrat, of Washington, who was accompanying him in that state, handed him a copy of that morning's *Spokane Spokesman-Review*. Magnuson remarked that the paper was as Republican as the *Chicago Tribune*. Actually, its play of the political news that morning was fair and the editorial page carried a friendly welcome to the president. When Truman stepped from the train, Rhea Felknor, a reporter, asked him. "How do you like being in a Republican stronghold?"

"Do you work for this paper, young man?" Truman countered. When Felknor said he did, Truman snapped:

"The *Chicago Tribune* and this newspaper are the worst in the United States. You've got just what you ought to have. You've got the worst Congress in the United States you have ever had and the papers—this paper—are responsible for it."[9]

Later that day Truman apologized to Felknor.

The Northwest had just been struck a blow by the worst flood of the Columbia River since 1894; and before a large audience in downtown Spokane Truman turned the disaster into a denunciation of Congress for skimping on reclamation projects. He said that "you are not going to get those projects as long as you have a Congress that believes in the theory of Daniel Webster: that the West is no good and there is no use wasting money on it. There are still men in Congress who are following Daniel Webster, and they are chairmen of key committees which make these appro-

priations." He insisted that he was trying to carry out the liberal Democratic platform of 1944 but was not getting help from Congress.

"That is partly your fault," he said. "In the election of 1946 you believed all
the lies that were published about your President. And two-thirds of you didn't even
go out and vote. Look what the other third gave you! You deserve it. Now, if you let
that sort of situation continue—you have got a chance to remedy it this fall—if you
let that sort of situation continue, I won't have any sympathy with you. You will get
just what you deserve."[10]

From there he drove to Grand Coulee Dam, where many of the traveling reporters who had already boarded the press bus at the Spokane station when Truman
was making his crack about the worst Congress caught up with him and sought an
explanation. The Eightieth, he told them, was the worst Congress since the days
when Thaddeus Stevens was a leader of the radical Republicans in the Reconstruction. This modified his earlier statement, already bulletined by the wire services. On
the roadway surmounting the dam, reporters were shouting at Truman to make
themselves heard above the waterfall, trying to establish just how bad he thought
the Eightieth Congress was.

"Can't we stand on your earlier statement?" one fairly yelled.

"Go right ahead," Truman said.

As "Worst Congress" filled the headlines, Republicans retorted that Truman
was the worst president in history. The *Chicago Tribune* called him a "nincom-
poop." He was a "nasty little gamin," a "Missouri jackass," said Representative
Cliff Clevenger, Republican, of Ohio. Taft went on radio and proposed that
Congress adjourn until a new president was elected. Then the senator put his foot in
it. Addressing the Union League Club of Philadelphia, he accused Truman of
"blackguarding Congress at every whistle station in the West." The Democratic
National Committee telegraphed officials of thirty-five cities and towns on Truman's itinerary to ask how they liked being called "whistle-stops," which was
railroad parlance for communities classified as too insignificant to enjoy regular
scheduled train service. Responses were unfavorable to Taft. "Must have the wrong
city," replied the mayor of Eugene, Oregon. Out of the incident grew the enduring
term for Truman's style of campaigning.*

Unmistakably, the blend of error, comedy, folksiness, and political head-
splitting was stirring great curiosity about Truman's itinerant Punch-and-Judy
show, and crowds grew larger as it moved along.

"You know, this Congress is interested in the welfare of the better classes,"
he said from the balcony of the Elks Club in Bremerton, Washington. "They are not
interested in the welfare of the common, everyday man."

"Pour it on, Harry," someone shouted.

"I'm going to—I'm going to," he replied.[11]

In Seattle a greater crowd turned out to see Truman than had welcomed Roosevelt. Moving on to Tacoma, Washington, Truman said, ". . . I had to come out
here and let you look at me and let you see for yourself what the facts are with

---

* See "whistle-stop," *Webster's Third New International Dictionary* (unabridged).

regard to what has been going on in the last three years. I don't think there is a President in the history of the United States who has been as thoroughly misrepresented as I have been."[12]

"Well, this certainly is a very great pleasure," he told the people of Albany, Oregon, from the rear platform. "I thought I saw all of Oregon in Portland and Salem. Apparently, I didn't."

"You're close enough to see your dimples," a woman exclaimed.

"Not dimples, they're wrinkles," Truman said. "You don't have dimples at sixty-four."[13]

On one of his last stops in Oregon that June 11 he took it into his head to tell the people of Eugene about Stalin and caused something of a sensation. Recalling Potsdam, he said:

I got very well acquainted with Joe Stalin, and I like old Joe. He is a decent fellow. But Joe is a prisoner of the Politiburo. He can't do what he wants to. He makes agreements, and if he could he would keep them. But the people who run the government are very specific in saying that he can't keep them.[14]

While this topsy-turvy analysis was similar to a comment he had made before the American Society of Newspaper Editors, the earlier remark, being off the record, was not reported. Furthermore that dinner was in mid-April. By June 11 the situation in Berlin was much more dangerous, and American policymakers, dismayed at the headlines out of Oregon, preferred to have Stalin perceived as a ruthless, aggressive dictator instead of as a decent chap and pal of the president of the United States. Lovett and Bohlen got in touch with Clifford to plead for an end to such folklore. Clifford agreed to try to persuade Truman not to reiterate how much he liked old Joe.[15] Truman dropped the tune.

On the next leg of the journey he breezed into California and told the people of Davis: "You know, I am on a non-political trip. I am going down here to Berkeley to get me a degree."[16] That afternoon he delivered a well-received foreign policy speech before fifty-five thousand persons at the commencement exercises in the stadium of the University of California. In view of the worsening situation in Berlin, the State Department hierarchy, the White House staff, and outsiders like Rosenman, Robert Sherwood, and Louis Nizer, an attorney, all had a hand in the seven drafts the speech went through.[17] Truman said:

The great issues of world peace and world recovery are sometimes portrayed as disputes solely between the United States and the Soviet Union. This is not the case. . . . We are not waging a "Cold War."

The cleavage that exists is not between the Soviet Union and the United States. It is between the Soviet Union and the rest of the world. . . .

The door is always open for honest negotiations looking toward genuine settlements . . .[18]

Monday, June 14, in Los Angeles was one of the outstanding days of the entire trip. The schedule included a motorcade from the railroad station to the Ambassador Hotel, a speech before the Greater Los Angeles Press Club and then private appointments. One of these was with James Roosevelt, who was going to take time out from trying to draft Eisenhower to pay his respects to Mr. Truman. This was bound to be interesting.

The welcome in Los Angeles was tremendous. Behind a mounted sheriff's posse the motorcade moved under showers of confetti through streets lined with perhaps a million people. "Honest John," a used-car dealer, sent up his own fleet of skywriters to emblazon "Welcome President Truman" above the city. Mexican-Americans turned out in native Mexican dress. At one corner a group of blacks displayed a sign: "The Sixty-second District Republicans Welcome President Truman—Thanks for the Civil Rights Program."

The Press Club luncheon was a spirited affair, with Dinah Shore serenading Truman with "You Made Me Love You." All this boded ill for the Eightieth Congress. Aroused for the fray, Truman listed eight measures that Congress should pass before adjournment. These were the Taft-Ellender-Wagner housing bill, a new appropriation for the Bureau of Labor Statistics, the administration's program to broaden Social Security, a federal health program, aid to education, the farm bill, stand-by economic controls and funds for reclamation, irrigation and public power.[19]

"On just about every important public issue," wrote Charles Lucey of the Scripps-Howard newspapers, analyzing Truman's trip, "the President has decided to carry the banner of Franklin Roosevelt."

At four o'clock Jimmy Roosevelt arrived at the presidential suite at the Ambassador. Matt Connelly received him, took him into the sitting room, and then left him alone with Truman and, always nearby, Henry Nicholson of the Secret Service. Roosevelt was an operator, a "man of no political ideals," Ickes once said.[20] Long addicted to fast cars and café society, he had been his father's assistant in the White House, making many enemies among the New Dealers. He was a marine officer during the war and was now maneuvering to be the Democratic bigwig in California, aiming for the governorship and perhaps beyond. Nicholson watched him as he strode up to Truman, affable and towering above the president in height. The next thing Nicholson saw was Truman's right forefinger jab into Roosevelt's chest.

"Your father asked me to take this job," Truman said, as Nicholson recalled his words. "I didn't want it. I was happy in the Senate. But your father asked me to take it, and I took it. And if your father knew what you are doing to me, he would turn over in his grave. But get this straight: whether you like it or not, I am going to be the next President of the United States. That will be all. Good day."

Truman turned and walked out on a silent James Roosevelt.[21]

Heading back to Washington that night, the train made a late operational stop in Barstow, California. No meeting had been scheduled, and Truman had already retired when he learned that a small crowd was waiting to see him. Appreciative, he went out on the rear platform in a blue bathrobe and blue pajamas for a neighborly chat. A woman remarked that he sounded hoarse. "That's because I ride around in the wind with my mouth open," he smiled. When the train reached Dodge City, Kansas, he said: "I think I have definitely fixed the issues which are before the country now. It is merely the facts: are the special privilege boys going to run the country, or are the people going to run it?"[22]

He returned to Washington June 18, three days before the Republican National Convention was to meet in Philadelphia and hear former Representative Clare Boothe Luce of Connecticut say: "Let us waste no time measuring the unfortunate man in the White House against our specifications. Mr. Truman's time is short; his situation is hopeless. Frankly, he is a gone goose."

Nothing seemed to justify her remarks more completely than the nomination of the ticket of Thomas Dewey and Earl Warren. Geographically, it was perfect, balanced by the governor of New York and the governor of California, states the loss of which would be crippling for Truman. Dewey and Warren were seasoned, respected politicians, each a moderate, each with a good record, each a poor target for campaign attacks, each a good campaigner in the past, and each a man of seemingly presidential stature. Even Truman's mother-in-law, Mrs. Wallace, is said to have told friends it was a waste of time for him to run against such a ticket.

On the day after the convention had adjourned, Truman strode out the northwest gate of the White House on his morning walk, accompanied by Nicholson. Truman asked him what he thought of the ticket. The Secret Service man ventured that a Warren-Dewey ticket would have been stronger. "That's right, Nick," Truman agreed. Reflecting on Dewey, he added: "Before this campaign is over I will take the mustache off that fellow, you can be sure of that."

As they walked, Truman said the Republicans had made a mistake in not nominating Taft.

"He was deserving of it, and he is an honorable man," Nicholson recalled Truman's saying. "They think he would be easy to defeat because he doesn't have labor support. Well, he has. He has plenty of labor support when he runs and wins in Ohio for the Senate. He would be a very much tougher opponent for me than Governor Dewey."[23]

Before Congress adjourned it passed only one of the eight measures Truman had designated in Los Angeles—the Agricultural Act of 1948. This measure, extending price supports, was by no means the heart of the political drama in the farm belt in 1948, however.

Rather, a routine bill that was to influence the outcome of the election, though no one imagined it at the time, was S. 1322. That June the charter of the Commodity Credit Corporation, the agency through which Federal farm loans and subsidies were extended, came up for renewal, provided for in S. 1322. Reflecting the influence of the grain lobby and the economy-minded House Banking and Currency Committee, Congress wrote into the bill an obscure provision that was potentially costly to farmers. To qualify for price supports farmers had always had to store their grain in facilities approved by the government, either in commercial bins or ones maintained by the Commodity Credit Corporation. The new provision, however, prohibited the CCC from acquiring new bins, the number of which already had been declining since the war. In the event of a moderate harvest the new provision would not have drastic effect because commercial storage facilities could handle the grain. But if bumper crops grew, then the CCC could not provide additional bins near the farms as in the past, and the farmers would stand to lose money for lack of storage space.

Ironically, the Democrats in Congress raised no objections, and Truman signed the bill without comment. When he also signed the Agricultural Act three days later, however, he issued a statement about it and noted in passing that the new restrictions in S. 1322 could cause financial injury to the farmers.[24] No one paid much attention then. As weeks passed, however, it became evident that the Republican party had a great deal riding on the size of the harvests in late summer and fall, just as the campaign would be hitting its stride.

The opening of the Democratic National Convention July 12, also in Philadelphia, was approaching with two issues still causing a furor. One was the problem of a civil rights plank that would not split the party. The other was the motley movement to nominate Eisenhower or, if that failed, Justice Douglas.

The rebelliousness in parts of the South that erupted after Truman's civil rights message February 2 had gathered momentum during the spring. Already faced with the Wallace defection, Truman began applying the brakes when the threat of a Southern decampment became unmistakable. Asked at his press conference March 11 whether he would send Congress bills to carry out his message, he replied: "Congress never feels very happy when the Executive sends them bills and says, 'This is it.' When I was in the Congress it was customary for the Congress to write its own bills. If they request me for suggestions, I will be glad to make them."[25] Cooled, too, was the ardor for executive orders, promised in the February message, to deal with racial discrimination in the civil service and the armed forces. Drafts had been attempted within the administration, but the effort lagged, as Elsey noted, with the approval of McGrath, Ewing and other "politicos."

Without reversing any of his positions, Truman was side-stepping to keep the South in line. While, for example, he had paraded almost every other imaginable liberal issue of the day on his California trip, he had scarcely mentioned civil rights. Back in Washington, he met with Representative Rankin of Mississippi. Leaving the White House, Rankin told reporters: "I am not without hope that the Democratic convention will reach a satisfactory agreement on civil rights. If that convention adopts the same plank that was inserted in the platform of 1944, I am assured that it will be adhered to." Carrying no specific recommendations, the 1944 plank said that racial and religious minorities had the right to live, develop, and vote equally with all citizens "and share the rights that are guaranteed in the Constitution. Congress should exert its full constitutional powers to protect those rights."

The liberals wanted to discard this vague language in favor of endorsement of specific proposals contained in Truman's civil rights message. Such a plank would have meant a showdown with the South that the White House wanted to avoid. In his meeting with the southern governors in February, McGrath had suggested the 1944 plank as a model for the 1948 platform. Unquestionably, Truman favored such a compromise, and a draft was prepared in the White House that was also acceptable to Senate Democratic leaders, including Myers, the platform committee chairman.

So on the weekend before the convention a subcommittee responsible for civil rights reported to the committee a plank that was a rewrite of 1944. What this compromise strategy overlooked, however, was that in 1948, partly because of Truman's policies, civil rights had become a much more crucial issue than it was in

1944. Even conservative southerners opposed the compromise, but an onslaught came from liberal delegates, foremost among them Mayor Hubert Humphrey and former Representative Andrew J. Biemiller of Wisconsin, officials of Americans for Democratic Action. The platform committee redrafted a somewhat stronger version, but only after rejecting the liberals' proposal for specific commitment to the terms of Truman's civil rights message. The fight, however, was only beginning.

The Eisenhower boom meanwhile had reached a crescendo in farcical scenes. Principles gurgled down the drain in a torrent of expediency, designed to nominate a winner. Led by Americans for Democratic Action, liberals were all over Philadelphia fighting for a hot civil rights plank while at the same time striving to replace Truman, a candidate in the Roosevelt tradition, with Eisenhower, who, six years later, as president, was to turn his back in disapproval on the *Brown* decision and refuse to utter a word of support for Chief Justice Warren and the Supreme Court for having outlawed racial segregation in the public schools.

At the instigation of an unchastened James Roosevelt and under the sponsorship of an incongruous coalition including Humphrey, Strom Thurmond, Governor Tuck of Virginia, Governor Laney of Arkansas, Senator Lister Hill of Alabama, Chester Bowles, Mayor William O'Dwyer of New York, and Colonel Jacob M. Arvey, Illinois Democratic leader, a caucus was scheduled in Philadelphia just before the convention to try to dump Truman. Common sense had fled. On July 5, the day after Mayor Hague had announced that he would throw New Jersey's thirty-six votes to Eisenhower, the general had issued a statement, again declining to run. "I will not at this time," he said, "identify myself with any political party and could not accept nomination for any public office or participate in a partisan political contest."

"In my first talk with the President this morning when I discussed the Eisenhower statement briefly with him," Assistant White House Press Secretary Eben Ayers noted in his diary July 6, "the President showed some disgust with what Eisenhower had said, indicating he felt it was weasel-worded and he referred to the General as a s – – – a – –."

Sure enough, Roosevelt, Hague, and Senator Pepper of Florida, bemused by Eisenhower's phrase "at this time," read the statement as meaning he would accept a draft.[26] Eisenhower had not said he would refuse to serve if elected, John M. Bailey, the Connecticut leader, pointed out. Pepper announced he would place the general's name in nomination. On July 9, before the caucus, Eisenhower blew the house of cards apart in a telegram to Pepper saying: "No matter under what terms, conditions or premises . . . I would refuse to accept. . . . I ask you to accept my refusal as final and complete, which it most emphatically is."[27] The shock waves were so great that even the minor boom for Douglas, led by Leon Henderson, ADA chairman, collapsed. One by one, most dissidents declared for Truman. Not so Pepper, however. The ultraliberal Senator announced that he would run for president in place of Eisenhower. "This is no time for politics as usual," he said.

On the evening of July 14—the Wednesday of convention week—Truman was back aboard the Ferdinand Magellan, bound for Philadelphia to deliver his acceptance speech if all went well in the balloting. For the moment, Truman and Charles Murphy were alone together by the radio in the presidential car, listening to a broadcast of the proceedings. Suddenly, Truman became perturbed. He complained to Murphy that Leslie Biffle in his role as sergeant at arms of the convention was trying to swing the presidential nomination to Alben Barkley, the Senate minority leader.[28] The thought had been hounding Truman all week. In notes he had made on Monday he commented: "My *"good"* friend Leslie Biffle spends all his time . . . running Barkley for President."[29]

The 1948 convention was the first ever televised. Thus Truman was the first President ever to be able to watch the proceedings from the White House. It appeared to him that a demonstration for Barkley after the latter's keynote speech had been promoted by Biffle.

The convention had opened in despair. Then the first night the delegates were born again with a dose of old-time Democratic religion administered in the galvanic keynote address by Barkley, a log-house-born Kentucky raconteur and spellbinder, a former Paducah prosecuting attorney, who had taken his seat in Congress the day Wilson was inaugurated president, on March 4, 1913. Having delivered the keynote addresses at two previous Democratic conventions, having seconded Alfred E. Smith's nomination in 1932 and having placed Roosevelt's name in nomination in 1944, Barkley was a seasoned orator, brimming with merciless ridicule of the Republican party. Not only did his performance revive the convention, but it made him an obvious candidate for vice-president—indeed, the only serious contender since Justice Douglas had rejected an offer by Truman of second place on the ticket.

During the preconvention troubles with the liberals in Philadelphia, McGrath had telephoned Truman and suggested that he deal with the problem by selecting Douglas as his running mate. Truman reached Douglas in an Oregon camp where he was vacationing and made the offer. After deliberating for a few days Douglas declined on the opening Monday of the convention, saying he did not believe the court should be used as a stepping stone to political office.[30] Doubtless he did not relish boarding the *Titanic,* either. In one of his private memorandums of those heated days Truman wrote:

I call him, tell him I'm doing what FDR did to me. He owes it to the country to accept.

He belongs to that crowd of Tommy Corcoran, Harold Ickes, Claude Pepper crackpots whose word is worth less than Jimmy Roosevelt's. I hope he has a more honorable political outlook. No professional liberal is intellectually honest. That's a real indictment—but true as the Ten Commandments. Professional liberals aren't familiar with the Ten Commandments or the Sermon on the Mount.

Most Roosevelts aren't either![31]

In his Monday memorandum, after Douglas had turned him down, Truman said:

I'm inclined to give some credence to Tommy Corcoran's crack to Burt Wheeler that Douglas had said he could "not" be a No. 2 man to a No. 2 man.[32]

John Snyder telephoned Truman on Monday or Tuesday to report that Roosevelt, Henderson, and Wilson Wyatt were backing Barkley for president. At that point Truman's suspicions were eased, for he noted in a Tuesday memorandum: "Maybe so, but Barkley is an honorable man. He won't give me the double cross, I am sure."[33] Something seems to have been going on in Barkley's head, however, and Truman was enough of a fox to know it. Having heard of Truman's offer to Douglas, Biffle told certain Democratic senators that if Barkley did not get the vice-presidential nomination, they might be surprised at what he would run for.

At about the time Douglas had declined Truman's offer, Biffle and Barkley telephoned the president from Philadelphia. Barkley asked if Truman would mind if he sought the vice-presidential nomination.[34] At first glance Barkley was not an ideal choice for Truman. The senator was seventy, six years older than the president. Furthermore Kentucky and Missouri were hardly a good balance compared with New York and California on the Republican ticket. But Truman assented, unenthusiastically. After the White House staff meeting July 13, Eben Ayers noted in his diary: "Talking about the vice-presidency the President said he never did care much who was nominated to run with him. . . . He indicated he did not feel Barkley was the best candidate but that if the delegates wanted him, let them have him."[35]

The good spirits of Monday night gave way to renewed bitterness over civil rights on Tuesday when the platform committee, supported by the Truman forces, recommended the moderate plank patterned after 1944 to prevent a southern bolt. Biemiller thereupon announced that the liberals would carry the fight for a stronger plank to the convention floor on Wednesday. By the time Truman got to town Wednesday night the Democratic party had been through an inferno. Frustrated in their efforts to dump Truman, the liberals carried the day in a wild fight to amend the civil rights plank.

Eliminating the vague language of 1944, the new plank commended Truman for his stand on civil rights. It called upon Congress to act on his proposals for full and equal political participation, equal opportunity in employment, the right to personal security, and "the right of equal treatment in the service and defense of our nation."

When he could get the floor, Handy Ellis, an Alabama delegate, told the convention, "We bid you good-bye." With that, thirteen members of the Alabama delegation and the entire twenty-three-member Mississippi delegation seized their state standards and marched out of the hall.

Truman then was nominated on the first ballot, receiving 947½ votes to 263 cast by southern delegates for Senator Russell of Georgia.* No one adhered to tradition and moved that the nomination of Truman be made unanimous. It was unlikely the South would have gone along. Thus, when Truman arrived the situation was that he was going to have to run against the powerful Dewey-Warren ticket with a northern Progressive faction of Democrats split away under Wallace and a Democratic southern Dixiecrat faction split away under the ultimate leadership of Governor Thurmond and his running mate, Governor Wright of Mississippi, who hoped to be able to throw the election into the House of Representatives.

In these seemingly hopeless circumstances Truman went before the bedraggled

* Former Governor Paul McNutt of Indiana received half a vote.

delegates and did the last thing anyone would have imagined possible at that wretched hour of 2 A.M. He electrified the convention.

"Senator Barkley and I," he said, "will win this election and make these Republicans like it—don't you forget that!"[36]

He laid it right on the line:

Never in the world were the farmers . . . as prosperous . . . and if they don't do their duty by the Democratic Party, they are the most ungrateful people in the world. . . .

And I say to labor what I have said to the farmers: they are the most ungrateful people in the world if they pass the Democratic Party by this year.

In those days before air conditioning Convention Hall was sweltering. The miserably managed convention had dragged on so long Truman had to wait downstairs for four hours. When he finally appeared on the rostrum in his white linen suit, Mrs. Emma Guffey Miller, sister of a former senator from Pennsylvania, released from a floral Liberty Bell a flock of white pigeons in the role of doves of peace. The place was turned into a flapping scene out of Alfred Hitchcock, with birds winging everywhere, crashing into balconies, and even alighting on the lectern within Rayburn's grasp.

Truman soon had the hall in a different kind of uproar, Democrats stamping and hollering as he sprang a trap on the Republicans. Speaking from an outline prepared chiefly by Murphy, Rosenman, and Clifford, he first laid down a barrage against "that worst Eightieth Congress" for all the things it had not done about economic controls, slum clearance, schools, and welfare. Then he recited the promises in the recently adopted Republican platform to deal with high prices and provide housing, aid to education, and increased Social Security benefits.

"My duty as President," he said, "requires that I use every means within my power to get the laws the people need on matters of such importance and urgency.

"I am, therefore, calling this Congress back into session July 26.

"On the twenty-sixth of July, which out in Missouri we call 'Turnip Day,'* I am going to call Congress back and ask them to pass laws to halt rising prices, to meet the housing crisis—which they say they are for in their platform. . . .

"I shall ask them to act upon other vitally needed measures such as aid to education, which they say they are for; a national health program, civil rights legislation, which they say they are for . . . extension of social security coverage and increased benefits, which they say they are for. . . .

"Now, my friends, if there is any reality behind that Republican platform, we ought to get some action from a short session of the Eightieth Congress. They can do this job in fifteen days, if they want to do it. . . ."

Republicans fumed at this impudent strategy, which had been under discussion in the White House for some time. It was a rather obvious and appealing device. The calling of special sessions is an option open to all presidents. Truman already had called the one in the fall of 1947 to deal with foreign aid and inflation. As

---

* Missourians differ as to whether Turnip Day was July 25 or 26. In any case the latter date served Truman's purposes better, since the twenty-sixth fell on a Monday that year—a logical day for the convening of a special session. An old Missouri saying was "On the twenty-sixth day of July"—assuming Truman was right—"sow your turnips, wet or dry."

Congress had balked at passing his program in 1948, speculation about a special session often appeared in the press. Reporters kept asking Truman about the possibility throughout the spring. The question was asked as recently as the press conference of July 1.[37]

The idea, therefore, was not arcane. Truman's most intimate political advisers favored it. An unsigned memorandum of June 29, later found among Rosenman's papers, though not written by him, reflected the thinking of the subject. The election, it said, could be won only by bold and daring action, such as the calling of a special session. The advantages of such a call were enumerated: (1) it "would focus attention on the rotten record of the Eightieth Congress," (2) it "would force Dewey and Warren to defend the actions of Congress and make them accept the Congress as a basic issue," (3) "it would keep a steady glare on the Neanderthal men of the Republican party . . . who will embarrass Dewey and Warren," (4) it would split the Republicans on major issues, and (5) it "would show the President *in action on Capitol Hill,* fighting for the people."[38] Cussing away, Truman announced his decision on the special session to his staff July 13, informing them that he was going to tell the Republicans: "Now, you sons of bitches, come and do your God-damndest."[39]

He was pleased with the excitement stirred by his speech, jotting in a memorandum July 16:

Editorials, columns and cartoons are gasping and wondering.
    None of the smart folks thought I would call the Congress. . .
    Dewey synthetically milks cows and pitches hay for the cameras just as that other faker Teddy Roosevelt did—but he never heard of "turnip day."[40]

While the public was concentrating on the conventions, the situation in Berlin had grown more serious. As was to be the case throughout the next four months, Truman was pulled between the spectacle of the campaign and the exigencies of Israel, Korea, China, and Germany, where the Soviet blockade remained clamped on Berlin as tightly as ever. Truman's decision to hold the United States zone of the German capital still stood. B-29s were being readied for movement to Germany and Great Britain. Fleets of American transport planes kept 2,500 tons of food and fuel flowing daily to the beleaguered Berlin population. Yet on July 3 Sokolovsky told the Western military governors that the blockade would continue until their countries abandoned plans for a West German government.[41] On July 10 General Clay made a drastic proposal. In a message to General Bradley he said:

. . . I am strongly of the view that if the blockade is not lifted . . . we should advise the Soviet Government that . . . we propose on a specific date to send in a convoy accompanied by the requisite bridge equipment to make our right of way into Berlin usable. There is of course an inherent risk . . . since once this convoy crosses the border it is committed to the movement to Berlin. . . .[42]

Convinced that the Soviets did not intend war, Clay repeated his request July 15, the day Truman returned from Philadelphia, and Bradley assured Clay the proposal was being weighed.[43]

While this question hung in the balance Truman approved a general position that Marshall communicated to the embassy in London July 20. The United States would maintain its place in Berlin and was "prepared to use any means that may be necessary" to discharge its rights of occupation in the German capital. However, Truman and his advisers did not believe that the Politburo was intent on war. "We do not feel, up to the present," Marshall said, "that the Soviet Government has committed itself so irretrievably to maintain the blockade as to preclude the possibility of some face-saving retreat on their part." The president and his advisers, therefore, had decided, if agreeable to London and Paris, to make a direct approach to Stalin.

If Stalin's attitude should prove negative, Marshall said, "we . . . would take the matter to the United Nations with a view to assuring our rights to Berlin."[44]

With Clay back in Washington, the National Security Council met July 22, and the president asked the general what risks would be involved in the dispatch of an armed convoy.

"The general said," Truman recalled, "he thought the initial reaction of the Russians would be to set up roadblocks. Our engineers would be able to clear such obstacles, provided there was no Russian interference, but the next step the Russians would take, General Clay thought, would be to meet the convoys with armed force."

Clay said he did not believe the Soviets would attack American planes unless Moscow already had made the decision to go to war.

Were there any indications the Soviets would go to war? Truman asked. Clay said not.

"I stated it as my judgment," Truman remembered, "that if we moved out of Berlin we would be losing everything we were fighting for. The main question was: How long could we remain in Berlin without risking all-out war?"

General Vandenberg of the air force said that the airlift would reduce air strength elsewhere, leaving the country exposed in an emergency. Truman disagreed.

"I asked him," he recounted, "if he would prefer to have us attempt to supply Berlin by ground convoy. Then, if the Russians resisted that effort and plunged the world into war, would not the Air Force have to contribute its share to the defense of the nation?"

The airlift, Truman declared, involved less risk than armed convoys. Therefore, being particularly cautious before the election, he directed the air force to do its utmost to supply Berlin.[45] With the Joint Chiefs also opposed to an attempted push to Berlin, at least until the United States had time to prepare for war, convoys were ruled out.[46] The Allies imposed a counterblockade, which halted shipments of industrial goods to Soviet-occupied East Germany.

At the same time that he was dealing with Berlin and trying to plan the fall's political campaign Truman was dragged into a dispute over custody of nuclear weapons. On the president's return from Philadelphia Forrestal requested a meeting to discuss whether custody should be transferred from the Atomic Energy Commission to the Pentagon, a question causing high feelings within the government.[47]

After the AEC had been formed it assumed custody under the Atomic Energy

Act of all fissionable materials and nuclear weapons. If such weapons were ever to be used, of course, they would be used by the military, not the AEC. The act provided that the president could direct the AEC to deliver to the armed forces such weapons as he considered necessary to the national defense. The Military Liaison Committee of the AEC had raised the issue of transfer as early as September, 1947, but Lilienthal and the AEC commissioners resisted. The European crisis brought the question to the fore again. When the news of Jan Masaryk's death arrived in March, Truman sternly told both sides of the custody debate he would tolerate no more squabbling, an element in which was the old issue of civilian versus military control of nuclear weapons.[48]

Truman at that point was infuriated by the fighting among the armed services and the inability of Forrestal, with his vague powers, to take charge and pull the Pentagon together. Budget Director Webb told Lilienthal, "The President is his own Secretary of Defense right now; he *has* to be because Forrestal won't take hold."[49] Turning custody of the atomic bomb over to a bevy of infighting admirals and generals was not a reassuring prospect.

Although Forrestal did not know it, Truman had told Clark Clifford earlier in the summer, "As long as I am in the White House I will be opposed to taking atomic weapons away from the hands they are now in, and they will only be delivered to the military by particular order of the President issued at a time when they are needed."[50] In response to Forrestal's request for a formal presidential decision, however, Truman assented to a meeting of all concerned July 21. He told Forrestal, however, that he was going to retain the power of decision on use of the bomb and did not intend "to have some dashing lieutenant colonel decide when would be the proper time to drop one."[51]

Evidently, Truman was grim and severe in presiding over the meeting. "I don't think," he said at one point, "we ought to use this thing unless we absolutely have to. It is a terrible thing to order the use of something that is so terribly destructive—destructive beyond anything we have ever had. You have got to understand that this isn't a military weapon. It is used to wipe out women and children and unarmed people and not for military uses. So we have got to treat this differently from rifles and cannon and ordinary things like that."[52]

Three days later he announced his decision in a public statement: "As President of the United States, I regard the continued control of all aspects of the atomic energy program, including research, development, and the custody of atomic weapons, as the proper functions of the civil authorities."[53]

As the Turnip Day session neared, Republicans were angry and divided. Many of them branded it a cheap trick, the act of a desperate man, as Representative Hugh Scott of Pennsylvania, Republican National Chairman, said. Some Republicans felt that Congress should hear Truman and then adjourn in contempt. Others wanted to receive his recommendations, denounce them as political gimmicks, pass a few minor measures and go home. As Truman had anticipated, Dewey was thrown into a dilemma epitomized by Harold Stassen's observation that the Republican nominee either should try to take charge of the session, however the governor of New York could manage that, or else wash his hands of it. Dewey went halfway. Herbert

Brownell, his campaign manager, announced that the governor thought Congress should give careful attention to the president's proposals.[54] Brownell and Scott recommended to Taft, privately, that the special session at least placate ethnic groups by liberalizing the Displaced Persons Act. "No," Taft retorted, as Brownell and Scott recalled, "We're not going to give that fellow anything."[55]

Even as Congress convened July 26 Truman pulled another surprise. Without warning he issued two executive orders, one to end discrimination in the armed forces and the other to guarantee fair employment practices in the civil service. The order on the military stated that equality of opportunity and treatment regardless of race or color was the policy of the president as commander in chief. It established in the Pentagon the President's Advisory Committee on Equality of Treatment and Opportunity in the Armed Services to examine rules and practices. The order applying to civil service forbade discrimination in hiring and conferred on the head of each department the responsibility for a program to prevent violations. A Fair Employment Board was established in the Civil Service Commission to hear appeals against departmental hiring practices and to oversee the new policy throughout the government.

These orders, of course, were the delayed fulfillment of promises Truman had made in his civil rights message in February, the further withholding of which was pointless after the strengthened civil rights plank in the Democratic platform. The Republican platform itself proclaimed opposition "to the idea of racial segregation in the armed services."

The order to the military did not encounter smooth sailing. Black leaders and the black press reacted against its failure to prohibit segregation. Inadvertently, General Bradley heightened their dissatisfaction by saying at a meeting in Fort Knox, Kentucky, the day after the order was issued that it was not up to the army to conduct social experiments. He commented that desegregation would occur in the army only as it spread throughout society. This was publicly interpreted as an indication that the army would not obey Truman's order if it required desegregation.

Bradley immediately wrote to Truman that "nothing is farther from our intent." While he felt it would be hazardous deliberately to use the army as a vehicle of social reform, he believed, he said, that the army must keep pace with the progress of the rest of the country in race relations. He added:

I had no intention whatsoever of embarrassing you in any way, and had I known the press was present, I would have avoided any mention of the segregation issue. At that time I had not seen the Executive Order.

"I understand the situation as it affects you very well," Truman replied, "and I know that you never would do anything that would stand to cut the ground from under me without first talking to me about it."[56]

At his next press conference Truman was asked whether his order envisioned the eventual end of segregation in the armed forces. "Yes," he replied.[57] With the Dixiecrats now in the field, black leaders had to think twice about how much they wanted to damage Truman. Satisfied that Truman meant to end segregation, Philip Randolph canceled his plans for a campaign of civil disobedience.

With relish and aplomb Truman went before a joint session of the reassembled Congress, whose Republican majority cursed the return to Washington's heat and gave him a silent reception.

"Our people," he said, "demand legislative action by their government to do two things: first, to check inflation and the rising cost of living and, second, to help in meeting the acute housing shortage. These are matters which affect every American family. . . . We cannot afford to wait for the next Congress to act."

Aware that the Republicans would scorn his program, yet eager to turn this disdain to his own advantage with the voters, Truman asked not only for antiinflation measures and the housing bill, but resubmitted practically the whole array of liberal proposals that had been rejected at the regular session.[58]

Dewey seems not to have sensed the possible danger to himself in Truman's initiative. Writing to his aunt the same day the president spoke, the Republican nominee said: "Mr. Truman's special session is a nuisance but I do not believe it will have much effect on the election."[59] After "more or less" consulting Dewey by telephone about the Truman speech, but receiving no recommendations, Republican congressional leaders went on radio to accuse Truman of demagoguery and to make it plain that no major legislation would be passed. The Republicans brought up an anti-poll tax bill in the Senate first in hope of getting southerners to embarrass Truman with a filibuster. In fact southern Democrats did get their wind up and the measure was eventually shelved.[60]

Five days after the session began Truman and Dewey met as speakers at the dedication of Idlewild (now John F. Kennedy) International Airport on Long Island. It was a handshake between a man who was president and another who was already presidential.

As always, Truman carried a plain, midwestern air about him. Dewey, although most of his career had been spent in public service and politics, had the prosperous, tailored, sophisticated look of a Wall Street attorney. For most people who knew him and favored him Dewey was an acquired taste. At forty-six, eighteen years Truman's junior, he was too egotistical, too lordly, too overbearing, too didactic, too cold to like easily. Though he had a kind side, he did not convey warmth. His mellowing came much later. He was not a part of the people in anything like the sense that Truman was. In contrast to Truman, his image was that of the good manager, the efficient executive, the tough lawyer. In private, his brown eyes aglow, he could be overpowering in his demands and enthusiasm. In public, however, he had a habit of stepping into a role: he became formal, restrained, even a shade tense and ill at ease. The most distinguishing feature of his handsome face was a black mustache in an age when mustaches were not so common as before or since. Together with his conservative clothes and stiff bearing, the mustache was apt to make him look fastidious or, as Mrs. Alice Roosevelt Longworth said, like the little groom on the wedding cake.

If that was the caricature, the reality was Dewey's capacity to be very hard, determined, relentless, and supercilious. He was a strong administrator, skillful in attracting competent men to his staff. Secure in his own talent, he regarded Truman as a poor executive, a bungler. On July 27 he had written to Samuel R. Guard, editor-publisher of *Breeder's Gazette* in Louisville:

I agree with you on Henry Wallace. He would destroy—I think knowingly—everything that has made this country great. Harry Truman might but because of ignorance.[61]

Conversely, the picture of his Republican opponent that seemed to linger in Truman's mind was that of the younger Dewey as special prosecutor, gangbuster, and district attorney of New York County. He told White House associates that Dewey was too much the aggressive courtroom practitioner to be a good president, especially in matters of foreign affairs.[62]

Consistent with the general appearance of the campaign, Dewey had the breaks at Idlewild. He made an uninterrupted speech. The speeches, however, had fallen behind schedule. When it came Truman's turn, a flight of military jets thundered overhead, drowning out his flat voice and causing him to rush through the text while the crowd gawked at the planes. Truman said something to Dewey, but reporters could not learn what it was. Years later Representative Leo W. O'Brien of New York, revealed that Dewey had confided that Truman said: "Tom, when you get to the White House, for God's sake do something about the plumbing."[63]

Even as Truman and Dewey were meeting, the country was being shaken by sensational testimony in Washington about Communist espionage.

On July 30 Elizabeth Bentley, the dowdy former Communist spy, then unknown to the public, testified before a Senate subcommittee that during the war she had received secret information directly from twenty government officials and indirectly from at least as many more. The next day before the House Un-American Activities Committee she swore that Harry Dexter White, whom Truman had appointed to the International Monetary Fund, and Lauchlin Currie, an assistant to President Roosevelt, had furnished information to Communist espionage rings identified as the "Silvermaster Group" and the "Perlo Group." The next week Whitaker Chambers emerged from the anonymity of *Time*'s editorial offices to implicate in Communist infiltration of the government Alger Hiss, former director of the Special Political Affairs Division of the State Department and now president of the Carnegie Endowment for International Peace. Chambers named Hiss, whose name at the time meant nothing outside the small diplomatic, political, and social circles in which he moved in New York and Washington, as one of a prewar Communist underground group, the mission of which was to place other Communists in sensitive Washington positions. At another proceeding—after the election—Chambers was to implicate Hiss in espionage as well.

These charges and others that followed, endlessly, were to pollute the national political atmosphere for a decade. The damage to be inflicted included irreparable cracks in the foundation of Truman's leadership. He might have limited the trouble by responding differently, or not at all, to the first sensations and by devising a better strategy for meeting the later attacks by Senator McCarthy and others as they came along. But at the very start he got off on the wrong foot, just two days after Chamber's testimony.

"Mr. President," a reporter asked him at his press conference August 5, "do you think that the Capitol Hill spy scare is a 'red herring' to divert public attention from inflation?"

When a reporter asks a question in that fashion, he is trying to lure the president into a specific answer that the reporter knows will make a headline. Truman snapped at the bait.

"Yes, I do," he said.[64]

For the rest of his presidency he was to bear the increasingly heavy political burden, exploited by his enemies, of having called investigation of communist espionage a red herring, even though he had not initially volunteered the characterization. His allowing a reporter to put words in his mouth—and not for the last time—produced the same unfortunate effect.

If the words were the reporter's, however, the attitude undeniably was Truman's, created partly by the growing hostility arising between himself and Congress. After answering the reporter's question, Truman read a prepared statement, outlining his policy toward requests by the congressional committees for records of government employees under scrutiny. The departments, he said, could furnish the committees unclassified routine papers. But no information relating to an employee's loyalty and no investigative data of any kind would be made available. Truman continued:

No information has been revealed by these committees' investigations that has not long since been presented to a Federal grand jury. No information has been disclosed in the past few days by the Congressional committees that has not long been known to the FBI. The Federal grand jury found this information insufficient to justify indictment of the Federal employees involved."

When the House Committee on Un-American Activities, investigating the loyalty of Dr. Edward U. Condon, director of the National Bureau of Standards, had demanded an FBI letter that spring, Truman, in refusing, took possession of it personally and told his staff, "Now let them come and get it."[65]

Still, the excitement over the hearings escalated. In a note to Clifford later in August Elsey commented that spies had become a major Republican issue, which was "getting worse, not better."[66] This was not entirely coincidental. Parnell Thomas, chairman of the Un-American Activities Committee, said later that Republican National Chairman Scott "was urging me in the Dewey campaign to set up the spy hearings. At the time he was urging me to stay in Washington to keep the heat on Harry Truman."[67]

Among the first Republicans to sense how the issue might be used against Truman in the campaign was Representative Nixon, a member of the Un-American Affairs Committee. Writing September 7 to John Foster Dulles, then a foreign policy adviser to Dewey, Nixon noted the absence of progress in strengthening the espionage laws. "The record of the administration is completely vulnerable and should be attacked," he said. The administration should be attacked also, he continued, for failing "to prosecute and to enforce vigorously the laws providing for deportation of alien Communists." Truman "should be charged with placing politics above the national security," Nixon advised, adding: "If it could be handled properly it would be the ideal answer to Truman's 'red herring' charge."[68]

Approvingly, Dulles forwarded the letter to Dewey, who neither answered it nor in fact ever made much of the alleged Communist menace in his campaign. For all his other handicaps Truman was lucky on this issue. Sensations like the revelation of the pumpkin papers on Chambers's Maryland farm and the indictment of Hiss for perjury came after the election. McCarthy had not yet stumbled onto the Communist issue. Nixon was not yet a major figure. China had not fallen to the Communists. And, curiously, the grand jury impaneled in New York to hear the testimony of Miss Bentley and others did not hand down any indictments. Committed to fostering national unity, Dewey avoided Red-baiting. He did not feel that he needed the issue to win. Still another factor was critical in getting Truman off the hook. Henry Wallace had become so entangled with Communists that, with generous help from the Democrats, the Communist issue was turned against him instead of Truman, as Dewey, too late, was ruefully to acknowledge.

In a postelection exchange of letters A. Augustus Low, chairman of the Hamilton County Republican Committee in New York, commented to Dewey that if Wallace had not run, "all of the extreme left wingers, screwballs etc. would have been in Truman's camp and he would have had a left-wing load to carry and explain."

"There is a lot to what you say about the Wallace candidacy," Dewey replied. "In many respects he helped the opposition more than he hurt them."[69]

Thirty years later leading historians agree with this assessment.

The Turnip Day session ground through eleven querulous days to a barren end. Rejecting Truman's antiinflation program, Congress passed a bill simply authorizing the Federal Reserve Board to raise reserve requirements of member banks and to reimpose controls on consumer credit. Truman signed the bill but denounced it as feeble and advantageous to "the ends of special privilege."[70]

The old deadlock on housing carried over into the special session. The House again rejected provisions in the Taft-Ellender-Wagner bill for low-rent public housing and urban redevelopment, and Truman had to settle for legislation easing the terms of federally insured mortages and of down payments. While signing the bill, he accused Congress of deliberately neglecting families forced to live in slums.[71]

At the end of the session he was pleased to let a reporter put more words in his mouth.

"Would you say it was a do-nothing session, Mr. President?"

"I would say it was entirely a 'do-nothing' session," he replied. "I think that's a good name for the Eightieth Congress."[72]

The Republican massacre of his program was fodder for the kind of campaign he planned to wage. In contrast to Dewey's comment to his aunt that the special session would not much affect the election was a memorandum to Truman August 13 from Clifford, reporting on a talk with Carey of the CIO:

He stated that there had been a decided change in feeling among the top officers of the CIO with reference to the coming election. The President's Speech at the Convention made a great impression on labor as did the decision to call a special Session of the Congress. The failure of the Congress to enact any legislation remotely beneficial to labor has helped crystallize the support of labor for the President.[73]

From another quarter worse trouble was creeping up on Dewey. As the summer progressed, the prospect of a tremendous harvest became unmistakable only weeks after Congress had changed the Commodity Credit Corporation charter so that it could not lease land for new storage bins. Commercial storage facilities that might have handled the grain in normal years were already overtaxed by the end of July. The new secretary of agriculture, Charles Brannan, successor to Clinton Anderson, who was running for United States senator in New Mexico, warned farmers that, lacking the usual help from the CCC, they would have to build their own bins or face loss of price supports. With harvest estimates constantly soaring, farm prices began to decline for the first time since the 1930s. The *Dayton Daily News* sensed the impending consequences of the new CCC charter from the plight of Ohio farmers who had large wheat and oats crops and were worrying about where they were going to store their corn. On August 27 the *Dayton Daily News* carried a front-page story by W. McNeil Lowry, its chief Washington correspondent, reporting: "The whole course of the 1948 political campaign in the great corn and wheat states may ultimately be affected. From Ohio through South Dakota, farmers are asking where they are going to store the record 1948 grain crop and what price it is going to bring."[74]

Much later, after the election, Dewey was to write to a friend:

I wish somehow that we had known that the farm vote was slipping away sooner. What we could have done I do not know, but we might have invented something beyond speeches.[75]

As August ended, however, the Republicans saw scarcely a cloud in the sky. Editorially, 65 percent of the daily newspapers, having 78 percent of the circulation, were about to support Dewey. Only 15 percent supported Truman. Ben Duffy of Batten, Barton, Durstine, and Osborn, Inc., which handled advertising for the Dewey campaign, wrote to Brownell: "We talked with George Gallup yesterday. . . . Gallup commented . . . 'Why does the Republican committee want to spend any money? The results are a foregone conclusion.' "[76]

But Truman wrote to his sister September 2:

It looks like another four years of slavery. I'd be much better off personally if we lose the election but I fear that the country would go to hell and I have to try to prevent that.[77]

42. *Whistle-Stop*

I N MICHIGAN huge crowds of working people turned out to hear Truman open his campaign on Labor Day with apocalyptic predictions of what would happen to labor if the Republicans should win the election. The Taft-Hartley Act "is only a foretaste of what you will get if the Republican reaction is allowed to continue to grow."[1]

While Dewey stayed home, confident that a later start would suffice, Truman rolled through Detroit, Grand Rapids, Lansing, Hamtramck, Pontiac, and Flint by train and motorcade, scathing the "do-nothing Eightieth Congress," giving his own highly colored version of the preceding three years and filling the air with simplistic economics.

In Cadillac Square in Detroit he preached labor solidarity. "If you let the Republican administration reactionaries get complete control of this government, the position of labor will be so greatly weakened that I would fear not only for wages and living standards of the American working man but even for our democratic institutions of free labor and free enterprise," he told a crowd estimated at 100,000 persons.[2] The Democratic organization in Michigan had been crippled by the 1946 defeats, but the United Automobile Workers and the CIO had effectively taken its place.

With portents of a Dewey victory emblazoned in the sky, many people who should have known better failed to see below the effective nationwide efforts being undertaken by labor to elect Democrats in 1948 in reaction to the Taft-Hartley Act. For the first time in its history the American Federation of Labor formally participated in a presidential campaign through a new organization, Labor's League for Political Education. Headed by Joseph Keenan, former secretary of the Chicago Federation of Labor, it was the counterpart of the CIO's Political Action Committee. While the AFL clung to its tradition of not endorsing a candidate, the League raised money for Democrats. Sometimes Keenan rode on the Truman train as an adviser; other times he preceded it to muster labor crowds for Truman's appearances.

Since the Democrats were the larger party, their best hope of victory lay in a large turnout on Election Day. The LLPE and PAC waged a strenuous campaign to get union members to register. After his fling with the Eisenhower movement Philip Murray came round with substantial help for Truman, including money for a national radio broadcast of a presidential speech from Pittsburgh when the Democrats could not afford it.[3] The CIO endorsed Truman. Among the country's principal labor leaders only Truman's old antagonists, Alvanley Johnston and, by indirection,

John L. Lewis, backed Dewey.

The biggest job done by labor, however, was not in the presidential campaign but in the cities and states where union officials, bent on electing a friendly Congress, helped local Democratic candidates. Truman was in a way an almost incidental beneficiary of labor's efforts.

In this connection, although its import was widely overlooked at the outset, the Democrats had nominated a particularly formidable group of candidates for other offices in 1948, most of whom received enthusiastic labor support.

These candidates included Adlai E. Stevenson, running for governor of Illinois; G. Mennen (Soapy) Williams, running for governor of Michigan; Frank Lausche, running for governor of Ohio, Chester Bowles, running for governor of Connecticut; Mayor Humphrey, running for senator from Minnesota; Paul H. Douglas, running for senator from Illinois; Estes Kefauver, running for senator from Tennessee; Representative Lyndon Johnson, running for senator from Texas; Robert S. Kerr, running for senator from Oklahoma, and Clinton Anderson, running for senator from New Mexico. In his tattered condition in 1948 Truman did not have anything like FDR's helpful coattails. He was in poor shape to pull others to victory. But the extraordinary group of Democratic gubernatorial and senatorial candidates was capable of attracting votes to the Democratic tickets in the various states and thus giving Truman a lift.

Although the cost of electioneering then was a pittance by today's standards, the Truman campaign was continually down to its last dollar. With the polls indicating a Dewey landslide (in September Elmo Roper stopped syndicating his polls on the presidential race because Dewey "is almost as good as elected"),[4] contributions to Truman were slow coming in. The bill for the broadcast of the Cadillac Square speech was paid by the Truman-Barkley Clubs of America because the Democratic National Committee had no money for it.[5] Earlier Secretary of the Treasury Snyder had had to ask Baruch for $2,500 for balloons and noisemakers for the convention.[6]

On August 19 Truman wrote to Baruch requesting that he serve on the finance committee. Baruch politely declined, explaining that his practice was not to serve on party committees nor make political statements—a course that Roosevelt had approved of, he said. Truman replied, vindictively: "A great many honors have passed your way, both to you and your family, and it seems when the going is rough it is a one-way street."[7] Baruch talked to Westbrook Pegler, who caused a deep breach between Truman and Baruch by quoting the financier in his newspaper column as having called the president "a rude, ignorant, uncouth man."

Truman had difficulty getting anyone to serve as chairman of the finance committee. He offered the post to Jesse Jones, Roosevelt's secretary of commerce, but the aging Texas tycoon begged off returning to Washington.[8] Democrats in and out of government were invited to White House teas with the Truman family, at which the president would state his need for funds. A guest at one of these receptions has recalled Truman's standing on a chair and speaking in this vein: He knew he had a hard fight on his hands. Most people thought he was going to lose. But as president he ought to have sufficient money to conduct enough of a campaign to tell the voters his views. As things stood he could not do that. In fact he could not even afford to get the train out of the station.

On this particular occasion the guests repaired to the Democratic headquarters. Albert M. Greenfield, a Philadelphia real estate operator and philanthropist, cried shame on the Democrats for the president's predicament and in effect passed the hat. Stuart Symington, for one, doubled his previous contribution. Out of such sessions came at last a finance chairman, Colonel Louis A. Johnson, a conservative, a highly paid corporation lawyer and businessman, a former national commander of the American Legion and a former assistant secretary of war under Roosevelt, who was destined for a stormy career in Truman's second term.

Among them, Johnson, the labor leaders and wealthy men and women acting from different motives kept Truman's head above water, although barely at times. Rumors circulated in Washington for years that Johnson got considerable cash from Juan Trippe, president of Pan American Airways. The airline was a client of the law firm of Steptoe and Johnson. Truman's friend, Milton S. Kronheim, Sr., a respected Washington wholesale liquor dealer, and T. Lamar Caudle, assistant attorney general, who was headed for grief in the second term, worked as a team soliciting funds. According to Kronheim, Abe Feinberg, a New York banker, paid for the broadcast of Truman's final campaign speech from St. Louis.[9]

Wealthy men who were or had been in the Truman administration wrote checks. Included among them were Ed Pauley, the brothers David and James K. E. Bruce, Harriman, Will Clayton, and ambassadors William Pawley, Robert Butler, and Laurence Steinhardt. David Dubinsky of the International Ladies Garment Workers paid for several broadcasts. An old friend of Truman's in Kansas City, Tom Evans, who owned a radio station and who was chairman of the board of the Crown Drug Company, dug into his pocket. Another, the Washington socialite, Mrs. Perle Mesta, became a star fund raiser.

Still others made contributions or loans because they were Democrats, or because they hoped for (and received) future Democratic favors, or because they made a practice of giving money to both parties to be safe, or because they yielded to the pressures of Johnson and Pauley. This group included Cornelius Vanderbilt (Sonny) Whitney, a founder, and J. Carroll Cone, an assistant vice president, of Pan American; Floyd B. Odlum, a Wall Street financier; Jacob Blaustein, industrialist and president of the American Jewish Committee; Nathan Lichtblau, a plastics manufacturer; William Helis—''the Golden Greek''—who was rich in oil money; Welburn Maycock, Ed Pauley's attorney; Curtis Calder, chairman of the board of Electric Bond and Share; George Luckey, vice-chairman of the Democratic State Central Committee in California and a friend of Pauley's, and George L. Killion, president of the American President Lines.[10] When the Truman train reached Oklahoma in September, not enough money was on hand to get it back to Washington. Two wealthy Oklahoma Democrats, Governor Roy J. Turner and W. Elmer Harber, gave a party in the Ferdinand Magellan and raised enough money not only for the rest of that trip but for the next one as well.[11] In Massachusetts, meanwhile, Joseph P. Kennedy refused to give the Truman campaign anything.[12] The broadcast of Truman's speech in Philadelphia October 6 had to be cut off the air before he had finished to avoid overtime costs. On other occasions checks had not been in the banks long enough for clearance and McGrath had to carry as much as $35,000 in cash to the radio studios to get Truman on the air.[13]

Accompanied as usual by Mrs. Truman and Margaret, the president departed September 17 on his first big coast-to-coast whistle-stop trip of the campaign, and Democratic bigwigs were at Union Staion to cheer him on. "Go out there and mow 'em down," Barkley told him.

Truman's reply was his epitaph. It was the definition of a role he was pleased to live up to for the rest of his life. "I'll mow 'em down, Alben," he said, "and I'll give 'em hell."

Because reporters on the train had nothing else to write that day but the departure story, newspapers and news broadcasts poured out the story of the underdog off to the battle, vowing to "give 'em hell." "Hell" was still a somewhat daring word then, and Margaret chided her father for using it.[14] But his comment, flashed across the country, caught on like "Remember the Maine!" Wherever Truman went someone would invariably shout, "Give 'em hell, Harry," and that would set him walloping Wall Street or slapping the special interests or chopping up the Eightieth Congress, which he was soon calling "good-for-nothing" as well as "do-nothing."

The role became good politics in the campaign, and, of course, when the election turned out as it did, Truman cherished it. It is too much to say that the "Give 'em hell" act changed his personality, but it affected his style in public. Forever after, he knew what audiences expected, and the temptation to perform was strong.

The first major appearance scheduled for the tour was a farm speech at the National Plowing Contest in Dexter, Iowa. Truman and Secretary of Agriculture Brannan were alert to the Republicans' problems in the Midwest and gave Dewey no quarter.

At just about the time farmers were realizing what the changed rules of the Commodity Credit Corporation meant to them, Harold Stassen visited Dewey in Albany September 2 and then made a statement that fell like manna on the White House. With the farmers increasingly worried about the sag in prices, Stassen attacked the Truman administration for having deliberately tried to keep food prices high. Blaming the administration for inflation generally, he continued that the Department of Agriculture in order to prevent lower food prices had made unnecessary grain purchases for export. Brannan, he charged, had implied he would increase such purchases.[15]

Long an obscure official in the Department of Agriculture who had caused little fuss and looked like a professor, Brannan turned out to be a political fireball as secretary. Within two hours of Stassen's statement he blew the issue sky-high by retorting that Dewey and Stassen were attacking the farm price-support system. Stassen had not mentioned price supports explicitly. Brushing this detail aside, the Democrats grabbed the issue in their teeth and shook it in the eyes of the farmers.

On September 4 Representative August H. Andresen, of Minnesota, second-ranking Republican on the House Agriculture Committee, wrote to Dewey from his home in Red Wing, warning him that Stassen had done much harm. The Truman administration was turning Stassen's statement to its advantage, Andresen said, adding: "I have been in Minnesota for the past two weeks, and I regret to state that many farmers do not intend to vote for the Republican ticket in the coming election. . . . We cannot win without the farm vote."

Dewey replied that he had been disturbed by similar reports but that a statement would be issued countering the fire from Washington.[16] Meanwhile Truman was westward-bound, and "give 'em hell" was a modest characterization of what he had in store for Dexter, Iowa.

His farm speech, echoing the era of William Jennings Bryan, was truly the last of a kind. Such prose has not been heard from the candidate of a major party in any presidential election campaign since. The lurid passages, however, were not Truman's creation but were the work of a little-known writer and former government employee named Albert Z. Carr. Carr had worked in the White House under Roosevelt and stayed on briefly in the Truman administration. He returned in the summer of 1948 when Truman brought in as a special speech writer David M. Noyes, and Noyes enlisted Carr's services. A former newspaper editor and public relations man, Noyes had known Senator Truman in Washington during the war. While the farm speech was the product of many hands in the White House and the Department of Agriculture, the style and tone were Carr's.[17]

Addressing 80,000 persons on Mrs. T. R. Agg's model farm, Truman zeroed in on Wall Street "gluttons of privilege." Fabulous sums were they contributing, he said, to turn the country back to the times when farmers suffered under Harding, Coolidge, and Hoover. When did "Wall Street Republican administrations" ever help the farmer? "The Republicans gave you that greatest of all depressions . . ." In the Eightieth Congress they had already "stuck a pitchfork in the farmer's back"—Carr's phrase.[18] Touching a raw nerve, Truman continued:

Many growers have sold wheat this summer at less than the support price because they could not find proper storage. When the Democratic administration had to face this problem in the past, the government set up grain bins all over the wheat and corn belts to provide storage. Now the farmers need such bins again.

But when the Republican Congress rewrote the [CCC] charter this year there were certain lobbyists in Washington representing the speculative grain trade—your old friend. These big-business lobbyists and speculators persuaded the Congress not to provide storage bins for the farmers.

Then he picked up where Brannan had left off and accused the Republicans of "attacking the whole structure of price supports." After that came the dividends from Stassen's visit to Albany:

Republican spokesmen are now complaining that my administration is trying to keep farm prices up. They have given themselves away. They have given you a plain hint of what they have in store for you if they come into power. They are obviously ready to let the bottom drop out of farm prices.[19]

Dewey's Victory Special had finally pulled out of Albany. The Republican nominee was on his way also to the traditionally Republican state of Iowa to deliver his first campaign speech in Des Moines forty-eight hours after Truman's blast at Dexter. After the Republican convention a stream of Republican leaders had flowed through Albany, giving the candidate advice on the forthcoming campaign. Unanimously, it seems, they urged Dewey to say as little as possible and avoid controversy. Dewey was seen as having enough votes to win; the problem was not to lose any of them by rash words. This advice coincided with his own instincts.

Aggressive campaigning against Roosevelt in 1944 appeared to have hurt Dewey by linking him with low tactics, and he was chary about repeating it.[20] The danger this time, as he saw it, was that aggressiveness on his part might arouse sympathy for the underdog Truman. Furthermore, if victory were as likely as it seemed, it was better for Dewey to adopt a presidential stance at once than to appear the perennial district attorney, because a high-minded campaign would help unify the country under a Dewey administration. While some Republicans wanted him to pick apart the conduct of foreign affairs under Roosevelt and Truman, Dewey persisted in a commitment to bipartisan foreign policy, under pressure from Vandenberg and Dulles.

A defect of this placid strategy was that once Dewey committed himself to an unaggressive campaign in September, when his prospects were unquestioned, it proved impractical to change in October, when doubts began to arise.

In his opening speech in Des Moines Dewey did not mention the Commodity Credit Corporation, storage bins, price supports, or the Eightieth Congress. He did not allude to the falling farm prices. Before leaving Albany he had issued a statement endorsing the principle of price supports, but it was drowned out by Truman and by Brannan, who was campaigning up and down the farm belt.

While Dewey was speaking in Des Moines and elsewhere of unity and a glorious future, Truman was running loose in the country heaping blame and ridicule on the "mossbacks" of the Eightieth Congress—"The Republicans are trying to sabotage the West."[21] "Old Taber, you know, said that the West was 'squealing like a stuck hog,' because he knifed appropriations for conservation and flood control and things of that sort."[22] "You have been crudely and wickedly cheated by the power lobby in Washington operating through the Eightieth Congress."[23]

After reading a draft of a speech Brownell planned to deliver, Dewey wrote him October 1 asking him to replace some passages "with a spirited defense of the Eightieth Congress."[24] Yet as the campaign progressed, Dewey himself did not attempt a sustained defense of Congress such as might have neutralized Truman's strategy. Certainly, Dewey could have made a case. It was the Eightieth Congress that had passed such landmarks as the Truman Doctrine, the Marshall Plan, and the Vandenberg Resolution, all of which commanded considerable public support then. And the administration's position on many of the domestic issues before the Congress was by no means unassailable.

Days passed, however, and Truman had a clear track. As his train sped across the prairies, crept through the Royal Gorge of the Colorado River, wound among the High Sierras, and rolled down the California valleys, he got away with murder in parceling out blame for the housing shortage, inflation, and the quality of national leadership. Any charge that came into his head ("They'll tear you apart.")[25] he flung without compunction at the Republicans. No nationally heard voice was raised against his tirades about Republican servitude to big business, as if the Truman administration had done anything to change the system under which corporations were bursting with profits.

Dewey's facility with the cutting remark, his courtroom skill, his talent for marshaling facts and figures could have bruised Truman, but he persisted in what Truman aptly called "high-sounding lectures."[26] The leaves turned red and gold, and still the president held the initiative, not only because of Dewey's determination to avoid controversy but also, it appears, because of Dewey's own attitude toward the Eightieth Congress. According to his chief speech writer, strategist, and close friend, Elliott V. Bell, who traveled at his side during the campaign, the governor, too, felt highly critical of Congress and for many of the same reasons that Truman voiced. Furthermore the governor was aware that many Republicans in Congress, especially the Old Guard, looked for leadership to his rival, Taft, and thus he felt no particular kinship with them.[27]

On September 30 Dewey sent Brownell another memorandum: "Attached is a poll from a Salt Lake paper which is so encouraging I do not believe it but send it along for your information."[28] The polls everywhere overwhelmingly provided reassurance that Dewey's strategy was right. Even in the farm belt both the Gallup and *Des Moines Register* polls indicated a Republican landslide. A closer look, however, might have raised questions. The price of corn was down, having fallen from $1.78 a bushel in September to $1.38 in mid-October.[29] Returning from California through the Midwest, Truman revived his attack on Republican farm policy at whistle-stops in Oklahoma and Illinois. "Wheat has been selling below parity," he said, "and they [the Republicans] want that to happen because they want to turn the farmer back to the speculators."[30] On October 3 Representative Andresen again warned Dewey.

"Many of the farmers," he wrote, "are on the fence, due to remarks made by Truman about Republicans wrecking the farm program."[31]

George Elsey has recalled that in the early weeks of the campaign Truman was frank to say, privately, that he was behind Dewey. "He knew he was behind and he said he was behind," Elsey said, "but he was catching up and he was confident that by Election Day he would be out front."[32] Neither in public nor in private did Truman ever betray doubt that he would win the election, or, if he did, the evidence has not survived. At the start of October he returned from the western trip exuding confidence. Obviously, however, he felt he was in a desperate fight, and his next move reflected this.

On Sunday, October 3, he summoned Chief Justice Vinson to the White House and made an astonishing proposal. Without a word to Secretary of State Marshall, who was in Paris for talks about Berlin on the eve of United Nations meetings, Truman asked the chief justice to go to Moscow and plead with Stalin the aspirations of the American people for peace. After the Soviets had blockaded Berlin, Truman had thought about sending Eisenhower on such a mission and then decided against it. When the campaign got under way, David Noyes and Albert Z. Carr, the two political speech writers Truman had brought in that fall, revived the idea.

As always during the second half of 1948, the Berlin blockade and airlift kept alive the danger of war and thus had a potential effect on the campaign, particularly because of Wallace's charges that Truman was a warmonger. Noyes believed that Wallace was making headway in New York and California with the war issue. He talked to Truman about dramatizing his desire for peace in a mission to Moscow and out of these talks came a decision by Truman to send Vinson.[33] The latter doubted the wisdom of involving the chief justice in such an undertaking. But when Truman put the matter to him in terms of a presidential request, he dutifully accepted.

Although Truman doubtless thought of the mission in terms of Vinson's making a plea to Stalin for mutual understanding and not in terms of diplomatic negotiation, circumventing Marshall, the whole history of the preceding sixty days militated against the likelihood of fruitful talks. In a renewed search for a Berlin settlement Ambassador Walter Bedell Smith and his British and French counterparts had twice conferred with Stalin in August. New talks were begun with Molotov. The military governors met again in Berlin. All the parleys, however, led only into a labyrinth of disagreements. When the three Western ambassadors asked Molotov September 14 for yet another meeting with Stalin, Molotov said with finality that Stalin was on vacation and could not be disturbed.[34]

By September 25 the Western powers had reached the end in negotiations with Moscow. Despite some earlier differences among them on procedure, Marshall now won in Paris an accord with the British and French foreign ministers to submit the Berlin question to the United Nations Security Council. The clear understanding at the end of September was that none of the Allies should continue negotiations in Moscow.[35] Nothing, therefore, could have seemed more out of harmony than for one of the three, acting without consultation with the others, to send a special emissary to Stalin.

Probably unaware of all these details during his incessant campaigning, Truman requested Lovett to arrange for a Stalin-Vinson meeting and instructed Ross to ask the radio networks for thirty minutes for the presidential announcement Tuesday night, October 5.[36] Noyes and Carr drafted a speech for the occasion, in which Truman would appeal for a new period of trust in Soviet-American relations.

During the day Tuesday Truman communicated with Marshall in Paris by teletype to prepare him for what was certain to be sensational news. Marshall was horrified. The objections were obvious. The mission would leave the British and French in the lurch. It would appear to circumvent the Security Council at a critical time. It would look, reasonably, like the injection of politics into diplomacy. Marshall simply put his foot down on the plan. Truman accepted his objections.

Crestfallen, he returned to a meeting of his political advisers in the cabinet room and said the plan was off and the request for the broadcast should be rescinded. When some of his aides tried to argue with him, he simply said, "We won't do it."[37]

That night he invited Connally and Vandenberg to the White House. To Connally, who arrived first, he told the story of his abandoned plan. He said nothing about it to Vandenberg, but he asked the two senators what they would think of his trying to ease the Berlin crisis by telephoning Stalin. They were cool to the idea, particularly since Truman and Stalin did not speak the same language, and he dropped this venture, too. Vandenberg departed with a sense that Truman was groping for something that would give his campaign a needed "shot in the arm."[38] That was true no doubt, but the whole truth surely involved Truman's worry, reflected in a private memorandum he had written September 13: "I have a terrible feeling . . . that we are very close to war."[39]

With the public knowing nothing of the aborted mission, Truman left Washington October 6 on another whistle-stop tour through Delaware, Pennsylvania,

New Jersey, and upstate New York. The crowds were remarkable; if nothing else, this suggested that local Democratic organizations and labor groups were on the job. Truman had put aside his chagrin for his usual verve. "The record of the Eightieth Congress," he said, "is the handwriting on the wall: *mene, mene, tekel, upharsin.* They better beware."[40]

It was the same old Truman campaign: sharp speeches fairly criticizing Republican policy and defending New Deal liberalism, mixed with sophistries, bunkum piled higher than haystacks, and demagoguery tooting merrily down the track. Truman's attacks were rough. Still a good deal of his rhetoric smacked of the blarney of old campaigns for Board of Aldermen, and seldom were his oratorical abilities up to the voltage of his allegations. His attacks were discounted, too, in the widespread feeling that he was just going through the motions in a hopeless cause. The impromptu air of his appearances were deceptive, however. Behind him was an organized group of writers and researchers—in Washington and on the train—who kept him constantly supplied with material for whistle-stop talks as well as for the formal speeches.

The Truman train was crossing New York State October 8 when the clouds burst. Walter Trohan of the *Chicago Tribune* had broken the story of the Vinson affair, and everyone who wanted to jump on Truman had new cause and new access to the press for airing his opinion. "Playing politics with the nation's foreign policy," said *Time,* epitomizing the critics' attitude.[41] Truman continued his day's schedule, but, after a speech in Buffalo that night, terminated the trip and returned to Washington for a meeting the next day with Marshall, who had flown from Paris for "consultations." Truman then issued a statement explaining the episode in terms of his desire for peace.[42] Publicly, Dewey treated the episode with statesmanlike reserve. Off the record, he said to reporters: "If Harry Truman would just keep his hands off things for another few weeks! Particularly, if he will keep his hands off foreign policy, about which he knows considerably less than nothing."[43]

Making speeches before Dewey was up in the morning and often still entertaining crowds along the way after Dewey had retired at night, Truman again went whistle-stopping through the Middle West in mid-October and again drew large crowds, the meaning of which was mystifying at the time. Except for Truman perhaps, no one could explain the discrepancy between the big crowds and his continuing lag in the polls.

With an increasing show of confidence he derided Dewey: "Of course we don't know what he means by unity because he won't tell the country where he stands on any of the issues. . . . He doesn't dare tell the country what the real plans of the Republican party are. He's afraid that if he says anything he'll give the whole show away." "Apparently, I have offended the Republican gentleman who wants to be President. . . . Republicans don't like people who talk about depressions. You can hardly blame them for that. You remember the old saying: Don't talk about rope in the house where somebody has been hanged."[44]

En route to St. Paul October 13 Truman dictated to Elsey his forecast of the election, predicting, excessively, that he would win with 340 electoral votes and correctly claiming he would carry Massachusetts, Rhode Island, West Virginia,

Kentucky, North Carolina, Tennessee, Georgia, Arkansas, Oklahoma, Texas, New Mexico, Arizona, Nevada, Washington, Montana, Wyoming, Illinois, Missouri, Iowa, Minnesota, and Ohio. He made some erroneous claims, notably Pennsylvania, New Jersey, Maryland, Michigan, and Indiana. On the other hand, he shortchanged himself by calling California and Wisconsin doubtful.[45]

Dewey was scheduled to speak in Kansas City October 14 and be introduced by Alf M. Landon, the 1936 Republican nominee. On the fourteenth Landon wrote to him: "If I thought you had a tough fight and I could be of any help by being present . . . I would be there. Since neither is the case . . . I will listen to you on the radio." Dewey replied:

"I am not so sure of the result of the election as your letter indicates, being a conservative on those matters."[46]

According to Elliott Bell, Dewey was having doubts at that point. He raised the question with Bell and others as to whether he should change tactics. But, overwhelmingly, the response from Republican leaders around the country was that this would be a mistake. Dewey's supposed unfortunate experience with changed tactics in 1944 had an inhibiting effect now. Suddenly to change tactics against Truman might appear a sign of weakness. Furthermore his advisors on and off the train kept stressing his lead in the polls.

"The general attitude of everybody was," Bell recalled, " 'What are you fussing around for? We can't lose.' We knew the farmers in the corn belt were dissatisfied, but our agricultural experts said, 'Yes, the farmers are mad, but don't try to do anything about it. You can't do anything about it anyhow, and when the chips are down they will vote Republican.' "[47]

Talking to reporters aboard his train October 16, Truman struck close to the truth. "These polls were all taken before the real 'war' started," he said.[48] In the closing days of the campaign the polls did show him narrowing the gap between himself and Dewey as it had existed during the conventions. But the pollsters had stopped interviewing too soon, in those precomputer days, to catch the extent of Truman's October spurt. They also miscalculated the direction of many of the early undecided voters.

As October progressed Truman had more going for him than was generally realized. The advantages of incumbency were one thing. Then, too, public loathing of the Communists over Czechoslovakia and the Berlin blockade devastated the Wallace movement, already impoverished by labor's decision to stay with the Democrats. The Dixiecrats turned out to be a ragtag band shunned by the South beyond Alabama, Mississippi, Louisiana, and South Carolina, which had a total of thirty-eight electoral votes. While Truman made only three speeches in the South outside Texas, he generally soft-pedaled civil rights. In the meantime Barkley, Rayburn, and other prominent southern Democrats campaigned effectively among southern voters.

Liberals, including Mrs. Roosevelt, who had been cool to his renomination, announced their support of Truman. Even Ickes came round. Above all, the Democratic party of Franklin Roosevelt remained a great force. Memories of the depression and the New Deal kept a powerful current flowing in American politics, which now bore Truman along. Loudly, he played on New Deal sentiment. Up and down the land he made himself the keeper of the flame and stirred anxieties about what would happen to the economic and social reforms of the 1930s if the Republicans should win. "You better get out and help me win this fight, or you're going to be the loser, not I," he told the Democrats of Jersey City.[49]

In an incident in mid-October Dewey stubbed his toe, and Truman gleefully stomped on it. As the governor had begun to speak from the rear platform in Beaucoup, Illinois, his train suddenly lurched a few feet backward toward the crowd in what might have been, if the movement had continued, a serious accident. However, the train stopped quickly, yet Dewey, momentarily losing his poise, exclaimed into the microphone, "That's the first lunatic I have had for an engineer. He probably ought to be shot at sunrise, but I guess we can let him off because no one was hurt." The Democrats trumpeted this as the true reflection of Dewey's feelings about the workingman. A day or so later the Truman train pulled into the yards at Logansport, Indiana, a rail center, where trainmen wearing peaked caps and carrying long-spout oilers made up a large part of the crowd. Losing no time in telling what a grand trip he was having, Truman said, "We have had wonderful train crews all around the country, and they've been just as kind to us as they could possibly be." Then in a radio talk attacking Dewey for his promises about government efficiency, he said:

You remember that Mr. Hoover was an "efficiency expert," too. Also, as the Republicans presented him, he was the "Great Engineer." We have been hearing about engineers again recently from the Republican candidate. He objects to having engineers back up. He doesn't mention, however, that under the "Great Engineer" we backed up into the worst depression in our history.[50]

Increasingly, on the home stretch Truman ran against Hoover. The former president, who had refrained from criticizing Truman in his own speech at the Republican convention, was hurt at the words of his new friend and complained to James H. Rowe, Jr., Washington lawyer and prominent Democrat. Rowe tried to console him with explanations of political necessities.[51] According to Steelman, Truman once confessed to him, "I don't mean a word of it. Hoover didn't have any more to do with the Depression than you and I did."[52]

In mid-fall an issue involving the boundaries of Israel burst into the campaign. In May, in the face of Arab-Israeli hostilities, the United Nations General Assembly had appointed Count Folke Bernadotte, president of the Swedish Red Cross, as a mediator in Palestine. A cease-fire was agreed to by the combatants to give the count a chance to propose peace terms. His first suggestions were presented to the two sides in Rhodes June 28. One of the points—the one pertinent to the later issue in the presidential campaign—was that the Negev, awarded to the Jews in the debate over partition in November 1947, should be transferred to the Arabs. At the same time, Bernadotte suggested, western Galilee should be included in Israel.

While these discussions were going on, the Democrats adopted in their platform at Philadelphia a plank which read: "We approve the claims of the State of Israel to the boundaries set forth in the United Nations resolution of November 29th

[1947] and consider that modification thereof should be made only if fully accept-able to the State of Israel." The possible conflict between this plank and Ber-nadotte's suggestions, if rejected by Israel, was obvious. The Republican platform also contained a similar plank. Furthermore Truman apparently had given Weiz-mann assurances in keeping with the Democratic pledge.[53]

As the summer wore on with no peace in sight, Marshall and Bevin, separately but in close communication, strove for a satisfactory settlement. In the main their views coincided. On September 1, while Bernadotte was still working on his final report, Marshall prepared a message for James G. McDonald, United States special representative in Israel, outlining the American position. Israel, Marshall said, should have boundaries that "will make it more homogenous and well integrated than the hourglass frontiers" delineated in the General Assembly resolution of November 29, 1947:

Specifically it would appear to us that Israel might expand into the rich area of Galilee, which it now holds in military occupation, in return for relinquishing a large portion of the Negev to Transjordan. This would leave the new State with materially improved frontiers and consider-ably enriched in terms of natural resources.

The draft of the message was sent to the White House. Truman noted his ap-proval in the margin. That same September 1, therefore, Marshall sent the message to McDonald.[54] Ten days later he dispatched Robert McClintock to Rhodes to acquaint Bernadotte with the American view.[55] On September 17 Bernadotte was assassinated by Israeli terrorists in Jerusalem. Three days later his previously com-pleted report was submitted to the General Assembly, meeting in Paris. It proposed awarding the Negev to the Arabs and western Galilee to Israel.[56]

Having obtained Truman's written approval of such a realignment, Marshall, who was in Paris for the General Assembly, decided to issue a statement September 21, calling the Bernadotte report a "generally fair basis for settlement of the Pales-tine question." The statement, which Marshall—in advance of its release—cabled to the White House for Truman's comment, added: "My government is of the opinion that the conclusions are sound and strongly urges the parties and the Gen-eral Assembly to accept them in their entirety as the best possible basis for bringing peace to a distracted land."[57] Truman registered no objection, if he ever saw the statement between whistle-stops.

Publication of the statement sent the Jews in America into a rage over the prospective transfer of the Negev to the Arabs. Democrats cringed. Pro-Israel audi-ences booed Emanuel Celler and Sol Bloom when they made campaign speeches. As Truman was heading back from California, William M. Boyle, Jr., a campaign official and an old friend of Truman's, sent Matt Connelly a message to the train, saying that the "Jewish situation in New York and large cities turned against us ter-rifically by Marshall and Bevin Bernadotte Plan."[58]

In the midst of the trouble Eddie Jacobson joined the presidential party while Truman was campaigning in Oklahoma. "H.S.T. told us," Jacobson noted in his diary, "he would not budge from the U. N. decision of November 29th, regardless of what Marshall-Lovett or anyone else said."[59] Again, as in the case of the switch from partition to trusteeship the previous March, the question recurs as to what

Truman had understood when he signed his approval of the message to McDonald, September 21, taking the same position on boundaries that Bernadotte was to take in his final report.

Aboard the train Truman wrote out a message to Marshall, saying that the secretary's statement on the report "requires clarification." This was necessary, Truman noted, because he personally, the United States government, and the Democratic platform had all endorsed the boundaries set forth in the 1947 General Assembly resolution. "I shall have to state that my position as to boundaries has not changed," Truman wrote. Clifford telephoned Lovett from the train in Tulsa September 29, and as a result the message was never sent to Marshall. Clifford said, according to Lovett, that "the pressure from the Jewish groups on the President was mounting and that it was as bad as the time of the trusteeship suggestion." Lovett informed Clifford, however, of Truman's written approval of the boundary change. To send the drafted message of reversal to Marshall now, Lovett warned, "would put the Secretary in an intolerable position and, because of the agreements made with other countries in the light of the agreed policy, would label this country as violating its agreements and as completely untrustworthy in international matters. The consequences could be absolutely disastrous to us in the United Nations and elsewhere."[60] Truman remained silent on the question.

But on October 22 Dewey brought the issue to a head in the campaign by writing a letter to Dean Alfange, chairman of the American Palestine Committee, accusing the Truman administration of vacillation on Palestine and reaffirming his own support of the Republican platform commitment on Israel's boundaries.

Thereupon on October 24, in a statement drafted by Clifford, Truman reversed his position of September 1 and, publicly undercutting Marshall, said, "I stand squarely on the provisions covering Israel in the Democratic platform." He added:

With reference to the granting of a loan or loans to the State of Israel, I have directed the departments and agencies of the Executive Branch of our Government to work together in expediting the consideration of any applications for loans which may be submitted by the State of Israel.[61]

As for the Negev, it remains to this day, of course, part of Israel.

Truman set out on his final whistle-stop tour that same October 24, with an itinerary calling for major speeches in Chicago, Cleveland, Boston, New York, and St. Louis before going to Independence to vote. Despite crowds that were spectacular, especially in Chicago and Boston, Truman's last swing lacked the drama of many campaign finales because the contest was without suspense. No thought of a close finish or a surprise ending excited the country. *Life* reflected the national consensus in a caption accompanying a photograph of Dewey: "The Next President Travels by Ferryboat over the Broad Waters of San Francisco Bay."

Alfred C. Gaunt of the Merrimac Mills Company of Methuen, Massachusetts wrote to Dewey:

You may want Mrs. Dewey to help you pick the pattern for the inaugural suit; so I am sending you herewith a swatch book which embraces several patterns of the type that might be pleasing to you and which would definitely be 'acceptable.' 25-53 is the plain blue serge in the dark blue and 23-46 is the same thing in a herringbone.

Gaunt had made suits for Coolidge and Hoover. His father had made them for William McKinley. Dewey replied October 25:

My difficulty is this: would I need an inaugural suit, I would undoubtedly use the cut-a-way I now have. It would be quite a waste to have another.[62]

In these last days Truman concentrated on identifying himself with the New Deal philosophy and intensified his appeal to elements of the Roosevelt coalition, including blacks, Jews, Catholics, labor unions, and voters of Eastern European origin. In Chicago he delivered a rather nasty speech. Written by Carr but softened by Clifford and Elsey, it likened Dewey by implication to Hitler and Mussolini in the sense that he was the front man for fascist elements that might destroy democracy in the United States.

"The Republican candidate has the gall to say, and I quote him verbatim," Truman declared, " 'The Eightieth Congress delivered as no other Congress ever did for the future of this country.'

"Well, I'll say it delivered. It delivered for the private power lobby. It delivered for the big oil company lobby. It delivered for the railroad lobby. It delivered for the real estate lobby. . . . Republican leaders stand ready to deliver to big business more and more control over the resources of this nation and the rights of the American people."

The next night in Cleveland Truman made a rollicking speech, comparing the current polls with the *Literary Digest* poll of 1936, which indicated that Roosevelt would lose to Landon, who in the end carried only Maine and Vermont. "These polls that the Republican candidate is putting out are like sleeping pills designed to lull the voters into sleeping on Election Day," Truman said. "You might call them sleeping polls. . . . My friends, we are going to win this election."

In Mechanics Hall in Boston the following night he attended to Catholic sentiment by charging that in 1928 the Republicans had resorted to bigotry against Alfred E. Smith, the Catholic Democratic nominee. "And now the Republican leaders tell us that they stand for unity. In the old days, Al Smith would have said, 'That's baloney.' Today I think he would say, 'That's a lot of hooey.' And if that rhymes with anything, it is not my fault."

"Wait until the morning of November 3," he said in South Norwalk, Connecticut, October 28 on the way to New York, "and you are going to see more red-faced pollsters than you ever looked at in your life." "We are winning this election," he told a sidewalk crowd in Manhattan. "Don't let anybody tell you anything different." At a Liberal party rally in the old Madison Square Garden that night his pitch was what he had done for Israel. Trying to squelch any lingering resentment over the Bernadotte plan, he said, "I have never changed my position on Palestine or Israel."

The next day Truman went to Harlem and delivered a civil rights speech in a public square where he was presented the Franklin D. Roosevelt Memorial Brotherhood Medal by the Interdenominational Ministers Alliance. As was the tradition for Democratic presidential candidates then, he ended his New York visit with a speech at the Brooklyn Academy of Music. He warned that the Communists wanted to end the Truman administration and for that purpose were trying to help Wallace capture enough votes to defeat the Democratic ticket. "My friends, that must not happen!"

The next day, Saturday, October 30, was the end of the line. As the first whistle-stop had been Crestline, Ohio, on a bright June morning, the last was Mattoon, Illinois, in a gloomy autumn drizzle before only a fair-sized, late-afternoon crowd. The general level of hope on the Truman train as it pulled away on the final lap to St. Louis was fairly well captured by a weary Charles Ross. "Win, lose, or draw," he told reporters, "we'll be going down to Key West right after the election."

That was not Truman's mood, however. For his final major broadcast speech of the campaign in St. Louis that night he discarded a prepared text that had gone through three drafts and tossed aside a prepared outline. With a few of his own notes, which he barely looked at on the rostrum, he delivered an extemporaneous, broadcast speech in a style that had Kiel Auditorium rocking.

"People are waking up that the tide is beginning to roll," he concluded, "and I am here to tell you that if you do your duty as citizens of the greatest Republic the sun has ever shone on, we will have a government that will be for your interests, that will be for peace in the world and for the welfare of all the people and not just a few."[63]

Truman went home to Independence. The final polls were published. The final columns on the election were written for the newspapers. Magazines were trucked to the post office to be delivered to subscribers the day after the election. *Changing Times,* published by the Kiplinger organization, featured on its cover "What Dewey Will Do." Government would remain large and expensive under President Dewey, the *Wall Street Journal* reported. Drew Pearson's column surveyed the Dewey advisers who would move into the White House in January. A column by Joseph and Stewart Alsop worried about "how the government can get through the next ten weeks" with the lameduck president. The *New York Times* foresaw a Dewey victory with 345 electoral votes. The predictions of fifty political writers queried by *Newsweek* averaged 366. "We're going to miss lil' ole Harry," wrote Frederick Othman, a Washington columnist for Scripps-Howard newspapers.

In their final versions the Gallup poll gave Dewey an edge of 49.5 to 44.5 and the Crossley poll 51 to 42. The *Chicago Tribune* poll showed Dewey swamping Truman in Illinois and the *Des Moines Register* poll showed Dewey running away with Iowa.

Returning from a fourteen-state tour, Representative Everett McKinley Dirksen, Republican, of Illinois, wired Dewey on election eve: "Your victory is assured and will be bigger than you think. . . . You have a date with destiny."[64] Typifying the lead stories in countless newspapers on Election Day, the *Evening Star* in Washington reported: "Unless all signs fail, the balloting will put Governor Dewey of New York in the White House, the first Republican President in 16 years." On some markets that day corn was selling for $1 a bushel, down from $1.78 in September.[65]

43. *Incredible Victory*

B<small>Y THE TIME THE</small> polling places had closed in the East on Election Night Republican fat cats, the men in dinner jackets, the women in evening gowns and jewels, were waiting in line to get into the impending Dewey victory celebration in the ballroom of the Hotel Roosevelt in New York. A plump man who was at the head of the line with his wife had heard a rumor that Truman was leading in some early returns. He asked a passing reporter if this were true and received confirmation just as his wife inquired of him where he had put her mink coat. "If Truman wins," he said, "you won't have a mink coat."[1]

Dewey and his advisers were in a suite upstairs in the Roosevelt. No one knew where Truman was. It had been assumed that he would spend the evening at home in Independence, but townspeople gathering outside the house were simply told, "The president is not here."

With three Secret Service men—James J. Rowley, chief of the White House detail, Henry Nicholson, and Frank J. Barry—Truman had slipped away by car and headed for The Elms, a hotel at Excelsior Springs, Missouri, thirty-two miles northeast of Kansas City. When he arrived he had a Turkish bath, then went up to his suite and dined alone on a ham sandwich and a glass of buttermilk. A radio was on a table next to his bed, and the management had left a bottle of Scotch and a bottle of bourbon on the dresser. The Secret Service men occupied the suite across the hall.[2]

By ten o'clock in the East it was clear that Truman had carried Philadelphia but by less than FDR's plurality in 1944. People around the news tickers in the Roosevelt ballroom rejoiced that Pennsylvania was safe for Dewey, which it was. "We may be out of the trenches by midnight, said James C. Hagerty, the governor's press secretary. Next came news that Truman had carried Baltimore, but again by less than Roosevelt's plurality of four years earlier.

. What was happening, it appeared to those at the Roosevelt, was that Truman was carrying the big, urban Democratic strongholds where the vote count was reported earliest. However, since he was winning by relatively small margins there, it was cheerfully assumed that when the count from the traditionally Republican small towns and rural areas came in, Truman's lead in the cities would be overtaken by Dewey. The Republicans itched to hear these returns. At 10:30 Republican National Chairman Scott said at his Washington headquarters, "Now we have come to the Republican half of the evening."[3]

As the minutes ticked away, however, Truman continued to hold the lead in the total popular vote.

Before midnight the Secret Service post in the Meuhlebach Hotel in Kansas City telephoned Rowley, Nicholson, and Barry at Excelsior Springs with word that Truman had won Massachusetts.

Nicholson stepped across the hall to ascertain if Truman had heard the news on the radio. The president was asleep. Nicholson noticed that the bottle of bourbon had been opened and that about an inch of whiskey was gone. He could not resist waking Truman with the news. "Nick, stop worrying," Truman said. "It's all over. You all go to sleep, and we'll get up early in the morning."

City rooms in newspapers across the nation were getting into a jam. Editors had supposed they would be able to go in early with victory editions. Layouts with Dewey's biography and photographs of his family were in hand. But, nationally, the result remained inconclusive, and Truman still clung to a lead in the popular vote. Since those were days before computer-based projections, it looked as though many hours would pass before the result was known.

The country having been mesmerized by the public opinion polls, everyone was incredulous. By midnight radio commentators were saying in surprised tones that the election was the closest since the Woodrow Willson-Charles Evans Hughes race of 1916.* CBS interviewed former Democratic National Chairman Jim Farley on the outlook in case no candidate should receive a majority of the electoral vote and the election should be thrown into the House of Representatives.

In New York State Truman took an early lead over Dewey. A large Wallace vote, however, cut into Democratic strength, and around midnight Dewey was ahead—after the years of agonizing in the White House over the Jewish vote and the Palestine question.

CBS switched to Hugh Scott in Washington.

"I think the Republican Party and the Dewey-Warren team are winning," he said. "With New York coming through as well as it did, I feel that we are going to be all right. Pennsylvania is for Dewey. Ohio is for Dewey. I have returns from Illinois—they are for Dewey, and we are in there fighting and we are going to win."[4]

Scott's conclusions were premature. In Illinois and Ohio the race was nip and tuck.

At about 1:30 A.M. at the Roosevelt word was passed to reporters that Herbert Brownell was on his way down from Dewey's suite with an important statement. When he appeared in the ballroom he was mobbed and had to stand on a chair to make himself visible.

"We now know," he said, "that Governor Dewey will carry New York State by at least 50,000 votes and is the next president of the United States."

A tremendous cheer went up, and some guests were bowled aside by reporters racing to the telephones. The happy crowd of Republicans drifted back to news tickers only to read with consummate annoyance that Truman was still leading in the popular vote. Furthermore returns from Ohio and Iowa, both of which Dewey had carried in 1944, began to look disturbing.

"This stuff is all from the cities," a Republican official explained, "Wait till

---

* Television had election night programs, but the principal electronic coverage was on radio.

the farm vote starts coming in.''

Votes were being counted in California, and CBS switched to Earl Warren's headquarters in the St. Francis Hotel in San Francisco for a comment from his chief political adviser, Senator Knowland.

"I firmly believe," he said, "that California is going to be in the Republican column. The returns which we have from various sections of the state so far indicate, I believe, that Governor Dewey and Governor Warren will carry California by at least a 250,000 margin.''

Alf Landon was standing by in Topeka. "The outcome is certain," he told CBS listeners. "Thomas E. Dewey is certain to be the next president of the United States. . . . With the world so near the abyss of war the interests of our country and our civilization demand that president-elect Dewey participate immediately in framing our foreign policy.''

Although they still had to contend with the nagging fact of Truman's lead in the popular vote, Republican politicians took heart from a drop being indicated in the size of the president's early plurality in some states. CBS sought an assessment from Edwin F. Jaeckel, an intimate Dewey adviser.

"Well, I think it's running about true to form," he said. "Matter of fact in other states where there were great majorities for the president, they have been reduced. . . . I notice that the last returns in from Illinois showed a remarkable decrease in the majority and that was also true in Indiana and some of the other Midwest states. As far as we are concerned, it looks as though it is very optimistic in a number of these states because any majority that's been shown at this time for the president has been greatly reduced.''

Some of the leaders at the Roosevelt allowed themselves to talk about appointments Dewey might soon make as president. Over a glass of champagne Representative Leonard W. Hall of New York suggested to Brownell that Victor Johnson, director of the Republican Senatorial Campaign Committee, be nominated as ambassador to Guatemala.[5]

It was growing very late. Dewey had still not overtaken Truman in the popular vote, although he had already won New York, New Jersey, Pennsylvania, Maryland, Connecticut, Delaware, Maine, Vermont, Indiana, and his native state of Michigan. How could a Republican candidate win those states and have the Republican farm belt yet to be heard from and lose an election? NBC turned to its famed commentator, H. V. Kaltenborn, for an analysis.

"All the figures that I have had which I have managed to compare with four years ago," he said in his authoritative, staccato voice, "indicate a gain of from 2, 3, 4, 5, up to 10 percent for Dewey. I am inclined to think that while it is a very close race, on the basis of the figures as they now stand on our board Dewey has the best chance.''

Nevertheless the big moment never seemed to arrive in the Roosevelt ballroom. Those who had come to revel were fed only crumbs of hopeful news. Sometimes they had to endure long stretches with no news at all except from the hated tickers telling of Truman's persistent lead in the popular vote. Guests became annoyed at being told to wait for the farm vote, especially when late returns from

Ohio, Illinois, Iowa, Wisconsin, and Minnesota suggested disaster for Dewey in many small towns.

Then, incredibly, California, despite the presence of Governor Warren on the ticket, began to turn sour for the Republicans, and CBS switched back to Knowland. Indifferently, the senator said he was scaling down his earlier prediction of a 250,000-vote plurality for the Republicans.

"I am still convinced," he declared, "that California is going to end up in the Republican column by more than 100,000—maybe between 100,000 and 175,000 would be a good estimate at the present time."

By three or four in the morning bewilderment and disgust had fallen over the Roosevelt ballroom. Weary Republicans left in droves. Dewey went to bed for a couple of hours of sleep. Ohio, Illinois, and California held the balance.

The telephone rang in the Secret Service agents' suite in Excelsior Springs. It was the Muehlebach calling again, this time to report that Illinois had gone for Truman. Rowley, Nicholson, and Barry could not resist telling the president. When they entered his room he woke up, squinting without his glasses. "That's it," he said when they gave him the word.

"Now let's go back to sleep, and we'll go downtown tomorrow early and wait for the telegram from the other fellow," he said. On second thought he added: "Well, boys, we'll have one and then we'll all go to sleep." He got the bottle of bourbon off the dresser. "I'll pour the first one," he said.

Rowley, Barry, and Nicholson, still unaware that Ohio and California also were going for Truman, drank the first toast to a victorious president, who in a superhuman effort for a man of his age had been elected in his own right. In the process the Republican majority of the Eightieth Congress had been wiped out. The Democrats won control of the House and the Senate.

Thousands assembled in front of the Jackson County Courthouse in Independence Wednesday night to cheer Truman's victory—"not my victory," he contradicted, "but a victory of the Democratic Party for the People."[6] The next morning he and his family departed for Washington by train, stopping at stations along the way for brief talks free of gloating. Ten thousand persons were waiting at Union Station in St. Louis. Someone handed Truman a copy of the *Chicago Tribune*. On strike for months, the paper had to meet midday deadlines for some of the next morning's editions. On the basis of fragmentary returns and the optimism of its Washington bureau chief, Arthur Sears Henning, the headline on a mail edition run off around lunch time on Election Day read: DEWEY DEFEATS TRUMAN. The president laughingly held it aloft to please the crowd.

"I do not feel elated at the victory," he said at the next stop in Vincennes, Indiana. "I feel overwhelmed with responsibility."[7]

Truman already had struggled through three and a half years of great events, a monumental burden for one man, especially one without previous training in policy-making and management, without advanced education or diplomatic experience. If Truman had come to office as a great statesman full of knowledge, foresight, finesse, and skill in national and international leadership, his role would have been absorbing enough. It was a remarkable personal drama because he was not a great statesman. Suddenly handed the helm at a turning point in history, the former senator and small-town politician had been forced upon the journey unprepared, without being enabled by some miracle to shed a certain personal narrowness, ineptness, ignorance, impetuosity, and crudeness. Along the way, however, he was able to draw upon the resources of his own spirit, his own courage, humor, hope, good instincts, capacity to learn, willingness to face large challenges, and faith in the people and the American system of government. While he entrusted to other men like Marshall, Acheson, Byrnes, Forrestal, Clay, and MacArthur wide discretion in their fields and thus gave them a deep influence on the policies of his administration, Truman was always the president.

Nearing Washington and a great welcome, he had cause for gratification.

Apart from the Employment Act of 1946, he had not succeeded in getting major domestic reforms through Congress. Yet the country was prosperous in the conventional sense, the sense in which not too close a look was taken at the plight of the blacks and the poor. More than sixty million Americans had jobs. After months of muddling through by Truman and his advisers, the administration had taken a firmer grip. The wartime dislocations of industry and commerce at home had been overcome. Military spending had been reduced drastically. With the report of the President's Committee on Civil Rights, the president's special message to the Congress on civil rights, and the executive orders banning discrimination in the civil service and the armed forces, the federal government was turning slowly away from the old era of racial segregation in the United States. The liberal reforms of the New Deal had been successfully defended in the first presidential election since Roosevelt's death. Control of atomic energy had been kept in civilian hands.

Abroad the United States had undertaken an initiative to help put Western Europe back on its feet. The Berlin airlift was sustaining the Western position in Germany. Under American occupation Japan was experiencing an extraordinary revival. The two recent enemies of the United States, Germany and Japan, were becoming increasingly strong friends and partners of the American people. Greece, Turkey, Iran, and the Eastern Mediterranean remained outside the Soviet sphere.

Rapidly growing in the United States, however, was a condition with a potential for great harm to democracy, to Truman and his administration, and to the civil liberties of individuals. It was an overblown, zealous, and all too often crackpot alarm over communism and Communists. Culmination of decades of hostility by the American people to the Russian revolution, this scare was fed by—among other things—repugnance at Stalin's ruthlessness at home and abroad, by suppression of religion and free speech in the Soviet Union, by evidence of Soviet espionage, by the unscrupulous tactics of American Communists, by frustration over the unsatisfactory nature of the peace, by the outrageous intrusions of the House Committee on Un-American Activities, by the effective demagoguery of some Republican leaders in smearing liberals and liberal reforms as "Communistic," and, finally, by the president's own rhetoric in such utterances as the Truman Doctrine and by such of his acts as the establishment of the loyalty program.

Since the war some of the politicians, the press, the churches, the organs of business, the veterans' groups, and civic and patriotic associations had been exploiting anti-Communist sentiment so indiscriminately as to threaten a form of sickness in American society. In Truman's first term the disease had fallen short of being a plague. But the infection was now widespread, susceptible of being inflamed by a combination of the right kind of demagogue and unwholesome circumstances, of which Communist seizure of China and a cruel, stalemated war in Korea would be perfect models.

More than three years after the end of the war the international situation remained troubled and dangerous. Soviet-American relations continued to deteriorate as a result of mistrust, ambition and shortsightedness on both sides. Over Asia, too, black clouds were forming. "Because of the recent military reverses due in part to shortage of equipment and ammuinition, I am appealing personally to you, Mr. President," Chiang Kai-shek had written to Truman during the campaign, "to use your influence by every means at your command to hasten the procurement and transportation to Chinese ports of weapons and ammunition. . . . These have now become imperative. I am gravely concerned that any further delay in their delivery will have a disastrous effect on the outcome of the present operations."[8] As Dewey was to observe in a letter to Dulles, "China is in dreadful straits."

The day Truman arrived in triumph in Washington, November 5, Lovett cabled Marshall in Paris counseling against early withdrawal of American forces from South Korea, scene of a Communist uprising October 28. Four days later John J. Muccio, United States special representative in Korea, sent Marshall a copy of Syngman Rhee's message to his own delegation in Paris: "Due to recent uprising and also to continued propaganda stories coming from north, people feel nervous for fear that Red Army might march down south the moment American forces pull out."[9]

Hundreds of thousands of persons cheered the president on his ride up Pennsylvania Avenue from Union Station to the White House. It was one of the greatest crowds ever seen in a capital that had not only an affection for Harry Truman but a professional interest in how he had contrived seemingly the greatest upset in an American presidential election.

Only 51.1 percent of the eligible voters cast their ballots, in a low turnout. Obviously, there was considerable dissatisfaction with the choice of candidates. Then the contest had seemed so one-sided as to make the electorate apathetic. The polls doubtless misled many Republicans into thinking that it was not worth the trouble to vote since the election was already won. "It appears that 2 or 3 million Republicans stayed home out of overconfidence," Dewey said in a postelection press conference.

Truman did not win a majority of the votes cast, because of the diversion of Democratic votes to Wallace and Thurmond. Of the popular vote Truman received 24,105,812—49.5 percent—against Dewey's 21,970,065—45.1 percent. Truman did better in the electoral vote: 303 as against 189 for Dewey and 39 for Thurmond. Wallace received none.

Nevertheless the election had been extremely close in the sense that a small shift of votes in Ohio, Illinois, and California would have elected Dewey. If Dewey had carried any two of these states, the election would have been thrown into the House. In the end it was the Midwest and West that bore Truman to victory. In some states, notably Illinois, where Stevenson swamped the opposition, Truman ran behind the ticket and was doubtless helped by the strength of other Democrats.

Above all, Truman had skillfully taken advantage throughout of the power of the majority Democratic party—a potency reflected in the fact that twenty-three of the twenty-eight states he carried had voted for Roosevelt every time FDR ran.

Everyone was asking how Truman had won. "Labor did it," he was reported to have told a visitor the morning after the election.[10]

"All you have to do," Dewey wrote to a friend, "is to note that I carried New York, Pennsylvania, New Jersey, Delaware, and Maryland, while I lost Iowa, Minnesota, Wisconsin, Illinois, and Ohio. Each was lost exclusively in the rural areas."[11]

He also wrote to Henry Luce: "The farm vote switched in the last ten days, and you can analyze the figures from now to kingdom come and all they will show is that we lost the farm vote which we had in 1944 and that lost the election."[12]

An explanation that has stood the test of time well was offered by Truman in an exchange of letters with Churchill right after the election. Churchill wrote:

My dear Harry:
    I sent you a cable of my hearty congratulations on your gallant fight and tremendous victory. I felt keenly the way you were treated by some of your party and in particular Wallace who seemed to us over here to be a greater danger than he proved. But all this has now become only the background of your personal triumph. Of course it is my business as a foreigner or half of a foreigner to keep out of American politics, but I am sure I can say now what a relief it has been to me and most of us here to feel that the long continued comradeship between us and also with the Democratic Party in peace and war will not be interrupted. This is most necessary and gives the best chance of preserving peace.

    Truman replied:

Dear Winston:
    . . . I had a terrific fight and had to carry it to the people almost lone handed but when they knew the facts they went along with me. It seemed to have been a terrific political upset when you read the papers here in this country. Really it was not—it was merely a continuation of the policies which had been in effect for the last sixteen years and the policies that the people wanted.[13]

The Roosevelt coalition had held together just long enough to elect Truman.

The Washington reception ended with a ceremony on the north portico of the White House, after which the Trumans went inside and tried to get back to normal somehow. The next morning when West, assistant to the chief usher, entered Mrs. Truman's study to offer congratulations she laughingly brandished a copy of a recent issue of *Time* with a portrait of Dewey on the cover.

"Well," she told West, "It looks like you're going to have to put up with us for another four years."[14]

Mrs. Truman could not have foreseen the toll to be exacted by those four years. There was a price to Truman's victory. It was the price that a president would have to pay in dealing with the Communist seizure of China; with the North Korean invasion of South Korea; with the insubordination of General MacArthur; with an attempted assassination at Blair House; with the decision to develop the hydrogen bomb and rearm Western Europe; with "5 percenters" and scandal within the Administration; with the "China lobby" and the rise of Senator McCarthy and Richard Nixon, and, finally, with the emergence of General Eisenhower as the Republican candidate for president in 1952.

BIBLIOGRAPHICAL NOTE
REFERENCES
INDEX

Bibliographical Note

The following abbreviations are used in the References.

FR *Foreign Relations of the United States, Diplomatic Papers,* cited by year and volume. These volumes, publications of the Department of State, contain diplomatic correspondence, cables, memorandums, reports of conversations, and the like. Generally, they are published twenty-five years after the events to which they pertain—and not less than twenty-five years. Several may be issued in any given year by the U.S. Government Printing Office in Washington, D.C. All have the title *Foreign Relations of the United States, Diplomatic Papers.*

HSTL Harry S Truman Library, Independence, Missouri.

OF Official File, Truman Papers. Harry S Truman Library.

OH Oral History Transcript, Harry S Truman Library. The transcripts are of interviews conducted under the auspices of the Library with former officials of the Truman Administration, journalists, friends of the President and others who had special reason to know him and to have seen the operations of his administration.

PP *Public Papers of the Presidents of the United States: Harry S Truman,* cited by year. Under the direction of the National Archives and Records Service, Office of the Federal Register, a book under this title is issued for each year a president is in office (sometimes in more than one volume). Each volume contains such papers for that year as presidential messages, addresses, certain correspondence, transcripts of presidential press conferences, and statements of one sort or another. The volumes are issued by the U.S. Government Printing Office in Washington, D.C.

PPF President's Personal File. Harry S Truman Library.

PSF President's Secretary's File. Harry S Truman Library.

References

PREFACE

1. Richard S. Kirkendall, "Harry Truman" in Morton Borden, ed., *America's Eleven Greatest Presidents* (Chicago, 1971), p. 260.
2. Harry S Truman, *Year of Decisions* (Garden City, N.Y., 1955), p. 159.
3. OH, James H. Rowe, Jr.
4. James F. Byrnes, *All in One Lifetime* (New York, 1958), pp. 221–28.
5. Ibid., p. 101.
6. Robert E. Sherwood, *Roosevelt and Hopkins: An Intimate History* (New York, 1948), p. 882.
7. OH, James H. Rowe, Jr.
8. Truman, *Year of Decisions*, pp. 192–93.
9. Papers of Eben A. Ayers. Box 12. Vice-presidency folder. HSTL.
10. Diary of Henry L. Stimson, entry March 13, 1944, Henry L. Stimson Papers, Yale University Library, New Haven, Conn. For a different version, see Truman, *Year of Decisions*, pp. 10–11. Identification of Pasco as the installation in question is in Elting E. Morison, *Turmoil and Tradition: A Study of the Life and Times of Henry L. Stimson* (Boston, 1960), p. 616.
11. Alfred Steinberg, *The Man from Missouri: The Life and Times of Harry S Truman* (New York, 1962), pp. 145–46; 150.
12. William Hillman, *Mr. President* (New York, 1952), pp. 189–90.
13. Ibid., p. 172.
14. Vice-president Truman's speech to Jefferson City High School, February 22, 1945, quoted in *Newsweek*, April 23, 1945.

1. CALL FROM THE WHITE HOUSE

1. Interview with Lewis Deschler, February 21, 1972.
2. Truman, *Year of Decisions*, p. 6.
3. Interview with Lewis Deschler. (Some accounts place Senator Lyndon B. Johnson in Rayburn's office at this time. Deschler assured me that Johnson did not arrive until after Truman had left. This was confirmed by D. B. Hardeman, aide to Rayburn, who, though not present himself, discussed the event many times with Truman and Rayburn.
4. Truman, *Year of Decisions*, pp. 4, 43. Also Hillman, *Mr. President*, pp. 109–10.
5. Joseph P. Lash, *Eleanor and Franklin* (New York, 1971) p. 721.
6. Truman, *Year of Decisions*, p. 4.
7. Interview with Maj. Gen. Harry H. Vaughan (ret.), March 3, 1972.
8. Lash, *Eleanor and Franklin*, p. 708.
9. Truman, *Year of Decisions*, p. 5.
10. An account of the reaction to Roosevelt's death is contained in Bernard Asbell, *When F.D.R. Died* (New York, 1961), passim.
11. Albert E. Speer, *Inside the Third Reich* (New York, 1970), p. 586.
12. The author was the "old soldier."
13. Margaret Truman, with Margaret Cousins, *Souvenir: Margaret Truman's Own Story* (New York, 1956), pp. 83–84.
14. Truman, *Year of Decisions*, p. 5.
15. Jonathan Daniels, *Frontier on the Potomac* (New York, 1946), p. 10.
16. J. B. West, with Mary Lynn Kotz, *Upstairs at the White House: My Life with the First Ladies* (New York, 1973), p. 54.
17. Margaret Truman, *Harry S Truman* (New York, 1973), p. 211.
18. Interview with Harry H. Vaughan op. cit.
19. OH, Edward D. McKim.
20. Interview with Harry H. Vaughan op cit.
21. Truman, *Year of Decisions*, p. 9.
22. Winston S. Churchill to Roosevelt, March 13, 1945, *FR*, 1945, vol. 5, pp. 158–60.
23. V. M. Molotov to W. Averell Harriman, March 16, 1945, *FR*, 1945. vol. 3, pp. 731–32.,
24. Roosevelt to Stalin, March 17, 1945, *FR*, 1945, vol. 5, p. 1082.
25. Molotov to Harriman, March 22, 1945, *FR*, 1945, vol. 3, pp. 736–37.
26. Roosevelt to Stalin, March 24, 1945, *FR*, 1945, vol. 3, pp. 737–39.
27. Letter, Anna Rosenberg to Harriman, quoted in Averell Harriman, "Russia and the Cold War," in Robert D. Marcus and David Burner, eds., *America Since 1945* (New York, 1972), p. 5n. (The reference is to "Mrs. Hoffman." Anna Rosenberg later married Paul G. Hoffman.)
28. Roosevelt to Stalin, March 24, 1945, *FR*, 1945, vol. 1, p. 156.
29. Stalin to Roosevelt, March 27, 1945, *FR*, 1945, vol. 1, p. 165.
30. Stalin to Roosevelt, March 29, 1945, *FR*, 1945, vol. 3, pp. 739–40.
31. Roosevelt to Stalin, April 1, 1945. *FR*, 1945, vol. 5, pp. 194–96.
32. Walter Millis, ed., with the collaboration of E. S. Duffield, *The Forrestal Diaries* (New York, 1951), p. 38.
33. Stalin to Roosevelt, April 3, 1945, *FR*, 1945, vol. 3, pp. 742–43.
34. Charles E. Bohlen, with Robert H. Phelps, *Witness to History* (New York, 1973), p. 209.
35. Harriman to Edward R. Stettinius, Jr., April 4, 1945, *FR*, 1945, vol. 5, pp. 817–20.
36. Roosevelt to Stalin, April 4, 1945, *FR*, 1945, vol. 3, pp. 745–46.
37. Churchill to Roosevelt, April 5, 1945, *FR*, 1945, vol. 3, pp. 746–47.
38. *New York Times*, March 27, 1972, p. 33-M.
39. Harriman to Stettinius, April 6, 1945, *FR*, 1945, vol. 5, pp. 812–14.
40. Stalin to Roosevelt, April 7, 1945, *FR*, 1945, vol. 3, pp. 749–51.
41. Stalin to Roosevelt, April 7, 1945, *FR*, 1945, vol. 5, pp. 201–4.
42. Harriman to Stettinius, April 11, 1945, *FR*, 1945, vol. 5, pp. 994–96.
43. Truman, *Year of Decisions*, p. 10.
44. Diary of Henry L. Stimson, entry April 12, 1945.
45. Francis Biddle, *In Brief Authority* (Garden City, N.Y., 1962), p. 360.
46. Quoted in Herbert S. Parmet, *The Democrats: The Years after FDR* (New York, 1976), p. 18.
47. Papers of Frank McNaughton, HSTL.
48. Diary of Harold L. Ickes, entry April 12, 1945 (dictated April 28, 1945), Diaries of Harold L. Ickes, Library of Congress, Washington, D.C.
49. Arthur H. Vandenberg, Jr., ed. with Joe Alex Morris, *The Private Papers of Senator Vandenberg* (Cambridge, 1952), p. 165.
50. David E. Lilienthal, *The Journals of David E. Lilienthal*, vol. 1, *The TVA Years, 1939–45* (New York, 1964), p. 690.
51. Hillman, *Mr. President*, p. 114.
52. OH, Edward D. McKim.

2. HONEYMOON FOR THE "MISSOURI GANG"

1. Interview with Sen. George D. Aiken, May 5, 1975.
2. Interview with Harry H. Vaughan, March 3, 1972.
3. Margaret Truman, *Souvenir*, p. 86.
4. Interview with John W. Snyder, March 2, 1972. Also Snyder's

address to the Harry S Truman Institute, April 11, 1970, HSTL.
5. William D. Leahy, quoted in Len Giovanneti and Fred Freed, *The Decision to Drop the Bomb* (New York, 1965), p. 30.
6. Truman, *Year of Decisions*, p. 29.
7. Hillman, *Mr. President*, p. 110.
8. Truman, *Year of Decisions*, p. 17.
9. Diary of Henry L. Stimson, entry April 13, 1945.
10. Vandenberg, ed., *The Private Papers of Senator Vandenberg*, p. 167.
11. Richard E. Neustadt, *Presidential Power: The Politics of Leadership* (New York, 1960), p. 173.
12. Truman, *Year of Decisions*, p. 19.
13. *Kansas City Star*, April 15, 1945, p. 1.
14. Notes of Harold D. Smith: conferences with President Truman, April 1945–December 1945, entry of June 14, 1945. Bureau of the Budget Library, Washington, D.C.
15. Diary of Harold L. Ickes, entry April 29, 1945.
16. Sherwood, *Roosevelt and Hopkins*, p. 881.
17. Merriman Smith, *Thank You, Mr. President: A White House Notebook* (New York, 1946), p. 205.
18. John Morton Blum, ed., *The Price of Vision: The Diary of Henry A. Wallace, 1942–1946* (Boston, 1973), p. 452.
19. Truman handwritten notes, undated. PSF: Speech file. October 14, 1946, folder. Box 47.
20. Margaret Truman, *Harry S Truman*, p. 15.
21. Note, no date. PSF: Presidential appointments File. April 1945 folder. Box 82.
22. *PP*, 1945, p. 1 ff.
23. George E. Allen, *Presidents Who Have Known Me* (New York, 1950), pp. 164–65.
24. Winston S. Churchill, *Triumph and Tragedy* (Cambridge, 1953), p. 484.
25. Ibid., p. 481.
26. Interview with Harry H. Vaughan, August 3, 1972.
27. Blum, ed., *The Price of Vision*, p. 448.
28. Sam Rayburn interview with Martin Agronsky, quoted in

Alfred Steinberg, *Sam Rayburn: A Biography* (New York, 1975), pp. 228–29.
29. Joseph C. Grew, *Turbulent Era: A Diplomatic Record of Forty Years, 1904–1945*, vol. 2 (Boston, 1952), p. 1485n.
30. Notes of Harold D. Smith, entry April 18, 1945.
31. *PP*, 1947, p. 471.
32. Dean Acheson, *Present at the Creation: My Years in the State Department* (New York, 1969), p. 730.
33. Robert T. Elson, *The World of Time Inc.: The Intimate History of a Publishing Enterprise*, vol. 2 (1941–1960), p. 128.
34. *United States News*, May 18, 1945.
35. Truman to Clinton P. Anderson, August 27, 1945. PSF: Subject file. Cabinet data folder. Box 154.
36. Truman, *Year of Decisions*, p. 328.
37. Notes of Harold D. Smith, entry, May 21, 1945.
38. Blum, ed., *The Price of Vision*, p. 440.
39. Cabell Phillips, *The Truman Presidency: The History of a Triumphant Succession* (New York, 1966), p. 145.
40. Arthur M. Schlesinger, Jr., *The Imperial Presidency* (Boston, 1973), p. 221. For Ford staff see Hugh Sidey, "The Presidency. Help Wanted: Manager," *Time*, November 3, 1975, p. 15.
41. Richard E. Neustadt, "The Constraining of the President." *New York Times Magazine*, October 14, 1973.
42. John W. Snyder, address to the Harry S Truman Institute (cited in n. 4).
43. Ibid.
44. Emmet John Hughes, *The Living Presidency: The Resources and Dilemmas of the American Presidential Office* (New York, 1972), p. 347.
45. Acheson, *Present at the Creation*, p. 731.
46. OH, Samuel I. Rosenman.
47. Herbert Feis, *From Trust To Terror: The Onset of the Cold War* (New York, 1970), p. 8.
48. Blum, ed., *The Price of Vision*, p. 437.
49. Hughes, *The Living Presidency*, p. 333.
50. Interview with Richard E. Neustadt, November 9, 1973.

3. PRO–NEW DEAL; ANTI–NEW DEALER

1. Alonzo L. Hamby, *Beyond The New Deal: Harry S Truman and American Liberalism* (New York, 1973), p. xix.
2. Charles S. Murphy, remarks at the Harry S. Truman Library, Independence, Mo., April 1967, p. 10. HSTL.
3. David E. Lilienthal, *The Journals of David E. Lilienthal*, vol. 2, *The Atomic Energy Years, 1945–1950* (New York, 1964), pp. 433–34.
4. Ibid., p. 434.
5. Jonathan Daniels, *White House Witness, 1942–1945* (New York, 1975), p. 286.
6. Lilienthal, *The TVA Years*, p. 693.
7. *Kansas City Star*, April 15, 1945, p. 1.
8. Hillman, *Mr. President*, p. 115.
9. Lilienthal, *The Atomic Energy Years*, p. 434.
10. Margaret Truman, *Harry S Truman*, p. 253.
11. Jonathan Daniels, *The Man of Independence* (Philadelphia, 1950), p. 301.
12. See "T.R.B.," *New Republic*, June 4, 1945, p. 789.
13. Diary of Eben A. Ayers (former assistant White House press secretary), entry September 14, 1945. HSTL.
14. Margaret Truman, *Harry S Truman*, p. 260.
15. Biddle, *In Brief Authority*, pp. 364–65. For a different version: Truman, *Year of Decisions*, pp. 324–25.
16. Interview with Lloyd K. Garrison, May 6, 1972.
17. Blum, ed., *The Price of Vision*, p. 374.
18. Senate Select Committee to Study Government Operations with Respect to Intelligence Activities (hereafter cited as the

Church Committee), Final Report, bk. 2, *Intelligence Activities and the Rights of Americans* (Washington, D.C., 1976), p. 37. While the name of the person referred to as having been under surveillance was not mentioned, committee staff members privately identified him as Thomas G. Corcoran.
19. *PP*, 1945, pp. 9, 10, 28, 38, 72 ff., 82.
20. Quoted in William C. Berman, *The Politics of Civil Rights in the Truman Administration* (Columbus, Ohio, 1970), pp. 8–9.
21. Ibid., pp. 11–12.
22. Ibid., p. 12.
23. Ibid., pp. 19–20.
24. *PP*, 1945, pp. 10–11.
25. Berman, *The Politics of Civil Rights in the Truman Administration*, p. 8 ff. Also Donald R. McCoy and Richard Ruetten, *Quest and Response: Minority Rights in the Truman Administration* (Lawrence, Kans., 1973), p. 14 ff.
26. Quoted in McCoy and Ruetten, *Quest and Response*, p. 13.
27. Quoted in Robert A. Garson, *The Democratic Party and the Politics of Sectionalism, 1941–1948* (Baton Rouge, 1974), p. 22.
28. Mary Hedge Hinchey, "The Frustration of the New Deal Revival" (Ph.D. dissertation, University of Missouri, 1965).
29. Truman to Adolph J. Sabath, *PP*, 1945, pp. 104–5.
30. The friend was Earl Mazo, at the time a reporter for *Stars and Stripes*.
31. OF: 40. 1945 Folder.

4. THE OMINOUS RIFT OVER POLAND

1. OH, N. T. Veatch.
2. Churchill, *Triumph and Tragedy*, p. 366.
3. Roosevelt to Churchill, March 29, 1945, *FR*, vol. 5, p. 189.
4. Roosevelt to Stalin, April 1, 1945, *FR*, vol. 5, pp. 194–96.
5. Roosevelt to Churchill, April 11, 1945, *FR*, vol. 5, p. 210.
6. Truman to Churchill, April 13, 1945, *FR*, vol. 5, pp. 211–12.
7. Truman, *Year of Decisions*, pp. 38–39.
8. Ibid., pp. 14–17.
9. John W. Snyder address to the Harry S Truman Institute, April 11, 1970.
10. *New York Times*, June 24, 1941, p. 7.
11. J. Joseph Huthmacher, ed., *The Truman Years: The Reconstruction of Postwar America* (Hinsdale, Ill., 1972), p. 3.
12. James F. Byrnes, *Speaking Frankly* (New York, 1947), p. 58.
13. William D. Leahy, *I Was There: The Personal Story of the Chief of Staff and Presidents Roosevelt and Truman Based on His Notes and Diaries Made at the Time* (New York, 1950), p. 349.
14. John R. Deane, *The Strange Alliance: The Story of Our Efforts at Wartime Cooperation with the Russians* (New York, 1947), p. 86.

15. John Lewis Gaddis, *The United States and the Origins of the Cold War* (New York, 1972), p. 202.
16. W. Averell Harriman and Elie Abel, *Special Envoy to Churchill and Stalin, 1941–1946* (New York, 1975), pp. 441–43.
17. Edward R. Stettinius, Jr., *Roosevelt and The Russians: The Yalta Conference*, ed. Walter Johnson (Garden City, N.Y., 1949), p. 302.
18. Truman, *Year of Decisions*, p. 50.
19. Harriman and Abel, *Special Envoy*, p. 317.
20. Harriman to Cordell Hull, February 14, 1944, *FR*, vol. 4, pp. 1054–55.
21. Harriman to Hull, March 13, 1944, *FR*, vol. 4, p. 951.
22. Harriman to Stettinius, April 4, 1945, *FR*, 1945, vol. 4, pp. 817–20.
23. John Morton Blum, *From the Morgenthau Diaries*, vol. 3, *Years of War, 1941–1945* (Boston, 1967), p. 305.
24. This account is drawn from Charles E. Bohlen's notes of the Truman-Harriman meeting in *FR*, 1945, vol. 5, pp. 231–34.
25. Byrnes, *Speaking Frankly*, p. 61.
26. This account is based on Bohlen's notes in *FR*, 1945, vol. 5, pp. 235–36.

27. Account based on Bohlen's notes, *FR*, 1945, vol. 5, pp. 252–55.
28. Diary of Henry L. Stimson, entry April 23, 1945.
29. Margaret Truman, *Harry S Truman*, p. 238.
30. Aleksandr I. Solzhenitsyn, *The Gulag Archipelago, 1918–1956: An Experiment in Literary Investigation, I–II* (New York, 1947), p. 176.
31. According to Ernest Bevin, quoted in Acheson, *Present at the Creation*, p. 234.
32. Account based on Bohlen's notes in *FR*, 1945, vol. 5, pp. 79–82, supplemented by his recollections in Bohlen, *Witness to History*, p. 213.
33. In Truman, *Year of Decisions*, p. 82, Truman relates that the meeting ended with this exchange: Molotov: "I have never been talked to like that in my life." Truman: "Carry out your agreements and you won't get talked to like that." Bohlen's official record indicates no such exchange, and he told me in an interview no such words were spoken.
34. Journal of Joseph E. Davies, entry April 30, 1945, Joseph E. Davies Papers, Library of Congress, Washington, D.C. Box 16.

35. Leahy, *I Was There*, p. 352.
36. Harriman and Abel, *Special Envoy*, p. 454.
37. Joseph C. Grew, "Memorandum for the President: Policy With Respect to China," April 27, 1945. PSF: Subject file. Secretary of State-Stettinius folder. Box 159.
38. Walter LaFeber, "Roosevelt, Churchill, and Indochina: 1942–1945," *American Historical Review*, December 1975, p. 1277 ff.
39. Blum, ed., *The Price of Vision*, p. 451.
40. Gaddis, *The United States and the Origins of the Cold War*, p. 191.
41. Bruce Kuklick, *American Policy and the Division of Germany: The Clash with Russia over Reparations* (Ithaca, N.Y., 1972), p. 184.
42. *Conference of Berlin (Potsdam)*, *FR*, 1945, vol. 1, p. 262.
43. Zbigniew K. Brzezinski, *The Soviet Bloc: Unity and Conflict*. Revised and enlarged edition (Cambridge, 1971), p. 5.
44. Harriman to Truman, June 8, 1945, *Conference of Berlin (Potsdam)*, *FR*, 1945, vol. 1, pp. 61–62.

5. "THE MOST TERRIBLE WEAPON"

1. Truman, *Year of Decisions*, p. 85.
2. Barton J. Bernstein, "Doomsday II," *New York Times Magazine*, July 27, 1975, p. 21.
3. Morison, *Turmoil and Tradition*, p. 620.
4. Henry L. Stimson, "The Decision to Use The Atomic Bomb," *Harper's Magazine*, February, 1947.
5. Henry L. Stimson, "Memorandum Discussed with the President, April 25, 1945." Text in Henry L. Stimson and McGeorge Bundy, *On Active Service in Peace and War* (New York, 1948), p. 635 ff.
6. James MacGregor Burns, *Roosevelt: The Soldier of Freedom* (New York, 1970), p. 456.
7. Martin J. Sherwin, *A World Destroyed: The Atomic Bomb and the Grand Alliance* (New York, 1975), pp. 13, 33, 39.
8. Dwight D. Eisenhower, *Crusade in Europe* (Garden City, N.Y., 1948), p. 443.
9. Memorandums of George L. Harrison and Ralph A. Bard, texts in Sherwin, *A World Destroyed*, pp. 307–8.
10. Stimson and Bundy, *On Active Service*, p. 613.
11. Sherwin, *A World Destroyed*, pp. 83–85.
12. Ibid., pp. 104–5.

13. Richard G. Hewlett and Oscar E. Anderson, Jr., *The New World, 1936–1946* (University Park, Pa. 1962), pp. 334–35 (vol. 1 of *A History of the United States Atomic Energy Commission*).
14. Sherwin, *A World Destroyed*, p. 133.
15. Diary of Henry L. Stimson, entry December 31, 1944.
16. Truman, *Year of Decisions*, p. 87.
17. Anthony Eden, *The Reckoning* (Boston, 1965), p. 612.
18. Truman, *Year of Decisions*, p. 417. Also Stimson and Bundy, *On Active Service*, p. 619.
19. Sherwin, *A World Destroyed*, p. 200.
20. Gen. Leslie R. Groves's memorandum, "Report of Meeting with the President," text in Sherwin, *A World Destroyed*, pp. 293–94.
21. OH, J. Leonard Reinsch, pp. 25–26.
22. *PP*, 1945, p. 22.
23. Allen, *Presidents Who Have Known Me*, p. 152.
24. Notes of Harold D. Smith, entry April 26, 1945.
25. *PP*, 1945, p. 151.
26. Merriman Smith, *Thank You, Mr. President*, p. 286.
27. Interview with John W. Snyder, December 17, 1974.

6. V-E DAY: TRIUMPH AND TROUBLE

1. Margaret Truman, *Harry S Truman*, p. 241.
2. West, *Upstairs at the White House*, pp. 56–57.
3. Truman, *Year of Decisions*, p. 206.
4. *PP*, 1945, pp. 48–49.
5. Herbert Feis, *The Atomic Bomb and the End of World War II* (Princeton, 1970), pp. 15–16. For Truman text, *PP*, 1945, p. 50.
6. Churchill, *Triumph and Tragedy*, pp. 511–12.
7. Ibid., p. 506.
8. *Conference of Berlin (Potsdam)*, *FR*, 1945, vol. 1, pp. 3–4.
9. Churchill, *Triumph and Tragedy*, pp. 573–74.
10. Truman, *Year of Decisions*, p. 203.
11. Ibid., p. 302.
12. Memorandum, Grew to Truman, May 1, 1945. PSF: Bulgaria and Rumania Folder. Box 172.
13. Truman, *Year of Decisions*, p. 255.
14. Gaddis, *The United States and the Origins of the Cold War*, p. 230.
15. George C. Herring, Jr., *Aid to Russia: Strategy, Diplomacy, the Origins of the Cold War* (New York, 1973), p. xiii.
16. Notes of Harold D. Smith, entry April 26, 1945.
17. Stettinius to Grew, May 9, 1945, *FR*, 1945, vol. 5, p. 998.
18. Herring, *Aid to Russia*, p. 204.
19. Truman, *Year of Decisions*, p. 228.
20. Herring, *Aid to Russia*, pp. 204–5.
21. Sherwood, *Roosevelt and Hopkins*, pp. 894, 896.
22. Blum, ed., *The Price of Vision*, p. 436.
23. William Hardy McNeill, *America, Britain, and Russia: Their Cooperation and Conflict* (New York, 1970), p. 554n.
24. Diary of Joseph E. Davies, entry May 13, 1945; journal of Joseph E. Davies, April 30, 1945; Joseph E. Davies PApers, Library of Congress, Washington, D.C. Box 16.
25. Bohlen, *Witness to History*, p. 215, and Harriman and Abel, *Special Envoy*, p. 459. For a different version see Truman, *Year of Decisions*, pp. 257–58.
26. Margaret Truman, *Harry S Truman*, p. 253.
27. Hillman, *Mr. President*, p. 116.
28. Churchill, *Triumph and Tragedy*, p. 578.
29. Hillman, *Mr. President*, p. 116.
30. Gaddis, *The United States and the Origins of the Cold War*, p. 232.
31. The Hopkins-Stalin talks are reported in Sherwood, *Roosevelt and Hopkins*, pp. 887–912.

32. Hopkins to Truman, May 31, 1945, *FR*, 1945, vol. 5, pp. 307–9.
33. Churchill, *Triumph and Tragedy*, pp. 582–83.
34. *PP*, 1945, pp. 120, 123, 126.
35. Truman, *Year of Decisions*, p. 244.
36. Grew, *Turbulent Era*, vol. 2, p. 1475.
37. Ibid., p. 1479.
38. Truman to Churchill, May 16, 1945. PSF: Churchill folder.
39. Truman to Charles de Gaulle, May 1, 1945, *FR*, 1945, vol. 4, p. 682.
40. Diary of Eben A. Ayers, entry May 4, 1945.
41. Henry L. Stimson, "Memorandum of Conference with President," June 6, 1945, Henry L. Stimson Papers, Yale University Library, New Haven, Conn. Also Stimson's diary entries of June 5 and 6, 1945.
42. Leahy, *I Was There*, p. 373.
43. Truman to de Gaulle, June 6, 1945, *FR*, 1945, vol. 4, pp. 734–35.
44. Howard M. Sachar, *Europe Leaves the Middle East, 1936–1954*. (New York, 1972), pp. 314–23.
45. Diary of Eben A. Ayers, entry May 31, 1945.
46. Ibid., July 7, 1945.
47. Exchange of telegrams, Truman to Stalin, June 14, 1945; Stalin to Truman, June 16, 1945, *FR*, 1945, vol. 3, pp. 135–37. Also Gabriel Kolko, *The Politics of War: The World and United States Foreign Policy, 1943–1945* (New York, 1968), p. 506.
48. LaFeber, Walter, "Roosevelt, Churchill, and Indochina: 1942–45" (cited in n. 38, chap. 4).
49. Senate Committee on Foreign Relations, *The United States and Vietnam: 1944–1947: A staff study based on the Pentagon Papers, Prepared for the Use of the Committee on Foreign Relations of the United States Senate, Study no. 2*, committee print (Washington, D.C., 1972) pp. 15–17.
50. Ibid., pp. 16–17.
51. Truman, *Year of Decisions*, p. 224.
52. Saul D. Alinsky, *John L. Lewis: An Unauthorized Biography* (New York, 1949), pp. 327–28.
53. *PP*, 1945, p. 111.
54. Hillman, *Mr. President*, pp. 121–22.
55. Truman, *Year of Decisions*, pp. 57–58.
56. James T. Patterson, *Mr. Republican: A Biography of Robert A. Taft* (Boston, 1972), p. 302.

57. Blum, ed., *The Price of Vision*, p. 454.
58. Notes of Harold D. Smith, entry May 4, 1945.
59. Joseph C. Grew, "Memorandum for the President: Policy with Respect To China" (cited in n. 37, chap. 4).
60. Russell D. Buhite, *Patrick J. Hurley and American Foreign Policy* (Ithaca, 1973), pp. 182–83.
61. John Paton Davies, Jr., *Dragon by the Tail: American, British, Japanese, and Russian Encounters with China and with One Another* (New York, 1972), p. 402.
62. John Stewart Service, *The Amerasia Papers: Some Problems in the History of U.S.-China Relations* (Berkeley, 1971), pp. 187–88.

63. Herbert Feis, *The China Tangle: The American Effort in China from Pearl Harbor to the Marshall Mission* (Princeton, 1953), p. 272.
64. E. J. Kahn, Jr., *The China Hands: America's Foreign Service Officers and What Befell Them* (New York, 1975), pp. 165–67.
65. Millis, ed., *The Forrestal Diaries*, p. 65.
66. Senate Committee on the Judiciary, Subcommittee to Investigate the Administration of the Internal Security Act and Other Internal Security Laws, *The Amerasia Papers: A Clue to the Catastrophe of China*, vol. 1, committee print (Washington, D.C., 1970), p. 42.

7. ATOMIC BOMB: THE FATEFUL MOMENTUM

1. Transcript of Truman's informal remarks before the opening of his press conference June 1, 1945. HSTL.
2. Hillman, *Mr. President*, pp. 117–18.
3. Gene Smith, *The Shattered Dream: Herbert Hoover and the Great Depression* (New York, 1970), pp. 233–35.
4. *PP*, 1945, p. 83 ff.
5. Stimson and Bundy, *On Active Service*, p. 617.
6. Jeremy Bernstein, "Profiles, Physicist—II," *New Yorker*, October 20, 1975, pp. 61–62.
7. Hewlett and Anderson, *The New World*, p. 358.
8. John Toland, *The Rising Sun: The Decline and Fall of The Japanese Empire 1936–1945* (New York, 1970), p. 794.
9. Stimson and Bundy, *On Active Service*, p. 617.
10. Byrnes, *All In One Lifetime*, p. 286.
11. Toland, *The Rising Sun*, chap. 29.
12. Henry L. Stimson, "Memo of Conference with the President, June 6, 1945," Henry L. Stimson Papers, Yale University Library, New Haven, Conn.
13. Diary of Henry L. Stimson, entries May 14 and 15, 1945.
14. Hewlett and Anderson, *The New World*, p. 361.

15. Toland, *The Rising Sun*, p. 50.
16. Bernard Brodie, *War and Politics* (New York, 1973), p. 51.
17. Hewlett and Anderson, *The New World*, p. 355–66. Also Barton J. Bernstein, ed., *The Atomic Bomb: The Critical Issues* (Boston, 1976), pp. 25–26.
18. Barton J. Bernstein and Allen J. Matusow, eds., *The Truman Administration: A Documentary History* (New York, 1966), p. 15.
19. Fletcher Knebel and Charles W. Bailey, "The Fight Over The A-Bomb," *Look*, August 13, 1963, p. 20.
20. Hewlett and Anderson, *The New World*, pp. 369, 371–72.
21. Leahy to the Joints Chiefs of Staff, memorandum June 14, 1945, in "The Entry of the Soviet Union into the War Against Japan: Military Plans, 1941–1945," Department of Defense release, October 19, 1955. The account of the June 18 meeting is based on the official minutes in *Conference of Berlin (Potsdam), FR*, 1945, vol. 1, p. 903 ff., and also on Hewlett and Anderson, *The New World*, pp. 363–64.
22. Text in Sherwin, *A World Destroyed*, p. 284.

8. TRUMAN, STALIN, CHURCHILL

1. Diary of Joseph E. Davies, entry May 21, 1945, Joseph E. Davies Papers, Box 17.
2. Truman, *Year of Decisions*, p. 331.
3. Diary of Harold L. Ickes, entry July 8, 1945.
4. Hillman, *Mr. President*, pp. 123.
5. Bohlen, *Witness to History*, p. 226.
6. Notes of Harold D. Smith, entry July 6, 1972.
7. Bohlen, *Witness To History*, p. 226.
8. Truman, *Year of Decisions*, p. 340. Also Churchill, *Triumph and Tragedy*, p. 630. Also Lord Moran, *Churchill: The Struggle for Survival, 1940–1965, Taken from the Diaries of Lord Moran* (Boston, 1966), p. 293.
9. Merriman Smith, *Thank You, Mr. President*, p. 244.
10. Unpublished manuscript by Harry H. Vaughan, recounting his years with Harry S Truman. Lent to the author by Vaughan. P. 63.
11. Groves, "Report on Alamogordo Atomic Bomb Test" (cited n. 20, ch. 5).
12. Hewlett and Anderson, *The New World*, p. 383.
13. Scene recounted to author by George M. Elsey, who was present as a communications officer.
14. Bohlen, *Witness to History*, p. 230.
15. This account is based on Charles E. Bohlen's notes in *Conference of Berlin (Potsdam), FR*, 1945, vol. 2, p. 43 ff. and p. 1582 ff.
16. Svetlana Alliluyeva, *Twenty Letters to a Friend* (New York, 1967), pp. 21–22, 28.
17. Interview with Harry H. Vaughan, March 2, 1972.

18. Truman, *Year of Decisions*, p. 341
19. Ibid., pp. 341–42.
20. Daniels, *The Man of Independence*, p. 278. Also PSF: Mr. President file. Interview folder, p. 3. Box 269.
21. Interview with John W. Snyder, December 17, 1974.
22. Interview with Harry H. Vaughan, March 2, 1972.
23. Leahy, *I Was There*, p. 368.
24. Gaddis, *The United States and the Origins of the Cold War*, p. 118.
25. Letter, Stimson to Truman, May 16, 1945. PSF: Subject file. Secretary of War folder. Box 157.
26. Truman, *Year of Decisions*, p. 235.
27. Ibid., p. 236.
28. Senate Committee on the Judiciary, Subcommittee to Investigate the Administration of the Internal Security Act and Other Internal Security Laws, *Morgenthau Diary (Germany)*, vol. 2, committee print (Washington, D.C., 1967), pp. 1223–24.
29. Harriman to Stettinius, April 3, 1945. *FR*, vol. 3, p. 186.
30. Truman, *Year of Decisions*, p. 308.
31. "Instructions for the United States Representative on the Allied Commission on Reparations," May 18, 1945, *FR*, 1945, vol. 3, p. 1222 ff.
32. Kuklick, *American Policy and the Division of Germany*, p. 140.
33. McNeill, *America, Britain, and Russia*, p. 614.
34. Byrnes, *All In One Lifetime*, p. 290.
35. Truman, *Year of Decisions*, p. 357.

9. THE POTSDAM CONFERENCE

1. Unless otherwise indicated this account of Potsdam is drawn from *Conference of Berlin (Potsdam), FR*, 1945, vols. 1–2. Also from the British minutes, Public Records Office, London, F.O. 371.50867, 1910, pp. 97–282.
2. Gaddis, *The United States and the Origins of the Cold War*, pp. 163–64.
3. Bohlen, *Witness To History*, (cited chap. 1), p. 228.
4. Margaret Truman, *Harry S Truman*, p. 269.
5. Moran, *Churchill: The Struggle for Survival*, p. 294.
6. Diary of Henry L. Stimson, entry July 22, 1945.
7. Churchill, *Triumph and Tragedy*, p. 648.
8. Truman, *Year of Decisions* (cited in Preface), p. 369.
9. Moran, *Churchill: The Struggle for Survival*, p. 298.
10. Truman, *Year of Decisions*, p. 369.
11. Journal of Joseph E. Davies, entry July 21, 1945.
12. Diary of Joseph E. Davies, entry July 21, 1945.
13. Truman, *Year of Decisions*, p. 384.
14. Diary of Joseph E. Davies, entry July 25, 1945.

15. Eisenhower, *Crusade in Europe*, p. 444.
16. Margaret Truman, *Harry S Truman*, p. 260, and Truman, *Year of Decisions*, p. 295.
17. Journal of Joseph E. Davies, entry July 29, 1945.
18. Truman, *Year of Decisions*, p. 402.
19. *Conference of Berlin (Potsdam), FR*, 1945, vol. 2, p. 279.
20. Kuklick, *American Policy and the Division of Germany*, pp. 155–63.
21. Robert Murphy, *Diplomat Among Warriors* (Garden City, 1964), pp. 278–79.
22. Interview with Harry H. Vaughan, June 21, 1973.
23. Letter to the author from Milton F. Perry, curator of the museum at the Harry S Truman Library, June 25, 1972.
24. Truman to Wallace, July 27, 1945. OF: 27-B.
25. Byrnes, *All in One Lifetime*, p. 313.
26. Adam B. Ulam, *Stalin: The Man and His Era* (New York, 1973), p. 626.
27. *PP*, 1945, p. 210.

10. "RELEASE WHEN READY"

1. Diary of Henry L. Stimson, entries July 18 and 21, 1945.
2. Churchill, *Triumph and Tragedy*, p. 639.
3. Grew, *The Turbulent Era*, vol. 2, p. 1450.
4. Ibid., p. 1424.
5. Henry L. Stimson, "Memorandum for the President," July 2, 1945, quoted in Stimson and Bundy, *On Active Service*, pp. 620–24.
6. *Conference of Berlin (Potsdam), FR*, 1945, vol. 1, pp. 893–94.
7. Cordell Hull, assisted by Andrew Berding, *Memoirs*, vol. 2 (New York, 1948), pp. 1593–94.
8. Telegram, Sen. Richard B. Russell, Jr., to Truman, August 7, 1945. OF: 197, Miscellaneous.
9. Hewlett and Anderson, *The New World*, p. 381.
10. *The Conference of Berlin (Potsdam), FR*, 1945, vol. 2, p. 1267.
11. Stimson and Bundy, *On Active Service*, p. 626.
12. Ibid., p. 618.
13. Forrest C. Pogue, *George C. Marshall: Organizer of Victory, 1943–1945* (New York, 1973), pp. 499–502.
14. Lilienthal, *The Atomic Energy Years*, p. 198.
15. Churchill, *Triumph and Tragedy*, p. 639.
16. Byrnes, *All in One Lifetime*, p. 292.
17. Department of Defense release: "The Entry of the Soviet Union into the War Against Japan" (cited in n. 21, ch. 7), pp. 85–88.
18. Stimson and Bundy, *On Active Service*, pp. 617–8.
19. Memorandum by Bohlen, *Conference of Berlin (Potsdam), FR*, 1945, vol. 2, pp. 1587–88.
20. Churchill, *Triumph and Tragedy*, p. 642.
21. Hewlett and Anderson, *The New World*, p. 369.
22. Truman, *Year of Decisions*, p. 416.
23. Interview with Harry H. Vaughan, March 3, 1972.
24. Ulam, *Stalin: The Man and His Era*, p. 625.
25. Stimson and Bundy, *On Active Service*, pp. 638–41.
26. Ibid., p. 637.
27. Hewlett and Anderson, *The New World*, pp. 391–92.
28. Truman to Ambassador Patrick J. Hurley in China, July 23, 1945, *Conference of Berlin (Potsdam), FR*, 1945, vol. 2, p. 1241. Also Byrnes, *All in One Lifetime*, p. 291.
29. "The Combined Chiefs of Staff to President Truman and Prime Minister Churchill," July 24, 1945, *Conference of Berlin (Potsdam), FR*, 1945, vol. 2, p. 1462.
30. Hewlett and Anderson, *The New World*, pp. 397–98.
31. Leslie R. Groves, *Now It Can Be Told: The Story of The Manhattan Project* (New York, 1962), p. 265.
32. Truman, *Year of Decisions*, pp. 420–21.
33. *Conference of Berlin (Potsdam), FR*, 1945, vol. 2, p. 1474 ff.
34. Ibid., pp. 1284, 449–50. Also Byrnes, *All In One Lifetime*, p. 296.
35. Feis, *The Atomic Bomb and the End of World War II*, p. 107.
36. Extracts, "Press Conference Statement by Prime Minister Suzuki," *Conference of Berlin (Potsdam), FR*, 1945, vol. 2, p. 1293.
37. Stimson and Bundy, *On Active Service*, p. 625.
38. Truman, *Year of Decisions*, p. 421.
39. Stimson to Truman, July 30, 1945, *Conference of Berlin (Potsdam), FR*, 1945, vol. 2, pp. 1374—75.
40. Interview with George Elsey, November 15, 1972. Truman's message is in the records of the Manhattan Engineer District (Harrison-Bundy folder no. 64), United States Atomic Energy Commission. Elsey possesses the original handwritten copy.
41. Groves, "Report on Alamogordo Atomic Bomb Test" (cited n. 20, ch. 5).
42. Lansing Lamont, *Day of Trinity* (New York, 1965), p. 238.
43. Jeremy Bernstein, "Profiles: Physicist—II," *New Yorker*, October 20, 1975, p. 58.
44. Merriman Smith, *Thank You, Mr. President*, pp. 257–58.
45. The United Press story filed from the *Augusta*, August 6, 1975, by Merriman Smith.
46. Fletcher Knebel and Charles W. Bailey, *No High Ground* (New York, 1960), pp. 230–31.
47. *PP*, 1945, p. 197 ff.
48. Ibid., p. 212.
49. Truman to Samuel McCrea Cavert, August 11, 1945. OF: 692-A, atomic Bomb folder.
50. Truman's handwritten draft of a speech to the Gridiron Dinner in Washington, December 15, 1945. PSF: Speech file. December 15, 1945, folder. Box 46.
51. Memorandum, Truman to Acheson, May 7, 1946. PSF: Subject file. Atomic tests folder. Box 201.
52. Barton J. Bernstein, ed., *The Atomic Bomb: The Critical Issues*, pp. 95–96.
53. Notes of Harold D. Smith, entry October 5, 1945.
54. Toland, *The Rising Sun*, p. 794.
55. Sherwood, *Roosevelt and Hopkins*, p. 902.
56. *PP*, 1945, p. 200.
57. Toland, *The Rising Sun*, pp. 806–7.
58. Lamont, *Day of Trinity*, pp. 304–5.
59. Sherwin, *A World Destroyed*, p. 209.
60. Ibid., p. 234.
61. George M. Elsey note, undated. 1945–46 folders. Papers of George M. Elsey. Atomic Energy folders. HSTL.
62. *PP*, 1945, p. 197 ff.
63. Patterson to Rosenman, letter and draft, August 9, 1945. Papers of Samuel I. Rosenman. August 9, 1945, folder. HSTL.
64. Barton J. Bernstein, "The Atomic Bomb and American Foreign Policy: The Route to Hiroshima." In Bernstein, ed., *The Atomic Bomb: The Critical Issues*, p. 115.
65. Toland, *The Rising Sun*, pp. 810–13.
66. Truman, *Year of Decisions*, p. 427.
67. Ibid., p. 428 ff.
68. Lisle A. Rose, *Dubious Victory: The United States and the End of World War II* (Kent State, 1973), p. 319.
69. Blum, ed., *The Price of Vision*, p. 474.
70. Ibid.
71. Russell to Truman. OF: 197. Miscellaneous.
72. Blum, ed., *The Price of Vision*, p. 475.
73. Truman, *Year of Decisions*, 430–32. Also "Memorandum by the Special Assistant to the Assistant Secretary of State," *Conference of Berlin (Potsdam), FR*, 1945, vol. 1, pp. 933–35.
74. Toland, *The Rising Sun*, p. 729–32.

11. VICTORY—AND THEN?

1. Sen. George D. Aiden, of Vermont, told me of a talk he had with Truman in May, 1945. Truman was worried as to whether the American people would be satisfied with a victory that did not include a triumphant invasion of Japan. Aiken, about to deliver some Memorial Day addresses in New England, said he would throw out the idea of victory without invasion to test people's reaction. He reported to Truman later that he had sensed no reaction at all.
2. Quoted in Barton J. Bernstein, ed., *The Atomic Bomb: The Critical Issues*, p. xiii.
3. Samuel Eliot Morison, "Why Japan Surrendered," *Atlantic Monthly*, October, 1960, reprinted in Barton J. Bernstein, ed., *The Atomic Bomb: The Critical Issues*, p. 41 ff.
4. *New York Times*, August 15, 1945.
5. Truman, *Year of Decisions*, p. 438.
6. Truman to Ambassador Hurley in China, August 1, 1945, *Conference of Berlin (Potsdam), FR*, 1945, vol. 2, p. 1321.
7. George M. Elsey memorandum, *The Conference of Berlin (Potsdam) 1945, FR*, vol. 1, pp. 309, 310.
8. "Korea: Occupation and Military Government: Composition of Forces," March 29, 1944, *FR*, 1944, vol. 5, pp. 1224–28.
9. *FR*, 1945, vol. 6, p. 1039.
10. Ulam, *Stalin: The Man and His Era*, p. 628.
11. Truman, *Year of Decisions*, p. 434.
12. Davies, *Dragon by the Tail*, p. 410.
13. Department of State, *United States Relations with China, with Special Reference to the Period 1944–1949*, Far Eastern Series 30, Document 3573 (Washington, D.C., 1949), p. 939 (hereafter cited as "China White Paper").
14. Ibid., pp. 311–12.

12. THE MORASS OF RECONVERSION

1. Darrel Robert Cady, "The Truman Administration's Reconversion Policies, 1945–1947" (Ph.D. dissertation, University of Kansas, 1974).
2. Herbert Stein, *The Fiscal Revolution in America* (Chicago, 1969), p. 169.
3. OF: 172-A.
4. Stephen K. Bailey, *Congress Makes a Law: The Story Behind the Employment Act of 1946* (New York, 1950), p. 93.
5. Cady, "The Truman Administration's Reconversion Policies" op. cit.
6. Stein, *The Fiscal Revolution in America*, p. 242.
7. OH, Samuel I. Rosenman.
8. Interview with John W. Snyder, October 6, 1972.
9. OH, Samuel I. Rosenman.
10. Interview with John W. Snyder, op. cit.
11. Craufurd D. Goodwin and R. Stanley Herren, "The Truman Administration: Problems and Policies Unfold," in Craufurd D. Goodwin, ed., *Exhortation and Control: The Search for a Wage-Price Policy, 1945–1971* (Washington, D.C.: Brookings Institution, 1975), pp. 13–14.
12. William H. Davis memorandum. OF: 407. Labor 1945 folder. Also *PP*, 1945, p. 220 ff.

13. Diary of Eben A. Ayers, entry September 17, 1945.
14. Ed O'Connell to Matthew J. Connelly, August 23, 1945. OF: 170. CIO 1945–46 folder.
15. Barton J. Bernstein, "The Truman Administration and Its Reconversion Wage Policy," *Labor History*, Fall 1965, p. 222.
16. Interview with W. Willard Wirtz, April 24, 1974.
17. *PP*, 1945, p. 263 ff.
18. Hinchey, "The Frustration of New Deal Revival," (cited n. 28, chap. 3).

19. *Congressional Record*, September 6, 1945, p. 1945.
20. Garson, *The Democratic Party and the Politics of Sectionalism*, p. 146.
21. Figures supplied by the Bureau of Labor Statistics.
22. Diary of Eben A. Ayers, entry September 21, 1945.
23. *Newsweek*, September 17, 1945, p. 30.

13. "PEACE IS HELL"

1. Blum, ed., *The Price of Vision*, p. 524.
2. Notes of Harold D. Smith, entry November 28, 1945.
3. Chester Bowles, *Promises to Keep: My Years in Public Life 1941–1969* (New York, 1971), p. 161.
4. Notes of Harold D. Smith, entry September 18, 1945.
5. *PP*, 1945, pp. 325–26.
6. Ibid., p. 272.
7. Barton J. Bernstein, "The Truman Administration and Its Reconversion Wage Policy" (cited n. 15, chap. 12).
8. Notes of Harold D. Smith, entry September 18, 1945.
9. Lilienthal, *The Atomic Energy Years, Journals*, pp. 4–5.
10. Truman to William H. Davis. OF: 96. OES. Also Diary of Eben A. Ayers, entry September 19, 1945.
11. Margaret Truman, *Harry S Truman*, p. 290.
12. Hillman, *Mr. President*, p. 127.
13. Blum, ed., *The Price of Vision*, pp. 489, 491. *Time*, October 1, 1945, p. 20.
14. Margaret Truman, *Harry S Truman*, p. 288.
15. *PP*, 1945, p. 394.
16. Barton J. Bernstein, "The Removal of War Production Controls on Business, 1945–1946," *Business History Review*, Summer 1965.
17. Lilienthal, *The Atomic Energy Years, Journals*, p. 7.
18. Diary of Harold L. Ickes, entry October 20, 1945.
19. Arthur S. Link, *American Epoch: A History of the United States Since The 1890s* (New York, 1958), p. 597.
20. Chester Bowles to Samuel I. Rosenman, October 29, 1945. Papers of Samuel I. Rosenman. Wages and Prices folder. HSTL.
21. *PP*, 1945, p. 439 ff.
22. Ibid., p. 458 ff.
23. See letter, Fred Smith to Matthew Connelly. OF: 407-C. November 1945, folder.
24. Benjamin F. Fairless to John W. Snyder, November 13, 1945. OF: 342. Steel 1945-February 1947 folder.
25. Truman memorandum, November 13, 1945. OF: 407-C. November 1945 folder. (There is no indication whether it was actually sent.)

26. *PP*, 1945, p. 516 ff.
27. *Time*, December 17, 1945, pp. 17–18.
28. Blum, ed., *The Price of Vision*, pp. 529, 553, 555, 575.
29. Diary of Eben A. Ayers, entries December 12 and 14, 1945.
30. Richard O. Davies, *Housing Reform during the Truman Administration* (Columbia, Mo., 1966), p. 43.
31. Bowles to Truman, December 17, 1945, quoted in Bernstein and Matusow, eds., *The Truman Administration: A Documentary History*, p. 62.
32. Blum, ed., *The Price of Vision*, p. 531.
33. *PP*, 1945, p. 508.
34. Interview with John W. Snyder, May 15, 1974. Also *PP*, 1945, p. 563.
35. Quoted in Bernstein and Matusow, eds., *The Truman Administration: A Documentary History*, p. 57.
36. This account draws on Bailey, *Congress Makes a Law*, chap. 8. Vinson's letter to Truman October 22, 1945, is in PSF: Subject file. Secretary of Treasury-Snyder folder. Box 160.
37. Diary of Harold L. Ickes, entries November 17 and 25 and December 2, 1945.
38. Alben W. Barkley, *That Reminds Me—The Autobiography of the Veep* (Garden City, 1954), p. 197.
39. Daniels, *The Man of Independence*, p. 298.
40. Diary of Harold L. Ickes, entry December 2, 1945.
41. *PP*, 1945, p. 569.
42. Allen J. Matusow, *Farm Policies and Politics in the Truman Years* (Cambridge, 1967), pp. 12–16.
43. Truman handwritten draft of his speech to the Gridiron Dinner in Washington, December 15, 1945. PSF: Speech file. December 15, 1945, folder. Box 46.
44. *PP*, 1945, p. 475 ff.
45. Diary of Harold L. Ickes, entry December 9, 1945.
46. Interview with John R. Steelman, August 23, 1974. Also OH, Steelman.
47. National Archives and Records Service, Office of the Federal Register, *Public Papers of the Presidents of the United States: Lyndon B. Johnson, 1965* (in two volumes), vol. 2 (June 1 to December 31, 1965), p. 811 ff.

14. TRUMAN AND THE MILITARY

1. Truman, *Year of Decisions*, p. 509.
2. *Congressional Record*, September 14, 1945, p. 8607.
3. Truman to E. E. Cox, September 12, 1945, OF: 190-R.
4. Interview with John W. Snyder, November 1, 1973.
5. Notes of Harold D. Smith, entry September 18, 1945.
6. *PP*, 1945, p. 326.
7. Ibid., p. 328.
8. Truman, *Year of Decisions*, pp. 520–21.
9. Millis, ed., *The Forrestal Diaries*, p. 102.
10. Diary of Henry L. Stimson, entry September 4, 1945.
11. Vandenberg, ed., *The Private Papers of Senator Vandenberg*, p. 221.
12. *PP*, 1945, pp. 212–13.
13. Hewlett and Anderson, *The New World*, p. 417.
14. See Averell Harriman report from Moscow, quoted in Barton J. Bernstein, ed., *The Atomic Bomb: The Critical Issues*, p. 133.
15. Henry L. Stimson, "Memorandum for the President," September 11, 1945. Text in Stimson and Bundy, *On Active Service*, pp. 642–46.
16. Hewlett and Anderson, *The New World*, p. 419.
17. Blum, ed., *The Price of Vision*, p. 481.
18. Joint Chiefs of Staff, "Memorandum for the President," October 23, 1945. PSF: General folder. Leahy file.
19. Joseph Davies's notes on a conversation, quoted in Gaddis, *The United States And the Origins of the Cold War*, p. 273.
20. This account is based on Truman, *Year of Decisions*, pp. 525–28; Acheson, *Present at the Creation*, pp. 123–24; Millis, ed., *The Forrestal Diaries*, pp. 94–96, and Blum, *The Price of Vision*, pp. 482–85.
21. *PP*, 1945, p. 362 ff.
22. Tris Coffin, *Missouri Compromise* (Boston, 1947), p. 17.
23. *PP*, 1945, pp. 380–81.
24. Ibid., 381 ff.
25. Blum, ed., *The Price of Vision*, p. 524.
26. For the history of the May-Johnson bill see Hewlett and Anderson, *The New World*, chaps. 12–14.

27. *PP*, 1945, p. 403.
28. Exchange of memorandums, October 22 and 24, 1945. OF: 692. Atomic energy.
29. Papers of George M. Elsey. Box 88. Atomic energy. HSTL.
30. Harry S Truman, *Years of Trial and Hope* (Garden City, 1956), pp. 3–4.
31. Richard F. Haynes, *The Awesome Power: Harry S Truman as Commander in Chief* (Baton Rouge, 1973), p. 72.
32. Hewlett and Anderson, *The New World*, p. 461.
33. Gaddis, *The United States and the Origins of the Cold War*, pp. 270–72.
34. "International Control of Atomic Energy: Memorandum by the Prime Minister," in *Documents Relating to the Meeting in Washington between the President of the United States of America, the Prime Minister of the United Kingdom, and the Prime Minister of Canada on the subject of Atomic Energy, November 1945* (London: British Public Record Office), p. 4.
35. Hewlett and Anderson, *The New World*, pp. 459–65.
36. *PP*, 1945, p. 472 ff.
37. Gaddis, *The United States and the Origins of the Cold War*, p. 272.
38. Margaret Truman, *Harry S Truman*, pp. 289–90.
39. Notes of Harold D. Smith, entry October 16, 1945.
40. Charles G. Ross to Arthur Krock, October 17, 1945. Correspondence folder. Ross Papers. HSTL.
41. Senate Committee on Foreign Relations, *The United States and Vietnam: 1944–1947* (cited n. 49, chap. 6), p. 9.
42. For background on UMT and Truman's attitude see Haynes, *The Awesome Power*, chap. 6.
43. Interview with George M. Elsey, August 6, 1974.
44. *PP*, 1945, p. 404 ff.
45. Memorandum for the President. Subject: "Basis for a Postwar Army." OF: 109. UMT.
46. Blum, ed., *The Price of Vision*, p. 502.
47. Gaddis, *The United States and the Origins of the Cold War*, p. 275.

48. Frederick C. Barghoorn, *The Soviet Image of The United States: A Study in Distortion* (Port Washington, N.Y., 1950), p. 143.
49. *PP*, 1945, p. 431 ff.
50. Barghoorn, *The Soviet Image of The United States*, p. 143.
51. Senate Committee on Foreign Relations, *The United States and Vietnam: 1944–1947* (cited n. 49, chap. 6), p. 9.
52. Truman's handwritten draft of his speech to the Gridiron Dinner in Washington, December 15, 1945. PSF speech file. December 15, 1945 folder. Box 46.
53. *PP*, 1945, p. 546 ff.
54. Millis, ed., *The Forrestal Diaries*, p. 118.
55. For a history of unification see Demetrios Caraley, *The Politics of Military Unification: A Study of Conflict and the Policy Process* (New York, 1966).
56. Papers of George M. Elsey. Box 82. Unification folder. HSTL.
57. Robert Greenhalgh Albion and Robert Howe Connery, *Forrestal and the Navy* (New York, 1962), p. 261.
58. Interview with George M. Elsey, August 6, 1974.
59. Interview with Harry H. Vaughan, March 3, 1972. Also Truman, *Year of Decisions*, p. 17.
60. Adam Yarmolinsky, *The Military Establishment: Its Impact on American Society* (New York, 1971), pp. 27–28.
61. Notes of Harold D. Smith, entry June 5, 1945.

62. Haynes, *The Awesome Power*, pp. 21–22.
63. Margaret Truman, *Harry S Truman*, p. 260.
64. Diary of Harold L. Ickes, entry August 26, 1945.
65. Margaret Truman, *Harry S Truman*, p. 293.
66. Churchill, *Triumph and Tragedy*, p. 481.
67. *PP*, 1948, p. 600.
68. Robert H. Ferrell, *George C. Marshall as Secretary of State, 1947–1949* (New York, 1966), p. 3.
69. Pogue, *George C. Marshall: Organizer of Victory*, p. 558.
70. James R. Shepley to George C. Marshall, March 7, 1946, *FR*, 1946, vol. 9, pp. 511–12.
71. John Lewis Gaddis, "Harry S. Truman and the Origins of Containment," in Frank J. Merli and Theodore A. Wilson, eds., *Makers of American Foreign Policy from Benjamin Franklin to Henry Kissinger* (New York, 1974), p. 511.
72. Haynes, *The Awesome Power*, pp. 265–66.
73. See Truman's Army Day speech, *PP*, 1946, p. 186.
74. Stephen E. Ambrose in *The Military and American Society: Essays and Readings*, Stephen E. Ambrose and James Alden Barber, Jr., eds. (New York, 1972), p. 5.
75. George E. Hopkins, "The Air Power Lobby and the Cold War" (Paper read at the annual meeting of the Organization of American Historians in Boston, April 19, 1975), p. 14.

15. THE TRUMANS AT HOME

1. West, *Upstairs at the White House*, p. 57.
2. Margaret Truman, *Souvenir*, p. 117.
3. Blum, *The Price of Vision*, p. 478.
4. Interview with Henry J. Nicholson, September 11, 1972.
5. Interview with George Aiken, May 5, 1972.
6. West, *Upstairs at the White House*, p. 59.
7. Carl Solberg, *Riding High: America in the Cold War* (New York, 1973), p. 12.
8. West, *Upstairs at the White House*, p. 86.

9. The exchange of telegrams between Adam Clayton Powell and Bess Truman is in OF: 93. DAR controversy, separate folder.
10. *PP*, 1945, p. 396.
11. Marianne Means, *The Woman in the White House: The Lives, Times, and Influence of Twelve Notable First Ladies* (New York, 1963), p. 229.
12. Diary of Eben A. Ayers, entry October 13, 1945.
13. Margaret Truman, *Souvenir*, p. 118.
14. West, *Upstairs at the White House*, p. 76.

16. THE HURLEY AFFAIR: AN OMEN

1. Blum, ed., *The Price of Vision*, p. 519.
2. Department of State, "China White Paper," pp. 581–84.
3. Blum, ed., *The Price of Vision*, p. 520. For an account of Hurley's motives and activities see Buhite, *Patrick J. Hurley and American Foreign Policy*, chap. 11.
4. *FR*, 1945, vol. 7, pp. 629–34. Also Ernest R. May, *The Truman Administration and China, 1945–1949* in The America's Alternatives Series, ed. Harold M. Hyman (Philadelphia, 1975), p. 8.
5. Truman's handwritten note, attached to November 15, 1945, appointments sheet. PSF: November, 1945, folder. Box 82.
6. Millis, ed., *The Forrestal Diaries*, p. 113. Also Blum, *The Price of Vision*, p. 522.
7. Kenneth S. Chern, "The Senate and the China Problem, 1945" (Paper read before the American Historical Association meeting in Chicago, December 28, 1974).
8. Papers of George M. Elsey. China folder. HSTL.
9. George C. Marshall memorandum of a conversation with Tru-

man, Byrnes, and Leahy, December 11, 1945, *FR*, 1945, vol. 7, pp. 767–69.
10. Truman to Will Durant, November 7, 1951. PSF: General file. D Folder.
11. Marshall memorandum of a conversation with Truman and Acheson, December 14, 1945, *FR*, 1945, vol. 7, p. 770.
12. *PP*, 1945, pp. 543–45.
13. Truman to Marshall, December 15, 1945, in Department of State, "China White Paper," pp. 605–6.
14. C. V. Cheriyan, "The United States and Korea: A Historical Study of Relations 1945" (Ph.D. dissertation, University of Kerala, India, 1970).
15. Frank Baldwin in *Without Parallel: The American-Korean Relationship Since 1945*, ed. Frank Baldwin (New York, 1973), p. 9.
16. MacArthur to the Joint Chiefs of Staff, December 16, 1945, *FR*, 1945, vol. 6, pp. 1144–48.

17. THE BEGINNING OF THE END FOR BYRNES

1. Diary of Harold L. Ickes, entry July 8, 1945.
2. Bohlen, *Witness to History*, p. 256.
3. Notes of Harold D. Smith, entry September 18, 1945.
4. Blum, *The Price of Vision*, p. 517.
5. Notes of Harold D. Smith, entries November 28 and December 5, 1945.
6. Diary of William D. Leahy, entry November 28, 1945. Papers of William D. Leahy, Library of Congress.
7. Journal of Joseph E. Davies, entry December 8, 1945.
8. Vandenberg, ed., *The Private Papers of Senator Vandenberg*, p. 228.
9. Harriman and Abel, *Special Envoy*, p. 524.
10. Diary of Eben A. Ayers, entry December 12, 1945.
11. Truman, *Year of Decisions*, p. 549.
12. Gary R. Hess, "The Iranian Crisis of 1945–46 and the Cold War," *Political Science Quarterly*, March 1974.
13. Truman, *Year of Decisions*, p. 551.
14. Interview with John W. Snyder, October 6, 1972.
15. David S. McLellan, *Dean Acheson: The State Department Years* (New York, 1976), pp. 75–76.

16. Exchange of telegrams between Byrnes and Truman. PSF: Presidential appointment file. January 1946, folder. Box 83.
17. Interview with John R. Steelman, August 23, 1974.
18. Acheson, *Present at the Creation*, p. 136.
19. Byrnes, *All in One Lifetime*, p. 343.
20. Truman, *Year of Decisions*, p. 550.
21. Daniels, *The Man of Independence*, p. 311.
22. Interviews with John W. Snyder, November 1, 1973; Harry H. Vaughan, May 3, 1973; Samuel I. Rosenman, November 11, 1972; and John R. Steelman, September 5, 1974.
23. *PP*, 1946, pp. 9, 10.
24. Hillman, *Mr. President*, pp. 21–23 (the same letter that appears in Truman, *Year of Decisions*, pp. 551–52).
25. Truman, *Year of Decisions*, pp. 551–52.
26. Byrnes, *All In One Lifetime*, 402.
27. PSF: Mr. President file. Drafts, no. 1 folder. Box 268.
28. Interview with John W. Snyder November 1, 1973.
29. *PP*, 1946, p. 102.
30. Millis, *The Forrestal Diaries*, pp. 127–28.
31. Blum, *The Price of Vision*, p. 536.

18. 1946: A DISASTROUS YEAR BEGINS

1. Transcript of pre-press conference remarks by the president, December 20, 1945. HSTL.
2. *Time*, January 27, 1946, p. 3.
3. *Statistical Abstract of the United States, 1948*, p. 224.
4. *PP*, 1946, p. 1 ff.
5. Patterson, *Mr. Republican*, p. 304.
6. Margaret Truman, *Harry S Truman*, p. 302.

7. Robert Sherwood to Rosenman, January 5, 1946. Papers of Samuel I. Rosenman. Sherwood folder. HSTL.
8. Truman notes, "Radio Address to the Nation." PSF: Speech file. January 3, 1946, folder. Box 46.
9. *PP*, 1946, pp. 15–16.
10. *Newsweek*, January 21, 1946.
11. Diary of Harold L. Ickes, entry January 12, 1946.

12. Interview with Henry J. Nicholson, September 11, 1972.
13. Diary of Harold L. Ickes, entry January 12, 1976.
14. Dwight D. Eisenhower memorandum for the president, "Soldier Demonstrations in Manila," undated. PSF: General file. Eisenhower folder. For "plain mutiny," see diary of Eben A. Ayers, entry January 8, 1946.
15. *PP*, 1946, p. 16.
16. Truman's handwritten notes on steel negotiations January 16 and 17, 1946. Charles Ross papers. HSTL.
17. *PP*, 1946, pp. 23–24.
18. Interview with John W. Snyder, November 4, 1974.
19. Bowles to Truman, January 24, 1946. PSF: General file. Bowles folder.
20. Interview with John W. Snyder, November 1, 1973.
21. Blum, ed., *The Price of Vision*, p. 555.
22. *PP*, 1946, p. 123.
23. Bowles, *Promises to Keep*, pp. 173–75.
24. *PP*, 1946, pp. 115–16.
25. Truman to Baruch, February 15, 1946. PSF: General file. Wage-price data folder.
26. *PP*, 1946, p. 123. Also Bernard M. Baruch, *Baruch: The Public Years* (New York, 1960), p. 387.
27. *PP*, 1946, pp. 116–19.
28. *New York Times*, February 3, 1946, p. 1.
29. Frank Cormier and William J. Eaton, *Reuther* (Englewood Cliffs, N.J., 1970), p. 229.
30. Millis, ed., *The Forrestal Diaries*, p. 143.
31. Ernest Gruening, *Many Battles: The Autobiography of Ernest R. Gruening* (New York, 1973), p. 341.
32. Notes of Harold D. Smith, entry January 4, 1946.
33. Bailey, *Congress Makes a Law*, p. 237.
34. Stein, *The Fiscal Revolution in America*, p. 197.

35. *PP*, 1946, pp. 125–26.
36. On Nourse appointment see OH, Charles S. Murphy. On offer to Monrowe see *PP*, 1948, p. 229.
37. Stein, *The Fiscal Revolution in America*, p. 205.
38. Truman to Senator Brien McMahon, February 2, 1946. *PP*, 1946, pp. 105–6.
39. Gaddis, *The United States and the Origins of the Cold War*, pp. 252–53.
40. Attlee cable mentioned in Truman, *Year of Decisions*, p. 467. Byrnes quoted in Matusow, *Farm Policies and Politics in the Truman Years*, p. 18. See Matusow, chaps. 1 and 2, for an account of the administration's handling of the food crisis.
41. *PP*, 1946, p. 106 ff.
42. Notes of Harold D. Smith, entries February 8 and 28, 1946.
43. Text of Truman's letter to Mrs. Roosevelt and the exchange of correspondence between him and Tom Clark are in OF: 197. Japan.
44. McCoy and Ruetten, *Quest and Response*, p. 11.
45. Garson, *The Democratic Party and the Politics of Sectionalism, 1941–1948*, p. 142.
46. *PP*, 1946, p. 94.
47. Copy of letter to the author by the FBI, April 3, 1975.
48. John Kenneth Galbraith, *Money: Whence It Came, Where It Went* (Boston, 1975), p. 258.
49. Telephone interview with George M. Elsey, May 2, 1976.
50. Notes of Harold D. Smith, entries May 4, May 11, July 6, and September 5, 1945.
51. Byrnes's statement, *New York Times*, November 13, 1953, p. 12.
52. *PP*, 1946, p. 21.
53. Ibid., pp. 90–91.
54. West, *Upstairs at the White House*, pp. 96–97.

19. ICKES QUITS

1. Diary of Harold L. Ickes, entry June 9, 1945.
2. Margaret Truman, *Harry S Truman*, p. 290.
3. *PP*, 1946, p. 90.
4. Joseph P. Lash, *Eleanor: The Years Alone* (New York, 1972), p. 123.
5. "Memorandum handed me by the President—February 1946." Papers of Charles G. Ross. HSTL.
6. Diary of Harold L. Ickes, entry April 29, 1945.
7. Ibid., entries June 2 and 9, 1945.
8. *PP*, 1945, pp. 352–54.
9. Diary of Harold L. Ickes, entry December 23, 1945.
10. *PP*, 1946, p. 121. Truman's recollection was that he had said, "Well, tell the truth, but be kind to Pauley."
11. Ibid., p. 111.

12. Diary of Harold L. Ickes, entries February 10 and 17, 1946.
13. "Memorandum by the President," Ross Papers (cited n. 5).
14. *PP*, 1946, pp. 119, 120.
15. Ibid., p. 128.
16. Ibid., 153, 154.
17. Coffin, *Missouri Compromise*, p. 58.
18. *PP*, 1946, p. 314. Also McNaughton and Hehmeyer, *Harry S. Truman, President*, pp. 222–23.
19. Hoover to Vaughan, December 6, 1946. PSF: Subject file. FBI. I folder. Box 168.
20. Forrestal to Truman, undated. PSF: General file. D folder.
21. Diary of Harold L. Ickes, entry June 2, 1945.
22. Blum, ed., *The Price of Vision*, p. 551.

20. SHARP TURN TOWARD THE COLD WAR

1. OF: 85-J. U.N. General Assembly, 1945–1946.
2. Blum, ed., *The Price of Vision*, p. 503.
3. *PP*, 1946, p. 97 ff.
4. Truman, *Year of Decisions*, p. 479.
5. Feis, *From Trust To Terror*, p. 230 n.
6. Blum, ed., *The Price of Vision*, p. 526.
7. Byrnes, *All In One Lifetime*, p. 310.
8. Gaddis, *The United States and the Origins of the Cold War*, pp. 259–60. For Stalin's negative reaction see Harriman and Abel, *Special Envoy*, p. 534.
9. "Memorandum prepared in the State Department," December 1, 1945, *FR*, 1946, vol. 1, p. 1138.
10. Harriman and Abel, *Special Envoy*, pp. 533–34.
11. Acheson, *Present at the Creation*, pp. 150–51.
12. Millis, ed., *The Forrestal Diaries*, p. 134.
13. Diary of William D. Leahy, entry February 20, 1946.
14. *PP*, 1946, p. 127.
15. George F. Kennan, *Memoirs, 1925–1950* (Boston, 1967), p. 547 ff. (excerpts from telegram).
16. Ibid., p. 294.
17. Harriman and Abel, *Special Envoy*, p. 548.
18. Millis, ed., *The Forrestal Diaries*, p. 136.
19. Kennan, *Memoirs, 1925–1950*, pp. 294–95.
20. Alexander L. George and Richard C. Smoke, *Deterrence in American Foreign Policy: Theory and Practice* (New York, 1974), pp. 21–22.
21. Robert Murphy to Byrnes, February 24, 1946, *FR*, 1946, vol. 5, pp. 505–7.
22. Vandenberg, ed., *The Private Papers of Senator Vandenberg*, p. 246.
23. Byrnes, *All in One Lifetime*, p. 351.
24. Truman, *Years of Trial and Hope*, p. 95.
25. Truman to Byrnes, October 13, 1945. PSF: Subject file. Secretary of State folder. Box 159.
26. Albion and Connery, *Forrestal and the Navy*, pp. 186–87.
27. OH, Harry H. Vaughan.
28. Churchill to Truman, November 8, 1945. PSF: Churchill folder.
29. Interview with Harry H. Vaughan, April 2, 1973.

30. Exchange of letters in PSF: General file. Churchill folder.
31. Feis, *From Trust To Terror*, pp. 76–78; Byrnes, *All In One Lifetime*, p. 349; Gaddis, *The United States and the Origins of the Cold War*, pp. 307–8. Also Richard L. Walker and George Curry, *Edward Stettinius, Jr., 1944–1945, and James F. Byrnes, 1945–1947*, in the American Secretaries of State and Their Diplomacy series (New York, 1965), p. 369.
32. OH, Harry H. Vaughan.
33. Margaret Truman, *Harry S Truman*, p. 312.
34. *PP*, 1946, p. 145.
35. Ibid., p. 156.
36. Harriman and Abel, *Special Envoy*, p. 550.
37. *PP*, 1946, p. 147.
38. Ibid., p. 155.
39. Walker and Curry, *Edward Stettinius and James F. Byrnes*, pp. 207–9; Truman, *Year of Decisions*, p. 553.
40. Notes of Harold D. Smith, entry May 2, 1946.
41. Byrnes, *All in One Lifetime*, pp. 353–55.
42. Acheson, *Present at the Creation*, p. 163.
43. Byrnes, *All in One Lifetime*, p. 354.
44. Interview with Benjamin V. Cohen, May 24, 1972.
45. Byrnes, *All in One Lifetime*, pp. 333–34.
46. Robert J. Rossow to Byrnes, March 5, 1946, *FR*, 1946, vol. 2, p. 340.
47. Kennan to Byrnes, March 17, 1946, *FR*, 1946, vol. 2, pp. 362–63.
48. *PP*, 1946, p. 164.
49. PSF: Presidential appointment file. Appointment sheet, March 23, 1946, folder. Box 83.
50. Beatrice Bishop Berle and Travis Beal Jacobs, eds., *Navigating the Rapids 1918–1971: From the Papers of Adolf A. Berle* (New York, 1973), p. 573.
51. *New York Times*, March 28, 1946, p. 1.
52. Firuz Kazemzadeh, "The Problem of Great Power Confrontation: Iran, the USSR, and the United States, 1946–1948" (Paper read at the American Historical Association meeting in Chicago, December 30, 1974).
53. Truman, *Year of Decisions*, pp. 555–56.
54. Thomas G. Paterson, *Soviet-American Confrontation: Postwar*

Reconstruction and the Origins of the Cold War (Baltimore, 1973), pp. 52–54.

55. Ernest R. May, *"Lessons" of the Past: The Use and Misuse of History in American Foreign Policy* (New York, 1973), p. 30.

21. BUILDING ON SAND: THE BARUCH PLAN

1. Transcript of Truman's pre-press conference remarks, May 16, 1946. HSTL.
2. Notes of Harold D. Smith, entry March 20, 1946.
3. *PP*, 1946, p. 53.
4. Ibid., p. 55.
5. Ulam, *Stalin: The Man and His Era*, p. 641.
6. *PP*, 1946, pp. 47–48.
7. Ibid.
8. Haynes, *The Awesome Power*, p. 120.
9. Notes of Harold D. Smith, entry March 10, 1946.
10. Millis, ed., *The Forrestal Diaries*, p. 148.
11. Caraley, *The Politics of Military Unification*, p. 135.
12. Millis, ed., *The Forrestal Diaries*, pp. 160–63.
13. Millis, ed., *The Forrestal Diaries*, pp. 160–63.
13. Ibid., pp. 168–70.
14. Stuart Symington, "Memorandum: Discussion With General MacArthur," July 18, 1946. PSF: Subject file. Air Force. Secretary of War for Air folder. Box 157.
15. Caraley, *The Politics of Military Unification*, p. 147n.
16. Truman, *Year of Decisions*, p. 469 ff.
17. *PP*, 1946, p. 136.
18. Ibid., p. 203.
19. Ibid., p. 212.
20. Ibid., p. 215.
21. Matusow, *Farm Policies and Politics in the Truman Years*, pp. 28–32.
22. Ibid., p. 36.
23. Lilienthal, *The Atomic Energy Years, Journals*, p. 10.
24. Hewlett and Anderson, *The New World*, p. 536 ff. Also Acheson, *Present at the Creation*, p. 153.
25. Hewlett and Anderson, *The New World*, pp. 545, 547.
26. Acheson, *Present at the Creation*, p. 155.
27. Ibid., p. 154. Also Lilienthal, *The Atomic Energy Years*, p. 30.
28. Truman, *Years of Trial and Hope*, pp. 7–8.
29. Baruch, *Baruch: The Public Years*, p. 361.
30. Truman, *Years of Trial and Hope*, pp. 8–10.
31. Baruch, *Baruch: The Public Years*, p. 369.
32. Acheson, *Present at the Creation*, p. 155.
33. Lilienthal, *The Atomic Energy Years*, p. 125.
34. Baruch, *Baruch: The Public Years*, pp. 367–68.

22. ONE WAY TO HANDLE A RAIL STRIKE

1. *PP*, 1946, p. 242. Also Alinsky, *John L. Lewis: An Unauthorized Biography*, p. 329.
2. Letter, Truman to Wallace, February 18, 1946. PSF: General file. Small business folder.
3. Truman to Charles Sawyer, May 13, 1946. PSF: General file. Sn-Sz folder.
4. *PP*, 1946, p. 247.
5. Ibid., p. 270.
6. Ibid., pp. 271–72.
7. *New York Times*, May 24, 1946, p. 6.
8. Daniels, *The Man of Independence*, p. 325.
9. OH, Clark Clifford.
10. *PP*, 1946, p. 225.
11. *New York Times* reported May 25, 1946, that the drafting of strikers had been recommended to Truman by Sen. Harry F. Byrd the day before. Byrd was at the White House at noon that May 24 but with a group for a bill-signing. The evidence suggests that Truman had the idea before this time—in fact, John Snyder assured me that this was the case.
12. Papers of Clark Clifford. Railroad speech. HSTL.
13. Ibid.
14. Ibid.
15. Bert Cochran, *Harry Truman and the Crisis Presidency* (New York, 1973), p. 206.
16. *PP*, 1946, pp. 274–77.
17. Interview with Tom C. Clark October 25, 1974.
18. Alvanley Johnston and A. F. Whitney to Truman, May 25, 1946. PSF: General file. Strikes-RR folder.
19. Blum, *The Price of Vision*, p. 575. Also OH, Clark Clifford.
20. For the chronology see "Memorandum by Charles G. Ross," Papers of Charles C. Ross. HSTL.
21. Interview with John R. Steelman, September 5, 1974.
22. *PP*, 1946, pp. 277–80.
23. OH, Clark Clifford.
24. *Congressional Record*, 79th Congress, 2nd Session, vol. 92, pt. 5 (May 25, 1946), p. 5760.
25. Exchange in OF: 1016. American Labor Party.
26. Hamby, *Beyond the New Deal*, pp. 77–78.
27. Eleanor Roosevelt to Truman, PPF: 460.
28. Interview with Tom Clark July 25, 1973. Also notes of Harold D. Smith, entry May 29, 1946.
29. J. Edgar Hoover to Harry H. Vaughan, June 5, 1946. PSF: Subject file. FBI-RR data folder. Box 169.
30. Blum, *The Price of Vision*, p. 575–76.
31. Papers of Clark Clifford. The Case Bill. Memorandum to the President. HSTL.
32. Blum, ed., *The Price of Vision*, pp. 577–79.
33. *PP*, 1946, pp. 289–97.
34. Truman to Sidney Hillman, June 15, 1946. PSF: General File. C folder.
35. Alinsky, *John L. Lewis: An Unauthorized Biography*, p. 330.

23. THE FIRING OF HENRY WALLACE

1. Papers of George M. Elsey. Box 63. HSTL.
2. Blum, ed., *The Price of Vision*, pp. 582, 588, 602.
3. Truman to Baruch, July 10, 1946. PSF: General file. Baruch folder.
4. Text in Blum, *The Price of Vision*, p. 589 ff.
5. Elsey note, July 24, 1946. Papers of George M. Elsey. Box 63. HSTL.
6. Ibid.
7. Memorandum, Clifford to Truman, September 1946. Russian no. 2 folder. Papers of Clark Clifford, HSTL.
8. Kennan, *Memoirs, 1925–1950*, pp. 301–4.
9. Papers of George M. Elsey. Box 63. Russia. HSTL.
10. Truman to John N. Garner, September 21, 1946. PSF: Subject file. Russia 1945–48 folder. Box 187.
11. Elsey note, July 27, 1946. Papers of George M. Elsey. Box 63. HSTL.
12. Hamby, *Beyond the New Deal*, pp. 127–28. Also Norman D. Markowitz, *The Rise and Fall of the People's Century: Henry A. Wallace and American Liberalism, 1941–1948* (New York, 1973), p. 181–82.
13. Richard J. Walton, *Henry Wallace, Harry Truman, and the Cold War* (New York, 1976), pp. 98–99.
14. For the two men's contrasting accounts see Truman, *Year of Decisions*, p. 557, and Blum, *The Price of Vision*, p. 612. In his oral history transcript, Clifford confirms that Wallace read through the speech for Truman.
15. "Conversations with Secretary Wallace." Papers of Bernard Gladieux. 1946 folder. HSTL.
16. Acheson, *Present at the Creation*, p. 190.
17. George M. Elsey note, September 14, 1946. Papers of George M. Elsey. Box 105: Henry Wallace. HSTL. Also, according to Clifford's oral history transcript, the speech clearance procedure at the White House was changed by Truman after the Wallace imbroglio. The new rule required that speeches be submitted a couple of days before delivery for review by the presidential staff.
18. *PP*, 1946, p. 426–28.
19. Millis, ed., *The Forrestal Diaries*, pp. 207–8.
20. *PP*, 1946, p. 427n.
21. Hewlett and Anderson, *The New World*, p. 600.
22. Margaret Truman, *Harry S Truman*, p. 317.
23. Wallace's account is in Blum, *The Price of Vision*, p. 617 ff.
24. *Newsweek*, September 9, 1946, p. 33.
25. Hillman, *Mr. President*, p. 128.
26. Byrnes to Truman, September 18, 1946. PSF: Presidential appointment file. September 15–30, 1946. folder. Box 84.
27. Teletype Conference, September 19, 1946. PSF: Presidential Appointment File. September 15–30, 1946, folder. Box 84.
28. Margaret Truman, *Harry S Truman*, p. 318.
29. Blum, ed., *The Price of Vision*, p. 629. Also interview with Clark Clifford, March 29, 1974.
30. Wallace to Truman, September 20, 1946. PSF: Political file. Wallace folder. Box 61.
31. Truman, *Year of Decisions*, p. 560.
32. *PP*, 1946, p. 431.
33. Truman to Roger T. Sermon, December 18, 1946. PSF: General file. C folder.
34. J. Edgar Hoover to George Allen, September 25, 1946. PSF: Subject file. FBI-Communists folder. Box 167.

24. THE BEEFSTEAK ELECTION OF 1946

1. Truman, *Year of Decisions*, p. 560.
2. Garson, *The Democratic Party and the Politics of Sectionalism*, pp. 161–64.
3. *PP*, 1946, pp. 371–72.
4. Garson, *The Democratic Party and the Politics of Sectionalism*, pp. 166–67.
5. Patterson, *Mr. Republican*, p. 313.
6. Stein, *The Fiscal Revolution in America*, p. 207.
7. *PP*, 1946, p. 439 ff.
8. Cady, "The Truman Administration's Reconversion Policies" (cited n. 1, chap. 12).
9. Susan M. Hartmann, *Truman and the 80th Congress* (Columbia, Mo., 1971), p. 9.
10. Coffin, *Missouri Compromise*, p. 297.
11. Patterson, *Mr. Republican*, p. 313.
12. Earl Mazo, *Richard Nixon: A Political and Personal Portrait* (New York, 1959), p. 47.
13. Hartmann, *Truman and the 80th Congress*, pp. 9–10.
14. Martin Dies, "Communist Influences In High Places" in David Brion Davis, ed., *The Fear of Conspiracy: Images of Un-American Subversion from the Revolution to the Present*, paperback ed. (Ithaca, 1972), p. 283.
15. H. Bradford Westerfield, *Foreign Policy and Party Politics, Pearl Harbor to Korea* (New York, 1972), pp. 189–90.
16. Church Committee (U.S. Senate), Final Report, bk. 3, *Supplementary Detailed Staff Reports on Intelligence Activities and the Rights of Americans* (Washington, D.C., 1976), pp. 282–83.

17. Donald F. Crosby, S.J., "The Politics of Religion. American Catholics and the Anti-Communist Impulse," in Robert Griffith and Athan Theoharis, eds., *The Specter: Original Essays on the Cold War and Origins of McCarthyism* (New York, 1974), p. 29.
18. Peter H. Irons, "American Business and the Origins of McCarthyism: The Cold War Crusade of the United States Chamber of Commerce," in Griffith and Theoharis, eds., *The Specter*, pp. 78–81.
19. Joseph C. Goulden, *The Best Years: 1945–1950* (New York, 1976), p. 226.
20. Richard M. Freeland, *The Truman Doctrine and the Origins of McCarthyism: Foreign Policy, Domestic Politics, and Internal Security, 1946–1948* (New York, 1972), p. 120.
21. William S. White, *The Taft Story* (New York, 1954), p. 56.
22. Matusow, *Farm Policies and Politics in the Truman Years*, pp. 56–59.
23. Clifford P. Case to Truman, OF: 327. May–December 1946, folder.
24. Herman P. Kopplemann et al. to Truman, October 8, 1946. PSF: General file. "Meat" folder.
25. *PP*, 1946, p. 451 ff.
26. Truman to Bowles, October 16, 1946, PPF: 2687-Bowles.
27. Truman handwritten notes. Undated. PSF: Speech file. October 14, 1946, folder.
28. Alinsky, *John L. Lewis: An Unauthorized Biography*, p. 331.

25. SHOWDOWN WITH JOHN L. LEWIS

1. Charles C. Ross to Ella Ross, November 13, 1946. Papers of Charles C. Ross. HSTL.
2. Hamby, *Beyond the New Deal*, p. 180.
3. Truman to Sherman Minton, November 14, 1946, PSF: General file. Mi-Mn folder.
4. Margaret Truman, *Harry S Truman*, p. 143.
5. Daniels, *The Man of Independence*, p. 226.
6. Truman, *Year of Decisions*, p. 224.
7. Goulden, *The Best Years, 1945–1950*, p. 125.
8. Figure supplied by the Bureau of Labor Statistics.
9. John L. Lewis to Julius A. Krug, October 21, 1946. Papers of Clark Clifford. Coal case no. 1. HSTL.
10. Krug to Truman, November 13, 1946. Papers of Clark Clifford. Coal case no. 1. HSTL.
11. Exchange of letters in papers of Warner L. Gardner. HSTL.
12. *PP*, 1946, pp. 481–82.
13. Hillman, *Mr. President*, pp. 128–29.
14. OH, John R. Steelman. Also interviews with the author in 1974.
15. Hillman, *Mr. President*, p. 129. Also OH, Edward T. Folliard, p. 63.

16. Diary of Eben A. Ayers, entry December 7, 1946.
17. *PP*, 1948, p. 508.
18. Margaret Truman, *Harry S Truman*, p. 325.
19. Church Committee (U.S. Senate) Final Report, bk. 3, *Supplementary Detailed Staff Reports on Intelligence Activities and the Rights of Americans*, p. 431.
20. Malcolm Ross memorandum to Truman, OF: 93-C (SF).
21. McCoy and Ruetten, *Quest and Response*, p. 44.
22. Exchange of correspondence is in OF: 93, May 1946-December 1946.
23. Garson, *The Democratic Party and the Politics of Sectionalism*, pp. 198–99.
24. *PP*, 1946, p. 368.
25. McCoy and Ruetten, *Quest and Response*, p. 43.
26. Berman, *The Politics of Civil Rights in the Truman Administration*, p. 51.
27. Truman to Clark, September 20, 1946. PSF: General file. Negro folder.
28. McCoy and Ruetten, *Quest and Response*, p. 48.

26. THE UNRAVELING OF THE OLD ORDER

1. Department of State, "China White Paper," pp. 136–41.
2. Truman to Hugh De Lacy, February 15, 1946. PSF: Subject file. China, 1946, folder. Box 173.
3. Marshall to Truman, May 6, 1946, *FR*, 1946, vol. 9, pp. 815–18.
4. Marshall to Truman, June 17, 1946, *FR*, 1946, vol. 9, pp. 1099–01.
5. Marshall to Truman, July 22, 1946, *FR*, 1946, vol. 9, pp. 1394–95.
6. Truman to Ambassador Koo (for Chiang Kai-shek), August 10, 1946, *FR*, 1946, vol. 9, pp. 2–3.
7. Blum, ed., *The Price of Vision*, p. 587.
8. Marshall to Truman, August 17, August 30, September 13, and September 23, 1946, *FR*, 1946, vol. 10, pp. 53–54, 109–11, 186–88, and 217–20. Also Marshall memorandum to Chiang Kai-shek, October 1, 1946, pp. 267–68.
9. Marshall to Acheson, October 2, 1946, and Marshall to Truman, October 5, 1946, *FR*, 1946, vol. 10, pp. 271–74 and 289–92.
10. George Marshall to Marshall S. Carter, October 6, 1946. Also minutes of a meeting between General Marshall and Chou Enlai, November 16, 1946, *FR*, 1946, vol. 10, pp. 298–99 and 544–47.
11. Marshall Carter to General Marshall, December 11, 1946, *FR*, 1946, vol. 10, 609–10.
12. *PP*, 1946, p. 499 ff.
13. Leopold W. Leopold, *The Growth of American Foreign Policy* (New York, 1962), p. 677.
14. Edwin W. Pauley to Truman, June 22, 1946. Truman to Pauley, July 16, 1946, *FR*, 1946, vol. 8, pp. 706–09 and 713–14.
15. *PP*, 1946, pp. 348.
16. Interview with Benjamin V. Cohen, November 11, 1974.
17. Bohlen, *Witness to History*, p. 248.
18. Acheson, *Present at the Creation*, pp. 195–96.

19. *FR*, 1946, vol. 7, pp. 840–42.
20. Joseph Marion Jones, *The Fifteen Weeks, February 21–June 5, 1947* (New York, 1955), p. 63. In an account of this meeting (pp. 63–64) Jones said that Eisenhower attended and whispered to Acheson to ask whether Truman really understood the gravity of his decision. Acheson, in *Present at the Creation*, and some other writers have repeated this version. White House records at the Truman Library do not list Eisenhower as a participant, and a story in the *New York Times* reported that he was in Mexico City August 15.
21. *FR*, 1946, vol. 7, pp. 847–48.
22. Byrnes to Clayton, *FR*, 1946, vol. 7, pp. 223–24.
23. "Memorandum Prepared in the Office of Near Eastern and African Affairs," October 21, 1946, *FR*, 1946, vol. 7, pp. 240–44.
24. Acheson to Lincoln MacVeigh, October 15, 1946, *FR*, 1946, vol. 7, pp. 235–37.
25. Acheson to Edward Wilson, November 8, 1946, *FR*, 1946, vol. 7, pp. 916–17.
26. Hewlett and Anderson, *The New World*, pp. 608–9.
27. Richard L. Sharp memorandum of a conversation, *FR*, 1946, vol. 8, pp. 15–20.
28. William Clayton to Charles S. Reed, *FR*, 1946, vol. 8, p. 57.
29. Jefferson Caffrey to Byrnes, November 29, 1946, *FR*, 1946, vol. 8, p. 63.
30. Acheson to Reed (for Moffat), December 8, 1946, *FR*, 1946, vol. 8, pp. 67–69.
31. Byrnes cable to certain missions abroad, December 17, 1946, *FR*, 1946, vol. 8, pp. 72–73.
32. Memorandum, John Carter Vincent to Acheson, December 23, 1946, *FR*, 1946, vol. 8, pp. 75–77.
33. Byrnes to Jefferson Caffrey, December 24, 1946, *FR*, 1946, vol. 8, pp. 77–78.

27. 1947: THE EIGHTIETH CONGRESS CONVENES

1. Richard H. Rovere, *The American Establishment and Other Reports, Opinions, and Speculations* (New York, 1962), pp. 186–87.
2. Diary of Eben A. Ayers, entry November 25, 1947.
3. Goulden, *The Best Years, 1945–1950*, p. 236.
4. Words and phrases culled from Republican platforms of the Roosevelt era.
5. Hartmann, *Truman and the 80th Congress*, p. 11.
6. *PP*, 1947, p. 1 ff.
7. George M. Elsey note, December 20, 1946. Correspondence folder. Papers of George M. Elsey. HSTL.
8. James E. Webb notes on conferences with the president, October 11, 1946, and October 28, 1946. Conference notes folders. Papers of James E. Webb. HSTL.
9. Tom Clark memorandum to the president, November 23, 1945.
09–11, PSF: General file. Labor-management folder.

10. Elsey note, January 1, 1947. Correspondence file. Papers of George M. Elsey, HSTL.
11. *PP*, 1946, p. 114.
12. Davies, *Housing Reform during the Truman Administration*, pp. 44–58.
13. "Homes & Juvenile Delinquency," Truman handwritten notes. PSF: Speech file. March 6, 1946, folder. Box 46.
14. Hamby, *Beyond the New Deal*, pp. 154–55.
15. Ibid., pp. 159–60.
16. Lash, *Eleanor: The Years Alone*, pp. 91–92.
17. *PP*, 1947, pp. 99–100.
18. George M. Elsey note to Clifford, undated. Unification folders. Papers of George M. Elsey, HSTL.

28. CHINA MISSION FAILS; MARSHALL SECRETARY OF STATE

1. Marshall to Truman, December 28, 1946, *FR*, 1946, vol. 10, pp. 661–65.
2. J. Leighton Stuart to Byrnes, December 21, 1946, *FR*, 1946, vol. 10, p. 651–52.
3. Two telegrams, Marshall Carter to George Marshall, January, 1947, *FR*, 1946, vol. 10, p. 680–81.
4. Truman, *Year of Decisions*, p. 552.
5. George Marshall to Marshall Carter, January 4, 1947, *FR*, 1946, vol. 10, p. 681.
6. *PP*, 1947, p. 104.
7. Interview with Benjamin V. Cohen. June 25, 1975.
8. Byrnes, *All in One Lifetime*, p. 387.
9. Acheson, *Present at the Creation*, p. 213.
10. PSF: Presidential appointment file. Appointment sheet, February 18, 1947. February 17–28 folder. Box 85.
11. Lloyd C. Gardner, *Architects of Illusion: Men and Ideas in American Foreign Policy, 1941–1949* (Chicago, 1972), pp. 204–5.
12. George M. Elsey note, June 23, 1947. Rent Control and Housing speech. June 30, 1947, folder. Papers of George M. Elsey. HSTL.
13. Commentaries culled at random from papers of George M. Elsey. HSTL.
14. Lilienthal, *The Atomic Energy Years*, p. 144.
15. Ibid.
16. *PP*, 1947, p. 158.
17. Richard G. Hewlett and Francis Duncan, *Atomic Shield, 1947–1952* (University Park, Pennsylvania, 1969), pp. 10, 49, 53 (vol. 2 of *A History of the United States Atomic Energy Commission*).
18. Margaret Truman, *Harry S Truman*, p. 349.

29. CRISIS IN EUROPE

1. The *Times* of London is the main source of this account of the winter of 1947 in Europe.
2. Leopold, *The Growth of American Foreign Policy*, p. 649.
3. Howard M. Sachar, *Europe Leaves the Middle East 1936–1954* (New York, 1972), p. 481.
4. Walter Bedell Smith to Byrnes, January 8, 1947, *FR*, 1947, vol. 5, pp. 2–3.
5. Mark F. Ethridge to Marshall, February 17, 1947, *FR*, 1947, vol. 5, pp. 23–25.
6. Lincoln McVeigh to Marshall, February 20, 1947, *FR*, 1947, vol. 5, pp. 28–29.
7. Acheson, *Present at the Creation*, p. 217.
8. Aide-Mémoire, British Embassy to the State Department, *FR*, 1947, vol. 5, pp. 32–35, 35–37.

9. Acheson memorandum to Marshall, February 21, 1947, *FR*, 1947, vol. 5, pp. 29–31. Also Jones, *The Fifteen Weeks*, p. 131.
10. Acheson testimony, March 13, 1947, in Senate Committee on Foreign Relations, *Legislative Origins of the Truman Doctrine*, Hearings Held in Executive Session on S.938, Eightieth Congress, First Session, Historical Series, committee print, (Washington, D.C., 1973), pp. 2–3.
11. Acheson, *Present at the Creation*, p. 217; Jones, *The Fifteen Weeks*, pp. 6, 7, 130; Truman, *Years of Trial and Hope*, pp. 98, 100; Kennan, *Memoirs, 1925–1950*, pp. 313–314.
12. Stein, *The Fiscal Revolution in America*, p. 210.
13. Acheson memorandum to Marshall, February 24, 1947, *FR*, 1947, vol. 5, pp. 44–45.

30. THE TRUMAN DOCTRINE AND THE MARSHALL PLAN

1. Millis, ed., *The Forrestal Diaries*, p. 245.
2. Marshall memorandum to Truman, February 26, 1947, *FR*, 1947, vol. 5, p. 58.
3. *FR*, 1947, vol. 5, p. 58 n.
4. Interview with John R. Steelman, August 24, 1974. Also OH, Steelman.
5. John Lewis Gaddis, "Reconsiderations: The Cold War. Was the Truman Doctrine a Real Turning Point?" *Foreign Affairs*, January 1974, p. 386 ff.
6. John Gimbel, *The Origins of the Marshall Plan* (Stanford, 1976), pp. 5, 179 ff, and 277–78.
7. "Statement By the Secretary of State," undated, *FR*, 1947, vol. 5, pp. 60–62.
8. Acheson, *Present at the Creation*, p. 219.
9. Jones, *The Fifteen Weeks*, pp. 141–42.
10. Acheson, *Present at the Creation*, p. 219.
11. Interview with W. Averell Harriman, February 24, 1974. Also Eric F. Goldman, *The Crucial Decade: America, 1945–1955* (New York, 1956), p. 59.
12. Jones, *The Fifteen Weeks*, pp. 146, 151.
13. Ibid., pp. 152–53. Text of Truman's March 12 speech in *PP*, 1947, p. 176 ff.
14. Papers of Joseph M. Jones. HSTL.
15. Jones, *The Fifteen Weeks*, p. 155. Also Kennan, *Memoirs, 1925–1950*, pp. 315–16, 320.
16. Acheson, *Present at the Creation*, p. 221, Bohlen, *Witness to History*, p. 261.
17. Elsey memorandum to Clifford, March 7, 1947. Papers of Clark Clifford. Greek speech folder. HSTL.
18. Notation, March 9, 1947. Papers of George M. Elsey. Truman Doctrine speech folder. HSTL.

19. Acheson to Robert P. Patterson, March 5, 1947, *FR*, 1947, vol. 5, pp. 94–95.
20. Memorandum. Papers of William L. Clayton. Confidential memo folder. HSTL.
21. Millis, ed., *The Forrestal Diaries*, pp. 250–51.
22. Interview with Clark Clifford, April 7, 1975.
23. Clifford quoted in Lilienthal, the Atomic Energy Years, p. 163.
24. Amy M. Gilbert, *Executive Agreements and Treaties, 1946–1973: Framework of the Foreign Policy of the Period* (Endicott, New York, 1973), p. 24.
25. Jones, *The Fifteen Weeks*, pp. 159–60.
26. David S. McLellan, *Dean Acheson: The State Department Years* (New York, 1976), p. 109.
27. Senate Committee on Foreign Relations, *Legislative Origins of the Truman Doctrine* (cited n.10, chap. 29), p. 15.
28. Margaret Truman, *Harry S Truman*, p. 343.
29. Excerpts from transcribed telephone conversation between Forrestal and Carl Vinson, March 13, 1947. Papers of Clark Clifford. HSTL.
30. Hartmann, *Truman and the 80th Congress*, p. 61.
31. Jones, *The Fifteen Weeks*, p. 190.
32. Senate Committee on Foreign Relations, *Legislative Origins of the Truman Doctrine* (cited n. 10, ch. 29) p. 95.
33. Exchange of correspondence between Eleanor Roosevelt and Truman. OF: 426. Aid to Greece and Turkey.
34. Interview with Clark Clifford, August 21, 1972.
35. Report of the Special Ad Hoc Committee of the State-War-Navy Coordinating Committee, April 21, 1947, *FR*, 1947, vol. 3, p. 209.
36. *FR*, 1947, vol. 3, p. 204 ff.

37. *FR*, 1947, vol. 2, p. 377 ff.
38. Bohlen, *Witness to History*, p. 263.
39. Gimbel, *The Origins of the Marshall Plan*, p. 189–93.
40. Lucius D. Clay, *Decision in Germany* (Garden City, 1950), p. 174.
41. Truman, *Years of Trial and Hope*, p. 112.
42. Walter LaFeber, *America, Russia, and The Cold War (1946–1971)*, 2nd ed., paperback (New York, 1972), pp. 47–48.
43. Kennan, *Memoirs, 1925–1950*, pp. 325–26.
44. Kennan memorandum, May 16, 1947, *FR*, 1947, vol. 3, pp. 220–23.
45. Kennan to Acheson, May 23, 1947, *FR*, 1947, vol. 3, pp. 223 ff.

46. Gimbel, *The Origins of the Marshall Plan*, pp. 248–49.
47. Text in *FR*, 1947, vol. 3, pp. 237–39.
48. Kennan, *Memoirs, 1925–1950*, p. 342.
49. Jones, *The Fifteen Weeks*, p. 253.
50. Benjamin V. Cohen memorandum of a conversation, undated, *FR*, 1947, vol. 3, pp. 260–261.
51. Joyce and Gabriel Kolko, *The Limits of Power: The World and United States Foreign Policy, 1945–1954* (New York, 1972), p. 386.
52. Bohlen memorandum of a conversation, August 30, 1947, *FR*, 1947, vol. 1, pp. 762–65.

31. THE MISGUIDED LOYALTY PROGRAM

1. Text in Eleanor Bontecou, *The Federal Loyalty-Security Program*, (Ithaca, 1953), p. 287.
2. Ibid., pp. 272–73.
3. Ibid., p. 307.
4. Jack Redding, *Inside the Democratic Party* (New York, 1958), p. 41.
5. Bontecou, *The Federal Loyalty-Security Program*, p. 300 ff.
6. Truman to George H. Earle, February 28, 1947, OF:263.
7. Richard M. Fried, *Men Against McCarthy* (New York, 1976), p. 9.
8. Fred J. Cook, *The Nightmare Decade: The Life and Times of Senator Joe McCarthy* (New York, 1971), p. 64.
9. Text in Bontecou, *The Federal Loyalty-Security Program*, p. 275 ff.
10. Telephone interview May 1, 1976, with Ugo Carusi, former executive assistant to Attorney General Francis Biddle.
11. George M. Elsey, "Truman's White House," *Washington Post*, June 5, 1974, p. A-26.
12. Church Committee (U.S. Senate), Final Report, bk. 2, *Intelligence Activities and the Rights of Americans*, p. 44.
13. Harry B. Mitchell and Frances Perkins to Truman, April 25,

1947. OF: 252-K. Government employees loyalty program.
14. James Webb memorandum to Truman, April 30, 1947; and Tom Clark memorandum to Truman, May 1, 1947. OF: 252-K. Government employees loyalty program.
15. George M. Elsey note, May 2, 1947. Papers of George M. Elsey. Internal security folder. Box 69. HSTL.
16. Letter, Truman to Mitchell, May 9, 1947. OF: 252-K. Government employees loyalty program.
17. Clifford memorandum to Truman, May 23, 1947. Papers of George M. Elsey. Internal security folder. Box 69. HSTL.
18. Church Committee (U.S. Senate), Final Report, bk. 2, *Intelligence Activities and the Rights of Americans*, p. 44.
19. Truman, *Years of Trial and Hope*, p. 281.
20. Philip Murray to Truman, April 14, 1947; and Truman to Philip Murray, April 15, 1947. OF: 252-K, Government employees loyalty program.
21. Bontecou, *The Federal Loyalty-Security Program*, pp. 239–40.
22. John Lord O'Brian, *National Security and Individual Freedom*, (originally the 1955 Godkin Lectures at Harvard) (Cambridge, 1955), p. 22.

32. TAFT-HARTLEY: TRUMAN ON THE OFFENSIVE

1. R. Alton Lee, "Harry S. Truman and The Taft-Hartley Act" (Ph.D. dissertation, the University of Oklahoma, 1962). A number of details in this chapter are drawn from that work.
2. Joseph C. Goulden, *Meany: The Unchallenged Strong Man of American Labor* (New York, 1972), p. 144.
3. *Time*, June 23, 1947.
4. Truman's remarks at the White House to Mutual Broadcasting System representatives, January 31, 1947. PSF: Appointment file. January 20–31, folder. Box 85.
5. Interview with John R. Steelman, August 23, 1974.

6. *PP*, 1947, p. 288 ff.
7. *Congressional Record*, 1947, vol. 93, pt. 6, p. 7398.
8. *PP*, 1947, pp. 298–301.
9. Ibid., p. 305.
10. A. H. Raskin, "Taft-Hartley at 25—How It's Worked," *New York Times*, June 18, 1972, sec. 3, p. 1.
11. Press release. Papers of John W. Gibson. Railroad trainman folder. HSTL.
12. Hamby, *Beyond the New Deal*, p. 185.

33. CIA

1. Presidential Commission on CIA Activities within the United States, *Report to the President* (Washington, D.C., June 1975), p. 54 (hereafter cited as "Rockefeller Report).
2. Ibid., p. 52.
3. David Wise, "In the Beginning the CIA Seemed Harmless Enough," *New York Times*, January 12, 1975, sec. 4, p. 4.
4. "Rockefeller Report," p. 51.
5. Roberta Wohlsetter, *Pearl Harbor: Warning and Decision* (Stanford, 1962), p. 56.
6. Acheson, *Present at the Creation*, p. 158.
7. Ibid., pp. 158–61.
8. Church Committee (U.S. Senate) Final Report, bk. 1 (Washington, D.C., 1976), p. 483.
9. *PP*, 1946, pp. 88–89.
10. George M. Elsey memorandum, July 17, 1946. Papers of Clark Clifford. National Intelligence Folder. HSTL.
11. Marshall memorandum for Truman, February 7, 1947. Papers of Clark Clifford. Box 17. Unification. Correspondence folder. HSTL.
12. *PP*, 1947, p. 153. Draft published in "National Defense Establishment." Hearings on S.758 before the Senate Armed Services Committee, 80th Congress, 1st Session.

13. Church Committee, Final Report, bk. 1 (cited n. 8), p. 481.
14. Ibid., p. 21.
15. Ibid., p. 508.
16. Ibid., p. 132.
17. Ibid., p. 138.
18. Ibid., p. 426.
19. For a description of "Shamrock" and for Senator Church's comment see his opening statement at his committee's hearing November 6, 1975, in Church Committee (U.S. Senate), *The National Security Agency and Fourth Amendment Rights*, Hearings, Ninety-fourth Congress, First Session, vol. 5, committee print (Washington, D.C., 1975), p. 57 ff.
20. Millis, ed., *The Forrestal Diaries*, p. 295.
21. Albion and Connery, *Forrestal and the Navy*, p. 285.
22. Interview with Clark Clifford, May 31, 1972.
23. *New York Times*, July 27, 1947, p. 1.
24. Adam B. Ulam, *Expansion and Coexistence: The History of Soviet Foreign Policy, 1917–1967* (New York, 1971), p. 436.
25. Text in *New York Times*, October 6, 1947, p. 3.
26. Clay, *Decision In Germany*, p. 239.
27. Church Committee, Final Report, bk. 1 (cited n. 8) pp. 132, 144.

34. PALESTINE

1. Statement, undated. Senatorial file. Jews, May, 1944, folder. HSTL.
2. Truman, *Years of Trial and Hope*, pp. 132–33.
3. Truman, *Year of Decisions*, pp. 68–69.
4. Truman, *Years of Trial and Hope*, p. 133.
5. Memorandum on Palestine. Papers of George M. Elsey. Box 3. HSTL.
6. Truman, *Years of Trial and Hope*, pp. 133–34.
7. OF: 204. Palestine.
8. OF: 204. Miscellaneous. Palestine.
9. Acheson, *Present at the Creation*, p. 170.
10. *PP*, 1945, p. 228.
11. Undated, unsigned memorandum on Palestine chronology.

Papers of George M. Elsey. Box 3. HSTL.
12. Truman, *Years of Trial and Hope*, pp. 136–37, 140.
13. Papers of Samuel I. Rosenman. Harrison folder. HSTL.
14. Truman, *Years of Trial and Hope*, pp. 137–39, 141–42.
15. Truman to Virginia C. Gildersleeve, October 15, 1946. OF: 204. Miscellaneous.
16. Emanuel Celler to Truman, November 15, 1945; Stephen S. Wise and Abba Hillel Silver to Truman, November 15, 1945, rabbis' petition to the president. OF: 204. Miscellaneous.
17. Unsent letter, Truman to Joseph H. Ball, November 24, 1945. PSF: General file. Ba-Bh folder.
18. Chaim Weizmann to Truman, December 12, 1945. OF: 204. Miscellaneous.

19. Walter Laqueur, *A History of Zionism* (New York, 1972), p. 561.
20. Herbert Feis, *The Birth of Israel: The Tousled Diplomatic Bed* (New York, 1969), pp. 22–23.
21. Acheson, *Present at the Creation*, p. 169.
22. *New York Times*, September 29, 1952, p. 23.
23. OH, Oscar R. Ewing, p. 134.
24. Myron C. Taylor to Truman, May 15, 1946; and Niles memorandum for the president, May 27, 1946. OF: 204.
25. *PP*, 1946, pp. 218–19.
26. Laqueur, *A History of Zionism*, p. 565.
27. Excerpts from Ernest Bevin's speech at Bournemouth in *New York Times*, June 13, 1946, p. 4.
28. Frank J. Adler, *Roots in a Moving Stream: The Centennial History of Congregation B'nai Jehudah of Kansas City, 1870–1970* (published by the Congregation, 1972), p. 199–201.
29. Truman, *Year of Decisions*, pp. 133–35.
30. Arthur J. Lelyveld to Edward Jacobson, July 13, 1946. Papers of Edward Jacobson (microfilm). HSTL.
31. Truman, *Years of Trial and Hope*, p. 149.
32. OF: 204, Miscellaneous. Palestine.
33. John Snetsinger, *Truman, the Jewish Vote, and the Creation of Israel* (Stanford, 1974), p. 40.
34. Interview with Samuel I. Rosenman, May 12, 1973.
35. *PP*, 1946, p. 335.
36. OF: 2.
37. Acheson *Present at the Creation*, p. 176; Blum, *The Price of Vision*, p. 607.
38. OF: 204. Miscellaneous.
39. James G. McDonald, *My Mission to Israel 1948–1951* (New York, 1951), p. 11.
40. Blum, ed., *The Price of Vision*, p. 605.
41. Truman to James G. McDonald, July 31, 1946. OF: 204. Miscellaneous.
42. Blum, *The Price of Vision*, pp. 605–6.
43. Memorandum, Truman to David Niles, May 13, 1947. PSF: Subject file. Palestine 1945–1947 folder. Box 184.
44. Patterson, *Mr. Republican*, pp. 280–81.
45. Blum, *The Price of Vision*, pp. 606–7.
46. Paul E. Fitzpatrick to Truman, August 2, 1946. OF: 204, Miscellaneous.
47. Truman to Clement R. Attlee, August 12, 1946. *FR*, 1946, vol. 7, pp. 682–83.
48. Truman to Edward J. Flynn, August 2, 1946. PSF: Subject file. Palestine-Jewish immigration folder. Box 184.
49. Eliahu Epstein to Nahum Goldmann, October 9, 1946. The Weizmann archives. HSTL.
50. Robert E. Hannegan to Truman, October 1, 1946. PSF: Secretary's file. Subject file. Palestine 1945–47 folder. Box 184.
51. Ernest Bevin's speech in the House of Commons February 25, 1947. Excerpts in *New York Times*, February 26, 1947, p. 15.
52. *New York Times*, October 7, 1946, p. 1.
53. Laqueur, *A History of Zionism*, p. 573.
54. *PP*, 1946, pp. 442–44.
55. Walter F. George to Truman, October 5, 1946. Truman to George, October 8, 1946. PSF: Subject file. Palestine 1945–47 folder. Box 184.
56. Truman to Pauley, October 22, 1946. PSF: Subject file. Palestine-Jewish immigration folder. Box 184.
57. Ibn Saud to Truman, October 15, 1946. OF: 204. Truman's message to Ibn Saud, *PP*, 1946, pp. 467–69.
58. George to Truman, October 14, 1946; Truman to George, October 17, 1946. OF: 204. Miscellaneous.
59. William A. Eddy, *F.D.R. Meets Ibn Saud* (Booklet published by the American Friends of the Middle East), pp. 36–37. Copy in HSTL.
60. Acheson to Henderson, *FR*, 1947, vol. 5, pp. 1048–49.
61. Truman to Huston Thompson, February 25, 1947. OF: 204. Miscellaneous.
62. *FR*, 1947, vol. 5, p. 1011 ff.
63. Bevin to Marshall, undated, *FR*, 1947, vol. 5, pp. 1035–37.
64. Excerpts in *New York Times*, February 26, 1947, p. 15.
65. Feis, *The Birth of Israel*, pp. 34–35.
66. Truman, *Years of Trial and Hope*, p. 154.
67. Laqueur, *A History of Zionism*, p. 579. Gromyko statement,

FR, 1947, vol. 5, pp. 1084–85.
68. Memorandum, Truman to David Niles, May 13, 1947. PSF: Subject file. Palestine 1945–47 folder. Box 184.
69. Excerpts from the meeting of the United States Delegation, September 15, 1947, *FR*, 1947, vol. 5, pp. 1147–51.
70. Samuel K. C. Kopper memorandum of a conversation, October 3, 1947, *FR*, 1947, vol. 5, pp. 1171–73.
71. John H. Hilldring memorandum, October 9, 1947, *FR*, 1947, vol. 5, 1177–78.
72. Snetsinger, *Truman, the Jewish Vote, and the Creation of Israel*, p. 54.
73. Margaret Truman, *Harry S Truman*, pp. 384–85.
74. Millis, ed., *The Forrestal Diaries*, pp. 309, 323.
75. Snetsinger, *Truman, the Jewish Vote, and the Creation of Israel*, pp. 54–55.
76. Truman to Claude Pepper, October 20, 1947. Confidential file. P folder. Box 59. HSTL.
77. Telephone interviews with Harry H. Vaughan and Rose Conway, May 21, 1976. John R. Steelman correspondence with author, May 1976.
78. "Memorandum Prepared in the State Department," September 30, 1947, *FR*, 1947, vol. 5, pp. 1166–70.
79. Marshall to Lovett, October 23, 1947, *FR*, 1947, vol. 5, 1200–01.
80. *FR*, 1947, vol. 5, pp. 1251, 1255–56.
81. Chaim Weizmann, *Trial and Error: An Autobiography* (New York, 1949), pp. 458–59.
82. Lovett to Warren R. Austin, *FR*, 1947, vol. 5, pp. 1269–70.
83. Robert M. McClintock memorandum, November 19, 1947, *FR*, 1947, vol. 5, pp. 1271–72, 1271n, 1272n.
84. Matthew Connelly memorandum to Truman, November 22, 1947. OF: 204. Miscellaneous.
85. Weizmann, *Trial and Error*, p. 459.
86. Ibn Saud to Truman, October 30, 1947, *FR*, 1947, vol. 5, pp. 1212–13. Truman to Ibn Saud November 21, 1947, ibid., pp. 1277–78.
87. Snetsinger, *Truman, the Jewish Vote and the Creation of Israel*, p. 66.
88. Lovett memorandum to Truman, (and Annex), December 10, 1947, *FR*, 1947, vol. 5, pp. 1305–7. For evidence that the U.S. "representative" was Clifford see Diary of Eben A. Ayers, entry November 28, 1947.
89. Millis, ed., *The Forrestal Diaries*, pp. 357–58.
90. Truman memorandum to Lovett, December 11, 1947, *FR*, 1947, vol. 5, p. 1309.
91. Lovett memorandum, November 24, 1947, *FR*, 1947, vol. 5, pp. 1283–84.
92. Feis, *The Birth of Israel*, p. 45.
93. Snetsinger, *Truman, the Jewish Vote, and the Creation of Israel*, pp. 70–71.
94. Notes unsigned, undated, attached to November 20, 1947, memorandum referring to the cabinet meeting November 11, 1947. PSF: Subject file. Cabinet data folder. Box 154.
95. Celler to Truman, November 27, 1947. OF: 204. Miscellaneous.
96. Millis, ed., *The Forrestal Diaries*, p. 346. Harvey S. Firestone, Jr., is identified in Larry Collins and Dominique Lapierre, *O Jerusalem!* (New York, 1972), p. 28.
97. Kennan memorandum to Lovett, January 19, 1948. Tab A, Policy Planning Staff no. 19, Diplomatic Branch, National Archives, Washington, D.C.
98. "Memorandum for the President" by M.J.C. [Matthew J. Connelly], November 27, 1947. PSF: Subject file. Palestine-Jewish immigration folder. Box 184.
99. Weizmann to Truman, November 27, 1947. PSF: Subject file. Palestine 1945–47 folder. Box 184.
100. Berle and Jacobs, eds., *Navigating the Rapids*, 579–80.
101. Llewellyn E. Thompson memorandum to Loy Henderson, December 18, 1947. Tab A, Policy Planning Staff no. 19, January 19, 1948, Diplomatic Branch, National Archives, Washington, D.C.
102. *FR*, 1947, vol. 5, p. 1307, n. 4.
103. Philip C. Jessup, *The Birth of Nations* (New York, 1974), p. 264.
104. Millis, ed., *The Forrestal Diaries*, p. 346.

35. THE HISTORIC CIVIL RIGHTS REPORT

1. McCoy and Ruetten, *Quest and Response*, p. 94.
2. *PP*, 1947, pp. 98–99.
3. Ibid., p. 105.
4. Niles to Connelly, June 16, 1947. Papers of Clark Clifford. Box 3. HSTL.
5. McCoy and Ruetten, *Quest and Response*, p. 73. Berman, *The Politics of Civil Rights in the Truman Administration*, p. 61.
6. *PP*, 1947, p. 311 ff.
7. Draft, civil rights speech. PSF: June 29, 1947 folder. Speech file. Box 47.
8. Garson, *The Democratic Party and the Politics of Sectionalism*, p. 221.
9. Note, Tom Clark to the author, March 1974.
10. The three communications are in OF: 596-A.
11. Berman, *The Politics of Civil Rights in the Truman Administration*, p. 72.
12. Garson, *The Democratic Party and the Politics of Sectionalism*, p. 226.
13. *PP*, 1947, p. 482.
14. McCoy and Ruetten, *Quest and Response*, p. 95.

36. WALLACE DECLARES

1. Interview with John W. Snyder, May 25, 1975.
2. Interview with Samuel I. Rosenman, November 11, 1972.
3. Interview with John R. Steelman, February 24, 1976.
4. Interview with Dr. Milton S. Eisenhower, October 12, 1972.
5. Millis, *The Forrestal Diaries,* pp. 343–44.
6. Truman, *Years of Trial and Hope,* p. 187.
7. Letter, Council of Economic Advisors to Truman, April 7, 1947. Papers of Clark Clifford. Associated Press speech file. HSTL.
8. *PP,* 1947, p. 201.
9. Ibid., pp. 263–64.
10. Ibid., p. 492 ff.
11. Craufird D. Goodwin, ed., *Exhortation and Controls: The Search for a Wage-Price Policy,* pp. 45–46.
12. Ibid., p. 46n.
13. Hartmann, *Truman and the 80th Congress,* pp. 123–24.
14. *PP,* 1947, pp. 532–34.

15. Vandenberg, ed., *The Private Papers of Senator Vandenberg,* p. 376.
16. Hartmann, *Truman and the 80th Congress,* p. 120.
17. Millis, ed., *The Forrestal Diaries,* p. 341.
18. *PP,* 1947, p. 515 ff.
19. The foregoing account on the Wallace situation draws on Hamby, *Beyond the New Deal,* chap. 8, and Markowitz, *The Rise and Fall of the People's Century,* chap. 7.
20. John Morton Blum, "Portrait of a Diarist" in Blum, ed., *The Price of Vision,* pp. 47–48.
21. Text in *New York Times,* December 30, 1947, p. 15.
22. Letter, Truman to Burton K. Wheeler, January 7, 1948. PSF: Political file. Montana folder. Box 59. Also Diary of Eben A. Ayers, entry January 4–9, 1948.
23. Letter, J. Edgar Hoover to Harry H. Vaughan, January 27, 1948. PSF: Subject file. FBI-Communist folder. Box 167.

37. A STORMY BEGINNING

1. Interview with Stanley Gewirtz, June 27, 1974.
2. Arthur M. Schlesinger, Jr., *The Politics of Upheaval* (Boston, 1960), p. 237.
3. Marriner S. Eccles, *Beckoning Frontiers: Personal and Public Recollections,* ed. Sidney Hyman (New York, 1951), p. 435 ff.
4. Telephone interview with John R. Steelman, February 24, 1976.
5. Francis Russell, *The Shadow of Blooming Grove: Warren G. Harding in His Times* (New York, 1968), p. 455.
6. Truman, *Year of Decisions,* p. 134.
7. John R. Steelman to the author, February 26, 1976.
8. Diary of Eben A. Ayers, entry May 6, 1948.
9. *PP,* 1947, p. 456.
10. Ibid., p. 536.
11. *PP,* 1948, pp. 99, 101.
12. Ibid., p. 217.
13. This account draws on the files of the *Washington Evening Star.*
14. Text in *PP,* 1948, p. 1 ff.
15. Letter, Council of Economic Advisers to Truman, December

13, 1947. Papers of George M. Elsey. State of the Union: Source material folder. Box 19. HSTL.
16. McCoy and Ruetten, *Quest and Response,* p. 99.
17. *PP,* 1948, p. 121 ff.
18. Diary of Eben A. Ayers, entry January 23, 1948, also Hillman, *Mr. President,* p. 134.
19. V. O. Key, Jr. with Alexander Heard, *Southern Politics in State and Nation,* paperback ed. (New York, 1949), p. 330.
20. Ibid., pp. 330–331.
21. McCoy and Ruetten, *Quest and Response,* p. 103.
22. Diary of Eben A. Ayers, entry February 3, 1948. Also, Truman to Speaker W. M. Beck, February 18, 1948. PSF: Political file. Alabama folder. Box 54.
23. *PP,* 1948, p. 147 ff.
24. Garson, *The Democratic Party and the Politics of Sectionalism,* p. 239; Redding, *Inside the Democratic Party,* p. 136–40; McCoy and Reutten, *Quest and Response,* p. 102.
25. *New York Times,* March 9, 1948, p. 1.
26. Robert A. Divine, *Foreign Policy and U.S. Presidential Elections 1940–1948* (New York, 1974), p. 178.

38. CZECHOSLOVAKIA AND THE BERLIN BLOCKADE

1. *PP,* 1948, p. 182 ff.
2. Laurence A. Steinhardt to Marshall, April 30, 1948, *FR,* 1948, vol. 4, p. 747 ff. (paragraph 10).
3. Marshall and Jefferson Caffrey, February 24, 1948, *FR,* 1948, vol. 4, pp. 735–36.
4. Steinhardt to Marshall, February 26, 1948, *FR,* 1948, vol. 4, pp. 738–41.
5. NSC-7, March 30, 1948. "The Position of the United States with Respect to Soviet-Directed World Communism." Box NSC 1/1-33, Modern Military Branch. National Archives, Washington, D.C.
6. Truman handwritten notes. PSF: Speech file. March 17, 1948, folder. Box 48.
7. *PP,* 1948, p. 166.
8. For origins of the Atlantic alliance see *FR,* 1948, vol. 3, pp. 1–12.
9. Truman handwritten note attached to Marshall memorandum to the president and the cabinet, March 5, 1948. PSF: Subject file. Cabinet data folder. Box 154.
10. Jean Edward Smith, ed., *The Papers of General Lucius D. Clay: Germany 1945–1949,* vol. 2, pp. 568–69.
11. Ibid., p. 569.
12. Millis, ed., *The Forrestal Diaries,* pp. 393–94.
13. Diary of Eben A. Ayers, entry March 16, 1948.
14. Interview with James E. Webb, December 19, 1974.
15. *PP,* 1948, p. 186 ff.
16. Hamby, *Beyond the New Deal,* p. 219.
17. John King Fairbank, *The United States and China,* 3rd ed., paperback (Cambridge, Mass., 1971), pp. 311–12.
18. *PP,* 1948, pp. 144–46.
19. Department of State, "China White Paper," pp. 380–84.
20. Marshall memorandum of a conversation, June 7, 1948, *FR,* 1948, vol. 8, pp. 84–86.

21. NSC-8, April 2, 1948. "The Position of the United States with Respect to Korea." Box NSC 1/1-33, Modern Military Branch. National Archives, Washington, D.C.
22. *FR,* 1948, vol. 3, pp. 46–48.
23. Robert Murphy to Marshall, March 20, 1948, *FR,* 1948, vol. 2, pp. 883–84.
24. Jean Edward Smith, ed., *The Papers of General Lucius D. Clay,* vol. 2, pp. 599–608.
25. Interview with John W. Snyder, June 10, 1972.
26. Truman, *Year of Decisions,* p. 306.
27. Truman, *Years of Trial and Hope,* pp. 122–23.
28. George and Smoke, *Deterrence in American Foreign Policy,* p. 123.
29. Jean Edward Smith, ed., *The Papers of General Lucius D. Clay,* vol. 2, p. 623.
30. NSC-9, April 13, 1948, "Report by the National Security Council on the Position of the United States with Respect to Support for Western Union and Other Related Countries." Box NSC 1/1-33, Modern Military Branch. National Archives, Washington, D.C.
31. *PP,* 1948, p. 231 ff.
32. Church Committee (U.S. Senate) Final Report, bk. 4, *Supplementary Detailed Staff Reports on Foreign and Military Intelligence,* pp. 29–31.
33. Editorial note, *FR,* 1948, vol. 2, pp. 909–10. Also Galbraith, *Money: Whence It Comes, Where It Went,* pp. 161, 251–52.
34. Murphy to Marshall, June 26, 1948, *FR,* 1948, vol. 2, pp. 919–21. Jacob D. Beam memorandum, June 28, 1948, ibid., pp. 928–29.
35. Marshall to the United States embassy in London, June 28, 1948, *FR,* 1948, vol. 2, pp. 930–31.
36. Information supplied by the Office of the Historian, Department of the Air Force, Washington, D.C.

39. TRUMAN AND THE STATE OF ISRAEL

1. Memorandum, Loy Henderson to Marshall, November 10, 1947, *FR,* 1947, vol. 5, p. 1249.
2. Editorial note, *FR,* 1947, vol. 5, pp. 1313–14.
3. "Memorandum Prepared in the State Department," June 4, 1947, *FR,* 1947, vol. 5, p. 1096 ff.
4. Robert Macatee to Marshall, December 31, 1947, *FR,* 1947, vol. 5, p. 1322 ff.
5. Sachar, *Europe Leaves the Middle East,* p. 513.
6. "Report by the Policy Planning Staff on Position of the United

States with Respect to Palestine," January 19, 1948, *FR,* 1948, vol. 5, pt. 2, p. 546 ff.
7. Millis, ed., *The Forrestal Diaries,* pp. 370–73.
8. Letter, Forrestal to Marshall, April 19, 1948, *FR,* 1948, vol. 5, pt. 2, pp. 832–33.
9. Clifford memorandum of a conference, March 24, 1948, *FR,* 1948, vol. 5, pt. 2, p. 755.
10. *PP,* 1948, p. 229.
11. Draft, "The Position of the United States with Respect to Pal-

estine,'' February 17, 1948. Papers of Clark Clifford. Palestine correspondence. Miscellaneous no. 1 folder. HSTL.

12. Undated memorandum, Wadsworth to Truman, *FR*, 1948, vol. 5, pt. 2, pp. 596–99.
13. Wadsworth memorandum of a conversation with Truman, February 4, 1948, *FR*, 1948, vol. 5, pt. 2, pp. 592–95.
14. "The Department of State to President Truman," February 21, 1948, *FR*, 1948, vol. 5, pt. 2, pp. 637–40.
15. Truman to Marshall, February 22, 1948, *FR*, 1948, vol. 5, pt. 2, p. 645.
16. "Paper Prepared in the Department of State for the President," undated, *FR*, 1948, vol. 5, pt. 2, pp. 648–49.
17. *New York Times*, February 25, 1948, p. 1.
18. *PP*, 1948, p. 164.
19. "Memorandum by the Director of the Executive Secretariat [Carlisle Humelsine]," March 22, 1948, *FR*, 1948, vol. 5, pt. 2, pp. 749–50.
20. Marshall to Warren R. Austin, March 8, 1948 (noon), *FR*, 1948, vol. 5, pt. 2, p. 697.
21. Papers of Clark Clifford. Notes dated May 4, 1948. Palestine correspondence. Miscellaneous no. 3 folder. Box 13. HSTL.
22. Truman, *Years of Trial and Hope*, p. 163.
23. Ibid., p. 160.
24. Matthew J. Connelly to Chaim Weizmann, February 12, 1948. Weizmann archives. Box 1. HSTL.
25. The account of Jacobson's call from Frank Goldman and Jacobson's subsequent meeting with Truman is contained in a letter from Jacobson to Josef Cohn, an aide to Weizmann, March 30, 1952, published in *American Jewish Archives*, April 1968. pp. 4–14.
26. Truman to Jacobson, February 27, 1948. Jacobson Papers. Correspondence, Truman, 1948–52, folder. Box 1. HSTL.
27. Author's correspondence with Robert A. Lovett, 1976.
28. Vera Weizmann (Mrs. Chaim Weizmann), with David Tutaev, *The Impossible Takes Longer* (Memoirs) (London, 1967), p. 228. Also Truman, *Years of Trial and Hope*, p. 161.
29. Text in *New York Times*, March 20, 1948, p. 2.
30. Vera Weizmann, *The Impossible Takes Longer*, p. 229.
31. Jacobson to Cohn in *American Jewish Archives* (cited n. 25).
32. Clark Clifford, "Factors Influencing President Truman's Decision to Support Partition and Recognize the State of Israel" (Address to the annual meeting of the American Historical Association in Washington, D.C., December 28, 1976), p. 12.
33. Margaret Truman, *Harry S Truman*, p. 388.
34. Interview with Samuel I. Rosemann, May 18, 1972.
35. Humelsine memorandum (cited n. 19).
36. Editorial note, *FR*, 1948, vol. 5, pt. 2, pp. 748–49.
37. Diary of Eben A. Ayers, entry March 20, 1948.
38. Charles G. Ross handwritten notes, March 29, 1948. Notes re: Palestine, etc., folder. Papers of Charles G. Ross. HSTL.
39. Interview with Charles E. Bohlen, January 25, 1973.
40. Marshall memorandum to Bohlen, March 22, 1948, *FR*, 1948, vol. 5, pt. 2, p. 750 n.
41. *PP*, 1948, pp. 190–91.
42. Truman, *Years of Trial and Hope*, p. 163.
43. Ross notes (cited n. 38).
44. See "The Department of State to President Truman," February

21, 1948 (cited n. 14), p. 640, par. 12. Also Humelsine memorandum (cited n. 19), par. 2.
45. Jessup, *The Birth of Nations*, p. 266.
46. Clark Clifford's address to the American Historical Association (cited n. 32), pp. 9, 12.
47. Ibid., p. 18.
48. *FR*, 1948, vol. 5, pt. 2, pp. 842–43.
49. Lovett memorandum of a conversation, *FR*, 1948, vol. 5, pt. 2, p. 761.
50. Macatee to Marshall, March 22, 1948, *FR*, 1948, vol. 5, pt. 2, p. 753.
51. Henderson memorandum of a conversation, March 26, 1948, *FR*, 1948, vol. 5, pt. 2, pp. 764–65.
52. Memorandum, Robert M. McClintock to Lovett, April 22, 1948, *FR*, 1948, vol. 5, pt. 2, pp. 845–46.
53. Lord Inverchapel to Marshall, May 5, 1948, *FR*, 1948, vol. 5, pt. 2, pp. 906–7.
54. Philip C. Jessup to Rusk, *FR*, 1948, vol. 5, pt. 2, p. 897.
55. Editorial Note, *FR*, 1948, vol. 5, pt. 2, p. 906.
56. "Memorandum of Conversation, by the Secretary of State," May 12, 1948, *FR*, 1948, vol. 5, pt. 2, pp. 972–76.
57. "Transcript of Remarks Made by Mr. Dean Rusk . . ." May 11, 1948, *FR*, 1948, vol. 5, pt. 2, pp. 965–69.
58. This account is based on "Memorandum of Conversation by the Secretary of State" (cited in n. 56); on George M. Elsey "notes," undated, Foreign Affairs-Palestine folder, Box 60, George M. Elsey Papers, HSTL; and on OH, Clark Clifford.
59. Editorial Note, *FR*, 1948, vol. 5, pt. 2, p. 976. Also author's correspondence with Lovett.
60. Lovett memorandum of conversations, May 17, 1948, *FR*, 1948, vol. 5, pt. 2, pp. 1005–7.
61. *PP*, 1948, p. 253.
62. Vera Weizmann, *The Impossible Takes Longer*, pp. 232–33.
63. Ernest A. Gross memorandum to Lovett, May 13, 1948, *FR*, 1948, vol. 5, pt. 2, pp. 960–65.
64. Jessup, *The Birth of Nations*, pp. 274, 284.
65. Weizmann to Truman, May 13, 1948, *FR*, 1948, vol. 5, pt. 2, pp. 982–83.
66. Lovett memorandum of conversations (cited n. 60).
67. Eliahu Epstein to Truman, May 14, 1948, *FR*, 1948, vol. 5, pt. 2, p. 989.
68. Lovett memorandum of conversations (cited n. 60).
69. Editorial Note, *FR*, 1948, vol. 5, pt. 2, p. 993.
70. Ibid.
71. Jessup, *The Birth of Nations*, pp. 279–81.
72. *PP*, 1948, p. 258.
73. Jessup, *The Birth of Nations*, pp. 280–81, and Editorial Note, *FR*, 1948, vol. 5, pt. 2, p. 993.
74. Editorial Note, *FR*, 1948, vol. 5, pt. 2, p. 993.
75. Eleanor Roosevelt to Marshall, May 16, 1948; Marshall to Mrs. Roosevelt, May 18, 1948: in Lash, *Eleanor: The Years Alone*, pp. 133–34.
76. Editorial Note, *FR*, 1948, vol. 5, pt. 2, p. 993.
77. Jacobson to Cohn (cited n. 25).
78. Memorandum, Marshall to Lovett, February 19, 1948, *FR*, 1948, vol. 5, pt. 2, p. 633. Also Rusk memorandum of a conversation, ibid., pp. 877–79.

40. THE LIBERALS VS. TRUMAN

1. Francis J. Myers to Truman, March 4, 1948. PSF: Subject file. 1948–52 folder. Box 184.
2. Unsigned memorandum on the stationery of the Secretary of Defense, March 26, 1948. PSF: Appointment file. March 14–31, 1948, folder. Box 88.
3. Hubert H. Humphrey, *The Education of a Public Man: My Life and Politics*, ed. Norman Sherman (Garden City, 1976), p. 110. Also Hamby, *Beyond the New Deal*, p. 238.
4. Hamby, *Beyond the New Deal*, p. 225.
5. Interview with Arthur J. Goldberg, June 13, 1974.
6. Harold L. Ickes to Truman, March 17, 1948. PSF: Subject file. Secretary of the Interior-Ickes folder. Box 158.
7. *New York Times*, March 28, 1948, sec. 4, p. 1.
8. Chester Bowles to Truman, April 1, 1948; Truman to Bowles, April 5, 1948. PSF: General file. Bowles folder.
9. Hoover to Vaughan, March 31, 1948. PSF: FBI-Truman folder. Box 169.
10. Interview with Arthur Goldberg (cited n. 5).
11. Telephone interview with Clark Clifford, January 27, 1976.
12. Truman to James W. Gerard, April 27, 1948. PSF: General file. Ga-Go folder.

13. Truman to Haysler A. Poague, April 27, 1948. PSF: Political file. Texas folder [*sic*]. Box 61.
14. This account draws extensively on Richard M. Dalfiume, *Desegregation of the U.S. Armed Forces: Fighting on Two Fronts 1939–1953* (Columbia, Mo., 1969), chap. 8.
15. *PP*, 1948, p. 466.
16. Ibid., p. 272 ff.
17. Ibid., p. 557.
18. Ibid., p. 867.
19. Ibid., pp. 330–32.
20. Ibid., pp. 276–77.
21. Ibid., p. 469.
22. Ibid., pp. 373–74.
23. Ibid., p. 867.
24. *Newsweek*, April 30, 1945, p. 93.
25. Text of off-the-record remarks is in the papers of Eben A. Ayers. Foreign policy–Russian relations folder. Box 6. HSTL.
26. *PP*, 1948, p. 259 ff.

41. A PRESIDENT COMES OUT FIGHTING

1. *PP*, 1948, pp. 284–85.
2. Ibid., pp. 285–87.
3. Irwin Ross, *The Loneliest Campaign: The Truman Victory of 1948* (New York, 1968), p. 78.
4. OH, Edward D. McKim.
5. Ibid.
6. *PP*, 1948, pp. 300–1.

7. OH, Charles S. Murphy, p. 9.
8. *PP*, 1948, pp. 304–7.
9. *Spokane Spokesman-Review*, June 10, 1948, p. 1.
10. *PP*, 1948, pp. 308–9.
11. Ibid., pp. 313–15.
12. Ibid., pp. 315–17.
13. Ibid., pp. 327–29.

14. Ibid., pp. 328–29.
15. Ross, *The Loneliest Campaign*, p. 85.
16. *PP*, 1948, p. 335.
17. Divine, *Foreign Policy in Presidential Elections 1940–1948*, p. 207.
18. *PP*, 1948, pp. 336–40.
19. Ibid., pp. 348–53.
20. Patrick Anderson, *The Presidents' Men*, paperback ed. (Garden City, 1969), p. 77.
21. Interview with Henry J. Nicholson, September 20, 1972.
22. *PP*, 1948, pp. 360–61.
23. Interview with Henry J. Nicholson, September 20, 1972.
24. *PP*, 1948, pp. 399–400.
25. Ibid., p. 179.
26. Interview with Claude R. Pepper, May 25, 1976.
27. Arthur Krock of the *New York Times*, in his *Memoirs: Sixty Years on the Firing Line* (New York, 1968), p. 243, said that Truman enlisted the help of Secretary of the Army Kenneth Royall in getting Eisenhower to issue this statement.
28. Interview with Charles S. Murphy, December 11, 1974.
29. Margaret Truman, *Harry S Truman*, p. 9.
30. Truman, *Years of Trial and Hope*, p. 190.
31. Margaret Truman, *Harry S Truman*, p. 8.
32. Ibid., p. 9.
33. Ibid., p. 10.
34. Truman, *Years of Trial and Hope, p. 190*.
35. *Diary of Eben A. Ayers, entry July 13, 1948*.
36. *PP*, 1948, p. 406 ff.
37. Ibid., p. 393.
38. Memorandum, "Should the President Call Congress Back?" Unsigned, June 29, 1948. Papers of Samuel I. Rosenman. HSTL.
39. Diary of Eben A. Ayers, entry July 13, 1948.
40. Margaret Truman, *Harry S Truman*, p. 14.
41. Clay, *Decision in Germany*, p. 367.
42. Jean Edward Smith, ed., *The Papers of General Lucius D. Clay*, vol. 2, pp. 733–35.
43. Ibid., pp. 739–740: Exchange of messages between Clay and Bradley.
44. Marshall to the United States Embassy in London, *FR*, 1948, vol. 2, pp. 971–73.
45. Truman, *Years of Trial and Hope*, pp. 125–26.
46. NSC-24, July 28, 1948. "U.S. Military Courses of Action with Respect to the Situation In Berlin." Box NSC 1/1–33, Modern Military Branch. National Archives, Washington, D.C.

47. Millis, ed., *The Forrestal Diaries*, p. 458.
48. Hewlett and Duncan, *Atomic Shield*, p. 158.
49. Lilienthal, *The Atomic Energy Years*, p. 386.
50. Ibid., p. 377.
51. Millis, ed., *The Forrestal Diaries*, p. 458.
52. Lilienthal, *The Atomic Energy Years*, pp. 388–92.
53. *PP*, 1948, pp. 414–16.
54. Hartmann, *Truman and the 80th Congress*, p. 197.
55. Patterson, *Mr. Republican*, p. 422.
56. Omar N. Bradley to Truman, July 30, 1948; Truman to Bradley, August 4, 1948. PSF: Subject file. Military-miscellaneous folder. Box 146.
57. *PP*, 1948, p. 422.
58. Ibid., p. 416 ff.
59. Thomas E. Dewey to E. Grace Dewey, July 27, 1948. Papers of Thomas E. Dewey. Personal correspondence. Series 5. Box 46, University of Rochester, Rochester, New York.
60. Hartmann, *Truman and the 80th Congress*, pp. 198–99.
61. Dewey to Sameul R. Guard, July 27, 1948. Papers of Thomas E. Dewey. Personal correspondence. Series 5. Box 77.
62. Interview with John R. Steelman, September 5, 1974.
63. Telephone interview with Leo O'Brien, July 18, 1976.
64. *PP*, 1948, p. 432.
65. Diary of Eben A. Ayers, entry April 30, 1948.
66. Fried, *Men Against McCarthy*, p. 18.
67. Goulden, *The Best Years*, p. 318.
68. Richard M. Nixon to John Foster Dulles, November 7, 1948, typescript copy. Papers of Thomas E. Dewey. Second term personal correspondence. Series 5. Box 140. Folder 11.
69. A. Augustus Low to Dewey, December 20, 1948; Dewey to Low, December 22, 1948. Papers of Thomas E. Dewey. Second term personal correspondence. Series 5. Box 92.
70. *PP*, 1948, pp. 451–52.
71. Ibid., pp. 436–37.
72. Ibid., p. 438.
73. PSF: General File. Clifford folder.
74. Ross, *The Loneliest Campaign*, pp. 185–86.
75. Dewey to W. Lloyd Adams. Papers of Thomas E. Dewey. Personal correspondence. Series 5. Box 1.
76. Ben Duffy to Herbert Brownell, August 25, 1948. Papers of Thomas E. Dewey. Personal correspondence. Series 10. Box 6. Folder 5.
77. Margaret Truman, *Harry S Truman*, pp. 19–20.

42. WHISTLE-STOP

1. *PP*, 1948, p. 477.
2. Ibid.
3. Interview with Joseph Keenan, May 21, 1974.
4. *Newsweek*, September 20, 1948, p. 28.
5. Redding, *Inside the Democratic Party*, p. 215.
6. Interview with John W. Snyder, January 8, 1976.
7. Exchange of letters in PSF: Political file. D folder. Box 156.
8. Interview with John W. Snyder, January 8, 1976.
9. Interview with Milton S. Kronheim, Sr., December 10, 1974.
10. *Time*, June 6, 1949, pp. 22–23.
11. Redding, *Inside the Democratic Party*, p. 273.
12. Kenneth P. O'Donnell and David F. Powers (with Joe McCarthy), *Johnny, We Hardly Knew Ye: Memories of John Fitzgerald Kennedy* (Boston, 1970), p. 10.
13. Ross, *The Loneliest Campaign*, p. 176.
14. *Time*, September 27, 1948, p. 23.
15. Matusow, *Farm Policies and Politics in the Truman Years*, pp. 177–80.
16. Exchange of letters. Papers of Thomas E. Dewey. Personal correspondence. Series 5. Box 7.
17. Memorandum, "Some Aspects of the Preparation of President Truman's Speeches for the 1948 Campaign" by Charles S. Murphy, December 6, 1948. Copy in Murphy's law office in Washington, D.C.
18. Interview with Charles S. Murphy, June 11, 1975.
19. *PP*, 1948, p. 503 ff.
20. Ross, *The Loneliest Campaign*, p. 167.
21. *PP*, 1948, p. 512.
22. Ibid., p. 600.
23. Ibid., p. 534.
24. Dewey to Brownell, October 1, 1948, Papers of Thomas E. Dewey. Personal correspondence. Series 10. Box 5. Folder 5.
25. *PP*, 1948, p. 562.
26. Ibid., p. 845.
27. Interview with Elliott V. Bell, June 25, 1976.
28. Dewey to Brownell, September 30, 1948. Papers of Thomas E. Dewey. Personal correspondence. Series 10. Box 6. Folder 5.
29. Matusow, *Farm Policies and Politics in the Truman Years*, p. 188.
30. *PP*, 1948, p. 643.
31. Andresen to Dewey, October 3, 1948. Papers of Thomas E. Dewey. Personal correspondence. Series 5. Box 7.

32. OH, George M. Elsey, pp. 65–66.
33. Telephone interview with David M. Noyes, April 29, 1975.
34. Walter Bedell Smith to Marshall, September 14, 1948, *FR*, 1948, vol. 2, p. 1157.
35. "Records of Meetings of the Secretary of State with the Foreign Ministers of the United Kingdom and France," Paris, September 26, 1948, *FR*, 1948, vol. 2, pp. 1184–86.
36. Truman, *Years of Trial and Hope*, pp. 212–17.
37. Daniels, *The Man of Independence*, p. 29.
38. Vandenberg, ed., *The Private Papers of Senator Vandenberg*, pp. 457–58.
39. Hillman, *Mr. President*, p. 141.
40. *PP*, 1948, p. 698.
41. *Time*, October 18, 1948, p. 24.
42. *PP*, 1948, pp. 724–25. The speech appealing for peace that was written to be delivered by Truman over radio in the planned announcement of the Vinson mission was instead delivered by the president at the American Legion Convention at Miami Beach, October 18. (Ibid., p. 815 ff.)
43. Goulden, *The Best Years*, p. 414. This remark was known to all the reporters on the Dewey and Truman trains but never reported at the time because Dewey had spoken off the record.
44. *PP*, 1948, pp. 726, 802.
45. Ross, *The Loneliest Campaign*, p. 221.
46. Exchange of letters in the papers of Thomas E. Dewey. Personal correspondence. Series 5. Box 106.
47. Interview with Elliott V. Bell, June 25, 1976.
48. *PP*, 1948, p. 813.
49. Ibid., p. 696.
50. Ibid., pp. 795, 828.
51. Interview with James H. Rowe, Jr., January 25, 1975.
52. Interview with John R. Steelman, August 23, 1974.
53. Truman, *Years of Trial and Hope*, p. 166.
54. "The Secretary of State to the Special Representative of the United States in Israel," September 1, 1948, *FR*, 1948, vol. 5, pt. 2, pp. 1366–69. See n. 4, p. 1369, for citation of Truman's approval.
55. Marshall to McClintock, *FR*, 1948, vol. 5, pt. 2, p. 1387.
56. *FR*, 1948, vol. 5, pt. 2, p. 1401 ff.
57. *FR*, 1948, vol. 5, pt. 2, p. 1415.
58. William M. Boyle, Jr., to Connelly. PSF: Subject file. Russia 1945–1948 folder. Box 187.

59. Diary of Edward Jacobson, entry September 28, 1948, p. 5. Papers of Edward Jacobson. HSTL.
60. Lovett, "Memorandum of a Telephone Conversation," September 29, 1948, *FR*, 1948, vol. 5, pt. 2, pp. 1430–31. See n. 2, p. 1430, for Truman's draft of a message to Marshall.
61. *PP*, 1948, pp. 843–44.
62. Exchange of letters is in Papers of Thomas E. Dewey. Personal correspondence. Series 5. Box 70.

63. *PP*, 1948, pp. 848 ff., 864, 882–84, 889, 901, 913, 923–24, 929, and 938–39.
64. Everett M. Dirksen to Dewey, November 1, 1948. Papers of Thomas E. Dewey. Personal correspondence. Series 5. Box 48.
65. Matusow, *Farm Policies and Politics in the Truman Years*, p. 188.

43. INCREDIBLE VICTORY

1. The passing reporter was the author.
2. The account of Truman's night at Excelsior Springs is based on interviews with Henry Nicholson.
3. *Newsweek,* November 8, 1948 (Special Election Edition), p. 4.
4. Quotations from election night broadcasts are taken from CBS and NBC tapes at the National Archives, Washington, D.C.
5. Donnie Radcliffe, "Taking the Chill Out of the Past," *Washington Post,* February 28, 1976, p. C-1.
6. *PP*, 1948, p. 940.
7. Ibid., p. 941.
8. Chiang Kai-shek to Truman (forwarded by the Chinese Embassy, September 28, 1948). Confidential File, State Department. No. 13 folder. Box 35. HSTL.
9. Lovett to Marshall, November 5, 1948, *FR,* 1948, vol. 6, p. 1319. Also John J. Muccio to Marshall, November 9, 1948, ibid., p. 1323.
10. *New York Times,* November 4, 1948, p. 7.
11. Dewey to E. G. Bennett, December 13, 1948. Papers of Thomas E. Dewey. Personal correspondence. Series 5. Box 15.
12. Dewey to Henry R. Luce, December 15, 1948, Box 113.
13. Churchill to Truman, November 8, 1948. Truman to Churchill, November 23, 1948. PSF: General File. Churchill folder.
14. West, *Upstairs at the White House,* p. 102.

Index

Poland (*continued*)
    Potsdam discussions of, 74, 82–85, 86, 87, 88
    underground in, 52
    U.S. reactions to issue of, 35, 39, 56
    Warsaw Provisional Government of, 34, 35, 37, 39, 42, 44, 47, 53, 55, 56
    Yalta discussions of, *see* Yalta Conference
    Yugoslav precedent and, 35, 39, 42
poll taxes, legislation on, 31–32, 245, 335, 354
Porter, Paul, 277, 278
Porter, Paul A., 167, 277*n*
postwar reconversion, 107–26, 231
    civilian production in, 107
    government intervention and, 112, 113–14
    inflation vs. unemployment in, 107–9, 111, 120
    labor problems in, 110–11, 114–15, 116, 119, 120–21, 122, 163, 164–65, 166–68, 198, 208–18
    liberals vs. conservatives and, 108, 109–10, 112–14, 118, 119, 230
    wage-price policies in, 108, 110, 111, 112, 117, 119–22, 166–68, 198–99
Potsdam Conference (1945), 72–89, 96, 107, 109, 221, 231, 285
    atomic bomb and, *see* atomic bomb
    background of, 52, 55–57
    character of leaders at, 72–76
    free waterways proposed at, 77, 85, 88
    German issue at, 76–79, 80, 82–84, 87–88, 89, 249–50, 359
    Italy discussed at, 80–82, 85–86, 87, 88
    Montreux Convention and, 85, 87, 189
    North African trusteeship sought at, 87, 89
    Palestine issue at, 313
    Polish issue at, 74, 82–85, 86, 88
    Truman's views on, 72, 74, 84, 89
    Vietnam divided at, 102
Potsdam Proclamation, 94–95, 97, 98–99, 101
Powell, Adam Clayton, Jr., 147–48
power, public vs. private, 273, 392–93
President's Committee on Civil Rights, 245, 332, 333, 353, 391
    report of, 334–36, 436
President's Temporary Commission on Employee Loyalty, 243, 292–94
price controls, 30, 111, 117, 120, 229, 340
    relaxation and removal of, 108, 110, 121, 166–68, 198–99, 235–37, 239, 261, 262
    vs. voluntary reduction, 339
price supports, 420, 422
production controls, 110, 111
Progressive Citizens of America (PCA), 263–64, 342–43, 361
Purnell, William R., 98

Quebec conferences (1943; 1944), 47, 68

Rabi, Isidor I., 66, 96
race relations, 6, 30–33, 147–48, 172–73, 332–37, 352–56
railroad strike, 199, 208, 210–18
Randolph, A. Philip, 390, 391, 411
Rankin, John E., 127, 171, 258–59, 403
Raskin, A. H., 303
rationing, 124–25, 171, 198, 340
Rauh, Joseph L., Jr., 264
Rayburn, Sam, 3, 4, 13, 18, 19–20, 25, 29, 123, 214, 235, 347, 390, 426

Reconstruction Finance Corporation, 177, 262
Rees, Edward H., 234
Reinsch, J. Leonard, 49
Republican party, 120, 142
    anti-Soviet policy in, 189, 228, 231, 273, 274, 286
    China policy in, 149, 151, 248, 341, 361, 437
    Communist issue in, 161, 231–33, 234, 242, 272, 273–74, 293
    in Congress, 113, 114, 115, 149, 151, 161, 180, 181, 215, 219, 222, 230, 237, 239, 242, 257–58, 259, 272–74, 278, 280–81, 287, 293, 294, 352, 356, 391–93, 403, 410–12
    in election of 1946, 115, 230, 231, 237–38, 242
    in election of 1948, 336, 349, 350, 388, 391, 393, 395–416, 421–23, 425, 427
    National Convention of (1948), 402, 428
    southern Democrats and, 113, 123, 299
Reston, James, 224, 372
Reuther, Walter P., 109, 120, 122, 166, 168, 388
Rhee, Syngman, 153, 362, 437
Richberg, Donald R., 272
Roberts, Roy A., 17, 27
Robeson, Paul, 245
Roosevelt, Eleanor, 3, 5, 7, 8, 18, 19, 51, 102, 298, 325, 333, 385, 388, 426
    ADA and, 264, 342
    civil rights and, 147, 243–44, 333
    Pauley opposed by, 178, 179
    Truman advised by, 216–17, 239, 286–87
Roosevelt, Elliott, 388
Roosevelt, Franklin Delano:
    atomic bomb policy of, 42, 43, 46, 47, 48, 71, 93, 98
    cabinet of, 9–10, 21–22, 27, 28, 29, 46, 179, 184, 220
    China policy of, 63, 64, 152
    civil rights issue under, 32, 173
    death of, 3–8, 9, 21, 26, 35
    de Gaulle and, 58, 59, 60
    health of, 5, 9, 20
    labor and, 61, 111, 240, 242
    legislative program of, 30, 109, 110, 112–13, 125, 216
    liberal attraction to, 263, 272, 356
    military and, 140, 141, 142
    Palestine issue under, 312–13, 318
    postwar planning of, 10, 76–77, 78
    security issue and, 232–34, 242, 292, 294, 296
    Soviet Union and, 10–13, 34, 36, 38, 39, 41, 42, 52, 55, 57, 71, 77, 82, 157–58, 186
    at Teheran conference, 10, 44, 53, 157–58
    Truman contrasted with, 19–22, 81, 117, 118, 119, 121, 125, 140, 146, 148, 164
    Truman's succession and, 3–14, 15–16, 17, 18–19, 24, 30, 36, 42–43, 52, 55, 56, 91, 109, 110, 112, 128, 140, 229, 401, 438
    Truman's views on, 18, 24, 52, 118, 236, 401, 405
    as war leader, 9, 10, 16, 18–19, 32, 35, 46, 47, 52, 107, 306
    Yalta and, 5, 10–11, 34, 77, 80, 82, 258
Roosevelt, Franklin D., Jr., 264, 301, 388
Roosevelt, James, 388, 390, 400–1, 404, 405
Roosevelt, Theodore, 26, 45
Rosenman, Samuel I., 109, 110, 120, 124, 125, 164, 178, 213, 214, 270, 318, 338, 376, 380, 386, 400, 407